The focus of this unique comparative study is on a form of political radicalism at its high point around the middle of the nineteenth century, but broad topics such as trade unionism, co-operation, socialism, and religion are also examined in depth. The author argues that French and English radicalism did not directly stem from or reflect work and workplace relations, but drew on a medley of work groups and organisations, material concerns, and social and religious groups. Radicalism, it is argued, was part of everyday social life, the daily concerns of which affected its practice – though usually not its programmes. Radicalism was also characterised by cultural diversity, although actual forms of organisation and action usually depended strongly upon the political context and strategic choices. The book also offers reinterpretations of specific developments and actions in both countries.

This book is based on a rich range of archival and printed primary source material and on many years of research in French and British archives. It therefore offers a major resource for anyone interested in the complex and diverse origins of modern political life.

Radical artisans in England and France, 1830–1870

# Radical artisans in England and France, 1830–1870

Iorwerth Prothero

*University of Manchester*

CAMBRIDGE
UNIVERSITY PRESS

PUBLISHED BY THE PRESS SYNDICATE OF THE UNIVERSITY OF CAMBRIDGE
The Pitt Building, Trumpington Street, Cambridge CB2 1RP, United Kingdom

CAMBRIDGE UNIVERSITY PRESS
The Edinburgh Building, Cambridge, CB2 2RU, United Kingdom
40 West 20th Street, New York, NY 10011–4211, USA
10 Stamford Road, Oakleigh, Melbourne 3166, Australia

First published 1997

Printed in the United Kingdom at the University Press, Cambridge

Typeset in Plantin 10/12 pt

*A catalogue record for this book is available from the British Library*

*Library of Congress Cataloguing in Publication data*

Prothero, I. J., 1939–
Radical artisans in England and France, 1830–1870 / Iorwerth Prothero.
     p.   cm.
Includes bibliographical references and index.
ISBN 0 521 58299 7 (hardback: alk. paper)
1. Labor movement – England – History – 19th century.
2. Labor movement – France – History – 19th century.
3. Trade-unions – England – History – 19th century.
4. Trade-unions – France – History – 19th century.
5. Artisans – England – Political activity – History – 19th century.
6. Artisans – France – Political activity – History – 19th century.
7. Radicalism – England – History – 19th century.
8. Radicalism – France – History – 19th century.   I. Title.
HD8399.E52P76   1997
322′.2′094109034–dc21   96–45550   CIP

ISBN 0 521 58299 7 hardback

CE

To my parents
Marjorie and Iorwerth Prothero

# Contents

# Acknowledgements

This work arises from an interest in comparative British and French labour history that developed in my early years as a lecturer in the History Department at the University of Manchester, where there was a tradition of English–French Special Subjects, one that I was strongly encouraged to continue by Professor Albert Goodwin. Later, on my first research trip to Paris, I was very fortunate to meet Rémi Gossez, who, showing no resentment at a foreign interloper, very generously shared with me his unrivalled knowledge of artisan trades and politics, and, above all, strongly encouraged me to put aside my doubts and embark on a comparative study of this magnitude. While I have not fulfilled his hope that I would exemplify the qualities of Edward Thompson and the English tradition of empirical economic history, I owe him an enormous debt. I am also grateful for help at the research stage from Maurice Agulhon, Scott Haine, Yves Lequin, Andrew Lincoln, Ian McKay, Barrie Ratcliffe, and Michael Sibalis. From my postgraduate students Tim Burns, Alan Little, David McNulty, John Sanders, Rob Sykes, and Tony Taylor I gained a wealth of information and references.

I wish to thank for their assistance the librarians and staff at the British Library; Public Record Office; Goldsmiths' Library, University of London; Library of Political Science, London School of Economics; Bishopsgate Institute, London; Bibliothèque Nationale; Bibliothèque de l'Arsénal; Archives Nationales; Bibliothèque Historique de la Ville de Paris; Archives de la Ville de Paris; Archives de la Préfecture de Police; Modern Records Centre, University of Warwick; John Rylands University of Manchester Library; Manchester Central Library; Co-operative Union Library, Manchester; Archives Municipales de Lyon; Bibliothèque Municipale de Lyon; Archives Départmentales du Rhône; Stockport Public Library.

Research in London, Paris and Coventry was financed by grants from the Social Science Research Council, Economic and Social Research Council, and British Academy. A Visiting Fellowship at the Research School of Social Sciences, Australian National University, enabled me to process my research materials and organise the arguments and structure of the book. Completion of the research was made possible by a grant from the Twenty-Seven Foundation, whilst a grant from the Faculty of Arts at the University of Manchester, which provided teaching relief, enabled me to do the bulk of the writing.

My colleague, Patrick Joyce, kindly read and commented on most of a draft of the book. With him, John Breuilly, and Sally Taylor, I have been engaged on a comparative study of urban culture in nineteenth-century Hamburg, Lyons, and Manchester, supported by generous grants from the British Academy and by a Social Science Research Fellowship from the Nuffield Foundation, and I have incorporated some research material from this project.

This book is based on many years of research that have put burdens on my family, and is of a type unfashionable now as it has necessitated a long 'unproductive' period. I am therefore grateful to the Department of History at the University of Manchester for allowing me to work on it to my own schedule and scope without any pressure to curtail or hurry it for the sake of earlier publication.

# Abbreviations

| | |
|---|---|
| *A* | *Atelier* |
| ADR | Archives Départementales du Rhône |
| AML | Archives Municipales de Lyon |
| AN | Archives Nationales |
| *APO* | *Associations Professionelles Ouvrières* |
| *APOT* | Fédération Française des Travailleurs du Livre, *Associations Professionelles Ouvrières Typographiques* |
| APP | Archives de la Préfecture de Police |
| *AR* | *Association Rémoise* |
| ASCJ | Amalgamated Society of Carpenters and Joiners |
| ASE | Amalgamated Society of Engineers |
| *ATWM* | *Apprentice and Trades' Weekly Messenger* |
| *ATWR* | *Apprentice and Trades' Weekly Register* |
| *BBCU* | *Book-Binders' Consolidated Union. Friendly Circular* |
| *BCUC* | *Bookbinders' Consolidated Union Circular* |
| *BFFC* | *Book-Finishers' Friendly Circular* |
| *BFP* | *Bolton Free Press* |
| *BH* | *Bee-Hive* |
| BHVP | Bibliothèque Historique de la Ville de Paris |
| BN | Bibliothèque Nationale |
| *BO* | *Bradford Observer* |
| *BTC* | *Bookbinders' Trade Circular* |
| *C* | *Commonwealth* (originally *Miner and Workman's Advocate*) |
| *CC* | *Cordwainers' Companion* |
| *CP* | *Commune de Paris* |
| *ECC* | *English Chartist Circular* |
| *EF* | *Eglise Française* |
| *EL* | *English Leader* |
| ELDA | East London Democratic Association |
| *EO* | *Echo des Ouvriers* |
| *ES* | *Evening Star* |

| | |
|---|---|
| *F* | *Fraternité* |
| *F 1845* | *Fraternité de 1845* |
| *FLA* | *Friends of Labour Association's Monthly Circular* |
| *FSA* | *Friendly Societies' Advocate* |
| FSOC | Friendly Society of Operative Carpenters and Joiners |
| *G* | *Gauntlet* |
| GNCTU | Grand National Consolidated Trades' Union |
| *GS* | *Glasgow Sentinel* |
| *GT* | *Gazette des Tribunaux* |
| *HHE* | *Halifax and Huddersfield Express* |
| HO | Home Office Papers |
| IWMA | International Working Men's Association |
| *JO* | *Journal des Ouvriers* |
| *JP* | *Journal du Peuple* |
| *JT* | *Journal des Tailleurs* |
| *JTA* | *Journal of the Typographic Arts* |
| *LD* | *London Dispatch* (originally *'Destructive' and Poor Man's Conservative*) |
| LDA | London Democratic Association |
| *LL* | *Labour League* |
| *LM* | *London Mercury* |
| *LN* | *London News* |
| LOTPA | London Operative Tailors' Protective Association |
| LSC | London Society of Compositors |
| *LT* | *Leeds Times* |
| LTC | London Trades' Council |
| *LYC* | *Lancashire and Yorkshire Co-operator* |
| *M* | *Marseillaise* |
| *MG* | *Manchester Guardian* |
| MRC | Modern Records Centre |
| *MWA* | *Miner and Workman's Advocate* |
| *NAUT* | *Monthly Report of the National Association of United Trades* |
| NAUT | National Association of United Trades for the Protection of Labour |
| NCA | National Charter Association |
| *NL* | *Northern Liberator* |
| *NMW* | *New Moral World* |
| *NP* | *Notes to the People* |
| *NR* | *National Reformer* |
| NRU | National Reform Union |
| *NS* | *Northern Star* |

| NU | *National Union* |
| NUTARLA | *National United Trades' Association Report and Labour's Advocate* |
| NUWC | National Union of the Working Classes |
| O | *Operative* |
| OBS | Operative Bricklayers' Society |
| OBSTC | *Operative Bricklayers' Society's Trade Circular* |
| ON | *Opinion Nationale* |
| OSM | *Operative Stonemasons' Fortnightly Returns* |
| OSM | Operative Stonemasons' Society |
| OT | *Organisation du Travail. Journal des Ouvriers* |
| P | *Peuple* |
| PC | *People's Conservative* |
| PD | *Père Duchêne* |
| PMG | *Poor Man's Guardian* |
| PMGRF | *Poor Man's Guardian and Repealer's Friend* |
| PN | *People's Newspaper* |
| Pop. | *Populaire* |
| PP | *People's Paper* |
| PRO | Public Record Office |
| PS | *Peuple Souverain* (Bordeaux) |
| PTA | Provincial Typographical Association |
| R | *Reasoner* |
| Réf | *Réformateur* |
| RL | Reform League |
| RN | *Reynolds's Newspaper* |
| RP | *Représentant du Peuple* |
| RR | *Réformateur Religieux* |
| Ruche | *Ruche Populaire* |
| RWN | *Reynolds's Weekly Newspaper* |
| SDH | Société des Droits de l'Homme et du Citoyen |
| SRI | *Sheffield and Rotherham Independent* |
| SS | *Southern Star* |
| TA | *Travail Affranchi* |
| TAHP | *Trades' Advocate and Herald of Progress* |
| TC | *Trades' Chronicle* |
| TN | *Trades' Newspaper* |
| TO | *Tribune Ouvrière* |
| TP | *Tribun du Peuple* |
| TPC | *Typographical Protection Circular* |
| TS | *True Sun* |
| TSMC | *Typographical Societies' Monthly Circular* |

| | |
|---|---|
| *TWM* | *Trades' Weekly Messenger* |
| *TWRA* | *Trades' Weekly Register and Apprentice* (originally *Apprentice and Trades' Weekly Register*) |
| *VP* | *Voix du Peuple* |
| *VR* | *Vraie République* |
| *WFP* | *Weekly Free Press* |
| *WA* | *Workman's Advocate* |
| *WM* | *Working Man* |
| WMA | Working Men's Association |
| *WMF* | *Working Man's Friend* |
| *WTS* | *Weekly True Sun* |

# Introduction

One of the great themes of nineteenth-century European history was the rise of labour, and this study looks at familiar elements in the process – trade unionism, political radicalism, co-operation, educational activities, and intellectual developments – in both Britain and France. But the period dealt with runs from the July Revolution in 1830 to the fall of the Second Empire in 1870, the period that preceded the rise of mass labour parties and trade unions, and the focus is on artisans, the male workers whose place in the formation of the modern European world is not always clear.

I am fully aware that the scope of such a large and ambitious topic runs the danger of superficial generality and cannot do justice to the complexity and detail of activities in every locality at every time. The aim, however, is not coverage but interpretation, and I have tried to explore what seem to me key general questions in relation to detailed instances. To avoid superficiality I have relied on my own primary research and not engaged in a distillation or reinterpretation of other secondary writings, but the unavoidable limits of this research mean that whole areas are not considered. The focus is primarily on some of the great cities, most of all the two capitals that were the main centres of labour politics in the period.

It is a defect of most historical research that it is confined to a single country, and as a Welshman living and working in England I am anxious to break free of such national limitations and parochialism, as well as being aware of the misleading nature of the title – Scotland is not considered, but some Welsh examples are drawn on, and Wales, of course, is not part of England. The transnational research-based character of this work is original and makes it an essay in comparative history, but I do not see the different countries as entities to be compared and contrasted, or find national character a helpful tool of analysis, even in its most plausible form of national political culture. While we might contrast the British and French 'economies' at a national level, we can also find great similarities in the structures,

1

technologies, developments, and experiences of artisan trades. In general, I would argue for the greater importance of political than economic factors in explaining differences between radicalism in the two countries. For example, in France, there is the more centralised and authoritarian political system, the political instability and fluctuations, and the periods of severe repression, while  English politics has a more open and participatory nature. But economy, society, state, or political culture are not usually helpful abstractions in looking at particular activities and movements, which were not all inter-connected, and the focus of my attention is at this more specific level. Instead of seeing England and France as two distinct and uniform blocks on which to construct national generalisations, I find similar differences and variations, and fluctuations according to circumstances, within each country. For me, the advantage of research on different countries lies not in arriving at a list of variables explaining the differences between their labour politics, but in the greater variety of instances I am forced to consider, the wider range of experience and frames of reference that have to be taken on board, and the way developments and interpretations in one case suggest ways of approaching and reinterpreting events and organisations in another.

While I do look at several different forms of labour activity, the main emphasis is on political radicalism, which was a very significant feature of this period. Artisans were always very prominent in 'popular' or 'plebeian' radicalism, but only alongside many other groups, especially other kinds of workers, such members of the lower middle class as shopkeepers, small dealers, and professionals, and what Max Weber called 'pariah intellectuals'.[1] While it is not difficult to show that artisans were a key, even dominant, element in urban radicalism and the movements this study is concerned with, artisan radical activity was not self-contained and was greatly influenced by potential or actual radical support elsewhere, just as growing politicisation and labour organisation among other workers, both urban and rural, was in the later nineteenth century to transform artisan labour politics.

The prominence of artisans in these movements justifies a focus on them, but it must be recognised that 'artisan' is an ambiguous term. Definitions are usually in terms of technology, expertise, and small-scale production, artisans being men working for wages in old specialised trades, and doing unmechanised, skilled work in workshops. These definitions do not completely fit: members of new trades, particularly working on iron, sometimes even in factories with power-driven machinery, can be regarded as artisans, engineers being the chief example; some units, such as shipyards and building yards, were big;

and skill was very varied and often subjectively defined, with many workers in trades such as shoemaking, tailoring, and cabinet-making being no more than semi-skilled, often domestic, workers. But the definition is serviceable enough as a descriptive category, and it is dangerous to construct a false precision, more rigorous definitions being usually artificial and too restrictive.[2] I take pains in several chapters to underline how varied and complicated were the attributes of workmen who can be called artisans.

Consistently with this, my study of artisans who were radicals does not reflect a commitment to a notion of a distinctive 'artisan radicalism', and indeed my general argument is that this is not the case, there being no distinctive artisan mentality, tradition, or set of values, still less an ideology. There is a well-established historiographical tradition that focuses on artisans and skilled workers as the basis of formal working-class organisations and movements, with the changes they experienced in the nature of their work leading to resistance and politicisation. While there is justified criticism of treating this process as in itself constituting the making of the working class, not least because it focuses on male workers alone, there is none the less no serious questioning of artisan predominance in the activities dealt with here, or the causal importance of conflicts in production. But I do not see artisan radicalism as the direct product of relations at the workplace, of role in production, economic exploitation, growing conflict between employers and wage-earners, or of the imposition of a new work discipline. A study of work relations and organisations reveals divisions, hierarchies and antagon-isms in the workforce, which were not natural bases for wider collective action. Craft particularity and labour solidarity cannot be treated as complementary. While capitalist economic developments did create pressures and problems, and therefore discontent and protest among artisans, this does not explain either why protest should take political forms or the nature of those political forms. People fervently supported political causes that were not related to their own interests, political ideologies cannot be tied to single socio-economic groups, and radical artisans were concerned with many things apart from work. Political movements were political movements and not reflections of socio-economic factors, and indeed operated precisely by transcending and ignoring work divisions and trade particularism. Political arguments had their own rationality, logic, and persuasiveness.

To say that radicalism did not stem from work is not original, although it is best demonstrated by studying both radicalism and work rather than by simple assertion and ignoring work in a self-justifying focus on politics. But the current stress on the 'autonomy of politics' and the view of political movements as dependent on politics and not material interests can have two unfortunate results. One is a self-contained study of political activity that ignores any links between political and social developments. The 'social' category is much wider than that of work, and indeed the workplace itself was not only where tasks were carried out but a social location, the site of social relations. My argument is that radicalism was not a wholly self-contained activity, and does need to be related to other aspects and concerns of artisan life, both material and non-material. Radicalism could articulate and fulfil individual needs and aspirations, and express and embody the daily efforts of people to cope with uncertainty, pursue their varied and often competing ambitions, endure hardship, gain respect and enjoy life.[3]

The second unfortunate result is to see politics just as ideas (even if they are called language) and, consequently, to confine the primary sources consulted largely to articles in newspapers and periodicals. A focus on radical ideas undoubtedly reveals a large degree of continuity during this period, but this is not helpful in explaining the fluctuations, forms, and divisions that characterised radical movements and campaigns. Ideas cannot be tied to particular movements or organisations, and do not in themselves explain their rise and fall. To show that Chartism was pervaded by certain enduring ideas is not to explain the Chartist movement, while its decline was the result neither of extensive socio-economic changes nor of a shift in ideas. Groups and individuals with the same ideas could support different and rival organisations, and engage in different or hostile activities and tactics.

A stress on the interrelation between aspects of social, political, and economic life, on identities that transcended the workplace and existed as much in the community, club, and pub, and were reinforced by political notions articulated by the radical press and popular cultural forms, can be seen as a cultural approach. But I do not see culture as shared values or treat radicalism as values, language, symbolism, and forms of communication. I do not deny the existence of underlying populist, liberal, or patriotic values shared by a variety of often antagonistic groups, but question their centrality as explanation or focus. It is no surprise that different and opposed groups, living at the same time in the same country and using the same language, shared and invoked certain ideas and conceptions, but a demonstration of what they had in common fails to explain the divisions and antagonisms among them, which seem to me far more important. A depiction of distinctive radical values can exaggerate the uniformity of radicalism, which was no more a simple reflection of values than it was of socio-economic relations, and both radicalism and liberalism were characterised by cultural diversity, not uniformity. Thus, in the activities I look at, I do not see a central, unilinear trend related to particular key developments such as mechanisation and factories, modernity, class formation, growth of party politics, commercialisation of leisure, separation of public and private, exclusion of women from the workplace, or rhetoric of domesticity. People's attitudes and behaviour fluctuated according to their readings of the situation.

My focus is on particular movements, activities, and organisations (all of which could contain a variety of cultural forms and practices), as well as on more specific questions: why certain forms of activity predominated at certain times, how and why organisation and action took the forms they did, and why certain strategic choices were made. These questions demand a constant attention to the context, and make it important to study what people did as well as what they said or wrote (as well as what they did not do or say). Of course action can only be studied through written documents, with all the problems of interpretation that historians have recognised for generations, but an excessive focus on the expression of ideas and values in written texts (which should not always be taken literally, for language is often used ironically or instrumentally, and its meaning is not fixed), carries the danger of privileging the role of the articulate who have left such traces, and in itself reveals nothing about their reception. An investigation of actions can thus both broaden the scope of the study and help uncover the reception of ideas, for as action is the product of thoughts, it is in itself potent evidence for thoughts. What people said, wrote, and did are all evidence for what they believed, and thus radical practice can help reveal differences in concerns, motivations, interests, cultural outlook, and perceptions of radicalism.

This book thus rests on the political importance of groups of artisans who were central to the development of the urban economies of the time and experienced problems that could lead them into radical political action, something for which they had the individual and collective capacities. Its main concern is with a range of benefit, trade, co-operative, credit, insurance, educational, and convivial clubs, of varying degrees of formality, and composed mostly of people connected with manufacturing industries. These clubs could, and many did, have strong political elements and orientations and were thus constituent elements of artisan radicalism, especially as they were unspecialised and multi-purpose, and radical clubs could meet the same needs and aspirations as they did. Nearly all of them promised material gains which were important motives for adhesion. The obstacles to commencing and continuing these organisations were severe and legion, and their form and operation depended on differing political circumstances, available organisational resources, and the organisational capacities and qualities of particular individuals, a source of tension lying in differences in outlook between ordinary members and the, usually more political, leaders. These institutions were of pivotal importance in nineteenth-century social developments and were foundations of political action. Such action led to political alliances that were not predetermined by economic or social strata, that depended very much on the overall political context, and that usually also included people from non-manual occupations. These alliances, with their usually slender material resources, were often temporary and fragile, and difficult to sustain. To understand artisan radicalism, therefore, we must consider not only the structure of work and workplace relations, and political ideas, but also the nature of politics, urban culture, strategic options, and the role of individuals.

While the different chapters deal in turn with different activities right through the whole period, there is a logic in their ordering. Chapter 1 looks at understandings and interpretations of artisans and their radicalism. Because the history of working-class agitation should not be separated from the cultural and intellectual history of the rest of the nation, and because artisan radicalism can be seen as derivative, the result of a 'trickling down', via 'culture-brokers', of ideas developed by higher and more educated groups, chapter 2 outlines the main themes within the common radicalism in which radical artisans shared, while at the same time stressing the variations and divisions within it that did not necessarily stem from intellectual principles. These first two chapters basically clear the ground for the more substantial ones that follow, although the latter part of the second chapter stresses the importance of the political context, a theme that runs through the book. The third chapter looks at trade unionism, and in arguing that even this did not directly reflect or develop from the workplace and work relations, indicates that the same was true of radicalism. The next chapter nevertheless argues that there were important ways in which radicalism was related to work, in practice if not in ideas. Chapter 5 argues that radicalism was not displaced by a new socialist ideology appropriate to new economic relations and the situation of workers, and this argument is continued in the next chapter, on co-operation, often seen as the chief application of socialism in the period. Chapter 7 draws these chapters together in a discussion of the possible class character of this radicalism.

Chapter 8 then looks at the main forms of political action, and argues that formal organisation was relatively unimportant, radical mobilisation depending on other, more informal bases, including, as was shown in chapter 4, work groups and trade societies. Some of the other bases are looked at in the remaining chapters, which also discuss more generally the importance in radicalism of education, religion, and various locations and institutions of popular culture.

# 1 Artisans

We are on the eve of great changes. The present system is worn out, and must give way. Every reasoning man admits this. Ask any one whose station or experience gives him the means of knowing what is going on in society, and he will tell you, that the present order of things cannot continue.[1]

Radicalism at the start of our period was characterised both by the confidence aroused by two epoch-making events, the July Revolution in France in 1830 and the Reform Crisis in Britain in 1831–2, and by bitter disappointment at the outcome, when the looked-for reforms had not occurred, and the people, whose action had made the changes possible, had been betrayed. Self-seeking politicians had used them to gain power and then turned against them.

I saw a man pretend to be
The advocate of Liberty –
I see him, in his power elate,
Uphold the evils of the State.[2]

Both the National Union of the Working Classes and Others in London (1831–5) and the Society of the Rights of Man in Paris (1832–4), fully expressed these feelings, and announced the appearance of labour, of the working classes, in politics and society. The sense of combining political action and popular grievances was conveyed at an early meeting of the National Union of the Working Classes by the respected veteran radical and trade union organiser, the shipwright John Gast:

Adverting to the destitute and hopeless condition of the working classes, he enquired, how it could be otherwise, seeing they were in no way represented in Parliament? There every measure adopted went directly to favour monopolists and capitalists, while it robbed the honest and industrious labourer of the fruits of his exertions; and it would be found, and, indeed, he defied contradiction when he asserted, that though there were hundreds of laws against the interests of the working classes, not a single law could be found on the statute book affording them the least protection. The people were beginning now to be aware of the power they would possess if they were intelligent and united – they saw clearly that by UNION their efforts to improve their condition would be successful, because it would enable them to enjoy the produce of their own labour instead of leaving that produce to be devoured, as it now is, by an unfeeling and rapacious aristocracy. By a union of their physical and moral energies, they would soon be able to command the repeal of all such laws as, at present, prevented them from enjoying the fruits of their labour.[3]

This popular democratic radicalism continued for the rest of our period, at times gaining widespread and mass support, but subject to great fluctuations, continuous activity being the work of minorities. 'We are', said the chief French workers' paper of the 1840s, 'the forlorn hope of the workers.'[4] It exhibited continuity in personnel and in ideas, as well as in the combination of an awareness of change, a conviction of the inevitability of reform, with a disappointment at the outcome of all the efforts made. The radical experience was recurrent defeat and, except for a brief spell in 1848 in France, radicalism was an ideology of opposition. No-one felt this more deeply than Auguste Blanqui, who spent forty of his seventy-six years in prison:

as for us, our destiny was to live in an age of change, one foot still on the ladder, and not belonging either to the world of the past or that of the future. It is a life full of hardship, of sorrow and bitterness; that of the Hebrews in the desert between Egypt and the Promised Land.[5]

The rise of popular radicalism was not a uniform process, or a simultaneous one, for it was well established in Britain by 1830, but was yet to develop in France, though soon to grow rapidly in Paris and Lyons. The two periods of the most dramatic extension of such radicalism were at different times, in England during and just after the Napoleonic wars, and in France during the Second Republic of 1848–52. Three factors are usually picked out to explain these expansions of radicalism: the 'trickling down' of radical ideas from higher social groups, through written and oral propaganda and participation in political and electoral campaigns; the generation of discontent by economic hardship, particularly in the cotton, woollen, and hosiery industries in England, and in the wine- and olive-producing areas of southern France; and the repression of popular activities, inspired by fears of popular sedition, a repression that often proved counter-productive and created political alienation and disaffection.[6] All these are relevant, but we must avoid the danger of looking for ideas coming only from above, and material motivations from below. It was a constant tendency among observers to see labour activity and popular radicalism as purely materialist in motivation, an example of how contemporary views have misled historical study of the poor.

Yet the people affected by these sudden extensions of radicalism lived mainly in villages, where industrial and agricultural activities were intermixed and combined, whilst it was urban artisans, more specialised and full-time handicraft workers, who seem the most continuous and persistent elements in popular radicalism. In 1833 'these Unions are now fast extending to all *crafts* in the kingdom'.[7] It was the artisans that were the mainstay of trade unionism and radicalism and predominated in the July Revolution, the Society of the Rights of Man, the National Charter Association, the Icarian movement, the June Days in Paris in 1848, the 1851 rising, the Reform League, and even in rural radicalism.

Three reasons are usually given for the predominance of artisans in collective action and protest, including political radicalism.[8] The first is their importance in the economy and workforce, for France and Britain were the first two industrial nations, with steadily growing manufacturing sectors. There were important differences between the two. France had slower population growth, a larger and more impoverished rural population with more peasant agriculture and rural industry, and a more restricted and less unified domestic market characterised by greater regional variations. She did not rely on imported food, and, having lost her colonies in the wars, exported far less. Britain had greater economic unity, a much larger and more uniform middle-class market, and was very dependent on overseas trade, importing between a quarter and a sixth of food needs, and relying on the production and export of a very limited range of staple manufactured items, especially cottons. France had higher industrial productivity, produced higher-quality manufactured commodities using traditional supplies of skilled labour, which formed a greater element in costs. Even the factory-made cottons of Alsace and woollens of Roubaix were of higher quality than British ones, and in exports France relied more than Britain on quality goods such as silks, gloves, or porcelain. Britain produced for a lower-quality market at home and abroad, and concentrated on intermediate goods, basic manufactures, and common, mass-consumption articles, especially textiles, using more unskilled labour and intensive production. Britain also provided a number of services to the rest of the world – shipping, banking, and commercial – which financed a surplus of imported commodities and, therefore, higher consumption. It was mainly in British towns and colonies that there were mass markets for cheap consumer goods, which led to some mass-production industries, such as cotton spinning and weaving, food processing, brewing, soap-making (Marseilles likewise produced 60 per cent of France's soap), and publishing. It was in these fields that most mechanisation occurred in Britain and France, with carding, spinning, shearing, combing, weaving, dyeing, and printing in cotton and wool; sawing, ropemaking, newspaper printing, stereotyping of standard works, sugar-refining, papermaking, wallpaper-printing, brickmaking; beating, cutting, and pressing in bookbinding; baking and, later, wood planing and grooving. But in both countries most industrial production was not of this kind, factories and powered machines being very much minority phenomena, and iron towns such as Merthyr, Tredegar, Rhymney, Gateshead, Décazeville, or Le Creusot, or areas such as Lancashire or the Stéphanois (the Loire basin around St Etienne) remained very untypical. Even in the Stéphanois, the cradle of France's industrial revolution, the largest industry was unmechanised and artisanal ribbon-weaving.

The lack of mass production and steady runs of orders was a disincentive to the costs of adopting machinery, especially when there was a plentiful supply of cheap labour, and mechanisation did not always increase productivity. The expansion of manufacturing in step with the expansion of both population and economy did not take the form of mechanisation so much as the employment of more and more labour, men and women and children, often with changes in speed of work, division of labour, and the gender and age of workers.

Technological change did continue after mid-century, in England, with the spread of machines in tailoring, shoemaking and printing, in France, with the rapid concentration in iron and chemicals, and the modernisation in cotton and extensive mechanisation in wool, but these were mostly at the end of, or after, our period. It was after 1875 that the steel revolution occurred in France and that steam power was massively applied in England.

In England, France and Wales throughout our period economic life remained dominated by agriculture, consumer-goods manufacture, small-scale commerce, and local banking, despite the growth of railways, coal-mines, a few department stores, and share-dealing, and the main industries were in textiles, clothing, food processing, building, leather (including footwear), and wood (including furniture), composed in the main of small firms. Thus the chief industries throughout our period were consumer ones, and small-scale production and handicraft labour, whether in workshop or at home, predominated, even in industries where some great firms did arise. 'The workmen of the great manufactures and great factories constitute, without any doubt, the great minority of workers.' [9]

The predominance of hand-labour naturally meant that such people should dominate working-class movements, the more 'modern' workers dominating later in the century. But it is one thing to establish the prevalence of hand-labour and another to regard its practitioners as a single group. Hand-labour is really a definition in terms of what it is not, namely operating powered machinery, as if this is the determinant factor. Handworkers were not uniform. Large numbers did not specialise in a single occupation, and indeed often combined agricultural and urban work. 'Behind the apparent specialisation, the great mass of workers in the region consisted of labourers who did not know how to do anything and were capable of doing everything.'[10] These were very different from more specialised and skilled workmen, mostly in towns, who did not usually seek work in another occupation (although their occupations might often change in the course of their lifetime). There was also a difference between those who worked at home in a family unit, and men who worked in workshops, again mostly in towns. But there was also a lot of domestic work in the towns, particularly in weaving and clothing, and although shoemakers tended to work at home, homework was in general associated with poverty and female and juvenile labour. In contrast, men working in all-male workshops might feel that the man should earn a wage to meet the basic needs of the whole family. This might be a plausible aspiration for some skilled men, and reinforce a distinction between 'productive' paid male work outside the home, and 'unproductive' unpaid female work in the home, and thus solidify the gender division of labour and tendency to confine women to domestic work. Thus in 1867 'in Paris, the workers live their own life separately, the husband one way, the wife another, as the workshops are often far from the workers' accommodation'.[11] But in fact there was a great gap between the womanly ideal and women's actual lives. Furthermore, a workman's standard of living depended not just on his wage, his wife's ability as a housekeeper, women's networks, credit access, and the extent of their financial self-discipline, foresight, and temperance, but usually also on paid women's and children's work, a lot of it informal and casual but still vital, though characterised by low levels of pay, skill and authority.

While everyone recognised a connexion between poverty and discontent, and 'those who are acquainted with the history of agitations for all great principles, need not be told of the lulling effects of comparative prosperity',[12] and radical movements and disturbances reached their peaks in years of economic distress, it was also clear that people could be so impoverished as to succumb to helplessness and hopelessness, fatalism and resignation. Forms of solidarity were needed to make collective action seem feasible and plausible, while poverty and isolation seemed to produce apathy, and so such action, whether industrial or political, tended to occur in occupations that needed a certain amount of skill to give some bargaining leverage, that contained a high proportion of adult male workers, and that were characterised by substantial geographical concentration. While certain factory and domestic workers and villagers might share these characteristics, most of them in the towns did not.[13] Thus in Leicester the mainstay of Chartism and contemporary trade unionism was the better-paid and more skilled glove-knitters, not the impoverished wrought framework-knitters, while the elastic web-weavers came to the fore in the 1860s. Although 'the silk weavers of Lyons were among the most socially aware and even socially self-conscious "working-class" groups in France – and on the European continent, for that matter – during the nineteenth century', this was true of the more skilled fancy weavers, not the impoverished plain weavers.[14] Thus, in addition to the artisans' continued numerical and economic importance, a second reason for their prominence in labour movements is seen in their special capacity for such a role, greater economic independence underpinning social and political independence. With a pride in their skill and feeling of superiority, they were less deferential than other workmen, were better educated, belonged to occupational communities, and had long traditions of organisation. They thus had the necessary individual and collective resources for collective action. They could, moreover, also induct into collective and labour activity newer groups of workers who, in the course of time, would come to displace them in such activity.

From identifying and explaining the prominence of artisans in the labour and radical movements of this period, it is a short step to identify a specific 'artisan radicalism', on the assumption that the artisans' position at work conditioned the nature of their radicalism. The earliest and most usual form has been to stress the proximity of small master to journeyman in artisan trades, and the resultant large degree of social mobility, close and harmonious relations, and absence of conflict between the two. The contrast here is with factory workers, working in large units, on mechanised tasks, separated by a great gulf from their employers and subject to much more discipline. In this view, artisans might well be radical but this radicalism was not extreme, or marked by class hostility or consciousness. On the other hand, being subject to greater control, factory workers might be less free to engage in independent activities. This typology is, however, dubious. Adult males were a minority in the labour force in many factories, and tended to be the more skilled and better paid workers there, often not doing the mechanised tasks that were the preserve of poorly paid and often female and child workers. Research on artisans also quickly reveals that the small size of firms was no obstacle to conflict or labour organisation, and that the common-sense sociology, whereby small masters would sympathise and have the best relations with their workmen, is unfounded. Small masters were often the worst employers, their petty resources and precarious position often meaning they could not afford good wages and were the most likely to reduce them, and attack and erode other standard practices. This was also true of those small masters who became dependent on capitalist firms, suffering competitive pressures from them and therefore desperately reducing their own labour costs, becoming the tragic villains as well as victims of the situation. Small firms were not necessarily independent units, for large and small firms were often tied in networks of credit and dependence. Thus in Birmingham in the mid-1830s all small master builders were dependent on one big firm.[15] In much industrial production, articles were not made entirely in one firm but by a series of separate enterprises and dispersed units, small shops specialising in one phase of production, their work co-ordinated by a merchant-manufacturer, who supplied credit and materials, and sold the final product. The Sheffield cutlery industry was a classic example, and knife-making in Thiers and Paris consisted of nineteen different specialisms. Not one of the great London coach-making firms made all the parts, and some made nothing at all but merely assembled. Industrial fragmentation and commercial co-ordination was the typical form. Large firms did not necessarily mean technological concentration, and the top capitalists were not the industrialists, but bankers, merchants, ironmasters, and builders. Sub-contracting was universal, involving delegation of authority, employment by workmen of their own assistants, a wide spectrum of dependence, often no sharp distinction between employer and employee, and a range of both harmonious and conflictual relations.

Paternalistic policies by employers were sometimes a means of extensive control of the workforce, but in fact factories were not usually very large, and were riven by different departments and sub-contracting. Discipline in workshops could be just as harsh as in factories, few being harsher than the London strapping-shops described by Henry Mayhew, where men worked in a silent race, each making as many desks as possible, at the end of each day the one who had made the least being sacked. Some groups in factories were highly skilled and saw their occupation as a 'trade'. They sought rewards commensurate with those of skilled artisans, and established societies on artisan models. Thus English factory workers' demands in the 1830s for a ten-hour day were because this was seen as a characteristic of respectable artisans. Artisans should therefore not be contrasted with factory workers on grounds of skill or discipline.

It also follows that 'modern' factory workers should not be seen as harbingers of a new world and artisans as survivors of an 'old' world. Small-scale industry was not 'traditional', static, or inefficient, being characterised by constant innovation in practices, flexibility in technology, and shifts in production. Some of this was related to mass production, like pegging or riveting boots and shoes instead of stitching (and, later, unpowered machine-sewing), the use of iron-work instead of wood in building or coopering, pasting instead of sewing clothes, and using larger ovens and fewer workers in baking. Iron replaced wood in printing presses and shipbuilding, new forms of cask appeared in coopering and new vehicles in coach-building. Tariff changes ruined the English silk industry. As industries grew in some areas they declined in others. The expansion of porcelain in Limoges led to the decline of the surrounding towns. As domestic outwork declined in northern England it grew in the Midlands, where boot and shoemaking expanded into the shrinking hosiery networks. St Etienne ribbon-weaving and Lyons silk-weaving spread into the countryside, using labour previously engaged in hemp, linen, and wool. Changes in fashion led to the growth of silk-hatting at the expense of felt hatters, until a revival after mid-century, while the dethronement of fancy silks in Paris fashion under the Second Empire helped transform the Lyons silk industry. This age of economic, industrial, and urban growth was thus characterised by constant changes and variety, in technology, division of labour, intensity of work, distinctions between men's, women's, and children's work, and in structures of employment.

The adaptability and flexibility of small-scale industry and hand-labour thus casts doubt on another view of artisans as a dying group, threatened with extinction by the spread of mechanisation and factories, and therefore, in contrast to the previous view, seen as a more 'revolutionary' group than factory workers. Artisans engaged in back-ward-looking resistance to a new order that threatened their very existence, while factory workers accepted the new industrial society and sought a better place for themselves in it. Thus there were two distinct labour movements, one replacing the other. But, as we have seen, it is not possible to see artisans as a disappearing group in this period. It was not just that there were still a lot of them left, for, given both the limited nature of mechanisation and the growth of population and economy, hand-labour did not just survive but expanded enormously in this period to meet the growing demand. Most artisans were not displaced by machinery, which usually replaced domestic and rural labour rather than workshop trades, and, since most mechanisation was in the preparatory stages of production, it could actually promote hand-labour in the later stages by cheapening and increasing the supply of materials, as the mechanisation of spinning did for hand-loom weaving. Thus mechanisation of one branch could promote the expansion of hand-labour in others. Mechanisation of spinning and weaving assisted the expansion of tailoring and dress-making, that of paper-making increased the number of wallpaper-stainers and (with machine-printing) the work and number of hand compositors, power-sawing promoted cabinet-making and (with mechanised brick-making) building. Later, in the 1860s, the mechanisation of sewing soles to the uppers of boots and shoes led to a mushroom growth of hand-labour in all other branches, including the key task of 'making', stitching the uppers. Steam locomotive railways meant more work for stonemasons (on stations, buildings, and bridges), textile factories promoted building and local machine shops, while factories often contracted work out to small firms or used outworkers to absorb extra demand at peak periods. Small-scale industry therefore *expanded*, not contracted in our period.

Yet these great changes in the artisans' trades brought costs and threats to their situation. Thus a third factor explaining artisans' radicalism is the various pressures and problems they faced, mainly in the forms of capitalist development, pressures to increase and cheapen production, and competition for markets and employment. There is a danger that analyses of these developments are based on an ignorance of the eighteenth century and consequent exaggeration of the novelty of some of these changes, rely too heavily on a conception of artisans as having been, before this period, members of skilled and regulated trades, and show excessive concern with the old guilds and a consequent corporate mentality. Nevertheless, these pressures are undoubted, although they did not usually involve deskilling technology or greater control by employers of production. One development was the use of cheaper labour, lads, unskilled men, or females. The use of lads as cheap apprentice labour, discharging them after a few years to take on fresh, cheap ones, without providing a proper training, helped swell the pool of available, poorly qualified labour. Female labour was usually in subsidiary and subordinate tasks, such as the preliminary work in bookbinding, and was widespread in tailoring and shoemaking. In the 1860s there were concerted efforts to introduce women into print shops. The use of female labour was often associated with homework, as women often preferred work that would not conflict so much with household tasks. But whether by males or females, homework was cheaper for employers, as it removed the need for sizeable premises, the workers bore the costs of heating and lighting, and it impeded uniformity and united action among the workforce. Use of cheaper, less skilled labour usually accompanied cheaper and inferior production, such as the low-price, low-quality ready-mades instead of bespoke clothing and footwear, the speculative building, and the mass production of cheap books. Trained adult workers could be forced to produce lower quality goods or 'scamp'.

Cheapening of production was assisted by sub-division of tasks, each performed by someone who was unqualified and lacked all-round skill. Efforts to increase productivity by having men work longer hours and at greater intensity did not usually involve greater direct control over production by employers. One means was payment through results, giving bonuses for greater output. 'Chasing' involved paying a very good workman extra to work very hard, and then making his pace or output the standard. Reliance on piece-work, whether with individuals or teams, was a way of increasing the intensity of work, although well-organised work groups could check this by controlling output. Where piece-work did not apply, attempts in building and engineering to introduce pay by the hour instead of by the day opened the way to longer working hours. Sub-contracting was also a means of increasing productivity, at no managerial costs to the employer, and sub-contractors, piece-masters (*marchandeurs*), and task-masters (*tâcherons*) would contract for a job or order for a certain sum, and then use workmen as cheaply or as hard as possible to increase their own take. In the 'farming system' in printing, especially of periodicals, the clickers (*metteurs en pages*) contracted for jobs, did the difficult parts themselves, such as making up, setting headlines and imposing, and employed boys and unskilled labour at low rates to do the rest. In tailoring, shoemaking, and cabinet-making, 'chamber-masters' and 'garrett-masters' (*appiéceurs*) tendered competitively for orders from warehouse firms dealing in ready-made clothing (*confection*), and met them either through their own or family labour at home, or by employing boys, females, or other cheap labour, or by becoming middlemen and giving out parts of the orders to others to do at their homes, in all cases falling into dependence on the capitalist trading firms. Sub-contracting was thus inextricably intertwined with the other means of cheapening labour and increasing productivity – low pay, homework, division of labour, longer hours, greater intensity, and piece-work.

It is, in fact, very dangerous to generalise on artisans and distinguish them clearly from other groups of workers, for research on artisans quickly reveals great variety and diversity. We should not associate specific social, political and cultural values with occupations or groups of occupations. We must also be on guard against such statements as 'the London mechanic for whom the injustices of life were less outrageous and who looked to patient and steady education as the true remedy for England's wrongs', or: 'skilled French workers often exhibited an almost severe moral rectitude and abhorred the lax morals and frivolous behaviour of their social betters'.[16] There are echoes here of the more traditional contrast of artisans, not with factory workers but, as 'tradesmen', with peasants and other agricultural workers, with domestic and other servants, and with unskilled labourers. That is to say, with people who were servile and tied to employers, not engaged in urban workmanship, or in possession of a skill. This had especially been the case when artisans had been organised in guilds and had been the settled 'core' in the urban labour force, with labourers the transient element, while servants were often of rural origin. But this is a poor basis for classification in the nineteenth century. Most workmen in artisan trades were life-long wage-earners not aspiring to a mastership, unless they set up for themselves in a desperate response to unemployment and poverty. Certainly, in our period the disdain for servants, who might be better off despite their lower earnings because they did not have the expenses of food, rent, or heating, but who had given up their dignity as men, might be extended to others who served or wore uniform, such as waiters or coachmen, who were not regarded as 'working men' (*ouvriers*), and even to bakers, who received part of their payment in kind, an attribute of domesticity and dependence. 'A *bona fide* working man may be said to be one who subsists upon the daily or weekly wages obtained by the sale of his labour to others.'[17] This also excluded seamen and costermongers, but artisans also often distinguished themselves from labourers who did not have a 'trade'. The whitesmith Holyoake regarded a description of him as a 'labourer' as an insult, and some disputes were provoked by treatment or pay that seemed characteristic of labourers or seamen.[18] These divisions often coincided with gender ones, for many domestic servants were women, and women workers were usually unskilled. But the security and superiority of artisans in our period should not be exaggerated, and increasing division of labour (Paris jewellery was divided into twenty-three trades), pressure on wages and output, underemployment, and the great growth of semi-skilled labour made traditional distinctions between artisans and others out of date. The poor, depressed workers of the East End of London, whom Mayhew characterised as unpolitical in contrast to the artisans of the West End, nevertheless included large numbers of fancy cabinet-makers and shoemakers, all by some definitions artisans. The old discourse of 'love of work' and the pleasure of the artisan in his intelligent activity was now dubious. Thus, rather than radicalism stemming from superiority and craft pride, these qualities, where they existed, seem to have been *obstacles* to participation in radical and wider movements, and radicalism can be seen as the result of their destruction. It is the insecurity of artisans that needs to be recognised, and artisan trade societies remained by and large weak organisations, the bulk of work-shop disputes not involving any formal organisation. The pressures on artisans did vary, and in general the members of superior and more secure artisan trades, such as compositors, bookbinders, coopers, shipwrights, or coachmakers, were not so active in radicalism or wider labour movements, although there might be some strong societies in these trades. But the security of artisans must not be exaggerated, and these trades were on the whole small ones. Contemporaries and historians picked out certain of the large universal urban trades as pre-eminent in their protest – cabinet-makers, carpenters and other building workers, and, above all, those proverbial politicians, the tailor and the shoemaker ('the Chartist snob').[19]

'Artisans', even if confined to adult, specialised and fairly skilled men employed in workshops, were thus a large, varied, and changing group, and it is very doubtful if they can be given a single or distinct identity. The established concepts of pre-industrial society, custom, moral economy, and traditional culture are also unlikely to be of much use in studying artisans in this period. Most generalisations about artisans seem to have been the result of being misled by a number of discourses current at the time. Edward Thompson warned against a tendency to divide the common people into two on the basis of contemporary classifications. He saw these as reinforced partly by a propertied fear of popular revolt and consequent identification of the moralisation of the people as the means of social salvation, and partly by the disapproval among self-educated working men of the main elements of the popular culture they rejected.[20] To these we may add the age-old distinction between work and labour, embodied in the languages spoken in England, France and Wales at this time – such as work/labour, *œuvre/travail*, or *gwaith/llafur*. Whereas 'labour' carried the notion of toil and effort, 'work' embodied notions of creativity, and the noun doubled as a description of both the process and the product created.[21] This traditional distinction between work, which was creative and enjoyed, and labour, which was not, was still very much current in our period. It produced a tendency, shared by many radicals, to divide the working population into two, artisans and labourers, with the former charac-terised by skill, security, intelligence, and education, a distinction that has misled historians into a false assessment of the experience of large numbers of 'artisans'.

Similarly, in the 1860s in Britain there was a liberal current, reinforced by the Social Science Association, to separate the 'intelligent artisan', involved in self-improvement, temperance, moderate craft unionism implementing benefit insurance, and co-operative societies characterised by rational and responsible management, from the rest. It was among these people, the 'aristocracy' of their class, that Henry Solly crusaded for working men's clubs.[22] This assessment was also reinforced from the ultra-radical side, where Chartists and advocates of working-class unity and common action, especially Ernest Jones, blamed the frequent failure of their appeals on the selfish contentment and exclusive aloofness of the better-off working men, to whom they gave the derogatory epithet 'aristocracy of labour'.[23] The concept was particularly prominent in the debates over parliamentary reform in the mid-1860s, when reformers such as John Bright waxed reassuring and lyrical over social progress, distinguishing intelligent artisans, who 'deserved' the vote, from the 'residuum', whose admission to the vote would swamp the middle-class electorate, and working-class radicals naturally played upon and used the 'Rochdale argument' on the respectability and responsibility of artisans. It was a crude analysis that the engineer Thomas Wright sought to demolish in the light of his experience, and, as Alastair Reid has shown, he argued that the classifications of workmen into skilled and unskilled, society and non-society, educated and ignorant, drunken and sober, radical and not radical, did not at all coincide.[24]

Yet this influential view also found a response among liberals in France in the 1860s, who looked to England for a model that combined freedom with stability, and argued that class antagonisms and bad industrial relations were the result of unjust laws.[25] To parallel the situation they believed obtained in England, they advocated the moralisation of workers through proper training, and argued that freedom of association and assembly would encourage co-operative, trade, friendly, and insurance societies on the British model, and thereby achieve security and an end to unrest and extremism. These views were reinforced by the reports of the delegates that the Paris trades were allowed to elect in 1862 to visit and report on the International Exhibition of that year in London. These delegates made contacts with trade societies in London, and were clearly impressed at their strength and solidity, and the liberality of the labour laws. They pressed for similar legislation in France and naturally, to strengthen their case, painted a picture of stable, moderate and responsible craft unions devoted to good industrial relations. It is the same division of the working population into two, with better-off, moderate, upper workers composing strongly organised craft unions, the power of which was widely exaggerated. But their experience of English trade societies was very limited, and they were arguing a case. These influential classifications were thus mostly based on imagination and calculated rhetoric rather than knowledge of workers' lives.

It is not possible to match up forms of employment, levels of wages, cultural pursuits and political views and behaviour. Popular radicalism was composed mainly of urban artisans, who were central to the urban economy and workforce, had the personal and collective resources for collective action, and were experiencing and reacting against a number of pressures and problems, and their radicalism embodied current ideas and responded to economic fluctuations and repression of their institutions. But these artisans were not a homogeneous group politically, socially, or culturally, while their radicalism did not stem directly from workplace experience and was not necessarily different from that of other groups of workers. Work could divide artisans, and radical artisans shared a mass of other concerns and influences. Their radicalism was not self-contained and needs to be related to their life more widely, the chief elements in which were work, family, and leisure. Work was important, of course, and needs attention, the most convenient way being through a focus on trade unionism, but an important concern for radical and other artisans was a tension between work and non-work time, and a resistance to work's exclusive dominance and monopoly of life. Political activity had to fit in with the demands of all three, an alternative activity that at the same time had to accommodate instead of clash with them, and even incorporate and build on them.

## 2    Radicalisms

### Radical themes

Radicalism is against privilege and for equality. These two fundamental elements are not unambiguous and can be understood in different ways, and radicals differed amongst themselves. Radicalism should therefore be seen not as a uniform philosophy or programme but as a diverse and contradictory array of people, concepts, and strategies leading to loose coalitions with broadly agreed outlooks and aims. One basic element was that power was unequal, and that the few who held it used it unfairly in their own interests at the expense of the many. Such inequality takes many forms, and resentment at them is age-old, but an essential second aspect of the radicalism that is the concern of this study focused on public institutions, in which the rich, privileged few, through corruption and favouritism, monopolised the top positions in the state, the remedy lying in representative democracy, open and accountable government, and certain basic negative freedoms that involved extensive limits on governmental power. Since this was not achieved in our period, except for a brief interlude in France in 1848–9, radicalism was characterised by a sustained critique of the existing unfair, unfree and privilege-ridden system, run by groups of which the landowning class was the most important, and fattening parasitically on a rather loosely defined and heterogeneous 'people'. The content of this radicalism was already established by 1830, and as new groups came into politics, they naturally adopted established vocabularies and organisational forms.

#### Privilege

One of the most powerful and constant elements in radicalism right through our period was resentment at and condemnation of 'corruption'. This was not just personal greed, venality, and dishonesty, but the perennial overlapping of economic, social, and political leadership; the personal rewards, favours, honours, patronage, and incentives that were the crucial constituents of politics; the jobs for friends, relatives, and clients; the personal rivalries and dislikes that seemed to dominate politics; the legitimisation of social leaders through local office; the whole structure, in short, that linked local notables to parliaments and parliaments to governments. The decrease in the number of scandals under the Second Empire, and the administrative and fiscal reforms and rejection of traditional jobbery in England, had little effect on the pervasive and systematic role of patronage or in reducing continued radical fury at such corruption.

Intrinsic to this corruption of the political establishment was its cost, and radicals condemned high salaries, sinecures, and pluralism (*cumul*), and the creation of posts simply to support members of upper-class families at public expense, seeing 'the whole executive establishment ashore as a huge system of sham labour test for national poor relief'.[1] The high burden of taxation was thus a second radical theme, a cause of distress and the result of government extravagance, waste, incompetence and indebtedness that involved high taxes to pay interest to idle speculators. Taxes should therefore be reduced by reducing government expenditure and personnel.

The privilege that radicals assailed was often seen in terms of groups or interests that pursued their selfish concerns at the expense of those of the general population, and these interests were often defined in economic terms. The chief element in the ranks of privilege was the great landowners, the traditional enemy who tended to hold the top posts in the state, a corrupt and selfish aristocracy. But 'aristocracy' was an epithet not reserved for nobles and landowners, and embraced a wider ruling class that could include placemen, slave-owners, merchants, stock-jobbers, bankers, money-mongers, usurers, barons of finance, forest-owners, ironmasters, coal-owners, railway kings, and, to a lesser extent, spinners and other factory-owners, all men who wielded local or national power and promoted policies in their own selfish interests, such as high customs duties on imported necessities.[2]

Given that the governing system was essentially exploitative, radicals usually wanted to reduce its power and favoured minimal government. Certain institutions were a particular concern here, such as the state churches and army. 'The two causes of Pauperism were the sabre and the cassock.'[3] Many favoured universal short-term military service to create a people in arms as a democratic citizen militia that would be a barrier to oppression, although the need for an army was more strongly accepted in France than in island Britain.

Opposition to the privileged few embodied a notion of the general good, and a concern for the Nation, or People, instead of the ruling elites. The reformers were the lovers of the Nation, the 'patriots'. Because patriotism implied national unity, public spirit, and the sacrifice of private interest to public duty, it was threatened by selfishness, an 'anti-national' exclusive possession of power by the few. In both countries radicals saw themselves as patriots, adhering to a concept of the nation in which everyone mattered and should participate in social and public life. English radical patriotism worked with the grain of the concept of England as a favoured Protestant home of liberty, while stressing that the constitution had been perverted and liberty was in danger. French radical patriotism drew on the French Revolution, a break with France's past that inaugurated and proclaimed a new liberty, but each could see their own country as having a unique mission to spread liberty in Europe.

Most opponents of privilege, corruption and oligarchy wanted the involvement of a wider section of the population in public affairs and politics, but not all radicals, however fierce their opposition to privilege, supported universal political rights in a democratic state, and there were disagreements on the required extent of political participation. Radicalism can therefore be seen as a spectrum, with an agreed hostile analysis of the structure of power but a constant tension over the relative importance of the two poles of privilege and democracy.

### Democracy

The right to the vote was an essential element of democracy, but democracy did not necessarily mean that everyone should have the vote in electing representative institutions, and there could be many exclusions on the basis of dependence (children, women, servants, prisoners, paupers, monks) and length of residence. 'Universal suffrage', that is, the vote to nearly all men, was already an established, familiar, and widely supported aim in Britain by the start of our period, but this was not at all the case in France, where radicals had doubted the readiness of the people for democracy and had conceived of a republican state and even a very temporary dictatorship to prepare them for it first. This difference was due to the extensive and popularly backed earlier campaigns for universal suffrage in Britain between 1816 and 1820, a popular support entirely lacking in France in the 1820s, and it was only the popular rising in Paris after the liberal victory in the 1827 general election and, especially, the July Revolution itself, that convinced some younger republicans, led by Godefroy Cavaignac, that the people were virtuous enough for immediate democracy.[4]

Yet democracy did not consist of the vote alone. Radicals had a very negative attitude to politics and the state, and there was little idea of establishing new governmental institutions to take on new roles. The scope and cost, and therefore level of taxation to support it, would have to be drastically shorn, and universal suffrage would serve not so much a positive function, leading the state to take on more functions, as a negative one, to stop the government from doing things, a democratic parliament being a barrier against tyranny and corruption. This also tended to imply decentralisation. While some French radicals were more worried at the local power and ascendancy of conservative notables and clergy, especially in rural areas, and therefore sometimes favoured a stronger and more centralised state to neutralise this,[5] radicals usually favoured strong local government, a tendency that reached its extreme in the French support at the end of our period for decentralisation into autonomous communes. 'We are of the opinion', declared the Executive of the National Charter Association, 'that the perfection of freedom consists in local government being unchecked in its workings.'[6] The difference here was that strong local government was an accepted and integral part of the British political system, but not in France.

It followed that the elected parliament should be independent of the government, and radicals favoured a weak executive. In the Second Republic they opposed a directly and democratically elected President, independent of the legislative. It is true that a distinctive feature in France was the association of patriotism with the cult of Napoleon, which was consciously used by liberals under the Restoration and republicans in the July Monarchy, but in itself this was not necessarily a sign of a wish for a strong executive. In 1848 Bonapartism certainly became a powerful, umbrella movement with strong radical and populist elements, although the Bonapartist pretender, Louis-Napoleon, also secured conservative support and projected himself as a man of stability, so it is impossible to generalise about his overwhelming support in the presidential election of December 1848. However, once in power he allied with the whites, and the *coup d'état* largely destroyed radical support. The Second Empire, despite its universal suffrage and plebiscites, was not democratic because the legislative body was not independent of the government or subject to popular scrutiny and accountability. Radicals tended to see those elected not as representatives but as delegates, bound by pledges made at elections, directly answerable to their constituents to whom they had to report, and even subject to recall, hence the support in Britain for annual parliaments. These views were at odds with later Chamberlainite radical conceptions of democracy where parties chose candidates and programmes democratically, controlled MPs and, on winning a general election, implemented their programme in an untrammelled way. Radicals in this period were in fact unhappy over liberal conceptions of politics as being of competing interests, and were generally hostile to 'parties' as sectional and selfish obstacles to unanimity.

The accountability of representatives to their electors was to be direct and continuous, not through party organisation, and this necessitated freedom of political activity for the people at large. For British radicals universal suffrage, annual parliaments, and secret ballot were not seen as substitutes for popular participation, or as closing down those extra-parliamentary campaigns that were a feature of politics, but, on the contrary, to make Parliament more open to them.

Such ideas remained strong throughout the period, despite some weakening in the 1860s, with the growth of party politics and, in Britain, with a decline in support for annual parliaments. Their relevance was shown in France, which from 1848 did have universal suffrage. For, in contrast to England, French civic liberties of freedom of press and association lagged behind the right to the vote. Thus in 1848 Auguste Blanqui condemned the deification of universal suffrage, for 'the poisoning of the vote by the press monopoly is the greatest of crimes'. His policy was 'the press and free speech, or the rifle'.[7] The manipulation by the authorities of the restored universal suffrage after the 1851 *coup* brought home to French radicals the inadequacy of universal suffrage in itself, and led radicals to place greater stress on parliamentary government and liberal freedoms. Similarly in England, the substantial extension of the vote in 1867 was followed by greater emphasis on the secret ballot, purity of election and the criminalisation of electoral corruption.

### Liberalism

Thus, from another point of view, radicalism can be seen as the extreme form of liberalism. Radicals shared liberal beliefs in a rational authority, subject to the scrutiny of the citizenry organised in a public body operating under the rule of law, in a constitutional state; the establishment of a meritocracy through the ending of monopolies and privileges of birth and of discrimination on the basis of religion; equal civil rights, and basic civic freedoms – from arbitrary arrest without trial (preferably by jury), and of thought, religion, speech, press, association, assembly; a faith in science and a confidence in the safety and utility of the extension of knowledge; free discussion and a free press, which would allow open debate so as to arrive at an understanding of the public interest through reason and argument; the release of individual initiative and energy, removal of patronage and charity, and the development instead of the self-made man relying on self-help.

Radicals were thus fully developing the ideas and implications of liberalism, but a very important difference was that most of the political aims of liberals were already in place at the start of our period in Britain while, although France had a constitutional monarchy from 1815 to 1848, there were far more restrictions on civic rights, press, associations and public activity, the state remained highly centralised and the police retained wide powers, which became far more rigorous under the authoritarian Second Empire. Britain had a liberal political system right through our period that was not subject to any serious challenge. In continental terms, nearly everyone was a liberal in Britain, and it was therefore much easier to be a liberal there than in France.

Liberalism contained radical and conservative elements, which could provide a defence or a critique of the existing order. Radicals stressed the inconsistency between the universalist language of liberalism and the practical limits most liberals put on full citizenship on grounds of reason, civilisation, independence, moral worth, responsibility, or property. They sought much wider freedom, in thought and expression, in publishing political and anti-religious works, in action safe from state or police interference, in religious equality and the independence of political activity from social status or economic power, and worked for a much more representative and less exclusive political system than most liberals would approve. These could be seen as differences over the meaning and use of shared concepts and values, so that British radicals were developing agreed terms and conceptions of representation and freedom, and arguing that they were not yet complete, while in France from 1830 the concepts of freedom and progress were also official ones. In England there was reference to a national history of freedom and the development of the Constitution, with radicalism as a continuation of the story, while in France reference was to the French Revolution, and all the French regimes after 1830 identified with the Revolution (or particular phases therein). Radicals were thus in both countries employing and appealing to official values, an effective strategy as these values could not be denied by the rulers without questioning the legitimacy of the regime.

This liberalism embodied a gendered view of reason and science as masculine characteristics, and a distinction between public and private spheres envisaging the former as male and the woman's place as in the family and home. Women were thus marginalised in liberal civil society, and freedom tended to be seen as a manly virtue, and slaves as effeminate, lacking the virile spirit and energy to fight for their liberties.

Radicals tended to share this liberal stress on manliness and the view of women's nature as governed more by feeling than reason, imagination rather than analysis, and possessed of distinctive moral qualities and instincts best served in the household.[8] While the ideology of separate spheres never corresponded to reality, and women operated in neighbourhood networks, engaged in paid labour outside as well as inside the home, contributed fully to urban culture and participated in politics, radicals 'wished to remain free, remain men' and urged their fellows to 'assert our rights as men',[9] and universal suffrage meant manhood suffrage. 'We do not understand a female *legislator* any more than we understand a male *nurse*.'[10] There were some efforts to involve women in radical organisations, though usually in a subordinate and auxiliary role; a female Chartist in 1843 criticised the rules of the National Charter Association for referring to members as 'men' instead of 'persons'; and a number of male radicals were in favour of votes for women, but it was manhood suffrage that was nearly always sought, the occasional exception usually being in local government. Even French women who raised women's issues and denounced their enslavement, often opposed giving them the vote because they were too much under the influence of religion.[11]

Yet the position of radicalism at the far end of liberalism in no way precluded strong disapproval by many liberals of their demands, aims, and methods as extreme and dangerous. Democracy, for instance, by presaging the end of all social distinctions, destruction of all aristocracies, even of intelligence, and giving power to those without property or education would produce the politics of flattery and the reverse of enlightenment, while radicals frequently condemned moderate liberals for selfishness, inconsistency, privilege and lack of principle, and conflicts among liberals and radicals were often fiercer than with conservatives.

One of the main occasions of radical disenchantment with, and opposition to, liberals was the disappointment engendered by their actions once they gained office, whether locally or nationally. Thus the new French monarchy established in 1830 disappointed many who had hoped for more extensive changes, and they moved into opposition to the government and often even to the regime. Similar disillusion with a new liberal government was to reappear in 1848 and 1870. Parallel disappointment in England at the new Whig government of 1830 was to foster the formation of radical organisations whose members would all have recognised the demands being made across the Channel, while the feeling of disillusion, that liberals out of office hypocritically advocated reforms that they abandoned once in office, was to lead to radical opposition in the late 1850s and mid-1860s, and to the increasingly unpopular Gladstone government after 1870. Conversely, as a Bristol radical remarked in 1863, when liberals were out of office they were more likely to adopt radical reforms to secure wider support.[12] This was particularly clear after electoral defeats or loss of office, nationally (in 1841, 1857, and 1866) and locally.

### Rights

Radical condemnation of moderate liberals was usually for their readiness to compromise, and therefore often for their insincerity and lack of principle. Most commonly radicals attacked compromises with reference to rights that were being denied, and a major feature of radicalism was the employment of the language of rights to reject moderation, sensible adjustment, common sense, and utility. Thus Cobdenites by the 1860s advocated the extension of the vote to working men for utilitarian reasons, to check the power of privilege and aristocracy, and thus were not concerned on principle with giving it to all working men, and this was criticised by other radicals on the basis of the right of all to the vote. The language of rights, especially 'natural rights', can be a very effective and exhilarating instrument which, by insisting that current legal powers are not the final court of appeal, and by providing a justification for opposition even to properly elected representative authorities, can facilitate a change in people's self-image and be a liberating and even revolutionary rhetoric, and it proved very effective in mobilising resistance. But rights were not only 'natural', they could be 'historical', 'constitutional,' or even 'legal', for reference to the past could be a basis for rejecting current legal or constitutional arrangements. This was particularly effective in England because of the widespread conception of an enduring free English Constitution and the fact that the reforms of vestry, parliamentary and municipal voting in 1818, 1832, and 1835, and the various improvement acts and New Poor Law, by tying political rights exclusively to property, frequently reduced the earlier level of popular participation in the official political process. But French as well as English radicals invoked past historical struggles against royal and aristocratic despotism. The overthrow of the free and democratic republican governments of the native Gauls or Anglo-Saxons, with their elected kings and annual assemblies, by Roman, Frankish or Norman invaders, had created the two classes of nobles and serfs from which the present aristocracy and people were descended. Both Norman Conquest and the reign of Clovis had despoiled the people and established private property in land.

Thus radicals, in their criticism of moderate reformers, invoked natural, constitutional, and historical rights in defence of an intransigent or extreme position and a refusal to compromise, but there was not always agreement on these rights; all rights come into conflict at times, and such language did not in fact preclude compromise. In England after 1850, support for manhood suffrage tended in practice to mean support for any reform bill as an 'instalment', as in the Reform League's grudging support for the very mild Liberal Reform Bill of 1866, and the great campaign in 1867 that preceded the Reform Act of that year. The insistence on manhood suffrage in a programme, with consequent quarrels with groups not willing to do so, was not so much in the hope of gaining its enactment, or a refusal to compromise, as a measure of social egalitarianism, a recognition of the worth of all men (even though there were always some exclusions).[13] Such compromises, coupled with the newer argument that working people had now advanced and improved so as to be fit for the vote, seem in marked contrast to the Chartists' refusal to abandon their six points and People's Charter when prospects of alliances with more moderate reformers arose in the early 1840s, but it was easier, of course, to adopt such a stance when there was no government measure in the offing. The situation in 1866–7 really parallels the years 1830–2, when ultra-radicals consistently opposed 'moderate reform' up until the introduction of the Whig Reform Bill, which most of them then supported as the most extensive change that could be hoped for. Unlike radicals in 1831–2 or 1866–7, the Chartists were never faced with a government reform bill likely to pass Parliament, so it is not clear what their attitude would have been. When the Whig bill was rejected by the House of Lords in 1831 and seemed lost, a number of ultra-radical groups did then form separate political unions to press for universal suffrage, until the reintroduction of the bill restored united action among reformers, while on the defeat of the Liberal bill in 1866 the Reform League returned to its campaign for manhood suffrage and was very hostile to the new conservative proposals until amendments produced a more radical measure than the 1866 one. There are clear parallels between the two periods, when the initial government measures were lost, even to the extent of proposals for a people's parliament and general strike.

Radicals were also much more likely to be republican in France than in Britain in our period, but this was only the case after 1830, as before then republicanism was stronger in England because radicalism was. Republicanism became significant after 1830 in France among radicals disappointed at the limited changes brought by a new dynasty that lacked deep-rooted popular loyalty, but it was limited mainly to Paris and Lyons until the Second Republic. There was a republican tradition in Britain which drew partly on historical precedents, and the number of republicans, which should not be underestimated, reached a peak at the end of our period in disillusionment with Gladstone's government. It was, however, more difficult to see the English monarchs as the real rulers of their realm, and the Chartist leader, O'Connor, while seeing true democracy as republican, felt democracy was far more important than the actual form of the regime.[14] In Britain the fear was of 'crown' (governmental) rather than royal tyranny, but in both countries the essential element was the same – fear of a strong executive, support for an independent legislature, and insistence that neither infringe basic rights.

### Producers

Another feature that radicals shared with liberalism was the long-term displacement of the old, indeed ancient, idea that participation in political affairs was the highest form of activity, by the view that non-political activity, such as commerce, was equally honourable, or even morally superior since politics was a matter of selfish struggles between privileged groups. Thus economic activity, or 'industry', was not a lowly activity but the foundation of society and the central activity of a nation. The economically active could be seen as the useful and productive members of society, and ruling groups, the idlers in army, navy, church, law, and state, as unproductive and parasitic. The indispensability of every man's labour to society gave a moral basis to the claim to the vote for all men, and meant that all who worked were superior to those who did not, and that it was wrong that some did not work. 'Labour' and 'productive' were understood in a number of different ways, usually gendered ones, such as all the economically active males, or all those engaged in manufacturing (as opposed to trade and finance), or those performing manual or waged work in manufacturing. But one important theme of the century was a rejection of the idea that manual labour was the meanest of all activities, devoid of all moral and spiritual elements, and many radicals therefore asserted the dignity, value and rights of manual 'working men' (*ouvriers*), who lived by the 'sweat of their brow'.

Radicals characteristically distinguished the people from privilege in three ways – rich and poor, rulers and ruled, those who worked and those who did not. Either one of the first two pairs was usually seen as causal, so that people with wealth therefore had political power and lived off the labour of the rest, or, more usually, those with political power were therefore rich and lived off the labour of others. Yet the third relationship could often be the key, morally charged one.[15] It also provided a rebuttal of the claim that property should be the basis for political representation, for if, as was commonly asserted, property was legitimate if the result of one's labour, it was clear that much property was not the result of the owner's labour; on the other hand, labour was itself a form of property.

### The poor

Among those supporting formal democracy, many radicals shared a particular concern with the poor and their sufferings, and this was a distinguishing issue within radicalism. Patriotism was threatened not only by the exclusive privileges of the selfish few, but also by the social divisions consequent on the indifference, disdain and exclusiveness towards the poor on the part of rulers who lacked a feeling of nationality. Equality and respect for the poor was not only an act of justice but the way to national political unity and was thus an act of patriotism. 'They would be loyal', said O'Connor, 'when they had something to be loyal to – when they had something in return for it; could they be loyal to a rattle-box, to a steam engine, a railroad, a Stock Exchange, or a palace? . . . there was patriotism, a higher word than loyalty, in those feelings [for the land] – there was love of country.' The materialism of the middle classes particularly threatened national unity and led to national decline. 'Their patriotism consists in money-getting and money-saving.'[16]

This distinctive concern for the poor among some radicals explains two apparent exceptions to the general radical negative attitude to the state and centralisation. There was a tendency for conservatives to support indirect taxation, including import tariffs, and for radicals to favour direct taxation. Some radicals disliked income tax because it made no distinction of sources of income, and preferred a property tax. While this seemed to embody an extension of the state, radicals not only saw indirect taxes as shifting the burden from the rich on to the poor (Gladstone's reduction of the burden of indirect taxation being a source of his popularity among them), and strongly opposed import duties on necessities such as corn, they also saw a reliance on tariffs for revenue as making the government the arena of corrupt pressure through competing selfish interests. There was thus a political, anti-government foundation for direct taxation and free trade as well as an economic one.

A national system of education was also a widespread radical aim. Education was a prime radical concern, as it made possible the opening of people's minds to the injustices and inequalities of society and thus could be a powerful means of change; rationalism would thus lead to reform and equality, while oppressive governments had a vested interest in ignorance, for 'education and moralisation render people wilful over accepting or supporting bad governments'.[17] Radicals engaged in a plethora of activities that they regarded as educational, including schools; and radical support for free, compulsory, non-denominational state education grew throughout our period, earlier in France, something that liberal devotees of popular schooling tended to baulk at. But the dangers of government-controlled 'Prussian' schooling were recognised, and in England, especially, there was a stress on local control. These two issues of progressive direct taxation and free, compulsory, non-sectarian, or secular national education tended to divide radicals from most liberals.

The five approved lecture topics of the Reform League were suffrage extension, ballot, British Constitution, taxation, and the Land Question. The land was a basic concern for radicals, because of the importance of landed wealth among the privileged classes, but its importance was much wider than that, and while the much greater concentration of land ownership in Britain meant there were far more attacks on the 'land monopoly' there, both British and French radicals were concerned at excessive immigration from the countryside into towns with consequent urban overcrowding and unemployment. Land should therefore be made available to the people, which would lead to much greater agricultural production and a more plentiful supply of food, and, by removing the 'surplus labour' from towns and manufactures, would reduce unemployment and competition for work and thus enable wages to rise. Support for common ownership or land nationalisation was much more widespread in Britain than in France, with its extensive peasantry, but most advocates of land nationalisation did not conceive of collective agriculture but of its being let out in small plots.

Nevertheless, for most radicals the sources of injustice and inequality were political. Wealth and privilege were due to political power that enabled its holders to live parasitically off the proceeds of taxes and other levies on the people, the useful and industrious part of the population. The 'people', the 'servile classes', created riches for 'the legions of royal leeches, aristocratic vampyres, sacerdotal slugs, and usurious locusts who prey upon the enslaved labour of England', so that 'the real contest will be, between those who pay taxes, and those who receive them'.[18]

### Action by the people

Support for full democracy and reforms to benefit the poor in particular is not the same as actually associating and campaigning with the common people, and it was often this rather than different ideas that distinguished some radicals from others. Those that aimed their message at the poor found a potential support in long-standing popular hostility to taxes (especially those on necessities), conscription, and usury. The biggest protest of all in France was the campaign in 1849 against the restoration of duties on drink, the petitions gaining six and a half million signatures. Some radicals thus looked to popular action as the means of gaining radical reform. This did not necessarily mean support for mass action, but the 'mass platform' strategy was established in Britain in the post-war radical agitation, while in France it was only after the 1830 revolution that younger republicans looked to the common people instead of attempting to seize power in a *coup* to gain a radical republic. Later the radical *Réforme* and *National* and others of the opposition press took advantage of the widespread subsistence riots of 1846–7 to launch a political campaign for universal suffrage.

The hope of achieving radical reform through popular action was often connected with a rejection of the characterisation of the masses as uncivilised and with a belief that the poor, or urban workers, or artisans, were more honest, virtuous, and moral than those above them. Christian themes and the Romantic and Rousseauist discovery and glorification of the People and its folklore were important influences here, with their stress on the dignity of simple folk and simple toil and a sense that workers, in their poetry, songs and struggles, obeyed simple instincts, uncorrupted by worn-out and cynical civilisation. It was thus logical to look to the poor to check corruption and centralisation of power in the corrupt metropolis. Thus the strand of radicalism that this book is concerned with is that which championed the interests of all, 'of the whole of society, of all members of society, of the whole people, of the workers at least as much as that of the idler',[19] which sought out the poor and pursued radical reform through popular action.

This, then, was the corpus of ideas and grievances of radicalism in England and France, not a systematic or coherent single doctrine, but a set of attitudes and beliefs held in different combinations and the source of disagreements. These themes included the vote to all men in a democratic state; reduction of government expenditure and taxation; a shift from indirect taxes on consumption to direct ones on wealth; opposition to standing armies and preference for a universal citizen militia; opposition to the state church; and support for basic freedoms of opinion, speech, press, association, and meeting. In France, with its larger state apparatus, there was more stress on the numbers and salaries of public servants, and questions of national defence were more acute. British radicals were more likely to advocate common ownership of the land, but these were in a minority, and the idea of settling the urban poor on waste lands to give them self-reliance and self-respect and reduce the urban labour surplus was strong in both countries. Radicals condemned privileged groups wielding political power, including not only aristocrats, landowners and prelates, but also business groups such as City of London financiers, the 'financial aristocracy' of the July Monarchy, railway magnates, bankers, and ironmasters, for example Hudson, Talabot, or Schneider. Radicalism contained a strong anti-state element, and wished not so much to establish new state institutions to take on new responsibilities as drastically to reduce the scope of government and state. Radicals tended not to see politics as a permanent, on-going activity involving manoeuvring, clashing, compromising interests, but to see reform as once-for-all negative changes and the implementation of justice. They saw themselves as part of an historical story of struggle, condemned the sufferings of the poor, looked forward to a free and united nation, saw the progress of knowledge as having a crucial role, and extolled the virtues of unity but also often sought popular action and mobilisation to achieve the reforms necessary for national unity and harmony. Despite the many common themes found on both sides of the Channel, radicalism was characterised by variety, and by divisions, although these were less over theoretical principles than tendencies, over the targets of concern and strategy, the relative weight of a focus on privilege, how far privilege was defined in economic terms, the commitment to democracy, the extent of the liberal freedoms sought, a specific concern with the poor, and over the seeking of political change through the common people themselves or through mass action. Moreover, radicalism was not just a matter of ideas but was also practice, and practice depended not only on inclinations but also on the political situation. The levels of freedom or repression profoundly affected the forms and timing of radical action; disillusion and disappointment at reformers who gained office led to breakaway radical campaigns and organisations; and radicals more often reacted to than created widespread political excitement, conflict or crisis. An understanding of radicalism is impossible without considering the wider political context.

## Revolutionary traditions

The radical tradition in Britain at the start of our period was also one of action – participation in elections, election pledges, public mass meetings, simultaneous meetings, tax refusals, runs on the banks, and general strikes – all considered by the Chartists. Most of these were also advocated in France, but it is here that the greatest contrast between the two seems apparent, in the famous French revolutionary tradition. France experienced not only revolutions in 1830 and 1848, but also several risings, as well as the various secret societies engaged in conspiracies in the intervening period. Unlike Britain, there were also rival plausible regimes competing for allegiance: legitimist, Orleanist, republican, and Bonapartist. But these enormous differences do not justify a bald characterisation of British radicalism as 'reformist' and French as 'revolutionary', the dichotomy itself being dubious and unhelpful.

In both Britain and France radicals claimed there was no obligation to obey laws in whose making they had had no say, that political systems not emanating from the will of the people lacked legitimacy, that resistance to assaults on their rights was justified, and that the sovereign people had the right to change the political system whenever they chose. 'A NATION never can rebel.'[20] Theoretical justification of revolution is, of course, not the same as engaging in it, and here France and Britain radically diverged. But revolutionaries actually played little part in the fall of the regimes in 1830, 1848 and 1870, while support for an alternative regime did not usually involve insurrectionary activity, although it did weaken loyalty to existing regimes. Revolutionaries and conspirators did play a role in the risings of 1832 in Paris and of 1834 in Paris and Lyons, but those of June 1848, June 1849, and December 1851 were in *defence* of the republic gained in February 1848.

The French secret societies are certainly a distinctive feature of French radicalism, but are to be explained not in terms of a revolutionary tradition but of the political situation. Under the Restoration, liberals joined secret societies, but when the July Revolution restored liberty of expression, radicals then engaged in open activity and propaganda. Public hostility, the conservative direction of the governments from 1831 and consequent clamp-down on radical political activity made radical and republican activity more secret, but it was the severe repression after 1834 that made open republican agitation no longer possible, and the result was secret societies. But at the same time Raspail, who had opposed revolutionary conspiracies in the early 1830s, set out in his journalism to identify republicanism with universal suffrage and not plot, insurrection, conspiracy, violence, or anarchy, and this stress on republicanism as liberty and fraternity for all was continued by Michelet and Lamartine. The failure of secret societies by 1840 and the greater freedom of speech and the press led to republican participation in more open activity, such as for parliamentary reform.

With the 1848 revolution, all republican societies and groups became open again, in the form of political unions or *clubs*, the Society of the Rights of Man being refounded as 'the peaceful continuation of the armed struggle'.[21] Thus Auguste Blanqui, a prominent radical since 1827, whose non-involvement in the 1834 rising left him, after the subsequent round-up, an unchallenged leader, became the chief figure in new secret societies planning seizures of power, that culminated in a disastrous attempt in 1839. Yet in 1848 one of the chief political clubs was Blanqui's Central Republican Society, for Blanqui, although exceedingly suspicious of the new authorities, to the extent even of wishing to exclude some members, and being very sensitive to the dangers to the new Republic from hostile officials, the army, and from the influence of the clergy and gentry over the rural population, was in this new situation no longer a conspirator and he exerted himself against sectarianism and in favour of a united front of all true radicals. His demands were complete democracy, complete freedom of speech, press, and association, repeal of all laws against trade unionism, admission of all unemployed to paid service in the National Guard, dismissal of all judges and magistrates of the former regime, and postponement of elections. His club was, in fact, one of the most open of all, allowing complete freedom of expression, and even when he was back in prison he supported Nadaud's parliamentary opposition.[22]

But after the June Days a steady increase in repression, which reduced political freedom to less than that under the July Monarchy, destroyed the public life of radicalism and drove it to privacy and clandestinity again, and the small, local, secret society became the main form of radical organisation, though this time over a far wider area of France than ever before. This secrecy was not a sign of exclusiveness or insurrectionism, merely a pragmatic response. After June 1849 these radical groups were part of a constitutional, extra-parliamentary opposition to the anti-republican legislature, government, and authorities, stressing legalism and reverence for the Constitution, and, while prefects were clearly in favour of provoking disorders, these groups urged a calm response to repression and a reliance on the vote, and confidently pinned their hopes on the 1852 election. Only with the new electoral law of May 1850 which ended universal suffrage by depriving three million working men of the vote through a stringent residential qualification, did some societies begin to work for an armed rising. But most republicans continued to await 1852 and avoid any excuse for repression. The president's *coup d'état* in 1851 brought methodical and massive repression, and the police state not only prevented all open political activity but also crushed nearly all secret societies, and there was very little support for conspiratorial revolution.

In fact the usual concept of revolution was very similar in France and Britain, not a planned insurrection or conspiracy with the date fixed in advance, but a reactive move in response to government attack, a spontaneous and not organised event. This, of course, was what characterised the revolutions of 1830 and 1848. A revolution would be collective spontaneous resistance to a particularly outrageous action by the authorities, and radical revolutionaries would therefore not organise a confrontation, but be united, armed, and ready to act when the time came. A member of the Rights of Man, interrogated after the 1834 rising, explained that their model was the recent 1830 revolution: 'today as then We counted on the mistakes of the Government, events and the chance of fate which could Serve us, as they served the Society *aide-toi le ciel t'aidera*.'[23] The same concept predominated in Britain, and the emphasis in the early, most excited phase of Chartism, in 1838–9, when an atmosphere of physical force predominated in some areas, was on mass mobilisation through open, confrontationalist, intimidating mass meetings, not on secret proceedings, and this was following an established radical strategy.

The general concept of revolution did not include conspiracies and it is important not to equate the two, or use the small numbers of actual conspirators in Britain as an index of the extent of revolutionary feeling. The general pattern in those peak years of radical activity – 1817, 1819, 1839, 1848 – was the same: an open, mass, confrontationalist campaign based on ever-growing enthusiasm through public meetings, with a constant expectation of violent attack; the puncturing of this enthusiasm and a rapid decline; a retreat by most of those who remained active radicals into educational or cultural activities and into support for political prisoners, with a small minority going instead into secret conspiracies planning an uprising or *coup*. Conspiracies thus only appeared late in the day as a reaction to defeat, decline, and repression, and involved small numbers, most of the revolutionary feeling having been earlier. The distinction between conspiracies and revolution was also stressed by Cavaignac and Cabet in France. The latter's Icarian movement in the 1840s was tolerated by the police because of its unambiguous emphasis on wholly peaceful means, but this was not a disavowal of revolution. What Cabet combated was not revolution but secret societies and conspiracies, and it was his assessment in 1846 that there was no chance of a revolution, because of the construction of forts around Paris, that led to his decision to leave France with his followers for the New World.[24]

The readiness of radicals to envisage a violent revolution was predicated on a belief that the authorities were not only repressive but also violent and weak. Despite their occasional verbal violence, radicals themselves were not very violent, and by the 1840s most of them opposed capital punishment. But the violence of the authorities meant that a complete commitment to seeking reform through peaceful means alone was not possible, for they might still be attacked. No radical who was engaged in political campaigning could therefore disavow violence. Memories of Peterloo reinforced this in England, where any repressive act at a peak time of excitement or agitation was seen as the start of a 'reign of Terror', and French radicals saw the Rouen 'massacres' in 1848 in the same light. The government's ban on a Reform League demonstration in Hyde Park in 1866 was seen as an attempt to provoke a riot to justify repression, and at the height of excitement in April-May 1867 the *Commonwealth* thought bloodshed and revolution likely, especially when a Hyde Park meeting was again forbidden.

If we mistake not, the Government has determined to stake its future on the result of a single issue, and of that issue we have little doubt and small concern. Let but a single drop of blood shed on Monday next, and, if we are not mistaken, the word will go forth, that such blood must be avenged. We at least shall be prepared to admit that the reign of terror has commenced and must be played out.[25]

The most popular republican journalist in France in the early 1830s, Cabet, recognised that 'we are only too sure of having to defend ourselves', but like his British counterparts he warned against provoking a clash and advocated waiting to wage a defensive war against 'the inevitable aggression of the authorities'; as the government became more violent, more and more people would be alienated. A Marseilles republican explained in 1834 that they had not been planning a clash: 'his observations and reading newspapers had convinced him that a conflict in which the Government would be the aggressor could begin sooner or later: he said this was why it was necessary to prepare people for an attack, which he was far from wishing to provoke'. The Chartist exile in France, M'Douall, conveyed the same message: 'we only recognise the right of *resistance*, which is the right to life: we want neither conspiracy nor riot; we stand on the *defensive*; and if our Aristocracy attacks us, we shall be in a position to crush it through the national will'.[26] This strategy necessitated the acquisition of arms, but only for use against attack, for 'violence must never be our weapon, unless compelled – unless driven to absolute desperation – and *then* only to be employed in *resisting* violence'.[27] The widespread Chartist open talk in 1839 of 'physical force' was nearly always in a defensive context.

Whatever the nature of the showdown, it would be short. The

basically negative view of the nature of politics fostered the conception, not of a long drawn-out struggle, but of a rapid, once-for-all implementation of justice. Since the corrupt system had no strength but itself, there could not be much resistance to a united people, and any struggle between tax-eaters and tax-payers would be short and sharp, especially if the troops would not act against the people. Thus advocates of, and participants in, insurrection did not actually expect to have to do much fighting. 'Physical force could not be carried out until the united voice of the people proclaimed that the time was coming for it, and then there would be no need to resort to it.' In the 1851 rising, 'the "authorities" would be swept aside with impunity. The rights of the people were about to triumph everywhere in France.'[28]

Thus British and French radicals had a broadly similar conception of revolution, and the occurrence of revolutions and risings in France was not due to a distinctive radical tradition but to different circumstances. More important than a revolutionary tradition was a revolutionary situation after the fall of a regime. The aftermath of the 1830 and 1848 revolutions was confused, with initially insecure regimes and everything put into question. Inevitably, many were disappointed at the extent of the changes that occurred, especially as in 1848 the new Provisional Government saw its role as a purely caretaker one until the Constituent Assembly should meet, any reforms being extracted from it unwillingly. In both years the new governments wanted to check the extent of democratisation, and the result was growing radical disillusion and bitterness at the fruits of the revolution and the meagre benefits to the common people. More important, however, was the fear of the continued power of the adherents of the previous regime and their desire to overthrow the new one. The Lyons radical, Joseph Benoit, recalled that as early as the third day after the 1848 revolution there were fears of a reactionary attack on the town hall.[29] Such fears led to calls for a purge of all servants of the previous regime, the death penalty for the ministers of Charles X for their treason against the nation so as to strike a death-blow against the legitimists and end political uncertainty, or the adoption of the red flag in 1848 to mark a complete break with Orleanism and prevent the establishment by the Provisional Government and old National Guard of a Regency under the Duchess of Orleans. These fears were compounded, especially in 1830–2, by expectations of invasion by foreign reactionary powers to undo the revolution, and led to condemnations of the weakness of the new governments and their failure to secure the new regime against enemies at home and abroad. Worried radicals therefore demanded an armed mass mobilisation of the people to defend the regime in a universal and democratic National Guard, as had happened to some extent in 1815 and was to happen again in 1870–1. One of the chief political issues in 1848 was control of armed power. The 17 March demonstration in Paris arose out of a campaign, led by Blanqui, to secure the sending of all troops away from Paris, the arming of the people, and a postponement of elections of new National Guard officers until everyone had been able to register in the Guard. In Lyons, two societies of silkworkers, the 'Voraces' and 'Unionistes' became workers' militias and occupied the forts overlooking the city so as to make the revolution safe.

At the same time other groups desired a return to security, order and normality, and were alarmed at the arming of the common people, and the result was a hardening of political positions between moderates and radicals. The increasing caution of the government in response to this reaction led to radical suspicions and accusations of bad faith, and in 1848 a fear of being tricked again, as in 1830. As radicals sensed they were failing they became more hostile to the government, becoming republican in the early 1830s, while in both the demonstrations on 17 March and 16 April 1848 there were elements seeking a purge of the government. Their increasing desperation provoked a further reaction. While radicals feared counter-revolutionary plots, moderates feared a radical *putsch*, and growing repression both embittered radicals and alienated others from the regime.

Yet at the same time the revolutions had created a permissive situation in which all sorts of antagonisms and grievances were allowed expression. The result was unrest and disturbances over food prices, taxes, tolls, forest-rights, railways, machines, wages, and hours of work. Especially important were the agitations among urban workers, above all in the capital, who shared in the initial euphoria over prospects of change but agitated in support of specific and limited aims, mainly wages and hours. Despite the moderate nature of these demands they were not well received by governments seeking economic recovery and re-establishment of order, especially as the revolutions had damaged business confidence and worsened the depression, and they called on the workers for patience and sacrifice. Much of the general population also wanted the government to end demonstrations and get the economy going again, and blamed workers and radicals for the continuing uncertainty. Workers' disappointment and anger at this negative response to their limited and practical demands fuelled suspicion of, and hostility to, the authorities. Closer links were therefore established between radicals and workers' organisations. In the June of 1848 excitement and alarm reached fever pitch,[30] and measures to check the growing demonstrations and gatherings further inflamed feelings, but an actual revolt needed an event that seemed a threat to all workers, however diverse, and this came with the order to dissolve the National Workshops.

These had been established in Paris and other cities as a refuge for unemployed workers, on the model of earlier charity workshops that were regularly opened in periods of unemployment, as in 1812, 1817, and 1830 in Paris, and 1830 and 1837 in Lyons. As in 1830, they also became centres of disorder when attempts were made to check recruitment, reduce pay, replace day-work with piece-work or close them down entirely. The June Days in Paris were also accompanied by a rising in Marseilles provoked by attacks on the ten-hour day in the national workshops there.

In England it was elections and withdrawal of public relief that were the two chief occasions for disorder. Threats to unemployed relief provoked disturbances, most dramatically and extremely in the late 1830s in opposition to the New Poor Law and its abolition of relief to paupers except in the workhouses, but they occurred also at other times. There were riots in Burnley in 1842 and 1878, when relief was not given, but not in the distress of 1852–3 and 1857–8, when policy was generous. The calm of Lancashire in 1857, when there was no attempt to restrict relief, contrasted with the disturbances in London in that year over attempts to cut down on relief, but there was violence in parts of Lancashire when the Poor Law Board tried to limit local relief in 1847, 1853, and, above all, in 1863, when the Ashton and Stalybridge riots provoked fears of a rising. As in the June Days, these riots did not consist mainly of people actually receiving relief. The same two issues, elections and withdrawal of relief, were also the main occasions for disorder in France in 1848.[31]

Thus the *withdrawal* (not absence) of a right to relief was likely to provoke resistance and disorder in both England and France. This is not to say that the June Days were just another riot over relief, for they were clearly on a different plane, but it is to stress that the key factor was the political situation in the aftermath of revolution, not any insurrectionary tradition. Rebels believed that, in attacking the last remaining gain secured for the poor after the February revolution, the reactionaries and royalists in the Assembly and the government were seeking to overthrow the Republic and provoke civil war. Important in legitimising this resistance was the fact that the National Guard itself split, those in eastern Paris supporting the protests and even fighting on the side of the insurgents.

Nevertheless, these views on revolution did change during the period. The defeat of the Chartists in 1839 and their strategy of intimidation through the mass platform and open talk of physical force, was a chastening one. The power of the state was clear, the troops stayed loyal, Chartists were imprisoned, and simplistic ideas of unplanned spontaneous uprisings were discredited. The whole rhetoric of Chartism changed, physical force was disavowed, and there were no more armed meetings. As the (Scotch) Chartist exile M'Douall told French readers:

Like a host of other Englishmen, I believed formerly that violence was necessary; but experience has shown me the madness and peril of conspiracy and riot; and I am now convinced that argument and reason are stronger than sword and cannon . . . The national will is the true sovereign. Violent struggle is a *game of chance*, and in this game the advantage lies always with the Government, which has organisation and concentration.[32]

In France, optimism over mass and armed action lasted longer, and the easy victory of February 1848 and radical successes in the 1849 general election (their failure to secure a majority attributed merely to the outlawing of political clubs, and government and police pressure in the elections) fed radical confidence in another victory when the troops would join the people. The easy defeat of the June 1849 risings in Paris and Lyons and the subsequent brutal repression cowed both cities and ended their illusions. June 1849 was the last attempt by the Second Republic radical opposition to achieve political victory through action on the streets, and henceforth they relied on legal and constitutional means. The urban protests against the *coup d'état* in 1851 were *unarmed* ones, and it was in rural areas in the south that armed protests occurred, but these armed demonstrations and military columns were not preceded by any military training or drilling and were really like village processions and did not envisage serious fighting. The outcome was so disastrous that the radical insurrectionary myth of the people in arms was finally discredited, rebellions and nearly all secret societies ceased despite the widespread bitterness against the regime, and the chief form of rural collective action was henceforth to be the *unarmed* demonstration.[33]

There was thus a change in radicalism in our period, away from armed protest and expectations of a short, armed clash in which the people would prevail, towards a greater appreciation of the power of the state, in 1839 in England and Wales, 1849 in the French cities, and 1851 in the French countryside.

Surviving Chartists took part in the formation in London of the Reform League in the mid-1860s. The rejection of even the moderate Liberal Reform Bill was followed by the accession of a Conservative government, whose action to prevent a League meeting in Hyde Park provoked clashes and an enormous reaction in both London and the provinces to this invasion of the people's rights. This led to a new era of mass public meetings, advocacy of a national convention ('people's parliament') and general strike, and talk of confrontation, of forcing the government to grant reform, of its wish for a showdown, and of revenge for any spilling of blood.[34] What did not take place was armed meetings, and the contrast with the atmosphere in 1839 was very great indeed. 1848 had also seen some mass meetings, arming and drilling, but the difference between 1848 and 1867 was the European situation in the former year, worry over which led to extensive arrests and then armed insurrectionary conspiracies. There were not the same widespread arrests in 1867 and the movement led not to total defeat but to a sort of success, and there were therefore no revolutionary conspiracies (although the question of Fenian violence later in the year did cause dissensions).

The disastrous repression by the French police state after 1851 destroyed the radical movement there, and so the most hated of all the regimes in the period experienced the least insurrectionary activity. Open republican political opposition to the regime revived in 1863, to reach a climax in the excited and extreme public meetings in Paris from 1868–70, when a sick emperor with a minor as heir led to a sense that the end of the regime was near. At these meetings, open-air demonstrations, and street disorders there were denunciations of the regime's illegal origins and, especially from March 1869, calls for violence and insurrection, but, despite brutal repression and even the arrest of the chief radical leaders in 1870, radicals generally worked to check the riots which the police were trying to provoke so as to justify repression, and the public meetings quietly ended.

A study of radical ideas, through pamphlets, newspaper articles, and (often edited) reported speeches, produces a picture of broad uniformity in democratic radical ideas throughout the period, and because so much of radicalism consisted of expounding ideas and arguments with opponents, artisan radicalism can easily be seen as the derivative absorption of such established ideas. Yet radicalism was also characterised by divisions and tensions over the degree of emphasis on privilege, democracy, the extending of liberal freedoms, the plight of the poor, and the seeking of changes through the actions of the common people. Undue concentration on the content of political programmes is wrong because radical activity consisted not only of expounding and canvassing ideas, but also of strategic alliances and choices, and political programmes did not alone determine political allegiances. It is not enough to focus on radical ideas as if they alone reveal the nature or essence of radicalism. Chartist assessments of the prospects of success could change very rapidly and drastically, and a narrow focus on the details of Chartist demands and analyses can miss the enormous, even millenarian, sense of confidence and hope in 1839 and 1842. Radical artisans certainly drew on and responded to a medley of familiar and enduring radical ideas, but they could still interpret them differently and have their own specific concerns and readings. The possibility and identity of particular artisan attitudes, values, interests, modes of behaviour, and understandings of the world may be approached through what would seem to be the most basic form of artisan activity and organisation, most closely tied to their position as artisans, most faithfully and directly reflecting their fundamental concerns and distinctiveness – trade unionism.

# 3  Trade unionism

In an approach that sees artisan radicalism as a response to working-class life, an important place is given to trade unions, as the classic institutions of the world of work. But this is not straightforward, for the multiplicity of actions, organisations, and functions that can be subsumed under the term 'trade unionism' makes generalisations very difficult, and, while the enduring importance of workplace activities and industrial action is evident, we must not assume that formal organisations had always the same concerns and functions as informal action, or that they were direct emanations from the workplace or working communities. What a study of these forcefully reveals is divisions and hierarchies in the workforce, and hostilities and conflicts between organisations, none of them obvious sources of strength for radicalism.

The essential starting-point in looking at trade unionism is the diversity and precarious existence of the working population, the male sector alone full of what were often antagonistic divisions between peasants, servants, labourers, masters, supervisory and clerical staff, and settled and mobile workers, and the urban trades themselves characterised by virtually permanent insecurity. Learning a trade was only done on the job, from experienced workmen through oral transmission, precept, and example. Finding and then keeping employment was not easy in a world of small units without long, steady runs of orders, so that men were not permanently employed by the same master but were taken on for short periods. While steady employment in a single firm over a long period of time might occur in some new industries, irregularity of employment was the norm, so much so that artisans often purposely worked for more than one employer. 'I always liked to have "two strings to my bow", and at that season full employment from one shop was not to be depended on.'[1] Constant changes of employment meant constant search for employment and loss of earning time. Levels of employment could fluctuate with the weather, the season (for nearly every trade had brisk and slack seasons), and the trade cycle. Accident and illness were ever-present menaces to the ability to earn, the arrival of children usually reduced the wife's earnings, while the approach of old age meant a decline in earnings, poverty, and often disaster. 'We are all', wrote the shoemaker James Devlin, 'in quest of the golden apple of security.'[2]

'Jem' Devlin himself, one of the very best boot-closers in early nineteenth-century London, able to do sixty stitches to an inch by hand, nevertheless experienced periods of great poverty, and died in a parish workhouse,[3] for skilled artisans were by no means protected from a life of hard material existence or chronic insecurity, nor were they necessarily better off than other workmen. A London baker, during a period of unemployment, took riverside work unloading wheat and was paid 8s 2d for a day's work, 'the highest sum I ever received in one day for hard labour', and the shoemaker O'Neill took a chandler's shop to be free of the endless drudgery of the seat.[4] 'Often good artisans (*ouvriers*), ruined and worn out by employment and loss of time caused by too frequent discharges (*livraisons*), leave the trade and become shopmen so as to have a secure wage.'[5]

A key factor in access to learning a trade was the role of relatives and family contacts in securing apprenticeship, this being by far the most important contribution a father could make to his son's future. 'We remember in our youth hearing fathers boast with something like honest pride that they had nothing of this world's gear to bequeath to their sons, but at least they had *that* which would *always* enable them to get an honest living – their father's trade at their finger ends.'[6] But this, of course, did not guarantee security of employment thereafter, and relatives, friends, and other contacts remained important in securing work, as did links based on area of origin or nationality. In such segmented labour markets, it was common for artisans to try to limit training to members of their families, the Paris pressmen being particularly successful,[7] and for groups to seek exclusive monopolies and control in certain firms. Norman stone-cutters tried to exclude all others from the Paris yards in which they worked, and hostilities between members of different nationalities or from different regions or even villages meant that in several Paris trades masters preferred to employ homogeneous labour forces.[8] In 1853 tailors struck at a firm in Paris for the right to choose who would be hired.[9] Such attempts to corner employment in a particular area were a response to poverty and insecurity, an aspect of that jealousy and division that characterised the world of labour.

There were divisions between artisan trades in the same industry, such as in printing, between compositors and pressmen, or in building. 'During the meal-hours the best fun was to hear the masons telling tales at the expense of the joiners. These in turn would have a go at the bricklayers or plasterers, while all hands relished a poke at the plumbers.'[10] There were divisions between different sections of the same trade, of gender and religion as well as nationality, and powerful antagonisms in such trades as tailoring, between 'indoor' workmen in the workshops and 'outdoor' workers at home (this was also partly a gender difference).[11] But there were also divisions within the workshop. The foreman looked down on the rest, the mechanic on the labourer, while masons despised the rough wallers (*limousins*) and would not eat with them.[12] In the tailoring shops the more skilled cutter was an elite workman, better paid and feeling superior, 'for he has the privilege, excessive in this trade, of being employed all the year and having less tiring work'.[13] The distinction between more stable and more casual workmen was important. In mid-century Paris there were about 1,500 whitesmiths (*ferblantiers*), of whom only a third were regularly employed; the rest, 'usually summoned as assistants when there is a hurry to meet an order, were discharged as soon as they were not needed. Always in search of work, they run from shop to shop, and sometimes from one town to another. This instability, entering their behaviour, has made part of the whitesmiths veritable nomads.'[14] There were divisions of age and seniority. Apprentice lads, particularly in their early years were treated by the men as servants or drudges, their life often a total misery.[15] Even after they finished their time, they often continued to suffer at the hands of their seniors. In French building yards older workmen rarely allowed young 'foxes' or 'spews' near them, kept the best work for themselves, and made the young ones do the work in the suburbs or out of town, while among Manchester building workers, it was only the wages of new hands that were reduced in the winter.[16]

And yet a very strong male camaraderie could also develop at the workplace, close relations established, workshop slang absorbed. 'We have always been surprised at the ease with which the workmen form friendships with one another. If you hire a workman on Tuesday, on Saturday he is tutoying all the fellow-workmen in his team; note that they did not know one another before.'[17] These relations were often regulated and enshrined in workshop rules and customs, related rather to rites of passage than to actual work, such as the often coarse celebration of a workman's marriage, the frequently burdensome 'footings' and *bienvenues* paid by lads coming out of their time (finishing their apprenticeship) or by new arrivals in the shop, which mainly took the form of buying drinks for the rest, although among bookbinders a new arrival experienced a rebirth through being given a new name and christened with his head in a pail.[18] The use of nicknames stressed the separation of the group from strangers. There were fines for transgressions, the proceeds of these and of collections often going to workmen in difficulties. This camaraderie was thus not necessarily based on shared economic 'interests', the solidarities not necessarily about work itself, for as the engineer Thomas Wright wrote, work itself was not the main element in workshop life:

> There are traditions, customs, and usages interwoven with, and indeed in a great measure constituting, the inner and social life of workshops, a knowledge of which is essential to the comfort of those whose lot is cast amongst them, as technical proficiency is necessary to obtaining or retaining employment. To these unwritten, but perfectly understood and all-powerful laws of workshop life, all workingmen – whatever may be their private opinion – must in some degree bow.[19]

Workmen thus had to fit into the general outlook and mentality. A shipwright in the north of England or a stonemason in Birmingham would be fined 'for coming to his work on a Monday with an unclean shirt', while bookbinders at a London shop sent a man to Coventry for reading a book instead of playing cards on a Monday, and there was always pressure on men to drink.[20] In Paris 'the *curriers* also know when hands are needed in a workshop through the continuous links that they have with one another and hiring is, in general, solely a matter of camaraderie; the workman who has not won the good will of his fellow-workmen, whether in not sharing their amusements or through defects in his character, remains unemployed in normal times and only finds work when *currying* business is brisk'.[21]

Yet unity in the workplace was precarious and fragile, and in any case often contributed to wider disunity, being based, as we have seen, on exclusion of, for example, non-relatives, strangers, foreigners, other religions, females, or 'prigs', while the radical Jules Leroux deplored the hostility between the workmen of different printing workshops in Paris.[22] It is in this context of insecurity and disunity that we can locate the various forms of organisation that artisans developed.

### Trade societies

The most widespread organisations were friendly or benefit societies (*sociétés de secours mutuels, sociétés de prévoyance, sociétés de bienfaisance, caisses de secours*). These addressed fundamental concerns of working men – loss of livelihood through accident or sickness, the disaster of old age, the deeply felt need for a decent funeral when one died, and a feeling of repugnance towards begging or seeking public relief.[23] Common features were limited membership, regular subscriptions, relief for sickness or injury, obligations to visit sick members in turn, grants toward and attendance at funerals of members, refusal of relief if injury or sickness were in some way the member's own fault, such as through drunkenness, fighting, or venereal disease, pensions, and the keeping of funds in a strong box with three locks, the keys held by three different people to prevent theft. Many were small and actuarially unsound, and the provision of pensions was a particular drain on finances, so sometimes there was a separate fund, which might only grant as many pensions as the funds could stand.[24]

To an extent, benefit societies were built on informal workplace activities, for it was very common to make collections or levies when a workmate was sick or injured, died or lost his wife, or to relieve people out of work.[25] A number of workshops did have benefit funds for which a levy was made on wages, but these were of limited value as workmen lost the right to benefit if they left the firm, however much they had contributed, and they were often imposed by masters as a form of control. Independent benefit societies were a way of combating this, although masters might try to secure control of these also.[26] Benefit societies could be pretty informal affairs. After the *coup d'état* of 1851, Paris shoe clickers took to meeting every Saturday, after pay-time, with their wives, for drinks, and made a collection for anyone in the group who was sick. In 1858 a rule was adopted whereby the shopmates of any member of the group who fell sick sent a letter round the other shops seeking contributions. 'For sixteen years this Society has had no regulation beyond its members' hearts and no resources save in the spontaneity of its five hundred and eighty members, who meet every Saturday in some public place.' Each Saturday everyone paid seven sous, and the resultant 200 francs were divided among all those currently sick, on average between eight and fourteen.[27] Many formal benefit societies were simple extensions of these activities, frequently combining material benefits with conviviality, in the form of drink, dinners, or songs, and some periodically shared out their funds.[28]

Many benefit societies were confined to members of a single trade, but these were nevertheless a minority, especially in England, and were often limited to providing insurance for tools of the trade, or they were confined to those members of dangerous or noxious trades who were not admitted to other societies because they were a risk.[29] Most societies did not admit people in their forties, for the same reason.[30] Such exclusions and strict conditions for entry limited the societies' effectiveness in relieving distress; in the eyes of the Paris cabinet-maker, Tartaret, 'to gain admission to mutual insurance against sickness, one had to be in the position of never being sick'.[31] Many people could not afford to make regular contributions to a society. But they remained the chief working-class institution, especially for artisans. Membership of legally registered societies alone in England and Wales was a million and a half in 1850 and four million in 1872, and 800,000 in France in 1870, but many societies were not registered and the real figure was therefore much higher, perhaps half the adult male working population in England and Wales in 1850 and two-thirds in 1870.[32]

A second form of organisation was concerned with placement. Given the irregularity of employment, masters did not have a stable labour force but hired men as needed, and journeymen did not have a regular employer, so for many the day started with an often long and trying tour of workshops looking for work, although many, no doubt, had a round of masters they were accustomed to try, often working for more than one at a time.[33] In the mid-1850s the leading Paris compositor, Gauthier, worked out the shortest itinerary whereby compositors could take in all eighty printing firms.[34] In many French towns there were specific places where wallers, hodmen, and house-painters gathered to be hired, while particular public-houses or eating-houses (*gargotes*) were patronised by certain trades as social centres where one could find out about vacancies and work. The proprietors might act as employment agents, even exploitative ones, often in league with the foremen, these last taking full advantage of the ample scope for favouritism and bribery in hiring men and distributing work, as they favoured those who bought them drink or forced them to buy their beer from the houses with which they were linked.[35] In French cities exploitative private agencies forced people to register and pay a fee to have any chance of employment. To meet these problems: the difficulty in finding men and work, and the exploitation, artisans ran their own agencies.

The trade house of call, usually a public-house, was a universal feature, where members out of work entered their names on a book and waited; masters in need of men sent to the house for the number required, and these were sent according to the order on the book.[36] In Paris the boot and shoemakers in the 1840s and in 1867, and the bakers in 1848, made great efforts to suppress or supplant the particularly bad private employment agencies in their trades, and in the temporary liberation of 1848 many Paris trades set up their own houses of call.[37]

The success of such houses of call depended on acceptance by the masters, which depended on the convenience of a supply of workmen whose ability was guaranteed. Thus men whom masters complained of for inferior work or theft, would be punished or expelled. This acceptance was easiest among trades whose scarcity or high level of skill put them in a strong position, as with the Paris engineers, who had the most powerful house of call in 1848. The bargaining power of houses of call in trades such as tailoring or shoemaking could not be based on indispensable skill, only on convenience to masters, whereby men of guaranteed competence and, equally important, with the ability to work fast, could be supplied immediately at any time for a job in hand. Such clubs therefore had to guarantee to make good any defective work. The Sheffield tailors were typical, in that 'our Society guarantees to every Master employing our Members, that each Garment made by any of them shall be suitable for any Gentlemen's wear, or we hold ourselves responsible, as a Society, to the Employer for the amount charged by him for any such Garment, not finished in a workmanlike manner by any of our Members'.[38]

Houses of call could overlap with benefit societies, but they could also reflect some of the work divisions mentioned above. The hierarchy according to age or seniority was reproduced in English tailors' houses of call, which had two or three books in which out-of-work members signed, according to their level of seniority, and calls for men were met first from the first book, with the most senior members. This was partly because acceptance of the house of call by masters depended on there nearly always being men available, which was only possible if there was a pool of unemployed men. Thus by having a lot of people, too many in fact, on the books, and by always giving priority to senior members, the house could guarantee men although this really meant an under-employed pool in the interests of the privileged senior men.[39] Such houses also exhibited the tendencies to exclusion and monopoly that characterised the insecure world of labour. Just as the specialist newspaper compositors in London and Paris allowed no apprentices in their printing shops, and the latter were an especially closed group who maintained an exclusive monopoly of newspaper work, so in London there were societies of compositors and pressmen called 'Gifts' that were limited in size and helped members find work, with the aim of securing monopolies of work in their areas.[40] In the Parisian engineering works there were societies called *dizaines*, each limited to ten members, who prevented the employment of people they opposed, by violence if necessary.[41] London tailors' call-houses tried to corner the labour supply in certain firms. Such societies were thus composed of small minorities of the trade, and their nature meant they wished to remain small and had no desire to encompass the majority of the trade.

The best known and most elaborate of such societies were the French *compagnonnages*, old journeymen trade societies, federated in different Orders (*Devoirs*) with complex traditions and ceremonies; the Toulon turners' rule book dated from 1731. They had many familiar functions, notably arrangements to help travelling journeymen, benefits, and instruction in drawing, but one of the chief ones was finding work for members, and excluding non-members and members of rival orders. All such efforts naturally bred resentment and opposition, and the *compagnonnages* were especially renowned for their violent battles, as well as for their rituals and regalia.[42] In fact these aspects have probably been exaggerated. Certainly brawls (*rixes*) and even pitched battles did occur, a number of them involving shoemakers or bakers, who had formed compagnonnic lodges and whose right to do so was rejected by other societies. Fights between groups of young men, for example from different areas or streets, were commonplace, and not 'archaic',[43] but most compagnonnic brawls were in fact between rival societies in the same trade, or between members and non-members in the same trade, which makes them much nearer to the English model. The worst hostilities arose over societies' efforts to secure monopolies of employment.[44] Thus there were fierce fights among stone-cutters, between 'wolves' (*loups, compagnons étrangers*, children of Solomon) and 'were-wolves' (*loups-garous, compagnons passants*, members of the Devoir), and among carpenters, between *gavots* or Indians, of the Order of Liberty, and those in the Devoir, called 'jolly fellows' (*bons drilles*), *devoirants*, and *dévorants*.

As with other such societies and monopolies, masters might accept or be favourable to them, and even be current or ex-members, sometimes controlling local lodges.[45] But the main compagnonnic trades were in the building industry, and here the leading man in the yard, or *gâcheur*, was the key figure. If he belonged to a compagnonnic society, he would hire members and exclude others. Thus the key function of such *compagnonnages* was a monopoly of hiring and a control of recruitment. This did not have to mean 100 per cent membership in any yard. The two carpenters' Orders divided Paris between them, the Carpenters of Liberty working on the left bank of the Seine, the *devoirants* on the right, but in all yards there were also many non-members, *limousins*, working in subordinate roles. Thus the Devoir 'is composed of the top workmen in the workshops'. The essential aim was *control* of hiring by members of the society, many of whom hoped to go on to become masters themselves. Yet when some *limousins* worked at lower wages than the rest, they were excluded by the society men from the yards.[46] The key role of the *gâcheur* meant that Paris masters hardly ever knew the real names of their carpenters, only their society ones.[47] Foremen in other trades favoured societies in similar ways. When stonemasons were hired to build a viaduct for the Birmingham and London Railway, 'our late president and now member of the G Committee is to be foreman so you may guess what sort of men he will employ'.[48]

In the less skilled artisan trades, such as tailoring, boot and shoe-making, house-painting, or carpentry and joinery, where members were more vulnerable and easily replaceable, the tendency in the cities was for a number of small competing societies trying to control employment in an area or group of firms. London carpenters and tailors were divided into a multitude of small, rival call-houses, the rivalry being such that London tailors' call-houses provided strike-breakers for firms blacked by rival societies.[49] Paris joiners were divided not only into *gavots* and *devoirants*, but also into Independents and Aspirants of Beneficence; Paris shoemakers into the Laborious, Fraternity, New Era, and two compagnonnic societies; and Marseilles shoemakers into hostile *compagnonnages*, *sociétaires*, and Independents.[50] Blackburn had two rival painters' societies, and London a score.[51] But there were also rivalries between societies in more skilled trades that had regional federations, for example amongst the stone-cutters. English hatters were divided between the London-based 'Lillies' and the Lancashire-based 'Blue Blank', an enmity extending to the provision of strike-breakers; French hatters between a *compagnonnage* and the Good Children or 'Dro-gains'.[52] Similar rivalries occurred in the 1860s between the Friendly Operative House Carpenters and Joiners, or 'General Union of Carpenters', and the new Amalgamated Society of Carpenters and Joiners, and between the Manchester Unity of Bricklayers and the London Order of Bricklayers, each trying to exclude the rival from firms and towns, and entice branches.

Placement, then, could be the chief function of trade societies. 'They have enabled the working man to keep a more independent position than he would if he had only his own efforts to fall back upon, for by the system of trades combinations he can learn at any moment where to find the best market for his labour.'[53] In the first half of 1848 many Paris trades tried to establish monopoly employment agencies, forbidding members to seek work from a master directly. But it was a very divisive function, involving the exclusion of labourers, members of other trades, or members of the same trade. Paris coachmakers excluded Germans from their society, Manchester packing-case makers struck against the employment of members of a rival society, there were two antagonistic societies of coopers in Liverpool, and engineers everywhere were divided into a multitude of societies.[54] London bookbinders had three societies, and the Edinburgh society sent strike-breakers during the 1839 and 1849 London strikes; London compositors had two rival societies in the 1820s and 1830s, while in the 1850s two societies of Paris compositors battled to take over workshops and expel the foe; and the three societies of lithographic-printers in Paris engaged in pitched battles to exclude the others from workshops.[55] The more exclusive a society was, the more likely it was to provoke a rival, which is what happened among London bookbinders and Birmingham cabinet-makers.[56]

A third feature of trade societies, after benefits and placement, was tramping. Wandering journeymen were a centuries-old phenomenon, composed particularly of young men before they married, partly to complete their training, and many came to the capital for a few years. Working-class mobility was extensive anyway, and not necessarily voluntary, yet many did travel out of choice, 'from a mere errant disposition, or for pleasure'.[57] Some trades were particularly mobile, such as stonemasons or the 'essentially migratory' shoemakers.[58] A Wolverhampton shoemaker referred to 'that incessant shoal of moving shoemakers who were always passing through such towns'.[59] So mobile were shoemakers that wives often accompanied them on tramp.[60] Tramping was also a very common recourse during unemployment, as men wandered in search of work, so that in the depression of 1847 'our high roads have resembled that of a mechanical workshop, or a mighty mass of moving human beings'.[61] Tramping, then, was a well-established activity and, although declining in the 1860s, remained widespread, as was informal relief for tramps looking for work. Out of this developed more formal organisations, partly in an attempt to check fraud and establish the *bona fides* of tramps, through mutual agreements between local clubs and houses of call to relieve one another's members and set up proper systems of tramp-relief or *viaticum*. These wider organisations arranged transfers of funds between lodges, each of which provided tramping members with board, lodging, and help in finding work or, if none was available, money so as to be able to proceed to the next town. There were often set tramping itineraries, such as the *compagnonnages*' Tour of France.[62]

Tramping was an important aspect of trade unionism, and indeed could form the main aspect. Men could be directed to areas where there was a shortage of labour, it was a means of unemployment relief, and people on strike, instead of being paid strike pay, could go on tramp.[63] Most of the national 'unions' in such trades as hatters, stonemasons, coachmakers, basket-makers, cabinet-makers, engineers, bookbinders, or compositors were really tramping federations, as was the secret Philanthropic Society of Tailors operating in parts of France in the 1830s, while among boot and shoemakers tramping districts 'may be looked upon as the very props of our trade'.[64] As a form of relief it was less than ideal, as it meant a man leaving his family and walking long distances. The stonemason Henry Broadhurst spent five years travelling, and in the terrible winter of 1858–9 tramped 1,200 miles without finding any work at all.[65] Yet, despite persistent criticism, it could not be dispensed with, for merely local relief schemes tended to attract surplus labour from elsewhere, and the ambitious attempt by the National Typographical Association in the 1840s to replace tramping with unemployment relief led to financial collapse.[66]

Given the frequency of misunderstandings about piece-work rates, privileges, custom, and practice, a common recourse was arbitration by respected and experienced men, such as by the Thames shipwright Gast, the Paris pressman Garde and the City of London tailor Neal. A formalisation of this was the 'trade committee', acting as arbitrator or tribunal and pronouncing on cases and practices. Based on consensus among different groups in 'the trade' on the need for stability and common understanding, they could, even if composed wholly of journeymen, exert a wide degree of authority. But they did not *enforce* their judgements, nor seek to have all those in the trade as 'members'.[67] The strong desire for agreed rules and decisions, established negotiating bodies, and agreed forms of arbitration incorporated basic ideas of 'the regulation of the trade', and some societies looked back to the models of the old guilds. Price scales, especially for piece-work, or a minimum, agreed uniform rate for day-work, were seen as ways of avoiding endless disputes and checking competitive reductions. Prominent here were the compositors, who in the chief European cities had written scales agreed with representatives of the employers. The London scale dated from 1810, but the London Trade Society committee had problems of interpretation submitted to it nearly every week, and in 1833 the two rival societies established a Union Committee of six from each to act as a committee of final appeal and consultation on important questions, while in the 1840s Paris compositors gained great prestige from an agreed scale with the employers and a standing arbitrating body to which questions were referred.[68] Such scales also existed among, for example, the Sheffield trades and shipwrights, hatters, coopers, coachmakers, tailors, shoemakers, and cabinet-makers.

Ideas of 'boards of trade', consisting of equal numbers of representatives of masters and men to fix wages for the area, were common among handloom weavers and framework-knitters, and there were efforts to secure them by legislation, on the model of the old Spitalfields Acts, or by the democratisation of the French Courts of Arbitration.[69] The almost universal desire of the Paris trades in 1848 was for public agreements with the employers, and, in contrast to its original remit, the government-established Luxembourg Commission became engaged in arranging such agreements.

With the liberalisation of the Second Empire in the 1860s 'syndical chambers' arose in many artisan trades. These were small bodies, essentially trade committees seeking to act as arbitrators and negotiators, and not aiming to recruit everyone in the trade as members. The movement was also strong in England in the 1860s.[70]

Coupled with the internal regulation of the trade was its defence against outsiders, and one function of trade committees was to act as political lobbies on behalf of the trade. The Thames Shipwrights' Provident Union in 1824 built on the organisation involved both in the support of Queen Caroline in 1820–1 and in the campaigning against reductions in tariffs in 1823, and the new union continued to oppose the Reciprocity Treaties. The origins of a Liverpool coopers' society in 1842 lay in a campaign in favour of tariff duties on foreign casks, a cause it continued to press.[71] Yet the best example was the compositors. The first case of widespread political action by a French trade was the Paris compositors' protests at the 1826 press and printing bill. In the early 1830s, during the Second Republic, and in the 1860s they pressed for the removal of all restrictions on printing, while English compositors also campaigned against the 'taxes on knowledge'.[72] The origins of a number of trade organisations in 1848 and in the 1860s and 1870s lay in the organisation of the election of delegates to the Luxembourg Commission, the international exhibitions at London (1862), Paris (1867), Lyons (1872), and Vienna (1873), and the official Court of Arbitration.

With a typical English trade society, 'its meeting-place, or club-house, is generally neither more nor less than an ordinary public-house, where the members, over beer and tobacco, discuss the gossip of the trade'.[73] The meeting-house often held raffles or concerts for hard-up or ill brothers.[74] Houses of call, benefit societies, and lodges were important social and convivial centres, with drinking expected and allowed for, even to the extent of using society funds for the purpose. There were often rituals, regalia, and near-masonic ceremonies on initiation, meetings, or funerals, and sometimes special dress.[75] There were annual dinners and anniversary celebrations, such as that of the founding of the club, or the celebration by bookbinders all over England of the release from prison of the five London bookbinders in 1787, or the day of the patron saint, for example the printers' St John and, especially, the shoemakers' St Crispin.[76] Thus in 1840 a Lyons boot and shoemakers' society, thirty-five strong, spent in the year 536f. on relief, and 473f. 15c. on 'administrative costs' connected with the annual St Crispin's Day dinner.[77] But they were probably outshone by the English trade clubs with their concerts, raffles, brass bands, cricket clubs, libraries, indoor games, sports days, rowing clubs, and theatre benefits.

Annual dinners, celebrations, and fine funerals might seem wasteful to outside observers, but they also served the utilitarian function of attracting members, indeed it was claimed that the abolition by the London bookbinders' society of the regular lodge meetings and the annual dinner had led to a decline in membership.[78] The same is true of benefits. These were often a very important aspect of trade societies, but few had an extensive range of them, the Sheffield trades and the few large English 'amalgamated' societies being most untypical, the latter only managing superannuation benefit through a steady expansion of members to fund it. Some people did prefer sick, accident, and funeral benefits through trade organisations, as these were more flexible and sympathetic to trade-related illness and accidents than were the restrictive benefit societies, while insurance against loss of tools was usually through trade societies. Unemployment benefit, too, prevented unemployed men from taking work at lower rates, and local plasterers' societies were often referred to as out-of-work societies.[79] But proper unemployed relief, rather than tramping, was expensive and usually only possible in stronger societies of well-paid trades such as hatters, bookbinders, compositors, pianoforte-makers, engineers, and ironfounders.[80] It was usually only given in the slack season of the trade, as with the London tailors' 'vacation money' and the painters' 'winter funds', and the amount was often not fixed but varied according to the finances.[81]

Trade societies thus encompassed a range of functions – benefits and relief, placement, tramping, arbitration and rule interpretation, political lobby, and conviviality. These were functions that were not usually easily organised in the workplace itself, and were in fact performed *outside* the workplace, and they tended to be less important than workplace life and relations, on which they impinged little. Trade societies were thus neither part of, nor alternatives to, workplace activities, but back-ups to them. In this sense they did not grow directly out of the workplace, and since it was not obvious what were the boundaries of the 'trade' that the society was concerned with, trade societies were, in fact, composed of different groups of workers, with different and often conflicting work concerns and interests. Examples were vellum binders, the more skilled finishers, and the ordinary forwarders in bookbinding; compositors and pressmen in printing; railway carriage makers in coach-building; coopers and packing-case makers; wood and building gilders; stone-cutters and wallers; men's and women's shoemakers; stitchmen and shoe-riveters; and indoor and outdoor workers. The famous Amalgamated Society of Engineers contained engineers, machinists, millwrights, smiths, and pattern-makers. 'The trades incorporated in this society bear about the same relation to each other as do those of the bricklayer, carpenter, and stone-mason in the building trade.'[82] 'Trades' were in fact composites, socio-cultural constructs not spontaneous realities or economic givens.

Trade societies could also reflect the basic division between the settled, usually married workers, and the migratory, often unmarried ones. This was seen in the *compagnonnages*, which mainly catered for young, unmarried, travelling journeymen; benefit societies, including single-trade ones, were for sedentary workers. When men finished their Tour of France they usually withdrew from active membership of the *compagnonnages* (the chief exception being the nomadic stone-cutters), but might join a benefit society of ex-companions, such as the Paris carpenters' *agrichons*.[83] The Operative Stonemasons' Society was basically a tramping federation, and it found recruitment hampered by 'the great objection to becoming members, (the want of an immediate perceivable benefit) raised by those of our trade who are residents'.[84] Indeed it met opposition from societies of settled masons, which it often called 'blacks'. Thus Leeds masons established a 'Black Society' which did not assist any tramps, while in 1856 Bolton 'blacks' struck against members of the OSM, and in 1835 Northwich 'blacks' attacked the OSM club-house and fought a pitched battle ('Waterloo was nothing to it.')[85] The Pudsey shoemakers' society declined because it was a tramping society and held little attraction for local shoemakers, while in 1863 the Paris shoemakers' branch of the tramping Fraternal Alliance seceded and became a local society for settled workmen.[86] The frequent opposition in trade unions to tramping was presumably largely among settled workmen, who were particularly annoyed at supporting the number who went on tramp through choice, and there were attempts to limit tramp relief to unemployed workmen only.[87]

Trade societies might also reflect the hierarchies of the workshop. The division between senior and junior workmen was institutionalised in *compagnonnages* and, as we have seen, tailors' call-books, and the Clichy tailors' society in 1848 discriminated against the younger workers.[88] In the shoemakers' *compagnonnage* the local lodge was often run by senior men. 'These leaders are usually the oldest working companions who, retired to their homes or married in the area, still hang around the lodging. They unite and concert among themselves so that they easily dominate the views of the young companions, trusting their experience. Woe, then, to those they take a dislike to or who, not being always of their views, manage to displease them.'[89] Leading hands in building or ship-building, or clickers in printing, were often the natural leaders. Nathaniel Clarke was the leader in the 1820s of an elite, exclusive shipwrights' work-gang called the 'Royals', who tried to secure the best work for themselves, but when the Thames Shipwrights' Provident Union was formed in 1824, Clarke became president.[90] Foremen and even masters could often join trade societies, such as the Amalgamated Society of Engineers. All but two Bury master cloggers belonged to the local society and only employed members.[91] Foremen were often prominent in their societies, such as Newton in the Amalgamated Society of Engineers, Applegarth in the Amalgamated Society of Carpenters and Joiners, and Parmentier and Viez among the Paris compositors. In 1864 some bricklayers in Salford struck against a foreman who belonged to the same society as they.[92]

But while trade societies were mainly engaged in extra-workplace activities and played little direct part in workplace practices, which were mainly a workshop concern, so that most disputes and disagreements arose within the workshop, with cases of ca'canny and industrial action usually being workplace initiatives, members of a strong society were naturally more confident over asserting their 'rights' and resisting 'infringements'. The Operative Bricklayers' Society and other London building unions enabled their members on their own initiative to end the practice of payment of wages at pubs, and the attendant pressure to patronise the pub linked with master or foreman.[93] Thus societies could back up workplace efforts *initiated* by members there, particularly over wage reductions and the defence of wage scales, and seek to establish common policies, such as insisting no one be employed who had not served a proper apprenticeship or training, limiting the number of apprentices (a common cause of disputes), opposing piece-work or sub-contracting, or seeking uniform wage rates, hours or overtime rates. The English boilermakers' society had a rule that no man could take job-work without telling his shopmates and stating the price he was receiving.[94] In such cases members might be withdrawn from a firm which was declared 'black' and all members forbidden to work there. But much of the bargaining and pursuit of uniform policies was informal and independent of institutional organisation. Key figures such as the 'father' or 'dean' (*doyen*) of printing chapels, or the clicker in printing works, or the leading hands (*gâcheurs*) in building and ship-building, or an inner ring of more senior workmen, often operated with a large degree of autonomy and with little reference to the society.

This relative importance and autonomy of the workplace was compounded by the irregular and unstructured nature of many societies. In unions such as those of the Thames shipwrights and ship-joiners, the key men were the delegates in each yard, who dealt with matters without consulting the committee.[95] English compositors' societies were exasperated that many unemployed members did not sign on the call-books but went direct to printing works to beg for work.[96] The habits of fixed and rigid rules, prompt attention to business, and recognition of authority from above were hard to learn.[97] But as long as the decisions were accepted, there was no need for a very strong trade union organisation, indeed they might be a substitute for it. The Paris paper-stainers had no formal society but 'in the paper trade, it is owing to the solidarity between workmen that has existed since 1826 that the piece prices have been maintained in a relatively good way', while among Limoges porcelain-workers, 'at the time of the "coup d'état" a heavy blow was struck at all combinations, but these men had always managed to have a sort of tacit understanding, by which they to a great extent (though under serious difficulty) had succeeded in upholding their wages'.[98] The Hand in Hand London coopers were a small, local, secret society, whose business was all conducted orally, while among the London wood and tin packing-case makers, 'although the trade was thus almost without any formal organization from 1867 to 1872, the men were still actually united. They continued to meet regularly at their known houses of call & discuss trade questions.'[99] Similar were the loosely organised Sheffield trades. In the Spring Knife Grinders' Association, 'these men seem to pay subscriptions when they choose & the collectors are allowed to compromise the bad debts of members by receiving half or 1/3rd. of the total &c.' Yet 'it was well known that Sheffield was the father of Trades' unions'; 'Sheffield was declared to be the stronghold of trade societies, and it was unknown that the average amount of earnings of the working classes in this town was higher than in any other towns in the country.'[100]

Trade unions were thus characterised by variety. In some old skilled trades such as hatters, coachmakers, farriers, or Morocco leather-finishers, there were strong but often rival societies, tramping federations, or *compagnonnages*, that exerted powerful controls, insisting on apprenticeship and limiting the number, imposing piece-work through a scale, controlling hiring, excluding non-members, insisting on proper workmanship and behaviour, sharing work, and controlling the choice of foremen. Similar controls were exercised by coopers, shipwrights, and the Sheffield trades, but they were less mobile and often opposed the employment of 'strangers'. Less strong, but often powerful and similar in their policies were stonemasons/cutters and compositors, both engaged in tramping. Among large, less skilled trades such as tailoring, shoemaking, and cabinet-making, organisation was weak except in the quality, bespoke sectors, and in the large towns there was a multiplicity of small, fractional societies which could not control apprenticeship and sought to operate leverage through placement functions and guarantees of attention and workmanship. Somewhat similar were carpenters, although in this trade and in bricklaying some extensive, if not powerful, societies did appear, in the former case able to exploit the dependence of all building works on the carpenters.

Employers were not always hostile to certain forms of trade unionism. Placement functions were often welcome, especially to small employers who did not have long runs of orders or a regular workforce, yet who might need men in a hurry. Many masters supported the idea of regulation of the trade, including wage scales,[101] so as to check competition. Small masters were not better or more favourable employers, for while they might belong to trade societies, they were themselves insecure and in constant danger of failing, and becoming a master was often a response to poverty and unemployment, not upward social mobility. The small masters were the source of many of the evils resulting from low pay, homework, and family and boy labour, and they were therefore often regarded as the worst employers of all.[102] Larger employers might be more favourable to checking under-cutting competition, and seek to attract the best men. When Neath carpenters formed a lodge, the chair was taken by one of the largest employers.[103]

Trade societies must therefore be related to the context of divisions, solidarities, camaraderie, hierarchies, variations in skill, fragmentation of authority, and sub-contracting. All of these could lead to conflicts, but the conflicts were usually confined to a single workplace, did not involve the trade society, and did not usually display worker solidarity, for they could be directed at foremen or other workers as well as at employers.

### Workplace conflicts

The joiner Perdiguier emphasised the constant tensions, verbal hostilities, and ambiguous jokes between employers and workmen, and conflicts in the workplace were recurrent.[104] One issue was recruitment and training. As we have seen, insecurity, labour surplus, and the desire to establish a corner in employment led to efforts to limit recruitment, and to prevent the employment of members of other trades, labourers, or women.[105] Apprenticeship was one source of resentment, for while the lads were usually apprenticed to the master, it was the men who trained them while the masters profited from their work, and masters, particularly small struggling ones, often used lads as cheap labour in place of men. There was a particular problem in the great cities of an influx of poorly trained young men from the country towns willing to work for low pay.[106] Efforts were therefore made to limit the number of apprentices, although such exclusive policies led to resentment from parents seeking to place their sons.[107]

Refusal to allow the employment of men who had not served a proper apprenticeship was a form of exclusion, but, as formal apprenticeship declined in the course of the century, an alternative was to insist on a certain level of competence, such as having worked at the trade for a number of years or having the ability to earn a certain rate. Insistence on the capability of workmen to perform the stint or 'log', the amount of work to be done in a day, was a form of exclusion.[108] Thus the tailors at the great Clichy co-operative works in Paris in 1848 worked for a standard fixed daily rate but imposed a stint and a level of quality that excluded many workmen.[109] Insisting on equal wages did not mean equality between workmen, for it meant that the less skilful were less likely to be hired or the first to be discharged, just as equal pay for much-resented female workers meant they would not be hired. Such exclusive policies are, however, best seen as strategies in the workplace only, and the divisions they engendered should not be seen as reflections of deeper social divisions in the outside world.

There were many other sources of conflict. Pay was a prime one, of course, in both its levels and form. Delays in pay were a constant source of dispute, as they forced workmen into debt.[110] Many preferred day-work to piece-work, as the latter could lead to an intensification of labour, to men taking on more work at the expense of others, to reductions in rates through competition, and to endless rivalry, disputes, and ill-feeling.[111] Piece-work also encouraged masters to keep men on the premises with nothing to do and therefore not paid, to be available when there was a rush of work.[112] There were therefore efforts to secure day-work instead of piece-work, or, if there had to be piece-work, to impose a stint, thus limiting the intensity of work as well as excluding cheaper labour.[113] In fact, of course, a stint meant that piece-work was really day-work, so the difference should not be exaggerated, 'day-work' often really being a form of calculation for piece-work. The essential thing was control and regulation, as the London bookbinder Dunning pointed out. 'The advantages to workmen of time and piece work are often reciprocal, if it can be shown that the fair price of work by the *piece* has often been set by what a man is paid working by *time*.'[114]

But there was no general agreement on this. Many were prepared to work over-long hours to increase their earnings, even at the expense of others thereby deprived of work.[115] In bigger printing firms, especially those of daily newspapers where speed was vital, men were grouped into companionships (*commandites*) under a clicker (*metteur en pages*), the collective pay to the team being divided up either according to equal hourly rates, which most compositors preferred, or by piece-work, which inferior, infirm, or older workers preferred 'as in the former they fear being expelled and regarded as inferior producers'.[116] Among London tailors, 'men who have once got accustomed to piecework always prefer it, as they feel the restraints of regular hours & other conditions in timework shops'.[117] Any effort at a uniform policy over these matters thus led to divisions within the workforce.

Foremen were another major source of conflict. Much work was performed in gangs or teams with an elected leader who made agreements with employers for work, such as in the printing companion-ships. At Nantes and elsewhere 'when the journeymen shipwrights work to contract, they join together and share according to their labour and usual wages. That is, each is paid according to the quality and quantity of his work.'[118] Masters were often dependent on particular workmen, 'leading hands' (*gâcheurs*) in building, 'captains' (*premiers garçons*) or cutters in tailoring, and *grosses culottes* in Paris engineering, whose indispensability gave them leverage or control over recruitment or over the running of the shop, while in larger firms or where employers concentrated on trading, foremen were a necessity.[119] There were, as we have seen, many opportunities for favouritism and bribery.[120] Foremen, then, might be representatives or leaders of the men, or they might be agents of employers against them, and very many disputes were the result of tyrannical, bullying, and abusive foremen. A notorious foreman in a Paris type-foundry reduced and finally abolished the three customary breaks when the men could leave the hot, fume-filled works for a while, and also reduced the wages, recruiting labour when he needed it by standing at the entrance and calling out 'who is hungry?' After a number of disputes in 1833 he was treated to 'rough music' (*charivari*).[121]

Discipline in the workshops was an obvious source of conflict, but it is important to recognise how limited this tended to be, in a general absence of managerial control. Employers and foremen had actually very little control over the pace of work or labour process. Perdiguier recalled working for a master in Moulanguet. 'One day, he arrived at the workshop and said to us: "You, Avignonian, you, Provençal, you, Vivarais, I am putting you together to make me a store. Here is the plan; here is the wood; work, and proceed as fast as you can." '[122] This lack of discipline distinguished artisans from servants.[123] The shoemaker O'Neill took work for a while as a gate-keeper, 'though I did not like it, it being contrary to my habits through life', 'being through a long life subject to no will but my own'; when he left this job, 'I felt myself like one released from a state of bondage.'[124] One attempt at control was the effort to have fixed hours of arrival and departure, and the reaction it evoked was an indication of the general lack of discipline. A master boot- and shoemaker's introduction of fixed hours was 'refined tyranny', a Paris engineer in 1841 provoked a strike by introducing fines for unauthorised absences, and there were riots among cabinet-makers in a Paris firm in 1846 'against the signal for entry and departure at the workshops by the sound of a bell, an innovation which the workmen considered an attack on their dignity'.[125] Paris tanners, who were not allowed to sing or smoke at work and for whom a bell did signal the beginning and end of work were described as subject to 'severe discipline'.[126] The Paris compositor Gauthier was horrified at the idea of a bell, and compositors struck in 1865 at a firm that lowered discs to signal the start of work and imposed fines for lateness.[127] Fines for other things, such as for flaws in workmanship, were equally resented.

For these reasons employers tended to try to control their workforce by other means such as shop relief funds, truck, and arrears in pay. Some masters had annual treats or celebrations, at which the workmen gave insincere votes of thanks, but employers of artisans could rarely aspire to the forms of paternalism implemented by some factory-owners, mine-owners or ironmasters, which were in any case of little effectiveness except where firms dominated the labour market in a relatively isolated area. Even the great paternalist, Robert Owen, had recognised this. 'Many years ago he had some thousands of operatives under his charge for nearly forty years. He did everything in his power to ameliorate their condition, but, after all his efforts, he found he was still their tyrant, and they his slaves.'[128]

Efforts to increase productivity by having people work longer hours and at greater intensity relied not usually on greater control but on such devices as paying bonuses for greater output and 'chasing'. Where time pay continued, pay by the hour could replace pay by the day, which meant paying only for the time actually worked and the possibility of longer hours. 'The men saw at once that if this system was carried out it would reduce them at once to the level of the labourers at the docks.'[129] However, some workmen preferred it because it left them free to work the hours they wished.[130]

Employers also tried to erode traditional privileges, such as the compositors' entitlement to full-page pay on magazine wrappers, building workers' pay for time spent 'grinding' (sharpening tools), or 'walking time' for work outside town. While most real craftsmen owned their tools, a frequently substantial investment that was a source of pride and independence, the insistence on men providing their own tools was detrimental to newcomers and to lads recently out of their time, and the lending of tools could be a means of reducing them to dependence, comparable to the lending of money or materials (joiners therefore often made their tools in working time).

While the artisan trades were subject to changes in our period, mechanisation was not usually one of them, any more than discipline or work. The introduction of machinery because of strikes was very untypical, the few examples including felt hatters, Manchester tailors, and Paris paste-board workers.[131] What characterised industry in general, including artisan sectors, was not machinery but the prevalence of sub-contracting. Sub-contracting was rife, but not necessarily opposed. Teams and gangs used it and often thereby controlled their hours and pace of work. It was an inevitable phenomenon, especially as so many masters could not afford a permanent workforce and preferred to engage sub-contractors when orders came. Thus Paris master curriers employed boot-blockers (*cambreurs*) in this way: they 'have used it up to now in fact to save themselves the costs of rent. They do not have enough work to occupy continually a certain number of workmen, and they prefer, when an order comes, to divide it between several *piece-masters* (*marchandeurs*).'[132] It freed the employer from the bother of detailed management and piece-work could provide the incentive to increase output. It could also be attractive to the men. Thus in printing 'what is most attractive in the *companionship* is the semi-independence which it assures them; the contacts between them and the employer are reduced to the absolute minimum; anyone who wishes to be away has no longer to ask permission, there are no more rebuffs to endure; he arranges a replacement for the time he wishes and that is all'.[133] But sub-contracting in printing could also be exploitative, and 'maroons' (*marrons*) in Paris were piece-masters who attached themselves to regular printing shops and paid low rates.[134] Larger mercantile firms handling large stocks used small masters and home-workers, and among Paris brushmakers 'most of the manufacturers, to reduce their costs, no longer have workshops, and workers who cannot work at home are forced to work at the contractors', who often exploit them disgracefully'.[135] Like cabinet and chair-makers, they also made things at home on speculation and tried to sell them to the public in the streets in the 'hawking system' (*trôle*) or 'Saturday truck or wheelbarrow business'.

The pressures arising from a surplus of labour, growth of large capitalist firms, and sub-contracting, led to the employment of cheaper labour – unskilled, lads or females – which swelled the labour pool, in cheaper and inferior production. 'We have been driven to seek the assistance of boys and women to perform that labour, which men alone ought to perform, depriving us of all domestic comforts and social happiness and adding to the already overstocked labour market, a still further means of reducing our wages, and preparing for ourselves and children a future too terrible to contemplate.'[136] Homework was cheaper for employers, although a number of journeymen might prefer it because of the freedom it brought, as did the bookbinder Eugene Varlin.[137] Among tailors 'a good minority of the men of course prefer it, as it gives them an opportunity to employ females & so earn more money than they otherwise could'.[138]

Cheaper labour was associated with lower-quality products, and was assisted by a sub-division of tasks, each section needing less skill. Thus in shoemaking 'the sub-division system of labour, as proposed by the Messrs. Bostock, was not only a great reduction in the wages, but an indirect means of ultimately destroying the independence of the shoe-maker, as the labour so allotted would render the completion of one shoe the work of many, and the operations of the skilled and unskilled would become so blended and identified, that it would be impossible to define the exact amount of individual merit (if any) in the aggregate production. We further believe that a contracted and diminished skill on the part of the workman would be the result.'[139]

All this was associated with those sub-contractors who treated for work and employed people to do it as cheaply as possible to increase their own profit, and were therefore agents in the cheapening of labour, the increasing of labour intensity, the division of labour, homework, and piece-work. 'We look with dread on the introduction of middlemen in any department of human industry. Those go-betweens are always more grasping, more sordid, more tyrannical than the real employers – always more ready to beat down prices, and to reduce wages. Whenever they have gained a footing they have been the heralds of misery and discontent.'[140] 'If there is one system that tends more than another to grind and overwork men, it is this system of large employers contracting with piecemasters, taskmasters, jobmasters, sub-contractors (or, as the colliers call them, the Butties) to get their work done for a certain figure, and for them, the Butties, &c., to realise their profits on the extra labour they can get out of the men.'[141] 'Subcontracting is the means of causing a most unnatural practice of competition amongst producers of wealth, which competition is always the means of keeping down the price of labour, inasmuch as the sub-contractor puts that into his pocket which ought to go into the pockets of the labourers, while at the same time it encourages a competitive system in the working department, which is injurious to the health and intellect of our members, for we cannot see any difference between sub-contracting, piece work, or tasking, beyond that of the name; and it is also our opinion, that it is the means of lengthening the hours of labour . . . no sooner do we find one of our class raised above us in the scale of society, than we almost uniformly find that man our greatest enemy.'[142] So closely allied were piece-work and sub-contracting, that Paris workmen in 1848 interpreted the government decree banning sub-contracting as the abolition of piece-work.[143]

All these pressures heightened the incidence of conflicts, and resistance to these practices was often in the name of the 'custom of the trade' against 'innovation'.[144] This did not denote a traditionalist or backward-looking ideology. Certainly there were many local traditions, and there were customary, if notional, ratios of apprentices to journeymen (1:10 among Paris compositors, 1:12 in London), differential rates in summer and winter, and stints. 'Custom' merely referred to established usage, not antiquity, as in the Woolwich and Plumstead building workers' reference in 1866 to stopping work at one o'clock on Saturdays as 'the custom now in the London district'.[145] The frequency of the word in England probably reflected the legal concept of customary law, and when work disputes came to courts of law the 'custom of the trade' was taken into account.[146] The usual term in France was *usage*.[147] The meaning was established practice, rules to which all workers, masters, and intermediaries should be subject, and these included notions of honour and respect – many conflicts were provoked by foremen's swearing and abuse of the men.[148]

Naturally, all these sources of conflict led to a variety of actions – go-slows, boycotts, absenteeism, protests, walk-outs, and strikes – and indeed it was often such resistance that made these pressures tolerable. 'Certain systems of exploitation cannot function if the workers do not resist. In the face of a tendency to impose unrestricted rhythms, if the workmen do not check it they collapse.'[149] But conflicts were not only between employers and employees, and were often among workers, and resentment was often greatest at the foremen (as for their abuse of hiring powers and their connexions with victuallers) or at employment agents. Sub-contractors, foremen, and small dependent masters might be targets of odium or be seen as victims of larger capitalist enterprises,[150] and foremen could act as leaders in disputes. The leader of a strike in 1855 by coach-makers in Paris was a foreman who had worked in the same shop for eighteen months and whose master was ready to re-employ him, and a violent figure in a strike in 1854 at a Thames shipbuilding yard was also a foreman.[151] But few of the issues leading to conflicts united all members of the trade, and the great majority of disputes were confined to single shops and firms, and for this reason, because they did not attract any outside attention, they remain unknown to us.

## Combinations

Thus trade societies were mainly extra-workplace institutions and did
not intervene much in the workplace, while most disputes and disagreements arose in the workplace, did not involve trade societies, and
occurred over a wide range of issues largely in reaction to changes. But
there were also wider movements, usually not reactive ones, for artisans
were very familiar with the most favourable circumstances for action –
years of high economic activity, the brisk season of the year, an
advantageous political situation, firms under pressure to meet orders. St
Malo shipwrights struck in the busy month of November in both 1846
and 1847.[152] Nearly all tailors' strikes were in April or May, at the start
of the brisk season, a time of 'that spirit of independence – amounting
pretty nearly to defiance, – which inspires our class at this season, and
prepares them for anything'.[153] In the wave of strikes in Paris in sixty-
nine trades in 1864–5, in each case the best time was chosen to put
demands with the threat of a strike.[154]

These wider movements tended to take place in waves, in times of
economic recovery. On both sides of the Channel these were concentrated in the years 1824–5, 1833–4, 1844–5, 1853–5 (to an unprecedented level in England), 1863–5, and from 1869 to the mid-1870s (this
last to an unprecedented level in both countries, but interrupted in
France for a while by the war). To these should be added waves in
1859–61 in England, and in 1830, 1840, and 1848 in France (the first
and last of these due to the favourable political situation and not the
economic one). These movements were not necessarily the work of
trade societies, indeed were nearly always much wider, involving both
society and non-society men, for while society men often disliked
working with non-society men, or joining with them in a common
organisation, they could easily co-operate in these temporary combinations. 'It was of no use for a number of men, even if they formed a
majority of the trade, to say that they would do this or that, unless they
had the moral support of the whole body of men – not only those who
belonged to the society alone.'[155] Society men did often take the
initiative in starting the movement, because of their standing and
reputation, and societies were often important in providing funds (at
least initially, for the main source was a general subscription), whilst the
existence of a trade or benefit society gave men greater confidence in
contributing to the fund, and other societies in making gifts or loans.
But this did not mean the societies ran the movement, for the initiative
might be taken by others, and a general committee or organisation
usually evolved before or during the movement, which presented the

demands and, if they were refused, organised 'rolling strikes' in a few firms at a time, the strikers being thereby paid from levies on those still at work; general simultaneous strikes were to be avoided.[156] But it was not just a question of uniting society and non-society men, it was also necessary to unite separate, rival, and often antagonistic societies, and it is remarkable how easily this was achieved. Thus in Paris the two rival *compagnonnages* organisations of carpenters combined in joint campaigns in 1822, 1832, 1833, 1836, 1837, 1840, 1843, and 1845, as did the two hostile farriers' clubs in 1830, the Nantes joiners' societies in 1840, or the three London bookbinders' societies in 1866.[157]

The reason why normally mutually hostile societies could combine in these temporary combinations was that the issues were different. Issues of securing a monopoly of work divided societies, but these wider combinations took place on other issues on which they were able to agree. The most common such uniting issue was wages. The general pattern in wages in the artisan trades was of rises in the Napoleonic Wars up to around 1812 and downward pressure thereafter, particularly from the later 1820s. Thus in the years of economic recovery 1824–5, 1833–4, 1844–5 there were attempts to restore wages to the earlier levels (usually, in fact, the rates established around 1812). A change came after mid-century, especially from the mid-1860s, when there were efforts to raise wages to unprecedented levels, and many trades gained the first rises for forty or more years, and this breakthrough was repeated on a greater scale in the early 1870s. The pattern was thus one of offensive movements in 'good' economic years (and, in France, in the good political years 1830 and 1848), for wage rises that, before the 1860s, were mainly to undo previous reductions.

A variant of attempts to secure general wage rises was efforts to raise wages in low-paying firms, to equalise up so as to remove competitive pressure on better paying firms to reduce their wages and equalise down.[158] Equality of wages was a means of preventing competitive wage-cutting but it did not, as we have seen, mean workers' equality, as it could mean that less skilled workers were less likely to be hired or the first to be dismissed. But the striking Paris carpenters explained in 1845 that they were not demanding 5 francs a day for every carpenter, young or old, skilled or unskilled, as the press had claimed. 'Such an absurd request has never occurred to a single one of us.' Five francs should be paid to every carpenter 'capable of fittingly proving and working carpentry'; after two or three days any employer could tell whether he was worth keeping. Old or less skilled men who 'do not fulfil the stipulated conditions for a 5fr. day's pay' could earn less, but only through proper agreements. Similarly the London tailors in 1834 demanded six shillings for a ten-hour day, but 'it never was contemplated by us that an idle and inefficient Man should have this rate of wages . . . we are now, or at any other good time ready to shew a Statement of what labour we were willing to perform in the 10 hours'. Aged and inferior workmen unable to meet this standard log would be paid less, but only by agreement with the men.[159] 'Equality of wages' was really a standard rate and a means of checking a general cheapening of labour, and could thus receive general support, and since superior men could earn more, it was often in fact a minimum rate, or a reference wage for calculating task or piece-rates.[160] An equalising up or a standard rate were often sought through a written agreed scale, preferably publicly promulgated and published.

Wage demands sometimes took other forms, such as the substitution of day rates for piece-rates, or for payment for hitherto unpaid time spent in connexion with work, such as shipwrights' 'docking money' (waiting to dock a ship), weavers' mounting looms, tailors' time spent waiting for the fitting of garments before making necessary alterations (*essayage*), or building workers' 'walking time' (going to work outside town), or else they were over having to pay for lighting or the use of tools or facilities (as with hatters' 'standing money').[161]

As the years went by, there was also growing reference to rates of pay in other towns. The scale achieved by the Paris carpenters in 1845 spread over France in 1848, the Manchester tailors' 'time log' or price list of 1865 was copied elsewhere and became the basis for a national organisation, while rises in building wages in Bristol and Cardiff in that year led Newport carpenters to strike for a rise 'to place us more on an equality with other branches of the building trade'.[162]

Apart from wages, the other main uniting issue in combinations was reductions of hours, especially when a uniform pay rate seemed unrealistic, indeed a reduction of hours in the day for the same day's pay was a form of wage rise.[163] But a reduction of hours was not only a way of reducing toil for, by sharing work and causing larger numbers to be hired, it reduced unemployment and thus competitive downward pressure on wages and thereby strengthened the bargaining position of labour. At the start of our period a ten hours' day was regarded as the mark of a respectable artisan. This was therefore the demand of the English factory movement, and was a regular demand in Paris in 1830, 1833, and 1840, and was achieved in a number of Paris trades early in 1848 before they secured a short-lived decree from the Provisional Government imposing it everywhere.[164] From 1847 English building workers pressed for a short Saturday, stopping at 4pm and later 1pm, and by the end of the 1850s were seeking a nine-hour day; these aims became generalised in the 1860s, while Paris workmen were still seeking a ten-hour day. Reduction of hours might meet the needs of trades not exercising craft control or apprenticeship and experiencing a surplus of labour, but it was not really applicable to workers paid according to a piece-work scale, especially workers at home, so hours demands were much less frequent than wage ones. Variations of this issue were attempts to stop systematic overtime work, one way being to establish higher rates for overtime beyond a standard day's work. This was common among engineers.[165] Bakers frequently tried to abolish or reduce night work and Sunday work.[166]

Thus while workplace conflicts occurred over a variety of issues, and were very often defensive, against new practices and impositions, wider combinations were aggressive, in favourable times, nearly all over wages and/or, to a lesser extent, hours.[167] This was true for the whole of our period. There were several reasons for this. Wages and hours were more likely to unite the different groups of workmen than divisive workplace issues. Employers were more willing to consider such claims than ones over apprenticeship, authority, piece-work, or sub-contracting, which they were more likely to see as dictation. External constraints, legislative and judicial, such as the combination laws of 1825 in England and 1864 in France, made action over wages and hours more legal. Such issues were also much more likely to secure public approval than restrictive practices over apprenticeship, demarcation, or machinery.[168] Masters were, in fact, sometimes ready to 'buy out' privileges and restrictions. While the achievement of a fixed scale could be much more difficult, and some masters saw it as a humiliation, others could see advantages in achieving stability and checking ruinous competition, and a large number of agreed scales were established in Britain in 1812, 1824, 1833, 1844–5, and the mid-1860s, as well as very many in France in 1848–9 when the revolution and republic made masters amenable to workers' demands. As in 1830, Paris workmen often tried to have these agreements officially ratified through the new authorities.

Small masters sometimes supported movements for better wages and hours, as among tailors, shoemakers, and building workers, and they took a leading role in pursuit of this aim among Lyons silk-weavers. The leader of the Paris tailors' movement in 1833 was the foreman Troncin, who also led the strike of 1840, the result being prison where harsh treatment led to his death.[169] The leader of the 1833 Paris carpenters' strike was the leading hand Albouisse, and the key role of the 'Compagnons du Devoir' in this strike and the one in 1845 reflected the role of the leading hands. They at first opposed the movement of the Foxes of Liberty in the mid-forties, and were asked to be intermediaries between men and masters, but in the end they took the lead in the 1845 strike.[170] Similarly a foreman, Mérot, led a Lyons joiners' strike in 1855 for the re-establishment of the 1848 scale.[171] Neither Troncin, Albouisse, nor Mérot stood to gain financially from the success of the movements they led, for they already earned more than was being requested. This is a reminder that demands over wages and hours reflected more than the 'material' concerns that outsiders tended to assume. These movements took on moral and crusading connotations, for such actions, numbers, and self-sacrifice would have been impossible without a sense of morality and justice, a conviction that employers should do, or be made to do, the decent thing.

There were occasionally some other uniting issues in certain trades, such as apprenticeship regulations, 'sweating' (exploitative sub-contracting), exploitative employment agencies, machinery, deductions for flaws in workmanship, and, in building, general contracting, over which small masters were often allies of the men.[172] One important example was tailors' opposition to homework and female labour.[173] But none of these was generally as important as wages and hours, and it should be stressed that they were 'uniting' issues in that they could unite workmen from different firms and societies, but not all workers in the trade; they were often opposed by sub-contractors, homeworkers, and female workers, and the London tailors' strike of 1866 was confined to men in the bespoke shops of the West End, who were nevertheless participating in an unusual and temporary collective action. Furthermore there were frequently disagreements in strikes over wages. Younger, more transient, unmarried workmen were much readier to take advantage of temporary favourable circumstances and strike for higher pay; if the strike failed, they would move on elsewhere; if it succeeded there would very likely be a counter-attack by employers when the favourable situation passed, and the transient workers could then move on. Domiciled workmen were much more concerned with stability than short-term gains, for they well knew that 'there is not a town in the kingdom that could not (at some period of the year) force an employer, if pushed with a job, to give additional wages; until that job was completed'.[174] As a baker explained, 'many a time and oft has my blood boiled under the tyranny of an employer, when the thought of my wife and little ones wanting food, has made me grin and bear it. Married men are lashed into submission by the fear of poverty, and as to their being more steady, well poverty is the patron saint of all the virtues.'[175] Strikes were frequently begun by transient workers.[176] In 1867 Huddersfield tailors decided by a small majority to strike, mainly because of 'a large number of strangers who happened to be in the town at the time who had neither stake not interest in it, and are always for going the "whole hog", and as soon as they get town into difficulties either leave or act dishonourably'.[177]

As we have seen, existing trade societies sometimes took the lead in these combinations, for example the compagnonnic societies in building. In 1832 three Paris tailors' societies united to launch a common movement which produced a special organisation for the 1833 strike,[178] while in London the various tailors' houses of call came together at the same time to form a special 'Grand Lodge', embracing society and non-society men, that launched the great strike of April 1834. London boot and shoemakers' societies also came together to form their own Grand Lodge, and in France shoemakers' movements, including members of rival societies, arose as temporary alliances.[179] It was a small engineers' society that in 1836 launched the general campaign in the London trade for a ten-hour day, a campaign consisting mainly of non-society men and headed by an elected *ad hoc* general committee, a small cabinet-makers' society that took the lead in the Bristol movement that gained a rise in 1845, and the small Progressive Society of Carpenters that began a London campaign for a nine-hour day, composed mainly of non-society men, that led on to the famous builders' strike of 1859.[180] Most strikes in the building industry involved non-society men. There were many such movements in France in 1848, and in the 1860s combinations, Paris compositors' votes were not confined to society members.[181] The London tailors' movement of 1833–4 was repeated in the mid-1840s, when the call-houses again came together with non-society men in opposition to homework. With economic recovery in the mid-1860s the tailors in the West End shops made another effort and established the London Operative Tailors' Protection Association to secure a rise and uniform 'log' for good quality work, that is an agreed list of time needed to make different articles as a basis for calculation of pay. The masters refused and imposed a lock-out, which was defeated with the support of provincial tailors, and the West End tailors gained a rise of a penny an hour. This victory had a tremendous impact, especially as provincial prices were often tied to London ones, and both the LOTPA, throughout the Home Counties, and the provincial Amalgamated Association formed a mass of new branches. These branches were clearly formed with the short-term aim of gaining a rise and did not in any way express a commitment to a longer-term organisation, so membership fluctuated greatly. But outworking was extensive in London, and in the 1866 dispute West End firms had been able to have a lot of work done by small masters desperate for orders, and journeymen working at home were delighted with the new better-paid orders which were 'quite a little harvest for them'. So when a new strike occurred in April 1867, the LOTPA this time made great efforts to organise outworkers, including women and east European Jews, to prevent them doing strike-breaking work. The LOTPA even expanded to such places as Brighton to stop London firms having work done there. With the defeat of the strike, this organisation naturally ended.[182] At the same time the Paris tailors, in preparation for their strike, formed a benefit society so as to raise funds for it, although the strike involved far greater numbers than the members of this society.[183]

Combinations involving members of different societies and non-society men thus often produced new organisations that were only intended to be temporary. Another variant was seen in the very good year of 1853, when shoemakers' societies all over England provisionally opened membership to non-society men to form temporary organisations in order to regain some of their position through wage rises; the carpenters' General Union had done the same in the early 1830s.[184]

Thus these wider movements or combinations involved temporary *ad hoc* organisations that might or might not be due to the initiative of some existing society or take the form of a temporary expansion of one. These organisations were distinct from the permanent benefit and trade societies and were not meant to supplant them or continue after the campaign was over, and if victory were gained and some of these organisations did in fact continue, this was only by changing their character into that of permanent benefit societies with a usually much smaller membership, such as the Thames shipwrights' union after the 1825 strike or a Paris wallers' society after the 1840 one.[185] This form of temporary organisation, distinct from trade societies, was called in France a 'resistance society' (*société de résistance*) and was usually wound up after the dispute.[186] In England most of the 'grand lodges' and 'united' and 'consolidated' unions of the early 1830s were meant as temporary resistance societies, the usual form of organisation in combinations.[187]

In discussing 'trade unionism' among artisans we must then distinguish between three separate phenomena: workplace conflicts, over a wide variety of issues and not usually involving a formal organisation; trade societies, concerned with a number of extra-workplace functions and rarely involved in workplace conflicts; and wider movements or combinations, mainly over wages or hours, seeking gains (often to undo previous losses) in favourable circumstances, economic or political, often involving temporary organisations, and setting employers against employees. This is to stress the similarities between England and France, even though it is usually a contrast that is made, between weak, discontinuous, or informal French labour organisations and strong, permanent British ones.

Many organisations in both countries were intended to be temporary, and the contrast is largely based on a misconception of British unions and an exaggeration of their strength, an impression influenced by the analysis by the Webbs in their standard history of trade unionism. They identified a 'gradual building up of the great "amalgamated" societies of skilled artisans, with their centralized administration, friendly society benefits, and the substitution, whenever possible, of industrial democracy for the ruder methods of the Class War'. These 'new model unions' were characterised by trained, salaried officials, high benefits and contributions, national organisation, conception of labour as a commodity, desire to control supply and demand through hours, conditions and apprenticeship, and support for political reform as a means to social advancement not as a mechanism for socio-economic transformation.[188]

This conception was drawn largely from an article by Professor Beesly in the *Fortnightly Review*, which contrasted the newer 'amalgamated' societies, such as the Amalgamated Society of Engineers or the Amalgamated Society of Carpenters and Joiners, with their high subscriptions, large range of benefits, and consequent large funds and more stable membership, with what he regarded as an 'older' type of society, with low subscriptions and few benefits; the latter he referred to as a 'striking society' whose membership fluctuated quite drastically.[189]

The distinction is a valid one, but it was not one between old and new, for there were many examples before 1850 of high benefit and high subscription societies, and it was not true that 'practically all unions with small contributions are strike societies'. Beesly failed to make the distinction between trade society and resistance society, and even branches of 'new' amalgamated societies were often formed precisely as resistance societies seeking short-term gains, through strikes if necessary. Swansea painters established a branch of the London-based General Association of Painters in their quest for a rise for 'country work', four miles from town, and eventually went on strike; Llanelly and Neath carpenters formed lodges of the General Union in a movement to secure wage rises and reductions in hours; while branches of the ASCJ were formed in Maidstone and Ashton with similar purposes.[190] While some of these lodges were to continue after success was gained, this was, in accordance with the usual pattern outlined above, no longer as resistance societies but largely as benefit societies. The ASE was originally formed in 1851 in an aggressive campaign against piece-work and systematic overtime. Only after the great defeat of 1852 did it revert to the more familiar benefit-type society that did not interfere much in the workplace.

### Strikes, employers, and the law

Great disputes, particularly defeats, could lead to new organisations, such as among Sheffield railway spring fitters in 1852–3 or London newspaper compositors in 1852, while the London builders' lock-out of 1859 led to the creation of the Amalgamated Society of Carpenters and Joiners and the short-lived Amalgamated Association of Painters, and to the remodelling of the Operative Bricklayers' Society.[191] After a bitter strike, the Paris hatters remodelled their organisation in 1868.[192] It was also true that large disputes could lead to the expansion of organisations and operations. This was partly because employers frequently sought to recruit men from elsewhere to replace those on strike, even from abroad, Germans being brought to London during strikes by pianoforte-makers in 1850, gas workers in 1859, and bakers in 1872.[193] Strikers therefore sought to dissuade such scabs on their arrival, or prevent their coming, by, for instance, notifying local tramping stations and houses of call.[194] The growing size of some enterprises and business connexions meant that firms experiencing a strike in one town could try to have the work done by a branch or business associates in another, and this led to sympathetic action in other towns.[195] The English compositors' societies had a regular correspondence to check men coming to work for blacklisted firms, and this was one of the functions of their trade journals, such as the *Typographical Societies' Monthly Circular*. The London West End tailors' LOTPA, as we have seen, expanded into the East End and into towns in the Home Counties to prevent work being done there for firms against which they were striking, while the Operative Bricklayers' Society, in the 1850s a London society, experienced a dramatic expansion outside London to become a national organisation, through the London strikes of 1859 and 1861, when lodges were formed in town after town to prevent the recruitment of blacklegs, and in the process of transformation it therefore gave up its earlier restrictive concern with apprenticeship.[196]

If negotiations failed, direct pressure could be put on employers. They might be harassed, their houses beset, or be subjected to 'rough music' (*charivari*).[197] Lancashire sawyers in the 1830s used arson, vitriol, and explosives.[198] If it came to a strike, the men preferred a 'rolling strike', in a few firms at a time, so that the relatively few strikers at any one time could be supported by those still at work. General strikes were usually the result of a concerted confrontational action by employers, such as the sacking of ringleaders, lock-outs, the refusal to employ members of an organisation or the imposition of a written renunciation of labour organisation, the 'document', as a condition of employment.

There were different means of enforcing a strike. Processions and tours of workshops were one way, mainly in the early years.[199] To prevent people working on the sly, there were several 'call times' in the day that all had to attend.[200] To prevent people taking away work to do at home and to stop blacklegs going to work, 'picquets' were used, but these often led to scuffles and clashes and then police or legal involvement. Sometimes homeworkers were prevented from working by taking away vital implements, such as weavers' shuttles or hatters' bows. Pressure, intimidation, and violence were obvious means. Hatred of 'scabs' was very marked and they were long remembered, and combining with members of rival societies was far more congenial than working with former 'black sheep'.[201]

While general strikes were the result of concerted action by employers, this was not usual. 'The spirit of jealousy and competition among masters in most trades, renders a union on their part, to oppose the unreasonable demands of their journeymen, a matter of great difficulty. Nothing but the pressure of extreme circumstances can, generally speaking, induce them to combine for such a purpose.'[202] This rivalry meant that the employers were in general less likely to combine than the workmen, the main exceptions being when there was a small number of employers, as with type-founders in Paris and London, or bookbinders in French provincial towns.[203] Sometimes employers encouraged strikes against rivals, or larger employers encouraged them to kill off smaller firms.[204] It was certainly true that smaller masters were more willing to concede to the demands of combinations, as among Paris and London tailors in 1833 and 1834, London builders in 1834 and 1861, or Paris carpenters in 1845.[205] This has commonly been attributed to their closeness to, and greater sympathy for, the men, as the republican lawyer defending tailors on trial in Paris in 1833 declared. 'A remarkable thing, adds he, the small masters agreed to the rise, only the large refused. This is because the former, nearer to the poor, still remember their journeymen, and agree to offer them a friendly hand.'[206] In fact it was because they did not have the means to resist a strike. It was often the actions of small masters, who bitterly resisted wage rises they could not afford, who provoked the strike in the first place. They were thus more likely to provoke a strike but the first to give in to one.[207]

United action by employers, even the formation of societies, did not, therefore, include all employers, and was usually a temporary reaction to a combination.[208] It could take several forms, such as blacklisting, lock-outs, the document, and the discharge note or quittance paper, whereby no man would be employed unless he presented one given by his former employer. Such measures were not usually deployed against trade societies but against what were (initially at least) new resistance societies, such as the Thames shipwrights and Bradford woolcombers in 1825, the Operative Builders in 1833–4, the Amalgamated Engineers in 1852, the London and Amalgamated Tailors in 1866, or the Paris fellmongers in 1869. This was particularly when the new combinations were thought to be part of a new powerful general inter-trade organisation, as was believed of the London tailors and the Consolidated Trades' Union in 1834, the building workers and the National Association of United Trades in 1846, or the Paris leather-dressers and the Paris Trades' Federation and International Working Men's Association in 1869.[209] The use of the document in such cases reflected an exaggerated or unfounded panic at some deep, wide, general movement and was not necessarily a rejection of membership of any kind of labour organisation. Thus the Manchester and Liverpool coachmakers' document in 1834 only bound employees not to belong to any 'illegal union' or secret committee of trades unions, and that of the builders in 1846 was only against national and general unions.[210]

Such actions were rare and not always effective, for the document and the discharge note provoked resistance, among non-society as well as society men,[211] revived strikes, as among defeated London bookbinders in 1849,[212] and tended to provoke support from other trades for those on strike. After the 1830s such resistance secured their withdrawal in nearly every case, although this often left the employers victorious over the original point at issue.

Given the usual failure of lock-outs and the document, and the relative weakness of employers, it was often through legal means that they tried to defeat combinations. They could use the English Master and Servant Acts, and clauses in the French Civil Code, both biased in favour of employers, to prosecute employees for stoppages and walk-outs (both were reformed in the late 1860s), while in France there was also an official legal equivalent of the discharge note, the *livret*, a pass-book which theoretically every workman had to possess and which had to be signed by each employer when he left his employment. It was a means of control, but use of it varied, and most industrial relations were little involved with the law. Thus when sawyers at Manchester came before magistrates because of a fight between society and non-society men, they received lenient sentences because it was a private 'trade row'.[213] But employers did often turn to legal repression and government help against wider combinations. The wave of demands and strikes in 1824–5 led to pleas by employers for a reimposition of the recently repealed Combination Laws, and the Thames shipbuilders provoked a general strike by the shipwrights to strengthen the case for legislation. Similar requests arose in 1833–4. In 1840 the Paris master tailors countered a rolling strike by uniting to impose the *livret*, hitherto little used in the trade, and this provoked a general strike.[214] In several strikes the headquarters were raided, picquets prosecuted, and government workmen supplied as strike-breakers.

The role of government and labour laws is thus an important element in trade union actions. The 1825 Combination Act made it lawful in Britain for workmen to meet to discuss and decide wages and hours, so that trade unions and strikes were legal in themselves, but any form of pressure on men to strike was illegal. Only in 1864 was a similar act passed in France. The actual use of such laws varied, and France was particularly prone to fluctuations in the attitudes of authorities. The 1830 revolution replaced existing authorities, removed restrictions for a while, and led to a permissive situation, which encouraged a variety of forms of popular action, including strikes, demonstrations, and machine-wrecking, and a number of trades asked the authorities to act over wages, hours, and other matters. The new authorities disliked these movements as threats to order, business confidence and political stability, and as they gained in confidence, they banned processions and moved against industrial agitation, a Paris hatters' strike being ended by 'the prompt & judicious use of the means of repression'.[215] The year 1834 brought the law against associations and widespread repression, and for the rest of the decade authorities were hostile to combinations. The Rennes Procurator-General in 1837 considered the real aim of tailors' societies to be 'a universal and simultaneous attack on a social order whose foundation is the principle of property', while his counterpart at Albi believed in 1847 that 'every combination can become a public danger, especially at the present time when so many men believe they have an interest in perverting workers' views and are on the watch to turn the problems of the urban industries to the profit of their political machinations'.[216] Thus a typical report ran:

I have the honour to inform you that at the start of this month the journeymen tailors of this town left their respective workshops for several days expressing the intention not to go back until they obtained a rise in wages.
   This action bearing all the character of a concerted combination and punished by art. 415 of the penal code, led immediately to judicial prosecutions. 14 workmen were straightaway summoned before the Poitiers Police Correctional Court and by the judgement of the 14th. of this month, 13 were sentenced, to

wit one to one month's prison, another to 15 days, three to six days and the eight others to 24 hours.

The tranquillity of the town was not disturbed for a single instant, no disorder was remarked, and the population did not seem very interested in the fate of these workmen who besides receive a proper wage.[217]

In fact local employers were often more conciliatory than officials.[218] There were, however, often differences between ministers, prefects, procurators, and mayors. Sometimes the authorities sympathised with the men; thus strikes among Lyons silk-weavers were blamed on the manufacturers' greed. 'In reality, the workmen's complaints were justified; but it was impossible to tolerate the means they employed for the satisfaction of their Grievances', and they were merely fined.[219] Crude repression could be counter-productive, and at Le Mans they proceeded against the tailors judiciously, 'because one might fear provoking irritation and spreading the mischief instead of destroying it. The decision was therefore taken to leave the workmen for a while to tire of being idle and exhaust their resources, after which an arrest was made of one of them, which was enough to bring about the immediate and total submission of the others.'[220] Just as Russell, who became Home Secretary in 1835, began a less repressive policy towards labour organisations, so as to avoid provoking secret combinations,[221] so in the calmer and more liberal 1840s French procurators often did not act but let combinations drag on, as long as there was no public disorder, and sometimes even put pressure on masters to give in.

In 1848 combinations were at first allowed, but this was reversed as the Republic became more repressive, the repression reaching its peak with the Second Empire, although efforts were also made to win over working-class support, through such means as the encouragement of controlled friendly societies. The situation changed again in the 1860s, and the act of 1864 was a real turning-point. Repression of strikes did continue but on a smaller scale, the authorities adopting a far more conciliatory attitude and even sometimes assisting strikes. The early years of the Third Republic, however, were less free.

Waves of combinations and strikes thus bore more relation to political fluctuations in France than in England and Wales, as in 1830, 1848, and 1864–5, but throughout the period trade organisations and activities adapted to the legal situation. One means was secrecy, with a covert choice of officers. Paris compositors had no headquarters and held their quarterly meetings on Sundays outside Paris. Secrecy was not only due to political repression, however, as the English cabinet-makers' federation had been appalled at 'the enormity of such a dastardly act' when Liverpool employers gained access to some of their balance sheets 'through the co-operation of some unprincipled members or member of ours'.[222] Trade organisations took the form of benefit societies partly as a front, for such societies were not only legal but officially encouraged from the 1840s. As the Paris Typographical Society told the London society, 'they had previously been obliged to have their Society enrolled as a Benevolent Institution only – as any Society for the maintenance of wages is not tolerated by the laws of France'. When they began to prepare a wages movement, they established a separate secret fund.[223] Working men knew perforce how to work the law. Those sought by the police were provided with passports and spirited away.[224] Because French authorities disliked single-trade benefit societies, many admitted a token number from other trades to give them an ostensibly mixed character.[225] While the official authorised rules might for form's sake confine activity strictly to sick and invalid relief, this was evaded by the Lyons compositors' society's conferral of special powers to the president or by the Paris hatters' 'auxiliary fund' for unemployment relief.[226] When some leaders of a ship-caulkers' strike at St Malo were arrested, the men returned to work to secure lenient sentences for them; this gained, they resumed their strike.[227] Paris trades on strike in the early 1830s avoided crowds so as not to fall foul of the law, 'and it would be difficult to proceed against a combination which does not reveal itself either through gatherings or any disorder'.[228] In a Paris cabinet-makers' dispute in 1847, each man left work only when he had finished his particular task, to avoid prosecution for breach of contract.[229] At the end of 1865 5,000 or 6,000 Paris goldsmiths (*bijoutiers*) struck, met at wine shops and paraded in the streets, but never more than twenty at a time so as to keep within the law.[230]

Trade organisations could rarely use the law in a positive way, they generally regarded judges, magistrates, and juries as biased against them and favourable to employers' organisations, and so wished to have as little to do with the law as possible. While there was widespread support for procedures for arbitration and conciliation, through representative bodies of masters and men, in equal numbers, there was reluctance in England to use magistrates, and much suspicion of binding arbitration under a judge. Magistrates were little more respected in France, and the official courts of arbitration (*conseils des prud'hommes*) were regarded as biased in their composition. With meetings banned, strikers sentenced for conspiracy, and picquets arrested, they had a negative attitude to the state and the law. Even in 1871 the Provincial Typographical Association decided not to register under the new trade union act and thereby gain legal security for their funds: 'the Council are sufficiently conservative to consider that these are matters affecting none outside the Association; and most of all do they feel disposed to repudiate the direct surveillance of Government officials in trade disputes or agreements, wherein they never had, nor should have now, any concern . . . the greatest boon that could be conferred was simply to be let alone'.[231] This was the general attitude, and in the few golden weeks of early 1848, the Paris trades succeeded for a while in imposing neutrality on the state, something never before experienced. Seeing the Republic as the guarantee of this neutrality, and alarmed at the growing forces of reaction, they allied with radicals in their campaigns, demonstrations, and election committees.

Support by workmen for men involved in disputes was common enough at the local level, and also among members of the same trade in different towns,[232] although a lack of response is also noticeable.[233] Yet certain disputes proved particularly emotive and aroused much wider support, such as those of the Bradford woolcombers in 1825, Kidderminster carpet-weavers in 1828, Derby silk-weavers in 1833–4, Staffordshire potters in 1836, London bookbinders in 1839, London stonemasons in 1841, Paris carpenters in 1845, Preston cotton-spinners in 1853, London builders in 1859, and the Paris leather-dressers in 1869. Sometimes the emotion was such that wider unions were the result, such as the Grand National Consolidated Trades' Union in 1834, the Central Committee of Paris Trades in 1845, the *Trades' Chronicle* in 1854, the London Trades' Council and the *Bee-Hive* after 1860. The Paris bronze-workers' strike in 1867 rallied the Paris trades and caused an expansion of the International Working Men's Association, while the marble-workers' and leather-dressers' strikes lay behind the formation and growth of the Federal Chamber of Workingmen's Associations in 1869.[234]

Why some disputes in particular aroused such emotion is not immediately obvious. It was not the *scale* of the dispute but the means used against the men that was crucial. Often it was because the employers presented the document. This did not only offend members of societies: non-society men and the wider public were often outraged by such an attack on liberty. Thus the imposition of the document when the 1834 London tailors' strike had begun to crumble actually revived it and for the first time brought support from other trades,[235] while the imposition of the *livret* on the Paris tailors in 1840 led to their general strike and wider support.[236] Even the greatly distressed Spitalfields silk-weavers sent help to engineers faced with the document in 1852.[237] Just as important in provoking support, or more so, was the hostile involvement of public authorities and officials. The widespread belief that the authorities were backing the employers, and, above all the transportation of the Dorchester agricultural labourers, fuelled the confrontational atmosphere of 1834 in England, and the Dorchester case remained an emotive one for the rest of the decade. Even the small society of Preston joiners gave money to both the Dorchester and Glasgow funds.[238] In 1835 a strike by coopers at Cette (Hérault) for a rise spread to other trades when some of the leaders were arrested.[239] In the great Paris carpenters' strike the masters were 'notoriously assisted by the authorities', who arrested strikers, raided two club houses and seized their funds, refused passports to strikers wishing to leave Paris on tramp, and supplied military carpenters to work for the masters. 'All the workers of Paris were aroused by this strike; they understood that the carpenters' cause was their own and, fearing that they would lose the struggle they were waging, they offered financial aid.'[240] The provision in 1861 by the War Office of sappers to replace building workers on strike led to the extension of the dispute, angry talk of a general strike, and greater support from other trades.[241] While in the 1860s governments on both sides of the Channel tried to be more neutral in such disputes, this was less true of local civil, military, and judicial officials, and the military support for the great Le Creusot ironmaster in the 1870 disputes provoked a furious reaction. It was a police raid on the strike headquarters of the successful marble-workers that angered the Paris trades into forming under Varlin the federal chamber which then came to the aid of the leather-dressers who were on strike and faced with the document.

This was not automatic solidarity with any working men on strike but anger at the injustice and 'unfairness' of the actions against them, often accompanied by the belief that the employers and authorities were concerting coercive legislation or trying to provoke clashes to give an excuse for repression. The Thames shipwrights correctly believed in 1825 that the shipbuilders were trying to provoke a general strike to help secure new laws against combinations, while after the arrests, raids, and seizures in the Paris carpenters' strike, 'everyone thinks and says that the wish is to push them into riot so as to crush them'.[242] There was a recurrent fear in large English disputes that the government was allying with the employers and planning coercive legislation.[243] This was George Potter's message at a meeting in protest at the notorious conviction of London tailors for peaceful picketing: 'Trades' unions were now occupying a very important position in this country, and both the press and the capitalists were very anxious to get the legislature to bring in something to limit their influence and action, or crush them out altogether.'[244] The repression of the Paris strikes in 1840 created very great bitterness indeed and effected a significant change in the attitudes of the working population.[245]

It was these aspects of disputes, the abuse of power by employers and the partisan intervention by authorities, that aroused the greatest emotions and broadened and radicalised the conflicts, and created one of those links between work and politics that is addressed in the next chapter.

### Leadership and reform

It was a common complaint that unsuitable people became officers 'in consequence of the apathy and indifference of the great majority of the men composing the society', while the bookbinder Dunning resented the fact that such people were often nominated 'out of a lark'.[246] The demands on time and the threats of victimisation must have been a deterrent. The Plymouth stonemasons' secretary, Shortt, was blacklisted and had to leave town.[247] 'To take a conspicuous part in trade society affairs a person must be prepared either to make great sacrifices, or he must be in such a position as to be independent of the trade.' Thus the leader of the Bristol cabinet-makers' society, Jacobs, was a bookseller, and a number of branch secretaries were publicans, while the president of a London boot-closers' society, Charles Murray, was a broker and auctioneer.[248]

Since labour organisations were not natural outgrowths from the workplace, the role of leaders was particularly important, especially as they had to be more independent than most workmen, while the long periods in office held by trade society secretaries indicates the rarity of the exceptional qualities needed.[249] One of the perennial concerns of such people was to avoid the divisions, rivalries, and rifts which threatened their societies, such as those related to privileged groups of senior workmen. They disapproved of footings and other forms of exploitation of young by old as divisive, a stance vindicated by the many revolts and breakaways by younger members of the *compagnonnages*. The London bookbinders' society was divided into lodges, such as the 'Dons' and 'White Stockings', and it was the divisive rivalry between them that led a new secretary, Thomas Dunning, to secure the abolition of these lodges and the separate finishers' sections in order to form a single unitary society.[250] It was also after a bitter strike that the Paris hatters in 1868 abolished the different categories of member.[251] Tailors' leaders in London and elsewhere opposed the exclusive call-houses, with their privileges to senior workmen, and organisations were formed in London in 1859 and the mid-1860s to replace them.[252] The London compositors' society disapproved of 'Gifts' and companionships because they led to privileged groups, and the Cette coopers' society forbade compagnonnic songs and, like many other societies, forbade the discussion of religious and political topics as divisive.[253]

Trade union leaders were usually keener to admit women than were most members, instead of merely opposing female labour, as in shoemaking societies in England in the 1830s, 1840s, and 1860s, and amongst tailors in the 1860s.[254] In the Bible controversy of 1849–50 Dunning assisted the women's strike, for which he was criticised by his members, while in the 1860s Varlin secured the admission on equal terms of women into the Paris bookbinders' society.[255]

Trade union leaders often tried to cut down 'waste' that drained society funds, such as the sums, that could be enormous, spent on entertainment. They regarded themselves as taking a broader view, and saw much of their task as educating and improving members. They often sought to exclude masters and foremen from membership, and advocated educational activities and libraries, and in England a number of trade journals appeared, partly aimed at widening the outlook of their members.[256] For the Paris bronze-chaser Tolain a trade society 'would be the trade academy' while the cabinet-maker Tartaret opposed closed shops and saw trade committees as a means of enlightenment.[257] They often sought reform through reducing drunkenness, footings, plank ales, and maiden garnish, and sometimes moved the society away from public-houses, and, to much local opposition, the ASE in 1857 forbade branch secretaries to be publicans. There were also efforts to check dishonesty, fraud, misconduct, bad workmanship, and bad behaviour to masters.[258] The Operative Stonemasons' Society adopted a rule that restricted tramp relief to the genuinely unemployed but the branches refused to implement a rule that 'amounted to sacrilege'.[259] The leaders often tried to avoid a blind opposition to machinery, preferring to secure good rates for working it, and while leaders of the Provincial Typographical Association disapproved of local refusals to admit printing-machine minders, the Amalgamated Cordwainers unsuccessfully tried to persuade lodges to admit the new riveters.[260]

Leaders often issued policy statements, and official rules were often an aspect of this, seeking to mould members' opinions rather than to govern activity, to express aspiration rather than reality. Rules insisting on proper apprenticeship or condemning piece-work were declaratory or educational, and little effort was made to enforce them. Leaders were often exasperated by the actions of their members. Since members would not attend meetings or hold office, it was sometimes by rotation that they served as officers or on committees, as with Manchester compositors, Paris hatters, or Newcastle cabinet-makers, or there were fines for not serving, as with Paris gilders.[261] The London Society of Compositors had to urge unemployed members to sign on the call books, lest masters cease sending to them for men.[262] A London carpenter complained that 'if they gave the men a Voting paper they would not Vote, and if they called a special Meeting they did not attend'. A Paris shoemaker felt the same, for 'after thinking he had sown solidarity and fraternity, he saw harvested only indifference and self-ishness . . . Always, always the struggle of a handful of convinced men struggling with the sarcasms of selfish workmen who complain inces-santly and are not willing to make any sacrifice, either of time or money, to help build solidarity.'[263]

'Selfishness' was indeed the abiding obstacle to 'building solidarity' and implementing policies for the good of the whole. Such selfishness hampered efforts to check systematic overtime, reduce working hours, or gain a Saturday half-day.[264] Trade union leaders persistently conducted steady propaganda in favour of shortening hours. This would lead to more men being hired and would therefore cause employment to be spread and the surplus of labour reduced. 'If in all trades the surplus quantity of work were properly partitioned, no man might be idle', for 'the suppression of extra hours will result in the employment of a larger number of workmen and in the reduction of periods of unemployment which are always heavy for those who endure them'.[265] This would, of course, increase the relative strength of the men. 'So long as men are willing to work 12 or 14 hours a day there will always be found a large amount of surplus hands in the market, who are unfortunately driven, through sheer necessity, to submit to the terms of grasping capitalists, who are encouraged to try more inroads on our trade customs, which often lead to expense and mischievous results.' 'Shorter hours of labour is the key-stone of all improvements in our social position.'[266] To an equal extent, they also criticised the men's lack of response to these arguments, and as the first Trades' Union Congress saw it, 'the avaricious disposition of many of the workmen for money was also a fruitful cause of this evil of long hours'.[267]

The identification of selfishness was perhaps strongest in relation to piece-work, which trade union leaders saw as leading to uncertainty over prices, encouraging men to work harder and longer to increase their earnings and thereby deprive others of work, putting men in competition with one another. For the General Committee of the Operative Stonemasons, 'tasking creates in the individually selfish, such a stimulant to individual competition, that invariably throws numbers out of employment', its spread due to 'the inordinate desire and unrestricted selfishness of our own class'.[268] 'If the workmen were virtuous enough, they would be strong enough because they would be united.'[269] As leaders often pointed out, cheap clothing and other articles produced by sweated labour, or cheap periodicals produced by 'black' firms, were bought mainly by working people.

This conception of the general good and of the trade society as an agency of morality, could be expressed in opposition to strikes. This was not necessarily a sign that leaders were more 'moderate' than the rank and file. Thomas Wright believed that more radical and militant men tended to be elected to trade union posts, while George Howell believed officers were usually against strikes.[270] There was no uniformity, but even in combinations the leaders' wider views, their concern that resources should not be depleted and their recognition that gains made at a favourable time would probably be transient, led to opposition to intransigence and 'no surrender' cries. As the tailor Matthew Lawrence, a founder of the LOTPA and member of the General Council of the International Working Men's Association, put it, 'the men may at the beginning of a busy season compel the masters to yield an advance, but as soon as that season is gone the masters will embrace their opportunity and neither have any principle to act upon'. The leaders of the Paris and London tailors in 1833–4 and 1867 seem on each occasion to have been against the strikes that occurred, and the secretary of the Amalgamated Tailors felt that some of the branches had acted with more zeal than discretion. Against the wishes of their leaders, in a display of selfishness, the rank and file Huddersfield tailors both pressed for a local strike and refused to back the union's support for the London strike.[271] In the 1830s the Operative Stonemasons' Executive, frequently vehement against employers and firm in opposition to any abuses, nevertheless warned constantly, for tactical reasons, against too many local strikes.

If it did come to a strike, trade union leaders wished to convey the issues as concerning wages and hours, because these were more likely to create united action among the men and would also have a better effect on public opinion. Wages and hours were 'good' issues in strikes, as were the document, the discharge note, and the right to belong to a trade union, but restrictions on apprenticeship, closed shops, or opposition to machinery were 'bad' issues. However, this does not mean that a stress on wages and hours was particularly the work of officers, for, as we have seen, these were the usual issues in wider combinations.[272] Officials did develop skills at putting public cases, arguing, for instance, that shorter hours would mean less toil, more time with the family, and opportunities for mental improvement and cultivation. Thus we have here another extra-workplace function of the trade society, the presentation of a public case. The movement for nine hours in the London building trade, that led to the great 1859 dispute, was begun by the small Progressive Society of Carpenters with a prize essay competition, and the distribution of 10,000 printed copies of the winning entry (written by the Chartist Leno).[273] Other prize essays organised by trade societies followed in the 1860s.

Thus trade unions did not passively express an underlying unity of sentiment or interests, for the trade was not an existing entity, as disagreements over which groups of workmen should be included showed. They were conscious creations which sought to construct this unity, emphasising the collective good and unselfishness, both as regards the public realm and the divided membership. One aspect of this was their frequent espousal of benefits, both as a way of reassuring agents of the state and public opinion, and as a means of welding members into a stable whole. Benefits were a way of committing people to the society and avoiding frequent fluctuations in membership. They would strengthen the society, attract members, and mean a more efficient use of funds than shop collections and *ad hoc* or casual arrangements.[274] The OSM Executive, militant in its defence of men's rights against encroachments in the 1830s, continually urged members to join its optional sick fund, and was annoyed that this was retarded by 'a great number of our fraternity making voluntary subscriptions for careless individuals', which amounted to more in total than would regular contributions to the fund; if everyone joined it, it would make keener members of 'those lukewarm individuals who now only support the trade by compulsion . . . Thus, by providing for a time of sickness, we should be erecting a barrier in defence of our trade which would enable us to set at nought the wily intrigues of those despotic tyrants, who would fain make our homes hovels of squalled [*sic*] poverty and wretchedness, to enable themselves to riot and feast on the vitals of our honest industry.' A compulsory sick fund would also attract non-migratory masons.[275] Large benefits and subscriptions explained the strength of the Sheffield societies, ironfounders, and engineers, and enabled the ASE to survive the total defeat of 1852.[276] The great prestige of the ASE led others to copy it in the 1860s, in pursuit of a large, more stable and committed membership, greater funds, and a means of disciplining members and keeping them in line, as they had more to lose by being expelled. But such organisations were not typical and the policy met strong opposition both because it meant high subscriptions and because so many were already members of benefit societies and preferred low-subscription trade societies. Trade society leaders were much keener than the membership on benefits, and members of the

London Society of Compositors objected to the leaders' establishment of unemployment relief in 1838 and the proposal for a funeral grant in 1839; 'the members of the Union objected to the principle of converting a Trade Society into a Society for the Relief of its Members'.[277] In 1850 the Paris compositors' society agreed to create both a library and a central relief fund to replace the workshop funds which gave relief to members and non-member 'saracens' alike, so as to force the latter into the society. The decision to make this new fund compulsory was opposed by those who were already members of benefit societies, and led to a secession under the former president, Parmentier, to form a 'daughter' Free Association of the Scale. But this had the same problem of tying members to it, so instead of benefits it established a lottery, in which only members not in subscription arrears could take part.[278] An attempt in 1859 to unite the London tailors' call-houses failed because of the compulsory sick benefits, and the issue divided the LOTPA and Amalgamated Tailors in the 1860s. The committee of the former favoured one, but 'the feeling in the trade was that the committee were striving more to establish a sick fund than to raise up an Association for trade protection purposes'.[279] There were similar criticisms of the ASE, and the new national shoemakers' unions formed in the 1840s and 1860s averted opposition by making their sick funds optional.[280]

Given their wider perspectives, trade union leaders tended to be more favourable to common action with other trade societies than was the general membership. While sympathy and support for a group in difficulties or in dispute was widespread, efforts to establish common formal organisations met resistance in what leaders often saw as 'trade selfishness' (*l'égoïsme de la corporation*). The National Association of United Trades, established in 1845, found great difficulties in 'inducing such a combination of trades, each having different pursuits, different rates of wages, and, at first sight, different interests, to unite in sufficiently large numbers to give these principles a fair trial'.[281] From the 1840s a number of trades' delegate committees did arise in several towns to facilitate such mutual help, including London and Paris, but common organisation usually proved easier to achieve over political rather than industrial issues, as this was an easier way of transcending trade and society divisions, whether or not the 'political' activity was on specifically trade union or labour issues or of a more general kind. An example was Paris in 1848, where after the February revolution the new Provisional Government established a Workers' Commission at the Luxembourg Palace, to be composed of delegates from the different trades, to study labour questions, and prepare draft legislation for the forthcoming Constituent Assembly. This institution, and the elections to it, encouraged a great wave of industrial activity, organisation, and demands among the Paris trades in the next few months, in fact a wave of combinations of the familiar kind, and the Luxembourg Commission became a central co-ordinating organisation for this labour movement. But the main activities of the Luxembourg delegates were political, with the great demonstrations of 17 March, 16 April, and 15 May, and, particularly, with the elections to the new Assembly. They drew up a list of candidates after putting ten questions to all those seeking nomination, the topics covered being religion, divorce, the army, European relations, the fiscal system, magistracy, and the 'organisation of work', not really a very specifically 'labour' programme. Although after May the Luxembourg delegates (no longer an official commission or allowed to meet at the Luxembourg Palace) did go on to drawing up a programme of economic organisation, they still continued their political activity, in the form of petitions to the Assembly, the establishment of a journal which dealt with political matters as much as industrial ones, and activities in alliance with radicals in subsequent elections. The short-lived co-operation in June with the delegates of workers at the National Workshops was confined to a joint political declaration.[282] 'Working men's committees' in other French towns in 1848 and 1849 were also mainly political or electoral organisations.[283] Similarly, in London and Manchester in these same years political organisations of trades were established, the London one continuing for a few years.[284] While the London Trades' Council emerged in 1860 out of the trades' delegate meetings of 1859–60 in support of the builders' strike and, like the earlier Central Association of London Trades and a Paris counterpart, issued recommendations of support for strikes after examining the issues, its main activity was in fact political, opposing the supply of government workmen to replace men on strike, and campaigning over reform of the Master and Servant Law, over legislation on courts of conciliation and arbitration, and on mines regulation, the American Civil War, and franchise reform.[285] Similarly the various provincial trades' councils of the 1850s and 1860s were mainly political bodies, active in local and electoral action and as political pressure groups, as was the Trades' Union Congress, formed in 1868 in anticipation of imminent legislation.

In general, the sort of political issues that artisan organisations were willing to unite over were reactive ones, responses not initiatives. There was little campaigning among British trades in favour of the 1824 repeal of the Combination Laws, but a large one against the threat in 1825 of new coercive legislation. A renewed threat in 1837–8 produced trades' committees and the establishment in London of two trade union newspapers, the *Operative* and the *Charter*, while the national protest campaign that raised nearly two million signatures and defeated a new Masters and Servants bill in 1844, was the main factor behind the formation in 1845 of the National Association of United Trades. The government repression of the Paris strikes in 1840 provoked the establishment of a new working men's newspaper, the *Atelier*. This paper's efforts to arouse a campaign in favour of workers' representation on a new Paris Court of Arbitration gained limited support, but a government bill in 1845 to make the pass-book (*livret*) compulsory for all workers provoked an opposition campaign that involved twenty-nine trades, and it was only now that they were willing to press for reform of the courts of arbitration, and repeal of the anti-combination clauses of the Penal Code and the 1834 law against associations.[286] Similar campaigns arose in England over the Wolverhampton tin-plate workers' trial in 1851, which seemed to put in jeopardy some of the provisions of the 1825 act, and new moves against trade unions on the later 1860s. It was their role in the latter that established the pre-eminence in the trade union world of the amalgamated unions, especially the ASE, ASCJ, and OBS. In the same way there were united campaigns among benefit societies against proposed restrictive legislation in 1827–8 and 1833–4, the former leading to the drawing up of an alternative bill which was passed by Parliament, the latter to a permanent organisation. While in the early 1850s the Christian Socialists gained little support in their efforts to reform friendly society legislation, the situation was transformed by a new coercive bill in 1854, which led to a two-year campaign that, in a repetition of 1828–9, secured the defeat of the offending bill and the enactment of a favourable one.[287]

A study of 'trade unionism' reveals a number of points that are themes in the rest of the book. One is the multitude of distinctions, divisions, and conflicts within the workforce, something that trade societies themselves accentuated. But trade societies were not direct emanations of the workplace or on the whole involved in the many conflicts there. This is therefore also likely to have been the case with radicalism. Radicals who criticised trade societies included men who sought positions of trade union leadership from a variety of motives, such as from a desire for esteem and influence, altruism, and a wish to educate and improve the general membership, and for whom radicalism more often led to trade union policies than *vice versa*. Yet trade societies were still responses to material concerns over such things as insecurity, illness, or old age, while also incorporating non-material concerns such as conviviality. The fact that wider joint action was mainly over wages indicates that these were one of the chief concerns of radical artisans, alongside unemployment and food prices. As in other organisations there was constant tension over priorities, one issue being the wish of many leaders for trade societies to adopt a more public role, and enter civil society and politics, things that very many others considered not their business.

# 4    Work and radicalism

The divisions, hierarchies, antagonisms and exclusiveness in the work-place and in labour organisations, and the fact that wider combinations were mainly over wages and hours, would seem a poor basis for movements for political democracy and egalitarianism. Yet trade union leaders were often radicals, seeking to reform their organisations, combat selfishness and educate the members. Furthermore it was easier to unite trade societies in common movements for political rather than economic goals. Not only were trade societies involved in politics, there were other important links between work and radicalism, including the language of industrial conflicts, and the importance of work groups and trade societies as means of mobilisation for radical political action.

### Trade unions and politics

As was indicated in the previous chapter, three features in trade unionism encouraged political action. The first was a tendency of trade societies to act as political lobbies in the interests of their industry. It was particularly common for depressed trades in Britain, including those of tailors, cabinet-makers and carpenters, to press for legislative protection because they could see no other ways of improving their position.[1] Bakers' societies engaged in repeated public campaigns to collect and publish evidence on their working conditions and to press for legislation.[2] This was particularly the case when the government or state was seen as the source of the evils complained of, such as the cheap labour in prisons, the armed forces, the poorhouses, and convents, or the government, military, naval, or police orders to low-paying or sweating firms.[3] But this function was not confined to any particular kind of artisan trade, and the failures of such campaigns could lead to support for radicalism through producing resentment and a wish to change those in authority.

A second feature of trade unionism that had political significance was the fact that many leaders of trade societies were rather detached from the general membership, wished for reforms in organisation and work-place practices, and were concerned with their societies' public face. Thus they tried to influence members not to break the law over such things as the treatment of strike-breakers.[4] The leaders of the Amalgamated Society of Engineers were very concerned with favourable press publicity and the need to educate both membership and public through it.[5] Through the efforts of the Executive there was, in the great unsuccessful strike of 1851–2, not one clash with the law.[6] This concern with public opinion led in England throughout our period to the establishment of newspapers backed by trade societies, and, from the 1850s, to a number of trade journals, aimed as much at people outside the trade as at those within it.[7]

Such efforts at public sympathy in England did sometimes have some success, for public hostility was very important in the defeat of the Lancashire engineers' quittance paper in 1844, the Liverpool and London builders' documents in 1846 and 1859, and the Midland builders' discharge note in 1864.[8] The 'publicity' role of trade societies proved very important in that trade union leaders had a degree of success, not so much in changing workplace activities or behaviour as in influencing press, politicians, liberal groups such as the Social Science Association, and other elements in public opinion, in favour of the idea that trade unions were acceptable or even beneficial institutions and that, if they were treated fairly, the better elements would expand at the expense of the undesirable. Similarly liberals in France in the 1860s contrasted moderate English trade unions with militant French extremism, and saw freedom for labour organisations as the means of solving the 'social question'.[9] Such attitudes also affected governments. When in 1859 the London master builders asked the government for an expression of support and action against trade unions, the reply was a refusal and a declaration that the government must be neutral between masters and men, a stance adhered to ostensibly in the 1860s, if not always in practice. The French Imperial government also tolerated and even encouraged workers' organisations, although the nature of the regime meant that it preserved restrictions on strikes, associations, and meetings.[10] These shifts should not be exaggerated or seen as general, for there was very widespread hostility both in public opinion and the press towards industrial action and organisation as coercive, authoritarian, selfish conspiracies, subversive of good order and discipline in the workshop and society at large, and led by self-serving radical demagogues. 'All the workmen think the press is slow to do them justice, how hard it is for them to get a hearing there, and how readily everything against them finds a place.'[11] This gave special importance to radical papers such as the *Glaneuse, Populaire, Northern Star, Démocratie Pacifique, Reynolds's,* or *Bee-Hive,* which were ready to present the men's case and report their meetings free of charge.[12] Public opinion in England was prone to 'moral panics' over combinations during waves such as those of 1824–5 or 1833–4, over attempts at general unions, as in 1834 or 1845–6, or over reports of violence, terrorism, and murder, as in 1824–5, 1837–8, or 1866–7, and there were similar fears in France that republicans in 1833 and Internationalists in 1869–70 were fomenting strikes.

It was trade union leaders, in many ways detached from workplace practices and divisions, who showed a greater awareness of the political, legal, and public developments that affected their societies and members. As the ASCJ said of the Master and Servant Law, 'probably few of our present members are aware of the recent state of the law affecting workmen under their contract of service, and although the law is admitted to be one of the most one-sided and unjust laws that ever disgraced our Statute Book, we doubt much whether working men generally are aware of the extent to which it affects them'.[13] The OSM Central Committee was certainly aware of, and sought to inform its members on the 1838 enquiry into combinations, the 1851 Wolverhampton case ('If this conspiracy against labour should be successful, farewell to trade combinations, in any form'), and the 1859 Combinations Act.[14] Similarly the PTA Executive complained at the lack of interest among the branches in its campaign against the taxes on knowledge.[15]

Thus trade society leaders were much more interested in changing the laws affecting working men and their organisations. There were, however, three elements in these labour laws. Firstly, there were those dealing with employment relations, apprenticeship and workshop regulations, and contracts and breach of contract. Secondly, there were laws against combinations, collective movements for improvements, and strikes. Thirdly, there were laws affecting the legality and security of trade societies (among other societies). Clearly, the first two sets affected working people, society and non-society men alike, much more widely than those giving legal security to trade society funds, and most labour laws campaigns were to resist changes in these two categories. They involved opposition in England to harsher laws against combinations in 1825 and 1838, a harsher Master and Servant Law in 1844, a renewed threat to combinations in 1866, the tailors' and spinners' cases in 1867 and 1868 which seemed to undermine the 1825 act, and the Criminal Law Amendment Act in 1871. But in such cases, trade unions and their leaders played the chief role in the campaigns. There was far less interest in giving trade societies legal security than in the legality of strikes and walk-outs. Such concern was more widespread in connexion with those more extensive institutions, benefit societies, but even here, in both England and France, many societies preferred not to register to secure legal recognition and the attendant advantages, coupled as they were with restrictions on their activities.

In general, then, trade societies played a key role in campaigns over the labour laws, but this reflected the absence of widespread interest in such laws, least of all in the legal status of societies, with what interest there was being provoked by proposed adverse changes in the law. Efforts to initiate positive improvements in the legal situation were largely confined to a few trade society leaders and officials, usually in alliance with political radicals. The 1863 national conference on the Master and Servant laws was poorly attended, with far fewer than at the meetings on radical reform, and while a number of trade union leaders urged members to make the labour laws an issue in the 1868 general election, there does not seem to have been much response.[16]

Such a preoccupation was most clearly and prominently displayed by a small group of key trade union leaders in London in the 1860s known to historians as the 'Junta'. Their particular concern to secure a better legal position and public acceptance of trade unions led them to try to influence trade unions and combinations generally in the direction of avoiding actions that were publicly damaging, as the violence, processions and bands in the 1864 South Staffordshire colliers' strike had been. They engaged in a bitter row with Potter, mainly because of Potter's vehement support for strikes that they considered ill prepared, inappropriately timed, characterised by unnecessary intemperance, and harmful to the process of national amalgamation and to the public perception of trade unions, and because of their belief that Potter was unrealistic over what could be achieved at that particular time.[17] It was their particular concern with legislation and public acceptance of trade unions that led to their 'moderation', and to opposition from such equally 'moderate' trade society leaders as Dunning, who were much less interested in securing labour legislation and who saw the LTC as too political. Much of the Junta's prestige in the trade union world stemmed from their key role in 1867–8 in defeating the attempts at more repressive legislation, rather than from any acceptance of the need to give trade unions legal recognition.[18] Their special concern with legal questions and the labour laws was not typical of the trade union world, and it is not clear that they had much support. Certainly their views should not be equated with those of 'organised labour'.[19]

In France, repression was much greater, but government initiatives were still crucial in Paris efforts to change the labour laws. It was through government sponsorship and funds that trades' delegates were elected to attend the international exhibitions of 1862 and 1867, and their proposals led to the legalisation of strikes in 1864 and the 'toleration' of workmen's trade organisations in 1868.

Thus trade societies did sometimes engage in political action connected with their legal position. But this political action was not necessarily political radicalism. William Newton certainly attributed the inequity of the labour laws to the limited electorate, and saw the remedy in universal suffrage,[20] but the ASE and most other trade societies usually steered clear of formal expressions of support for radicalism. The distinction was made clear in the Chartist Ernest Jones' comments on the London compositors. 'Like most trades, they are highly conservative, conserving old forms and conditions of things, keeping themselves to themselves, taking no heed of public questions, *except as far as they may seem to disturb their own selves* – the Masters' and Servants' Bill for example – or may obviously tend to the Trade Welfare – Abolition of Paper Duties for example.'[21] But the London compositors' society's committee had good trade union reasons other than 'conservatism' for opposing political questions, 'for it must be obvious to you that in our ranks will be found men of all shades of politics, and were we to make it a practice to entertain questions of that character we are satisfied that the primary object for which we associate might be lost sight of in the tumult of political passions and the very existence of our Society endangered'.[22] Many trade society leaders who were themselves radicals and were very keen for their societies to be aware of labour laws and to support efforts for their reform (and often disappointed at the members' response), nevertheless opposed political radical activity within their societies, because it would arouse opposition and cause disunity.[23] As Dunning explained, political questions, apart from legislative threats to trade unions, were divisive, as workmen were divided into conservatives, liberals, and radicals, with the bulk being non-political and antipathetic to political agitators.[24] Thus in the 1830s the OSM leaders, despite their radicalism, a number of them being Chartists, still strongly urged the 'no-politics' rule.[25] All members of the central committee of the London Operative Tailors' Association were in favour of the reform demonstration in February 1867, but still opposed participating as a union.[26] Coulson, a member of the Junta, was an active radical, and the Operative Bricklayers' Executive even supported parliamentary reform and labour candidates at elections, but he still enforced the no-politics rule.[27]

The third aspect of trade unionism that could lead to politics, alongside the trade societies acting as specific-interest lobbies and the leaders' concern over the public position and legal situation of trade societies, was the radicalising effect of some combinations. In themselves, strikes were not political, but, as was indicated above, one of the features that was most likely to lead to wider emotion and support was the authorities' intervention against the strikes and then siding with the employers.[28] This clearly had radical implications. Thus the London builders' struggle in 1859 aroused trade society, radical, and Chartist support. It was also the case that those who emerged as leading figures in these combinations were often not leaders, or even members, of the existing trade societies, of which they were often critical, and were more likely to be political or social radicals. Thus radicals took the lead in forming the new London tailors' Grand Lodge in 1833, republicans set up the Paris resistance societies of the same year, and Chartists were prominent in launching new national tailors' and shoemakers' movements in England in the mid-1840s.[29] Combinations were far more likely than trade societies to involve people in radical, as opposed to special interest, politics.[30] During the Reform campaign in England in 1866–7, a few people did relate parliamentary reform to labour legislation, and the Hornby versus Close judgement in 1867, which undid the legal protection of trade society funds granted in the 1855 act, persuaded Allen and Applegarth to lead the ASE and ASCJ into supporting a Reform League demonstration officially as societies, but this was unusual, and in general the labour laws seem to have had little effect on the Reform campaign. Nor were labour issues of much importance in the 1868 election. It was much more the case that emotions over industrial disputes, particularly at 'unfair' actions by authorities, fuelled opposition to privilege and support for radicalism. In the north there was little trade union support for the Reform League, but the many strikes in the winter of 1866–7 did increase support for both radicalism and the League. Similarly, it was a meeting in Birmingham in March 1865 on the Staffordshire lock-out, attended by George Potter, that led to the formation of a branch of the Reform League.[31] Labour disputes could fuel radicalism, but mainly in terms of evoking support for the poor and unprivileged who were only seeking justice in the face of wealthy and well-connected employers and biased authorities, and this led to support not for changes in the labour laws but for radical reform to end privilege.

Radicalism did not usually spring from trade unionism, but rather the reverse. Applegarth was a radical *before* he joined the local Sheffield carpenters' society, and immediately set about reforming it – through meetings at a reading room instead of a public-house, discussions on political and social issues, and by joining the new Amalgamated

Carpenters' Society. When he became the ASCJ General Secretary and moved to London, it was through the Chartist Leno that he entered the world of the radical clubs.[32] George Howell and George Odger were Chartists in the 1840s, and, like Cremer, only entered trade union activity through rallying *as radicals* to the builders in 1859. These three then all became leaders in new trade unions. Similarly, London Chartists had been prominent in establishing the new general union, the National Association of United Trades, in 1845, while Peter Henriette was a leading London Chartist in the 1850s before becoming a leader of the new London tailors' union in the 1860s. Most artisan radicalism was not concerned with the labour laws, and was accurately expressed in the great workmen's paper, *Reynolds's Newspaper*, which combined support for the men's side in every single industrial dispute with a radicalism that constantly assailed aristocracy, privilege and corruption.[33] Of course in many cases opposition politicians defended men on trial for striking.[34] Radicals often condemned the inequity of labour laws and advocated freedom for trade unions and strikes,[35] sometimes supporting them,[36] and gaining gratitude through the stance taken by such papers as the *Northern Star*, 'that friend of man and advocate of labour'.[37] But, like trade society leaders, radicals were also critical of aspects of trade unionism – the hostility between societies, trade particularism, and the culture of drink,[38] while some radicals aroused criticism of their employment and industrial practices.

Thus labour activists and political radicals were not created by their occupational position, and radicalism was not so much a response to workshop problems and values as a demand for the widening of social life and the public sphere beyond an exclusive propertied civil society. But trade society leaders, including, or especially, 'reforming' ones, were frequently radicals, and the values and emotions expressed in combinations were very consistent with those of radicalism.

### The language of conflict

This language was expressed by Dunning in relation to the inequity of the law on labour activity:

They had had painful experience of middle-class juries, but what they had to fear now was from middle-class judges; that is, judges who were imbued with middle-class prejudices and opinions in favour of wealth and those who possess it, and a sovereign contempt for the workmen who produced it, regarding them as mere serfs, having no privileges or rights, as opposed to those who possessed wealth.[39]

But a language that drew on basic liberal values and was so consonant with radical expression was not confined to discussions of legal and political constrictions. The terminology of freedom, tyranny, and slavery suffused trade societies, disputes, and strikes, for strikes were caused by 'despotic encroachments', and 'even a foolish strike is a defence of free labour'.[40] Workmen subject to low pay and long hours, or at the mercy of their employers were 'white slaves'.[41] 'Talk no more of black slavery or the *liberty* of Englishmen', retorted the Bristol masons, while the rules of Manchester master shoemakers were 'well calculated to reduce them to the most abject state of slavery', and a union of all trades would 'be a means of redeeming the mechanics and artisans of our country from that position of slavery and serfdom to which tyranny has confined them'.[42] Men who refused to stand up for themselves were slaves: masons were sacked by a master in Accrington 'because they refused to become his willing slaves by giving up their right to think for themselves', and two blacklegs at a firm in Little Heywood 'are well known to all the Masons who have worked in his employment, as deceitful fawning slaves, who would lick the dust from their tyrant's shoes rather than follow the example of their shopmates, by standing up for their rights'.[43] The engineers' dispute of 1851–2 'is a struggle of vital importance to the producing classes of this country, inasmuch as it is a question of liberty of thought, word, and action; and indeed, whether the "British bee" shall be a slave or a free man'.[44] 'The employers of labour would, if they could, reduce the British operative to the condition of a serf.'[45] Bordeaux tailors struck against 'tyrants', and master coopers in Lunel also wished to be despots, two terms regularly used by the Operative Stonemasons, especially in the 1830s and 1840s.[46] Sacking men for belonging to a society was an 'act of barbarism'.[47] Birmingham carpenters resisting the discharge note declared that disputes were 'each occasioned by the attempts of the employers to make further encroachments upon the little of liberty that is left to them, and that should this discharge note become an established rule of the trade, there would be an end at once to all freedom of action', and Swansea carpenters agreed it was an infringement of the rights and liberties of every working man.[48] Havre compositors in 1869 opposed Sunday work as 'anti-social and contrary to man's aspirations to liberty'.[49]

Defence of liberty and rejection of tyranny was an act of self-respect; men deserved respectful treatment from employers, and the 1866 London tailors' dispute 'was not simply a question of wages, but one of better treatment towards the men. Many employers and many foremen had been too much in the habit of treating their men with a vast amount of contumely, in the belief that they would always find plenty of men to work for them; but this would not be the case if the men would exercise that self-respect they ought to do.'[50] Tyranny by masters and foremen infringed workmen's independence and honour, and there should be honourable behaviour between them.[51] The usual term in England was 'respectability', a term which impinged on a number of aspects – proper training for lads, keeping wages at a decent level and not working for low pay, keeping out unqualified workmen, maintaining aged members, and burying the dead, and not bringing a society into discredit through bad language, defective work, or letting the employer down.[52] The Maidstone carpenters decided that 'Br. Edward Jordan be excluded for bringing the Society into discredit in making Common 4 panel doors for 6–6d. and finding materials'.[53] The equivalent terms in French were *digne* and *dignité*. The Paris gilders agreed that 'one must no longer work by the year for any master in gilding and painting, as the *dignité* of the worker in the 19th century, no longer allows him to be the most obedient servant of another'.[54] The Paris tailors in 1840 rejected the *livret* 'and see it as a blow to their dignity' ('pensent voir leur dignité compromise'), while the Paris trades in 1867 rallied to the support of the locked-out calico-printers, feeling 'attacked in our dignity and independence'.[55] 'Let the workman respect himself and become respected, let him at last understand his worth, his rights and his dignity!'[56]

Accordingly, trade societies adopted a high moral tone, as defenders of principle and opponents of selfishness. Masters who opposed them were 'unprincipled', selfish, and mercenary, strike-breakers were 'men devoid of all principle', an attack on a trade society 'is to leave the ground open to selfishness'.[57]

They thus championed the rights of labour and sons of toil. Labour was a form of property which should therefore be protected.[58] It was the creator of wealth, for 'our brother toilers' were 'working *Bees*', and masters 'these crafty drones on the vitals of our industry'.[59] Workmen should 'wring from the privileged idlers of society, a sufficiency to keep soul and body together, of the wealth which they themselves produce'.[60] 'We have a right to live by the "sweat of our brow".'[61] With these claims for consideration, respect, recognition, and equality they rejected their characterisation as lackeys or servants in the Master and Servants Law and articles of the Criminal Code.[62] 'We grasp the hand of friendship not as hirelings, but as men who feel they have social rights and a social position.'[63]

This was to stress their character as men. Oppressive foremen imposed servility on workmen, so that they did not have dignity 'or act like men'.[64] 'We are not dogs . . . we object to be mere tools.'[65] The Paris tailors' poverty and insecurity meant 'we are not men like others', they should strike and not humiliate themselves 'at the price of honour and infamy', and one of their leaders showed 'his manly (*mâle*) courage in the battle'.[66] Manliness embodied notions of independence, self-reliance, and respect. The Sunderland tailors' society was a 'means of promoting a fraternal spirit amongst them, cherishing sentiments of manly independence, (free from the insolence of ignorance)'.[67] Exploitative sub-contracting was 'unmanly', men who left the Operative Stonemasons were 'instances of unmanliness', Manchester bricklayers struck in 1841, for 'we esteem our character as men', the Bristol trades' delegates agreed that the striking London masons 'acted as men', and Exeter shoemakers in 1853 acted to improve their situation through a 'sense of our dignity as men'.[68] A London baker in 1871 did not regret having taken part in a strike in 1835 despite being victimised for it, for 'I had the courage to stand up for my right like a man, and preserve my self respect for so doing.'[69] Compositors offered the choice of leaving their society or losing their jobs, 'chose the manly part', in 1864 plasterers in Hull decided to strike and 'came out like men', and when Manchester bakers were finally goaded into action, they had 'asserted their manhood at last'.[70]

Manliness was also associated with patriotism. Master painters in Chester 'are taking advantage of the winter season to wreak an Un-English and unmanly vengeance on the leading officers of the Society', while Lyons weavers were urged 'let us unite with perseverance and show ourselves worthy of the French people. We are not cowards or *ceresfin* or beggars.'[71]

Thus trade unions 'were devised and established solely for the purpose of bringing about a spirit of manly independence – to foster a spirit of brotherly love – and to seek the enlightenment and moral elevation of its members. They seek the independence of their members . . .'[72] The values of freedom, independence, self-respect, dignity, fraternity, worth of labour, manliness, and patriotism were all linked, and were also basic values of radicalism. Thus in the statements of trade society leaders and, especially, during combinations, we find a common radical language based far more on the wish to be admitted to civil society than on an analysis of economic and work functions. Such statements are far more plentiful in England and Wales than in France because of the more repressed and restricted area for public activity and pronouncements, but the general consonance between supra-workshop values and concepts and those of radicalism seems clear, and is well expressed in these three statements from the Operative Stonemasons, not intended for public perusal. 'Our society by the utmost perseverance and ardour have resisted the incessant attacks of power and tyranny to oppress the labourer and defraud him of his well-earned hire, they have surmounted the baneful treachery of unprincipled members, and are united to protect not to injure, the public approbation of a Body professing such patriotic principles is the highest honour which can be conferred on any man.'[73] During a strike, the Manchester masons, in a letter 'expressing the sentiments of our society with manful and becoming dignity', explained that 'we are determined to maintain the legitimate rights and privileges of our trade . . . the turnouts are determined manfully and zealously to defend their position, conscious their liberty, their interest – and all that is dear to them is at stake'. They were opposed by the masters, 'the combining despots. . . that they may, with impunity, treat those by whom they are kept in affluence with their wanted barbarity'.[74] The Weedon and Coventry masons sought a pay rise in 1837. 'Good God, is it inconsistent in working men to better their condition? Men who are the real producers of wealth; men who, after toiling and bleeding to keep a set of lazy and insolent plunderers in luxury, are very frequently doomed to pass their declining years in some accursed Bastille, or in obscurity, starvation and wretchedness! Ah! worthy brothers, we have hitherto been used worse than brutes, let us now strive to be men.'[75]

Such written statements emanate from leaders of trade societies and combinations, many of whom were involved in radicalism. They are therefore not necessarily expressions of a language of the workplace, and might be seen as the views of a small, untypical minority. But since, as we have seen, the most emotion and support was aroused by conflicts involving the 'tyranny' of the document, discharge note, or *livret*, or by the intervention of authorities on the side of employers, this suggests these radical values had a much more widespread resonance.

### Political mobilisation

There was a third form of connexion between work and radicalism, alongside forms of trade union political action and shared language. This lay in the bases for political mobilisation. Clearly the workplace itself, or the place where work was sought and found was a useful place for collecting signatures to petitions or subscriptions to organisations, or for selling publications. Thus the republican Friends of the People in the early 1830s sought to base its activity on the colleges, offices, and workshops, the workplaces of the three main groups it looked to for support – students, clerks, and artisans,[76] and it was through the workshops that republicans in the 1840s gained 130,000 signatures to a petition calling for an enquiry into the poverty of workers. The *Atelier* regarded the most influential location of propaganda as the workshops, though it was not always happy about 'this tendency for workshops to become little *political clubs*, where political and social questions are debated, at the expense of work, where often perhaps one is corrupted more than educated'.[77] Sometimes the employer led workplace radical activity.[78] Whole workshops participated in the June Days in 1848; it was compositors working on the *Leeds Mercury* who in 1860 established the Leeds Working Men's Parliamentary Reform Association; while the public works yards were centres of political activity in France in 1848 and 1870.[79] Workplace organisation was also very useful in clandestine activity, as in South Wales before the 1839 rising, and in France in the later Second Republic and after the *coup d'état*, when, for example, the revolutionary secret society 'Militante' in Bordeaux recruited whole workshops.[80]

Trade and benefit societies and club houses could perform the same functions, and mobilise people around political values external to the trade.[81] 'When society business is concluded, and the meeting has been formally closed, it is not unusual for the members to remain sitting, with the same chairman, to discuss social and political questions.'[82] Some trade societies were virtually political clubs, such as the Silver Cup Society of Carpenters in London, and a number formed Chartist or Reform League branches.[83] Unlike the preceding secret society of the 'Families', composed of students and, especially, soldiers, the 'Seasons' in Paris in the late 1830 had sections composed wholly of members of one trade, namely boot-blockers (*cambreurs*), carpenters, tailors, cooks, smiths, and hatters.[84]

The importance of trade clubs as agents of political mobilisation is shown by the attention paid to them in elections when their members had the vote, as in the English freeman boroughs before 1832, and in France after 1848.[85] This was not only true of radical candidates, and the trades were used to organise support for non-partisan events, such as the coronation processions in Manchester in 1821, 1831, and 1837.[86] Inevitably, then, radicals looked to trade organisations as a means of securing mass support for demonstrations and campaigns.[87] After defeat in 1839 and their consequent regroupment, the Chartists directed their efforts towards trade societies.[88] This was especially true in the great city of London, whose large distances and diversified nature made it notoriously difficult to mobilise.[89] Thus trade societies and clubs were key elements there in the 1831–2 Reform agitation and Chartism.[90] When in 1864 a new reform league was being attempted, Holyoake attributed the small numbers at the first public meeting to a failure to canvass the trades, and it was clearly recognised by radicals that visiting such societies was the way to secure support. 'Without the TRADES UNIONS', wrote Marx, ' no MASS MEETING is possible.'[91] Thus trade societies played a vital role in the campaigns on behalf of both the North in the American Civil War and the Poles, in those for the opening of museums and galleries on Sundays, and, especially, in those for parliamentary reform, with the radical mobilisation of trade societies in London a great contrast to the situation in Manchester.[92] Similarly, in Paris in the first half of 1848, when open political campaigning was possible, trade organisations were crucial in the great radical demonstrations of 25 and 28 February, 17 March, 16 April, and 15 May, and thereafter in radical voting in elections, when other forms of political expression were checked.[93]

However, the importance of workplace groups and club houses in political mobilisation does not mean that the radicalism was about workplace and trade questions, and the extent to which it was not so made it possible for artisans to combine with other groups in political activity. They were effective *locations* for, and means of, political organisation for a radicalism that asserted the right of the common people to speak and think for themselves, to enter fully into civil society. Nevertheless the actual activities and practices of radical groups could indeed reflect work and club concerns, and this could lead to tensions with other radicals in the movement. These points can be illustrated through a consideration of two particular radical organisations, the Society of the Rights of Man in Paris in 1832–4, and the International Working Men's Association of the later 1860s.

### Practice

As has been indicated earlier, the July Monarchy established in the 1830 revolution disappointed many who hoped for more extensive changes (and, often, for posts for themselves), and they moved into opposition to a government that demobilised the National Guard, did not provide education for all, introduced greater controls of the press, made its peace with the church, did nothing to help the Poles or Italians, and became increasingly conservative and repressive. Such opposition, in branches of the 'Aide-toi' association, patriotic associations, and societies in defence of the press, often moved into republican opposition to the new regime itself, whose king seemed to be playing a more active role. Much of this republicanism was really part of a wider liberal opposition, as was shown in electoral alliances, but more radical and democratic organisations appeared in the early 1830s, condemning the continuities from the previous regime, the revision of the constitution by the Chambers alone instead of by the people through a national convention, the abandonment of the principles of 1789 and of the promises of a 'republican monarchy', and the ascendancy of new privileged groups. They demanded administrative decentralisation, universal service in the National Guard, reduction of government expenditure and salaries, reform of customs and excise to help the poor, provision of free education for all, freedom of association, extension of trial by jury, cheap state credit, and a single legislative chamber elected by universal suffrage.[94] The chief republican organisation, the Friends of the People, actively sought working-class support, especially when reorganised and purged by Raspail.[95] It was this positive attitude towards workmen and the acceptance of them as equals that was so radical, and overwhelmed those workmen who did join.[96]

However, they had little success at first and republican societies remained small. Workmen were generally hostile to republican students who caused trouble and, by creating uncertainty, hampered economic recovery.[97] In striking contrast to England, there seems in 1830 to have been no working-class demand for the vote or for political participation. Yet great hopes had nevertheless been pinned on the new regime, and there were expectations of gratitude, consideration, and sympathy from the new authorities towards their plight, their grievances, and their limited desires over prices, wages, hours and unemployment. The shattering of these hopes and the *worsening* of economic depression after the revolution clearly made for discontent, especially as the revolution was universally regarded as the work and achievement of the Paris 'people'. There were disturbances, unemployed workmen took part in some radical and republican demonstrations, and the hardening of lines and antagonisms radicalised some of the working population, especially in Paris and Lyons.[98] While the Friends of the People remained small, a few sections composed of workers were formed, which were more radical, and these developed into a separate society of the Rights of Man which supplanted and absorbed the Friends of the People in 1832.[99] The Rights of Man sought to attract workmen and stressed the injustice and sufferings of the 'proletarians', although they had few specific proposals. Their aim was action 'to teach the working men, to penetrate the workshops so as to enlighten them', and 'the political education of the working class and the improvement thereby of the lot of this class'.[100] Yet membership was not large, and even in decline after July 1833.

The situation was transformed by the wave of industrial demands and strikes in the autumn of 1833. These were combinations in a period of economic activity of the type already described, often involving

temporary organisations and the co-operation of already existing trade
societies.[101] As explained earlier, in such combinations new men often
emerged as the leading figures, especially from among the political
radicals, and so it was that a number of members of the Rights of Man
were leaders of these combinations. For example, there were Efrahem,
Courtais, Rigal, and Pechoutre among the shoemakers; Grignon,
Maurin, Troncin, and Nepireu among the tailors; Royer of the cabinet-
makers; Dupuy of the boot-blockers; Allard of the smiths; Bourrière of
the cotton-spinners; Rubin of the paper-stainers; Seigneurgens of the
bonnet-makers; Pérard of the glove-makers; and Pasquier-Labruyère of
the compositors.[102] A number of other men were active in both
combinations and republican activity.[103] The Rights of Man leadership
responded by establishing a propaganda committee in which the law
students Marc Dufraise and Félix Mathé met regularly with these
leaders of the combinations, to organise propaganda aimed at the
workmen involved. Mathé toured trades meetings, and republicans
helped artisans draw up appeals.[104] The Central Committee issued a
statement identifying with the workers and applauding their attempts 'to
improve their position and break the yoke of their exploiting masters',
and opened a subscription to help those arrested and prosecuted.[105]
Other radicals also criticised the harsh punishments of strikers, and
radical papers were established aimed specifically at a working-class
readership.[106] The Rights of Man were not, as the authorities claimed,
the instigators of the combinations and strikes. However, the outcome,
especially with their defeat and repression and the radicalising experience of prison, was a revival of the society, mainly through the adhesion
of artisan groups.[107]

The nature and composition of different sections varied; while one,
for instance, 'was mainly concerned with discussing the Saint-Simonian
system, of which several were adherents',[108] in others work organisations
and groups were clearly important. Some were persuaded to go to
meetings by fellow-members of their trade.[109] One section, composed
mainly of cooks and eating-house keepers, met at a hotel where a
member was head of the kitchen.[110] It is not, then, surprising that a
number of sections were composed wholly or mainly of members of a
single trade: these were four of shoemakers (Mucius Scaevola, Peace to
the Cottages, Fifth and Sixth of June, War on the Mansions), five of
tailors (Right of Revision, Phocion, Lebas, Maurin, and another), two of
coach-makers (sections 2 and 5 of District 1), one of compositors
(Cordelliers) and one of goldsmiths (Three Days), while a number of
others had a large proportion from a single trade, for example shoemakers (Barricade), bootmakers (Cimber), cooks (Phocion, Marcus

Brutus), saddlers (Frankfurt, no. 5 of District 1), joiners (Passy), tailors (Washington), gold and silversmiths (Abolition of Ill-Acquired Property), dyers (Barricade of Méry), and porcelain-painters (Radicals).[111] Kersausie's secret and semi-separate Action Society also consisted mainly of shoemakers.[112] Clearly this development was not planned by the society leadership but arose out of occupational contacts. Although working men formed the bulk of the membership, this was not true of the officials, the Central Committee, and the quarter commissioners and sub-commissioners, none of whom were working men except for the currier Delente, the token (and illiterate) proletarian on the Central Committee, whose election was due to votes from the student sections, not from workers. Yet the leadership had to come to terms with this development, and in January 1834 ordered the section leaders to draw up lists of members, giving their trade or occupation. 'The Committee will then remodel the sections so as to make them of a single trade; though taking care not to move members of one district or even one quarter to another', so that members would be more united and 'the Committee will thereby have revived the *compagnonnage*, while sloughing off all the ceremonies bequeathed by XIII century barbarism'.[113] The last remark, reflecting a sudden awareness of the *compagnonnages* because of the carpenters' strike in September 1833,[114] revealed an unfamiliarity with the world of work that led to tensions between the leadership and the sections. In the eyes of the former, the function of the sections was to further political education by distributing republican literature and discussing political topics and committee resolutions, to collect subscriptions, and to organise men so as to be ready to act immediately to resist any move by the government against liberty. But the motives that led men to join seem more varied, some citing a desire for general education,[115] and even, in the case of a German tailor, to learn French.[116] Others sought help in finding work, unemployment relief, other benefits, and trade advantages, as well as convivial activities.[117] Not surprisingly, several sections did carry out benefit and placement functions, and held collections for unfortunate members, just like other journeymen's societies, and the Central Committee also had to accept this, and advocate sick relief and loans to those out of work 'to organise labour and mutual assistance'.[118]

These working men's sections were thus revealing a variety of concerns apart from the strictly political ones, and imported activities familiar from other organisations, to turn the branches into multi-purpose institutions, thereby illustrating a difference in outlook from the middle-class leadership, a difference not welcome to them that could lead to tensions. In particular, republicans were worried about labour disputes that caused divisions between masters and men and thereby brought harm to the political unity between them that they were trying to create. While sympathising with the 'proletarians', denouncing their poverty, seeking their support, and asserting their right to combine, they found it easier to condemn the repression of combinations by authorities than actively to support combinations. Whatever happened in the sections, the collection they ordered in November 1883 was not actually to support strikes as such but to help those arrested and prosecuted.

A pamphlet was issued during these strikes in the name of Grignon, the leader of the tailors' combination, although it seems that he did not actually write it. While it detailed the sufferings of workmen and called for better wages and shorter hours, equal relations between masters and men, and the formation of trade committees linked with one another, it nevertheless declared that the real evil was not the masters but the laws:

> It is not so much the masters for whom we work as the laws of our land which prevent the improvement of our position; it is the taxes on necessities that take away the greatest part of our wages; it is the monopolies which forbid us entry into profitable professions. Let us not forget that the rich alone make the law, and that we cannot fully emancipate ourselves from the yoke of poverty without having, like them, the right of citizenship.[119]

This pamphlet, which was also circulated among tailors in the provinces, carried a good republican political message, but even this was opposed by middle-class members of the propaganda committee of the Rights of Man as too favourable to combinations, one of them, Mathé, urging the shoemakers to form a political society instead of a combination. The publications committee also commissioned Marc Dufraise to write a pamphlet in favour of combinations. He produced one that condemned low wages and the idle rich, and called for the formation in each trade of a society to produce a wage scale and organise co-operative production, and then a union of all such societies for unemployment relief, and ended by calling for political reform. But when this came before the Central Committee it was rejected and it was decided to call only for political societies and to oppose combinations, and the cabinet-maker, Royer, wrote to Vignerte urging a publication in which 'you will set forth all the benefits of association. But you will say that we want neither combination, nor scale, nor wage rise, and workmen and masters to come to an amicable understanding.' Accordingly, while his original piece was now published in the name of the shoemakers' leader, Efrahem, and not in that of the society, Dufraise now produced a second pamphlet *opposing* combinations: strikes and scales could achieve nothing, strikes brought hardship to workers, and relief would come from reforms in taxation and through attacking the bourgeois and financial aristocracy through a democratic political system. Like the *Tribune*, the pamphlet stressed how the rich made the laws, in their own interests, and that industrial action could not succeed. 'The people, in order really to improve their situation, *must recover the exercise of their sovereignty.*'[120]

The republicans also sought to side-step the question of labour disputes by advocating '*association*', by which they meant co-operative production, for which only a democratic state could provide the necessary protection and funds. Workers, therefore, instead of supporting trade unions and strikes, should work for a democratic republic which would then solve the labour question by promoting co-operative production. But, as we shall see, this message had little effect.[121]

The Society of the Rights of Man, with its largely artisan membership, thus reveals the importance of work organisations to radicalism as a basis of recruitment and organisation, and how this could also influence radical practice, with the consequent tensions with other radicals. This feature continued. Republicans were divided on how to respond to the strikes in 1840.[122] With new political freedom in 1848, a new Society of the Rights of Man appeared, which included members from the old one, and again there was unease at the combinations around them. One member called for a ban on all trades' demonstrations as they harmed commercial confidence, while the veteran Napoleon Lebon, one of the chief and most radical and revolutionary leaders of the old Rights of Man, who had in 1833 opposed combinations and Grignon's pamphlet, resumed his opposition to combinations over wages and hours:

A rise in wages, reduction in work, all that is a cause of ruin for manufacturers (*entrepreneurs*), and only gains insignificant relief. Furthermore, these actions have the harmful quality of perpetuating differences between classes.[123]

The Society of the Rights of Man thus illustrates a general theme of this book, that politics was not autonomous and artisan radicalism was not separate from social life generally. In this social life, material and non-material concerns were both important, and work was only one of the several material concerns. The local branches of the Chartist and Republican Solidarity movements show the same.

The second example is the International Working Men's Association, or First International, founded in London in 1864. This was a radical organisation which expressed the different 'internationalist' themes that were an enduring element in radicalism. The many suffered in the interests of the privileged few, and so the people fought wars on behalf of their rulers, even though they had no real quarrel with one another.

Wars were instigated to check liberty, but the people's interests lay in peace, which democracy would secure.

National jealousy, educational prejudice, and all animosity fostered by kings, priests, and lords, fell before the all-powerful genius of Democracy.[124]

Another element was enthusiasm for foreign causes. British radicals' admiration for France was not usually reciprocated, but both supported Polish efforts at independence and the Italian Risorgimento (especially as this was anti-Papal). The hero of the latter, Mazzini, particularly expressed the radical goals of an independent, republican Italy responsive to the needs and wishes of labour, an alliance between subject peoples to achieve liberation, and social and international relations based on morality and reciprocal rights and duties. Such support for foreign movements of national liberation and unification was not necessarily a policy of peace, for radicals often wanted active intervention against reactionaries, including war with Russia, that bastion of European reaction. The common radical idea that the working people, uncorrupted by wealth and privilege, had a clearer view of moral issues, led to a conception of their special mission in achieving international peace and harmony. Much less important was the view that the working classes of all countries had united interests opposed to all other classes, enthusiasm for foreign causes being often undiscriminating. The establishment of actual internationalist organisations reflected these themes and relied largely on personal contacts through political exiles, particularly the groups of political refugees in London, such as the Fraternal Democrats in the 1840s, typically a metropolitan educational and propagandist body concerned not with practical efforts but with changing the ideological meaning of Chartism.

Another relevant feature was that the repressive nature of the late Second Republic, Second Empire, and early Third Republic left few outlets for open radical or trade union activity, and canalised them into activities that were allowed. One of these few avenues was the election and organisation of delegates to visit the international exhibitions, as happened for those in London in 1851 and 1862, Paris in 1867 and Lyons in 1872. The 1862 and 1867 delegates then went on to labour political and co-operative activity. One of the few means of trade organisation was thus in connexion with international events.

The International Working Men's Association initially exemplified of all these features. The Polish Rising of 1863 produced in London the radical National League for Polish Independence seeking intervention by Britain and France in support of the Poles, and in Paris a group of radical artisans, who had originally come together under the leadership of the bronze-chaser Tolain in connexion with the Exhibition delegation to London the previous year, circulated a pro-Polish petition among the workshops and sent Tolain and four other delegates to a great pro-Polish meeting in London in July. The enthusiasm for the exploits of that hero of the people, Garibaldi, culminated in his triumphant entry in to London in 1864, drawing the greatest crowds there since those in support of Queen Caroline in 1820–1, and a committee in Paris sent another delegation to London.

There was much overlap between the Polish League, Working Men's Garibaldi Committee and the Reform League. The origins of the last lay in protest meetings against the sudden departure of Garibaldi; one of its founders, Mason Jones, had fought in Garibaldi's English Legion; and its president, Edmund Beales, had been head of the Polish League. All three involved trade society leaders, and the first two had included contacts with like-minded people in Paris. This was the context of the formation of the IWMA in September 1864, which relied very much on the French political refugees in London, such as the O'Brienite Joseph Collett, and on their personal contacts in both London and Paris.[125]

The IWMA was thus one of several overlapping radical organisations operating in London in the 1860s, and it expressed the usual Mazzinian ideals over cruelty to Poland, the responsibility of criminal despotic governments for wars, the need for a foreign policy based on reason and morality, and the goal of peace and harmony between peoples. It did not stress working-class interests but was universalistic in its appeal, championing humanity and the good of mankind, opposing the selfish ruling classes and national prejudices, and seeing progress as coming through fraternity.[126] The Paris group was also made up of radicals. Although influenced by Proudhon, they did not share his opposition to political activity or strikes. In 1863 they formed a Paris workers' committee that displaced the initial largely Bonapartist committee of the London delegation, they were allied with a group of radical republicans, and they put up 'labour' candidates in Paris in the 1863 general election and 1864 by-elections.[127] Tolain's so-called Proudhonian address at the 1864 IWMA foundation meeting seems like the last part of the booklet he produced justifying the labour candidatures, a basically political work.[128] But the nature of the Empire meant that organisations could only operate openly if they were non-political. Thus one of the 1862 delegates who supported labour candidates and was on the 1863 delegation to the Polish demonstration was Cohadon, who was manager of the wallers' co-operative society, which he kept so strictly non-political that he would not welcome back into it the co-founder and republican refugee Nadaud when the amnesty gave him the possibility of returning to Paris.[129] The French group thought it essential to keep the IWMA non-political so as to be allowed to operate in France, and therefore experienced attacks from republicans, who regarded the overthrow of the Empire as a priority overriding all else, suspected the Tolain group's links with Prince Napoleon and his Palais-Royal Bonapartist group, and saw their support for labour candidates and an exclusively working-class character for the IWMA as dividing republicans and thereby helping the Empire. The radical nature of the Paris committee, and the good grounds for their cautious policy, were both confirmed when in November 1867 they did join with radical republicans in a demonstration at the tombs of Godefroy Cavaignac and the Italian patriot Manin, in support, that is, of republicanism and Italian liberties, the result being that the committee was prosecuted and a new committee had to replace them.[130]

Like the other radical organisations in London in the 1860s, the IWMA sought trade union support, the key means of mobilisation in the metropolis, which had been crucial in the mass welcome of Garibaldi (and, earlier, of Kossuth). Right from the start the Reform League set out to win support from the trades. It arranged deputations to societies and workshops, trade society leaders were active in the leadership, and trades' delegates came to League meetings, conferences, and deputations to ministers.[131] As in Chartism, a number of branches in London were composed of members of a single trade – six of shoemakers, eight from the building trades, and one each of tailors, cabinet-makers, coachmakers, and goldsmiths and jewellers. Above all, the trades were crucial in organising participation in the great demonstrations such as George Potter's in December 1866 and the League's in February 1867.[132]

The other great centre of the Reform League was Birmingham, for of the 440 known branches, 112 were in London, 60 in Birmingham, 29 in the rest of Warwickshire, 61 in the West Riding, 37 in Lancashire, 41 in Staffordshire, and 21 in Worcestershire.[133] Trade societies and the local trades' council were crucial in Birmingham too, 42 of the branches being trade societies or single firms, and the trades were vital in the monster demonstrations of October 1866 and April 1867.[134] There was also trade society support for the Reform League in Liverpool, Bristol, Stafford, and Cardiff, and vital involvement in the great Reform demonstrations at Leeds, Edinburgh, Newcastle, Sunderland, Manchester, and many smaller places.

The great difference between the Reform agitation of the mid-1860s and those of the late 1850s was this involvement of trade societies, but it was not achieved through stressing trade union issues, as the emphasis was on the exclusion of working men from the vote and their right to equality. While a few speakers did relate parliamentary reform to labour laws,[135] to the outcry over the 'Sheffield outrages', the establishment of a Royal Commission on trade unions, and to the Hornby versus Close decision, these developments seem to have had little effect on the Reform campaign generally. The League's address to the working classes based their claim to the vote on their role as producers of wealth, fighters of wars, payers of taxes, and subjects of laws, their degraded and humiliating position, and the denial of rights that were given to working people elsewhere (the USA, Canada, and Victoria were most commonly cited, France and North Germany less so).[136] George Howell, the League's secretary, stressed that democracy meant not the predominance of one class over another but the equality of all before the law.[137] In the League's special appeal to trade unionists, he did cite the injustice of the Master and Servant Law, the sentences on strikers and pickets, and government help to employers in strikes, but the main stress was on unjust and excessive taxation, government extravagance, Parliament's indifference to labour, and working men's fitness for the vote. The laws are 'made by a class, for a class; and the taxation most oppressive upon those least able to bear it'.[138] 'Manhood suffrage', said Odger, 'made a man self-reliant. With his rights he would feel his responsibilities, and his duties would be performed with manly self-respect.'[139] There was less interest in the Master and Servant Law than in the alleged vilification of working people by Lord Elcho, the ally of the Glasgow Trades' Council in seeking reform of this very law.[140]

It was then inevitable that the IWMA would also seek trade society support, and this was indeed gained, starting, as with the Reform League, with building trades and shoemakers. Similarly, some special arguments were also used to interest trade societies. Odger's original address had stated that an international association could stop the importation of foreign blacklegs, but this point was not greatly emphasised, and although at the St Martin's Hall foundation meeting this address was read out, the issue was not otherwise even referred to. It was, naturally, included in the leaflet issued to trade societies, but the appeal was really as a radical political body, and it was precisely this political character that led the London Society of Compositors to rescind its initial decision to send a delegate to the IWMA conference at Geneva.[141]

Yet, despite the initial intentions of the founders, trade union concerns did come to dominate. Some trades affiliated during disputes, such as pattern-drawers and basket-makers, and the chief role of the IWMA in England came to be the mobilisation of international support for strikes and preventing the import of continental strike-breakers. This had already been happening, with the help of contacts established by foreign workmen and refugees who found employment in London, as with the compositor Vasbenter, a member of the London Society of Compositors. The society agreed to send money to the one in Paris both in 1852 and during the general strike in 1862 (Vasbenter acting as interpreter for the two delegates from Paris).[142] Some Paris building workers sent help to the London builders in 1860.[143] There were also attempts in the 1850s at bilingual trade journals, such as the printers' *Gutenberg* and shoemakers' *Innovator*. Just before the IWMA began, the Limoges potters on strike appealed to the Staffordshire potters for help, and through the efforts of the exile Talandier the case was taken up by the *Bee-Hive* and the London Trades' Council.[144]

The recruiting of blacklegs by employers could extend abroad, as in the strikes by tin-plate workers in Wolverhampton in 1851 and Birmingham in 1853, and gas-stokers, bakers, cigar-makers, tailors, and pianoforte-makers in London.[145] Sometimes this was prevented. The London type-founders on strike in 1850 appealed to the Paris society, who agreed to stop men being recruited, and circularised all type-foundries in France, Germany, Belgium, the Netherlands, and Switzerland to this effect.[146] During the great London builders' strike, 'the employers threatened to import foreign workmen in mass. The English workmen immediately wrote to all the foreign working men's associations', but were unable to prevent any from coming.[147]

This development of international aid in strikes was independent of the IWMA, and in the wave of Paris strikes in 1865 the hatters and saddlers received aid from their London fellows.[148] The turning-point for the IWMA was the London tailors' dispute of 1866, the first industrial dispute with which it was involved. In the usual month of April, a new tailors' combination for a general rise of a penny an hour led to a general lock-out. In such cases, it was normal for the masters to seek blacklegs from Germany, but while the Amalgamated Tailors prevented recruitment in the provinces, the IWMA helped prevent recruitment in Hamburg and Berlin, 'thus stopping the usual resources of the employers'. The Paris tailors also sent help, and the masters quickly gave in and agreed to a rise. The links thereby established between the London and Paris tailors and the role of the IWMA led the Operative Tailors to affiliate.[149] This was the beginning of the IWMA's involvement, through international contacts, in industrial disputes, and it became its main function.[150] The tailors' links were strengthened when the Paris tailors struck in 1867 for a log, in April of course, and the London tailors acted to stop any work being done in London for Paris firms, and sent their president and secretary over to Paris to sign an alliance with the Paris tailors.[151] The Paris victory, in the form of a 10 per cent rise and the end of basting in the men's own time, was followed by the London tailors' new general strike for a log, and they now in turn received help from tailors in Paris and other French towns, while the IWMA raised funds on the Continent and America.[152]

Thus the IWMA recruited trade society support and what became its chief activity was something not intended at first, and this led to wider trade society, trades council, and TUC support in England (but not Wales).[153] Members later looked back and believed this had been the aim from the start. For some English trade unionists, such as Applegarth, the Association was also seen as a way of encouraging the formation and spread of trade unions in Europe, especially if this led to higher wages and thereby reduced both the pool of cheap blackleg labour and cheap competition with British goods. Thus such 'internationalism' consisted of promoting British ways, trade unions, and liberty. As Odger saw it, 'on the Continent they are raising up trade societies on the model of our English ones.'[154]

A similar change occurred in the Paris section of the IWMA which, like other continental branches, was almost independent of the General Council in London. Initially it was not a trade body at all, but a small group of political radicals organised in an educational and co-operative society, open to all tendencies, including veteran republicans from the Second Republic and with links with young republican students in the Latin Quarter. It supported co-operation, universal association, and a universal language, and in 1864 typically issued a declaration against war and in favour of general peace.[155] Outside Paris the IWMA had little strength in France, with only small groups in Rouen and Marseilles, but in Lyons the delegates to the 1862 Exhibition had remained active, and they came together in 1865 with groups of republicans to form a section of the IWMA, which engaged in open political discussions and propaganda, until in 1867 they split into three groups and the branch ended.[156] However, the Paris section did form working men's associations, particularly co-operative stores, and prior to the 1866 Geneva Congress it agitated among the Paris trades for support. Although only a few of them affiliated, notably the bronze-workers, enough financial support was gained to enable delegates to be sent to Geneva, and the Paris section then went on to encourage the formation of trade committees (*chambres syndicales*), the emphasis being on organisation, not industrial conflict.[157] However, in 1867 there was a large strike by the Roubaix spinners, at first against the employers' regulations and then against machinery, and the Paris section issued a declaration opposing machine-wrecking but also condemning the masters' regulations and the use of police against the strikes. The emphasis, then, was on freedom and non-intervention by the authorities, not on economic conflict.[158] The real turning-point was the strike early in 1867 of the Paris bronze-workers, a strongly organised trade society affiliated to the IWMA. Since the employers were trying to destroy the organisation this was just the sort of conflict likely to arouse wider support, and aid came from other trades in Paris and the provinces, and also from London, through the agency of the IWMA. The consequent rumours of the availability of inexhaustible English funds led the masters to give in, and this was accompanied by the victory of the Paris tailors, largely attributed to a belief in extensive English support – there were rumours that English tailors had sent 200,000 francs. These successes gave the French IWMA great prestige, trade society support took off, and membership soared.[159] After the trial and fine of the committee,[160] a second one was elected in March 1868, the leading figure being the bookbinder Varlin, whose society had joined in December 1866, and when the Geneva building workers went on strike, the committee prevented the recruitment of blacklegs in France and in two weeks raised 10,000 francs among the Paris trades. Although this saved the strike from defeat, this second committee was, as a result, in turn now prosecuted and imprisoned, and the IWMA in France was destroyed. At the same time English trade union affiliation to the IWMA fell, although they still responded to calls for aid, and the Amalgamated Cordwainers made a tramping relief agreement with the Paris shoemakers.[161]

The revival of the IWMA in France in 1869 was the work mainly of Varlin and Malon in Paris, Albert Richard in Lyons, and Emile Aubry in Rouen, in the form of a not particularly strong and a wholly political body.[162] But what brought the IWMA a new importance was the great wave of combinations and strikes over France in 1869 and 1870. Many members of the IWMA played leading roles in them, and the Association was carried along on the wave and in the process developed systematic financial aid. Strikers and societies joined, encouraged by hopes of English support, although the nature of their adherence was often very vague. In Paris Varlin threw himself into sustained activity – writing articles, collecting funds, and helping found organisations. The leather-dressers' strike of July to December 1869, because it involved the document, aroused great support among the Paris trades, and enabled Varlin to group them in a Federal Committee of Working Men's Societies, with the same leaders and premises as the Paris IWMA, although the two were officially separate. Similar federations were formed in Lyons and Marseilles. In this situation a panic developed, and the hand of the IWMA was seen in every dispute, just as had happened with the Consolidated Trades' Union in England in 1834. In fact the strike wave was not controlled by the IWMA and was a separate movement which swept the IWMA along with it, some resistance societies joining just prior to their strike solely in the hope of help. But the extent of such 'membership' was hazy, the Paris and Lyons federations stayed separate, and the IWMA itself was rather diffuse. Its independent strength should not be exaggerated, for the arrest of twenty-odd activists in Lyons in May and the flight of Richard to Switzerland meant the virtual end of the IWMA there, while in Paris the arrest of the IWMA leaders in April and imprisonment of thirty-nine of them in June more or less destroyed it there again. This reinforced the radical element in the Paris sections which tended to fall under the control of the Blanquists who, though at first hostile to the IWMA had, with the apparent decay of the regime and, especially, with the street protests over the Victor Noir affair, started to enter the IWMA sections and push them into an insurrectionary direction. The removal of the leaders now enabled the Blanquists to achieve dominance in the Paris IWMA federal council and to separate it from both the London General Council and the Paris trades' federation (which the war badly disrupted). Similarly the IWMA in London lost its trade union element and became more of a radical body, its basis now the various ultra-radical and republican clubs and organisations. The failure of the Commune brought another wave of French refugees to London, and the Blanquists allied with the German refugee Dr Marx, whose ascendancy in the IWMA was also a source of alienation.[163]

Recurrent concerns and practices thus greatly modified the operation of the IWMA in ways not foreshadowed in its foundation or programme. It showed how trade groupings were important as a basis for mobilising support, and how they might follow their own concerns apart from the formal aims of the organisation. Radicalism consisted of practice as much as programmes. It did not reflect or grow out of work or workplace relations, although radical movements often relied on workplace and work organisation for mobilisation and in the process responded to the concerns behind trade societies, so changing both the practice and meaning of radicalism.

# 5    Socialism

Radicalism, as we have seen, can be viewed as an inherited ideology, not emanating from the world of work, though modified in its practice by artisan concerns. Yet it is argued that experience at work produced a 'new ideology' that challenged or supplanted traditional radicalism in ways more relevant to workers' situations. Ideas on the evils of competition, the workers' right to property in their labour, bourgeois exploitation, and the need for a new socialist economic organisation are seen as seeping up from workers and modifying a purely political radicalism.[1] Thus at the start of our period Owen and O'Brien declared that 'mere' political reform was no good, and at the end of it Varlin predicted that the next revolution would not be a merely political one, but would free workers from all exploitation, political and capitalist, so that the workers could control the means of production and exchange.[2] It is particularly in France that the influence of the new socialist creed is recognised, its strength there in fact marking a contrast to England.

To assess the content and importance of socialism among popular movements, we should not look mainly at the various socialist schools. Saint-Simonism and Fourierism had little popular impact, and while some of their few working-class adherents did run a few periodicals, their small readership consisted of non-workers at least as much as workers. While an important Owenite 'Socialist' movement grew after 1834, to reach a peak in 1840, it rapidly declined thereafter, and the most distinctive element in Owenite thought, communitarianism, was the least influential. O'Brien developed his socialist ideas mainly after he had been marginalised from the Chartist movement, his followers forming a small sectarian group.

The person who undoubtedly had the largest radical audience in France in the 1840s was the communist Etienne Cabet, head of the Icarian movement, whose *Populaire* newspaper far outsold all other socialist or communist journals. But much of Cabet's renown was as a radical,[3] while the success of the *Populaire* was not due to Icarianism, which it hardly dealt with, but to Cabet's skilful and effective journalism.[4] 'It was', said a reader, 'the first that I could read in its entirety.'[5] Similar success met Cabet's *History of the French Revolution* and his annual almanacs. Cabet's split from Ledru-Rollin and the *Réforme* group of radicals in the autumn of 1845 nevertheless led to a fall in the *Populaire's* circulation and a decline in the Icarian movement, so that in 1846–7 Cabet gave up hope of success and decided instead on emigration to the New World to found a community there.[6]

The apparent prominence of Icarian groups in the 1840s should also be related to the context of political defeat, quiescence and unlikelihood of radical change (the *Populaire's* sale was only 4,500 per month). It was normal in such contexts for there to be an emphasis on enlightening the people, intellectual purity, and theoretical speculation detached from practical and tactical considerations; it was also usually safer. A parallel to the Icarian movement lay in England, after the end of the mass radical campaign in 1819, in the prominence in the 1820s of the fearless radical publisher Richard Carlile, with his freethinking journals *Republican* and *Lion* and his regular contact with a network of 'infidel' groups over the country. The general quiescence gave them a greater relative importance, and, in reaction to the unsuccessful post-war radical campaigns, Carlile emphasised doctrinal purity over numerical support. O'Brien was to do the same in the late 1840s, and, like Carlile earlier, came to oppose granting universal suffrage before the people were enlightened, and to support a household suffrage movement in 1848 and later advocate giving people extra votes according to the amount of taxes they paid.[7] The failure of Chartism also led in the 1850s to a greater intellectual curiosity in social theories and to organs for ex-Chartists and Owenites interested in intellectual debate, not practical politics. The same is true of French socialist and communist journals in the late 1830s and early 1840s, with their small readership, while the failure of radicalism in the Second Republic led Pottier and Lachambeaudie into Fourierism.

The influence of Saint-Simonian, Owenite, Fourierite, Icarian, Proudhonian, or O'Brienite ideas was therefore greatest among educated minorities that had a disproportionate role in popular radicalism, and the images of alternative societies were certainly important in encouraging dissent, and thus had an emancipating role. But they did not usually guide or inform actual radical campaigns and action, and in fact support for socialism was often a combination of intellectual boldness with practical inactivity in periods of political quiescence. Thus socialists often stressed changing consciousness rather than conflict, reason and fraternity rather than denunciation, and feared radical violence and mass movements, and O'Brien was typical of many socialists in asserting that democracy was of no use if the people did not understand socialism and that it would even be positively harmful.[8]

When radical political activity revived in Britain in 1830, Carlile was virtually eclipsed. Similarly, although the 1848 revolution led Cabet initially to drop his emigration plan, his club was more concerned with the National Guard question than Icarianism. He soon sank into insignificance, the Icarian movement ended in April–May 1848 and Cabet in despair returned to emigration, and the disastrous settlement in Texas.[9]

Another apparently influential French socialist was Louis Blanc, a radical republican journalist, who gained great renown in the 1840s through his articles and his book which advocated state loans to finance co-operative firms which would compete with and gradually kill off private firms. In these 'social workshops' members would work for wages (there would be a fixed minimum wage), and the profits would be used for sick and old-age relief, and for the purchase of equipment and materials, with the remainder shared equally among members. The 1848 revolution made him a member of the Provisional Government and unleashed a strong workers' movement, essentially an unprecedented wave of combinations of the nevertheless familiar kind in favourable circumstances. The demands were overwhelmingly for improvements in wages and hours, through solemn agreements by joint committees of masters and men. Other common demands were for the suppression of exploitative private employment agencies, freedom of combination, meeting and association, the neutrality of the state in industrial matters, and the provision of work for the unemployed, all of which seemed to be guaranteed by a democratic republic. This was clearly an autonomous movement of industrial demands, and although socialist phrases were used, they were interpreted differently: 'organisation of work' usually meaning wage scales agreed by mixed committees composed of representatives of masters and men in equal number, and the 'right to work' being action against unemployment and freedom from dependence on public relief or religious charity.[10] Faced with a constant barrage of such demands, the government sought to divert the agitation by establishing the labour commission, meeting at the Luxembourg Palace, with Blanc as chairman. The trades' delegates in this commission secured government decrees on the shortening of hours of work, the abolition of piece-mastering, the registration of offers and requests for work, and the abolition of work in prisons and convents, but Blanc felt the delegates were making exorbitant demands, and their interest in immediate, tangible reforms clashed with his conception of the commission as a means of investigation and indoctrination. His overriding concern was the creation of a labour ministry, or 'Ministry of Progress', under himself, and he expected the severe depression to bring the wholesale collapse of firms so that they would beg the state to take them over for free, and thus make possible state reorganisations of industries under his control.

The commission thus became a focus for the combinations over wages and hours, for concerns that were quite different from those of Blanc. Of the 331 petitions received, all were on practical aims, above all wages, and none were concerned with socialism. The main function of the commission lay in ratifying formal and public wage scales (although some trades, such as the bakers, instead used the offices of the radical Prefect of Police, Caussidière, just as in the provinces trades looked to the new sympathetic local officials). After the successful 17 March demonstration the delegates' new directing Central Committee of Workers of the Seine Department, mostly radicals, became preoccupied with elections and the growing counter-revolution, but after the electoral disaster a new committee worked to promote trade and working men's associations and produced its own plan for industrial reorganisation in which Blanc's influence was not very apparent.[11]

What needs to be reiterated is the strength and continuity of radicalism, and the popular support for a radicalism that stressed political rights and injustice, and which attributed material suffering and even economic evils to political causes. 'The chartists did not want social equality, but political equality. They knew that there would always be rich and poor, but they did not see why one man should be living on the coarsest food, while another should be living in idleness and luxury at the expense of industrious classes.'[12] Even political leaders supposedly influenced by socialism, such as Marx's friend Ernest Jones, saw political inequality as the cause of social antagonisms, while democracy would lead to harmony and to the acceptable resolution of differences. O'Brien himself agreed that 'all the evils they complained of were caused by acts of parliament'.[13]

This is true even of the extremist 'socialist' public meetings that flourished in Paris after a new act in 1868 legalised 'non-political' public meetings under certain restrictions. Over 1300 were held in Paris in two years from July 1868 and they were also important in Marseilles. In these Paris meetings twenty-odd socialist speakers were very prominent, including members of the IWMA and Blanquists, who openly pro-claimed their 'socialism' and 'communism', and there was much condemnation of pauperism, the exploitation of man by men, sub-contractors, employers, and the bourgeoisie, and calls for social reform, emancipation of labour, equality, social revolution, 'social commune', and 'revolutionary commune', though Fourier, Icarianism and Blanc were never invoked, and Proudhon rarely. However, because political and religious topics were forbidden, the official misleading topics of meetings necessarily concerned social and economic questions. Equally extreme statements could be found in the London radical clubs at the same time but they did not receive the same publicity. A perusal of reports reveals that, after an initial unsuccessful attempt by liberal economists to use the meetings, the overwhelming tone was one of political ultra-radicalism and bitter hostility to the regime, not socialism. Political questions far outweighed social ones. The main targets were the army, clergy, rentiers, financiers and speculators, and other parasites, robbers, and criminals at the top of society; they condemned poverty, which was blamed on low wages, and unemployment, stressed the right to work, and declared that everyone should work; they called for freedom of press and meeting, for the abolition of militarism, privileges, titles and monopolies, for fraternity between peoples, and the legalisation of divorce. But mostly, they condemned the government, the regime and their agents, the police, and the scandals and corruption.[14] Moreover, when the elections drew near, republican candidates began to attend, and the tone changed. The two-stage electoral system enabled candidates to stand in the first stage without any hope of winning or of affecting the final outcome, a form of publicity in fact, and a number of the public-meeting orators did stand in the first round, but they were swept aside and radical candidates were elected who ignored social questions. The only triumph the public-meeting radicals gained was the defeat of Garnier-Pagès (one of the traitors of 1848 hated for his denunciation of the meetings) by the aged Raspail. The latter was no socialist but the bitter foe of priests, police, and spies, which were key themes in the meetings. With war in 1870, the meetings were repressed, and after the fall of the regime the revived public meetings were less extreme and more exclusively political than before, for now they could openly broach political questions and were engaged in strategic choices and efforts to secure unity instead of mere opposition, and the same was true of the Commune itself.

However, all this by no means shows that socialism was not important, and it is too easy to take a set of theorists and show that their ideas had limited impact. The real question is what socialism was. As we have seen, there was no single socialist ideology, just as there was no single radical one. 'The communism of Cabet was not the socialism of Blanqui, any more than the socialism of Blanqui was that of Louis Blanc. The democracy of Barbès, Raspail and Ledru-Rollin was quite different than that of Godefroy Cavaignac, Bastide and Marrast.'[15]

It is undoubtedly true that the term 'socialism' was far more widespread in France than in England, but this is not necessarily a sign of actual differences in ideas. The themes of the French socialist workers' journals of the 1840s, particularly those of love, fraternity, and the potentially liberating role of machines, were certainly paralleled by the non-socialist Thomas Cooper in England.

I would not give a fig for the Charter, if I did not believe it would lead to our deliverance from Kingcraft and priestcraft; to the grand Community; the Universal brotherhood; the diffusion of such real Equality that none should be privileged to revel in splendour while others starve; none should claim the land exclusively for them . . . none should be exempt from labour of some kind, and consequently labour itself, by being equally and generally shared should become mere exercise, especially now science is so rapidly disclosing to mankind the means of existing without bodily slavery that has degraded the human race for ages.[16]

The term was widely used in France by anti-radicals. This was partly an extreme and exaggerated reaction to any popular movement or to one for greater social justice. The Lyons rising of 1831 gave it a reputation for 'socialism'. Priests urged the wives of Icarians to leave them, in England crime was attributed to Owenism, and conservatives in France called criminals 'Proudhonians'. In early 1848, the conservatives whipped up a real scare against the government that was born of socialism, through portraying Paris as being in the hands of opponents of property, family, and religion, picking out 'communists' as an easy target, and vilifying any democrat as a 'communist'. For it was a 'magical, cabalistic word, accusation from which a man in the provinces never recovers'.[17] The authorities regularly used the term 'anarchists'. Similarly, during the public meetings of 1868–70, 'the sycophantic press rushed to highlight the speakers' extravagance and, through its hints, troubled the minds of the partisans of *absolute tranquillity*', by picking out odd statements and portraying the meetings as being in favour of atheism, regicide, assassination, concubinage, abolition of the family and property, hatred of the bourgeoisie, and imposition of communism by force, so as to arouse fears of the 'social peril' in the approaching election and to taint the liberal opposition with socialism.

Socialism was, then, far more common as an epithet in France, reflecting the bitter political divisions, and could be applied to all sorts of radical measures, such as free compulsory education, and attacks on property through taxation. A radical journal claimed in 1848 that French conservatives would call the measures of the English Conservative government 'socialist',[18] for Peel had indeed introduced the 'socialist' measure of an income tax.

Because the term 'socialist' was widely used as one of abuse in France, its prevalence is thus no guide to its strength. But there was also, of course, positive support for socialism, and it is important to be clear that what we have here is not a single ideology but a number of different elements, all of which were found in England as well as France.

### Social reform

The first, and perhaps most important, meaning and aspect of socialism was 'social reform'. This derived its significance from the great interest in the 'social question' that characterised the 1830s and 1840s, and the problems of relating liberal principles to industrial society. 'Social' came to denote sympathy for the poor, with humanitarian and romantic impulses often prominent. Radicals, like others, were affected by 'social novels', often serialised in newspapers, offering vivid and frank accounts of the life of the poor, criminals, and outcasts. Blanc and the chief Fourierite, Considérant, were haunted by crime, Cabet's *Populaire* gained readers through its vivid portrayal of poverty, savagery, and moral collapse, and the revelations of appalling conditions inspired the Christian Socialists in England. But it was poverty above all, rather than sanitary reform or urban renewal, that concerned such socialists. As we have seen, particular concern for the poor was one distinctive form of radicalism, and a definition of this form of socialism would be a radicalism more concerned with poverty than privilege. Thus the miserabilist realism of portrayals of the poor in Eugene Sue's novel *The Mysteries of Paris* and Felix Pyat's play *The Rag-Picker of Paris* was interpreted as social protest and admired by all socialist schools, and gave the authors reputations as socialists.

The 'social republicanism' of the 1830s, especially in the Society of the Rights of Man, consisted of democracy; progressive taxation; free, secular, compulsory universal education; Robespierre's' commitment to total and direct popular sovereignty, his view that extremes of wealth could nullify political equality, and even his conception of property as a conventional, not a natural right. But the most distinctive feature was their acceptance of working people as equals, their identification with the poor, and their active search for 'proletarian' support.

Such features characterised radical republicanism under the July Monarchy, to be largely continued in the socialism of the Second Republic. Essentially, the republic was to be a 'social' republic, that is, one that really did something for the poor. In practice, in 1848, this meant defending and preserving the measures extracted from the Provisional Government in the early days: the 'right to work' (interpreted as public provision of work for all unemployed in their own occupation), the Luxembourg Commission, the ten-hour day, the abolition of piece-mastering, the freedom of combination, and the negotiation of binding wage scales. Yet these gains were steadily eroded and the 'social republic' dismantled in the course of the year. 'Socialism' tended to mean a defence of these measures and a conviction that purely political reforms were inadequate, as well as a caring about the poor, support for 'association', and general fraternity, rather than a particular set of theories. 'Socialism is the son of fraternity. It is not a system excluding all others, it does not call for unity in belief.'[19]

After June 1848, the increasingly anti-radical direction of the government led the ousted Ledru-Rollin and his associates to adopt a more radical stance and seek to unite all radicals under their leadership around the usual programme with the addition, to secure wider support, of the right to work, of provision of public credit to small producers (especially peasants) and to co-operatives, and of the nationalisation of railways, mines, canals, and other 'social property'. Despite Ledru's reluctance, on Lamennais' insistence they adopted the phrase 'democratic and social republic'. This led on to the formation in November of 'Republican Solidarity' to mobilise support for Ledru-Rollin's candidacy in the forthcoming presidential election. Despite support in the provinces, this was opposed by ultra-radical groups in Paris and Lyons, who could not forgive the Mountain (the radical group in the Assembly), and especially Ledru-Rollin, for their roles in bringing troops back to Paris, checking the 16 April Paris demonstration, voting for the law against processions, opposing the June rebels, and supporting the prosecutions of Proudhon and Raspail. Opposing the whole idea of a presidency, they put up instead the imprisoned Raspail as an anti-president candidate (though his programme was no different). In their bitterness at the exclusion of the right of work from the constitution in November, they held 'socialist dinners', especially one of 'socialist workers' on 3 December, the chairman being the absent imprisoned Blanqui, who sent a written toast that was a long diatribe against the Ledru-Rollin group.[20]

Thus the 'socialists' were the ultra-radicals opposed to Ledru-Rollin, but the increasingly reactionary and repressive policy followed under the new president, Louis-Napoleon, led the two radical wings to unite for the 1849 election under the name 'socialist democrat', with a programme laboriously negotiated by Pyat. This called for universal suffrage, and subordination of the executive to the Assembly; freedom of press, meeting, and association; right to work; relief for the infirm and old; common, free, compulsory education, and better pay for teachers;

free and simplified justice, and abolition of the death penalty and imprisonment for debt; universal military service for all, with no exemption, and better conditions for soldiers, and revision of the military code; reduction in government expenditure, abolition of taxes on salt and drinks, and of tolls, excise, and forced labour on roads, and revision of land and business taxes; state loans; state assistance for cultivating waste lands, irrigation and afforestation, and the establishment of agricultural colonies in France and abroad; state encouragement of agricultural and industrial co-operation; establishment of national emporia and bazaars; and nationalisation of insurance, banking, railways, canals, roads, and mines. These were to be the main radical demands for the rest of the republic.[21] With the exception of the last few measures, most of which were recent additions to win peasant support, these were familiar French and British radical demands. Socialist-democrats were thus supporters of this radical programme in the great polarisation of political alinement in France.

The programme was also to influence Chartism, after its final defeat and the discrediting of all its strategies. In fact, 'democracy' came to mean this sort of programme. Such demands reappeared in the Paris public meetings of 1868–70 and in the campaign of the radical Gambetta in his great, popular victory at Belleville in the 1869 election. Socialism basically expressed not a theoretical programme, but support for 'social reform' and an identification with the poor and their lot, as in the 'socialist' agitation in London in 1869 over unemployment and against the Liberal Party. The hero of the Paris public meetings was Henri Rochefort, who sat in the Legislative Body on the extreme left with Raspail, but neither had a distinctive programme. 'How strange! Rochefort, former man of the boulevards, friend of Hugo, stranger to socialist doctrines, simple expression of the hatred of Bonaparte, free of all question of principle, becomes the candidate of Socialism, etc., suburbs, Revolution.'[22] Nothing in all this kind of socialism was incompatible with radicalism, but it is nevertheless a distinctive kind of radicalism, which rejected the distinction made by liberals and other radicals between political and social matters. Social reform meant help for the poor, through tax reform, national secular education, unemployment relief, and public works.

### State socialism

The conception of socialism advocated in the radical Rheims paper, *Association Rémoise*, in 1849, was a fairer system of taxation that did not fall on the poor, action to lower prices, the abolition of monopolies, guarantee of work for all, and also state take-over of utilities, the revenue from which would allow lower taxation. The last measure relates to a second element of socialism, namely state intervention in the economy, and we have seen that this did figure, if not centrally, in the socialist-democrats' programme.

State socialism has two sides, social justice and removal of privilege, and efficient management of economic activities. One of the commonest conceptions of state economic activity was in finance, with a national bank replacing private ones to manage currency and credit in an impartial way in the national interest.[23] Nationalisation of railways was also a fairly common call, inspired in Britain by the unedifying spectacle of the 'railway mania' of the 1840s, with its competing and unsound speculations, and the corrupt, privileged monopolistic 'railway kings' gaining their goals through bribing politicians.[24] A liberal official at the Board of Trade was certain that the *laissez-faire* system in English railway construction (where private land could nevertheless be expropriated by law) had been wasteful and harmful, private interests triumphing over national needs, and the Board's president, Gladstone, favoured nationa-lisation of railways, just as in 1866 he set up a government life insurance scheme through the post offices, another of the French 'socialist' demands of 1848.[25] A number of English businessmen, fervent adherents of a market economy and a minimalist state, were nevertheless in favour of state provision of an infrastructure of telegraphs, post offices, and railways, and opposition to the quasi-monopolistic telegraph companies led to their nationalisation in 1870.[26] In France support for modernisation through the state was much stronger, and the July Monarchy actively promoted the 'national interest' in the fields of education, banking, communications, railways, and forced mergers, so that radicals were directly affected by the talk of economic progress and material improvement, the benefits of mechanisation, railways, agricul-tural colonies, and model farms, and the belief in a better society characterised by technologically and commercially based opulence. French radicals therefore tended to support government action to improve communications, including the compulsory expropriation of land to do so, and the government railway bills of 1838 and 1842 to enable state construction of railways, their support only reinforced by the furious opposition from private business to measures that were in fact no more extreme than liberal plans for state old-age pensions and saving banks. But a number of these radicals soon grew unhappy at the growth of 'financial feudalism', the financiers and stock-jobbers securing railway concessions and making profitable loans to an increasingly indebted state.

The two aspects of state socialism, enabling the liberal economy to operate better, and checking privilege, were particularly prominent in France in 1848, in the special circumstances of severe unemployment, acute economic depression, and, initially at least, a democratic state. This background coloured most of what discussion of 'socialism' there was in the Paris political unions (*clubs*) of early 1848, although this never dominated. Workers clamoured for relief from unemployment, one response to which was the traditional 'charity workshop' yards that had always been opened in periods of unemployment (and were to reappear in later years), a number having already been opened in the winter of 1847–8. The 'national workshops' of 1848 were to most people the same institution under another name. However, there was also workers' pressure, especially in Paris, for the government to take over and reopen firms that had closed down or been abandoned, so as to create work, and these considerations naturally reinforced ideas of state workshops, on the model of the military ones and naval yards, all in the short-term interest of ending unemployment.[27] However, a number of republicans in authority, including some ministers and the director of the Paris National Workshops, conceived of the national workshops as a means of reorganising Paris industry, of social regeneration through workers' housing, building, railways, and navigation improvements, and of ending the depression through restarting production. They particularly tended to combine them with the idea of a state take-over and construction of railways, which industrialists were also pressing for, and, indeed, the government did take over two railway companies danger-ously low in funds in response to pressure from their workers who feared they would not be paid, and they considered nationalising the others. Lamartine, who had come out in opposition to the government in the 1840s on the issue of the state's obligation to act to reduce working-class poverty, believed strongly in 1848 that it was the duty of the state to provide employment, and saw the national workshops and state railway construction as the means of achieving this and reflating the economy. This was all at a time when industrialists themselves were pressing for state help on the lines followed in 1830.[28] These were not particularly radical concerns, but it is not surprising that many radicals, such as Barbès and his Revolution Club, supported a state take-over (with compensation) not only of banks and railways, but also of canals, mines, salt-works, and insurance companies (not life insurance), from the big, privileged joint-stock companies, nearly all of them set up in the July Monarchy. They also advocated public works, specialised national workshops, the purchase of bankrupt factories, and state orders to industry. Short-term considerations were very important in all this, but there was also a concern to remedy the inefficiencies as well as the injustices of a liberal economy, to benefit employers, and end cyclical crises. Such ideas gained a lot of moderate support.[29]

With the ending of the depression and the increasingly reactionary nature of the regime radical support for such measures declined rapidly, but when the demise of the Empire seemed near, support was to revive among French radicals for the nationalisation of banks, canals, railways, insurance, and mines (though not land).[30] These demands were also adopted by the IWMA at the end of the 1860s.

With the exception of the 1848 crisis in France, ideas of state take-over and intervention did not extend to production. There were very few advocates of nationalisation of manufacturing, or even of state manufacturing firms. The emphasis was on public utilities, which 'should be constructed, or executed only at the public cost, and the public only, should have the advantage. They should not be suffered to fall into the hands of private speculators, for whom they are only a legal disguise to enable them to rob the public.'[31] State control of these was different from collectivisation of production. Thus even nationalisation of land was, in the eyes of O'Brien and continental members of the IWMA, quite compatible with individual peasant production, and O'Brien envisaged peasant and artisan private production, assisted by fair rents for land, state warehouses for exchanges, and a fair state-controlled currency. In general, state socialism was mainly concerned with distribution or circulation, not production, the prime concern of political economy. Indeed, it can certainly be argued that the main form of socialist production in Europe, at least up to the 1870s, was not state socialism but co-operative socialism, and many socialists combined state ownership of land and utilities with co-operative organisation of industry. Co-operation might seem to be the most popular and important form of socialism, and is therefore examined in the next chapter.

Thus ideas of state control, ownership or planning were quite compatible with political radicalism, and did not necessarily mean a fundamental change in its analysis. Yet they remained a minority stand, fatally weakened by the fundamental distrust of the state and concern for minimal government.

### Laissez-faire

A third understanding of socialism, probably the most familiar one, is one that sees economic rather than political explanations for suffering, and offers a critique of an economic system characterised by exploitation. For a Lancashire weavers' leader, 'taxation is, certainly, an evil; but it sinks into nothing when compared with the effects of the grinding system'.[32] There certainly was a widespread criticism of the prevailing economic arrangements and trends, right through our period and on both sides of the Channel, but it is equally clear that it was by no means confined to people that can obviously be called 'socialist'.

First, there was widespread condemnation of unrestricted competition, which led employers to seek to produce as cheaply as possible. Shoemakers were urged to 'protect yourselves from the absorbing influence of that Hydra-headed monster-competition, which is tearing asunder the sacred bonds of civil society, arraying man against his fellow-man, spreading privation and misery throughout the land, and ultimately threatens the destruction of our trade'.[33] Competition between masters forced them to cut costs, including labour costs through wage reductions, and once some 'dishonourable' or 'unprincipled' masters did so, the rest were forced, by competition, to follow, so as not to be undersold. They also extracted more work from the men for the same pay, so that *the tendency of competition is to increase both time and labour*.[34] 'Master is underselling master, and the journeyman is fighting with all', so that workmen had to accept lower pay, which led to overwork to compensate.[35]

Such competition led masters to produce inferior articles, through cheaper materials and labour, often using a greater division of labour. 'Competition is ruining fine work, what you may call skilled labour; for there's not the time allowed to do it.'[36]

Yet this competition was in fact ruinous for masters, for it forced them into continued efforts to produce ever more cheaply, the consequence being failure or dependence on warehouse firms. Thus competition and 'monopoly' went together, and men suffered from 'the pressure of monopoly and competition', 'the present individual and monopolising system of competition'.[37] The result was social polarisation that 'would ultimately result that the end would be to reduce society to two classes – lords and slaves'.[38]

In such a situation, machinery, which should have had beneficial effects in reducing toil, in fact had bad effects in throwing men out of work. Distress arising from low pay also restricted the market for products and thereby caused economic fluctuations, while better pay would enlarge the domestic market and thereby benefit industry through greater sales and stability. 'Thus competition rapidly lessens the demand for labour, reduces the wages of those employed to almost nothing, and destroys the profitable employment which would ensue from an extensive consumption at home, by depriving the industrious poor of the ability to satisfy their natural wants.'[39]

This stress on the home market was linked to a suspicion of free trade, though a distinction was often made between foodstuffs, necessities, and raw materials, and manufactured products. A drive for exports was seen as a motive for cheapening production, and in both Britain and France free trade was seen as unfair because foreign goods were cheaper and would therefore undersell home-produced ones and cause unemployment and wage cuts, and there were campaigns in many English trades against reductions in duties on foreign manufactured goods.

The result of a competitive, *laissez-faire* economic system was thus pauperism, industrial crises, 'these gluts at warehouses and stores, this choking up of all markets which swallow all products, which bring sales at the lowest prices, fall in profits and wages, failures and bankruptcies', rural immigration, and 'surplus of labour', 'these strange alternations that we witness, of feverish labour and forced unemployment, these concentrations of workmen at a given point and these sudden discharges, this perpetual under-bidding between starving men without employ, and finally these fluctuations which reduce the wage-earners of our manufactures to all the horrors of distress'.[40] And this meant continual conflicts in industry, 'the various attempts at the reduction of wages, and the seeming opposite interests of master and men'. 'There is war in the factory, and the workshop where the worker, frightened at the continual fall in wages, fights, inch by inch, the reduction imposed by the master.' 'With free trade you will arrive at two classes in society: the robber and the robbed.'[41]

However, this widespread critique of the competitive system was not usually one of all forms of competition, but rather of 'unprincipled competition', 'unfair competition', 'reckless and unprincipled competition', 'unlimited competition, sometimes unfair (*déloyale*) and always disastrous'.[42] Hence the frequent support for remedies such as minimum wages, wage scales agreed by masters and men, systems of arbitration, taxation of machinery and relief for those displaced by it, reduction of hours of work (to spread work and thereby reduce unemployment, distress, competition for work, and acceptance of lower pay), public relief, public works, and making agreed wage scales legally binding. Hence, also, the frequently canvassed idea of settling a section of the population on the extensive waste lands (land that could be cultivated but was not), so as to reduce unemployment and the competition for work that kept wages low. This was the rationale behind O'Connor's Chartist Land Plan in the 1840s. While there was a general rejection of Malthusian explanations of pauperism in terms of excessive population, and it was asserted that the country could support a much larger population, it was recognised that there was a severe 'surplus of labour', due to an unjust distribution of wealth, competition, and a lack of access to the land. Against emigration schemes, they supported 'home colonisation', to remove the labour surplus. Yet, declared O'Connor, 'I tell you that my plan has no more to do with Socialism than it has to do with the comet.'[43]

## Political economy

Many of these ideas ran counter to orthodox forms of political economy, the supposed value-free science, which dominated respectable debate over economic and social issues. Socialist theorists, from Marx downwards, saw it as an essential task to rebut this philosophy. While this can be seen as an essential element in socialism, in fact it went much wider. Certainly, its prestige in England was such that trade union spokesmen there often felt they had to come to terms with it, especially after mid-century, though this does not mean it affected trade union practice. Sometimes it was argued that political economy justified trade unions, 'for no principle of political economy favours haphazard dealing'; Potter would quote Smith or M'Culloch in favour of high wages, and obeisance might be made to the 'immutable laws of political economy', such as the dependence of wages on supply and demand, while concentrating mainly on establishing bargaining power between masters and men; 'acknowledging then, as we are reluctantly compelled to do, that the great principle of supply and demand regulates the wages of labour, the duty and interest of all workmen is to keep labour as fully employed as possible'.[44] While it was difficult to condemn free trade and support protection after the 1850s, they could oppose 'unfair' free trade and insist on terms of reciprocity, which the *Times* portrayed as being in reality, opposition to free trade.[45]

Yet there was also an explicit rejection of political economy, for 'local boards of trade were in themselves utterly opposed to the philosophy of the Manchester school of economists', and 'anything for the benefit of working men or to ameliorate the condition of women or children is sure to be opposed to political economy; but if political economy is always opposed to us, then let us be opposed to political economy'.[46] The rejection was on several grounds.

First, they rejected the denial of conflicting interests. 'It was', said Cremer, 'absurd to talk of the identity of interests between capital and labour, since the employer's object was to get the maximum of labour for the minimum of wages, while the workmen's aim was the maximum of wages for the minimum of work.'[47]

Secondly, materialistic political economy dealt in abstractions and figures, and conceived of people as things. As Dunning put it, 'if they can prove production is accelerated, no matter by what means, they are perfectly at ease, though in the process thousands are ruined', for a political economist 'separates labour and capital from labourers and capitalists'. 'In all these discussions', wrote another, 'the advocates of capital speak and write constantly about their fellow-men, as so much "materiel", to be dealt with in the "market" according to the immutable principles of "supply and demand" – like Ostend rabbits or Christmas logs.'[48] For political economy was partisan, on the side of employers. 'Free Trade was only a free lie, maintained for the benefit of landowners and capitalists, manufacturers and annuitants, while labourers of all countries were pitted against each other, continually working harder and getting less in return, and one of the first practical lessons which the working men of this country had to learn was to work less. The practical meaning of the political economists, who taught the free trade theory, was simply that the capitalists should grow richer, while labourers should grow poorer.'[49]

Political economy was rejected, explicitly or implicitly, through a stress on 'rights' and a concept of justice which refused to see labour as a commodity; 'let masters not seek to introduce Free Trade in human labour, as in the commodities of life. Labour and human energies are no more marketable articles than is the person of an upright and honourable man', and 'The whole world will perish if selfishness alone is to regulate it . . . We need sincere desires for public good.'[50]

'The wages of labour ought to be such as would enable an industrious and prudent man, marrying at the age of five-and-twenty, to bring up a family, or to lay by a decent and comfortable provision for his old age if he remains single.'[51] Disunited men could not achieve this, but 'union brings strength'.[52] As Dunning argued, if working men were disunited, the contract or bargain with the employer was unequal, and what he termed the 'predatory instinct' led masters to take advantage of their position and keep wages down, so that wages did *not* follow supply and demand. The system of supply and demand only occurred if the men were united so that bargaining was on equal terms. Thus Lyons tailors were forced to 'join together to struggle against the spirit of rapacity which would exploit our poverty if we remained isolated'.[53] Strikes were justified, and even unsuccessful ones were useful in checking later reductions, for 'it was very hard indeed to find a cause where any amelioration or change in the condition of the workmen had been conceded without a strike'. 'As long as capital tries to overreach labour, and demands more than the lion's share of the joint produce, strikes will continue and should continue whenever workmen are free.'[54]

There was, therefore, a continuous critique of unrestricted competition and political economy right through our period, based on certain consistent themes. Yet, as the references of the previous pages show, they were expressed not only by 'socialists' but also by others, such as mid-Victorian English trade union leaders, who have never been regarded as socialist, which suggests that, while they were a fundamental and influential element in socialism, they were not distinctively socialist. 'For us', declared Proudhon and his colleagues in 1848, 'socialism is not at all a system; it is simply a protest', and what socialists agreed on was a critique of existing economic arrangements.[55] The same ideas were found in both England and France, but were far more likely to be called socialist in the latter. While after mid-century there was greater confidence in the stability of the commercial economy, the ideas of an alternative political economy had never been necessarily opposed to competitive production as such, nor to existing property rights, waged labour or profit accumulation. Rather, they involved reducing competition through regulation, shortening the hours, and reducing the labour surplus (the resultant higher wages producing an extension of the home market and greater stability for all). The aim was regulation of supply and demand to secure a fairer distribution of wealth, the stress being on inequitable exchange relations rather than the means of production, and this was compatible with capitalist economics. Nor were such ideas an alternative to political radicalism. Radicals who identified with the common people denied the alleged mission of the rich to lead society and rule because they alone could recognise the interests of the country. This denial was easily combined with one of their alleged positive economic role, either as consumers (whereby their expenditure gave bread and work to the poor, so that the luxury of the rich saved the poor from poverty), or as producers (whereby they were workers with the same interests as the employees to whom they gave work by running businesses, providing wages and the instruments of working, and by risking their wealth to provide employment for the poor). All could throw up at such statements as this in the *Times*:

If the rich are so hard-hearted, who has founded all the hospitals and charitable institutions? Who bears the greater share of the expenses for schools in England and Wales? How is it that when a well-ascertained case of destitution and misery is reported in the newspapers, before 48 hours have elapsed money enough is thrown in by anonymous hands most effectually to relieve the sufferers? What took place at the time of the Irish famine?[56]

Radicalism thus easily incorporated the ideas that the hardships of the trade cycle were caused by under-consumption due to the workers' poverty, itself the result of receiving an unfair share of the fruits of production, and that this was an artificial situation, upheld only through the control by the landed and monied interests of the making of law and the machinery of law and order. Political democracy was the only real solution to this. Nor did such views imply a great extension of the role of the state, for it was a current theme of popular radicalism that once the poverty caused by taxes, low wages, and dear food was removed, men would see to the security and education of their families and society would improve.

### Anti-capitalism

Related to this were two other elements, those of anti-capitalism and the labour theory of value. Hostility to capitalists was certainly a widespread theme throughout our period. 'It was the wealthy capitalist that we had to compete with; and through them, all had been compelled to compete with each other.'[57] There were, of course, some socialists who condemned the wage system and 'wage slavery' completely, seeing the wage-earning 'proletarian' as the successor of the slave and the serf in different stages of historical development.[58] However, the 'capitalists' whom socialists criticised were not usually the employers. They were the large landowners, rentiers, financiers, bankers, 'usurers', Jewish money-lenders, stock-brokers, fund-holders, land and railway speculators, and merchant capitalists, the idle, monied classes who lived on interest from capital and thus lived off the productive classes, an idle aristocracy of money and monopoly in a system of financial and commercial feudalism. These were distinct from manufacturing employers, especially smaller ones, who were useful and productive, and themselves often dependent on and exploited by the capitalists.[59] This, of course, was consonant with the widespread trade union analyses which condemned not employers as such, but the mercantile middlemen 'speculating' capitalists, especially those from outside the trade, such as the general building contractors, footwear and clothing wholesale firms, silk mercers or booksellers. 'Whenever you find the speculating capitalist, there you find slavery in all its forms.'[60] But even large manufacturers, industrialists, and factory-owners might be classed among the industrious instead of among the idle capitalists, who were external to production, parasitic, and unproductive, levying large profits on productive manufacturers, both employers and employees.

This analysis was easily absorbed by radicals, who saw political influence, privileged position and links with the state as the basis of the power of such capitalists as bankers, financiers, war contractors, or railway magnates such as Hudson. These were merely added to the rest of the radicals' list of privileged parasites. Under the July Monarchy, Lamartine, Ledru-Rollin and others condemned the 'financial aristocracy', 'bourgeois aristocracy', and 'financial feudalism', including some very visible Protestants and Jews, while under the Empire the targets were the few great firms and families running France, such as Rothschild, Péreire, and Talabot. Nor were such feelings confined to active radicals, for there was always widespread resentment at the Imperial government's promotion of industrial concentration, monopoly, and great joint-stock companies in mining, banking, textiles, metallurgy, transport, and the scandals that accompanied them. The Prefect of Police reported in 1856 on the widespread criticism of the Péreires' 'Crédit Mobilier' bank, whose existence and vast wealth was attributed to support and privileged concessions from a government which, instead of helping small manufacturers and traders, allowed fat bankers to exploit trade and industry and send capital abroad.[61] Undoubtedly radical condemnations of such capitalists' privileges and monopolies was far more effective than any socialist critique of the profits of capital.

So capitalists were not employers, and in fact socialists opposed to the economic role of capitalists tended not to favour conflicts between masters and workmen, seeing them as petty and irrelevant to social transformation. Efforts to raise wages were futile and doomed to failure, and even if successful brought no benefits, because of the liberal economists' iron law of wages. In England, O'Brien and his followers were particularly hostile to strikes and trade unions, and to radical efforts to arouse social antagonism and class passions.[62] Trade unions were greedy, and 'the "Beehive" is the mouthpiece of those worst of monopolists – the Trade Unionists'.[63] Even such socialists who supported the idea of a general strike opposed all actual 'partial' strikes as a diversion, selfish, and harmful to other workers if they succeeded.[64] It was other radicals who found it easier to approve strikes as responses to provocation, unwillingness to compromise, greed, and profiteering on the part of employers.

This is not to deny that there were frequent attacks on industrial capitalists and millowners, the 'suzerains of industry', but this was usually for their actual behaviour rather than for their role in production, with their harsh attitudes to their workforce (especially women and children), opposition to factory legislation, and a control of their workforce through housing, shops, water, and fuel supply that reduced them to 'slavery' (not wage slavery). The English epithets of 'cotton lord', 'steam lord', and 'millocrat' emphasised their local power and transferred some of the odium attached to aristocracy. It was their political behaviour that was more often attacked than their economic function. Thus Howell condemned industrialists who manufactured arms and ships for the Confederacy in the American Civil War. A particular target in the Paris public meetings at the end of the 1860s was the great ironmaster Schneider, who controlled the lives of the thousand-odd workers he had under him at Le Creusot (indeed the whole Saône-et-Loire department was almost his fief), and was also the chairman of the ironmasters' committee and president of the Legislative Body, tied to the regime through his reliance on government orders. His oppressive regulations and control of benefits provoked strikes early in 1870 that he then suppressed with troops.

### Labour and property

The 'labour theory of value' can be seen as another element in socialism whereby capital is seen as stored-up or stolen labour, the result of depriving the labourer of a fair reward through exploitation. The basic idea that labour was the source of all wealth, and that the actual producers of wealth were robbed by the idlers who lived on the produce of others, was common enough. It followed that everyone should work, and those that did not did not deserve to consume. Far more important than any opposition to property or capitalism was that deep, abiding dislike of the idle scrounger, whether at the top or the bottom. 'I have no theories', said the Blanquist ironfounder Duval,' I am neither socialist, nor communist; I say that everyone who does not work lives off the sweat of the workers.'[65]

Such emphases on labour and the right to its whole produce were in fact basic ones in radicalism, where labour was seen as the chief title to political rights. But the definitions of 'labour' and 'productive' were vague, and did not usually only refer to waged or manual work, but embraced a whole range of useful activities. The robbery of labour was often conceived of as being through taxation rather than through economic exploitation.[66]

The ideas 'that LABOUR is the source of wealth; for there could be NO PROPERTY if there were no labour',[67] that labour was the working man's property, and that labour legitimated property, were old ones that could lead in our period to very radical conclusions, in that any property that was *not* the product of one's own labour was illegitimate; this was the basis of Proudhon's attack on property as theft. The most usual application of this, however, was in relation to property that was not the creation of labour but was given by God or Nature, especially land. 'God did not create the world and its use for some only to the exclusion of the rest. All men have the same right to property in the soil.'[68] Thus, common ownership of land was a familiar radical aim that reflected a widespread view, even among liberals, that land was a special kind of property, to which normal justifications for exclusive individual ownership did not necessarily apply.[69] It could also be extended to other gifts of nature, such as rivers, seas, fisheries, or mines. But a commitment to common ownership of 'natural wealth' usually made a clear distinction between this and all other wealth that was the product of labour, and therefore should be privately owned. Moreover, support for common ownership of land was much more extensive in British radicalism than in France, where there was much wider peasant proprietorship, and it was against the wishes of French delegates that the IWMA at the end of the 1860s adapted land nationalisation as one of its aims. It should also be stressed that such arguments, and the identification of the origins of inequality, property, and even of wages, with the forcible appropriation of the land by a few people at some time in the distant past, did not necessarily lead to calls for the collective ownership of all land in the present but were used to justify the more important right of *access* to the land for all who wished it, who were then not compelled to work for wages. As O'Connor put it:

when one man employs another, and makes profit of his labour, let others call it what they please, I call it slavery. That is, provided the man is compelled to work for another, because he has not the means of working for himself. The case is far different, when both doors are open, and when the workman may enter at which he pleases – the natural door, which is the land, or the artificial door, which is the factory. In such cases, the standard of wages established in the free labour, or natural, market, renders the man who works in the artificial market from choice just as independent as his neighbour.

Thus people who supported themselves on the land were receiving the full produce of their labour and this provided the goal which all other workers should reach, thereby also receiving the full value of their labour, and because settlement of some on the land would remove the surplus of labour, all those working in manufacture could achieve it.[70] Even those who, unlike O'Connor, believed in land nationalisation, did not envisage the collectivisation of agriculture but rather the letting of land in plots to individual producers, for in the words of O'Brien, an advocate of land nationalisation, 'the hope of individual reward is the most natural incentive to labour'.[71] Thus the issue here was not socialism but *access* to land for all (not settlement of all on land), which, whether or not achieved through land nationalisation, would eliminate poverty, provide equality of opportunity, rehabilitate labour, and secure a full reward for workers in manufactures, and would be a check on unfettered competition without being a restraint on individual enterprise, and was quite compatible with private ownership and division of labour in industry.[72]

O'Brien was one of those who favoured the nationalisation of other things apart from land and natural wealth, but these were all forms of property already regulated by legislation and so were not totally private forms of property. O'Brien argued that the various parliamentary acts empowering rich groups to build railways, canals, bridges, and other public works were all examples of political power being used to profiteer off the people, and therefore wanted all these forms of 'public' property directly owned by the state.[73] A similar programme was advocated by the Lyons Babeuvian, Benoit, and other French radicals in 1848.[74] These were forms of property that were neither the result of labour nor forms of manufacture.

There were also some who advocated the abolition of all private property of any kind, either in separate communities where all would live, work, and share in common, as in Owenism or Fourierism, or in a communist state, as in Icarianism or Babeuvianism. But it is not difficult to show that there was never widespread support for such a total abolition of property. Of the few who did support it, a number were religious in some form or another, their theories based on moral preoccupations. Their concern was not particularly with production and its socialisation, but with property *per se*, because it divided mankind and prevented harmony.[75] Hence we find that communists were also frequently opposed to established religions and to the family as well as property, because they also divided mankind. Whereas most radicals opposed women's paid work and wished to make it possible for women to stay at home for their natural and essential duties there, and emphasised productive males and manliness, Cabet's club in 1848 discussed the woman question. It was certain kinds of socialists and communists who were most interested in either abolishing the family or changing the place of women.

### Altruism

Another important element of socialism was a condemnation of competition on moral rather than economic grounds. A society founded on competition was characterised by jealousy, division, distrust, and hatred, which all made happiness impossible, even for the rich. Many socialists thus saw exploitation as the absence of social harmony and of a sense of community, and looked to education to allow the ascendancy of reason over ignorance and to end the situation whereby 'we are, from having a spirit of emulation and ambition instilled into our minds from infancy, pleased with the competitive strife of the men of wealth or ambition'.[76] Thus, in contrast to selfishness, 'socialism' meant altruism, the original meaning of the term in the previous century. The workers' journals and poetry of the 1840s were particularly pervaded with this language of harmony, brotherhood, fraternity, love, and social benevolence in place of selfishness and materialism.

Through selfishness, men were always stirred up to live in conflict.- Through selfishness, the strong enslaved the weak. – Through selfishness, the fruits of the earth were appropriated by the former, against the rights of the latter – Through selfishness, finally, distress, poverty, and slavery were the people's lot, and all was disorder, war, enmity.[77]

Disapproval of materialism was by no means confined to socialists, and was shared by many Christian manufacturers in England, but they tended to distinguish the world of work, where competition was and should be supreme, from the world of the family, characterised by mutual love and support. Socialists condemning competition on ethical grounds were opposing this distinction and seeking to extend the ethos of the family to society at large, to stress mutual dependence and the need for social co-operation and fraternity.[78]

Perhaps the best example of the importance of this theme is Lamennais, undoubtedly the most popular writer in France during the July Monarchy. His *Words of a Believer* of 1834 had an electrifying effect, to become one of the most influential works of the time, read everywhere and going through a hundred editions and translations within a few years (Mazzini was only one of the many foreign radicals influenced by him). The *Book of the People* in 1837 had an impact little less. These consist not of concrete proposals for social and economic change, but of long tirades against the injustices of society and treatment of the workers, and the materialism, selfishness, and lack of compassion of the rich. They were radical works that passionately denounced kings, rulers, and lawyers, condemned the July Monarchy for its weakness internally and externally, and championed liberty, equality, fraternity, the perfectibility of man, and the sovereignty of the people through universal suffrage. It was in this respect that Nadaud remembered the *Words*,[79] 'an astounding book of boldness, of vigour of style and well known above all for leading the people to hate kings'. Lamennais typically blamed the power held by oppressors who had abandoned morality on the people's lack of education, enlightenment, and unity, and asserted their right to unite in order to defend themselves against oppression. He condemned material suffering, and championed the suffering people in all countries, the poor, those without property who lived simple lives and were dignified by their labour, the real basis of society, who had remained moral and were forced to work for their rulers. He asserted the right of everyone to possess the fruits of his industry, condemned the oppression of the poor and even the wages system itself as a form of slavery which prevented social progress, declared that the land had been given freely to all and that private ownership of land and money had led to the ills of poverty, denounced the laws against combinations in defence of wages, and saw the remedy in the association of the people to change things and free themselves from dependence on the rich. Yet his specific proposals were few, beyond the abolition of monopoly, and the diffusion of capital and free credit, so as to make property through labour available to more people, and he specifically rejected taking the wealth of the rich. The real impact came from his moral critique: his overriding concern for humanity, assertions that material change was not enough in itself, attribution of misery and want to the disappearance of justice and charity, stress on conscience and duties, declaration that improvement can come through goodness and labour, and insistence that love unites and hatred and selfishness divide. The rich should be kind to the poor, and reform would come through the moralisation of society to drive away materialism and selfishness. He rejected 'socialism' as tyrannical and materialistic, but his impact, so much greater than that of any socialist theorist, indicates that the chief popular impact of Owenism and Saint-Simonism lay precisely in this moral condemnation of competition and assertion of harmony, where one would 'drown the self in an Ocean of Sociability'.[80]

We can, therefore see socialism, like radicalism, not as an ideology but as a set of themes, concerning poverty and welfare, state intervention in the economy, critiques of a competitive economy and orthodox political economy, anti-capitalism, the labour theory of value, common owner-ship of land and natural wealth, moral condemnation of a society based on selfishness and materialism, co-operative production, and the abolition of private property. While all might in some way be concerned with production, they did not really, except for the last one, offer alternative theories or analyses to radicalism, to which they could be assimilated without challenging a basically political identification of the sources of inequality and injustice. Socialist theories do not seem to have had a very popular distinctive appeal, but working men were very concerned with poverty, security, food prices, wages, and public relief, criticism of political economy was widespread, and the condemnation of materialism, selfishness, and injustice certainly struck deep chords. Thus the socialism that had a popular impact was not an alternative to radicalism but a particular form of radicalism.

# 6    Co-operation

It is not difficult to see co-operation as the most important aspect of socialism, for co-operative societies were a recurrent feature during the whole period, and there were times when they particularly flourished – a national movement in England and Wales around 1830, extending to over 400 societies in communication with one another, a number of co-operative periodicals, and national congresses; a similar upsurge during the Second Republic in France; and a revival in both countries in the 1860s, to a large extent on the model of the Rochdale Pioneers founded in 1844, the movement continuing to grow in subsequent decades.

There are three obvious reasons why co-operation may be seen as a form of socialism. Firstly, socialists were actively involved in co-operative societies. Secondly, socialists advocated co-operation. Thirdly, co-operative societies declared their socialism. A Paris bronze-workers' co-operative society in 1850 sought 'the growth of the welfare of the producers through the suppression of parasitic intermediaries and usurious capital, by means of the socialisation of the instruments of labour', and 'the emancipation of the workers by the abolition of employers (*patronat*)', to achieve 'the Republic in the workshops', while the Stockport Working Man's Redemption Society announced 'their object was to work for themselves instead of for masters'.[1]

Underlying all this, of course, is the fact that co-operation, through replacing private businesses with democratic control by groups, was effecting an economic and social transformation. There were, however, several forms of co-operation. 'The English prefer trading, the Germans credit and the French production.'[2] Co-operative trading on the Rochdale model has, in fact, been seen as a non-socialist form in contrast to the early socialist co-operative movement of the late 1820s and early 1830s.[3] Similarly the growth of co-operative stores in France from the 1860s has been seen as a fragmentation of the socialist vision.[4] It is co-operative production which has been seen as the most socialist and transformative form.[5]

It has also been seen as an ideology particularly appropriate to artisans. While there were some examples of co-operative mining, calico-printing, and cotton spinning or weaving,[6] it was generally recognised that co-operative production was the most practicable, attractive, and practised in the artisan trades, where less capital was needed to set up.[7] The slower industrialisation of France has thus been used to explain the much greater importance of co-operative production there, so that the artisanal structure of French industry is responsible for the co-operative 'trade socialism' or 'socialism of skilled workers' that is even seen as the dominant ideological component of the French labour movement in our period.[8]

However, 'socialism' is a limited and restricting approach to what were undoubtedly important movements. Not only were there several forms of co-operation, we need also to recognise the variety of impulses and goals within each form, and be aware of how these were all affected by readings of and readjustments to the political situation.

## Co-operative trading (coopération de consommation)

It is easy to relate this form of co-operation to a long-established and abiding consumer consciousness concerned especially with the prices and adulteration of food.[9] The best known expression of such concerns were the food riots that characterised Britain and France in the eighteenth century, which had all but died out in central England by 1830, and in France by the 1860s. One replacement for food riots in England was 'exclusive dealing', boycotting exploitative dealers and only buying at shops that charged fair prices. From exclusive dealing to buying only in a co-operative store that sold unadulterated goods at fair prices was not a big step, especially as the store often employed a shopkeeper to run it. Many co-operative societies in Belgium, southern Germany and Strasbourg did not even have a store, but made contracts with private shops with whom members dealt, using society tokens. The co-operative movement that arose in England at the end of the 1820s consisted overwhelmingly of trading stores and occurred at the very same time as the movements, especially in Lancashire and Yorkshire, to boycott shops charging high prices for beef, butter, or milk, and to deal only with fair ones. Other periods of distress provoked the formation of co-operative societies. Co-operative trading thus incorporated exclusive dealing and bulk-buying to retail at cost or little more (the Rochdale Pioneers began in the collective purchase, and dividing out, of a bag of meal).[10] Food was not the only concern – coal clubs were common in England, and such a club was the starting point of the United Workers at Lyons.[11]

As well as the bulk-buying of food and fuel, co-operatives might produce food themselves, particularly flour and bread. Some of the very earliest English co-operative societies were flour mills, and collective buying of live beasts was a well-established practice in parts of Germany, but in the towns co-operative bakeries and butcheries were more common.[12] It was the rise in meat prices because of the cattle plague in the mid-1860s that led the artisans at the naval arsenal at Woolwich to set up the famous Woolwich Royal Arsenal Co-operative Society.[13]

These stores aimed to free members from the malpractices of private dealers, particularly adulteration, an abiding concern.[14] A variant was a society in Chaumont to provide clean drinking water.[15] It is not then surprising that co-operative stores were common where there was a sudden rise in population and only a few tradesmen, who exploited their position.[16] One of the bases of shopkeepers' hold on working families was through credit, though the motives might well be humanitarian, and shopkeepers often had to give credit to keep their clientele. Co-operative stores aimed to free people of such credit dependence, for 'the normal condition of a workman who is not a co-operator is to be in debt'.[17]

A further variant was co-operative eating-houses, utilising large-scale purchase and cooking to produce cheaper as well as more wholesome food. There was a movement for them in London in the 1860s, but it was above all in Second Republic Paris that they flourished, there being about sixty fraternal restaurants and cafés scattered through the city.[18]

It seems fairly easy to understand these activities without reference to socialist ideas. This has always been the case with Rochdalian co-operation, though we should recognise the continuing and important role of Owenites and freethinkers, in this movement.[19] 'We have no doubt', wrote William Newton in 1851, 'that many stores have been established purely for the sake of the profits arising from them.'[20] But this was not new, and in the years around 1830 Owenites had also recognised that the co-operation societies they were involved with had similar concerns.[21] Rochdale principles and practices were not original, and had been anticipated earlier,[22] but this in itself does not render such societies purely commercial and there were frequent tensions over the relative weight of commercial, democratic, and solidarity emphases. Most societies were very local and run by working people. In 1864 the group of middle-class ex-socialists in Paris who ran the *Association* journal set up a big new store which evolved into 'Sincerity', a flourishing limited-liability commercial enterprise selling cheap food to the public and paying a dividend to shareholders on profits. This was criticised by many labour activists, such as Tartaret (an original member) and Varlin, as a commercial, profit-making body. They preferred the usual kind of store, selling only to members and paying a dividend on purchases, run by small, local societies of working people who elected the managers. Supporters of Sincerity and other such societies saw this as an expression of class antagonism and as sharpening class divisions. In 1866 there arose Working Economy in opposition to Sincerity, and henceforth all societies in Paris dealt only with members and paid a dividend on purchases.[23] These differences partly reflected legal constraints,[24] which, while restricting the activities of co-operative societies, left them choices on the degree of freedom, democratic control, exclusivity, legal security, commercialism, and profitability.[25]

The exclusivity was often reinforced by the fact that working-class shopping was overwhelmingly local, through little purchases at a nearby shop, and co-operative trading was only able to succeed through small local branches, as a neighbourhood-based movement. This was very clear in Lyons, a great centre of successful co-operative trading, where the societies each had large numbers of local stores, and efforts at larger commercial ones failed. The relative failure of co-operative trading in Paris was mainly due to the lack of such small, local grocery stores, and it is significant that the most successful co-operative sale there was of wine which, unlike other goods, was delivered. Thus in the 1840s the Rochdale Pioneers were only one of several societies in and near the town, with only one store and a membership limited to 500. Only in the 1850s did they expand, through absorbing the other small local societies as branches. It was therefore natural that a new co-operative society in Manchester in 1850 declared 'their design was to open a shop in every street'.[26]

It was also obvious that co-operative trading could only succeed if it had the support of the women. Given that running the home and the domestic budget were usually regarded as the women's sphere, it was they who organised and decided where and how to shop, and they might well not wish to have their purchases subject to the husband's oversight at a co-operative store, while, given the many demands on their time, they would be loth to make sizeable journeys for small purchases. Male co-operators therefore recognised that their support was essential, and tended to see the problem as one of educating them into a more extended view, though one Parisian suggested winning them over by buying them a dress from the dividends received for dealing at the store. The extent to which women were involved in the running and decisions of societies was limited, and though they did take part in cultural and social events, it was not as organisers but as listeners to speeches and providers of refreshments. At one co-operative tea-party the Chartist James Finlen told stories in verse as appropriate to an audience that included ladies (he preferred the 'Saxon' word 'women', but best of all liked 'household goddesses').[27]

Despite the undoubted importance of co-operative trading, particularly in the 1860s, it tended to be concentrated not only in time but also in place, the main centres of strength being the textile areas. Its spectacular expansion in England, to occupy a central place in working-class activity, was largely in Lancashire, Yorkshire, and, to a lesser extent, Cheshire. In 1850 there were only about fifty societies, mostly in Lancashire. It was really in the later 1850s that the movement really began to grow, but at the end of the 1860s, when there were about 600 societies, with nearly 200,000 members, around two-thirds were still in Lancashire, Cheshire, and the West Riding, with the Rochdale society as the dominant one. The other areas where the movement was also strong were mostly dominated by single industries, such as boot and shoe-making or coal and iron in the East Midlands, and the coalfields and steel and shipbuilding areas of the North East, but it was weak in southern England, Birmingham, or the West Midlands, while the failure of the Cardiff Stores led to the bankruptcy of the National Industrial and Provident Society, and the movement remained weak in Wales.[28]

In France the initial freedom created by the Second Republic led to an expansion of co-operative trading, the main centres, apart from the silk area of Lyons, being, as in England, the woollen, worsted, and cotton areas. Lille and Rheims had large, strong, and successful societies which led to imitations in the neighbouring towns, and both areas saw a revival in the 1860s.[29] But during the period as a whole, the two chief areas were probably Alsace and the Lyonnese. The former was a great centre of cotton-spinning, weaving and calico-printing, which experienced a real industrial revolution in the first half of the century. It was also distinctive in being a largely German area, with dynasties of great, largely Protestant, liberal, paternalistic employers, who encouraged co-operative stores. But Lyons was the strongest centre of co-operation under the July Monarchy, and the movement thrived in the Second Republic, mainly on the Croix-Rousse, the great silk-weaving district. All its societies were suppressed with the *coup d'état* of 1851, but secret co-operative trading continued in the 1850s, and the movement revived after 1859, especially in the widespread distress caused by the loss of American markets because of the American Civil War. Lyons therefore became again the chief French centre of co-operative trading, as before mostly in the Croix-Rousse, and the movement was also strong in nearby St. Etienne.[30]

On the other hand, co-operative trading remained weak in the two capital cities. London was an important centre around 1830, but new efforts in the 1860s produced only about thirty societies. The sixty-odd societies in Paris in the mid-1860s, with about 3,000 members had fallen to a mere half-dozen by the end of the decade, which compared feebly with Lyons, which, with a fifth of its population, had nearly thirty stores and over 5,000 members. In both cases, the lack of a dominant industry, a reluctance of clients to travel, a failure to establish enough local stores or big really central ones that could compete with private shopkeepers' know-how were problems; even Working Economy suffered from its position. It is significant that the few successful ones in London were in areas dominated by a single workplace – railway works in Stratford and the Arsenal at Woolwich.[31]

The extent and persistence of co-operative trading, even in informal forms during the dangerous repression of the 1850s in France,[32] shows that it met basic needs and concerns. But it was not a completely distinct form of activity. Like trade and benefit societies, co-operative societies could be concerned with legislation and therefore with political actions to change it. Basically, their desire was to be left alone, free of official interference, but their trading character made legal recognition more attractive than it was to benefit and trade societies. Society campaigns preceded the two British acts of 1852 and 1862, especially the latter, and there were campaigns in France in the mid-1860s against the various restrictive government bills between 1863 and 1867, the outcome being regarded as unsatisfactory.[33]

Co-operative trading was often used as a means of raising funds for other activities, whether welfare, educational or political. A number of Chartist branches opened stores, and the policy was officially adopted at the 1845 Chartist Convention, partly as a means of self-government and to teach the shopkeepers a lesson.[34] The links with benefit societies were particularly strong. 'We regard members of Friendly Societies as brother Co-operators.'[35] The origins of the co-operative movement in Leeds in 1829 lay in benefit societies, co-operative propaganda was aimed at benefit societies, some benefit societies opened co-operative stores, many co-operative societies, in France particularly, combined benefits with co-operative trading, while the Rochdale Pioneers saw their role of freeing members from credit and enabling them to save as akin to that of friendly societies, of which they set up one of their own in 1861. In 1866 Rheims benefit societies combined to set up a co-operative trading organisation confined to the members of their societies.[36]

There were also other reasons than prices and adulteration for exclusive dealing. It could be, alongside an exchange of services, a means of reinforcing solidarity, as among religious sects or among radical political groups during a period of quiescence or decline.[37] In

England it was a well-established technique during elections, whereby, in a system of open voting, non-electors could bring pressure on electors to vote the right way. It was thus one of the approved Chartist 'ulterior measures' in 1839.[38] The origins of the Jersey Street store in Manchester lay in a group of Chartists. 'Their primary objects were to supersede the shopkeepers, and to get votes for members of parliament; for they found on carrying round the petition for the Charter, that the shopkeepers treated them very saucily, and they therefore determined to be their own shopkeepers.'[39] Non-electors' anger at the way electors voted led to boycotts and co-operative trading. 'After an election has transpired, three out of every four of the co-operative stores, amongst working class non-electors have arisen from this source; and I make bold to assert, that co-operative stores and individual exclusive dealing, thus operating, have been the best escapement for non-electoral excitement and indignation during the transient enthusiasm of an election contest.'[40]

Co-operative trading thus overlapped with other concerns and activities. Strikes are a good example, for in a large strike the attitude of shopkeepers, and whether they would extend credit to strikers, was vital. London tradesmen organised exclusive dealing in support of the builders' strike in 1834, in their great strikes of 1833 and 1840 the Paris tailors set up kitchens to provide food for those on strike, and co-operative stores would support strikes.[41] The Rochdale Pioneers' store itself began in a three-month weavers' strike in 1844 that was costing £36 a week in strike pay. 'The store was an effort to help wages.'[42]

## Mutuality

Co-operation, said an O'Brienite boot-closer, should not just be for trading but also for housing and loans.[43] The last was particularly exemplified in the German movement under Schulze-Delitszch, and was also important in France in the 1860s. The appeal of such enterprises must be related to the universality of credit amongst the working population, and also to the prevalence of small, often informal clubs organising savings for Christmas, clothing, furniture, clocks, burials, tontines, or lotteries. These were all self-help efforts to cope with the uncertainties and hazards of life that, like co-operative trading, overlapped with friendly societies.[44] A particular feature that developed in England was emigration funds, to enable members to afford their passage across the Atlantic.[45] A number of such schemes were started by trade unions as both a form of relief and a way of reducing the labour surplus.[46]

The Staffordshire potters' fund provided both for emigration and the erection of cottage homes on freehold land, and a number of co-operative societies envisaged retirement cottages for members. Housing was a basic need, and the Lyons co-operative United Workers provided lodgings for members, while freehold and building societies were much in vogue in England from the late 1840s.[47] In 1843, an associate of O'Brien, Dr Thomas Bowkett, also an active Chartist and secularist, produced a plan to make building society loans available to poorer people, through forming small societies that used the income from subscriptions to make interest-free loans to each member in turn so that he could buy a house; when all members had secured one, the society was wound up. This democratisation of building societies, as modified by Richard Starr, became very popular, and large numbers of Starr-Bowkett societies were formed in the next decades,[48] with many imitators.[49] Starr also ran a co-operative coal society, and some Bowkett societies had co-operative stores and loan funds, for, as Bowkett said, his plan was a form of co-operation, and a number of co-operative building societies appeared. Similarly, in Paris in 1849 a number of co-operative societies began to use their funds to buy or erect houses for members.[50]

A similar movement of democratisation and access for the poor lay in insurance, where the big commercial companies did not cater for working people. A pioneer here was the dyer Ruffey Ridley (later D. W. Ruffey), a leading figure in the Consolidated Trades' Union in 1834 and in London Chartism, who in 1843 founded a United Patriots' Benefit and Co-operative Society to provide low cost insurance for working people to cover against sickness, loss by fire, a wife's lying-in, imprisonment for debt, being drawn for the militia, old-age relief, and funerals. It received strong Chartist support, as part of the policy of welfare schemes as a means of strength, and flourished, even building its own Athenaeum.[51] Appropriately, Ruffey also founded a land and building society 'for the working millions'.[52]

With the decline of Chartism at the end of the 1840s, Chartists in the provinces often went into co-operative trading or freehold land movements, but this did not happen in London, where in any case Chartism remained fairly strong throughout the 1850s, but a number did go into insurance.[53] Particularly important here were O'Connor's partners on the Executive of the National Charter Association and Board of Directors of the Land Company, all of whom became active in insurance in the 1850s, M'Grath ultimately becoming prominent in the Prudential.[54]

An outcome of Ernest Jones' Labour Parliament of 1853 was the United Brothers' Industrial Sick Benefit and Fire and Life Insurance Company, run by London Chartists such as Leno and Finlen, the directors being unpaid working men who continued working at their trades, with only the secretary receiving a working man's wage. 'This company was pre-eminently a working man's company. It had been originated, planned, and conducted by working men, for the amelioration of the wants of their order.' They saw themselves as pioneers: 'Life assurance is fast ceasing to be the exclusive affair it formerly was. The heavy premiums which were once demanded every year of the wealthy (who alone could afford to pay them) prevented the poorer classes from enjoying the benefits of assurance. The formation of the industrial assurance companies changed the whole character of assurance business and popularised it.'[55]

The most successful of these societies was run by the ex-Owenite and General Secretary of the NCA, Thomas Martin Wheeler, a friend (and fellow cricketer) of Leno, the joint author of O'Connor's book *On the Practical Management of Small Farms*, a prominent member of Ruffey's Patriots' Society, organiser in 1846 of insurance for people who refused to serve in the militia, and a founder in 1856 of the co-operative 'Labour League'. In 1853 Wheeler joined an old, ailing building society, the 'Friend-in-Need' (run by another Chartist), and transformed it into an insurance society that operated beyond the local sphere and provided sick, accident, fire and death insurance, on the principles that 'working men and tradesmen long connected with the workings of Benefit and Burial Societies, were competent to manage the affairs of an Assurance Society', and that 'working men and women should attend to their own business. If they could not, no one else could do it for them.' 'Its object is to meet the wants of the working classes by enabling its members to insure for any amount, large or small, against sickness, death, fire or other accidents. The large offices do not care to transact this kind of business, although well aware of its safety. They act like merchants who will not condescend to the retail system, but the Friend-in-Need meets the wants of all.' With Wheeler as general manager and secretary it grew rapidly to become a national concern, open to men and women, one of the biggest of its kind, with an agent in nearly every town, and an income in 1861–2 of £45,800. It was staffed almost entirely by Chartists, and on Wheeler's death in 1861 he was succeeded by his Chartist brother, George, who was also chief clerk of the United Patriots.[56]

Wheeler saw the United Patriots and Friend-in-Need as bringing the principle of self-government into every-day affairs. This democratisation led their promoters to campaign in 1864 against Gladstone's Annuities Bill which, in an effort to promote working-class thrift, made post offices agents for risk-free government-guaranteed insurance. It was a threat from the state to independent friendly and insurance companies, in an effort to gain hold of their money. By raising revenue for the government, it was a form of state-controlled taxation of poor savers, the profits to the Exchequer subsidising rich taxpayers. Similar feelings had earlier fuelled benefit societies' reluctance to invest in government funds. In each case, the working classes should be left alone to run their own organisations. 'The Government', said Leno, 'was getting jealous of the power of the working classes, through their trade and other organisations, and desired to cripple that power by the blighting influence of centralisation.'[57]

Thus in insurance, as in building societies, we find radical efforts at democratisation and mutuality, as well as that reform of working-class practices also found among trade societies – the United Brothers were 'superseding the old-fashioned and ineffectual system of benefit societies', while the Friend-in-Need operated 'without the aid of sounding titles and lavish expenditure'.[58] Similarly, in France in the later 1860s radicals in Paris advocated insurance run by the working class instead of the robbery and exploitation of commercial concerns.[59]

Because debt and the need for funds were a constant part of artisan life and a means of control, loan societies developed as a defence against paternalistic practices, usurious money-lenders, and high-interest loan societies.[60] Trade societies often made loans to members.[61] As with co-operative trading, building societies, and insurance, it was from the later 1850s that loan societies proliferated and federated in England and Wales, and by 1865 there were over 800 of them, 500 in London.[62] Particularly important in the metropolis was the Friends of Labour, founded in 1851 by a few working men in Pentonville, with a weekly subscription of at first a penny, later twopence, to make loans at 5 per cent interest for such purposes as buying tools, redeeming tools pledged at a pawnbroker's during unemployment, medical expenses, and benefit society payments during unemployment. It also paid death benefit. Growing rapidly, it established very many small branches in London at public-houses, and spread all over the country, to reach 500 branches in 1862, with 80,000 members, nearly all working men and the majority mechanics. By 1865 it was circulating nearly a million pounds a year. True to their democratic character, members had only one vote, however large their deposits, 'to prevent a monopoly by capitalists'.[63]

There were obvious points of contact here with co-operative trading, which also aimed to free members from shopkeepers' credit, and some co-operative societies, such as Rochdale and Halifax, made loans to members.[64] Furthermore, the Friends of Labour made loans to enable direct purchase of coal from a wholesaler to save costs, supported legislation against adulteration, provided in its rules for co-operative dealing, and in 1861 changed the title of its periodical to *The Friends of Labour Association's Monthly Circular and Co-operative Journal*. Having supported the London builders' strike in 1859 (as did Wheeler's Friend-in-Need insurance society), it also backed the co-operative campaign for legislation in 1862.[65]

Loan funds also existed in France, much more closely linked to co-operation.[66] As in Britain, there was an expansion of loan societies from the later 1850s.[67] With the depression that began in 1862 and the consequent business failures, the problem of credit became acute for all working men and many small investors, and a number of credit societies appeared to cater for them. By 1866 there were 120 mutual credit societies in Paris, and in the next three years the number nearly trebled. Co-operative credit was in fact the chief form of co-operation in Paris in the 1860s, and it was also important in Lyons and Alsace (where two-thirds of co-operative societies were credit ones, reflecting the influence of the German movement, whose congresses were attended by Alsatians).[68]

Co-operative trading, building, popular insurance, and loan societies all, like friendly societies, met basic needs of their members, and all experienced an expansion from the later 1850s, with radicals tending to take the lead, and mutual societies were one of the century's great legacies. All impinged on and overlapped with one another, and all can be seen as different forms of co-operation, as indeed they came to be seen at law, whether or not they took the name (loan societies were much more likely to do so in France). Their basic appeal and popularity is clear, and was far greater than that of the savings banks, so earnestly promulgated by philanthropists, reformers, liberals, and the state, partly as a way of checking more independent organisations. Most of those who used savings banks were not artisans but people with fixed jobs and pay, such as servants or clerks, for it was not thrift but self-help and mutuality that aroused the greatest response among artisans.[69] While these concerns involved commercial activities or considerations that could become dominant, as the IWMA feared, on the whole they kept their mutual, associationist, and friendly society tone during our period.

### Co-operative production

Co-operative production can be seen as the most important and radical form of co-operation, as it meant the displacement of private employers. But it was not a uniform phenomenon, and embraced a variety of practices and aims. One of the most important was its function as a strike weapon. In many artisan trades, men on strike could work for themselves and seek to sell what they made. 'When journeymen tailors, shoemakers, hatters, leave off work, they can on the day after which they struck, work on their own account. Some did this and their efforts were crowned with success.'[70] It was not then a big step to collective working, and it was a well-established technique in strikes to use strike funds to employ strikers to make things for sale instead of merely paying them strike pay, the proceeds reducing the drain on funds.[71] Tailors and shoemakers were particularly prone to 'temporary associations in which, to gain rights, the journeymen form themselves during a stoppage'.[72] It was in fact the Paris tailors' strike co-operative in 1833 that gave Louis Blanc the basis of his plans.[73] The device was put into operation on both sides of the Channel in the strikes of 1833–4. 'The Trades' Unions had now begun to feel the folly of keeping their men idle when on strike, and out of work, and pressing heavily on the trades' funds. No, said they, it must be altered, we must set them to work.'[74] Such expedients, especially the plans of the Consolidated Trades Union to employ members on strike, heightened the feeling that the new unions were permeated by socialist and Owenite ideas of replacing the employing class, but in fact the tactic was a familiar one, 'to raise enough to employ parties on strike, or other victims of oppression',[75] usually as a temporary device in aid of a strike, though a few such enterprises attempted to continue afterwards. The strategy was not even confined to artisans.[76] Sometimes a threat of co-operative production was a way of putting pressure on employers during a strike, and sometimes when, in the aftermath of a strike, a number of men, especially leaders, were blacklisted and unable to find work, they were set up collectively for a while, but these were all variants on a form of co-operative production that was a familiar and recognised temporary adjunct to strikes. It therefore figured in the plans of federations of trade unions such as the Consolidated Trades' Union of 1834, the National Association of United Trades in 1845, and the International Working Men's Association federations in 1869.[77]

While this form of co-operative production was linked to industrial conflict, a second was linked more to benefit and trade societies, as a form of unemployment relief, instead of tramping or cash payments, which were ineffective or impracticable during a depression, 'where, instead of men being sustained from the funds of the society, they might be set to work'.[78] Like strike pay, it was seen as a way of maintaining members at the lowest cost. It might be done at particular times of the year, as with the London bricklayers in the winter months, or among particularly distressed trades, such as the Spitalfields silk-weavers.[79] It was found in periods of general depression or times of difficulty for particular trades, including the defeat of efforts to raise pay.[80] Such schemes were often intended to be temporary, as with the London carpenters' societies' employment of out-of-work members to construct a house during times of depression, then discontinuing such employment when recovery came.[81] The Paris bookbinders started production in 1848, employing a few members at a time in rotation, and those in London were considering the same in 1861. In 1840 the Denton hatters established a company 'by which work, instead of money, will be given to those thrown out of employment', as did those in Lyons in 1865.[82] Around the Owenite Labour Exchanges established in London and Birmingham in the early 1830s arose a number of co-operative production societies, each composed of members of a single trade and producing goods for the Exchange bazaar, but they did not seek to employ all their members, only those who were unemployed.[83] Similarly, in the later 1840s several English compositors' societies were considering co-operative production relief, and one group of unemployed men actually launched a short-lived very radical newspaper, while in 1845 the Paris compositors set up a workshop under their president, Parmentier, to employ unemployed members to do orders from other trades, one of its rules insisting 'that the Social Workshop was considered only a provisional work asylum'.[84]

The links between this kind of co-operative production and benefit societies were clear, and the two overlapped.[85] A good example is the Paris boot and shoemakers' society, 'Industrious Humanity' ('Humanité Laborieuse'), founded in 1840 after the big strike, which combined sick and superannuation benefits with a large and efficient placement agency (with a guaranteed level of workmanship), as well as offering unemployment relief, mainly in money but sometimes in work. In 1848 co-operative production was extended, not for all members but for those out of work, a few at a time in rotation.[86] There were many other such boot and shoemakers' societies in Paris and the provinces in 1848, such as the one at Marseilles to help members 'by preserving them above all against the disastrous effects of unemployment'.[87] Again, tailors were also very prominent in this kind of co-operative production, as in Paris in 1833 'with a view to creating a work establishment so as to avoid in future the problems resulting from the slack season'.[88]

While such co-operative production could overlap with co-operative employment of strikers, both being temporary expedients and not permanent aspirations, it was also seen as an alternative to strikes, even emanating from a conviction of the futility of strikes, and some attempts, such as among the Paris tailors in 1833, the London stonemasons in 1841, the Paris shoemakers' 'Industrious' in 1840, and the Amalgamated Engineers in 1852, arose in the wake of unsuccessful strikes. The 'Industrious' was in 1848 quite distinct from the shoemakers' 'General Society' combination.[89] Such co-operative production that rejected strikes, instead of aiding them, was also much more likely to gain the approval of socialists and liberals.[90] It could also link up with co-operative trading as a form of relief – a Nantes society in 1849 employed out-of-work members and also set up a co-operative bakery, while a Salford co-operative store began employing unemployed members in production.[91]

A third form of co-operative production lay in sub-contracting which, as we have seen, pervaded manufacture in our period and opened the way to highly exploitative piece-masters and sweaters. However, in many trades, such as shipwrights, sub-contracting could take the form of collective contracts for jobs by groups of workers, which might come together just for one specific job, or might stay together for a longer time. A gang-leader or 'leading hand', whose position rested on the men's consent or election, acted as their spokesman in making an agreement with the employer for a job, allocated the work amongst the men, and handled the pay so that members of the group received regular amounts according to their work, with any balance at the end divided among them. Workers at the Toulon royal dockyard pressed for the introduction of such a system in the 1840s.[92] This form of sub-contracting was not exploitative.[93] It was what compositors' companion-ships (*commandites*) were, replacing the oppressive 'farming system' under clickers (*metteurs en pages*), and in a number of the Paris building trades, particularly after the great strikes of 1840 against task-mastering, small, often temporary, societies appeared using a gang-contract system instead of a task-master (*tâcheron*).[94] Thus many of the co-operative production societies of the early Second Republic were either continuations of these previous efforts, encouraged by the government decree abolishing piece-mastering, or were temporary groups that came together to execute particular tasks in public works, particularly among paviours.[95] The pianoforte-makers' society was a good example, for in this industry big establishments used sub-contractors and sub-sub-contractors, whom co-operative production now replaced.[96] Similarly, there was a proposal at a conference of Lancashire iron trade societies at Bolton in 1844 to equalise piece-work in this way. 'The equalisation system was deemed democratically radical in its character, therefore it received much opposition.' But collective contracting was begun as an experiment at an engineering firm in Oldham and was a great success; each group of men chose their own foreman, or piece 'gaffer', who contracted on their behalf; wages rose, minor disputes were settled by an elected works committee, and pay disagreements were decided by the whole shop.[97] Employers in the iron trades were often favourable to such systems that relieved them of many management chores, as in the great locomotive and machine-building works at Le Creusot.[98] In Paris in 1848 the system was also adopted at the great Cail engineering works – the employer provided workshops, tools, coal and foundry, and societies of engineers took on tasks at agreed prices through an elected leader, who divided the work and wages. It was a great success, and the system spread to several railway workshops.[99] Co-operative production could thus be a way of adapting and democratising sub-contracting, for 'sub-contracting can become a means of emancipation if it is practised by associated workers'.[100]

Similar in some ways to this form of co-operative production was profit-sharing, which was included in the Cail system. Profit-sharing schemes were sometimes called co-operative, and leading advocates of co-operative production in England tended in the 1860s and 1870s to concentrate on profit-sharing industrial partnerships.[101] The Rochdale Pioneers opened a co-operative spinning mill in 1855, the capital coming from paid-up shares, and each year the profits, after paying wages and a 5 per cent dividend to shareholders, were divided among both shareholders and employees. But in 1862 the 'bounty on labour' was ended and it became a simple joint-stock company, which is what many co-operative firms really were.[102] A common motive for profit-sharing was lack of capital, and employees who paid a sum to the firm in return for a share of the profits were really becoming creditors or sleeping partners, the management remaining in the hands of the employer. This was common among cabinet-making firms in the north of England, a number of hatting firms in Paris, or the famous Oldham 'Working Class Limiteds'.[103] The best known was the house-painting co-operative set up in Paris in 1842 by the Fourierite Leclaire, who retained complete control, which lasted the full intended fifty years, when each worker received the princely sum of 250,000 francs.[104] In another case, in 1848, the employees ran a hatting firm, which paid wages according to the agreed scale, shared profits half to the employer and half to the men, and developed into a full co-operative society in 1850.[105] However, trade society leaders were usually opposed to such schemes, seeing them as a way of increasing the employers' control through tying employees to the firm in the same way as single-firm benefit funds, and as akin to piece-work in activating men to work harder. One was operated by the printer Dupont, against whom the compositors struck in 1862; 'he gives the workmen an interest in it because he knows that the man who has an interest is more zealous', though the return each received was paltry.[106] In general profit-sharing that required capital from employees was only possible for foremen, who were seeking to become masters themselves. Such co-operative societies were thus a form of joint-stock enterprise by workmen hoping to become masters, and labour activists made a clear distinction between this and other forms of co-operative production.[107]

In many artisan trades both masters and journeymen suffered from dependence on great warehouse and mercantile firms, and from the increasing, cheapening, and ruinous competition which forced unemployed journeymen in slack periods to set up as chamber-masters (*appiéceurs*) and to increase the pressures. The London and Birmingham Labour Exchanges of the early 1830s were used as much, or more, by small masters as by journeymen, as a market for their goods and as a way of freeing the small producer from the large merchant, while it was only with masters' help that workmen could challenge the warehouses. Thus Paris basket-makers in 1848 wanted a central warehouse to receive the products of homework, just like the English Labour Exchanges. At a village near Tours, a co-operative society was formed, ending the thraldom of the inhabitants: distressed basket-makers who had had to hire a horse and cart to take their wares to the city, where they had been at the mercy of merchants who had paid them rock-bottom prices.[108] It was mainly in shoemaking, cabinet-making, and, above all (again), in tailoring that this action was found, and there were movements among tailors, in London and Paris especially, in the late 1840s and early 1850s, in favour of co-operative production as a way of linking the flexibility of small-scale production with an independence from the slop (*confection*) trade.[109]

There were also co-operative endeavours to help members acquire tools and other necessities for their work – Lyons silk-weavers organised loans of weaving tools, a society of carpenters in London bought tools in bulk at Sheffield and sold them to members at low rates, the Rennes tailors in the 1830s bought fine trimmings in bulk for members, Paris cabinet-makers bought wood, and Lyons bootmakers leather, while Paris brushmakers in 1870 helped members secure both equipment and cheap lodgings where they could work and not be at the mercy of the manufacturers.[110]

While these forms of co-operative production, none of them new to the century, might be adjuncts to labour conflicts, none of them in themselves challenged the economic system, all being compatible with private ownership, capitalism and a liberal economy. The democratisation of sub-contracting, for instance, was an adaptation to the prevailing economic structure which might barely change relations between employers and workmen, but might change relations among workers.[111]

In the new freedom of early 1848, co-operative production in France continued to take these three main forms: support of strikes (though here there was for a time an alternative in the national workshops in Paris and other cities, which, as in earlier periods, could act as havens for men on strike), democratisation of sub-contracting (as with Paris pianoforte-makers, Cail engineers, or groups of building workers contracting with local authorities), and unemployment relief.

The last was important because of the severe depression that followed the revolution. Some employers, in desperation, tried to associate their workers with them in providing capital and sharing profits, but leaving themselves as managers. Other employers and shop-owners told Blanc that they were unable to carry on and offered their firms to the state on condition that they remain managers or that they associate with their workers. Others closed down or abandoned their firms, which prompted efforts by their workforces to take them over and continue them, as had been done by some compositors in 1835 and was to happen again under the Commune. About twenty trades also petitioned the Luxembourg to be allowed to take over such firms, and some asked for state involvement. It was these pressures by employers and workers that encouraged Blanc to seize the opportunity to put forward his ideas of social reform.[112]

The famous tailors' co-operative works should be seen in this context. There had been several co-operative unemployment relief schemes among Paris tailors in the 1840s, and there were renewed efforts early in 1848, especially as this was also the slack season. At the same time the leading cloth-manufacturing towns asked the government for state orders to keep their works going, so on 9 March it was decreed that every borough should provide uniforms for its new, democratic National Guard, and the Paris municipality therefore ordered cloth from manufacturers at Sedan, Louviers, and Elbeuf. Through Blanc and the republican General Lamoricière, the Paris tailors' leader, Philippe Bérard, who had been involved in the *Atelier*, secured the Paris order for all 100,000 uniforms, as well as one from the Ministry of the Interior for 10,800 uniforms for the newly formed Mobile Guard, all to be made co-operatively by the Paris tailors. Blanc gained for them the Clichy debtors' prison which was by then empty, and the master tailors provided funds, fearful that otherwise the order would go to the slop-shops. It was executed by 800 to 1600 workers at the Clichy premises and by another 2,000 working at home, all for the sum of two francs for a ten-hour day. This co-operative enterprise should therefore be seen purely as a temporary relief organisation, open to anyone of a certain competence, male or female, with no classifications by skill or variations in pay (against Blanc's wishes), the hours limited so as to share work round for everyone, and members doing work for private firms whenever it became available. It was never intended to be a permanent or viable commercial concern, although afterwards a group of about fifty of them did unsuccessfully set up such an enterprise. It had no particular links with Blanc, but he also helped establish co-operative societies of spinners and braid-makers (*passementiers*) to make the National Guard epaulettes, and reinforced pressure from the Luxembourg which removed the old grievance of cheap labour in prisons, garrisons, and a military saddlery workshop, whereupon Blanc also secured an order for a Paris saddlers' association. But, like Clichy, these were all temporary organisations to arrange work for the unemployed.[113]

All the foregoing suggests there was not a great deal of difference between co-operation in France and England and Wales, apart from the obvious ones of the generally much greater repression of workers' organisations in France and a brief period of greater freedom and influence in 1848. France does not seem distinctive in the popularity of co-operation, but it is undoubtedly the case that it had much more extensive radical *propaganda* in favour of co-operative production (*association*). This became evident when republicans in the early 1830s were seeking to build up popular support, from the working people, amongst others, who had forced themselves on public notice through their role in the July Revolution, again in the wave of industrial demands that followed it, and then in the renewed industrial movements in 1833. While sympathetic to the plight of the poor and the injustices they suffered, and seeing workers' organisations and movements as bases of support, they were, as we have seen, not very happy at demands and strikes over wages and hours and the conflicts with employers that resulted, for they wanted united action by the people, the useful and industrious, including masters, against privilege. Conflict between employers and workmen would therefore fracture popular republican unity. This was reflected in the uncertainty of the Society of the Rights of Man over how to react to the strikes in late 1833, and the two different drafts of the address they issued.[114] The message in the end was that workers should not fight against employers but should attack the true, political, source of distress and the real, common, political enemy. They therefore focused on opposition to the arrests and prosecutions of strikers, and on collections for their families, instead of on support for the strikes. Radical republicans therefore supported co-operative production as the solution to the dilemma, and as a way of by-passing industrial conflict, for it would conciliate capital and labour, end social hostility, and unite the people. They also tended to believe, erroneously, that the 'proletarians' could not be won over to republicanism by political appeals alone, and that the way to make 'the republic descend into the workshop' was to relate it to material interests and gains through co-operative production, and so radical republicans steadily advocated 'association'.[115]

Particularly important here was Philippe Buchez, the ex-Saint-Simonian who became after the July Revolution a leading member of the chief, though still small, republican society, the Friends of the People. Here he advocated a policy of industrial harmony through three means: in big firms, elected boards of representatives of manufacturers, foremen and workmen, to fix wages, organise placement and benefits, and arbitrate in disputes; public credit banks to provide capital; and co-operative production in small-scale artisanal industry. Here he recognised the development of mercantile capitalism, such as general contracting in building, also under attack in England:

The working men whose skill forms their main capital and whom we therefore designate free, that is joiners, carpenters, etc., these working men are not in the towns in direct contact with those who order the work. Between the former and the latter are intermediaries whom we call contractors (*entrepreneurs*). It should not be thought that these intermediaries contribute to the good execution of the work which they seem to direct: they are not usually even concerned with this; it is a workman, an overseer who is charged with putting the drawings into execution, dividing and bringing together the different parts of the operation needed to complete it. The contractor only intervenes as a capitalist, or, in other words, as a tenderer, as possessor of premises which serve as a workshop, and provider of raw materials; in return for this, apart from all the other profits which he can receive through a contract more or less skilfully made, he levies on the net value of the labour of each of the workmen he employs, a sum of at least thirty sous to two francs per day. . . These contractors are pure parasites, whose involvement, of no use to producer or consumer, is nevertheless so dearly paid, that they rarely fail to make a large or small fortune.[116]

The real conflict, Buchez insisted, was not between employers and wage-earners, but between both and the non-productive, external speculating middleman who was, as we have seen, easily assimilated into the radical category of the rich, privileged, parasites, while the employers and wage-earners were both part of the people. The workman's enemy was not his employer but the capitalist, and this economic analysis served the political purpose of a united people.[117] But while radical republicans supported co-operative production with enthusiasm, it is doubtful if it had much impact among the artisans it was meant to attract. The workers' movement of 1833 was concerned with wages and hours, and the few attempts at co-operation were in connexion with strikes and unemployment, not what leading republicans had envisaged. When Jules Leroux urged the compositors to focus on co-operative production instead of on wage rises, he was ignored. Artisan republicans, as we have seen, followed their own concerns, not those of republican leaders, and although they used the same word, *association*, they gave it their own meaning, namely 'union', in pursuit of various goals, rather than co-operative production. The period 1830 to 1834 thus saw much republican propaganda but little artisan response, and working-class radicalism was not imbued with co-operative socialism.[118]

After 1834 and the repression of open republican activity, radicalism, as we have seen, either resorted to secret and even seditious activity, or took the form of more educational, theoretical, and legal activity. Republicans, including Louis Blanc, supported co-operative production as before,[119] and the repression of combinations also steered activities in this direction, co-operative and benefit societies acting as fronts or refuges for radical activists. With the defeat of insurrectionary conspiracies in 1839 and the greater liberalisation of a more confident regime, the various journals run by groups of workmen advocated co-operative production as a means of a class harmonisation that recognised the equal rights of the working classes. In particular, co-operative production was consistently advocated by the most important one of them, the *Atelier*, begun after the 1840 strikes by some former members of secret societies who were inspired by Buchez's Christian socialism. But this is not a sign of popular support, for the readership of this and the other workers' journals lay mainly in the middle classes, particularly amongst the liberal professions.

Co-operative production may thus be seen as more of a middle-class than working-class ideal. It remained a cardinal French radical republican article of faith, and it was no surprise that the new republican regime in 1848 was favourable to it. A number of local authorities did give public works contracts to societies of working men, usually transient ones,[120] while the Constituent Assembly voted a fund to make loans to co-operative production societies. But this is not a sign of artisan interest. Early in 1848, now that combination laws were in abeyance and industrial activity unprecedentedly, though temporarily, freed, the state neutral, and the press unshackled, workers' combinations proliferated, while the very fact of popular revolution in Paris and a widespread perception and fear of working-class strength there meant that for a few months insecure and fearful authorities and employers were very ready to conciliate workers and meet their demands, and a large number of agreements and conventions were concluded. But, as we have seen, workers' demands, when they could be freely made, were not for co-operative production but were overwhelmingly over wages and hours – higher and uniform pay rates recognised in agreed, written scales, and shorter hours without loss of pay. Co-operative production was not a prime interest, and was limited to the three usual forms of strike support, unemployment relief, and reform of sub-contracting.

Specific practices can always give rise to more ambitious projects. The Luxembourg Commission, as we have seen, was mainly concerned with questions of wages and hours and, especially from 20 March, with political questions. But with the total defeat of its political campaigns and its dissolution by the new Assembly, the delegates on 20 May elected a new committee, under Pierre Vinçard, which organised a new Society of United Trades and in June issued a remarkable manifesto outlining an ambitious organisation of all trades. In each trade an elected committee would establish a wage scale and organise its defence, study new technical processes, organise placement, and establish trades workshops run by workers. This was clearly a much more ambitious conception of co-operative production, but it does not seem that it was intended that all workers should be thus employed, and what was really being advocated here was a single co-operative firm in each trade to give work to those on strike or who were unemployed, to take over and reopen idle works, and thus regulate the labour market, something quite different from Blanc's conception and in fact something of a rejection of his statist tendencies. It is not clear either how much support among the trades there was for this new post-Luxembourg organisation, and in any case the June Days and subsequent repression checked it.[121]

In the distress of 1848 the United Kingdom Coach-Makers tried to organise co-operative production, but when this failed, turned instead to emigration.[122] These were two ways of reducing that 'surplus of labour' that was the bane of so many trades. Thus co-operative production was often advocated as a way of preventing those wage reductions that masters could enforce by exploiting the competition among men for work.[123] The ambitious attempt in England in 1845 at a new federation of trade unions, the National Association of United Trades, was intended as a political lobby to prevent legislation unfavourable to labour, and as an organisation of mutual support in strikes. In aid of the latter, there would also be co-operative production by members on strike, and also by those out of work (other measures to reduce unemployment being a statutory ten hours' day to share work, and public works). Thus, through employment of out-of-work members, the National Association of United Trades offered 'to the Trades, in their corporate capacity, the means of drafting from the labour-market that "surplus labour" which is the great, proximate cause of all reductions of wages, and of setting it to work on their own estates, in their own workshops, by means of their own capital and machinery, under circumstances which will make those funds reproductive and beneficial, which, by the old system of strikes, were totally lost, or positively injurious', so as to gain thereby 'the power of regulating the market at any time, and of equalising the supply with the demand – a power which would speedily put an end to all the tyranny which the working classes have to submit at the present time'. Similarly, a new national union of tailors in 1846 began co-operative production to employ 'surplus hands' so as to break the power of the Jewish monopolists and restrict the power of unprincipled capitalists.[124] The four main aims of the Consolidated Trades' Union formed in 1834 were similar: benefits, mutual support, in strikes, co-operative employment of members on strike, and employment of out-of-work members. Thus in the GNCTU, NAUT, and Paris Association of United Trades in 1848, we find a very similar strategy, one that, in intention and potential at least, posed the greatest challenge to capitalist economic organisation, a challenge not repeated after mid-century, even though the strategy never got off the ground, and the GNCTU and the Paris United Trades were very short-lived. All were expressions of an 'alternative political economy' which, as we have seen, accepted the wages system and was concerned with high wages and full employment as the means to economic stability and high consumption. Co-operative production was a key element in their strategy, not as a replacement of private employment, but as a means of reforming it, of making it work properly. The NAUT planned to have land as well as workshops, and this linked up with other schemes, such as the Chartist Land Plan (whose first title contained the word 'co-operative'), to acquire land on which to settle members, sometimes temporarily, in order to remove the labour surplus. Its founder, O'Connor, hoped that 'the working classes generally would agree upon some plan by which they could so adjust the number working at each trade to the amount of produce required from each as to insure a healthy settlement of demand and supply'.[125]

### The political context

Co-operative production, then, was mainly confined to three main forms, with very specific immediate purposes, and this was shown in the freedom of early 1848 in France. But the June Days in 1848 and subsequent repression rendered the Luxembourg delegates' plan still-born, and a different kind of co-operative production came to dominate, as small, separate co-operative societies were perforce the norm in France. There is no doubt that they flourished numerically. Because they were often informal, and therefore hard to trace, it is difficult to calculate the numbers. There were probably between 300 and 400 co-operative trading or production societies in total during the Second Republic, but many were short-lived and the nature of many of them is not clear. Probably at any time there were in the provinces around forty production societies (the bulk of them in Lyons), and fifty trading ones, and in Paris over 100 of all kinds, over half of them production societies, most of the rest being small societies of cooks and hairdressers.[126]

Many of these societies continued the established forms of co-operation, namely as a form of unemployment relief (and therefore not seeking to employ all members) or as alternatives to piece-mastering (such as societies of building workers contracting for public work), and economic recovery in 1850 meant that many of the societies seeking to mitigate unemployment were wound up. However, there were two special reasons for the growth in co-operative societies in the second half of 1848. Firstly, it was usual for political radicals, on the defeat of their campaigns, to diversify their activities into several fields, of which co-operation could be one. This happened among British radicals in 1833, and Chartists after defeat in 1839, 1842 (several of the original Rochdale Pioneers were Chartists), and 1848, when, in Lancashire especially, Chartists played a leading role in the expansion of the co-operative movement.[127] Secondly, after the June Days, arrests and deportations of rebels, imposition of martial law, closures of clubs and periodicals, restrictions on rights of meeting, and the restoration of stamp duty and caution money for newspapers all meant a check to the popular radical movement. Trade union activity also met defeat, as employers recovered their nerve and repudiated the agreements of a few months before, prosecutions for combinations were resumed, trade organisations could no longer operate openly or even put demands, private employment agencies revived, and the intended elections to new, democratic, and equitable Courts of Arbitration were never held. Yet in July the Assembly voted a fund to encourage co-operative societies, while a number of decrees from July to September gave the right to co-operative societies of workmen or employers to tender for public works contracts to supply labour only, not materials, and even gave them further advantages by freeing them of the need to lodge a deposit and by limiting the discount a sub-contractor could offer. Municipal orders often went to co-operative societies. Thus, on the one hand, industrial and political activity was repressed, and on the other, co-operative production was allowed and even encouraged. Not surprisingly, then, most attempts at co-operative production were after June 1848, though this did not reflect widespread support for the idea, but its status as a second-best, fall-back activity. The Typographical Society had eschewed co-operative production in 1848, but in October 1849 opened a social workshop for its unemployed. 'At present, the operation of the [co-operative] associations has as its immediate concern the defence of the interests of labour.'[128] It was not new for co-operative societies to be refuges for radicals, and this was now repeated. As the socialist teacher Lefrançais explained:

The socialist activists understood that they could use them to draw together again the feeble strength of the proletariat and thus give the movement a cohesion without which its claims will always end in defeat.

Indeed organisation in the form of working men's associations is far preferable to secret societies – always under the impact of legal bans and most often being only a weapon at the service of narrow interests and unhealthy ambitions.[129]

Co-operative production was not the only refuge, for co-operative trading and benefit societies were also used, and these were often linked. Many co-operative production societies included sick and superannuation relief, perhaps as a way of attracting members.[130] It was the veteran of the 1834 Lyons rising and leading radical in Paris early in 1848, Bressy, who was the chief figure in the Rheims trading co-operative, while in Lyons members of a radical club took the lead in October 1848 in forming the trading Fraternal Association of French Industries, a breakaway from which later founded a Democratic Association of United Industries, with its 'Renaissance' café, while the radical Jandard club formed the Fraternal Association of United Workers. All three were trading co-operatives led by radicals and they played important roles in the June 1849 rising, after which such societies resumed as refuges for radicals. As the Procurator-General reported: 'commercially, there is nothing serious in these associations formed with shares of one franc and renunciation of profits. Politically, they harbour a great danger. Logically, one can only see them as a disguised subscription for the benefit of socialism and a devious way of founding a political association.'[131]

Co-operative production was not really a national phenomenon but very much focused on Paris, where the number of societies was very large, though the size of many was very small. The successful co-operation in Lyons, despite the twenty-odd little production societies there, was trading, particularly the Fraternal Association of French Industries, and nationally trading was more important than production.

Co-operation was thus promoted by radicals after June 1848, and many of the Paris societies were more like political than industrial clubs. In these difficult times, radicals exchanged services and patronised co-operative restaurants, cafés, and hairdressers and bought co-operative wares as a form of radical solidarity, just as the National Union of the Working Classes in London had schemes of exchange of services and exclusive dealing after the Reform Crisis had passed.[132] Co-operative production had perforce to adapt to the official concept of small, separate societies, and even make a virtue out of the necessity, as in the Paris hatters' espousal of rival societies. 'We are for free competition. We believe, with all true Socialists, that freedom is nowhere bad, and that, in labour in particular, it is a condition of progress and emulation.'[133] While this necessarily marked a departure from the concept enunciated by the delegate organisation originating in the Luxembourg Commission, this organisation nevertheless continued, and at the end of 1848 began a systematic policy of promoting and assisting co-operation associations, and of drawing them together in a federal organisation that allied with Proudhon's People's Bank, in an effort to recreate the united radical movement begun at the Luxembourg.[134]

This close identification of co-operation with radicalism continued as propertied opinion recovered its nerve and grew increasingly hostile to co-operative societies as subversive and 'socialist', and the growing conservative confidence, especially with the election of Louis-Napoleon as President and his alliance with the Right, was expressed in persecution. Thus the political polarisation between radical reds and conservative whites saw co-operation identified with the former, the societies taking radical newspapers and making radical petitions available for signature. Conservative hostility to co-operation grew, and the much more conservative Legislative Assembly in January 1850 approved a report by Thiers that co-operative production was 'industrial anarchy', and later rejected a radical proposal to favour co-operative societies in public works contracts. Co-operative societies were harassed by the authorities and police. All were suppressed in Lyons after the 1849 rising, and while some were later allowed to reopen, these were joined by the strictly non-political Beavers.[135]

The final blow came with the 1851 *coup d'état* which led to widespread suppression, only about fifteen societies managing to survive in Paris, and then only by dropping the title 'fraternal' and hiding behind ordinary business activity; in a meeting of their delegates emigration was seen as the only recourse. In others, managers seized the firms as their own, and the members dared not protest lest they be branded as republicans. In the provinces repression was even more severe, and nearly all societies ended. Only a few continued in the repressive 1850s, often in secret, engaged in co-operative trading or credit, evidence that these aroused more real popular support than production.[136]

However, the more tolerant attitude of authorities from the later 1850s was followed by more open and extensive co-operative trading and credit, while co-operative production revived strongly in 1863, so that all three forms were flourishing again, and co-operation was the main popular movement in France in the mid-1860s. By the end of the decade it was estimated that there were in France 350 co-operative trading societies, 330 savings and loan societies, 125 production societies, six buying raw materials in bulk, and five selling a single commodity.[137]

The influence of the co-operative movements in Germany and England was clearly important, and the terms '*coopératif*' and *Store Coopératif* replaced the previous '*sociétaire*' and *association de consommation*.[138] But, again, there are reasons to doubt the real attraction of co-operative production, for there was little support for and some opposition to it in the very few open expressions of labour opinion that occurred in the early 1860s, as in the 'workers' pamphlets' of 1861, or the reports of trades' delegates to the 1862 and 1867 Exhibitions, their emphasis, as in the early 1848, being on trade grievances, wages, and freedom of industrial action.[139]

As before, the main reason for this co-operative efflorescence was that, after massive repression in the 1850s had checked nearly all forms of radicalism and labour activism, the limited liberalisation in the 1860s meant that co-operation was one of the few activities that was allowed, so that efforts by popular radicals and labour activists tended again, as in the later Second Republic, to focus on this form of activity. This was explained by French delegates at the first congress of the IWMA.

Citizen Tolain said that in Britain, thanks to the genius of British liberty, the class movement manifested itself by a policy of resistance, whereas in France by reason of the shackles imposed upon the organisation of the working classes, a strike has only been a rare and extreme measure and co-operation has been there deemed to be the only means of working class emancipation.[140]

Furthermore, the liberal and radical opposition to the Second Empire, both Orleanist and republican, took up co-operation as a way of gaining working-class support and to avert their recurring nightmare of the working class being won over to Imperialism.[141] Some large businessmen were also attracted to co-operation as the means to the social stability and harmony it was believed to have effected in England, and used Rochdalian co-operation as part of a paternalist strategy that often also included cheap housing; almshouses; sick, maternity, and retirement benefits; primary and technical schooling; libraries; low-price shops selling bread, food, and clothing; savings banks; cheap baths and wash-houses; shorter hours; and restrictions on child labour. Many co-operative shops were in fact company stores intended to promote wise spending and thrift, with the workers holding shares.[142]

Co-operation was also encouraged for a while by the Imperial authorities as part of Napoleon III's policy of preventing working-class political action while encouraging non-political movements that sought to improve material conditions. It was encouraged so as to divert the workers from politics and in the process gain some control over them (benefit societies were another example). For the prefect of Limoges, it 'gives the working class a peaceful concern and acts as a diversion from bad attitudes'. Thus official encouragement as well as toleration led to a focus on co-operative societies.[143]

The importance of co-operation as a fall-back activity, a refuge for radicals, and a means of preserving solidarity when other forms of activity were closed, was underlined when the government moved in 1867 against the IWMA, which it had hitherto tolerated. With open activity now impossible, its members supported co-operation as a legal base for propaganda and activity. Thus early in 1868, during a harsh winter characterised by a food crisis and high unemployment, Varlin and some colleagues established a food society, the 'Cooking Pot' ('Marmite'), which opened a kitchen-restaurant, and soon had fifteen branches; 'the goal is to provide, at cost price, for all members, healthy and ample food to consume on the premises or to take away'. It was registered under the Civil Code and could therefore only deal with members, who all belonged to the IWMA, and Varlin's main purpose was 'to have a permanent place to escape police surveillance'. The premises were also made available to radicals, socialists, and combinations, and thus fulfilled the roles of the co-operative restaurants of the Second Republic. In the same way later, in the repression of 1872, the resurrected Working Economy was to serve as a political refuge and site of secret meetings.[144]

Of course, liberals and radicals found it easy to support co-operation because they saw it as compatible with their social and economic philosophy, a form of self-help, without state involvement, that ended antagonisms between employer and employee, dealer and consumer, banker and client. It helped moralise the economic system, promoted values of thrift, self-restraint, and morality among members, and assisted upward mobility through these means. Even co-operative production societies, where shareholders elected managers, were like small, collective, joint-stock private firms, quite compatible with capitalism, free trade, and economic liberalism. For the great mine-owner and leading Orleanist Casimir-Périer, 'co-operative societies are the surest and most generous cure for the errors and perils of socialism', just as the radical *Réforme* had earlier praised 'this system, which denies none of the economic law established by science, and which at the same time corresponds to the most exalted aspirations'.[145] Co-operation was also a means whereby small firms could combine flexibility with the demands of mass production, and radicals thus saw co-operation as a check to dangerously excessive capitalist concentration, and as a way of preserving that wide spread of property that was essential to a healthy social system.[146] There was thus much common ground between advanced liberals in Britain and France over co-operation and its relation to social questions, linked to the prevalent conception of the 'intelligent artisan' as the key to social stability and harmony.[147] On the other hand, there was some radical criticism of co-operative production as of no benefit to the mass of the workers, as merely collective instead of individual exploitation, as divisive selfishness.[148]

Despite the very similar advanced liberal approval of, and support for, co-operative production in both Britain and France, little was practised in the former, where the Positivist Beesly contrasted the propaganda myth with reality. Very few British trade unionists supported it.[149] The co-operative movement itself remained overwhelmingly one of trading. The Christian Socialists, who saw co-operative production as the desirable form and were only interested in co-operative trading as an outlet for co-operative products, disapproved of the dominant co-operative trading stores and their dividend, and grew increasingly exasperated as their conception of self-governing, profit-sharing workshops was rejected by most co-operators as a French idea.[150]

Thus the same liberal case for co-operative production was made in both England and France in the 1860s, but was practised much more in the latter. The reason was not wider support for it but the political situation, in many ways similar to that obtaining after June 1848. The strength of co-operative production in France depended on particular circumstances, and when these did not obtain, it was much less important, as in the greater freedom of early 1848, late 1860s, and later 1870s. Co-operation in the mid-1860s was the result of toleration, with trading 'issuing from the empiricism of working class consumption', and with production promoted by politicians, but it declined rapidly in importance after 1867. This was partly due to the disasters of 1868, with the collapse of Sincerity, Working Economy, and the banks established to help co-operative societies; they dragged down some production societies with them, and the journal *Coopération* consequently ended. But more important was the further liberalisation and weakening of the regime, to allow not only strikes but trade societies, public meetings, and a freer press. The focus of labour activity therefore changed again, towards strikes, trade unions, and political action, which evoked far more popular support than did co-operative production, although Varlin's 'Cooking-Pot' did establish a federation of Paris trading societies in 1870.[151] Trades' delegates at the 1867 meetings declared that workers were indifferent to co-operative production and were much readier to contribute to strike funds, and the economist Molinari noted that speakers at the radical public meetings in Paris in 1869 had turned against co-operation. Co-operative production did not die out, and some new societies were formed, but these were now reversions to the familiar kinds, in support of strikes and against unemployment and sweating.[152]

Co-operative production was, then, never a high working-class priority, even in France. In the mid-1860s there were fifty to sixty production societies in Paris, and perhaps a hundred in the whole of the provinces, so it was only really of significance in the capital, where co-operative trading was weak. But by 1868 the number of loan societies was four times that of production societies. Thus co-operative trading (in the provinces) and credit (Paris and provinces) had much more support than co-operative production.[153] It was co-operative trading that was to be important, alongside trade unions and socialist clubs, in the socialist movements that arose after the 1870s.[154] In general, then, we can say that in both Britain and France co-operative trading gained steadier and more extensive support (alongside benefit and loan societies), while co-operative production, apart from the temporary strategies connected with strikes and unemployment, was only significant when particular political conditions obtained in France, and, as Beesly and the advocate of co-operation, Greening, admitted, it nearly always failed.[155]

While co-operative trading was more important, it was not purely material in its concerns. The Christian Socialists in the 1860s tended to see the co-operative production they favoured as alone characterised by high ideals and morality, and regarded trading as animal and selfish, but Holyoake protested against seeing a member of the latter as a 'guzzler – a person all throat and gastric juice' instead of someone rejecting the materialism of competition.[156]

Co-operation overlapped with other activities. Societies provided resources and premises where political activities could be organised. Alongside a rejection of competitiveness and consumerism, of parasitic commerce and speculation by intermediaries, as selfish, wasteful, and the means whereby the rich crushed the poor and wealth became concentrated, they asserted values of honesty and fair-dealing, mutuality, fellowship, and associationism.[157] While activities in trading, credit, insurance, building and production could all lead to the predominance of commercialism and consumerism (and indeed pioneer new forms), the radical input and the extent to which these were resisted also needs to be recognised. Co-operation incorporated those concerns for good wages and low food prices, the stress on fairness, and the critique of the bad material and moral effects of unlimited competition that characterised the other movements we are concerned with.

# 7 Class and radicalism

> You must be well aware that the cause of all your oppression is *Class Legislation*; it therefore behoves you to *unite* for your mutual protection, to demand your rights, to get protection for your labour, which is the foundation of all property, to be determined to leave an home of freedom for your children.[1]

Such sentiments as these permeated movements which sought to mobilise working people against their enemies. 'Chartism', said the *Annual Register*, 'is in fact an insurrection directed against the middle classes.' And yet the class character of such movements is widely questioned.

The case against an extensive and significant working-class radicalism can be easily stated, incorporating points already made in this study. The male 'working class' was not united but divided by occupation, skill and a myriad other factors. The workplace was characterised by compromise and agreement as much as by conflict, and conflicts often set workmen against workmen instead of wage-earners against employers, and, if employers were condemned, it was the bad or dishonourable ones, not the whole class. Hostility was directed less at the masters than at middlemen seen as their common enemy. It was tyrannical or oppressive behaviour, not economic exploitation, that aroused most anger, and violence was more likely against police than employers. Trade societies performed extra-workplace functions, were not predicated on conflicts of interest between employers and employees, and divided the working class, not only between trades but also within trades. Popular institutions and movements were by no means confined to working people but had varied social composition, radicalism only touched a small minority of the working population and only certain kinds of workers, while politically active workers did not always tend to support the most radical groups – many workers fought in Paris in June 1848 against the rising. Radicalism was not a working-class creation and came from higher up, and radical movements tended to have middle-class or gentlemen leaders. Even the National Association of United Trades in the 1840s was known as the Duncombe Union because of its aristocratic president.[2] Radicalism was the result of many other factors apart from social origin and occupational position, and it created as much as it reflected identities. It was concerned with political, not economic grievances, and directed its appeal not just to workers but to a broader and vaguer 'people' in opposition to privilege, and saw the sources of this people's grievances as political, not economic. Economic conflicts were not reflected in radicalism, and there were no widespread theories of economic exploitation.

The issue here is how far class explains or characterises the radicalism of the period with which this study is concerned, rather than more general questions – it is, after all, perfectly possible to argue that the working class did develop with industrial capitalism, but that this happened after our period, in the last quarter of the century, and that we should not expect to find it before 1870. Moreover, the understanding of class in these arguments is usually an economic one, and one should therefore not expect political movements to be class movements, class being operative in the economic field, so a study of political radicalism will neither establish nor disprove the existence of class and class struggle in other fields.[3] For many nineteenth-century historians, 'class consciousness' has been the main aspect of class, but a focus on the 'subjective' aspects of class means that 'class' explanation is through reference not to external relationships and position, but to what people thought. Class thus becomes a form of explanation akin to religious belief. While it is argued that the logic of economic relationships impels people in certain directions, it may be that the logical, 'rational' response of a sweated tailor was to make himself and his family work longer hours and to employ defenceless juvenile assistants, rather than to engage in uncertain enterprises such as trade unions or strikes, for such action involved those elements of selflessness, sacrifice, and idealism that have always been stressed in labour movements. Class, in this understanding, becomes a way of looking at things and constitutes only one identity alongside several other possible ones, such as religious, political, national, corporate, occupational, ethnic, regional, or gendered, and it is not necessarily the most important one.[4] The question of class, then, becomes a matter of empirical investigation into the relative importance of competing loyalties and identities. Moreover, if it is the subjective nature of class that is stressed, there is no external yardstick defining whether an attitude really is or is not a class one, beyond an 'ideal-type' construction; hence the tendency to rely on actual class terminology as the test. Yet such terminology might itself be indeterminate, ambiguous, and varied.

There is, of course, ample evidence that radical democratic movements had a wide and mixed social composition, included many artisans and small dealers, and were not always composed mainly of manual wage-earners, while leadership often went to upper-class figures or great industrialists.[5] It is also clear that radicals focused on political grievances and targets, stressed how the privileged, rich, idle few ran the state in their own interests, and laboured to end this through political reforms and democratisation. Even the 1851 rising in some southern rural areas against the *coup d'état*, portrayed by conservatives as a new *jacquerie*, was in fact driven far more by political tensions and leadership than by economic grievances, and it did not engage in expressions of social antagonism, there being no looting or other outrages, and only whites were arrested, not other rich people.[6] The stress on the 'industrious' and 'useful', and on labour as the source of wealth, embodied conceptions that extended beyond wage-earners. Nevertheless, radical movements seeking mass support recognised that this necessitated the involvement of working men, because of both their numbers and their institutional bases for mobilisation, and they could even be seen as the nucleus for any sustainable campaign. Radicals did at times express concern for the plight and sufferings of the working people, condemn the indifference of the more fortunate sections of the population, and make specific appeals for working-class support.[7] Yet they still tended to stress the political injustices of the working classes, such as their exclusion from political rights, the unfair burden of taxes they bore, the repression of their organisations and combinations, or the imposition in France of the pass-book (*livret*) which the workers' newspaper, the *Atelier*, saw as separating working men politically from the rest of the nation.[8] It was these special laws against workers and their activities that led radicals to see class divisions as the creation of political injustice and inequality, the removal of which was therefore the means to social harmony. It was thus believed in the radical Paris political clubs in early 1848 that the establishment of the Republic had abolished classes.[9] While they frequently showed an awareness of other injustices, including that of exploitation by masters, they strove to concentrate on political injustices and reforms, and often saw action over wages or rents as sectional and divisive.[10] It is not at all true to say that radicals ignored economic issues, but a linking of political and economic analyses did not necessarily lead to the conclusion that the working and middle classes, or the employers and wage-earners, had opposed interests – it could justify common action by masters and journeymen, or by shopkeepers and working people, against landowners, mercantile capitalists, or middlemen.

Yet we should avoid an ideal definition of what a truly working-class movement should be. Some radicals were distinguished from others, with whom they might share identical programmes, arguments, and terminology, by their explicit appeal to the working people for support and their concern for their situation. Moreover, because political movements are necessarily alliances of different groups and people who do not share uniform attitudes, the desire to maintain unity and achieve more extensive and effective support means that certain arguments or points, more likely to be unifying, acceptable, or persuasive, are stressed at the expense of others held by some supporters. Thus artisan support for a radical movement that ignored certain issues is not in itself evidence that these issues were not important to them or even to their radicalism. Language is not only used to convey ideas and construct identities but also to persuade.

Clearly, there were movements composed mainly of wage-earning working men, particularly Chartism, the workers' movement in Paris in the first half of 1848, or the Reform League in London in the mid-1860s. Moreover, the social composition of some movements changed; Chartism after mid-1839 shed most of its propertied leaders and supporters, while the repression of radicalism in France in 1848–9, by skimming off much of the leadership, led to greater participation by humbler people,[11] and the working population in the main urban centres voted red in the 1848 and 1849 elections.[12] Radical movements often drew, as we have seen, on such bases as work groups and benefit, trade, and co-operative societies, and, despite the intentions of the founders and leaders of radical organisations, their members pursued practices and concerns familiar in these milieux. Repression of political and other activities, particularly in France, worked to reinforce the interrelation between political, trade union, workplace, educational, and leisure actions. Political change, and participation in radical movements, embodied far more than the formal political demands. The political revolution of 1830 touched off a wave of hopes of better times, and encouraged popular actions over food prices, taxes, wages, and machinery. The process was repeated on a greater scale in the new period of hope and confidence in 1848; despite rapid defeat, such confidence could revive – the reds' triumph at Lyons in the 1849 election encouraged weavers to be rude to the merchants' clerks. Such hopes were also aroused in Chartism in 1839 and, in some areas, 1842, and the change thereafter lay not in political ideas but in the decline of this sense of success and optimism, and the growth of strategic adaptations.[13]

## Material concerns

Class explanations are often seen as a form of 'materialism', but the term is misleading, and unacceptable if it means that certain situations determine actions, as action can only result from people's seeing and responding to situations, and their assessments and understandings are by no means inevitable. Thus all action is mental in origin. Yet it is also true that nearly all people do distinguish between the material and the non-material, and that the former can seem the more important. It can be plausibly argued that for most of the working population material concerns such as wages, food prices, and unemployment were always prime ones, if never exclusively so, and they were not only male concerns.

Radicalism could thus incorporate those age-old popular concerns with taxes, especially indirect ones, and with food prices. Food riots were still important in France at the start of our period, and were often linked to politics. Chartists were prominent in agitations in London over food prices and in the formation of a People's Provision League in 1855.[14] At the same time, high rents and food prices led to nightly gatherings of workmen in Paris, and placards against the Emperor. High food prices were also a factor in the rapid expansion of the Reform League in the second half of 1866 and the first half of 1867. In Paris and other cities after the 1830 and 1848 revolutions, hopes of better pay were aroused and pursued. Thus, alongside the support for political democracy and the hostility to idle landowners and other privileged groups, food prices and wages can be seen as consistently important concerns in working-class radicalism, revealed as much, or more, in radical practice as in ideology. To these should be added a concern with unemployment, that great scourge of working men. It was lack of work, not the wage relation itself, that reduced them to slavery and deprived them of freedom of choice when they were offered employment by tyrannical masters or foremen. In the depression after the July Revolution there were disturbances over unemployment,[15] and in 1848 the cries in the political clubs (containing a large minority of working men) included: 'No more bourgeoisie! No more noble aristocracy! No more financial, commercial and industrial aristocracy! Work, work for the people, for the working man.' Working-class pressure at times secured responses from the authorities, such as the government orders for silks in Lyons, full employment in the Toulon dockyard, and state-financed 'national workshops' open to anyone in Paris, Lyons, Marseilles, Lille, St Etienne, Roubaix, and Tourcoing. Where such extensive workshops were not secured, in Rouen and Limoges, there were serious violent protests in April, and, as we have seen, withdrawal of relief provoked disorders and risings in both England and France. The working-class radicals of the public meetings in 1868–70 also laid great stress on poverty, low wages, and unemployment. The question of unemployment relief was a divisive one in radicalism. A Committee of Unemployed Artisans was important in the formation late in 1832 of a breakaway from the Birmingham Political Union.[16] When the Chartist engineer Newton stood as a 'labour' candidate for the Tower Hamlets in the 1852 election, he did not, of course, confine his appeal to working men alone; his programme consisted mainly of unoriginal political and business reforms; he did, however, also oppose the Master and Servant laws and call for the freedom of trade unions, and his only other distinctive demand was action to help the unemployed.[17]

Working men were fully capable of relating radicalism to their situation and economic concerns, although none of these issues (food prices, wages, unemployment relief) had inevitably to mean conflict with all other social groups, or that political action had to be confined solely to working men. Gladstone's budgets in the 1850s and 1860s were popular because they sought to reduce prices, secure full employment, and keep taxation to the minimum. Radical papers relying on the support of working men, such as the *Northern Star*, Lyons *Glaneuse*, or Toulon *Démocrate*, supported their combinations and they printed the workers' protests that were sent to them. And while radicals might stress how working people suffered from the *political* power of 'capitalists' and employers, and their consequent inability to further their own interests without political reform, this was not to deny that such groups did have interests opposed to those of working people, or that democracy would affect economic power.

He considered that not much good would accrue to the working classes, until they had a voice in the election of their representatives. At present, the labourer was not sufficiently remunerated for his labour; that it was the aim of masters to purchase labour as cheap as possible, and to attain their end they exercised undue influence over their workmen. He dwelt upon the benefits that would result to society; if laws were enacted to regulate wages, and to protect the property of the working man, which was his labour; and concluded by bringing forward arguments to prove that the burdens which occasionally pressed so heavily upon the tradesman and society at large, would be very greatly alleviated by the introduction of such a legislative enactment.[18]

### Middle classes

As the above statement by Jacobs, in the *Bath Guardian*, indicates, democracy would not benefit working men alone, and shopkeepers were of particular concern. The terms 'middle class' and 'bourgeoisie' were frequently used, but with little precision or consistency. 'Middle class' usually referred not to industrialists and factory owners or to a single economic class, but to the broad band of urban propertied groups, including, and sometimes especially, the lower middle class. Similarly, 'bourgeois' in France did not refer particularly to capitalists or industrialists, but could mean the rich and powerful non-nobles, or the urban population between the rich and powerful and the common people, or the landowners, or (in common parlance) the employer or the husband. Thus the use of the terms did not in itself usually embody a conception of a clear economic class.[19]

A short-lived newspaper in Paris in 1830, run by, and aimed at, working men, expressed their concerns and demands for work, but did not condemn employers, who were workers like them.[20] Condemnation of employers as a class was most prevalent in large, bitter, and emotional strikes, and this was reflected in radicalism, as in O'Connor's assertion during the great London stonemasons' strike of 1841–2 that it was not so much the aristocracy as the middle classes who trampled on the people.[21] But the language of such temporary episodes should not be taken as typical, and radicals did not specifically seek to restrict their support to a particular social constituency and they portrayed democracy as beneficial to the whole nation, except to the corrupt few running things.

Nevertheless, there were frequent and recurrent bitter attacks on the middle classes. This was not because their interests were seen as opposed to those of working people, but because of their political behaviour, their failure to join with the people, and their readiness even to ally with the enemy. Ultra-radicals who in 1831–2 opposed the Reform Bill, which was specifically advocated as enfranchising the responsible, propertied 'middle classes', saw it as a measure to deny democracy and to strengthen aristocratic institutions through middle-class reinforcements.

While there was, in fact, general radical support for the Bill, hopes were cruelly dashed after 1832 by the lack of further constitutional reform and the oppressive and unjust measures that issued from the new Parliament. The stance of the Bill's radical opponents seemed vindicated and there were furious denunciations of the middle classes for supporting measures hostile to working people, turning against the people, and allying with the oppressors. It was not their economic activities or interests that were being assailed but their politics. As Hetherington, one of the chief opponents of the Bill, explained, he never opposed master manufacturers on account of their calling, but only as enemies of workmen's political rights; no man should be blamed for his vocation as long as he supported equal political rights.[22] The coming to power of such people in northern towns could also fuel attacks on them as the new rulers.[23] But in general, since it was their political behaviour, and not their economic interests, that was condemned, there was always the possibility that this could change, especially as it seemed that the middle classes had not really gained political power and had been duped by the upper classes, and there was always the chance that they would come to their senses and see that their real interests lay in joining with the people to secure radical reform. The question of an alliance with members of the middle classes was thus never a closed one during Chartism, but specific attempts at such alliances were marked by a refusal to compromise in order to accommodate them and bedevilled by recurrent suspicions that they would again use the people and let them down, as in 1832:

The working classes had been made the tool of all parties and had been deceived by all. If the men of wealth in the country are in earnest in their desire to redress the grievance of the people, it can be accomplished whenever they think proper to effect a real union with us.[24]

Such fears reappeared when Reform was again an immediate issue in the 1860s, and the new organisation in London was bitter when Bright, his allies, and other parliamentary radicals dashed hopes raised in earlier speeches by refusing to support manhood suffrage, and the Londoners angrily decided to go it alone with their own Reform League.[25]

Similarly, the July Revolution, seen as bringing the 'bourgeoisie' to power, was followed by radical bitterness at the consolidation of a new privileged bourgeois elite, and at the abandonment of the people by the bourgeoisie.[26] Similar sentiments greeted propertied opposition to the reds in the Second Republic, when reaction had restored the division of the nation into two camps, and 'the struggle between the bourgeoisie and the proletariat is resuming'.[27] Propertied support for the moderate republican opposition in the 1860s and lack of support for public campaigns fuelled the condemnation of the bourgeoisie in the ultra-radical public meetings.

The recurrent sense of betrayal by self-serving political leaders, by 'great men, or men professing greatness', could secure wider support for political and cultural organisations confined exclusively to working men, for 'working men were so often betrayed, deceived, and deluded by their leaders, that his spirits were cast down'.[28] The coolness and reticence shown by workers to the surprised Flora Tristan led to the savage portraits of Perdiguier, Poncy, Jasmin, Reboul, Lapointe, and Vinçard in her diary.[29]

Yet such condemnations of non-workers were qualified by a view that support from such people was essential for the success of radical reform, a view that gained greater currency when there was a consciousness of weakness, as after the Chartist defeats of 1839, 1842, and 1848. Moreover, a distinction between a good and a bad middle class was often given an economic definition. While the 'cotton lords, capitalists, bankers, manufacturers, millocrats, merchants and all wholesale dealers' were, with landowners, part of the rich, powerful, privileged rulers, the lower middle class of small property owners, master artisans, small dealers, and lower professionals, was useful and industrious, by sentiment close to the people from whom it had largely sprung, and it suffered severely from monopoly, taxation, corruption, and specula-tion.[30] The shopkeepers particularly were seen as the natural allies of working people, for the more the workers earned, the more they could spend in the shops. Thus shopkeepers, in a desire for more generous poor relief, would sometimes clash with urban elites. As O'Connor explained:

Now, bear in mind, in speaking of the middle classes, great and flagrant errors have been committed. The question has been argued as though the interests of all the middle classes were identical, whereas, the interests of shop-keepers and that of manufacturers are the very antipodes one to the other. The interest of the manufacturer is to have cheap labour; while the interest of the shopkeeper is to have dear labour. You must enlighten the shopkeepers and tradesmen of all denominations, and fight them against the real enemy – the steam lords.[31]

O'Connor's consistent strategy throughout the 1840s was an alliance with the 'industrious portion of the middle classes', an aim encouraged by signs of shopkeeper discontent or radicalism. Ernest Jones continued the same distinction between the middle and monied classes. 'All taxation comes out of the pocket of the working man, and of the small retail shopkeeper dependent on home trade.'

By middle class I understand those who are equally removed from the great employer, and the poor employed – it is not the millowner and mineowner, the banker and landlord, the great capitalist of physic, law, or religion, – but it is the farmer, and the retail shopkeeper, who are comprised under the denomination – and these, I say, are becoming the sufferers under the system.

Even at the time of the Preston lock-out, 'it is the struggle of the wages' slaves – not against the middle classes – not against the small retailers of the country – but the bloated factory kings, usurers, and gigantic profit-mongers of our land'. 'The interests of the shop-keeper consists in the prosperity of the working classes – since high wages, or prosperous and independent labour, can alone create and maintain home-trade.'[32]

Similarly, the radical trades' committee in Rheims appealed to the shopkeepers on grounds of common interests:

The central committee, convinced that your interests are identical with those of the working man, and that on the fate of one depends the future of the other, and that the most complete solidarity should exist between the two classes whose interests are the same, appeals to the fraternal sentiments which must animate you, and in the absence of these, to your material interests that are already so injured and likely each day to be more so.[33]

But the end of Chartism as a national movement in the middle of the century resulted in a reduced confidence that weakened the previous refusal to compromise on the Six Points and led to a readiness to accept partial reforms instead of sticking to a manhood suffrage that was unlikely to be achieved, a stance reinforced by the more extensive, organised, and intense middle-class radicalism with which Chartists had to come to terms.[34] If the middle classes would not join the people, then they should go it alone, but the attitude here was one of suspicion rather than of outright hostility, and depended largely on the attitudes and behaviour of these middle classes. It was the reaction of members of the lower middle classes as much as anything else that determined the social composition and class nature of popular radicalism.

The radical view of the lower middle classes as part of the people did not necessarily reflect actual social and economic relations between them and the working people. While they were often dependent on merchant and industrial capitalists for credit, raw materials, and sales, and could engage in opposition to the rich and powerful, to high finance and bankers, and to the state, they also had direct relations with working people in their capacity as employers, dealers, and providers of working-class housing. The closeness of these relations, and the small means and working-class origins of many of the lower middle class (change of position indeed often being a reaction to poverty) did not in any way prevent such relations from being often very fraught, involving disputes and bitterness over wages and working conditions, prices and adulteration, and rents and evictions.[35] While working people engaged in work disputes, combinations, food riots, exclusive dealing, co-operative trading, flits to avoid rent, and rent strikes, these issues were not on the whole reflected in radical movements based on popular alliances, even though working-class radicals were personally very concerned with such issues. Wages were not necessarily the most important of these contentious concerns. As Gossez showed, small masters were not all hostile to the wages movements in Paris early in 1848, and they did not fight on the barricades against the June rising, preferring to protect their premises (from either side), although a number did fight on the rebels' side, and often opposed the repression that followed – testimony by employers of insurgents tried by court-martial tended to be favourable.[36] In great contrast was the usually hostile testimony of the landlords and of the chief-tenants who collected rents from fellow-tenants for the landlord, which suggested that tension over accommodation was greater than that over employment. The rapid growth of the Paris population under the July Monarchy had produced a housing shortage, rising rents, and arrears, and the revolution in February 1848 was followed by a spontaneous agitation, in eastern Paris especially, which secured the cancellation of the half-yearly rent payments in April and mobilised a demonstration involving perhaps 100,000 people. Yet the radical press and clubs hardly noticed this extensive agitation. In London, urban improvements meant the destruction of working-class housing and greater overcrowding, but this was exceeded in Paris by extensive changes under Haussmann which created an acute housing crisis, much higher rents, many disputes, and displacement to suburbs that lacked roads and water and involved lengthy travel to work. These all aroused great popular resentment, and radicals at the public meetings in 1869 and 1870 took up the idea of a rent strike when the April payment fell due, and during the siege of 1870–1 radical clubs did enforce controls of rent and food.[37] Thus the strategy of radical movements tended to filter out such issues, but they remained of great importance to working-class radicals, and the strength of radicalism encouraged action over them.

It is true that radicals also often attacked the middle classes for their occupations, but this was not a condemnation of their economic roles as such. It reflected a political opposition to or disenchantment with them, and was partly a riposte to the moderate reformers' anti-democratic praise of a very vaguely defined 'middle class', untainted by aristocratic luxury and corruption or by working-class brutalisation and excess, a morally rather than socially defined core of society, composed of right-thinking and upright men. The radical criticism attributed their failure to support radicalism to occupations that made them narrow-minded, subservient, unmanly, ignorant, and prejudiced, unable to recognise their own real interests or the true needs of the nation, or to see that they would all gain from radical reform.

All that is mean, and grovelling, and selfish, and sordid, and rapacious, and harsh, and cold, and cruel, and usurious, belongs to this huxtering race. Taken in the mass they are utter strangers to enthusiasm and to all the generous passions.[38]

These were *moral* critiques of the middle classes and bourgeoisie, for their selfishness and materialism,[39] which reflected a radical bitterness at their incapacity to support radicalism, rather than revealing a class outlook. Philosophical Radicals expressed the same disillusion, and the chief one of them, Harriet Grote, wondered 'who can do any good with such a pack of rotten quacks and a stupid middle class who dream only of shop', while Francis Place considered the middle classes 'among the most despicable people in the nation in a public point of view'.[40]

Thus denunciations of the middle classes or the bourgeoisie did not usually express class antagonisms but rather criticism of their political behaviour, often coupled with an unflattering moral analysis of their character. In all this, 1830 and 1832 were pivotal for radicalism, for they were the occasions when the middle classes had used the people to gain political admission for themselves, and had then turned against them, allied with corruption, and broken their promises, a betrayal compounded by their actions as special constables and National Guardsmen against the popular protests.

### Class terminology

The widespread stress on the need for class conciliation was in itself a recognition of the existence and peril of class divisions, but we must not assume that everyone meant the same by the same terms. Partly, as we have seen, class language was one of political strategy and criticism, not one of social description.[41] Class could be used in disputes over who should be included in the political nation and therefore be defined in political terms. 'Working class' and 'people' could be interchangeable, as in the 'class of workmen, the people', 'the great people of workmen', 'the workers, the real people'.[42] 'Working class' or 'proletarian' could mean the same as the people, the ruled, those excluded from the vote in 1832, or Blanqui's thirty-odd million proletarians who supported the political rulers through taxation. Or it could mean the poor, just as 'bourgeois' could mean the rich.[43] The extensive radical use of the term 'people' does not indicate a shared understanding of the term's meaning, while new terminology does not have to denote new conceptions; the 'proletarians' of the London Democratic Association in 1838 were not wage-earners but those without property.[44] 'People' could indeed also be an alternative to 'working class', and mean the middle class, reputable and responsible. For radicals, the term was often a way of stressing a wider message or appeal; thus the trade unionists who took over the *Workman's Advocate* changed its title to the *Commonwealth* to stress it was not the champion of a particular class, while the ultra-radical *Marseillaise* championed 'the people – and by that word we understand whoever owns to democratic principles, without distinction of classes'.[45] Journalists of the Commune appealed to 'bourgeois, working men, workers of all classes, men of sincerity' to join 'our revolution'.[46] But for others, the term 'represents all those who possess nothing, and those who only possess a little. These people are in modern society what the slaves were in ancient society.'[47] 'People' could thus mean working class, as in Cabet's call for unity between People and Bourgeoisie, partly as an act of class assertiveness, making the interests of the class central to the nation instead of being marginal or sectional.[48]

For a Paris workers' paper in 1830, 'in our eyes, the people are nothing other than the working class' which was the creator of wealth, but it also championed 'the industrious class of artisans'. The Rights of Man Society sought 'the political education of the working class and the improvement by this means of the lot of this class', and radical republicans of the July Monarchy and Second Republic, generally appealed to and advocated the cause of proletarians, but they saw this class as including small masters, dealers, and professional, intellectual, and artistic workers. The working class (or people) thus consisted not only of manual wage-earners, but of all those who worked, while the bourgeois enemy was not the employer but the rich, idle gentleman who lived well and inhabited a different world. Thus class language was an expression of the old emphasis on the industrious/idle distinction. 'It is the people that produces, it is the bourgeois that devours.'[49] Similarly, in the public meetings at the end of the 1860s, the *travailleur* they championed was not necessarily a manual wage-earning *ouvrier*.[50]

Class could also be used by radicals in a negative way, as by a group of Chartist women.

Let us reject their Church and State offers of education for our children, which is only calculated to debase the mind, and render it subservient to class interest; let us teach our offspring to do to others as they would others should do unto them.[51]

Many other radicals opposed, instead of asserted class. Radicals condemned '*class legislation*, – meaning by the term, predominant – nay, exclusive, – power in the House of Commons, and in the election of its members, by certain classes',[52] but this was not a wish to replace them with a different class legislation or representation, for such elements of class were associated with caste and privilege, and were obstacles to the unity, harmony, and progress of society. Class was associated with the selfishness and materialism of elites not primarily identified as the owners of the means of production, who denied the moral worth of the mass of the people and the unity of mankind. Radical reform would not place a new class in power or bring about socio-economic upheaval, but it would abolish classes and effect the liberalisation of society, social harmony and unity, and human brotherhood.[53]

But, just as Cobden's belief that free trade would ultimately lead to the harmonious reconciliation of all interests did not dispel his conviction of the inevitability of social conflict in the meantime,[54] so these radical analyses did not exclude a particular concern with working people and their situation. Thus many issues could be given a class dimension, for example the Sabbatarians' efforts to check activities on Sundays such as trading or the opening of museums and parks; the death penalty; and the prohibition on marrying one's dead wife's sister, ('of its importance to the working classes every domesticated individual must be aware').[55] Such inclusive radicalism could also embody a sense that the working classes had a special mission, for, freed from the corruption of opulence and political chicanery, forming the honest mainstay of state and society, and aware, through personal experience, of pervasive injustices, only they could end class legislation and unfairness and, in the interests of all, bring about reform and redemption.

A different understanding of class arose out of political economy and its categories of land, capital, and labour, which led to the idea of three main classes: landowners, capitalists, and workers. This was used by English trade unionists in the 1860s in presenting a public case for their organisations, as they stressed the mutual dependence of these classes and hence the importance and positive role of labour, and at the same time demonstrated that labour also had interests distinct from those of capital. There was no idea here of ending classes, but the analysis was used in the 1860s (and even in the 1820s by John Gast, a radical shipwright very aware of political economy) to justify extending the vote to working men, on the grounds that labour was a sectional interest that deserved representation along with other interests. This usually meant that it was only one interest among many, and could justify an extension of the franchise short of manhood suffrage, on the grounds that full radical reform would make labour the predominant interest. Thus radical MPs who regularly consulted a few London trade union leaders could be seen as the representatives of labour.[56] Yet an observation of the world purely in terms of economic categories always diverges from reality, and the use of such arguments by a few men, especially some trade unionists in London, should not blind us to the fact that this was not the usual language of popular radicalism. Such men as Howell and Applegarth joined with some radicals in supporting a scheme for proportional representation, that would have enabled large affiliated friendly societies, amalgamated trade unions, or co-operative societies to organise the election of their own candidates as MPs, but the vast majority of plebeian radicals gave no support to a scheme which ran directly counter to their conceptions.[57]

### Class identity

A far more common use of class terminology was to identify rank and stratification in society. While social scientists frequently distinguish class from status, in fact the English terminology of upper class, upper middle class, lower middle class, and working or lower class has usually referred to status groups, incorporating the age-old social distinctions between, at the top, those engaged in trade and those not, and, at the bottom, between manual and non-manual work. Thus the working class consisted of manual workers, including working masters, while white-collar workers were (lower) middle class. This class language referred to status distinctions based on male occupation and (often assumed) differences in way of life, morality, education, residence, and culture, perhaps especially in the desire of shopkeepers and clerks to assert their superiority over manual workers often earning more than them, and to preserve their precarious respectability through sacrifices and restrictions on their expenditure and behaviour. *Tait's Magazine* referred to 'the fashion for "respectable" people who do not work with their hands, to exhibit aristocratic contempt for those who do', and a bookbinders' periodical optimistically felt 'the old prejudices against manual labour, as debasing the man, as placing him in a lower grade of society than those who are not necessitated to toil, is wearing away; the day of consummation is at hand which will remove all the old barriers created between the different classes, and which shall destroy all the old aristocratic notions of contempt of toil'. These differences could include dress, the distinctive mark of a French working man being the blouse, originally a peasant garment which after 1830 displaced the short jacket in the towns, as rural immigration grew and it was rendered cheaper by the spread of power-loom weaving. Thus class could be a purely descriptive term, implying no sharing or conflicts of interests, and working-class radicals were radicals who belonged to the working class, and middle-class radicals those who were members of the middle class.[58]

Yet these social divisions could be reflected in radicalism. Committed republicans who sincerely championed the rights of the people might still regard them as incapable of running things. 'Do you realise', said one in surprise, 'that these *working men* have great good sense and are *really* intelligent?'[59] When Holyoake read a paper to a Social Science

Congress, 'those who expected an uncouth monster of a man were, we need not say, not a little surprised to see before them a gentlemen slight in figure, most gentle in manner and speaking in a voice that would alone disarm terror'.[60] Artisans traditionally despised domestic servants as unfree, subservient lackeys (though they were often more secure in their employment, and consequently better off) and objected to pass-books and pay by the hour as characteristics of servants and labourers. Their feeling ill at ease in the presence of non-artisans such as clerks was an obstacle to artisan involvement in English mechanics' institutions and in Paris Saint-Simonian meetings and political clubs.[61] A problem in reviving secret societies after the 1839 fiasco was that 'the workmen only obey men wearing cloaks', while a radical Toulon shipwright who sat on the municipal council in 1848 was not a friend of a fellow radical, 'since his social position is different from mine'. Working-class members of the Rights of Man who were put in prison resented privileges granted to prisoners according to their social rank, while Paris radical artisans in 1849 distrusted the men of letters, and money sent from Paris to French refugees in London tended not to go to the working men.[62] Particularly important was resentment on the part of artisans and small masters at snobbish clerks who treated them with disdain and, in France, tutoyed them whatever their age. In the early 1830s, an important section of the Paris National Guard was composed of clerks eager to please their superiors and far readier to act against disturbances. 'At the slightest sound of the quarter's drum, the bourgeois man shuts his shop and cowers in the bosom of his family. The clerk, for his part, rushes for his accoutrement and runs to his post next to his superior; the grades were according to rank at work.' Similarly, in the June Days there was far greater mutual hostility between workmen and clerks and students than between workmen and employers, and there was savage fighting between them. In vain in 1869 Varlin tried to 'break with that tradition so disastrous to democratic progress, which hitherto made clerks and workmen into two different classes'.[63]

## Social equality

Systems of stratification are not based on uniform consensus and involve a strategic playing of roles, resentment, and hostility. It was arrogance, contempt, and a hurtful lack of respect for manual workers and their families that aroused most resentment. As the shoemaker Lapointe pointed out: 'What alienates men from one another is not so much the inequality in situation as the haughtiness, the disdain and the prejudices which accompany the inequalities of these situations. In a word, it is the contempt (*inconsidération*) which wounds the classes of the poor.'[64] The Bury trades boycotted a procession to lay the corner-stone of a new Atheneum because of its rule excluding working men from using its lecture room for discussions.[65] Not only did people in superior stations look down on manual workers as inferior, they also often treated them as infantile, savage, brutalised, animal, and not fully human. A Leicester hosiery employer in 1871 defended levying frame rents on stockingers who were ill and unable to work on the grounds that illness was usually caused by drink or malingering, and Victorian law embodied and justified views on the latent fickleness and immorality of manual workers and the latent industry and honesty of the property-owning classes. Such entrenched prejudices on the inferior character, morals, and behaviour of the manual working class resulted in a deeply resented differential treatment of rich and poor debtors (the poor had to pay all and could be imprisoned if they did not, the rich were relieved of much of the debt by bankruptcy and limited liability laws) and in restrictions on working-class insurance to avoid the temptations there might be for parents to murder their children for money.[66]

Such social arrogance and contempt fuelled working-class radicalism. When the Reform Bill was introduced in 1831, a Bolton radical warned that 'if the middle classes obtained what they were now seeking for, they would in two years from this time join the aristocracy, and again call them a rabble and swinish multitude',[67] and indeed by 1833 there was great bitterness at the marked change from glorifying the 'estimable artisans, respectable workmen' for their role in the July Revolution, and praising the 'patriotic' efforts for the Reform Bill, to abuse and vilification.

> Of old, when long Petitions came
>     From Tom and Dick, who brew and bake,
> We used to hear the Press proclaim
>     That all the nation was awake.
> If Dick and Tom, who bake and brew,
>     Today petition to be free –
> '*The nation*', roared in thirty-two;
>     It's just '*the mob*' in thirty-three!![68]

The phrase 'swinish multitude' was one frequently repeated by radicals as a calumny on the people, comparable to Thiers' long-remembered reference to 'the multitude, the vile multitude'. It was the vituperative language and epithets used of the working classes by opponents of the Reform Bill in 1866 that really aroused working-class agitation for parliamentary reform, seeking, as a song went,

That Working-men shall be esteemed
No longer 'vile and low'
But have the vote and praise the League
As marching on we go.[69]

Thus class could again be seen in a negative light, and the abolition of class distinctions meant social equality, so 'that the absurdities and usurpations of ranks and classes should disappear, and MEN be the equal lords of this earth'.[70]

As *Reynolds's Newspaper* said in 1866, working men were so used to rude and insolent treatment that they admired to an exaggerated degree the few gentlemen and aristocrats who showed them respect. In the early 1830s working men who met the young well-born Saint-Simonians felt it miraculous that they treated them with such respect, while the young waller Nadaud was bowled over when young republican students treated him as an equal, the first members of the middle class ever to shake his hand, and he joined the Rights of Man. When, in a debate in the Chamber in 1840 on electoral reform, the republican Arago expressed concern over the miseries of the poor, he was thanked by a large deputation of workmen in an almost incredible display of gratitude. Yet Cabet broke with followers among the Lyons workers over his dictatorial manner, his insistence on unquestioning obedience, and his refusal to accept their wish to become theorists and treat themselves as his equal. In July 1841 the radical republican lawyer Ledru-Rollin was elected deputy, and it was not his unexceptional programme of electoral and taxation reform but his expression of concern over the conditions of the working people that made him at one stroke a leader of the radical republicans. 'These words produced in the workshops and yards the effect of a trail of gunpowder', and it was 'Ledru' who proposed a motion on the petition originated by the *Réforme* newspaper for an enquiry into the state of the workers, the popularity he gained standing him in good stead in 1848.[71] In general, middle-class people who did not adopt the usual harsh, arrogant, and disdainful attitude, aroused by their cordial or even merely respectful stance an enthusiastic response which is almost incomprehensible.[72] This partly explains the phenomenon of the 'gentleman leader', who gave up the privileges and prejudices of his class and sacrificed himself by coming among the common people to exhibit his nobility of heart and simplicity. Paris working men in the 1863–4 elections did not vote for the labour candidates but preferred Opposition men of leisure, education, political experience, oratory, and wealth (and consequent independence).[73] Generosity with money as well as time was appreciated, as was shown by the wives of Lamartine and Marie in 1848. Thus John Bright and

Gladstone were in the 1860s able to surmount the widespread popular distrust hitherto displayed, through the warmth of their sentiments towards working men and their development of the ideas that all great reforms started with them. The latter's very unclear and ambiguous statement in favour of parliamentary reform in 1864 had a quite disproportionate impact.[74]

The insistence on a programme of manhood suffrage could be an assertion of social equality rather than any realistic aspiration of gaining it, and it was in reaction to the prevalent contemptuous attitude to working men, and in assertion of their equality, dignity, worth, and manliness, that separate working-class organisations appeared. It was the refusal in the later 1830s of the Bath Radical Association, the Bolton Reform Association, and the Birmingham Political Union to admit working men on to their committees as equals that led to breakaway organisations that became Chartist in 1838–9. The same was true of separate working-class liberal organisations after 1868.[75] These did not necessarily have different programmes or ideologies, they were different *organisations* that asserted the equality of working men. The same is true of labour representation. It was the Paris republican leaders' initial ignoring of workers' organisations in their preparations for the 1863 general election, and their high-handed and undemocratic action over the choosing of candidates, that led the radical bronze-chaser Tolain and a group of working men to put up three 'labour' candidates at the election, and follow it up by issuing the famous 'Manifesto of the Sixty', whose programme was nevertheless pretty indistinguishable from radical republicanism except for the legalisation of strikes and establishment of trade committees. Labour representation also became an issue in England in the 1860s, and its advocates supported not distinctive programmes but rather the full recognition of working men as citizens.[76] In both countries, there was radical, republican, and socialist opposition to such candidacies.[77]

Tolain condemned the middle-class republicans' attitude to working men, for they 'look with ill humour and distrust on those among us who claim their place in the sun',[78] and the Manifesto specifically rejected a confinement of working men to the position of clients or subordinates. It was this stress on equality and participation in civil society, and the objection to class legislation and privilege, that underlay so much working-class radicalism, and was misinterpreted by contemporaries as a rejection of their economic position as workers or as an exclusive claim to power. They stressed equality in law, political rights and manners, fraternity, and their full admission into society as men, not as workers or producers. While Saint-Simonians divided society economically into the producers and the idle, their working-class adherents objected to being treated as subordinates in the Saint-Simonian hierarchy. Radical workers opposed the legislative outcomes of such prejudices, for example the Master and Servant Law and Civil Code, which, by regarding their word as inferior to the masters, did not recognise them fully as men; or they opposed the official paternalistic interference in their benefit societies and other activities or organisations. They resented the insensitivity of the rich and the humiliations of poverty, or the behaviour of charitable and relief institutions, for 'many of the poor, bashful and ashamed, prefer the cruellest hunger to the harsh and humiliating slavery which it imposes' so that 'they feel they abdicate their personal dignity', and they resented the English Poor Law, which served to 'point the finger of derision at honest artisans'.[79] All this could produce a distinctive form of radicalism. This (gendered) demand for social equality and full participation in public life was expressed in the various workers' journals that appeared, especially in France in the 1830s and 1840s. The very fact of journals run and produced by workers was, as the English *Trades' Newspaper* had declared in 1825 and the *Ruche Populaire* repeated in 1839, an assertion of the workers' place in civil society and public life.

It is a fact of great importance and high morality that must be registered, the existence of newspapers produced by Working men!
We have also taken possession of political life; we have sat down worthily at the feast of minds, and no-one can now say to us Go away, we do not know you.[80]

The radical *Bon Sens* also created astonishment among its readers at its inclusion of letters from working men.[81]

Aristocratic disdain led Cobden and Bright to stress the nobility and dignity of commerce, while English businessmen's rejection of a purely business education and their pursuit of a wider, even classical, education, and acceptance of honours, titles, and appointments was not necessarily flunkeyism and a servile aping of landowners but could instead reflect a wish to raise their self-respect and public ambition and to assert themselves as persons of consequence.[82] Similarly, these workers' journals strove to remove upper and middle-class disdain towards working men, and to show that they were more than mere workers (or savages), they were also fully human, respectable (*digne*) men of probity who deserved treatment as equals. Thus their character as men was frequently stressed.[83] Since the aim was to secure the full acceptance into society of working men, the 'poor wights whom nobody heeds',[84] these periodicals were aimed just as much at a non-working-class readership, to convince them of working men's intellectual and moral quality. The process would contribute to national unity.

The working people seek the enlightenment of intelligence; they seek the dignity of discussion; they seek, in fine, the happiness and glory of the country (*patrie*); they will be able to realise their powerful will through courage, resignation and labour.[85]

'Let the working man respect himself and gain respect from others, let him at last understand his worth, his rights and his respectability!'[86] The enterprise was aimed not only at securing respect for working men from others, but also self-respect among working men themselves, so that they no longer felt themselves inferior. As Nadaud saw it, 'the working man had travelled through such long and painful hardships, that he had become timorous, and in many cases, the fear of being thrown out of work took away his pride and shrank his character and the fine qualities that form the greatness of free peoples'. Poverty and ignorance were the scourges of the working class. Thus radical journalists sought to remove working men's shame in their position, their looking up to those above them, that inveterate humility which led them to believe they were fit for nothing but manual work, their failure to vote in elections because they felt politics a middle-class affair, or their decision to vote for employers instead of for working men such as Odger.[87] But this, and the need to secure recognition as civilised partners in social life, usually meant changes among working people themselves, and so the project involved efforts to reform working people, in education, moralisation, and self-control so that they would deserve equality and respect:

The workers, lacking self-respect, not respecting one another at all, waging war with one another, preying upon one another, have lost their position, freedom and well-being. This is an evil. But a new sun will shine in the world; they will rise in enlightenment, intelligence, virtue, wisdom, activity, authority (*droit*); and a renewed society will render back to them with interest what they have lost. Let them develop their reason, constantly heed the voice of their conscience, be champions of fraternity, love their neighbour, have hope: justice will be rendered them one day.[88]

The issue of combinations and strikes aroused fierce liberal opposition to working people, and their repression was, as we have seen, a potent source of radicalisation.[89] It was a small group of workers, especially printers, some of them veterans of secret societies in the 1830s but now disciples of Buchez, who in the aftermath of the general hostility to and repression of the combinations of 1840 in Paris, established a newspaper to be run exclusively by working men. The *Atelier* was the chief and most famous of the workers' papers of the 1840s, but its readers were nearly all non-workers. The stress on equality, respect, manliness, and reform we have already encountered in the public statements of trade union leaders, and these efforts to secure social equality for workmen involved *changing* working men's perceptions of themselves in the direction of a conviction of their rights and full humanity, and could thus lead to intellectual and moral elitism. Thus most of this class language of social equality was not a reflection of workshop practice or trade attitudes but the utterance of those combating the pejorative moral analyses of other writers. Their stress on the industry, productivity, nobility, and dignity of labour was not an emanation of a love of work or pride in skill but was, like an assertion of the moral superiority of working men, an attempt to throw back middle-class epithets, to turn the terminological tables, just like referring to the Poor Law Board as the 'ruffian crew at Somerset House'.[90] Thus 'class' was here a construction by activists in relation to middle-class attitudes and criticisms, not a reflection of widely held attitudes. It was the work of those attracted to utopian socialist visions, the 'dreamers' that Leno hymned.

> Only a dreamer, only a dreamer,
>     Pass him by, pass him by;
> Why should we trouble our heads about him?
>     You and I?
>
> Let the fool cherish his visioned tomorrow,
>     And fill in his pictures in rhythm and rhyme,
> Careless of grief, and careless of sorrow,
>     The world only moves at its own set time . . .

It was the work of

> the migrants who move at the borders between classes, individuals and groups who develop capabilities within themselves which are useless for the improvement of their material lives and which in fact are liable to make them despise material concerns. It was minority dreamers like these who were in turn encouraging the masses to dream.[91]

### Social fear

Efforts to achieve not domination or the overthrow of the economic system but equality and fairness might, from some theoretical standpoints, seem 'moderate', and could secure some support from radical liberals, especially those who came into contact with working men. But this is misleading, for the hostility to working-class equality and democracy made such a goal not moderate but subversive. The Reform League recognised that one of the chief obstacles to democracy was middle-class fear of the working classes.[92] The widespread middle-class perception of working people was as dangerous barbarians, nomadic threats to civilisation, brutish, incapable of discipline and reason, immoral, violent, and disorderly if not controlled.[93] Such perceptions were based on ignorance rather than on contact and experience, for it was often not 'our' workers but others that were the problem.[94] Furthermore, they were deeply marked by sensationalist and biased social investigations and the growth, especially in the 1840s, of social novels portraying ever-growing numbers and areas in the cities of people characterised by poverty, idleness, drunkenness, gambling, crime, vagabondage, and prostitution, against which the police were the only defence. Images of the working class were of factory workers, miners, doltish agricultural labourers, and the inhabitants of city slums, all untypical members of the working population whom most members of the middle class would never know; it was his horrified and uninformed perception of factory workers that confirmed Richard Carlile's decision to drop his previous support for universal suffrage. Conversely, urban Chartists subscribed to the idealisation of rural cottage family life in the myth of handloom-weavers and the poetry of Burns as a measure of social criticism, and, even if they had never seen factories, mines, or poor law workhouses, employed the imagery of women and children in mills and underground and in the Bastilles (poor law workhouses). 'Will you be cajoled', said the dyer Ridley to a meeting of artisans in London, a city almost devoid of factories, 'by the factory lords, by those who have amassed their wealth from the blood and marrow of the factory children? Will you be knocked down at such a price?'[95]

'We see with pain', ran a Paris police report, 'many individuals belonging to the working class, in blouses, with beard and moustache, apparently spending more time on politics than their labours, reading republican newspapers and detestable pamphlets published for distribution among them so as to lead them astray and gradually push them in the most deplorable direction.'[96] Radical political activity among working people was seen as a threat to civilisation, for hungry people were inevitably inclined to loot and plunder, combinations were 'mutinies',[97] and 'demagogues' aroused their 'animal passions'.

The rise of Chartism led to middle-class fears of Chartist violence and prompted *Blackwood's* to declare that 'it is now established beyond all doubt that universal suffrage in reality means nothing else but universal pillage . . . what the working classes understand by political power is just the means of putting their hands in their neighbours' pockets . . .'[98] In 1839 the forbearance of the government and local authorities led middle and propertied opinion to see the Chartists as the violent party (in contrast to 1819, when the authorities were seen as the initiators of violence), and there was a propertied reaction against Chartist violence and illegality, and the withdrawal of middle-class radicals from Chartism in most places. In their reaction to the defeat of 1839, the whole rhetoric of Chartism changed, in a disavowal of violent language that had not worked and had alienated potential support. But O'Connor's strategy of an alliance was doomed for most of the 1840s by an irremovable middle-class association of Chartism and the Charter with 'armed violence, intolerance, abuse and slander'.[99] Any middle-class sympathy for the Chartist revival early in 1848 was again dissipated by the apparent identification of Chartism with riot and outrage,[100] and the only newspaper to support the 1855 Sunday trading riots were *Reynolds's Newspaper* and Jones' *People's Paper*.

It was especially in periods of acute political tension that such moral panics developed, as in the aftermath of the July Revolution, when street demonstrations produced fears of 'anarchy' and calls for repression, and a judge declared that 'Republic and pillage were synonymous'.[101] After the Lyons rising in 1831 there was a panic at the slightest disorder. 'The days of November will leave in the public mind of Lyons a feeling of fear of the working classes which will show itself at the slightest occasion and often without reason.'[102] Disturbances at the French election results in 1869 and attacks on property and bread prices produced propertied stupor and panic,[103] while around the same time there was a panic in England over Fenianism and its links with English radicals. It is clear that governments could try to take advantage such emotions. The Second Empire allowed strikes, violent public meetings, and even assisted extreme candidates in 1869 as a way of provoking a reaction that would gain a rallying of support, but once it had secured a favourable result in the 1870 plebiscite it moved to repress these movements. The English government in 1848 created a sham confrontation over the Kennington Common meeting on 10 April, and secured a mass mobilisation of property-owners as special constables, as one of them later recalled.

> The government and its newspaper organs frightened us out of our wits. I confess that I was one of the tremblers on that occasion, and that the *Times* succeeded in throwing me into as complete a panic with its anti-chartist articles in 1848, as it did with its Cholera-lists in 1849. I will frankly confess, too, that I went and got sworn in as a special constable at Bow Street; but I have since bitterly repeated that I allowed the Government and the hireling portion of the press to make such a complete fool of me.[104]

The period of greatest tension was the Second Republic in France. The revolution, republic, and establishment of democracy set off a social fear, even among 'the small dealers and small capitalists who, in fact, have always professed liberal opinions'.[105] Fuelled by the literature of the 'dangerous classes' there was an obsession with bloodshed, the Terror, and the guillotine (police often searched radicals' homes for guillotines) and a fascination with horror and excess which fuelled an inability to believe that socialists were sincere or even sane, and spawned slanderous, anti-republican polemic. The February revolution, of course, did touch off a wave of working-class activity, claims, and a new feeling of strength, and although there were few attacks on property and workmen were often its best defenders, and workers' industrial demands were traditional, restrained, limited, and in search of agreement and conciliation, the hysterical reaction to these 'communist' threats to property and actions of civil war rendered such aims extreme and subversive. As a radical paper said of a strike by Paris paper-stainers, 'in the eyes of the reactionaries, these workmen are revolutionaries'.[106] Propertied groups also panicked over the tone (rather than the actual demands) of the political clubs, the right to work, the mobilisation of workers around the Luxembourg Commission, and the municipal workshops established in many towns, and were particularly alarmed at popular open-air demonstrations, an unfamiliar phenomenon in France (in contrast to Britain), which they assumed inevitably meant disorder and violence. Fuelled by a reactionary press there was terror in Paris and the provinces at the reds, brigands, and 'communists' believed to be conspiring to take over France.[107] This produced a political polarisation, made agreement and the establishment of harmony and fraternity impossible, forced workers in the 'communist' relief workshops to mobilise in self-defence and provoked corresponding intransigence against the 'pot-bellied, the satisfied, the exploiters of the poor, the devourers of the people'.[108] As a Luxembourg delegate lamented:

Thus we, who preach fraternity, we, who wish all theories put forward with equal freedom, we, who only ask the *progressive* application of the rights we hold from nature, and of which fraud and usurpation have deprived us until now, we, who have never uttered a single cry either against persons or property, it is we who are accused of excess . . . It is us they want to *exterminate*.
Moderate republicans, the fury of your moderation is as ridiculous as it is unwise.[109]

Radicals constantly and sarcastically employed conservatives' terminology for themselves as 'respectable' and 'moderate' but, as Pottier sang, if men advocated equality they were called drinkers of blood, whilst really 'the drinkers of gold are the drinkers of blood',[110] and once the popular movement had been defeated in mid-1848, governments manipulated the social fear, which flared up again at any radical election successes, to motivate repression, including the pitiless repression after the 1851 rising.[111]

The political conflicts and middle-class images and fear of the working classes thus led to extreme political polarisation and bitter social hatreds that were not mainly revealed in employer–employee relations. The chief issue of social conflict in 1848 was, in fact, probably the National Guard. This institution had revived after the July Revolution, ostensibly open to most of the adult male population, though those who could afford their own uniform and weapons looked down on those who had none – in Lyons they were called Bedouins. In practice, however, most rural units only existed on paper, and urban ones tended to become moribund, those that did continue consisting, especially after 1837, mainly of lower middle-class people who provided their own uniforms and arms, a propertied militia who acted against disorder and savages, and a 'bourgeois aristocracy' of pretentious shopkeepers, the butt of popular dislike and frequent ridicule in popular theatres.[112] In 1847 the Limoges National Guard tried to organise a movement within the Guard to exclude all those who could not provide their own equipment, a move that aroused local working-class uproar and bitterness at the insult.[113] With the Republic in 1848 the National Guard was democratised and open to all, and radicals and workers saw a democratic Republic as the guarantor of freedom of association and combination and of relief for the unemployed, and a truly popular armed National Guard as the bulwark of the democratic Republic against its enemies. But the prospect of the barbarians being armed filled propertied classes with horror, especially as in the early months there was a plurality of power, a number of radical paramilitary organisations emerged in Paris and Lyons, including the notorious 'Voraces' on the Croix-Rousse, and the regular troops were sent away from Paris after the successful 17 March demonstration. The greatest middle-class alarm seems to have been not over workers' economic demands, but the spectacle of armed workers and street demonstrations, and most of the clashes were over the control of arms. In fact the authorities managed to thwart mass registration in the National Guard, and provided weapons only to the propertied sections. From April 1848 the paramilitary units were dissolved, workers were purged from the Guard, and from 1849 whole units were wholly or partially dissolved or disarmed, membership was restricted to men who could provide their own uniform, and unofficial and illegal armed propertied militias were formed.[114] While the social composition of radical movements and actions was indeed varied, the repression tended to be on the basis of class, and sometimes in the name of morality, (although after the 1851 rising, middle-class participants were punished more harshly than peasants). The fear of a migratory, unsettled, dangerous population meant that many innocent inhabitants of low lodging houses were seized after the June Days, while the authorities' obsession with class struggle led them to regard the radical Mountain as the party of the working class, and to harass all workers' organisations as red (and thereby turn a lot of them red).[115]

In this way the perception of workers as a class came from outside rather than inside, and was keenest in periods of social fear and political crisis.[116] It was not based on direct contact. Millowners, who knew and controlled their workforce much more, were more confident over the danger, so that class antagonisms might be less obvious in factory districts.

Thus there was not a complete fit between the different uses of class terminology and analyses, in political strategies, moral critiques, categories from political economy, status distinctions, or claims for social equality. Yet in practice if not in ideology they related democracy to abiding concerns with poverty, wages, food prices, unemployment, and security. Thus the great workman's Sunday paper of the 1850s and 1860s, *Reynolds's Newspaper*, in continuation of much of the earlier *Northern Star*, gave extensive space to political corruption and was pervaded by hostility to privilege, aristocracy, bankers, speculators, professionals (especially lawyers), police, the legal system, flogging, and Sabbatarianism. Indifferent to temperance, it gave a lot of attention to poor relief, and gave unreflective support to trade union activity, especially strikes against the 'grasping avarice and implacable tyranny of employers under the existing order of things'.[117] Political radicals naturally concentrated mainly on political issues and the holders of political power, but this does not make their ideas incompatible with other analyses, preoccupations, and targets. In opposing 'class legislation' and asserting claims for the social equality of manual workers, it was the social, not economic, aspects of class that were their chief concern.

# 8    Political action and organisation

Political action was not a simple reflection of occupations, communities, or social forces, but created its own identities, procedures, and means and forms of communication. Organisation seems the crucial element in this, and French republicans in the early 1830s saw associations of citizens as the most effective form of opposition to governments. 'The right of association is a sacred right, it is the sole asylum of the weak.' After the re-election in 1857 of the republican Hénon to the Legislature, the Procurator-General of Lyons could see only two remedies for such a deplorable situation: one would be to abolish universal suffrage; the other

would consist of carefully removing from these masses all cohesion, all organisation, of stifling into silence the socialist ideas which agitate and influence them. Organisation, be it in the name of philanthropic society, be it attached to a professional journal, be it formed in one shape or another, constitutes the real power of ideas and what are called parties.[1]

As a French radical commented in 1849, England was different from France in its powerfully organised interest groups which acted collectively over issues that affected them and, as permanent checks on government, had made possible a series of liberal gains over the past two centuries. 'The rulers, in England, have for a long time chosen the slowest and gentlest form of death, and this explains their long life.'[2] Voluntary associations were central to the development of urban, especially bourgeois, culture, and operated with much greater freedom in Britain, while in France any association needed authorisation.[3] Liberals argued that this led to greater extremism in France. Thus the English Prime Minister, Grey, resisted great pressure from the King in 1832 to suppress the political unions: 'if not irritated by an injudicious interference, these Unions will die away . . . nothing, as it appears to Earl Grey, could be more impolitic than to unite them all in a common cause by an attempt to suppress them'.[4]

Coupled with this was the much greater importance of extra-parliamentary agitation in Britain. 'Public opinion' was recognised as an intrinsic element in the Constitution, and extra-parliamentary single-issue campaigns, involving non-voters as well as voters, based on platform, press, and petition, were a normal part of political life in a way they never were in France. Thus in Britain these forms of mobilisation were replicated by popular radicals, who had their own meetings, newspapers, and petitions (the Chartists secured two to three million signatures to petitions in 1841, 1842, and 1848), although they met greater obstacles from the authorities and suffered from the unavailability of premises or locations for meetings. However, a change in parliamentary procedure in the 1830s severely cut down the attention given to petitions and therefore reduced their effectiveness, and a growing gulf between Parliament and people was stressed by the Chartists, so that 'those House of Commons patriots, who selected their own questions for public discussion, but never joined the people in their agitation, were the people's deadliest enemies'.[5]

Nevertheless, these three forms of activity were far more restricted in France. The press was less extensive and under much stricter control. Petitions were a less central focus of campaigning, only systematically developed by Cabet in the 1840s, and the later radical campaign against the 1850 electoral law secured 500,000 signatures.[6] But the greatest difference was over public meetings, for in France any meeting not of an authorised association was illegal. The period of political freedom in 1848 was very short-lived, and the Empire banned any meeting without prior authorisation. The law of 1868 did change this, and 'it was in the dance-hall, at the Waux-Hall, behind the Waterworks garrison, that on Sunday 28 June 1868, the workers regained possession of the right to meet and discuss their interests'.[7] In a veritable wave of meetings, especially the 933 'non-political' ones held in Paris, political topics were in practice discussed.[8] But this situation was untypical of the period as a whole, and radicals had to operate within severe constraints, and adapt to a situation where open meetings were not possible.

## Meetings

Meetings helped people to constitute themselves and make others see them as groups. They gave participants a feeling of strength, and enabled them to set the boundaries of the general lines of policy and confer a mandate on leaders by applause or hooting.

Since radicals largely replicated forms of campaigning already established within the political system, the reason why public meetings, including outdoor ones, were so prevalent in Britain, was that parish vestry, township, town, and county meetings were established and legally and officially sanctioned institutions, in practice open to anyone.[9] 'It has been the practice of the people of England', said the radical MP John Fielden at the great Chartist meeting at Manchester's Kersal Moor, 'from time immemorial, to assemble in large numbers, to make known their grievances to the nobles and rulers of the people, and to demand redress.'[10]

This British peculiarity was brought home to the Chartist leader, O'Connor, on a tour of the Continent in 1845.

> Even now, in the midst of the most degrading slavery, we possess advantages which no other people in Europe do possess – the advantage of meeting and saying what we like, without more danger than the chance of being prosecuted for sedition, which, although bad enough, the Lancaster triumph has put out of fashion . . . In no other country do the people meet.[11]

Radicals in France had to explore alternatives to public meetings. They could risk meeting in secret, and Lyons radicals during the July Monarchy met in groups of twenty to thirty in the open air in summer and in workshops in winter, and in provincial towns it might be best to meet in suburban townships, or villages, where there was less control.[12] Republicans in the early 1830s, alongside petitions, associations for such specific purposes as a free press, patriotic subscriptions (to pay press fines or support Polish refugees), lotteries, and balls, used dinners (*banquets*) which involved 'toasts' that were in fact speeches, as a way of evading the ban on meetings.[13] Political dinners were also a well-established phenomenon in England, and with the repression of radicalism and meetings after Peterloo in 1819 there was an upsurge in radical dinners and toasts.[14] Early Chartism also had public dinners, but after 1839 they tended to give way to tea parties, soirées, and balls, which were cheaper, alcohol-free, and involved the whole family, although the first joint events between London Chartists and foreign political exiles in the mid-1840s took the familiar continental form of dinners or suppers.[15] In 1840 the French republicans ran an ineffective campaign of dinners in favour of electoral reform,[16] but in 1847 members of the liberal opposition organised a more extensive series, and radicals then joined in with dinners of their own. But it is a measure of the novelty and unfamiliarity of extra-parliamentary meetings that many members of the opposition held aloof from this dinner campaign because of its 'seditious' nature, and total attendance at all seventy dinners came to fewer than 100,000. With the repression after the June Days and then the law of 1849 against clubs and meetings, it was dinners that the reds concentrated on, until this device was in turn virtually stamped out.[17]

The ban on public meetings in France could also be evaded by outdoor demonstrations, which were allowed as long as they dispersed when told to by the legal authority, in a procedure similar to the English Riot Act, and there were adaptations of traditional occasions such as welcomes to visitors to the city, as with Lafayette on his tour of 1829, or accompanying the departure of individuals or groups, as with radical volunteers leaving to fight for freedom abroad. But these actions were steadily contained, and a much harsher law of 1848 made the legality of any open-air demonstrations very marginal.[18] By the latter part of 1849 republicans had been deprived of most means of public expression, but where they kept their popular support they were still able to employ other activities as demonstrations of radical strength. Thus in Lyons they organised large public dinners on the anniversaries of the first French Republic, the execution of Louis XVI, and the 1848 revolution; large civil burials with long processions through the streets; dancing and singing around liberty trees; burning symbols of their political adversaries; and processions with a boy representing the 'Man of the People'. Radicals also took advantage of traditional and folkloric outdoor occasions such as rough music (*charivari*), Carnival, and fairs. Far from revealing a 'traditionalist' mentality, it was a tactical choice when other forms of expression were closed down, and when the authorities then moved to check these forms as well, they ended, again not a sign of a transformation to a 'modern' mentality, merely another tactical choice.[19]

In the 1850s, when radical dinners, election meetings, café discussions, demonstrations, songs, shouts, red ties, and Phrygian caps were all repressed, republican groups would meet every anniversary of the 1848 revolution for a simple dinner, and in 1853 the Croix-Rousse weavers stopped their looms for a short while on that day. Republicans in Paris organised processions at the funerals of republican heroes or symbols, and even at those of their relatives, as for Ledru-Rollin's mother in 1852; Marrast, Arago, and Raspail's wife in 1853; Lamennais in 1854; and Beranger and Cavaignac in 1857.[20] Funerals were very impressive forms of demonstration, and were used by London trade unionists in 1834 to evade the ban on meetings on Sundays, and by Chartists.[21] In the 1860s republican students and workers in Paris held demonstrations at the tombs of republicans such as Manin, Godefroy Cavaignac, and Baudin (a deputy killed while resisting the *coup d'état* in 1851, a demonstration at his newly discovered tomb clearly putting into question the origins of the regime). Trials of republicans were another form of publicity, as they were among British radicals, and the performance of defence lawyers such as Favre, Gambetta, and Ferry made their radical reputations. Radicals then went on to organise civil burials as anti-clerical and hence anti-Imperial demonstrations, and in January 1870 100,000 angry people attended the funeral in Paris of the journalist, Victor Noir, murdered by the Emperor's cousin.

Meetings were thus more central to politics in Britain, where the right of meeting was regarded as a much more fundamental right than in France, where it was not a concern of the liberal, Orleanist, or republican opposition, who did not include it in their list of 'necessary freedoms'. It was regarded as much more of a working-class concern, the chief demand of the Paris trades' delegates in 1867 being the right of meeting (mainly to discuss trade questions), while the 'labour' candidate in the 1863 election, Jean Blanc, stood for free public and private meetings.[22] When public meetings began under the law of 1868, the republican press joined in the criticism and distrust of 'these gatherings of workmen'.[23]

The contrast between Britain and France lies not only in the much greater importance of public meetings in the former, exemplified by the occasional use in France of the English word 'meeting',[24] but also in the much greater extent of outdoor political activity there, and the less alarm aroused by it. The great Chartist procession that in 1842 in London accompanied the National Petition to Parliament, passed through such fashionable streets as Oxford Street, Regent Street, and Pall Mall, and

in many places the procession was greeted with immense cheering from the assembled multitude, and with waving of handkerchiefs, &c. from the windows and house-tops. Omnibuses and cabs sported the tricolour; and all seemed to be aware of the respect due to such a demonstration of the party of the people. The balconies of the various club-houses in Pall Mall and its neighbourhood were crowded with Members of Parliament and other persons of distinction.[25]

The French exile, Louis Blanc, who thought that the orderliness of the 1853 Preston strike was impossible anywhere else than England, was surprised at the tone of the great Reform demonstration in London at the opening of Parliament in February 1867, with its banners and bands, and Reform cigars on sale.

What gave the demonstration a somewhat English appearance was the humour that was to be seen in the choice of certain inscriptions and incidents in the machinery. The shoemakers, for instance, making a pun on the word 'last' (shoemaker's last), implying that they desired a Reform which should be the last. Quibbles and puns of this kind were numerous, and contributed in no small degree to efface what in the movement might have been considered as threatening in the minds of alarmists . . . People smiled – People cheered.[26]

In fact, however, French demonstrations were not necessarily disorderly and were equally disciplined, drawing on familiarity with established forms of open-air activity, such as benefit society, *compagnonnages*, religious, Carnival, and fair processions. It was not that French demonstrations were more disorderly, but that they were feared more, partly through that fear of the lower orders referred to in the previous chapter, and as authority was restored in 1830, 1848, and 1871, they were quickly stamped out, such hostility itself rendering them more threatening and seditious. However, there was also much disapproval in Britain of popular public meetings as rowdy and disorderly, and vestry meetings were often the sites of ferocious battles over church rates and the targets for capture by radicals. Like other continental observers, Blanc was unduly impressed by the freedom and harmony of British politics, for in periods of great political tension, the atmosphere was far less relaxed, and in the latter part of 1839 and 1848, all Chartist open-air activity was checked.

Public meetings were often very structured and ritualised, with a stress on unity and therefore compromise.[27] This is particularly true of the open-air meetings, particularly in the earlier part of the period. Much popular life took place out of doors, and, in the age-old tradition of the *agora*, one went outside to find out what was happening in the world, but whereas in France there were only indoor public meetings and open-air demonstrations, in Britain the two were combined in distinctive structured public meetings held in the open air, with previously arranged chairmen, speakers (who could not always be heard), resolutions, and votes. Chartism came together as a platform movement, for meetings were a crucial element in radicalism, and could be great events of unity, drawing people from miles around, as with the blind basket-maker who walked ten miles to a meeting in Swansea to adopt the People's Charter.[28] The relationship between crowd and speaker could be extremely intense. The Reform League did not attract much public attention until it began its great open-air meetings, especially the huge one in Trafalgar Square on 2 July 1866, initially banned by the police who were forced to give way, and attended by about 60,000. This was quickly followed by the great demonstration to Hyde Park, and the League, now much more confident, expanded its activities in the country for the rest of the year, and a series of monster meetings in provincial towns and cities gave the Reform movement a huge momentum and galvanised working-class opinion.

All public meetings had a large participatory element, mainly through expressions of approval and disapproval, but organised public meetings, with speakers and resolutions arranged beforehand, were very different from, for instance, the spontaneous, give and take character of regular

Sunday meetings at Hyde Park, Clerkenwell, Green or Bishop Bonner's Fields in London, where Charles Bradlaugh established his reputation, or from the indoor public meetings in Paris at the end of the 1860s, where unity was increasingly achieved by shouting down opponents, making the occasions like popular theatres. But the large British set-piece outdoor meetings seeking extensive popular involvement also embodied other aspects of popular culture, with their fairground atmosphere, side-shows, and entertainments, and sellers of gingerbread and other wares. Mass meetings were the essential element in the British radical strategy of mobilising and uniting the people as an irresistible force against their oppressors, and this, together with a conviction that the authorities would not concede power peacefully and were ready to use violence, and the consequent need for the people to be armed against attack, gave the early Chartist meetings, especially the armed and night-time torchlight ones, an unmistakable air of confrontation, polarisation, intimidation, and menace. After the defeat of 1839 armed meetings ceased, as we have seen, and although public meetings remained a key element in Chartist activity, the tone changed. Renewed defeat in 1848 meant the death of the policy of the mass platform, so much so that when it reappeared in 1866–7, it was seen by some not as the revival of an earlier tactic but the importation of an American one. But despite all these changes and fluctuations, all radical public meetings throughout our period, with the exception of a few non-Chartist ones in 1848, even the very largest (which necessitated a very large amount of planning and organisation) and the most excited, generally acted as *checks* to disorder and rowdiness, and there is a great contrast between organised radical and Chartist meetings and demonstrations, with their great efforts to avoid violence or saturnalia and consequent ridicule and criticism, and the direct action of election, anti-Poor Law, or Sunday trading riots.[29] Thus by the 1860s some French liberals saw English public meetings as a force for order and stability.[30]

There was, however, a long-term development in Britain inimical to outdoor political meetings. While the phenomenon of public meetings grew originally out of participatory elements in the Constitution, these were gradually closed down, with the introduction of multiple votes according to property in vestry and Poor Law elections, the incorporation of towns into municipal boroughs with an electorate in effect smaller than the parliamentary one, and the decline of township and town meetings.[31] Public meetings became mainly privately arranged, and at the same time there was a steady move away from outdoor to indoor meetings, perhaps latest of all in London. Indoor meetings were free of the weather and also had a more closed nature, in that only people who wanted to go there did so, for one did not end up there by accident, and it was possible to keep out undesirables and easier to maintain order. This, of course, depended on the availability of meeting places, which was often a difficulty for popular radical groups, as premises were often refused or too costly. Plans in London in 1840 and the mid-1860s for a 'Trades' Hall' and for a central meeting-place in Paris in 1848 all came to nothing, and radical premises were not usually preserved for long. Nevertheless, public meetings became more private or specialised, particularly with ticket-only meetings, which became by the 1860s a general British tactic.[32] Dilke's republican campaign in 1871 resorted to ticketed indoor meetings to keep out monarchist mobs.[33] This tended to reduce the fairground and entertainment tone of meetings, and render them more specialised as well as exclusive concerns.

Paralleling this, a number of radical leaders came to disapprove of outdoor meetings and demonstrations as open to disruption and high-jacking by enemies or trouble-makers, inevitably attended by criminals, and bringing on radicals the stigma of rabble. The Chartist Executive in 1844 condemned outdoor meetings as dangerous and ineffective, and the disturbances that arose at meetings in London in 1848 caused Chartists to despair at 'the ruffians committing depredations' and 'the bad odour into which all meetings of the working class have been thrown by the very unwise policy of certain political agitators'.[34] While the trades and trades' delegates organised the demonstrations in Paris of 25 and 28 February, 17 March and 16 April, many of the leaders of political clubs opposed street gatherings, or the plan in June for a great open-air People's Dinner, as easy prey for reactionaries and because it was impossible to keep such large numbers orderly and calm, as the disaster of 15 May showed. 'The people begin to tire of the speeches, they are hungry, and it could well turn out that the society of the Rights of Man would not be strong enough to keep the movement orderly. The mission of the Society is to place itself between those who possess and those who suffer; it does not wish to provoke a crusade of the poor against the rich, but to organise legally a fair restitution. When the masses are in the street, it only needs a few ill-intentioned people to rouse them and provoke terrible events; it is a very dangerous game which must not be risked too often.'[35] In June 1848 working men did grow tired of the long harangues at the remaining clubs, and the efforts to limit participation by imposing an agenda and to discipline discussion, and took to gathering in the streets and squares, especially the Place du Panthéon, numbers of them shouting for the 'little Louis' (Napoleon).[36] Outside gatherings were seen as a characteristic of working people. The French 1868 law stipulated that public meetings must be indoors, and, despite the turbulence and extremism of the meetings, a few people thought they still acted to reduce disturbances by concentrating radicals in a small number of supervised locations and ending street disorders, although in fact the difficulty of getting rooms did lead to street disturbances which the ultra-radical *Marseillaise* nevertheless took care not to report. In contrast to Paris, there were few public meetings in Lyons. 'The Lyons socialists instead of meeting in the great noisy assemblies, with all the revolutionary ostentation in use elsewhere, organised small meetings in each trade',[37] and even the radical demonstrations there in 1870 did not invade urban space in the same way as in 1848.

Open-air demonstrations and meetings were thus a divisive issue among radicals, supported usually by more plebeian groups than by the propertied, partly because it was more difficult for the former to secure indoor premises. Moreover, urban development put pressure on urban space. However, the growth of indoor and ticketed meetings represented not a taming of popular politics but a recognition of its untameability and the worries at a lack of popular support; outdoor activity remained common and contest over public space remained important in politics. Thus, despite the disciplined and structured nature of open-air events, popular radical resentment in Britain at exclusion from access to public places such as streets, open areas, or parks, which was seen as an attack on popular liberties and a denial of ancient rights and birthright, could polarise opinion and promote confrontation and disorder in defence of rights under attack, as in the Birmingham Chartist Bull Ring clashes in 1839. It was not the meetings themselves but the suppression of London Chartist meetings on Stepney Green, London Fields, and, especially, Bishop Bonner's Fields in 1848 and, even more, in 1852 that provoked disorder. By the 1860s the royal parks had become particularly important as the remaining places of meeting, and efforts to check meetings here were a source of great contention. The fighting arising out of Irish attacks on meetings in Hyde Park in 1862 in favour of Garibaldi led the police to forbid the use of London parks for public meetings and thereby arouse radical protests, for 'a Hyde Park meeting is the *ultima ratio populi* – it is the right to hold them we cannot surrender'.[38] Since nearly every patch of open ground in the metropolis could be classified as a 'park', it was seen as a move against any out-door public meeting in London. Matters came to a head in 1864 after the triumph of Garibaldi's welcome to London and the anger at the government for cutting short his visit to England, when the police stepped in to disperse a protest meeting on the issue at Primrose Hill, the bitterness intensified by the fact that an earlier meeting there to celebrate the Shakespeare Tercentenary, participated in by many of the same people, was allowed (though the use of Hyde Park was forbidden). Edmund Beales, the leader of the pro-Polish agitation in 1863, now fused the two issues of support for Garibaldi and defence of the rights of assembly into a radical campaign, and because there was no overall authority ruling London, the issue was a contest between an unjust government and the people's ancient, constitutional rights. It was in this parks campaign that the first proposals were made to establish a new political organisation, which led to the Reform League.[39]

After the League was founded in February 1865, Beales, its president, resisted pressure for big open-air demonstrations, and the first was not until May 1866, and because of its open-air character, not one of the MPs invited came. A group of Chartists led by Lucraft ran a series of public meetings on Clerkenwell Green and then forced the pace by moving them to Trafalgar Square, so that the Executive had to step in and take over their running. The issue came to a head when the new Conservative government that came into office after the defeat of the Liberal Reform Bill and resignation of the Liberal government, was seen as adopting a new oppressive parks policy and police terrorism in line with its Peterloo traditions. The League decided to expand its successful policy of large open-air meetings by holding one in Hyde Park, and persisted when the government forbade it, in a direct test of strength. A section of the multitude forced its way in, and for three days crowds overran the park and clashed with troops and police. This Hyde Park affair transformed the situation of the Reform movement, for it made the League's reputation and it was now that its branches multiplied. Moreover, the National Reform Union also took a very strong anti-government line on the issue, and this made possible united Reform demonstrations. John Bright now toured the country condemning the police action as war against the people, moved closer to manhood suffrage, and established himself as the figurehead of the Reform movement, appearing on Reform League and Reform Union platforms alike and calling for unity. The usual pattern in the monster meetings late in 1866 was for a large parade in the afternoon through the streets to the town hall or to a large park, a large outdoor meeting with several platforms proposing identical resolutions, and then an indoor meeting in the evening. It was at the last that Bright would speak, taking care to give copies of his speech to the press reporters.

In February 1867 the League held a great demonstration on the day Parliament opened. It decided to hold the meeting in the Agricultural Hall so as to avoid an outdoor challenge to the government and thus alienate support, but this was preceded by a huge procession from

Trafalgar Square to the Hall which, despite Blanc's favourable impression, spread alarm and was opposed even by the radical press. A new stridency in the League at the inadequate Conservative Reform Bill in March led to weekly Trafalgar Square demonstrations, against the reluctance of Beales and the secretary, Howell, and the climax to the Reform campaign came with another confrontation with the government over a Hyde Park demonstration. The League decided, again against the wishes of Beales and Howell, to hold a meeting in the park on 6 May, and, when the government banned it, the weekly meeting of London delegates voted to defy the ban, despite efforts by MPs to the contrary. The authorities gave in, and in a great triumph, several hundred thousand people entered the park to take part in ten meetings. Soon after, liberals secured the rejection of the government's new Royal Parks Bill.

It was the continued lack of indoor premises that forced Beales and Odger to use open spaces in their election campaigns in 1868–70, and there was more opposition and defiance in the early 1870s to unsuccessful attempts, this time by the new Liberal government, to restrict meetings in the public parks, and in the 1880s one of the issues dividing radical clubs from the Liberal Party was again the use of the parks, the issue not free speech as such but open-air meetings.[40]

### Elections

Public meetings overlapped with elections. In France, most extremely under the Second Empire, there were concerted efforts to make voting a substitute for politics. The established norms of extra-parliamentary agitation in Britain militated against such a situation, but there was nevertheless a tendency to confine politics more and more to elections, a process resisted by popular radicals with their constant campaigns and stress on participation. The Anti-Corn Law League in its later phase set the model for subsequent single-issue pressure-group campaigns focusing on the electorate alone.[41] Similarly, after the defeat of the mass platform methods of 1838–9, O'Connor tried to lead the Chartists into greater participation in electoral activity. Moreover, elections in Britain were often such important, outdoor occasions, involving such large proportions of the local population, voters and non-voters alike, that they provided opportunities for radical action in which the actual result of the poll was not necessarily the chief concern. As meetings tended to become more specialised and exclusive, this meant that groups without the means or support to run meetings of their own, often tried to take advantage of public meetings called by others, as at meetings in London in 1855 and 1857 over high bread prices or restrictive poor relief policies.

This was why many disapproved of open-air meetings, as we have seen. As vestry and other official public meetings declined, elections were left as the chief official public gatherings, and Chartists, particularly with the decline of the movement after 1842, used the excitement, interest, and numbers generated by the hustings to reach an audience and public they could not otherwise attain. This was particularly true of the general election of 1847. Radicals and Chartists would often stand, appear, and speak at the hustings to the crowds gathered, but withdraw before the actual poll with its exclusive electorate. Similarly, the two-stage process in French elections under the Empire enabled ultra-radicals to stand in the first stage of the 1869 general election without any chance of affecting the run-off stage, and thereby gain much wider attention and public. Thus the peak time for the Paris public meetings of 1868–70 was the election period of May–June 1869, when attendances were larger and real popular mobilisation was achieved. The by-elections in November were even more passionate, especially the election of the ultra-radical hero Rochefort, a success which encouraged radicals into stronger criticism of the Empire.[42]

The legality of elections and election meetings was also an important attraction for radicals as a means of open activity and publicity. This was especially so in France, once universal suffrage was gained (interest in general elections during the July Monarchy was low, but republicans did use National Guard elections in some towns).[43] With the clamp-down on political meetings and clubs in the repression after June 1848, radicals focused on electoral committees and meetings as legal forms of operation, and the June 1849 law against clubs still allowed meetings during a twenty-day election period, until this concession disappeared in 1850.[44] Electoral meetings were tolerated again in the 1863 election, even though few were actually held. The 1868 public meetings law also allowed electoral meetings, and in 1869 200 electoral meetings were held in Paris to make this the first ever free electoral campaign of the regime.[45]

But while election meetings had the advantage of legality, freedom and numbers, they were also much more likely than more exclusive meetings to result in disorder. While demonstrations and set-piece meetings stressed unity and consensus, elections did the opposite. The first armed clashes under the Second Republic were at the end of the elections of April in Rouen and Limoges, while May–June 1869 was not only the peak period of Paris public meetings, it was also a time of street disorders.[46]

Elections were also an important stimulus to political organisation, but this had an episodic character, as in the short-lived republican associations that were established during the July Monarchy in the course of elections, especially local ones. After the February revolution, political unions and clubs proliferated in Paris and some other cities. The earliest in Paris were formed around established radical figures such as Cabet, Raspail, Blanqui, and veterans of the Society of the Rights of Man, but a group around Barbès soon established an electoral committee which became the Revolution Club, and the vast majority of the many clubs formed in Paris were local, neighbourhood, and not always radical organisations, mainly concerned with the elections, first of National Guard officers, and then of representatives in the Constituent Assembly. Because they were temporary, *ad hoc* organisations, the great decline in the number of clubs after the April election was predictable. Attempts to federate clubs were also temporary in relation to this election and the June by-elections.

After the traumas of June 1848, the group around Ledru-Rollin tried to rally all Paris radicals in a united campaign for the September by-election, in which Raspail was elected (though, being in prison, he was unable to take his seat), and they then went on to organise the national organisation, Republican Solidarity, to work for the election of Ledru-Rollin as President. This strategy failed, as we have seen, in that some ultra-radicals formed a rival organisation which chose Raspail as a rival anti-presidential candidate. However, the landslide victory of Louis-Napoleon and the dissolution of Republican Solidarity by the government provoked effective radical unity for the April 1849 election. Radical organisations also tended to reappear at subsequent elections, and temporary organisations for elections were also a feature of the Empire. The National Guard Federation and the Central Committee of the Twenty Districts, which played such key roles in the Paris Commune, both originated in the 1871 election.

The connexion between political organisations and elections is also clear in England, as in organisations to secure the elections of Odger and Dilke in 1869. It is illustrated by the Reform League itself. While this grew out of the campaign over meetings in the public parks, the real impetus for a new association in 1864 came from the expectation of general election. The effort was therefore begun, under Beales, to establish a new political organisation to launch a national movement to make manhood suffrage, or at least a significant extension of the vote, an issue at the forthcoming election.[47] This movement dried up when an election did not transpire, although similar considerations did lead other established groups of reformers, based particularly in Manchester and

Bradford, to set up a National Reform Union, which followed the Anti-Corn Law League model of ticketed indoor meetings and electoral machines.

The London movement was resumed in February 1865, when an election was clearly not far away, and the new Reform League's address to trade unions was concerned with action in the coming election. The League was, of course, to develop into much more than an electoral organisation, and was pressed into outdoor campaigning. It was the great change in the situation in the middle of 1866, after the failure of the Liberal Reform Bill, the parliamentary insults of working people, the liberation of Gladstone from the restraints and compromises of office, and the advent of an anti-Reform Conservative government whose repressive tendencies seemed revealed in its Hyde Park policy, in a context of economic distress and industrial disputes in the north, that the Reform League, National Reform Union, and Bright had to adapt to growing plebeian pressure and co-operate in a series of great outdoor demonstrations, even though, as we have seen, Bright confined his speeches to indoor meetings. After the modified Conservative Reform Bill was passed in 1867 and political excitement ended, the Reform League reverted again to an almost entirely electoral temporary organisation.

Elections and electoral organisations were local and episodic. While there was a tendency for them to become more important and permanent in Britain, this was far less true of plebeian groups, for whom elections were a smaller part of politics. It was mainly at the end of our period that concerted attempts were made at permanent working-class party institutions, and elections and electoral organisations could be relatively more important in France, where open political campaigning and activity was more difficult.

## The press

A radical journal in 1834 singled out the three democratic institutions in France as elections, the National Guard, and the press.[48] The importance of the press in British politics and political movements has already been noted, and with the continual growth of the 'fourth estate' throughout the period it played a crucial role in creating local, provincial, and party (especially liberal party) identities, and its political importance probably grew at the expense of other elements in the public sphere, such as meetings.[49] In 1841 Thomas Cooper found it impossible to keep Chartism alive in the Leicester area without a paper.[50] The more restricted situation in France and paucity of meetings made the press even more important, and the role of newspapers in the July Revolution, the subsequent abolition of press censorship, and the introduction of trial by jury for press offences were followed by an enormous growth of the newspaper press, both national and, especially, provincial, at first mostly political, to become likewise the 'fourth power'.[51] Only three of the important national papers supported the regime, and while a cheaper and more commercial and entertaining and less political press did develop in the capital, the unprofitability of the provincial press meant it was run for political reasons, and nearly all the papers were either legitimist or republican.[52] There was a bitter warfare between the new republican press and the government in the early 1830s, and much republican activity was focused on this activity, with subscriptions to finance newspapers, arrange defences at trials, pay fines and support imprisoned journalists, Cabet being the leading figure here.

Radical artisans read these liberal and radical papers, and large readerships were gained by some aimed at working people. However, newspapers were expensive to run, and their high price was an obstacle to large sales – one week the editor of the *Commonwealth* had to pawn his flat iron to be able to buy a candle so that he could finish the leading article.[53] The stamp duty on newspapers, the duties on paper and advertisements all raised the cost of English newspapers, which typically sold at 7d at the start of our period, far too expensive for a working man to buy. In addition, newspapers needed propertied bondholders to guarantee that taxes would be paid and seditious matter would not be included. It was radical condemnation of these 'taxes on knowledge', which put newspapers out of the reach of the poor, that was behind the sustained and courageous 'war of the unstamped' which in the early 1830s produced, distributed, and sold unstamped and therefore illegal highly political and radical periodicals, especially the *Poor Man's Guardian*, and supported the families of the hundreds imprisoned for the work.[54] Similarly, in France newspapers had to pay a heavy bond (*caution*) and a stamp duty, newspapers such as the republican *Glaneuse* were prosecuted for breaching their bond, attempts were made to evade it by producing papers at irregular intervals, while Raspail, after remodelling the Friends of the People, produced a cheap simply written press organ paying no bond or stamp duty and sold by street-vendors which led to so many imitators that the authorities were for a while helpless. The Rights of Man also produced very short cheap pamphlets, and republicans saw the spread of political information through the cheap press as the means of generalising radicalism and uniting the people to secure radical reform, for, as the *Poor Man's Guardian* declared, 'Knowledge is Power'. 'The press killed the Restoration which tried to destroy it; the new counter-revolution will perish at the hands of the repressed press which will blow up the detached forts of arbitrary legality.'[55]

This rapid spread of political ideas through low-priced publications was checked in France in 1834 by the Laws of September, which killed off the cheap radical press, while an act of 1836 in Britain, although reducing the stamp duty to a penny, did the same there. Laponneraye was imprisoned in 1838 for producing a newspaper without a bond, and while a loophole in the law enabled the *Atelier* to publish monthly without one, more frequent cheap journals were not possible in France or Britain – a fortnightly Llangollen Welsh-language penny paper being killed by the penny stamp in 1851.[56]

Thus it was that on the morrow of the February revolution, Blanqui's club put forward a list of demands which he considered essential for a truly popular and democratic republic. Alongside complete freedom of association and meeting, replacement of the entire magistracy, enrolment of all wage-earners in the National Guard, with a payment of two francs for every day of active service, and repeal of laws against combinations, they demanded complete freedom of the press, abolition of the bond and stamp and postal duties, free circulation for all printed works through the post, pedlars, or street-hawkers, freedom for anyone to engage in printing, and freedom of printers from any liability for works they produced.[57] The Provisional Government's abolition of the September Laws and the stamp duty, and suspension of the bond, unleashed a wave of periodicals, pamphlets, almanacs, and printed songs which played a big role in popular exposure to political questions. The group that for three months had been vainly trying to raise enough money for a bond were now able to start the daily *Représentant du Peuple*, which became the radical paper most widely read by working men. While later in the year the bond and stamp duty were restored, periodicals and other printed works played, as in England, a key role in extending radical ideas, despite multiple press convictions, and just as the cheap unstamped papers of the early 1830s had reached people hitherto unaccustomed to reading, so new socialist-democratic newspapers and propaganda became the first regular reading for many of the French labouring poor.[58]

During the Empire, of course, in contrast to the gradual removal of the remaining taxes on knowledge in Britain, the press was restricted and reduced to servility if not support. This changed with a new press law in 1868, which produced a new flood of newspapers and a barrage of criticism of the regime. However, suspensions and refusals of permissions to sell on public highways were used against the ultra-radical press, until the fall of the Empire in 1870 led to the freeing of printing and publishing, and the abolition of stamp duty and bond.

The contribution of the press to radicalism was enormous. Clearly the extent of literacy was important,[59] but both illiteracy and high prices were circumvented by newspapers being available at public and coffee-houses and wine shops, and by groups clubbing together to buy or hire them to be read aloud and discussed at workshops, clubs, or out of doors. Thus, among the tailors, 'in every shop they had the chief newspapers and periodicals of the day, and these were read to them while they were at work'. It was in recognition of these practices and with the aim of reaching a new and different audience that the cheap republican *Journal du Peuple* appeared in 1834, aimed at those deprived of these means of collective reading, 'at those in the little towns where artisans do not get into the sole reading-room in the place, at those in large villages where there is no reading club, above all at those in the countryside where there is neither club, circulating library, cafés or newspapers', and it hoped to be bought by individuals and 'not be lent, not pass from hand to hand'.[60] Few people bought newspapers for themselves alone, and the number of 'readers' was far greater than the numbers sold. The repeal of the stamp duty on newspapers in England in 1855 certainly put newspapers in the reach of more pockets and led to larger sales, but it may not have meant they reached a wider audience, rather that reading become less public and collective and more private and individual.[61]

The importance of the press lay partly in the relative importance of meetings and organisations, but it was not just an alternative to these for it had a symbiotic relationship with them. The press reported meetings and the activities of organisations, and organisations promoted the sale of the press, and radicals became newsagents and news-vendors specifically to assist the press. The *Poor Man's Guardian* and other unstamped papers reported the National Union of the Working Classes, which drew support from its involvement in support of the unstamped war, the *Northern Star* and Chartist movement mutually strengthened each other, and a number of Paris papers in 1848 were allied to particular clubs. The *Northern Star's* reports on Chartist activities in every corner of the country enlarged the market for its sales, just as Paris papers were bought by members of political clubs to read 'the reports of the speeches they had heard, especially of those they had given themselves'.[62] While the *Commonwealth* acted more or less as the organ of the Reform League in London, the League suffered in the north of England from a lack of press support and outlets, except for the *Leeds Express* of the ex-Chartist Carter, while the rival National Reform Union had a newspaper supporting it in nearly every town.[63]

Radical newsagents and bookshops often became radical rendez-vous and centres of discussion, and the network of agents and communication established in the circulation of unstamped papers was crucial to subsequent radical campaigns in the decade. The basis of Cabet's Icarian movement was the publication and distribution of the *Populaire*, with local correspondents collecting subscriptions, reading Cabet's works, distributing the paper, organising collections, petitions, and shareholders' meetings to discuss practical and doctrinal matters, and acting as local leaders. The *Northern Star* fulfilled a similar function for Chartism. During the Second Republic Cabet's methods were copied, and a network of local correspondents sold subscriptions and shares for radical papers, read copies aloud in cafés and clubs, and introduced travelling agents to local radicals. With the banning of Republican Solidarity and public meetings, local newspapers often became the organisational centres, frequently turning themselves into joint-stock enterprises able to hold meetings of shareholders. 'The role closest to that of the offices, committees and headquarters of the twentieth-century political "parties" was played throughout the nineteenth century by the editorial offices of the newspapers: permanent areas of discussion and sometimes of organisation.' With press liberalisation after 1868, provincial opposition newspapers and their vendors become again foci for agitation and election activity.

By employing radicals as part-time reporters, and by supporting a web of newsagents or booksellers, newspapers were maintaining a network of centres of radical activity, and by helping radical activists to combine earning a living with activity on behalf of radicalism, they were creating a group of nearly full-time radical politicians. Thus the two radical leaders of the Toulon shipwrights' strike of 1845, Arambide and Langomazino, became in the Second Republic agents for the Toulon *Démocrate du Var* and the Marseilles *Voix du Peuple* respectively, the latter becoming thereby one of the most important radical figures in the whole of south-east France. 'And indeed the chief role of the newspaper was really to give these activists, through employing them, an occupation which enabled them to subsist while doubling in political activity.'[64]

Another key role of the press lay in giving readers a sense of being part of a national movement. While political activity was, necessarily, local, as were most of the newspapers, truly national ones being very difficult to sustain – the *Réforme* only had about 2,000 subscribers, and the *Northern Star* was very unusual among Chartist papers – nevertheless local radical papers could, by reporting and commenting on events all over the country, help create a national perspective. This was especially if radicals were sent from the capital to edit provincial newspapers, for example O'Brien to Birmingham in 1831 and radicals from Paris in the 1830s and 1840s. The press was the closest thing to a national republican organisation.[65]

National movements, then, did not depend on national organisations, but on two other things. One was the press, the other was political leaders. The continued tendency to see politics in terms of personalities gave political heroes great significance and popularity and a central place in politics. Examples were General Manuel, the republican General Lafayette, Garibaldi, Palmerston, Rochefort, the Tichborne claimant, or Louis-Napoleon. Particularly important in England, as we have seen, was the 'gentleman leader', whose wealth enabled him to be independent of party, place, and patronage, who was incorruptible, gave up the privileges of his birth and sacrificed himself for the people. This theme was used by Hunt and especially O'Connor, who emphasised their sufferings in the cause of the people, including prison and danger of death, or by Ernest Jones, who sacrificed his legal career,[66] or by Edmund Beales, who, as president of the Reform League lost his post as Revising Barrister for Middlesex and thereby most of his legal practice.[67] Somewhat similar was the upper-class Romantic poet Lamartine, who in the 1840s went into total opposition to the government and regime, in the grand and verbally extravagant manner, for betraying its principles and selling out to the greedy, materialist rich, and he expressed a humanitarian, nostalgic, and sentimental concern over poverty. He became a popular hero, vast crowds gathered wherever he spoke, and in the 1848 election he was elected in no fewer than ten departments.[68]

While oratory was important for political leaders, as they used a melodramatic style of innate Manichaean conflict between good and bad (Michel de Bourges being another exemplar), the press was equally important in creating national heroes, O'Connor's *Northern Star* being a classic example, as it enabled him to address his readers, and report his suffering and efforts. Lamartine's speeches were not effective in the Chamber, but through the press they went down very well in the country, while Bright reached a national audience through the reports of his prepared speeches.

The adulation of such leaders could be very intense, with celebrations of their birthdays, releases from prison, or local visits, and they were the object of presents, ballads, music, songs, devotion, reverence, and gratitude. Henry Hunt, who was seen as having stood firm and almost alone for the people's full political rights at the time of the Great Reform Bill and as having been hastened to the grave by the people's ingratitude, was the object of a cult. An important factor in the rise of the *Northern Star* was the enclosure in some numbers of pictures of popular platform heroes such as Oastler and Stephens, while one number of the *Commonwealth* was completely sold out because it contained a portrait of Beales.[69]

Such leaders as Hunt played an essential role in drawing together local radical groups through their tours and public oratory and their status in the radical press. While the outstanding oratory of Henry Vincent spread Chartism in the West Country and South Wales, it was O'Connor who did more than anyone else to bring radicals together in a national Chartist movement in 1838, through his *Northern Star* and ceaseless platform activity. While such platform campaigns did not take place in France, the triumphal tours of the veteran republican Lafayette in 1824 and 1829 were important in developing a national liberal opposition to the Restoration. It was in the Second Republic that Ledru-Rollin emerged as a true platform orator, and the elections of 1849, in which he was elected in five departments and received more votes than anyone else, made him the national leader of the democrats. His exile, with Felix Pyat and other leaders, after June 1849, left Michel de Bourges and such other figures as Nadaud, Perdiguier, Lamennais and even Hugo, to sustain the socialist-democratic movement by their constant travels to provincial capitals where they made speeches, presided at dinners, and, if lawyers, defended radicals at trials.[70] Shortly before the 1863 elections the veteran republican Garnier-Pages toured sixty towns for dinners and private meetings in which he urged republicans to participate in the elections, and this was important in helping republicans come out into the open after years of fearful silence.[71]

The new radical hero in the 1860s was John Bright, whose platform oratory in 1866–7 showed continuity with earlier gentleman radicals and established him as an unrivalled agitator and demagogue who was above party, and his tours, with meetings that were like civic pageants, were a great boost to the Reform agitation. The chief beneficiary of this was Gladstone, but however extreme the adulation of political leaders might seem, it was never unconditional, and depended not only on rhetorical powers and public credulity, but also on empathy, message, and reputations based on actual behaviour. It thus tended to focus on people out of office who were more easily seen as independent, uncorrupted, and above faction, as Louis-Napoleon soon found on attaining office. He therefore sought when Emperor to present himself as separate from and above parties and politicians. By December 1869 there were even complaints that the newly elected Rochefort had become 'too distant from the meetings'.[72] Gladstone's status as a Reform icon was greatly assisted by his departure from office in 1866, and despite the enthusiasm for him in the 1868 election, much of this was dissipated after a couple of years in office, to be restored by renewed campaigns in the 1870s when out of office again.[73]

## Associations

Formal organisations such as the National Union of the Working Classes, Society of the Rights of Man, or socialist-democratic societies had a similar form, with weekly subscriptions, an elected general committee which provided resolutions for discussion, and the membership divided into classes of ten who met at the class leaders' residence. The local focus of radical political organisations, and the reliance of national movements on the press and national leaders rather than on organisation is emphasised by an examination of some of the national organisations that did occur. The basic story is one of the continuity of local radical groups, acting informally or as a series of successive formal organisations, for example educational associations, political clubs, co-operative societies, electoral or non-electors' organisations, and sometimes coming together in wider campaigns and even formally as branches of the National Charter Association, Republican Solidarity, or Reform League.

Early Chartism consisted of the coming together of existing radical groups and organisations in a national platform movement which reached a peak of intensity and emotion in late 1838 and 1839, with a near-millennial tone of optimism in which it was expected that the Charter would be gained very quickly, in a matter of months or even weeks. This reliance on enthusiasm and members meant that organisation was neglected. Total defeat led to a new rhetoric and to a reassessment of tactics, and the conclusion that it would take a long time, years of steady work, to gain the Charter, led to the formation at Manchester in 1840 of the first national organisation, the National Charter Association, which grew to incorporate most Chartist groups in the country.[74]

The National Charter Association expanded to over 400 branches by mid-1842, containing 50,000 members, and was able to organise two million signatures to a petition in 1841 for the release of Chartist prisoners, and three million to a second petition for the Charter in 1842. It was an impressive organisation, with membership cards and regular subscriptions, local branches each with their own elected secretary and committee (although this was not officially the case as branches were illegal), a five-man Executive elected annually by the whole membership, and an annual delegate convention. However, this formal framework is misleading. The reality and vitality of the local branches or 'localities' is clear, but members did not regularly participate in elections or pay subscriptions. It seems clear that most members did not renew their cards every quarter, as they should, but tended to buy a card once and not renew it. Having a card, 'this mark of integrity and worth', was not seen as an aspect of participating in the running of a national organisation but rather as a declaration of allegiance and an assertion of where one stood, much like signing the National Petition. The National Charter Association address in December 1840 stressed that its main aim was the diffusion of political knowledge, and a member of the Executive defined that body's duties as concentrating Chartist energies, creating unanimity and allaying divisions, managing the finances, giving aid to Chartist victims, and creating a favourable public opinion by appointing lectures and spending most of the time acting as travelling missionaries.[75] The Executive thus administered the association and had a largely educational role of enunciating and elucidating the principles of the Charter. What it did not do was devise policy or consider strategy. Below the level of the Executive, the National Charter Association had district councils, composed of delegates from localities of the area, and these seem to have been more regularly supported financially, but, again, their main role was to organise corps of lecturers for the area, and indeed the NCA was often remembered as a lecturing association.[76] The National Charter Association was therefore a rather loose national organisation, its structure consisting of a remote Executive with administrative, financial, and lecturing functions, a stronger group of regional councils organising missionary work, and a very large number of very active localities. But these localities engaged in a mass of activities that were mostly not directly related to Chartism or to its political programme. There were lectures, debates, evening and Sunday classes, religious services, balls, soirées, outings, river excursions, band recitals, magic lantern displays, dramatic performances, co-operative stores, benefit societies, and choirs. Thus political, religious, educational, cultural, and convivial activities were mingled, and 'as much as possible of human life was being taken into working class movements'.[77] In many of these activities families were involved. Such social activities were always likely to reveal themselves in popular movements and could act as diversions from the official purpose. The very successful social festivals and choir (social harmonic society) were an attraction at Robert Owen's Institution in the early 1830s, but, by popular request, lectures on social science were changed to ones on natural science. Later, the branches of the Owenite Rational Society not only resisted Owen's paternal system in favour of democracy, but also engaged in a varied range of cultural activities, the educational classes studying not only Owenism but science, phrenology, the brain, and electrical theory. There were worries that these activities might be a diversion from the Owenite message, and it is a measure of O'Connor's strength as a popular leader that he encouraged all the Chartist social activities as long as they stayed within the framework of the National Charter Association. Here he can be contrasted with Cabet, who was faced with a similar growth of local group activities, including night schools, libraries, discussions of works, dinners, celebrations, songs, Sunday outings, games, and the participation of women and children but, unlike O'Connor, adopted a far more negative attitude to such activities and tried to restrict and control what was done.[78]

The formal element of national organisations should not be exaggerated, and it is better to think of the continuing local radical groups and centres as being loosely associated in a national movement. At the end of 1848 the French radicals set up two national organisations to carry out the familiar radical practices, with very limited central control or co-ordination. One, European Democratic and Social Propaganda, organised the national distribution and sale of newspaper subscriptions, cheap books, pamphlets, engravings, lithographs, songs, drawings, portraits, busts, cartoons, statuettes, medals, and medallions.[79] The other, Republican Solidarity, was established as the first national radical organisation in France, with the aims of electoral activity, support for the radical press, promotion of education, provision of defence in trials, and distribution of literature. By the end of 1849 it had 353 branches, with about 30,000 members, in sixty-two of the total eighty-six departments. But many of these branches had already existed as groups, and Republican Solidarity was really superimposed on a network of local political and literary clubs, electoral committees, and co-operative societies. While its condemnation and dissolution as a secret society removed any national leadership, the local branches and national links between them continued, though formal organisation was loose. 'In many communes, however, financial contributions were rare or non-existent, and organisational sub-units had at best symbolic significance.'[80] Since the most familiar and acceptable form of formal and regular subscriptions was in benefit societies, Republican Solidarity branches gave sick and unemployment relief as a way of securing regular financial contributions.[81]

In London, after the ending of the National Charter Association in 1859, there were a number of short-lived and loosely linked manhood suffrage associations, and the Reform League established in 1865 was really a coalition of already existing London reform associations, sects, groups, clubs, and trade organisations, meeting at public- and coffee-houses and secularist halls, and the rules recognised this by allowing the formation of autonomous branches and the affiliation of existing bodies. Early League lectures included old Chartists such as Mantle and Finlen, both already very popular in the metropolitan debating clubs and public meetings. As excitement grew, so did the number of branches, to sixty-seven at the end of 1866 and to over a hundred by the summer of 1867. But most of these had a stronger radical character than the leadership, and the Executive Committee condemned resolutions passed in the branches that did not adhere to League policy. The Clerkenwell and Holborn members operated autonomously in holding public meetings on Clerkenwell Green and in organising a church occupation in April 1867 to disrupt the sermon, and a number of Chartists and secularists pressed for mass demonstrations, mass petitioning, the National Convention, a general strike, and tax-refusal. The League was thus an *ad hoc* alliance of radical groups to secure parliamentary reform, and in the end leadership passed from the official Executive to weekly meetings of delegates from branches and trade and other societies, on the model of meetings begun by George Potter. Once parliamentary reform was gained, these various groups fell apart again, a number of the leaders going into worthy liberal causes and pressure-groups, such as those for national education and labour representation, while Odger organised the branches he had built up in Fulham and Hammersmith into a Working Men's Parliamentary Electoral Association which was the springboard for his electoral candidacy for Chelsea. However, others were engaged in activity in favour of causes disapproved of by most liberals, such as secularism, amnesty for Fenians, republicanism, and land nationalisation.[82]

The Reform League also spread into the provinces, first to Birmingham and then elsewhere, especially after the Hyde Park riots, to reach a total of 440 branches, but here again it built on existing radical groups and organisations. Non-electors' organisations in Coventry, Bradford, and Halifax, the Nottingham Reform Union and Wolverhampton Working Men's Liberal Association all become branches. A weak Manhood Suffrage League in Manchester also joined and became the nucleus of the Northern Department. In Leeds in 1866 the ex-Chartist leader of the advanced liberal party, Alderman Carter, joined with the Leeds Working Men's Parliamentary Reform Association to establish the Leeds Manhood Suffrage Association, which then joined the Reform League and became the Yorkshire Department. Late in 1866 the Northern Political Union in Newcastle became the North Eastern Department. (There was also a very weak Welsh Reform League formed at Denbigh.)[83] The branches gave the League the appearance of a national organisation, though most of them were small, run by local middle-class liberals and radicals, such as Walton in Brecon. Initially, the lecturers sent out by the League played a basic role, but few were sent after February 1867 as the branches were now doing their own work, for, despite the secretary Howell's voluminous correspondence, the Executive had little control over or regular contact with the branches, which remained very autonomous, with their own banners, flags, fly-sheets, pamphlets, and lectures. As in the NCA, many members merely paid an entry fee and no more subscriptions, and branches did not regularly pay dues to the departments, and even less to London. Thus in the country, also, the Reform League was basically a temporary *ad hoc* alliance in favour of parliamentary reform, which fell apart once this was gained, and branches dissolved or fused with liberal associations, especially for electoral campaigns.

Formal radical organisation was thus not very strong, and consisted more of an affirmation of unity, commitment, and fellowship, and served to create confidence and a set of traditions which, for example, enabled members of the National Charter Association in 1842 to feel strong enough to reject an alliance with Joseph Sturge's Complete Suffrage movement if it meant giving up the name of the Charter, something the Chartists of the 1850s were no longer able to do. But organisations were not necessarily identified with particular ideologies or programmes. Early Chartism built on earlier organisations, some of them radical associations formed as a result of O'Connor's tours between 1835 and 1838, others working men's associations founded by missionaries of the London Working Man's Association, but the latter were formed not in rivalry with radical associations but where these did not exist, and the quarrel between O'Connor and the London Working Men's Association in 1838 was not reproduced among the local radical and working men's associations.

Similarly, the Reform League was weak in Lancashire. The National Reform Union had already been formed in 1864 and had so taken the initiative, establishing strong roots in the Lancashire towns, and there-fore monopolising Reform organisation and sentiment and gaining extensive working-class support. This prevented a significant Reform League presence, which was confined to some small cotton towns (and even here the members were mainly shopkeepers and small tradesmen, not trade unionists or cotton operatives). There was little difference between the NRU and League branches, and even joint membership in some places.[84]

While there were only thirty-eight Reform League branches in

Lancashire, there were sixty-one in the West Riding where, apart from Bradford, the National Reform Union presence was much weaker, leaving the way clear for the Reform League. While there was certainly a stronger Chartist and manhood suffrage tradition here, as in London, this was not a clear dividing issue between the two organisations. At the conference that established the NRU in 1864, most of the delegates from outside Manchester voted for Beales' motion for manhood suffrage, while the Reform League included many members who were not committed to manhood suffrage, even in Yorkshire. This was also the case in Birmingham, where the Reform League was very large, strongly supported the mild Liberal bill of 1866, and co-operated closely with the Birmingham Liberal Association.

Political organisation was seen as a male preserve. Tommy Hepburn, the leader of the north-eastern miners in 1831–2, preferred formal trade union organisation of men instead of demonstrations which involved women who were usually prone to violence, and in the 1832 strike he urged the miners to stop their wives from 'interfering in matters which had nothing to do with them'.[85] Women were always prominent in direct action protest. This was most obvious in food riots, in which they might be more directly concerned, including those that took on a radical colouring, as at Metz in 1832. 'The women above all seem to have played a very big role in this affair; many were seen with tricolour flags marching to the tune of *the Marseillaise*.'[86] But Perdiguier recalled how in popular fury at Bordeaux over a death sentence on a soldier, it was the women who incited a rescue.[87] They could be important in neighbourhood pressures such as exclusive dealing or the pressure on people not to act as witnesses against radicals.[88] Women were very active in Lyons in the rising of 1831, the demonstrations and effigy-burning of 1848, and the civil burials and demonstrations of 1869–70. They were also prominent in anti-Poor Law riots, and while Plug Strikes in Lancashire in 1842 were very peaceful and orderly on the whole, there was some violence by women. In the June Days women were involved nearly as much as men, although very few were arrested, and they also played an important role in the 1851 rising, the Paris disturbances in May 1869, and on the Commune barricades.

Thus outdoor demonstrations, direct community-based political action, and violence involved women in a prominent role, and as organisation became more disciplined, structured, less open, and spontaneous there was greater male exclusiveness. Even though women might be involved in indoor and organised activities, it was in a more subordinate role. A London Chartist tea-party was a failure as the women would not come out because of the heavy rain, which might spoil 'the very nice dresses which even the democratic wives and daughters love to appear in'.[89] As this implies, women participated not independently but as members of male Chartists' families. It was not actually the strength of formal organisation that reduced the role of females, rather the development of more planned, structured, indoor, and exclusive activities, but the process was not complete, and outdoor demonstrations remained an important feature right to the end of our period.[90]

This paralleled the general weakness of party organisation, and extensive political organisation was thus not an important element of radicalism. Ambitious plans for premises, newspapers, or extensive activity were always checked by a lack of means. Even the Reform League received half of its income from donations, its activities were regularly hampered by lack of funds, and the dependence on middle-class donors made its failure to act independently in the 1868 election almost inevitable.[91] Radical strength could thus not depend on formal organisation, and lack of resources means that movements of the poor are usually unable to continue for long. This makes the actual extent of popular radicalism impressive. Despite the great variations in support for Chartism, its persistence as a national movement for ten years is astonishing. The socialist-democrats of the Second Republic had a shorter life only because of the armed *coup*. One of the most arresting demonstrations of popular radical strength was in Manchester in the Plug Strikes of 1842. These began among powerloom weavers in the Ashton area but spread systematically to other cotton towns, largely over wages and hours, Chartist leaders of the strike fairly uniformly opposing ideas of a general strike for the People's Charter. Yet when they spread to Manchester, a grass-roots movement among the Manchester trades, factory and non-factory alike, brought the city to a standstill in a general strike which, against the wishes of the local Chartist leaders, was a political one for the Charter, a lead then taken up in the other towns.[92] Clearly radicalism had other sources of strength than formal organisation, but general factors such as material distress or class-consciousness will not explain this. The press and public meetings had played their part, but they were not enough. As this chapter, and chapters 4 and 6 have argued, a variety of material and non-material concerns and activities were incorporated into plebeian radicalism, and the actual form of organisation and action depended very much on the political situation at the time. Political mobilisation was based on numbers at markets, church, or theatre, and on bloc recruitment, the incorporation of pre-existing groups that already possessed high degrees of group identity and extensive interpersonal ties, such as units in the National

Guard or national workshops, prison solidarities, trade societies, political clubs, educational groups, and clients of certain cafés and public-houses. These 'unpolitical' bases of radicalism were vital, and radicalism was largely unspecialised, incorporating social and convivial activities. Radical political activity had to be compatible with the demands of life, particularly work, family, and leisure. These could all be rivals and obstacles to radical action, but, as we have seen, work groups and organisations could be a basis for radical activities, and families could also be involved. Yet it was above all leisure solidarities and activities that needed to be incorporated within radicalism. When Saint-Simonians sought to proselytise workers, they found this was best done not through the workshops or trades but through education, friendship, neighbourhood and family ties, and the gospel of love. The remaining chapters examine how radicalism related to education, religion, and popular culture.

## Radicalism as education

Education is a particularly obvious element in and source of support for radicalism, because radicals constantly stressed its importance and advocated and promoted it. A rationalist contempt for a past full of the frauds perpetrated by self-seeking oppressors, and a belief that reformation could be achieved through transforming the people, meant education was of prime importance. It would enlighten the people, open their eyes to the abuses, oppression, and injustice of the present system, enable them to know their rights, make them aware of their true worth and power, and thus lead them to reject those who used tyranny, superstition, and fanaticism to preserve their unjust rule. Science had a key role in this, so that 'science and liberty are inseparable sisters. Tyrants have never been able to stifle one without the other.'[1] Once the people were enlightened, they would deem the present situation intolerable and, united in this conviction, their wish would be irresistible and the system would collapse. As a joiner in Aix sang in 1839:

> Know, great ones of the earth,
> That man is free when he wills.[2]

If ignorance was thus the obstacle to overthrowing tyranny, radicals could see their main work as educational. In 1848 'the political clubs are the fertile source where will come to imbibe those who lack the enlightenment necessary to accomplish fully the great work that is in preparation'. In the most extreme view, such educational activity could be seen as the *only* activity necessary. For as that uncompromising enemy of all political associations and mass campaigns, Richard Carlile, said: 'that is the great point to be ascertained. Do they read? Do they think? Do they enquire?' But the stress on education and enlightenment permeated all forms of radicalism, including insurrectionary ones.[3]

While it would serve radicalism that the people were as educated and informed as possible, it was in the interests of the rulers to keep the people ignorant, and 'one of the chief objects of the British Government and its supporters is to prevent the people from thinking'.[4] Repression of the press, booksellers, and libraries, and restriction of newspapers through stamp duty and bonds only reinforced the conviction that knowledge was power and ignorance favoured tyranny.

Education was thus a necessity and a right, and radicals pressed for its availability for all (women often included), irrespective of wealth and free of church or employer control. While this usually implied, as we have seen, schooling provision by public authorities, they were alive to the dangers of education controlled by the government, 'which is merely a lesson in the art of being slaves',[5] and favoured local, democratic control.[6]

The radical confidence that education could serve radicalism embodied liberal conceptions of progress, of rejection of superstitious fears, cruel sports, heavy drinking, and sexual laxity as characteristic of an older culture and time, and of support for sobriety, planning, and saving as the attributes of a modern, more stable age.

> Go it boys, the world's a-jogging,
> Freedom, it will out at last.[7]

Education and the spread of reason would reduce vice, greed, and social conflicts. 'The most ignorant nations are always the most wretched and depraved.'[8] The growth of civilisation lay through the supremacy of the rational over the 'animal' passions of man, and liberals in both Britain and France generally supported education and the extension of improving literature. 'What is education?' asked the *Northern Star*. 'It is the cultivation of the moral and intellectual faculties, and the depression of the baser propensities.'[9] The French hairdresser poet Jasmin affirmed that the people's duty is to be men in order to be free, and the stress on masculine independence, personal responsibility, progress, and moral reform was conveyed by the Chartist shoemaker, James Devlin:

> Choice have we, if we like, to work or play;
> And choice to choose the comrade of our side;
> We're neither slaves of time, nor must obey
> The growl of passion, or the fret of pride.[10]

Artisan autobiographies often express this sense of progress. 'When I look back on those days, and compare my condition and surroundings with the present time, it is like a peep into the Dark Ages.' This reference by the stonemason Henry Broadhurst was not to the 'hungry forties' but to the *1850s*. Partly the gains in their lifetime were material, but they also stressed the superstition and frightful stories of their childhood, the growth of education and available reading matter, and the decline of violence.[11] For them, progress was a lived experience, and they were particularly responsive to the liberal message of improvement, education, and the discarding of the past.

'Education, which gives man respect for his worth', was seen as a means of that self-respect that, as we have seen, labour leaders tried to foster or instil. 'Education will teach man his own value, and how to respect himself', 'it alone can elevate man, and make him conscious of his worth and understand his duties'.[12] Radicals tended to blame a lack of support for radicalism on the selfishness, egotism, and moral failings of the people as well as on their ignorance, saw education as a means of moral reform and both of these as enemies of bad government, and sometimes even insisted on a morality test for members of societies and the exclusion of roughs.

Not only liberals encouraged education, for rivalry between Anglicans and Dissenters in England and between liberals and clericalists in France led both sides to promote schooling, libraries, and cheap literature in order to enlarge their influence at the expense of each other, to encourage civilisation, and to check dangerous radicalism. Education was thus never an exclusively radical concern, but the provision was often ill conceived and ineffective, and therefore criticised by radicals, who also stressed that it should be really useful and include knowledge of their rights, and not be a means of indoctrination by the ruling classes. In 1831 Buchez pressed for a Workingmen's Athenaeum to remedy the defects of the existing courses put on for workers, for 'they seem to us in general rather removed from the Goal they set themselves, because they deal with material that is too difficult; because they are too often alien to the Needs and interests of those for whom they are Destined; finally because they omit important instruction'.[13]

Radicals thus set themselves educational tasks. The teacher, Armand Marrast, established in 1828 an Athenaeum providing free education and in 1831 became joint editor of the now republican *Tribune*. Other radicals in 1832 established a newspaper aimed specifically at working men.

To multiply the echoes of the *Bon Sens*, distribute it over the whole surface of France, pass from the towns to the countryside, accelerate the circulation of ideas and enlightenment, in step with the need that everyone feels today to enlighten and educate himself, such was the continual goal of our wishes and efforts.[14]

Radicals and republicans in post-July Revolution France supported not only a flourishing press and the publication of cheap books, but also an organisation that broke away from the liberal Polytechnic Association on the issue of dealing with political and social questions, and the new association, of which the radical deputy Cabet became organiser, was soon running sixty free adult classes, for men and women, in Paris. Cabet was also head of the Paris society for a free press.[15] In Lyons Saint-Simonians ran classes for workers in mathematics, and a dismissed republican teacher gave history lessons.[16] Raspail meanwhile was in Paris running a course at the Medical Union on organic chemistry, developing cellular theories which anticipated Pasteur and were acclaimed by an English Owenite as confirming Owen's doctrine of circumstances. Made president of the republican Friends of the People, Raspail conducted a series of purges of irresponsible hotheads and transformed its character. He introduced discussions on economic and moral questions, entrusted each member with the care and assistance of half a dozen poor families, including finding the means of education, and organised adult schools in different parts of Paris teaching singing, grammar, writing, arithmetic, history, and hygiene, as well as organising children's schools, practical classes, and a course of lectures on the French Revolution by Laponneraye. Laponneraye had already opened a free school for workers after the July Revolution, and now distributed free printed copies of his lectures to the 'working class'. Because the *Tribune* refused to act as the society's organ, Raspail also established a newspaper of his own, publicised through easy-to-read posters and sold in the streets. Students at his chemistry classes were recruited for the society, and when in prison he wrote a highly successful volume on agriculture for Hachette's series of books for primary schools.[17] Such work to combat the ignorance that served subjection was continued by the larger and more important Rights of Man. At section meetings newspaper articles, the 1793 Declaration of the Rights of Man, and the short pamphlets produced by the Central Committee were read out and discussed in the interests of political education, but members were also taught to read and write and whole sections participated in Cabet's education society. Some people, as we have seen, joined because of these educational activities.[18] At the same time, the National Union of the Working Classes in London, in addition to its weekly public meetings discussing resolutions drawn up by the committee, was, in the same way as the earlier London Corresponding Society, divided into classes which met each week for discussion and 'mutual improvement'.[19] Education was one of the chief activities in the Owenite movement, and radical educational and discussion groups were a recurrent phenomenon. Chartists also ran schools and Sunday schools for adults and children, circulating libraries, reading rooms, tract distribution, discussion groups, and educational lectures.[20] Similar activities were found in the Reform League and in the Second Republic, for example the free evening classes in Paris in 1848 that developed into a Popular Athenaeum running a library and holding courses in French history and geography, grammar, composition, arithmetic, the metric system, linear drawing, practical geometry, chemistry, physics, and hygiene.[21] In the 1860s an ex-teacher and a veteran of 1848, Jean Macé, author of many children's science books, joined with some liberal paternalistic industrialists, radical teachers, and co-operative leaders, and, with support from some authorities, launched a movement to found popular libraries. In 1866 he also founded an Education League which developed a dense network of educational clubs all over the country, with libraries, classes, exhibitions, and, especially, adult evening courses. Although he stressed the non-political nature of the organisation, it was backed by freemasons, Voltaireans, moderate republicans, radicals, socialists, and anti-clericalists and opposed by the church, and the clubs were vital centres of radicalism.[22]

The concentration on education was most evident when radicalism was in decline or suffering repression, for education and other cultural activities were safer activities less prone to suppression. One feature of periods of defeat and decline was a wish to learn from failure and the mistakes that had brought it about, one conclusion often being that the people had not been ready to achieve radical reform, had failed to see where their true interests lay, and had been easily led astray or been too concerned with 'sensual gratification'. They clearly needed educating and moralising to ensure victory in the future. Thus after the defeats of 1834 Raspail began a new daily journal, the *Réformateur* aimed at providing easy education for working men and children, consisting of elementary science, history, hygiene, arithmetic, geography, and chemistry.[23] After defeat in 1842 Chartists tended to drop notions of nation-wide agitation, their conceptions of strategy confined to how to respond to government or middle-class actions, their press seeing themselves as radical educators, not as the national, campaigning voices of a movement.[24] The same is broadly true of the French radical press after the June 1849 rising. In the 1850s French government purges of teachers and professors led them to open free schools, and radical liberals concentrated on enlightening the masses through schools and books, and avoiding the perils of overt opposition to the Empire.[25]

### Emancipation and distinction

But radical educational efforts only had an effect because of the response they met. While schooling for the children of poor families was often very defective, and parents' poverty meant that time spent there was limited, literacy did grow very fast, especially in the first two decades of the period, and parents were much more desirous of education for their children if they could afford it.[26] Radicals often argued that if the people had fair wages and enough time, they would see to their instruction.[27] But there was still also a demand for very basic and elementary adult education, as well as for more advanced and specialised tuition. Clearly the burgeoning book, tract, and periodical literature supplied by newsagents, booksellers, and lenders could exert political and moral influences, as could the schooling available, though people seem to have operated a large degree of choice over institutions they patronised. Radicals, philanthropists, religious groups, moral reformers, public authorities and commercial enterprises vied to meet this demand. Technical education for skilled workmen was one form particularly promoted and encouraged, and it received some radical and labour support as preferable to apprenticeship, although others saw it as a device to keep workers in their place and incarcerated in a trade.[28] But such educational institutions, like Mechanics' Institutions in Britain, were often inappropriately targeted and failed to meet working men's requirements, as well as being too costly, and there was clearly also a great demand among the working population for entertainment in their reading and education.

Thus education was not only a radical strategy and activity, it was also a means of recruiting for radicalism, though the reverse process was also possible – it was the 1848 revolution that filled the illiterate Truquin with a desire to learn; and while some people joined the Rights of Man because of its educational activities, it was *after* joining that the waller, Nadaud, not wishing to seem gauche among the students, set about educating himself. Nadaud later supplemented his earnings by opening a school for fellow-workmen, and used Lamennais' *Words of a Believer* and other radical works as texts. 'For, while giving my pupils the first notions of elementary education, I taught them to love the Republic and see this form of government as alone capable of gradually raising the people to the level of the other classes of society in both the moral point of view and in political and social rights.' He raised republican topics for discussion. 'What I was seeking was to educate myself and do harm to the government of Louis-Philippe whom we considered the chief author of our national shame and our poverty as workers.'[29] It was his quest for education that led the London cabinet-maker, William Lovett, to join a discussion society called 'The Liberals', and the radical and freethinking emphasis of the group was the beginning of his radical career.[30] Thomas Cooper also recruited Chartists at Leicester through his adult classes on current affairs, literature, history, and geography. Similarly, the growth of popular lecturing, no longer on dry scientific subjects and containing a large entertainment element, was reflected in the prominence of lecturing in the NCA. In Cooper's history lectures, as in the historical novels of Reynolds, a strong antimonarchical, political liberation content was combined with entertainment.

The impact of radical educational activities was thus not confined to the well educated, and the level must not be exaggerated. It is most clearly revealed in the lives of working men who became prominent radicals, and in those who wrote autobiographies. These reveal the awesome and heroic efforts and deprivations involved in finding the time and money to pursue their quest. For them, literacy led on to a love of books painfully acquired piecemeal, to voracious, compulsive, and often unsystematic reading, in spare time and at mealtime, and to going without food, efforts whose excesses led Perdiguier and Cooper to illness and breakdown.[31] The compositor Henry Vincent and the bookbinder Eugene Varlin acquired a passion for reading at their work, and Varlin's thirst for knowledge led to great sacrifices in youth that were followed, on his arrival in Paris, by attendance in 1860–1 at the free classes of the Philotechnic Association, and by further self-education, including the study of Latin, together with his partially paralysed brother. All this was made possible through avoiding alcohol and tobacco and buying only basic food and clothing.[32]

But we must never generalise from such people, or from what is revealed in autobiographies, as to the working-class experience in general, or to education and radicalism in particular. Writers of autobiographies were unusual men, and self-educated men were a small minority of the working population, in many ways separated and even isolated from the rest. Thomas Wright stressed the poor education and low literacy of his fellow-workmen, and how few had a real taste for reading, and saw the distinction between the educated and the uneducated as one of the central ones in the working population. Those that did read had usually begun with religious works because these had been the only ones available: the Bible, religious tales and commentaries, and, in France, lives of the saints. Some might then go on to the classic works of religious imagination such as *Paradise Lost* and *Pilgrim's Progress* in England and the *Imitation of Christ* in France (Lamennais' translation of this brought him an income for the rest of his life),[33] *Robinson Crusoe*, and (in France) a life of Napoleon. But most of those who continued reading went on to almanacs, broadsides and broadsheets, police news in Sunday newspapers, and cheap tales and (often serialised) novels, which might include Dickens, Dumas, Hugo, and, especially, Sue, but were mainly sensational, fantastic, or licentious, full of brigands, vampires, violence, murders, and rapes. Few were those who stuck to the 'classics', for example to Shakespeare, Milton, Corneille, Racine, Aesop, La Fontaine, Voltaire and Rousseau, or to newer poets such as Shelley, Byron, Hugo, or Lamartine.[34] Thus a turning-point came for Gilland, a self-taught smith whose great efforts to acquire things to read initially only secured cheap, obscene tales and serial instalments of great novels. Then 'one day I opened Jean Jacques and I was saved', and he went on to read the great moralists – Socrates, Marcus Aurelius, Vincent de Paul, and Fénelon.[35] Others were attracted more to science, for this was the golden age of the amateur scientist, second-hand scientific publications were readily available, and groups of working-class botanists, zoologists, and geologists walked in the nearby countryside, all seeking emancipation from folk superstition and ignorance and a discovery of the real world behind superficial appearances through the scientific investigation of natural phenomena.[36]

This pursuit of 'useful knowledge' was not the concomitant of the training and education required by craft skills, for the aim of the self-educated was not to become better workmen (though Odger did work for Goodyear and help him in patents for indiarubber boots and shoes) or necessarily to rise socially, but to acquire the freedom that came from knowledge and understanding of the world, and the enjoyment that followed. 'What pleasure study gives us!' wrote the weaver Magu.[37] As such, it could isolate such men from their fellows. 'When work was over for the day, my mates used to spend their evenings at the public-house. I used to go straight home and read Chamber's Journal.' The thirst for self-education could lead to a retreat into solitary privacy, to permanent tensions in relations with fellow-workmen, to the rejection of many of the features of popular culture, for example superstition and drink (although an alcoholic London bookbinder who died in 1861 read Latin and Italian works extensively). Thus Perdiguier gave up going on country rambles with his friends and instead went alone in the mountains, works by Voltaire in his hand.[38] The pursuit of knowledge was very much a minority tradition, but the difficulties in pursuing it and acquiring books could bring men together and establish very close friendships between 'readers' that were the basis of mutual improvement societies that rejected many of the prevailing elements in popular culture.[39] Thus much of the real demand for full education was met by groups of working men running things themselves,[40] compositors often prominent in such attempts.[41] Yet such groups could also be filled with a desire for the uplifting of their fellows through literacy and education, and be led to campaign for working-class access to education and culture through public schooling, access to libraries, Sunday opening of museums, and public exhibitions.[42]

Moreover, the distinctiveness of such men often gave them a position of standing among working people, just as the somewhat more educated café-keepers, publicans, shopkeepers and money-lenders could be leaders of local urban neighbourhood communities. Thomas Wright described how the few educated workmen, while regarded as haughty prigs because of their aloofness from much social activity and their dislike of the tone of life in workshop and locality, were nevertheless looked up to and regarded by their fellows, and referred to to decide disputes, write things, run meetings and associations, and act as their spokesmen. As readers and writers of letters, readers aloud of newspapers, local preachers, teachers, or doctors, they could become natural leaders and key figures in organisation.[43]

The pursuit of knowledge could be a way of coping with the insecurity of life and lead to escapism and a retreat from a world rendered unattractive. Yet the voracious reading of such people meant that the medley of ideas they assimilated included radical ones. Their sense of breaking with the past, the cult of reason and science instead of superstition and irrationality, their attachment to enlightenment and intellectual freedom, and their desire to understand society, could lead to freethinking and support for radical reform, and a rejection of middle-class cultural and educational control and institutionalised religion. Reading and discussing politics was a natural extension of the pursuit of knowledge. Thus many readers moved on to works questioning the established order, such as Moliere's *Tartuffe*, to the literature of the Enlightenment, particularly Voltaire, Rousseau, Volney, Paine, Godwin, or Dupuis, to histories of the Inquisition, French Revolution, and priestcraft, to the songs of Beranger, the poetry of Byron, Shelley (whose *Queen Mab* was a formative text of popular radicalism), and Burns, and to histories by Lamartine, Blanc, Michelet, or Quinet, especially with the development of publishers and booksellers specialising in radical works.[44] Applegarth became a radical through reading Chartist literature in America.[45] Self-improvement was thus an important element in radicalism, whether pursued individually or collectively, and it was a Paris compositors' mutual improvement group that published pamphlets on labour questions in 1847 and helped establish the chief radical paper of the Second Republic, the *Représentant du Peuple*, while the Uxbridge Young Men's Improvement Society, led by Leno and Massey, ran the violently Chartist *Uxbridge Pioneer* in 1848.[46]

Artisan radicalism thus relied heavily on unusual men such as a Paris tailor wounded on the barricades in the July Revolution who became active in republicanism and the tailors' combination of 1833. 'There is no complaint about his morals and conduct but he is an extreme republican and there was no mistake in locking him up as such.'[47] Such self-educated and articulate workmen became leading figures in radicalism, trade societies, and other organisations, played key roles in running them, defining terms of debate, producing literature, resolutions, and toasts, and thus exerted an influence out of all proportion to their numbers.[48] It was among such people that Owenite, Saint-Simonian, and Fourierite ideas were most influential, as much as forms of philosophical and social enquiry, speculation and analysis as practical goals. Yet their stress on sobriety, self-discipline, and rational enquiry could also set them apart from their fellows. As we have already seen with trade union and other leaders, they sought to change working men's behaviour and outlook, and could indulge in very high-minded criticism of their customs, particularly drinking. 'Negative estimation of the rank and file and emphasis on education was the general feeling of worker leaders, regardless of whether they were revolutionaries or reformists.'[49] Many were sickened by the hostilities and conflicts within and between work-groups and trade societies.[50] They tended to reject dialect language as a vulgar and trivial embodiment of an irrational and custom-ridden state of mind, and stressed standard English or French as the vehicle of progress whereby they would authenticate their cultural aspirations.[51] Because they had made such sacrifices to improve themselves, they resented the failure of those that did not do the same, expressing 'the self-made man's contempt of the feckless, and the autodidact's impatience with those who did not take up the opportunities of self-improvement which were offered'.[52] This could produce bitterness at those who did not follow their example, or who preferred pleasure to radical effort, especially if, for the sake of the cause, these people had taken on commitments such as cafés, coffee-houses, public houses, halls, or periodicals, which became liabilities when support was not forthcoming, the lack of support attributed to selfishness, ignorance, drink, immorality, and 'sensual pleasures'. Whereas when a movement was strong, they tended to defend the people against charges of drunkenness, immorality, or crime by blaming poverty and lack of educational provision, when it went into decline and support evaporated and they were left high and dry, they were then prone themselves to condemn the people for not following their lead and making the same efforts, and could see the moralisation of the people as necessary to avoid more failure and defeat.[53] As always, the political context was of vital importance. Independent radical education was always precarious, and only really possible when there was a strong movement. At other times, as after the decline of the Chartist movement after 1848, such piecemeal and isolated activities easily merged with more moderate liberal groups and took on a less political content, centring on individual self-improvement, responsibility, self-advancement, and civilising the poor rather than political equality and the raising of the position of the masses.

Many such people sought some fulfilment and part-time work as school and Sunday school teachers, Methodist preachers, co-operative storekeepers, friendly and trade society officials, and political lecturers, and a key element in labour politics was

these secretaries of workingmen's societies, burdened with defending the interests of colleagues in little hurry to pay their subscriptions; these great-hearted working men, constantly importuned over the distress of unemployed fathers of families or mothers of families whose husbands spent the housekeeping money at the pot-house; these pioneers of co-operative association, burdened with members more interested in future profits than the extra efforts needed to launch the firm; these working men journalists who had to represent to others – bourgeois, writers, politicians – a working population whose coarseness they themselves deplored; all those whose position in the workshop, trade, quarter, organisation, or newspaper forced them every day to confront their dream of abolition with the shabbiness of the working and domestic order.[54]

These roles all allowed such radicals to combine earning a living with radical activity, but it was chiefly as teachers, newsagents, booksellers, librarians, printers, publishers, and journalists that this was done, all aspects of the knowledge industry that reinforced their commitment to education. Thus the Birmingham whitesmith, Holyoake, became an Owenite and secularist lecturer, teacher of grammar, logic, and rhetoric at a mechanics' institution, author of a *Practical Grammar* and *Mathematics no Mystery*, and a journalist. While some did seek complete escape from the hated world of work, such as through employment by Saint-Simonians or the People's Bank,[55] and Perdiguier begged Sand to find employment for his wife and longed to leave manual work, more realistically it was the chance for partial and intermittent independence from unending manual labour that was hoped for. 'Never', advised the weaver Magu, 'neglect the labour which brings a living . . . work is certain – poetry is a dream; the one provides for our needs, the other lifts us to God.'[56] While manual work was often not enjoyed, being for Cooper a dark penalty, for Pottier boredom and a denial of life, for Corbon a daily forced labour, the hope was not so much to leave the world of labour as to secure access to a world other than that of labour, to avoid a life totally dominated by labour, to rise above the oppressive dullness and slavery of the world of labour, to share in the world of culture from which working men had been excluded. The *Atelier* was founded because 'the labour of the workshop takes up almost the whole life of the workingman', and the group around Tolain and Varlin founded the *Tribune Ouvrière* to enable workers to share in the nation's intellectual heritage.[57] It is this refusal to be dominated exclusively by labour that pervades working-class radicalism.

### Poetry

The Chartist journals had poetry columns, mainly with works by the Romantics and other poets of the day, and most of the self-educated working men seem to have been drawn to poetry.[58] Perdiguier described how he took to rambles in the countryside alone, giving himself up to a love of nature and a love of humanity. 'I became one with all beings, the earth, the sky, men, God, limitless space.' He began to think he was a poet, and to compose verses. Many autodidacts had literary pretensions, as did the Chartist Wheeler, who wrote novels, and the shoemaker O'Neill, who wrote eight plays, but it was poetry that attracted most autodidacts,[59] encouraged by the Romantic view of the poet as set apart from the community by the intensity of his sensibility, and of poetry as a sacred language that was a contrast to daily talk. The *Northern Star* was deluged with amateur verse,[60] and Chartist poetry was voluminous, the most famous figures including the ex-shoemakers Cooper and Leno, and the ex-factory worker Massey, while in 1839 a group of Saint-Simonian working men came together to found a workers' paper, the *Ruche Populaire*, which contained many of their compositions in verse (later published as a book), and the 1840s saw a veritable efflorescence of 'worker-poets' in France.[61]

For some, poetry-composition was a form of escapism:

> In the still night how sweet to leave behind
> The common world, the work-day throng
> And pass to the calm regions unconfined
> Of Phantasy and song.[62]

Indeed it was in opposition to the worker-poets of the *Ruche Populaire* that another group of artisans, a number of them veterans of secret societies, founded the *Atelier* in 1840 to arouse the workers in support of *practical* solutions. The worker-poets mainly based themselves on the established models, for example Shelley, Hugo, and Lamartine, and replicated the love of nature, extravagance, idealisation, and floods of emotion of the Romantics. Some French practitioners used plodding, prosaic, rhymed alexandrines, the shoemaker Savinien Lapointe alone being occasionally successful, and the only ones using more popular forms and idioms were Dupont, Magu, and Jasmin (who gained great fame and popularity by writing in Gascon).

Michelet disapproved of the French worker-poets because they copied the upper classes, and it is this feature of Chartist and worker-poetry that has also proved a disappointment to historians, who seem to have wished them to deal with work, poverty, and the working-class condition. But 'escapism', so as to enjoy nature or engage in study, was a rejection of the tyranny of work and the prison of the workshop, and it is surely misguided and a misinterpretation of their purposes to criticise them for a lack of proto-socialist realism or to wish for a wholly independent working-class literary culture. Since the aim of autodidacts was to escape from the domination of work and enter the world of culture, it is to be expected that they would adopt the dominant modes and themes, for 'a worker-poet is not necessarily a poet of the working class'. Yet, as Perdiguier pointed out, the new worker-poets' works were a contrast to popular songs on wine and prostitution, while Chartist poetry was replete with the theme of freedom, and often contained fierce invective, with a recurrent imagery of gold, blood, fire, light, productive labour, hunger, and poverty. Thomas Hood's 'Song of the Shirt' did more for the cause of the needlewomen than all the efforts of philanthropy.[63] The general context was, of course, important – with the end of the Chartist movement, Chartist poets dropped explicitly political appeals, and treated of more universal themes of rural England, nature, or personal enlightenment. Moreover the Romantics, especially in France after 1830, often followed a modish radical, even socialist course, concerned with the lot of the poor they hardly knew, a new religion of work, and visions of a fresher, happier, and peaceful world. Cooper and the Leicester house-painter Whitmore used Romantic forms to praise 'patriots of liberty', European nationalism, and that rural, republican bastion of resistance to slavery, Switzerland. Similar themes and images to those of Chartist poets were deployed in France, as in these words on the 1832 rising by the poverty-stricken Paris printer, Hegesippe Moreau:

> The people, eyes opened at last
> Murmured: my cause is betrayed,
> On my hunger a king now grows fat
> In a house that is watered with blood.
> I, whose bare feet have trampled down gold,
> I whose hand dashed to pieces a throne;
> When it's time for the fight to resume,
> Do you think it's for alms that I'll ask![64]

Patronage was important for worker-poets. A lack of it meant that Moreau published little before his early death, when his body was saved from anatomical dissection by Felix Pyat who then saw to the publication of his verses. These aroused a storm of comment in Paris and the feeling that the materialism of the age had allowed a rare spirit to die, and his work went through many editions and inspired imitators. This interest in worker-writers was a characteristic of Paris in the later 1830s and 1840s. The cabinet-maker Agricole Perdiguier, ill in Paris from an excessive regimen of self-instruction, wrote verses on political radicalism and against the ridiculous hostilities and antagonisms within the *compagnonnage*, intended as substitutes for the prevalent violent and aggressive compagnonnic songs, but it was only the latter that he succeeded in publishing in 1836. Because of poverty consequent on unemployment due to an eye complaint and arm injury, he was reliant, apart from cheap, low-quality cabinet work, on subscriptions to his publications, running a lodging-house, and teaching empirical geometry to wood-workers. During this time he also wrote a number of works: a fable on conflicts and reconciliation between two members of the *compagnonnages* who find they are long-lost brothers; an account of the history, organisations, functions, and rituals of the *compagnonnages*; and a technical essay on cabinet work. In 1839 all these were published in a single book which was also serialised in the *National* and became a sensation in literary circles, as the revelation of a world of which they were ignorant, partly because of the contemporary fashion for low-life and the fascination with ritual. For a time Perdiguier was lionised in the Paris literary world, being the model for Pierre Huguenin in George Sand's first socialist novel, *The Companion of the Tour of France*, and Agricol Beaudouin in Sue's *Wandering Jew*. Other worker-poets also received encouragement and help. Sand's characters Audebert in her *The Black Tower* and Arsène in *Horace* were the poets Magu and Gilland, while Jasmin took Paris by storm in 1842 as the French Burns. Similar fame greeted Thomas Cooper on his *Purgatory of Suicides*, and Magu received pensions from the government and the Crown (and a legacy from Chopin), Massey a government pension, and O'Neill several donations from the Literary Fund.

Despite such vital encouragement and patronage, few worker-poets were able to earn a living from their writings In some cases this was through choice – Gilland and Magu had no wish to cease to be a workmen, even if they were able to, and Magu wrote a poem to his shuttle, while despite all his fame Jasmin always returned to his work and his home town and gave away all the millions he received. While they proudly would not compromise their independence or radicalism –

Perdiguier deprived himself of a prize from the French Academy by refusing to exclude some republican sentences, Cooper always proudly described himself as 'Thomas Cooper, the Chartist', Magu was 'full proud of my independence', and Tourte declared 'I do not want your charity' – it was the sufferings of existence, rather than work itself that they affirmed. While O'Neill ran a short-lived journal on the shoemaking trade, the *Craft*, his compositions were not about the trade.

Worker-poetry could thus be seen not as expressing working-class attitudes and values but rather as a minor element in polite, respectable culture. It might be that this was due to the difficulties in getting work published, and the power and patronage of literary figures and journals, in filtering out true workers' poetry in favour of acceptable themes, a subtle censorship of potential class expression in favour of uncontroversial roles.[65] But it should be remembered that established circles did not necessarily want reproductions and imitations of established culture, and were interested in the special characteristics and values of urban low-life and 'authentic' popular culture, the 'other' unaffected by civilisation. While this might still serve to influence worker-poets in the direction of traditional, natural, and unsophisticated 'bards', a review of Perdiguier's songs in favour of reconciliation and fraternity among *compagnonnages* criticised them for their detachment from true popular culture. 'The only poetry of the *Compagnonnage* is war poetry; it is atrocious, but it has a genuine and original character.'[66]

The most famous and successful of the French worker-poets of the 1840s, Charles Poncy, produced poems that followed the dominant language, themes, and ideas of Romanticism, including its social criticism. It was George Sand, who took him up as a poet of the people, who urged him to write more about working men and to be a political, not a middle-class poet. 'The poet of the people has lessons of virtue to give to our corrupted classes and if he is not more austere, more pure and more truly a lover of good than our poets, he is merely their imitator, their ape, their inferior.' It was at her insistence, not through his own inclinations, that Poncy wrote his *Song of Each Trade*, endowing each worker in turn with the mentality public opinion attributed to his trade.[67] Thus there was established pressure in favour of a distinctive and more authentic popular poetry, and *Jerrold's Weekly* saw 'The Spirit' by the Leicester glovemaker, William Jones, as inappropriate verse for a working man.

Thus the content of worker-poetry should not be seen as a betrayal but as typical illustration of the autodidact and reading minority in the working population. Their concern was not to convey their experience as workers, but to escape the slavery of work, to share in nature or culture, to enter a new world in which they were part of articulate humanity. In the process they saw themselves as breaking working men's sense of inferiority, showing that they were as good as anyone else, and able to dress, write, and behave correctly, demonstrating that there was no contradiction between lowly labour and lofty creativity, and 'making the world of the working man itself contribute to that miracle of the discovery of a new mind which Cooper defined as the highest intellectual joy'.[68] Thus they were admired by other working men not for defending their class through militant writings, but for bringing honour to their class by the quality of their writings.[69] Characteristically, alongside anti-urbanism and pastoral lyricism, there was the familiar view of poverty and the plight of working people as due to the people's own folly, ignorance, and moral failings, and a stress on enlightenment and education and rejection of violence. But they also expressed social hopes, the lack of any necessity for conflict, and those ideas of the basic harmony of the people, who should all be good to one another. The return of fraternity instead of selfishness was also envisaged by Cooper:

> When Brotherhood returns, and hearts do feed
> On richest bliss, toiling in disregard
> Of self, and viewing their toil's fruit by brethren shared;[70]

By the late 1840s, representatives of the revolt against romanticism and in favour of realism, such as Pierre Dupont, were active in radicalism, but many artists and writers became apolitical and aloof under the Second Empire. One direction, in contrast to the earlier attitude, was a retreat into Provençal and dialect non-political poetry, something moreover tolerated by the regime as harmless. As poetry lost its position in the age of high romanticism as the most esteemed of the arts, worker poetry declined. Popular taste turned from literature to practical science, artisan attendance at vocational evening schools grew, and such men as Varlin or Malon, both born in 1840, did not write poetry.[71]

Thus, while education was important as a basis for radicalism, we must not generalise from the small self-educated minority or those of them who left autobiographies, even though we know most about them. This does not mean that such people were not of enormous and disproportionate importance in popular radicalism. But they were not enough in themselves to sustain significant popular radicalism. 'If we are concerned with historical change we must attend to the articulate minorities. But these minorities arise from a less articulate majority.'[72]

# 10    Religions and philosophy

In the later 1840s a group of radical artisan friends met weekly at the Crown Tavern, near Fleet Street in London, all of them Chartists and men of real significance in labour politics. The leading figure was Thomas Cooper, originally a shoemaker, who in the early years of the decade had been the fervent, dynamic, and fiery leader of the Chartists in Leicester. Julian Harney, an ex-sailor, had also been a notorious Chartist firebrand, and was now editor of the *Northern Star*, the great Chartist newspaper. James Devlin and John Skelton were both shoemakers, the latter an early member of the Working Men's Association and in the 1840s one of the leading Chartists in London. Both were active in their trade societies, and Skelton played a leading role in the establishment in the mid-1840s of a new national shoemakers' union, whose organ was for a while run by Devlin, and of the new national organisation to unite different trades all over the country, the National Association of United Trades, of which he became the first paid missionary. Thomas Shorter, a watch-case finisher, was a leader of the Finsbury Owenites, and Walter Cooper, a Scotch tailor, was in the early 1850s a leading figure in the co-operative production movement. Thomas Cooper, Harney, and Skelton were also prominent in international associations linking Chartists with the groups of foreign political refugees in London.

The group illustrates a number of the features outlined in the last chapter. The main purpose of the meetings was to hear and help Willie Thom, the Inverury weaver-poet. Thomas Cooper was an outstanding example of the artisan autodidact, joining in his youth with a friend to procure works to read, and attending mutual improvement societies and Mechanics' Institutions. Through intense effort, perseverance, and sacrifice, which at one point brought about a breakdown, he read voraciously and assiduously, and learned French, German, Italian, Latin, Greek, and Hebrew. He had also adopted temperance, became filled with a love of nature and poetry, tried his hand at verse himself, discarded dialect, become a teacher and then journalist, and organised the Leicester Chartists in a wide range of educational activities. 'Unless there were some stirring local or political topic, I lectured on Milton, and repeated portions of the "Paradise Lost", or on Shakespeare, and repeated portions of "Hamlet", or on Burns and repeated "Tom o'Shanter"; or I recited the history of England, and set the portraits of great Englishmen before young Chartists, who listened with intense interest; or I took up Geology, or even Phrenology, and made the young men acquainted, elementally, with the knowledge of the time.' Moving to London after two years in prison, he had secured the publication of his epic poem, the *Purgatory of Suicides*, and revealed his prodigious learning in lectures at a range of radical educational institutions. In 1850 he ran *Cooper's Journal*, which included verse by Shorter and some of the first compositions of Gerald Massey, the violent Chartist of 1848 who was soon to become one of the chief and most popular poets of the people. Skelton also wrote verse while, despite his great skill in shoemaking, Devlin became a journalist and writer, his real love and ambition being in poetry, and he formed with some fellow-shoemakers a literary group later joined by younger figures such as Leno.[1]

But there are other features of this group that repay attention. Like most autodidacts, Cooper longed to remove the power of superstition from the lives of ignorant workers. Overwhelmed at the age of fourteen with an anguished sense of sin, he had become a Primitive Methodist, then changed to Wesleyanism. However, his thirst for reading then led him on to Paine, Volney, and Voltaire and the conviction that at least some of the Old Testament was fable, and he ceased public worship. A breakdown at the age of twenty-two led him to religion again and a new overwhelming sense of sin, and after sampling several sects, like other such enquiring artisans, he chose the Wesleyans and became a very successful local preacher. These gifts he had then put to use as a leader of Leicester Chartism, when he included a large religious element into his meetings and speeches, organised Chartist hymn-singing and produced a Chartist hymn-book, most of the hymns in it composed by the framework-knitter, Bramwich, and the glove-hand, William Jones (whose poetry Cooper was also later to publish in his journal). Yet in 1843 he lost his faith and was won over by Strauss's *Life of Jesus*. The 'Crown' group was in fact one of religious dissidents, and Devlin was soon to produce an anti-Sabbatarian pamphlet in defence of the opening of Crystal Palace to the public on Sundays.[2]

Cooper's spiritual pilgrimage had not ended, for he was in the 1850s to regain his faith in Christianity, miracles, resurrection, and Christ's divinity, resume preaching, and join the General Baptists, and spend the rest of his life as a religious lecturer and writer. Cooper thus

exemplifies both the importance of religious Dissent in British radicalism (and in his case a republicanism drawn from Milton and
seventeenth-century Puritanism), and the spiritual pilgrimage and quest
so distinctive of autodidacts. Even at the time of the Crown meetings,
he held up Jesus as a model to follow, yet Skelton denied his actual
existence and was an active secularist with Harney, who was nevertheless strongly influenced by the French religious writer Lamennais.
Their quest for truth also led them into other interests. Cooper
regarded phrenology as part of 'the knowledge of the time'. In 1848
Skelton trained under the frighteningly named Dr Coffin, who
introduced American Thomsonian herbal medicine into England, and
spent the rest of his life as a practitioner of 'botanic medicine'.[3] Cooper
was also a friend of another medical reformer, Garth Wilkinson, a
Swedenborgian and sometime Fourierite physician who participated in
a range of social crusades, used herbal medicine, water cures,
mesmerism, and homoeopathy, and fought a lifelong battle against
medical authority and orthodoxy.[4] Walter Cooper was a freethinker
but, like Shorter, Massey, and Leno, joined the Christian Socialists in
the early 1850s. In 1855 the Christian Socialist leader, Maurice, was
deprived of his chair at London University for expressing doubts over
eternal damnation and suggesting the possibility of mercy for the
wicked hereafter, and the Christian Socialists then moved on to
concentrate on adult education, Shorter becoming secretary of their
Working Men's College. But in the 1850s Shorter also followed Robert
Owen into spiritualism, which Wilkinson had already embraced, and in
the 1860s he was editor of the *Spiritual Magazine*, while Massey
devoted the rest of his life to spiritualist writings.[5] While there was no
identity between political and religious views, any form of political
belief capable of being held by persons of any religious persuasion,
religion was important in radicalism, but this small group alone
indicates the complexity and range of the question.

### Lay religion

There are obvious reasons for the prominence of religion in radicalism.
The first is the general importance of religion, church attendance being
an inappropriate guide to working-class religious belief.[6] In religious
countries, radicalism inevitably had a religious content. But religion was
characterised by controversy and division, and these were often reflected
in political alinements. Thus the second reason why religion was
important in radicalism was that religious and political divisions often
coincided, Dissent being important among liberals in England, and

Protestantism, anti-clericalism, and Voltaireanism important in France, and these were sources of popular support.

There is no doubting the extent of popular anti-clericalism in both Britain and France, which weakened the political efficacy of the official clergy, and this was not confined to the clergymen of the Anglican and Roman Catholic Churches, but could also extend to Dissenting ministers and Protestant pastors, the new presbyter being but the old priest writ large.[7] There was dislike of the privilege, power, and pretensions of the clergy, their charges for seats and for performing key services, their refusal to officiate at funerals of those who died outside God's Grace, such as suicides, their denunciations of unmarried mothers, and their enforcement of religious practices on those in their power in schools, charities, hospitals, or prisons. Clerical interference in popular practices and amusements such as drinking and dancing, their insistence on Sunday observance, their conception of idleness as wicked and of misfortune as the consequence of sin, and their religion of fear, which was obsessed with death and happiness in the next world, and preoccupied with a vengeful and authoritarian God and the torments of hell-fire and eternal damnation, were all sources of opposition. Such strict, sin-obsessed killjoy religion ('Jesus never laughed') could be very alienating, and a Lancashire engineer in 1850 recalled the misery and thraldom of the strict religious home in which he grew up, when any shout, loud laugh, run, or fall received a severe rebuke, so that whenever the father was at home the children made excuses to go out and resort to the happy household of a local brewer.[8]

Important also was the frequent gulf between popular and elite religion. It was not just that clergymen objected to popular perceptions of churches as mainly instruments for providing public rites, especially baptism, confirmation, marriage, and, above all, burial, or to the popular tendencies to turn these events and religious holidays and festivals into profane occasions of enjoyment, feasting, dancing, drinking, and sex. There was also the very widespread 'pagan' and 'superstitious' character of popular or 'natural' religion, which saw the natural world as animate and saturated with magical forces – providence, fate, boggarts, spirits, Devil, demons, and ghosts – with the attendant importance of magic, astrology, augury, sorcerers, witches, and wise men. It was therefore concerned with coping with sickness, epidemic, and disaster, with interpreting dreams and omens, with predicting the future, with this world, not the next, and with manipulating it by spiritual means. French Protestantism, like Methodism, often absorbed and accommodated these beliefs, and in the early part of our period in France Roman Catholic priests were more active in opposing them than pastors.[9]

Popular radicalism therefore operated in a context of the strength of religion, the political power and privilege of official churches, the frequent coincidence of religious and political divisions, widespread anti-clericalism, and the gap between official religion and popular beliefs. However, there were, of course, important religious differences between France and Britain, in the latter's Protestantism and higher literacy, its religious pluralism and voluntarism, the strength of Dissent, its stress on lay participation and preaching, and the steady appearance of new sects. This lay religion was very important in British radicalism. However, while it is true that France was overwhelmingly Roman Catholic and that the dominant Tridentine form of Roman Catholicism emphasised the distinct and sacerdotal role of a hierarchical clergy, superior kinds of being who should control all forms of devotion and check all forms of spontaneous religious experience by laymen, this view had for centuries conflicted with forms and institutions of religious practice outside priestly authority and even involvement, so that the regional politico-religious division during the French Revolution was not one of religious vitality but was between clericalist and non-clericalist religion.[10] The Ancien Régime church was destroyed by the Revolution and replaced, on the one hand, by a non-sacerdotal Constitutional Church which went on to experiment with the use of the vernacular and the involvement of the laity,[11] and, on the other, by an often clandestine refractory church, in which communities of laymen essentially established and ran the religion they preferred, a practice continued after the 1801 Concordat in the small dissident 'Little Church'. While Napoleon destroyed both Constitutional and refractory churches and established a reclericalised Tridentine Roman Catholic Church as in effect a state church, these practices of lay control were not easily stamped out, especially because of the weakness of the new official church and its serious shortage of priests until the 1840s, which left very many lay congregations in practice still in control of their church and faith, accustomed to practising religion as they wished, while much religious teaching was in the hands of lay teachers free of priestly control whose religious views and interpretations often departed from orthodoxy. Thus in both countries there was a strong continuing current of lay religion, but in Britain this was met by Dissenting congregations whilst in France in the early part of our period lay religion was possible and more usual inside the church and produced frequent conflicts between priests and parishioners. However, it could also be met by French Protestantism, which was also a lay religion, and there were in the 1840s some spontaneous conversions to Protestantism by villages at odds with their local priest and attracted by humble pastors who were married and participated in communal life. This phenomenon of lay religion, by opening the way to more democratic practice and beliefs, was fundamental to artisan religious radicalism.

### Anti-clericalism

Anti-clericalism was a concomitant of lay religion, and the village cadres of anti-clericals were key elements in the radical movement of the Second Republic, and in general radicals on both sides of the Channel condemned the political power of the official dominant churches, those reactionary bodies, allies of rulers and oppressors, repositories of privilege, luxury, and wealth drawn from the people, institutions that forgot Christ's calling and used influence, fear, and superstition to make the people suffer and accept the present state of things. But while English Whigs and French liberal notables combined anti-clericalism with support for state control of the dominant churches, radicals wished them to lose their official positions and wealth, so that all churches would be voluntary organisations.

In the view of the Earl of Mulgrave, political influence was more likely to be wielded by 'the illiterate and extemporising artisan' than by a clergyman.[12] Anti-clericalism is important in understanding popular radicalism, but anti-clericalism was not necessarily anti-religious, and radicalism was able to embody a lay religion that tended to religious voluntarism, freedom, and equality, and that particularly opposed Roman Catholicism and High Church Anglicanism, the two sacerdotal religions with their hierarchical clergy between man and God possessed of authoritarian powers, characterised by ritualism, and holding official or privileged positions which made them allies of ruling elites (though with greater fluctuations in church–state relations in France). Both attracted strong liberal and radical opposition which in England and Wales was centred in other and rival Christian denominations far more than in France,[13] for the less autonomous and rich but more powerful Church of Rome was in France undoubtedly the target of much greater hatred as the enemy of the achievements and ideals of the French Revolution. Thus French radicals took part in anti-clerical demonstrations and disturbances, and in mockery of missions and parades, and the brief periods when radicals were in power saw measures to stop religious processions and close church schools, in 1830, 1848, and, above all, 1870–1 (after the close alliance of church with Second Empire). This hatred meant a more widespread rejection of Christianity in France than in Britain. 'In the Parisian workshop, the very few faithful which the

Church can number are exposed no less to sarcasm than the very few opponents of democracy.'[14]

Although many British radicals were Dissenters, and all shared the Dissenting belief in religious freedom and voluntarism, they could also often oppose the Nonconformists' social exclusiveness, hierarchies, full-time paid ministers, intolerance, and sectarianism, for all denominations were

> inculcating 'sound' and 'wholesome' doctrine, but each of them denying the orthodoxy of all the rest, and all of them agreeing only in one thing – to hate one another most cordially in the name of a God of peace, and to consign one another to eternal damnation in the name of an all-saving redeemer.[15]

Thus they could oppose the imposition of religious education, 'the evil effect of which had caused the ignorance, bigotry, and intolerance that had hindered the progress of the nation in the past, and opposes its best interests at the present'.[16]

Radicals identified 'priestcraft' as their enemy, characterised by the hypocrisy of those who attributed poverty, suffering, and injustice to God's will, by the intolerance of Sabbatarianism, and by attempts to check literature seen as endangering religion and morality. Chartists knew that churches were seen and used as antidotes to Chartism.[17]

> We meet, as in the oldest time
>   Our fathers met before;
> We teach those glorious truths sublime
>   Which Jesus taught of yore.

> The priest to the oppressor cries
>   Peace, when there is no peace!
> Awards them crowns to realise
>   An earthly *benefice*!

> O! early dawn delightful day
>   Bright o'er the moral skies,
> When truth shall sweep, like webs, away
>   Those refuges of lies![18]

## Christian radicalism

Christian aspects of radicalism were, in fact, very important.[19] As well as funerals, radicals sometimes used church premises as arenas for political demonstrations, especially when open expression of political sympathies was restricted. Thus, after the Chartist abandonment of a general strike in 1839 and the prevention of open-air demonstrations in many areas, there were waves of mass Chartist attendance at churches, a tactic repeated by Clerkenwell members of the Reform League in 1867. More generally, Chartists used the established New Dissenting techniques of prayer-meetings, love-feasts, camp meetings, and Sunday schools. They also established democratic chapels that incurred great hostility from religious denominations.[20] Religious lay preachers and Sunday school teachers, though not many clergymen, played a prominent part in the movement. Chartist meetings had hymns, prayers, and sermons, and used religious ceremonial and biblical inscriptions on their banners. Chartism, and radicalism generally in both countries, was pervaded by the language of Christianity and of a Christian view of the world. Radical songs were dominated by Christian imagery and by the themes of the perversion of God's justice and equal love for all humanity, and the wasting of the abundance of creation, by human cruelty and greed.[21] Chartists distinguished the corrupted church from the true church, and French radicalism during the Second Republic was filled with ideas of a return to primitive Christianity and a primitive liturgy. Ideas of justice were based on biblical writ: all were equal before God who never ordained that a few would have nearly all the wealth while the rest toiled for them, for everyone should be industrious and 'he who will not work should not eat'. The Bible showed that the rich and powerful were guilty of sins against God's purpose in denying the manhood of the people by taking away their God-given rights to the vote, work, sufficient pay, and freedom from arbitrary power, and by thwarting fraternity. Radicalism was portrayed as the religion of Christ opposed to the religion of hypocrites who forgot Christ's calling and message. For Jesus, 'the son of an artisan, contemplated the great revolution while at work in the workshop', 'son of a carpenter, himself a carpenter, found his most fervent and intelligent disciples among poor fishermen', 'the friend of the people, was at first nothing but an orator of the cross-roads and the desert'. A vagabond who would not be allowed to vote if alive today, he associated with the lowest element in society, and was a poor social reformer who championed the poor against the rich. The 'democrat of Galilee' was 'the first of the republicans', the first Chartist, 'the consoler of the poor, the enemy of the powerful', the founder of liberty and equality, who was received gladly by the common people, associated with extreme reformers and revolutionaries, was hated by the plunderers, and 'was crucified because he taught human fraternity and preached the abolition of slavery', and so became the first radical martyr.[22] Radicals likened themselves to the apostles and early Christians, who had preached 'the equality of human-kind, the brotherhood of humanity'; both were the agents on earth of God's will, and both were persecuted for their beliefs.[23] Thus in general, radical movements expressed an uninstitutionalised and undenominational radical Christianity, rejecting ecclesiasticism and the power and pretensions of priests, popes, and ministers, opposing religious animosities, and stressing individual conscience, humanitarianism, and the true nature of primitive Christianity.

There is no doubt that these radical Christian arguments, through using established and familiar concepts and examples, were very effective, and an important source of support for radicalism. One illustration is the tremendous impact of the religious writer Lamennais, already referred to. Both *Words of a Believer* and *Book of the People* were pervaded by religion and faith. Equality was the law of God, and it was the Devil who had brought about a division into kings and slaves. Jesus, the carpenter's son, was supported by the people but killed by their oppressors, and society must reform itself by rooting out sin. But just as important was the book's tone, quite unlike his earlier work. The *Words*, in particular, was like a biblical poem, full of power, high religious faith, mystical, emotional and concrete imagery, allegories, parables, visions of evil and the City of God, exhortations, and lyrical scenes.

There were also specifically religious radical organisations. Some radical ministers in Britain, who were suspended by their organisations, established their own separate radical churches. Around 1840 there were about fifty Chartist churches, clearly very religious, some of them in fact originating in existing congregations' dissatisfaction with the failure of their minister to support Chartism.[24] In addition to these there were religious localities and chapels, and religious meetings, within the mainstream National Charter Association.[25] Radical churches were also attempted in the Second Republic.[26]

However, we need to be clear on what all this shows. Specifically religious groups and organisations in radicalism, while important, were not typical, and do not in themselves demonstrate that radicalism was essentially religious; the existence of separate religious radical groups may suggest that the rest were not religious. Most Chartist organisations were not churches, and it is not at all clear that localities of the National Charter Association did resist a separation of religion from the rest of social, economic, and political life, for most radicals had no difficulty in separating religious from political questions.[27] The prominence of religious figures in radical movements does not make them religious, any more than radical leadership of trade societies or strikes makes them radical.

Praise of Jesus' teaching and life was not necessarily a sign of a recognition of his divinity, or an acceptance of Christian theology, or of a divine purpose, or even of any religion at all. The use of Christian language, imagery, and themes is not in itself a sign of religion but was the employment of widespread, commonplace rhetoric and shared idioms. It was always serviceable to legitimate claims through officially recognised points of reference, standards, and values. It was common for radicals to meet their opponents' arguments on their own terms, British radicals, for instance, using the general rhetoric of British freedom, representative government, and an enduring constitution, without believing it, as French radicals used the rhetoric of France as the beacon of progress in giving the world the principles of liberty, equality, and fraternity through the actions of the people. Thus radical use of Christianity could be a calculated way of fighting fire with fire. Chartist sermons in 1839 tended to be concentrated in the latter part of the year, when repression was closing down other outlets, and Chartist sermons, like Chartist church attendance, were a safer form of action and more difficult to forbid. The harassing pressure of police attendance could be neutralised by insisting they uncover during prayers.[28]

The dominant ideology conveyed in radical journalism was overwhelmingly secular, including that of the first editor of the *Northern Star*, a Swedenborgian minister. This may be a misleading impression of the actual movements, for the language of the press cannot be appropriated uncritically as *the* language of radicalism.[29] It is clear that religious elements were much stronger in meetings, songs, and tracts, so journalism can give an inaccurately secular picture of radicalism. Yet this does not mean that meetings or songs somehow conveyed people's feelings more directly or faithfully, for these also had their own models, imperatives, and structures – the ritual declarations of unity in the meetings, the emotional effect of religious language and banners, the use of simple-metre songs based on hymns, and the New Dissenting religious models for rallies and camp-meetings. Thus, where journalism underplays the strength of religious radicalism, meetings and demonstrations may overplay it.

On the other hand, rejection of Jesus' divinity and indifference to Christian theology does not in itself denote a lack of religion. There clearly was a recurrent radical form of religion, which denied ideas of predestination and an angry, vengeful, vindictive, and cruelly punitive God.[30] A belief in a just and benevolent God was consistent with radicalism, as it meant that cruelty and iniquity could be attributed not to God's will but to human actions, and were therefore remedial. But while radicals did stress a kind God, the message of Lamennais and others that all should love one another, and that it was the disunity resulting from the absence of such love that gave kings and oppressors their power, tended to lead to a concentration on Jesus rather than God, on the tolerant and forgiving figure who held out the promise of life eternal in the light of God's love, the greatest teacher and moral guide of a practical religion. A Chartist called on people to

advocate practical religion, and this not in mere attendance upon the outward means of grace, but following the spirit and example of our Lord Jesus sharing love, sympathy and kindness, to all around, moving and acting from the central point of moral justice, doing unto others as we would they should do unto us.[31]

It is thus characteristic that in his *Words of a Believer* Lamennais made Jesus much more prominent than in his earlier writings.

This led to an emphasis on the New Testament instead of the Calvinist preference for the Old. The gospel of fraternity, of humanity united by love, runs right through radicalism, sometimes seeing co-operation as a religion of solidarity, or trade unionism as a crusade against 'selfism' for mutual good. It was as a new religion of love opposed to the hated old one that Saint-Simonism made converts among artisans.[32]

This was consistent with the widespread popular religion concerned with commonsense morality and the simple religion of Jesus, rather than theology, personal sin, and disciplining behaviour. Corbon wrote that there were hardly any anti-Christian ideas in the Paris workshops, that Paris workmen supported church baptism, marriages, and funerals, and other external religious expression and ceremonies, and believed in God, but had no belief in the effectiveness of the sacraments or the divinity of Christ, did not share the church's constant preoccupation with the salvation of the soul, and saw religion as enjoining that all should help one another as brothers; 'religious sentiment is independent of all practice of external worship'.[33] 'The people therefore remain spiritualist, whatever one would like to say, and despite their separation from external worship.'[34]

While radicals tended to stress Jesus rather than God, it was usually an emphasis not on the Atonement or his intercession with a wrathful God on Man's behalf, but on Jesus the man and his life and work on Earth, his teaching and example that showed the way to a proper life in this world, a view that does not have to be religious. Yet at other times, radicalism could adopt the tone of religious revivalism, conversion, and evangelical fervour, engaged in a holy war against evil, and Bright and, especially, Gladstone were later to use these forms to great effect with a prophetic evangelical tone of invective and anathema against injustice, and a stress on the God of Battles and Lord of Hosts who would smite his enemies.[35] The apocalyptic, millennial tone was shown in an address by Hull Female Chartists, containing sixteen biblical quotations, calling for a mass national pray-in to regain their rights.[36] This form of radical religion, often drawing on the Old Testament, used biblical ideals of justice to condemn evils and abuses, and the image of God, rather than Jesus, as the redresser of wrongs and bringer of retribution, an image which itself justified the people's violent retaliation against their oppressors. This contrasted with the form of radical religion almost wholly drawn from the New Testament, an ethical religion following the precepts of Jesus, with golden rules such as behaving to others as you would like them to do to you.[37] The emphasis might change with the circumstances. The former was a generalised rhetoric in the ascendant Chartism of 1838–9 and, in some places, 1842,[38] the latter characterised the religious Chartist organisations after defeat, the French workers' press in the political quiescence of the 1840s, and, to a large extent, the radical socialist-democratic movement facing a conservative regime after 1849. In the short period of popular ascendancy in 1848, when religious rhetoric was less evident, it took a different form.

Thus radicals used the image of Jesus (a man, admiration of whom was not necessarily religious) particularly in sermons, stories, and parables, and of God (the Creator or Father whose benevolent purpose was being thwarted, or a redresser of wrongs) particularly in speeches, hymns, and songs. In addition to these two poles of Christianity,[39] there was in Roman Catholic France the growing cult of the Virgin Mary, and radical representations of the Republic as a woman were modelled on those of Mary, again in itself no sign of religiosity. But in addition there was the conception of 'Christ', differing from that of Jesus in its emphasis on a majestic, divine, and superhuman figure, associated with the Crucifixion, Resurrection, Messiahship, the King of Kings, and the return on a throne of glory on the Day of Judgement. It is important to distinguish Jesus the teacher from Christ the judge. Christ is not usually a radical figure in itself, and was employed by the authoritarian regimes of Louis XIV, Napoleon, and the Restoration during the ultra-royalist ascendancy, hence the eighteenth-century liberal emphasis on a deity instead, but, like the terrible God, Christ could be put to radical uses, as in 1838–9 in England,[40] or in the turmoil of 1848–9 in France, when 'Christianity is a great prophecy whose fulfilment is approaching.'[41] The dominant religious theme in early 1848 France was, in fact, that of the revolutionary and vengeful Christ identified with the crucifixion and resurrection of the French people, the People-Christ.[42]

This apocalyptic language did, of course, characterise much of the New Testament, and that continuing restlessness and fascination with prophecies, warnings about the present and predictions of the future and signs below the surface which has always been an element in

Christianity, had for centuries been a feature, alongside astrology, of popular chapbooks and almanacs, and in the nineteenth century influenced evangelical, especially Nonconformist, religion, and also produced movements such as the Southcottians or the French legitimist-inspired waves of strange tales, apparitions, ghosts, and miracles in 1815, 1830, 1839, and in the 1870s.[43] Lamennais' works were also full of prophecies and anathemas; the reign of Satan must precede that of God and the emancipation of the race, but the empire of despotism would soon end, the great battle was near, when a violent rising of the people and the return of the Messiah would be followed by a reign of peace and goodness.

In France, millenarian speculations found a home in the 1830s and 1840s in Romanticism, which often looked elsewhere than traditional religion to fill the religious and moral vacuum they felt, to pantheism, fascination with the supernatural and irrational, themes of the current of history and the end of days. Important figures in the Parisian literary and artistic bohemian milieu of students, dancers, theatre-stars, and nightlife were Ganneau and two followers, Esquiros and Constant, who all shared millennialist ideas based on the books of Daniel and Revelation, the sudden destruction of a world of sin and its rich rulers, to be replaced by an egalitarian New Jerusalem. Alphonse Esquiros was a republican activist in a range of struggles from the 1830s to 1870s, successor in 1849 as editor to the former police spy Laponneraye of the leading Marseilles radical paper *Voix du Peuple* until elected to the Legislative Assembly in 1850, and author of a range of radical books and pamphlets. The ex-Roman Catholic priest Constant went through recurrent phases of teaching, painting, intense Mariolatry, studies of animal magnetism, and Joachimite philosophy of history, and was also an admirer of the Protestant revolutionary, Thomas Munzer, with his advocacy of violence.[44]

In 1840–1 Esquiros, Constant, and their publisher, Le Gallois, were in prison, together with Lamennais, the religious communist Pillot, and Thoré, a leading republican journalist and art critic, whose first published article was a prophetic religious one.[45] These six radical millenarians confirmed and developed their ideas, one result being Esquiros' very influential radical and millennial *People's Gospel*.

Yet while millenarianism was a constant thread in radical religion, such ideas were likely to be much more emotional and make a much bigger impact in times of crisis. In the excited period of the Reform Crisis in London, millenarian tracts and speakers appeared at the radical centres, the star at the Borough Chapel and then the Rotunda being the well-known 'Zion' Ward.[46] There were millenarian elements in

Chartism in 1839 and, to a lesser extent, in 1842, with apocalyptic language and a sense of events of cosmic importance. It was in 1840, with the imminence of a new European war, when the 'Marseillaise' was sung all over France, that Pillot and others preached a messianic communism and Ganneau issued millenarian tracts to 'THE FRENCH PEOPLE, THE MESSIAH OF PEOPLES'.[47] Such language was also prominent in the early part of 1848. 'Hear now the counsel which the great agitator Jesus has told me to communicate to you; . . . preach that the new society is near.'[48] This was the tone in his violent *Prophecy of Bloody Days* of Louis Pujol, secretary of a political club, publisher of Thoré's paper, and brigadier in the National Workshops, who organised the demonstration on 22 June that led to the great rising of which he was a leader.[49]

Followers of Ganneau in 1848 included Sobrier, who had been a leader with Kersausie and Barbès of an insurrectionary group in the Society of the Rights of Man and of the 1834 rising, and was said to have fired the first shot on 23 February 1848 that started the revolution. For a while in charge of the Paris police, he then amassed a cache of arms in preparation for a new rising which he hoped the 15 May demonstration would provoke. Another was Felix Pyat, one of the leaders of the socialist-democratic movement later prominent in the Commune.[50] Ordinary events in 1848 were given a spiritual significance, and everywhere the image of the revolutionary Christ, crucified and risen in glory, merged with the theme of the crucifixion and resurrection of the People-France. It was now that Ganneau expressed to the full his apocalyptic and millenarian beliefs, in support of the Republic and the 'Christ-People':

The February Revolution is more than human, more than heroic. It is divine!
. . . spirit
Daughter of the Holy Spirit (the spirit of love), the Republic has descended from the sky to transfigure the earth.

It was Ganneau who was responsible for that extraordinary episode in the great triumphant demonstration of 17 March, when he passed a loaf of bread around the hungry crowd to the words 'Bread of God, give to all to eat!', a cry taken up from end to end in a massive holy communion.[51]

Constant also produced particularly extreme versions of this theme of the crucified People-Christ, insisting on the necessity and significance of martyrdom and violence, and he was to fight in the June Days. With Esquiros, Le Gallois, and Ganneau he founded the Club of the Mountain, which was very unusual in being composed mainly of working men. Its organ championed 'the great principles of love and charity so simply professed by the Christ, our master in everything concerning socialism'. Constant's 'The Justice of the People-Christ', published in the *Montagne de la Fraternité*, exulted at the revolution, for 'this day was the realisation of the predictions of the Christ', who was 'the first of the republicans'.

> In the name of Him who reigns in Eternity, the end of days predicted by the Christ has arrived, and the peoples and the kings are to be judged by their works.
> Rumours of war are noised by everybody.[52]

But after June this language of the radical revolutionary Christ disappeared, and the tone of religious radicalism for the rest of the Republic was like Chartism after 1839, an ethical stress on the teachings and example of Jesus, although in some Protestant areas a radical prophetism was aroused by the approach of the 1852 elections and the rising against the *coup*.[53]

### Sects of rational religion

Christian history contains that recurrent element of dissent, often expressed by Prophets of the Word, that looked back to the earliest days of the faith to revive the simplicity of the apostolic ideal of poverty and love of one's neighbour, and used evangelical preaching in a direct and easily understandable language. This had led in Britain to various artisan sects that were often anti-authoritarian and democratic, stressed inner experience rather than institutionalised practices, laid less emphasis on Original Sin, and were imbued with a sense of mission and a doctrine of universal atonement whereby Christ died for all, not just the elect.[54] A similar stress on simplification of worship, rationalism, reading the Bible, personal belief, and education and instruction as much as worship was also found in French Protestantism, which in a number of areas experienced a popular pietist revivalism that produced dissident churches, independent of all civil authority, opposed to the Concordat, and often sympathetic to radicalism.[55]

Chartist churches and religious localities in the National Charter Association were in many ways aspects of this phenomenon, and the formation of such breakaway radical sects and churches was a much more natural occurrence in a Protestant Britain already characterised by religious pluralism and a variety of sects. But in fact the nature of the July Monarchy, and, most of all, the shock of the July Revolution and the ferment that followed it, gave some encouragement to new churches, for example the Protestant revival mentioned above. The Prefect of

Police was exasperated by the uncontrolled anarchy threatened by 'the pretensions every sectary had of taking in turn the character of pastor or priest, of opening and officiating at a temple, of making whatever changes they judged proper in the new ritual'.[56] The most important was a new 'French Catholic Church' founded by a renegade priest, Chatel. Some of his 'priests' were even forcibly installed for a while in parish churches, and by the mid-1830s there were some nine of his churches in the Paris region, ten in the provinces, and one in Brussels. Although some of the new authorities at first encouraged Chatel as a check to the power of the clergy, this phase soon ended, his priests were evicted from parish churches, some of his churches were suppressed, and in the early 1840s all remaining ones were closed down and Chatel himself imprisoned, whereupon some of the congregations embraced Protestantism. He also tried, without much success, to revive his church in the Second Republic and harangued the crowd during the 15 May demonstration. It was quite an important movement in the 1830s, and a sizeable number of the insurgents of the June Days in 1848 had been in Chatel's church.[57]

His priests were accepted in provincial villages which lacked their own church or priest, or were at odds with the one they had, and his congregations were classic expressions of that abiding lay religion referred to above, especially as he introduced the early church principle of popular election of priests, and fell foul of the authorities through not seeking authorisation for the erection of new churches.

His church very faithfully reflected the main features of anti-clericalism. Services were in French instead of Latin, there was Mass at every service, but no need to fast before it, and for a while the highly unpopular charges for seats, and for conducting baptisms, weddings, and burials, were dispensed with. The much distrusted and allegedly abused confession was made purely voluntary, weddings were conducted without confessions, and people who died outside God's grace were none the less given funerals, even at home. Chatel rejected clerical celibacy, the ever-growing religious orders, and the hell-fire that preoccupied Roman Catholicism, recognising only Heaven and Purgatory in which people expiated their sins for a while, so that in the end all would reach Heaven. Consistently with this denial of Hell, Chatel expounded a religion of love, not terror and revenge, gloom and doom, fear and despair, a practical religion concerned with the here and now, rather than the next life.

Chatel also condemned Papal Infallibility, state salaries to churches, and persecutions of non-Catholics, and supported religious voluntarism. His was clearly a radical church, and he regularly celebrated the July

Revolution and the 1832 rising, supported help for the Polish revolt, a free press and universal suffrage, criticised royalty, opposed the death penalty, and became involved with the opposition, most of his congregation being republicans.

The process in breakaway sects of simplification and the stress on individual belief could lead to substantial shifts in the content of the religion, and the frequency of such sects in Britain meant that some developed unorthodox and even bizarre ideas. Some were overtly radical, such as the Swedenborgian Bible Christians in Manchester, whose chapel the Chartists used, or the Freethinking Christians in London, a number of whom, like Hetherington, were prominent radicals and Owenites,[58] while Lamennais was to go on to reject any supernatural order. Two common directions were towards humanistic rationalism and esoteric theosophy, both of which could limit their popular appeal, but they could still have vital initiating and organising roles in wider popular radicalism – it was mainly a group of Freethinking Christians that took the lead in the formation of the National Union of the Working Classes in 1831. The humanistic rationalism involved absorbing many of the ideas of the Enlightenment which were such an important element in radicalism, including the later Enlightenment view of the political and religious institutions as a conspiracy against the people, and which extended to criticisms of Christianity.

Since 'each religious sect finds its own allegory; each priest his own moral; and each tyrant his precedent, in the pages of the Bible,'[59] the rejection of clerical sectarianism and intolerance and an attitude of a plague on all your houses could lead to a rejection of Christianity altogether, both as untrue and, as a blind faith based on texts full of absurdities and contradictions and on an irrational belief in Original Sin, a 'fanatical' superstition that clouded men's minds, that was an obstacle to knowledge of the truth and one's rights and thus to radical reform. Christianity could thus be seen as the main reason why people did not accept radicalism: a conspiracy, an invention to keep people in thraldom. Reason and Science, the agents of progress and reform, disproved it, and this reiteration of the eighteenth-century combination of Enlightenment scepticism, rationalism, and scientific optimism led to the continual republication of the classic freethinking works, especially Voltaire, Paine, Volney, and Palmer, by freethinking publishers, and their sale by a network of secularist booksellers. G. W. M. Reynolds began his radical writing career with an attack on Christianity.[60] Self-educated working men, with their sense of progress and escape from the grip of tradition and superstition, and their determination to work out their own conclusions for themselves, tended towards a freethinking hostility to religious beliefs and practices, especially as their pursuit of rational investigation led, like Cooper, to reading biblical criticism and the great Enlightenment critiques of religion.[61]

> Religions are those codes and rules,
> Devised by PRIESTS to plunder FOOLS.[62]

For the self-taught follower of Owen, the tailor George Petrie,

the ruthless impostor condemns human Reason, and cunningly supplies its place by Faith; he threatens all with eternal torments hereafter who do not receive his dogmas through faith, and renounce the last vestige of reason; he promises you a heaven hereafter, but takes especial care to have himself the full enjoyment of that heaven here, a particle of which you are not permitted to taste.[63]

A Blanquist engineer thought the same:

What has produced despotism and slavery is that, in education, a supernatural being was introduced who does as he likes, and one is concerned with the enjoyment of a pretended future life to which humanity is sacrificed.[64]

Yet while secularism was often the chief issue dividing radicals from liberals in Britain, this could limit its appeal, for opposition to Christianity was very much a minority strand. The attacks on Christianity by Petrie and others in the co-operative movement and National Union of the Working Classes were divisive, and the leaders of the National Union moved to check them.[65] In France, rejection of Christianity was much more widespread, and British radicals did not openly mock religious ceremonies, seek to close churches down, or even, as happened at Lyons in 1838, try to seize a saint's remains to throw them in the river. But rejection of Christianity was not a rejection of religion, and even at the height of Cooper's rejection of Christianity, he never espoused full atheism but was nearer to pantheism or theism, and always stressed Christ's perfection and moral beauty.[66] Even in France, few republicans were atheists like Blanqui. Enlightenment writers themselves were mostly deists, believers in a wise and benevolent deity who was known through his works, so that a scientific study of nature's laws was the only way to God, through revealing his beneficence and design. Most French republicans tended to a vague Rousseauist deism, including an immortal soul and afterlife, a natural religion free of dogma or worship and based on morality.[67] One of the most successful of all the Reform League speakers, Philip Perfitt, was a leader of a theist society of religious reformers.[68]

It would be a mistake not to see this as genuine religion, and, drawing on Enlightenment notions of an original 'natural religion' underlying all existing faiths, deists could often regard themselves as restoring original

Christianity, especially if, like Cooper, they admired Jesus the man. By the 1820s deism was in Britain a radical belief, and there were in London several deist congregations that often involved an intense religious experience, and were supported by the former Lancashire Dissenting preacher, William Benbow, as the means by which 'religion itself will, sooner or later, be restored to its native purity, loveliness, and simplicity'.[69]

During the Reform Crisis and after in London there were several meeting places that held discussions on religion, most of them used at some time by the National Union of the Working Classes for its meetings. The Rotunda was a centre of republicanism and the group around the notorious infidel Richard Carlile. The leaders of the National Union in Finsbury were a group of Spenceans, deists, and freethinkers who used a couple of chapels in the area. The Borough Chapel in Southwark was another, but for a while the chief one was run by Benbow, one of the most violent and extreme members of the National Union, who in 1832 published a famous pamphlet advocating a one month's general strike by the people, a 'Grand National Holiday' which he justified by biblical quotations and references to the Levitical Jubilee. At his Institution of the Working Classes he and others preached political sermons, something he was later to do in the Chartist movement.[70] Soon this centre of religious radicalism was joined by the notorious Robert Taylor, a former Anglican vicar who had lost his faith, organised discussions and criticisms and 'services', and with Carlile held theological as well as political meetings at the Rotunda in 1830 until both were imprisoned in turn in 1831. Taylor did not share Carlile's atheism. Like Chatel he rejected a guilt-ridden faith for a cheerful, sensual religion, retained the existing order of church services, because of the grandeur, oratory, and poetry of their language, and developed an intellectual critique of Christianity that drew on Dupuis. He therefore saw all religions as rooted in sun worship and the same basic mythologies that illustrated scientific principles, the Gospel stories being allegories of the astrological beliefs that underlay all creeds. Organised churches Taylor denounced as a state trick to enslave the many. On his release from prison he quarrelled with Carlile and allied with Benbow, who became his publisher, and held his entertaining sermons and meetings at Benbow's institution. Here they also founded a Republican Association, other prominent members being the South-cottian James Smith, who had come to prominence through religious lectures at the Borough Chapel, and James Lorymer, editor of two of Hetherington's illegal unstamped papers. Smith may have been the translator for the first English edition of Lamennais' *Words of a Believer*, and Lorymer was certainly the first (bad) translator of the *Book of the People*.[71]

At the same time, whereas at first Chatel's church had exactly the same ceremonies, forms, vestments, and (translated) texts as the Roman Church, he soon modified its theology in the direction of a reformed, rational religion, influenced by Voltaire, Dupuis, and theophilanthropy. He rejected adoration of saints and images, denied the Real Presence, and sought a return to a primitive Christianity free of Romish superstition. With a denial of the Trinity, the divinity of Jesus, and the Resurrection, his religion became a form of deism, a 'natural religion', based on reason and opposed to superstition.

The radical desire to demystify the conspiracies of ruling elites led to other features. Benbow's fame in the 1820s was as a publisher of a mixture of Puritan, radical, scurrilously anti-clerical, and pornographic works, the different categories overlapping. Chatel and Taylor both resorted to satire and ridicule, akin to that continuing current of mockery and entertainment that had characterised the tone of the 'Radical underworld' of post-war London and the popular ex-Methodist preacher and lecturer Wedderburn.[72] When in the later 1820s Taylor established a deist liturgy and ceremonial in London, he coupled it with entertaining performances and parodies of church services, which proved far more attractive than the dry writings and discussions of Carlile. Taylor at the Rotunda in 1830, after the unsuccessful infidel tour, increased this showmanship aspect and moved nearer to Wedderburn's style of grossness and buffoonery, with ribald and profane mock-services which included reciting the Lord's Prayer backwards and ceremonies of raising the dead and the Devil. He took the titles of 'Devil's Chaplain', 'Archbishop of Pandemonium', and 'Primate of All Hell', claimed to be in a state of 'holy ejaculation', declared that Jesus was a thief, who was born in a stable, lived on the highway, and died on the gallows, and gave a 'Vindication of the Character of Saint Judas Iscariot'. Similarly, the Southcottian James Smith made his name in London by even greater abuse of Christianity, in lectures on 'Religion, and its mischievous Consequences', or 'The Devil; and a defence of his character'.[73] Benbow's Institution was clearly very similar, and Chatel and his priests undoubtedly also attracted support from the liveliness, vehemence, bluntness, and strength of their language against clergy, rulers, and their detractors, their public flouting of Roman dietary rules, and their patronage of cafés and dances. Chatel's words were 'harsh, ironic, incisive', 'caustic and jeering', 'biting, rough', and he was felt to lack tact and gravitas, and be a vulgar preacher.[74] The importance in radicalism of blasphemy as well as theoretical infidelism needs to be stressed.

### Aspects of religious socialism: harmony, property, feminism, and messianism

It was the stress on the gospel of love that composed the 'true socialism' of Chatel and the Saint-Simonians who established a church in the early 1830s. Later in the decade, some ex-Saint-Simonians, for example Pillot and Robert of the Var, became priests in Chatel's church, but also important, and more influential on Chatel himself, was Fourierism.[75] Chatel rejected existing economic relations, for 'commerce, as it is carried out, is nothing but legally organised fraud. Antagonism is everywhere, emulation nowhere.'[76] He was on good terms with the Saint-Simonian workers' papers *Ruche Populaire* and *Union*.[77] The socialism of the Second Republic seemed even more religious in character, with religious ceremonies of 'socialism, which is the new religion'.[78] Inevitably, Chatel himself then tried to revive his church as a socialist one, in praise of 'Jesus Christ, the great apostle of socialism'.[79]

As we have seen in chapter 5, socialism encompassed many different aspects and the aspect that had the greatest religious tone was the condemnation of the materialism and selfishness of commercial society and its political economy, and the insistence that people should love one another.

> Let us unite,
> Jesus commands it;
> Love, said he, and you shall be absolved.[80]

However, there is a distinctive aspect of socialism where the religious inspiration seems much more direct, namely the abolition of private property. This was not typical of most socialists, and of those who subscribed to it, some wanted the abolition of some forms of private property, others of all forms. The chief form of the former was land, because individual property was legitimate if the result of labour, so anything not the result of labour should not be individually owned; since God had given the earth to all, as He had the air and sea, it belonged to all in common and could not be individually appropriated. However, the religious impulse was stronger among those who wanted to abolish all private property, the 'communists'. Chatel's priest Jean-Jacques Pillot opened in 1836 his own unauthorised church near Versailles, but this was closed by the authorities and Pillot was imprisoned, the case becoming a *cause célèbre* among liberals over religious freedom. On his release he became one of those preaching a state-enforced communism, and in a number of publications based the abolition of private property on the Bible, the early Christians ('the first communists'), and the religious element Buonarroti had added to Babeuvianism. After another spell in prison, Pillot was one of the organisers of the famous communist dinner in 1840 in opposition to the radical republican one.[81]

Pillot's basing of communism on religious foundations, and a concern not with production but with divisions, selfishness, antagonism, and unhappiness caused by inequality of property, is typical of most of the communism of our period, which argued that Christianity could only be established in a social community, and that Jesus had opposed private property. They also invoked the models of the first Christians, monasteries, Jesuits in Paraguay, and the communal settlements of Protestant sects such as the Moravians. It was his involvement at Geneva with a religious and mystical group, including Swedenborgians, who practised equal sharing and community of goods that led the Lyons weaver Joseph Benoit to become a Babeuvian.[82]

The religious elements in Owenism are thus easily comprehensible, and the same is true of Cabet, who supported Chatel's church and from 1842 began to stress that communism was the true Christianity, putting this at the heart of his doctrine in 1846. He attracted communist Christian mystics, became the 'divine apostle of Christ' to a following that had strong religious elements, including the Swedenborgian painter Gouhenant in Toulouse, and from 1845 the Icarian movement became more sectarian, an exclusive fellowship of true believers with strong religious emphases.[83]

To some extent arising from the socialist element in Chatel's church is the position of women. Churches, of course, were one of the main institutions offering women an important role outside the home, and often had stronger female than male support. Chatel did attract a strong female following, as did Taylor in London, and the Saint-Simonians in Paris and London in the early 1830s when they became a religious cult and resurrected the ancient heresy of a female messiah. Benbow's religious Institution was also the centre of a radical women's society, the Friends of the Oppressed.[84] Whereas most radicals opposed women's paid work and wished to make it possible for women to stay at home for their natural and essential duties there, and emphasised male productive work, it is argued that religious radical movements offered more to women than labour movements.[85] Chatel addressed his congregation as 'my dear brothers, my dear sisters', supported an enlargement of females' role in public life, advocated equality between the sexes, and condemned the present system of marriage as involving the subordination of women and allowing the marginalisation of women generally.[86] He was even more explicit in his brief revival as a socialist in 1848, encouraging women to attend his social and religious dinners, and participating in the discussions that year of the 'female' problem of marriage and divorce and the slavery of marriages of convenience.[87] Cabet's club also discussed these questions.

Shakers, Swedenborgians, Owenites, Saint-Simonians, Fourierites, and millenarians often criticised the family and the position of women, and sometimes used the notion of an androgynous deity, evolutionist cosmology, and a sexualised vision of the universe and copulating planets, where the masculine and feminine principles, polar opposites with strong mutual attraction, were united in the Divine.[88] Ganneau founded a new 'Evadist' religion of Eve and Adam to reconstitute human unity in worship of a male–female God in a hermaphrodite doctrine of which he was the 'Mapah' (both father and mother). His associate, Constant, had also in 1838 entered Flora Tristan's circle of revolutionaries, feminists, and advocates of social renovation through the liberation of women.

Victorian spiritualists also used the belief in women's innate spirituality to have female mediums and healers (medical practice being closed to them).[89] However, a condemnation of the position of women in society is not the same as actively changing the role of women. The socialists most concerned with women's place were those whose socialism consisted mainly of a concern for harmony and solidarity. This often marked a rejection of the liberal view of society as a voluntary association where human relationships are reduced to contacts between autonomous individuals, and a stress instead on interdependence and non-instrumental ties, such as family, kinship, and friendship. These could be seen as a female moral perspective, based not on abstract principles of justice or rights, but on an ethic of care and responsibility. But, as in Evangelicalism, this assertion of female superiority through the essentialisation of the feminine, with mothering and caring seen as a natural, and superior, female activity, could imply a reduction of woman's experience and a legitimisation of gender differences as inevitable and natural, and thus reinforce female subordination. While Constant's Mariolatry and cult of woman led him to condemn the position of women and look forward to a merging of the two sexes in the future, in the meantime he did not envisage women being active thinkers or managers, their role remaining that of giving birth and engaging in charity, not working or taking part in politics. Their rule through love condemned them to mystical inactivity, woman being an idealised abstraction whose role lay in the future, not the present. Thus while at the Club of the Mountain in 1848 some supported female political activity and proper pay for female work, others felt 'that woman's grace and decency constitute her sovereignty; that she must not therefore be involved in public and political discussions'. James Smith, Southcottian, Owenite, and later Fourierite, followed an identical development.[90]

Constant and 'Shepherd' Smith also demonstrate the millenarian element in socialism. Owen, Saint-Simon, Enfantin, and Cabet all used prophetic language and ideas, and attracted chiliastic elements. For the millenarian Lamennais, private ownership of land had brought about avarice, murder, and bloodshed.[91] The chief champion of common ownership of land in England was Thomas Spence, who responded, on his arrival in the capital, to the London millenarian milieu to become much more religious in his emphasis, and stress Christ and the New Testament. After his death in 1814 the new leaders of the Spenceans, Thomas Evans, Robert Wedderburn, and Thomas Preston (the 'Bishop'), much more clearly identified Spenceanism as a new Christianity.[92]

In the later part of our period, the radicals in Britain most closely identified with land nationalisation were the disciples of James 'Bronterre' O'Brien, the journalist who from the 1830s gained a devoted following in London among a group of ultra-radicals centred on some Spencean veterans from the post-war period, who came together in the later 1830s in the London Democratic Association, which, like O'Brien, showed great concern over a millenarian movement among agricultural workers in Kent, led by a Spencean.[93] There was some continuity between these and the group of O'Brienites who maintained a radical presence in London right through the 1850s and 1860s, and continued to push the master's ideas, or crotchets as others saw them, particularly on land nationalisation and currency reform. Thus the O'Brienites were in some ways the heirs of the earlier Spenceans, and from being a radical journalist and leader of national stature, O'Brien became the leader of a small sect, although both Spenceans and O'Brienites were significant and influential in a range of London radical activities.[94]

Like Spence, O'Brien first developed his views on secular bases but seems to have changed because of the milieu to which he found himself confined, and by the late 1840s he had moved much closer to radical religion. His 1849 journal, the *Social Reformer*, used biblical language, and had a series of religious articles by an ex-clergyman. O'Brien himself also became a lecturer on religion and the true Christian principles of the Book, opposing atheism because it meant that people would not be punished for their misdeeds, and calling for support in 'our conflict with the powers of darkness'. 'The battle said to be once fought in heaven, has now to be fought on earth, ere his will can be done on earth as it is in heaven. The powers of darkness shall not prevail.' Whereas he had earlier supported the granting of equal civic rights to Jews, his new religious bent now led him to oppose Jewish emancipation because they had crucified Jesus.[95] His pamphlet of 1852 used religious language and quotations, and saw religious and political truth as inseparable. Several O'Brienites were disciples of Smith, whom this pamphlet specifically praised, sharing his view that religion was universal and natural and must be the basis of every social institution, and that the Second Coming would be effected by a minority of persecuted reformers.[96] 'And when these thoughts shall have been taught to the people, a "new heaven" and a "new earth" will be opened to their investigations.' The pamphlet declared its support for prophetic and doctrinal mysteries and clairvoyants, and one of the O'Brienites, the ex-Owenite tailor George Harris, was an active supporter of spiritualism.[97] The O'Brienites were an unorthodox religious sect, prominent in the republican Land and Labour League and in its journal, the *Republican*, which was run by Maccall, an ex-Unitarian minister and leader of the pantheistic Brotherhood of the Religious Life. In this journal they criticised Bradlaugh's atheism and based common ownership of land on Christian principles.[98]

Messianism and millenarianism could also focus on other figures. The radical sects of the July Monarchy shared the concept of a providential man serving the cause of progress, and an admiration for Napoleon, who was the object of a virtual cult in Chatel's church.[99] Napoleon was annexed to the 'blue' or liberal cause and was the object of an enormous and spontaneous popular enthusiasm, with prints portraying him as a secular saint. He was also the object of fantastic rumours. In Lyons after the rising of November 1831 a poor girl, Little Mary of the Terreaux, communicated her Bonapartist divine revelations and visions, was worshipped as the Holy Virgin, and predicted the fall of the July Monarchy.[100] Others circulated strange dying speeches attributed to the Napoleon-Messiah.[101] The inauguration of the Arc de Triomphe in 1836 touched off a wave of demonstrations and verse, but nothing could equal the emotion and frenzy aroused in 1840 by the return of Napoleon's remains to Paris, accompanied by the greatest crowds the city had ever seen. Coupled with the expectations of war, it seems to have set off millenarian and chiliastic excitement and hopes of a Messiah,[102] and it seems that the upsurge in communism of that year, including the messianic preaching of Pillot (who had lectured on Napoleon in Chatel's church) and his fellows, was set off by Napoleonic millenarianism.[103]

Who has not heard of the universal expectation that was the object of the famous year of 1840? What oracles were announced for that year, mysterious events! What anxiety everywhere! what foreboding! The world seemed to stop and await some great unknown.[104]

In the 1840s the Romantic cult of Napoleon was reinforced by eastern European mysticism, and Constant, a friend of the Swedenborgian Cheneau who had spoken to Napoleon in 1841, was one of those who saw Louis-Napoleon (who himself shared some of the ideas of the radical sects) as a revolutionary social 'prophet', inheritor of the genius of his uncle ('the God of the People'), who would pacify the country and re-establish the broken balance between spiritual and temporal authority.[105]

The question of religious radicalism is thus a very complex and varied one, which embraces political anti-clericalism, rationalist Christianity, and Enlightenment rationalism, common-sense scepticism and materialism, provocative blasphemy, radical sectarianism, the use of the Bible as a radical text, invocation of the ancient levelling Christ, a belief that God gave the land to all, social prophecy, and millenarianism.[106] The last two are most obvious before 1850 in France, after which prophets tended to disappear.[107] The drying up of Romanticism, with its strong religious impulse, was important here, as was the rapid decline of the chapbook trade, with its large religious content, before the rise of popular novels and serial magazines.[108] Perhaps the most obvious point is continuity in Britain and discontinuity in France, for the *coup* and its severe subsequent repression created a hiatus between 1851 and the 1860s absent from Britain. The close alliance between Empire and Church intensified radical hatred for the latter and led to a resurgence in publications of Voltaire, while the repression of deviance included religious deviance. As the increasingly ultramontane Roman Catholic Church adapted and strengthened itself, and was more successful at meeting the religious needs of the population through its softened tone, its change to a good God, the development of the cult of Mary, and compromises with popular beliefs and practices (thereby incurring greater rationalist ridicule), this was all under firm clerical control. The possibility of Protestantism filling the gap was prevented by repression and a loss of evangelical fervour.[109] In England, though not Wales, the Anglican Church reformed and revived, with a more active and visible priesthood, while Nonconformity tended to move away from its evangelical emphasis and stress on preaching, and concentrated more on buildings and developed institutions. This all meant a decline in the practice of a lay religion of the humble, and this led in turn to a decline in religious radicalism, particularly in France. Thus when French radicalism revived in the 1860s it was not religious. The tone and language at the Paris public meetings was overwhelmingly secular, and when the old veteran republican from the 1830s, Berryer-Fontaine, tried to invoke religion and Jesus he was shouted down.[110] As the new activist Malon explained in 1881:

Neither the God of Rousseau or the Jesus of the socialists of 1848 have been able to attract my political faith. Diderot, Spinoza, Hegel, Schopenhauer and the modern materialists are the object of my predeliction. My generation wishes it too . . .[111]

This marked a difference from Britain, where forms of Nonconformity such as Congregationalism remained important among labour leaders, religious impulses continued in the Labour Church movement and socialist Sunday schools, and one can still talk of a 'religion of socialism' in the late nineteenth century.[112]

## Science of the spirit

The decline in lay religion was part of a long-term process of professionalisation, so that religious radicalism became mainly a matter of radical clergymen, and thus in the earlier period lay religion was accompanied by lay philosophy and lay science, which therefore did not embody the later orthodoxy of materialistic science antithetical to religion. The change was recognised by the veteran Lefrançais, writing in 1886 about his views in the 1840s:

In religion I was atheist; only scholars, still in small numbers, were avowed materialists. At this time, one could be both atheist and spiritualist at one and the same time, however strange that may seem today.[113]

Freethinkers on both sides of the Channel opposed science to religion, as freedom to tyranny, and were naturally interested in scientific studies that undermined the Bible over the age of the Earth, and the evolution and antiquity of man, but 'science' itself was not uniform and was characterised by enormous changes, novelties, confusions, and uncertainties. Thus among radical artisans, for most of our period, a rationalist rejection of Christianity did not usually lead to atheism or to a mechanistic Newtonian view of the universe. We should note that Chatel held sessions and consultations in animal magnetism, that he and some of his priests became advocates of phrenology, and that Pillot became a homoeopathic doctor.[114] These were all seen as forms of science, and Chatel was combining religion with science. Self-educated working men had great faith in the scientific investigation of natural phenomena as leading to emancipation from folk wisdom and to progress, and rational religion was *ipso facto* in harmony with science, but still allowed the existence and scientific discovery of invisible and immaterial forces, substances, and worlds. To generalise from a small group of atheist journals in the 1840s and portray 'artisan science' as typically materialist is misleading,[115] for most were not atheists, and subscribed to a watchmaker God or diffuse, often pantheistic, beliefs in a power outside themselves, beliefs often not clearly thought out and even idiosyncratic. 'Many of the political reformers, nearly all the political reformers of Europe, appear to be neither Christians nor avowed Unbelievers. They seem to believe in God and immortality, but to have no faith in supernaturalism.'[116]

Radicals were often drawn into 'unorthodox' science, for the spirit of enquiry, intellectual independence, and reliance on one's own judgement could lead to revolts against hierarchical epistemology in unpredictable directions, so that, as Logie Barrow has said, heresy in one field attracted heretics from another.[117] As the radical Nonconformist and homoeopath, Miall, wrote: 'as a Protestant Dissenter I feel a natural sympathy for all those who hold opinions, whether theological or scientific, which are under the ban of legally-favoured professionals'.[118] Thus 'artisan science' was characterised not by uniformity but by extreme variety and flux, having in common only that they tended to annoy or threaten those who regarded themselves as more enlightened, as people shifted positions in search of a satisfying understanding of man's place in the world and universe, questions that were of much greater interest to members of mutual discussion groups than was economics. Thus Carlile shifted from atheism to support for Taylor's allegorical interpretation of Christianity to a conversion to Christianity.

The Abergavenny secularists held readings from Byron, Shelley, Burns, and Shakespeare, for secularist halls had a wide range of activities and views, and a glance at the secularist press shows that secularism was by no means a narrow, materialistic creed. They developed their own rituals and ceremonial, held constant debates with Christians as well as lectures by them, including unorthodox Christians such as the Mormons, and, like their press, were open to a whole range of different ideas and views. In the vast field between extreme idealism and extreme materialism, and in the 'popular version of Enlightenment, opposed generally to the religion of condemnation and the science of the learned',[119] there was no polarity between rationalism and millenarianism, religion and secularism, the material and the immaterial.

Secularists, Owenites, and Fourierites were very interested in phrenology, while the radical educational society in Paris arranging classes for workers after the July Revolution had a phrenology course, and the art critic Thoré related phrenology to art.[120] Phrenology had great appeal in the 1820s and 1830s as a progressive, reformist philosophy that challenged established privileged groups and old orthodoxies, including traditional religion, denied Original Sin or intrinsic human moral failings, and allowed for human improvement. While it could have materialist implications, these were not usually drawn out.

By the 1840s Owenites were also interested in mesmerism or animal magnetism, a philosophy based on an invisible, superfine fluid around all objects in the universe, its distribution explaining illness, which could be treated by activating human magnetic poles and the flow of magnetic fluid.[121]

Phrenology and mesmerism aroused similar debates, and, as their physiological bases were discredited, became (often linked) unorthodox beliefs. Both, especially the more vitalistic mesmerism, embodied the old idea that patients should be cured by restoring them to equilibrium, both within their bodies and with the external world, because sickness was not an isolated problem needing the chemical treatment of a material, malfunctioning human machine, man being connected with the world of nature in many ways. Phrenology and mesmerism, especially the latter, posed a special challenge to the medical profession in the form of lower-class, untrained amateurs who charged much less, and sought to make information on the mind and body accessible to the public instead of being the exclusive knowledge of a closed and self-perpetuating elite. With increasing medical regulation, alternative medicine became officially divided from regular practitioners who nevertheless did not enjoy an all-embracing hegemony, and were not, in fact, very effective, and tapped the widespread suspicion of doctors as using poisons as medicine and purposely keeping people ill to assure a continuing clientele.[122]

Doctors were prominent in radicalism for a number of reasons, but a number of them were also radical physicians, at odds with the medical establishments. Thus the saintly Raspail, who aroused such devotion among Paris workmen, developed an unorthodox medicine based on camphor, which was practised by a number of doctors. A staunch republican, he saw healing the material and moral illnesses of the poor and the ills of society as a combined process, was opposed to any registration of doctors, and ignored a fine in 1846 for illegal exercise of the profession.[123]

An important form of alternative medicine in Britain was medical botany, using herbal medicines in simple form, rather than refined chemical extracts, 'unnatural' mineral medicines, or poisonous doses. Brought to England in 1838 by Coffin, its chief figure was soon the Chartist shoemaker John Skelton.[124] Medical botanists opposed orthodox doctors as 'druggists' and poisoners who had a vested interest in ill-health. They remained overwhelmingly plebeian, and sought to free medicine from the bondage of the wealthier classes, and to democratise it both by instructing the poorer classes in the laws of health, thereby simplifying and popularising medicine, and by liberating them from the thraldom of 'legally qualified, money made and college-taught doctors'. For Skelton, 'to mystify, shut up in the schools, and make private property of that knowledge, which of all others ought to be universally taught, is a wrong the deepest and most injurious to society'. Medical botanists also criticised the fashionable movements in favour of the health of towns because they ignored the real reasons for ill health (wages, hours, and food) and gave too much power to doctors.

Raspail's use of camphor was shared by the 'Luther of Medecine', Hahnemann, the founder of homoeopathy, and while there were not many herbalists in France, it is striking how many French radicals were homoeopathic doctors. Homoeopathy stressed the patient's total equilibrium and relied on the curative powers of the 'life force' to help the body heal itself by quelling disease and by recreating internal balance. In using, for the most part, natural medicines, in regarding disease as not an isolated occurrence, and in stressing temperance, purity of diet and conduct, and the right mental condition, it had much in common with botanic medicine, though it was far less plebeian.

These movements often overlapped with other alternative medicines such as hydropathy (the water cure), and with vegetarianism. They were in conflict with medical establishments, in seeing disease as due to a violation of nature's laws and therefore avoidable, in regarding druggist medicine as a drastic, unnatural, and self-defeating attack on the body instead of as a way to assist it, in rejecting the reductionist treatment of isolated symptoms rather than of integrated wholes, in their optimist confidence in the healing power of nature, and in their democratic organisation and stress on democratic mutual caring in a medicine that all could practise cheaply as part-time amateurs.

The mesmeric practice of induced hypnosis was usually explained as a state in which the inner sense made contact with the spiritual world, and was freed to wander in space and time while the body remained fixed in a trance, and this practice came to dominate, so that mesmerism merged with clairvoyance, predicting the future, interpreting dreams, contact with the dead, and table-rapping and charcoal drawings by spirits. It thus became virtually indistinguishable from the new movement from America that spread fast in both Britain and France in the 1850s, spiritualism, which often used mesmerist fluidist theories to explain thought transference, and, like mesmerism, had services which involved sitting in a circle holding hands to allow invisible forces to work.[125] Notable adherents were Robert Owen, Esquiros, Fourierites such as James Smith, the very influential anti-clerical writer William Howitt, some old Spenceans such as Jennerson, and two of the three men who did most to accustom the English reading public to ideas of evolution, Robert Chambers and Alfred Wallace. Spiritualism portrayed itself as a science, and was also very much a movement of healing, opposing the tyranny of the medical professions over the bodies of their patients, for they should be helped to control them themselves through natural medicine. But it also absorbed older traditions of Swedenborgianism, fortune-telling, astrology, star-worship, pantheism, theocracy, millenarianism, and primitive religion. While some combined spiritualism with Christianity, most plebeian spiritualists were anti-Christian. In Britain, in fact, it became a surrogate faith, tapping into one of the main elements of popular religious belief, the afterlife and immortality of the soul, and it developed its own churches, choirs, hymns, lectures, prayers, and services by trance mediums.[126] There was much overlap with the secularist movement, which prospered in the 1850s, 1860s, and 1870s, but began to decline at the end of the 1880s, the decade when spiritualism really took off. The *National Reformer* showed great interest in phrenology and spiritualism, while spiritualists were great admirers of Bradlaugh.[127]

Thus, as in the shadowy, illuminist 'counter-Enlightenment' of the 1780s and 1790s,[128] there was great overlap between secularism, phrenology, mesmerism, medical botany, homoeopathy, astrology, and spiritualism (and also temperance, vegetarianism, and opposition to capital punishment, vivisection, and vaccination). All tended to reject materialist and physiological explanations of volition, emotions, imagination, and intellect, to see the mind as a distinct and fundamental reality, intangible and imponderable, and believe that each person had an intangible vital essence. While some of these movements drew support from all elements of society, for a while at least, the bulk of the support tended to be from small tradesmen, shopkeepers, a few professionals, and, especially, artisans and other educated workmen.[129]

They tended, also, to have links not only with radicalism but with socialist groups. The links between Owenism and phrenology, mesmerism, water-cure, spiritualism, nudism, laughing-gas, and new religions are well established, and Coffin was a socialist lecturer as well as a botanic physician. The influence of socialist schools on small groups of self-educated artisans extended to their religious, philosophical, and cosmological ideas.

Illuminist doctrines of pantheism and the transmigration of souls in progressive existences in a sexualised cosmos were taken over by Saint-Simonians and, especially, Fourierites (including Smith).[130] In 1848 the ex-Saint-Simonians Jean Reynaud and Ange Guépin identified their theology of successive and steadily purer lives on different planets, with the religion of the Druids, and this accorded with republican identification with Gauls against Frankish oppressors, expounded most of all in the histories of Thoré's friend Martin.[131] The members of a Fusionist church founded after the July Revolution proclaimed themselves the new Druids, seeking to undo the Roman and Frankish conquest of Gaul. One adherent of Reynaud's planetary-Gaulish theology was the highly religious veteran of secret societies, Armand Barbès, who in 1848 founded a religious radical club, the Club of the Revolution. Leading members were Sobrier, the fanatically religious disciple of Ganneau, Théophile Thoré, whose *Vraie République* publicised the club, and the secretary, Millière, a religious communist whose writings at the end of the 1860s crystallised the socialist ideas that had an impact during the Commune. In advocating self-governing communes which would own everything within them collectively, Millière gave full vent to a widespread pastoral strain as he sought to reverse rural depopulation, reject city life, and establish a stable, natural existence in natural units.[132]

All these ideas clashed with the ontological foundations of orthodox science, which was committed to a physicist's view of the mind–body relation and regarded such ideas as forms of 'superstition' and occultism. There was also an inevitable tension with a democratic epistemology, whereby knowledge was defined as being open to anybody and not mystified and shut up in academies as the preserve of intellectuals and professions. As a supporter wrote of Proudhon (himself, like Fourier, strongly influenced by the religious writer Martin Bucer on regaining the lost paradise of unity and harmony of nature):

He seeks to turn us uninstructed proletarians into *scholars* (savans), he does for social sickness what another *devoted* and *learned* citizen, Raspail, has done for sickness of the body; he wishes us to save ourselves without the aid of *doctors*, empiricists, *slaves of routine*.[133]

A democratic epistemology does not have to accompany democratic politics, but John Harrison has indicated a number of common themes shared in Britain by Chartists, Owenites, radical religion, fringe medicine, vegetarianism, and spiritualism (and, we may add, secularism).[134] Apart from the overlap in personnel, and the appeal to the same social constituency (labouring people, artisans, tradesmen, some of the lower middle class, and a few professionals), there are a number of common strands: democratic doctrines and assumptions; a stress on self-help and doing things themselves (expressed also in friendly, co-operative, and trade societies, and in opposition to charity or state schools); hostility to professionals and the elitism of those in authority (such as doctors, hireling priests, or lawyers); holism; a concern with religion and the place of man in society and the universe; a central concern with the relationship of mind and matter; a populist anti-intellectualism; a desire for esoteric knowledge; and, finally, an often semi-mystical concern with nature (shown in medicine, vegetarianism, the conceptions of natural and artificial society and of abundance for all wasted and perverted by man, the communist wish to return to a state of nature, and the pastoralism of ideal societies and communities).[135]

Beliefs such as homoeopathy were seeking to redraw the boundaries between science, medicine, and religion, and the above set of beliefs seemed to be opposed to a liberal culture of reason, science, individualism, professionalisation, and a civilisation or civil society founded on the conquest of nature and the suppression of natural savagery and instincts both within oneself and, in the eyes of elites, in certain sections of society. But this conception was also challenged by Romanticism and its view of nature as the repository of moral values corrupted by a new, materialistic society. Romantics shared in currents of religious revival, spirituality, Polish mysticism, eschatological thought, dreams of utopia, the cult of woman as the new redemptress of the world, harmonies, occultism, and the pantheism of such spiritual fathers of workers' poetry as Shelley, Lamennais, and Hugo (a believer in the transmigration of souls, hierarchy of invisible spirits, primitive religion, and universal harmony of sun, moon, and stars in the vital fluid).[136] Constant became a prime figure in occultism under the Jewish form of his name, Eliphas Lévi, but although he developed his ideas in a romantic, literary, and artistic world, not that of artisans, he was in fact the most popular of the magical writers, and he shows how religion, millenarianism, and magic could be a means of securing support for radicalism,[137] but these beliefs had much deeper and older roots than Romanticism, which itself had a natural affinity with Platonism.[138]

Particularly important here was pantheism. The belief that God or Spirit dwells in nature, that God is divine energy dispersed through all life, that man and nature are not independent of God but are modes or elements of his Being, can be seen as a derivation of God's infinity and omnipotence, but is difficult to reconcile with a belief in God as Christ and is usually opposed by Christians because the identification of God and nature is dangerously close to atheism. Yet it is not compatible with the Newtonian deist view that God controls nature from outside through laws. Pantheism can lead to virtual materialism and to seeing nature as in itself a sufficient explanation or cause for existence and the workings of the world, or to a denial of a separation of matter from spirit, or to a conception of men and women as divine and so on to mysticism and a magical view of the universe as alive.[139] It thus merged with a set of ancient beliefs whose most influential expressions lay in the late Renaissance.

These included persistent Gnostic notions of a dualism between the spiritual and material worlds, the eternity of matter and spirit, and of esoteric knowledge revealed to initiates; and hermetic philosophy incorporating alchemy and astrology (both regarded as higher forms of magic and male preserves distinct from witchcraft), symbolism, occult cosmology, and the transmigration of souls. They were complemented and reinforced by Renaissance neo-Platonism, with its vitalism and many spheres of being, system of spiritual hierarchy within nature, and magical and occult system of sympathies and correspondences with spiritual forces that could be comprehended or controlled.

Such beliefs gave way in the seventeenth century to modern science, Calvinism, and anatomical beliefs in the body as a wonderful but unmysterious machine, but they were overlain rather than wholly displaced (O'Brien's religious contributor used the same *nom de plume*, 'Philalethes', as that of the American alchemist who influenced Newton, Boyle, and Leibnitz),[140] and they remained important, and were reinforced by the Jewish mysticism of the Kabbalah, Romanticism, and Polish mysticism. They thus fed alternative intellectual traditions to rationalism, political economy, utilitarianism, modern science, and liberalism, and they reinforced a stress on experience alongside learning, with a consequent strong self-confidence, impulse towards system-building, and a repudiation of the authority of 'experts'.[141] They strongly influenced Fourier, whose influence on Chatel included his cosmological ideas, so that both believed in the transmigration of souls. Thus even the notorious Blanqui combined his atheism with praise of Jesus and with Platonic Idealism, and was influenced by hermeticism and its interest in life on other planets. Without necessarily approving of all of them, he condemned the Roman Church's opposition to all the innovations of the century.

Catholicism, eternal, implacable enemy of all forms of progress, enlightenment, perfectability. Who could forget the anathemas against vaccine, against chloroform, against railways, against steam, against all the discoveries of the human spirit? And mesmerism! And phrenology! and table-turning!

His club in 1848 included the religious radicals Esquiros and Pujol, and his later followers saw their beliefs as descended from Greco-Roman polytheism, a benign religion of natural processes.[142]

The links of such enduring beliefs with religion are shown in the Radical Reformation, English revolutionary sects such as the Shakers, and in Swedenborgianism. Perhaps the best new example in our period is the religion that Bramwich joined, Mormonism, an American religion of primitive communism, secret rites, and polygamy, which made 50,000 converts in Britain by 1856 alone, and also spread rapidly among southern French Protestants.[143]

Such ideas were not confined to small elites or sects, for folklore and the popular literature of chapbooks and almanacs were full of them.[144] They had many points of contact with widespread aspects of popular culture – there were suspicions of professional doctors and a reliance on midwives and folk herbal remedies (Skelton was at pains to stress the long roots of medical botany), mesmerism overlapped with traditional laying-on of hands and fortune-telling, and it and spiritualism were easily equated in the popular mind with the faith-healing and miracles of the New Testament.[145] But we should not see these ideas as exemplifications of a pre-scientific popular culture lagging behind modern rationality, or as the means whereby radicalism gained support from the illiterate, ignorant, or credulous. They were not held only by plebeians, and while radicalism certainly did tie in with aspects of popular religion such as opposition to gloom, doom, and hell-fire, stress on enjoyment, entertainment, and lay involvement, and concern for this rather than the next world, these attitudes were not confined to any particular section of the poor. Religion is manifestly not a characteristic only of the less educated. Mesmerists stressed that their doctrine was a science, not folklore, and there seems no evidence that popular superstition was a source of support for radicalism, or that religious motifs attracted to radicalism the undiscerning and ignorant in particular. Millenarianism did not appeal to the very poorest, and radical millenarianism in our period seems to be found among the highly educated. Thus all these currents, that so often interlocked with radicalism, were most obvious among more educated members of the working population, though never confined to them, for ordinary people leading simple lives do not necessarily hold simple beliefs and are capable of complicated ways of thinking, and these ideas were spread not only through written matter but orally through evening lectures, doctors' classes, and the practice of amateur scientists.[146] Thus, as Jacques Rancière says, we should pay attention to this 'parallel' philosophy, that diffuse religiosity that Corbon described, opposed to both the religion of original sin and the Voltaireanism of elites, and by no means just an echo of Romanticism, a philosophy

of the marginal, this rational mysticism or enchanted rationalism which is like the popular underbelly of the philosophy of the Enlightenment; philosophy linked to linguistic speculations, to innovating medicines, to parallel religions. A philosophy little known whose underground history has nevertheless often weighed much more heavily than the spectacular political and social theories.[147]

# 11 The culture of radical clubs

Radical political activity among artisans cannot be separated from other aspects of their lives. As in the French Revolution, it faced the rival demands of work, home, and pleasure-seeking at the cabaret, so that often, as Cobb said, 'billiards and women had the final say'.[1] Radicals thus competed with aspects of popular culture. Yet mobilisation is more successful if it builds on existing social relationships, shared structures of communication, and routine interaction, the community ties built up by social intercourse and conversation. Radicalism could thus be based on groupings existing in often very localised areas of social exchange and sociability. Work was one such location and basis for radicalism, and, as a commentator in Birmingham noted, 'the manufactories, my friends, have their politicians and republicans as well as the barber-shops and alehouses'.[2] But, as Corbon remarked, 'daily labour is therefore for our working man merely the forced labour imposed each day; and having generally no serious or lasting love for his labour at all, he only devotes to it the smallest portion of his intellectual weight', and he stressed, behind the apparent resignation of the working population, 'a devouring need for an outside life', 'this great and legitimate need of an outside life that characterises the Paris working man', which he saw expressed in an interest in novels, theatre, drinking places, gaming, easy women, and political events.[3] Dunning stressed how trade union newspapers always failed, because the working classes wished to read not about matters relating to working men but for amusement, to get as far away as possible from their daily toil, and his *Bookbinders' Trade Circular* only survived through subscriptions, including those of non-working people.[4] Radicals could also operate in fairs, sports gatherings, or dance-halls, but taverns and cafés were the especially important channels of sociability and sites of neighbourhood social clubs. Radicalism thus not only used leisure activities but, in giving people a sense of involvement and interest, had also to become a leisure activity, and thus take forms often different from those of the self-improving articulate minorities, and incorporate elements of a vivid tavern- and fair-going plebeian culture.

'Popular culture' should not be seen as hermetically sealed from any other culture, elite or otherwise nor as a uniform set of values or attitudes, but rather as an ensemble of practices in usually small social worlds, such as family, neighbourhood, clubs, or ethnic groups. These were not static, and the radical London jeweller Morrell wrote in 1866 of the great cultural changes that had taken place since his youth:

Many of us can remember the time when there were no public parks as we have now; when the working man was not thought worthy of entering Kensington Gardens; when cheap excursions by rail or boat did not offer the mechanic and his family the ready means of reaching, if only for a day, the pure and bracing atmosphere and the country scenery, and when Hampton Court Palace and its Picture Galleries, Kew Gardens and its Museums were not accessible.

Then the tastes and habits of the people were coarse and ignorant; dog-fighting, wrestling, and other brutal sports were common on the Sunday. To pass the day undressed, or to while away the time by fadding at home, was a custom; whilst great numbers who could work at home at their business, did so, that they might make holiday on Monday. Now we know that all this has been changed or is fast disappearing. The purer and more rational enjoyment of the Sunday is more appreciated, shops for unnecessary Sunday trading have been shut, and streets, once like fairs, are now quiet and closed.[5]

But these changes were in process, and on Sundays, and there were great continuities, reinforced by constant rural immigration, but there was also growing commercialisation, social separation of leisure, and pressure on public space. Many changes focused activities even more fully on the indoor public-houses, beer-houses, cabarets and cafés, steadily growing in number as centres for a whole range of activities, the sites where modern popular recreation originated.

One can see popular culture as characterised by resistance to efforts from above to control or change it, and by contempt for the law and its agents, and see assertions of the people's right to pleasure as resistance to discipline. There were disturbances in Bordeaux nearly every time a ball, play, or fireworks display was forbidden.[6] This resentment could be linked with political radicalisation, especially as radicals often resisted such attempts at control – Chartist opponents of Sabbatarianism were prominent in the Sunday trading riots in London in 1855.[7] 'Have we not seen the commons of our fathers endorsed by insolent cupidity, – our sports converted into crimes, – our holidays into fast days?'[8] But the association is not straightforward, for other political groups could associate themselves with popular culture, such as British Tories, while many radicals were opposed to those elements of popular culture which they saw as buttresses to the existing system, the drunkenness and immorality of Carnival and similar festivals, the coarse and obscene, or inane and anodyne, songs and plays, the 'gross and pernicious pleasures of the public-house',[9] music-halls and their scantily-clad females. For the O'Brienite Murray, 'the great want among trades' societies was sobriety', while Tolain condemned popular novels, 'these public poisoners, whose language, adorned with barbarities, ornamented with slang, oozes the pot-house, the prostitute and the convict-hulk'.[10] Thus many thought 'the socialists must intervene to use and moralise the People's amusements by giving them a becoming direction',[11] and they engaged in a number of alternative forms of sociability similar to those of middle-class moralists, including temperance, excursions, balls, tea-parties, soirees, readings, duets, glees, concerts, and field sports, in most of which the involvement of the family was sought.[12]

## Locations

A French republican declared in 1839 that the radicals would use the whole gamut of means open to them – papers, pamphlets, petitions, trials, and preaching in inns, streets, and squares.[13] Certainly radicals used the locations and occasions of popular cultural activities. The 1839 rising of the Seasons society in Paris took place on the Sunday when crowds were out for the races, while the Reform League demonstrations on Primrose Hill in 1866 and Blackheath in 1867 were arranged to coincide with the Whit Monday recreations. As the open spaces became lost or unavailable, the streets became the main arena of outdoor radical activity, of speaking, singing, hawking sheets and tracts, and processions, and the police measures to clear this last resort of popular assembly aroused tremendous resentment. In the early 1830s, 'each street in Paris was in turn the Waterloo of our public liberties'.[14] When street demonstrations were not allowed at all, as under the July Monarchy and in the latter years of the Second Republic, or on certain days, such as Sundays in Britain, radicals used other forms of action that had a certain legitimacy which hampered suppression, such as funerals, open-air preaching, or folkloric festivals. It was during Shrovetide in 1831 that a crowd, reacting to a legitimist ceremony, sacked a church and the Archbishop's Palace. The 1848 revolution began in Paris at the time of Carnival with the bodies of those demonstrators killed by the troops paraded on Carnival floats, and a radical 'funeral' in Lyons commemorating the death of legitimism was reminiscent of Carnival rituals. In 1832 radicals at Metz subjected the authorities to 'rough-music' (*charivari*), with bells, whistles, cornets, and pots and pans, singing the 'Marseillaise' and shouting 'shame on the proposer of the act against the Poles! Down with the renegade liberal! Down with the *juste-milieu*! Long live liberty!'[15]

Growing difficulties over outdoor activity made the available indoor sites more important. In the early part of our period churches and theatres were the two main buildings in which large numbers of the general public gathered. Churches were sometimes used for radical demonstrations, as in the wave of mass Chartist attendance at parish churches in the latter part of 1839, when outdoor gatherings were prevented, a tactic that reappeared in 1866, but far more important in England was the establishing of radical meeting-places as 'chapels' able to hold indoor meetings on Sundays. Public theatres, on the other hand, were well established as arenas for political expression. The large establishments were attended by both rich and poor (in separate parts of the auditorium), but in addition were the numerous other shows which drew popular audiences, with a large amount of interchange and banter between performers and audience, and much heckling and harassing. 'If anything is truly popular in France, and above all in Paris, it is without any doubt the show, less, perhaps, the great than the little: those, for example, in which they sing ballads.'[16] London and Paris compositors had theatre troupes and put on benefit performances.[17] It was because of its popularity that Pierre Vinçard felt 'the theatre above all can moralise the people' and Louis Blanc saw state control of the theatre as the most effective way of influencing the population.[18]

Radicals also exploited exclusive theatrical privilege and resentment at the closures of unauthorised theatres.[19] Theatre disorders, over plays, performers, prices, and seats were frequent, usually taking the form of conflict between the occupants of the rich and poor seats, particularly in periods of high social tension, as in 1848 in France. Audience participation made theatres subversive, as it was difficult to control them. Both plays and audience reactions were politically laden, and gave a priceless opportunity for political expression. In the early 1830s French audiences insisted on the singing of the 'Marseillaise' and loudly applauded radical sentiments, such as praise of Belgians or Poles. At a royal visit to Drury Lane theatre during the political excitement in 1831, it was judged prudent to replace the revolutionary opera *Masaniello* by the harmless *Marriage of Figaro*. Even anti-radical sentiments were dangerous, as the audience was free to protest – thus a play was hissed in London in 1866 for lines criticising the Hyde Park Reform meeting, and under the Second Empire pro-Imperial sentiments were excluded from theatre performances because they provoked a reaction.[20]

Theatres might also be hired for political meetings, and the universal popularity of dancing, especially among the young, led to the development in our period of large public dance-halls (where shows were often also performed) which provided another large indoor location important in popular leisure that could create spaces, free of the elements and seasons, for a democratic political urban life that radicals could utilise. Since they were very familiar places to the population at large and were not used three or four days a week, they were often let to societies or meetings, their musical stage providing a platform.[21]

However, much dramatics, entertainment, and dancing, as well as a myriad other activities, took place at public-houses, to make these places central institutions in popular culture. Their importance grew as the streets became unavailable, and 'the popular festivals became less splendid, the public-house was "the working man's church"'.[22] Their importance partly reflected the importance of drink in working-class life, and while this led often to drunkenness and violence, and the London Society of Compositors, for instance, received a continuous series of claims from members who lost their frames through drink, drinking was not the same as drunkenness and was seen as good for health and essential for any heavy labour.[23] The main reason for going to public-houses was not to get drunk but for the companionship and sociability that accompanied drinking. Nor was time in the pub a purely leisure activity, for much business was conducted there, including hiring and pay, and workmen often found relationships in a pub useful for information on employment, prices, and conditions, and for getting in the good books of those that mattered.

The basically artisan character of public-houses, beer-houses, and cabarets continued in the nineteenth century, and even increased, as richer groups progressively withdrew into more private clubs, fashionable cafés, the drawing room, and home, while those labourers, semi-skilled, and women who could afford to drink, often went rather to the dram shops and wine shops.[24] The largely male character of pubs, beer-houses and cabarets, especially on weekdays, and the consequent lack of respectability of females who went there, especially alone, meant that after a long walk Nadaud could not persuade his mother to go into a cabaret, even accompanied by him, while when in 1867 the London tailors' union set out to attract women and established a ladies' branch, with a committee sitting at a pub, a special side-door entrance had to be made available for women to use.[25]

The large number of pubs and cafés meant specialisation, in clientele and function, for example for members of a particular trade or interest, and for particular activities. 'Café life was powerful and ubiquitous because it was multiple and varied.'[26] As Lowery said of Newcastle in the 1830s, there were pubs for singers and musicians, freethinkers, literati, artists, scientists, and for each political party.[27] Cafés and pubs therefore provided building blocks for social movements, and constituted a privileged site where resistance was conceptualised and enacted, and they were centres for trade committees, societies, and combinations.[28] Since such institutions were often identified by their politics, they were very important in such radical activities as conspiracies, Chartist branches, sections of the Rights of Man, signatures to radical petitions, or meetings of socialist-democratic groups in the Second Republic. They largely explain how radical movements and upsurges were possible despite rather rudimentary and undeveloped formal organisation. But their largely male character reinforced the male character of radicalism, especially with the decline of outdoor actions in which women had usually been prominent.

The ancient association between tavern gatherings and anti-authoritarianism and the ease with which they could be a cover for clandestine and political radical activity meant that the authorities were always suspicious of such places and tried to control and limit them, though such actions often provoked great unpopularity and could alienate whole communities. While Napoleon was fairly tolerant of plebeian café life, the repression under the clericalist Restoration politicised the cafés in Paris, and the July Revolution was followed by an upsurge in café-based radicalism, both in the city and the suburban tea-gardens (*guinguettes*). Thus Raspail described republicans in the early 1830s plotting in the street, tap-room (*estaminet*), tea-gardens (*guinguettes*), billiard rooms, shops, and National Guard units.[29] The Second Empire brought severe and extensive repression of cafés (alongside other signs of working-class independence), and the total number in France fell from 350,000 to 290,000, only to rise again to 360,000 in the liberalisation of the 1860s, but this anti-café policy was a dead letter in Paris, where the number continued to grow, and the regime failed to stamp out café radicalism, as the Commune was to show.[30]

Both outdoor locations and cafés and pubs were regarded by many as unrespectable sites, but the importance of both was underlined by the failure of the 'infidel tour' of England in 1829 by Carlile and Taylor. Taylor's year in prison for his parodies of Christian services now led him to share Carlile's obsession with a respectable image and to insist that they did not preach outdoors or in public houses. The fatal result was the need to hire expensive rooms and usually thin attendance.

Some of the functions of pubs and cafés were increasingly also met by specialist institutions, such as cookshops (*gargottes*), eating-houses (*crêmeries*), and low lodging-houses (*garnis*). From the 1820s, cafés, with their range of beverages, grew at the expense of cabarets in French towns,[31] and the popular coffee-houses which multiplied in English towns, especially in London, supplied a range of non-alcoholic drinks, papers, and even books, with the great advantage that they were free of control by landlords, brewers, or magistrates. All these were also important outlets for radical publications and centres of radical activity.[32]

As other indoor premises became available, radicals increasingly used them. Early hopes of the Mechanics Institutions were not on the whole fulfilled and they were not usually open to hire by radicals. It was because of the unavailability of mechanics' institutions, and their exclusion of political discussion or female participation, as well as clerical campaigns in 1839–40 to prevent them from finding anywhere to meet, that the Owenites established their own 'Halls of Science'. Chartists also opened some of their own halls, and both were also available for use by other groups, while radicals could also often hire the halls run by friendly societies (especially the Oddfellows), temperance groups, and co-operative societies. In France, political clubs in early 1848 were able to rent private halls, but this was a short-lived facility, though there were some efforts to construct their own halls in 1849. As such places did become available in England, there were growing efforts to move away from reliance on pubs, among both radicals and trade societies, especially printers (in 1850 the Paris Typographical Society also rented a small building to house an office and a reading room away from cafés). Radicals' search for alternatives to pubs also accompanied efforts to increase female and family involvement in radical activities.[33] However, the extent of these developments was limited before the end of our period, especially in London and France, and the pub or café remained of central importance to popular radicalism.

### Media

All political groups had symbolic features – legitimists always commemorated the execution of Louis XVI, while republican students in the early 1830s were distinguished by their careless dress, beards, and long hair, and as a fervent republican the workman Nadaud wore a Phrygian bonnet.[34] Radicals necessarily used not only the locations but also the forms of popular culture. As we have seen, they appropriated the occasions and symbols of fairs, Carnival, rough music, effigy-burning, and funerals, and established forms of publicity and attraction. Radical shoemakers adapted the drunken 'prize-boot' contests traditional in their trade to raise funds.[35] Chatel, in seeking to draw attention to his church, 'resorted to the same expedients as troupes of strolling players', while Dr Coffin organised processions with bands.[36] Radicals collected, treasured, distributed, and sported white hats (associated with Hunt),

Phrygian caps of liberty, tricolour ribbons, medals, medallions, busts, statuettes, pipes, tokens, and pictures and mugs of heroes such as Garibaldi, Ledru-Rollin, or Jesus the Worker.[37]

Alongside visual forms, radicals used the main forms of popular printed literature, such as the ancient staple reading, the almanac, often including political verse and satire.[38] In the towns, especially, almanacs and chapbooks were supplemented or supplanted by popular literature in the form of broadsides, broadsheets, hand bills, squibs, and posters sold and distributed by patterers and ballad-singers, and fixed to walls and doors, and 'put in tripe shops, fish shops, barbers shops, beer-houses',[39] and radicals produced theirs alongside commercial ones.

Particularly important in France at the start of our period were Bonapartists and devotees of Napoleon who, deprived of direct access through the written word, brilliantly used tricolour ribbons, snuff boxes in the shape of Napoleon's hat, walking sticks with his face at the top, statuettes, trinkets, jugs, pipes, and medallions. Cheap prints portrayed him as the of hero the people, in the uniform of a corporal (later pictures in the Second Republic showed him blessing his nephew, or the nephew in prison writing about the sufferings of the poor).[40] These devices were copied by Cabet in his Icarian movement, his annual almanac a great success, and were then taken up very successfully by the socialist-democrats in the Second Republic, with almanacs, and pictures of radical heroes and of the Republic as a blooming woman, on the model of pictures of the saints, the Virgin, or Napoleon.

The growth of popular, cheap reading matter in our period was to modify these elements in popular culture in important ways, although the popular themes of fate, luck, romance, the lives and loves of the famous, and notorious crimes all endured in the rising popular fiction, often sold in cheap instalments or serialised in newspapers, an important element in the growth of a popular press. All these were used by radicals. Hetherington's illegal *Twopenny Dispatch* in the mid-1830s included full coverage of crimes and court cases, and pirated serialised novels, and his friend Cleave moved further into more entertaining and satirical radical publications. The outstanding success in France was Eugene Sue's serialised low-life novel depicting an underworld of crime and prostitution, the *Mysteries of Paris*. This apparent social realism aroused great emotion among working-class readers and was seen as a depiction of the oppression of the proletarians. Such serialised novels were used by radicals as a way of circumventing the 1835 press laws, and appeared in radical papers, such as Cabet's *Populaire*, whose success also owed much to its criticism of society through titillating short reports on crime, degraded artisans, and fallen women. Sue's novels, and Pyat's play *The*

*Rag-Picker of Paris* were among the most potent forms of radical propaganda, although some radicals deplored this commercialisation and sensationalism.[41]

An English shoemakers' journal, recognising that most members of the trade liked novelty and light reading, serialised Sue's *Mysteries of Paris*.[42] The chief imitator of Sue in England was Reynolds, whose serialised Gothic novels and entertainment magazine gave a radical tone to lively, sensationalist, and pornographic narratives of urban low-life, brutality, and murder, the often virtuous and heroic poor of the old ballads, the scandal, corruption and sex in high places, the parasitic upper class, and the conspiracies among the evil aristocrats and Jesuits that revealed the class nature of society. *Reynolds's Newspaper* was the largest of all the popular Sunday papers, with a weekly sale of 300,000 by the mid-1860s, and had the same blend of popular sensationalism and radicalism, with extensive coverage of crime and court cases, a persistent emphasis on the personal failings and immorality of aristocrats, and a democratic, republican radicalism that championed working men.[43]

Satire and caricature was also often an effective way of puncturing authority. With the press laws of 1835, the French republican press resorted more to innuendo and satire to evade the law, and the *Charivari* did more to spread republican ideas than any of the serious papers.[44] The same device was used under the Empire, and with the new liberalising press law of 1868, the only successful new extreme republican papers in Paris were satirical ones, especially the sensational *Lanterne* of Henri Rochefort. With its tone of boisterous gaiety, polemic, satire, poking fun at everyone, including the Emperor and his government, it was a prodigious success, selling 500,000 per month. Elected in 1869 to the Legislative Body, Rochefort sat with Raspail on the extreme left, and became the hero of the public meetings, combining with the Paris socialists and internationalists to launch a new newspaper, the *Marseillaise*, an alliance nevertheless opposed by radicals outside Paris.[45]

Thus the explosion in 1848 of almanacs, printed songs, pictures, pamphlets, and periodicals played a key role in mass exposure to political questions and challenges to the local dominance of the rich and elevated, but radicals relied largely on the established means of distribution – hawkers in streets, workshops, cabarets, cafés, tobacconists and barbers, and chapmen (especially in rural France), although in the towns radical bookshops, newsagents, and reading rooms grew in importance. In times of repression, as in wartime and post-war England, or in France after 1848, when political chapmen were suppressed, reliance was on the underground distribution of republican literature, through tramping artisans, seasonal migrants, itinerant musicians, removal men, stagecoach drivers, postal and railway workers, and commercial travellers. Radicals thus used the expanding commercial infrastructure of railways, postal system and sales agents, and both Republican Solidarity and Reform League used the insurance company technique of travelling agents who were funded through commissions on the new branches they established or the subscriptions they collected.[46]

Oral culture remained important, and it was really through former soldiers of Napoleon's armies that memories of the French Revolution were transmitted.[47] In recognition of the restrictions of written work, radicals such as Spence and Varlin wanted spelling reform to demystify literature and make it truly available to the people.[48] Radicals relied largely on speeches, lectures, and songs,[49] and drama was another important oral form. Chatel made a particular place for theatre artists in his church: 'comedians, citizens like other Frenchmen, and missionaries of the arts and progress, outrageously rejected by the Church of Rome, come to the temple of reform to unite with their brother artists, industrious like them'.[50] Radicals often put on dramatic pieces, for example *Wat Tyler*, *The Trial of Robert Emmett*, *Property is Theft*, and *Napoleon and Josephine*.[51] Melodrama, the dominant popular theatrical form, was easily given a radical slant.

Reading aloud at work or leisure was a universal element in popular culture, and Perdiguier was influenced by a Swiss comrade who read tragedies and other plays aloud. Penny readings were very popular among working people, and John O'Neill in the 1820s and Leno in the 1850s became well known in the London pubs as reciters of written works.[52] Thus radicals relied very heavily on the reading aloud of their literature, at workshops, lodging-houses, and, above all, pubs. But this was not just a reflection of limited literacy, for radicals often preferred to hear works read out and commented on, so that the 'reading' of radical work was not passive but collective, involving discussion and criticism. The French radical press, with Cabet again the pioneer, was therefore often written in an 'oral' style suitable for reading aloud, with entertainment, sensation, and a personal tone.[53] Radical literature could also take popular oral forms, like proverbs and, especially, fables. The various books of fables produced by the Saint-Simonian Lachambeaudie went through several editions and were recited in the workshops.[54]

## Singing

But the most popular oral medium was undoubtedly song, the main, universal form of music in popular culture. Songs were popular, easy to understand and remember, and did not require literacy. Singing was a recourse for beggars, and there were many street ballad-singers and patterers, singing and selling songs printed on single sheets of low-grade paper, and catering for popular taste.

The content of popular songs varied enormously – laments, a life of hunger and insecurity, the pain of things, love, and sentimental, dramatic, bacchic, comic, martial, marital, didactic, rude, scandalous, and satirical themes, for 'song partakes of both the chameleon and Proteus – it is impregnated with the influence and willingly makes itself the echo of the changes that take place in the environment in which it hums'.[55] The most effective technique used by the great Restoration religious missions in the 1820s was the singing of canticles, in which religious lyrics were set to popular tunes, even revolutionary ones, and they were often also printed on very cheap broadsides accompanied by pictures.[56] The products of the French worker-poets that had most impact were their songs.[57] Perdiguier thought the workers' papers of the 1840s failed to reach a popular readership because of their tone and content, and he himself looked to song as the main medium. Thus when he tried to end the destructive antagonisms and hatreds between the different compagnonnic orders, he focused on their harsh, savage, frenzied, warlike songs, and sought to replace them with reformed, acceptable ones with a message of fraternity and harmony; 'he perceived the real place of the song as a form of expression for the workers'.[58]

'Let me make the ballads, and who will may make the laws.' Song was put to all political uses. During the French Revolution and Restoration, opposing groups sang rival songs, while Napoleon, Louis XVIII, and Charles X employed songsters to produce suitable songs for the street singers.[59] Inevitably, then, radicals seeking popular support had to make use of song as the main means of linking radicalism and popular culture, for, as Kingsley said, 'the man who makes the people's songs is a true popular preacher'.[60] Moreover, popular song had always had elements of sharpness, satire, humour, and complaint, abuse and ridicule of the rich and powerful, and rejection of all injustice, unscrupulousness, and unmerited glory. 'In all ages', wrote Nicholas Brazier, 'the people has mocked. Although the ballad yields to all forms, the form that seems to suit it the best, is the satirical one. The ballad must always be in opposition, at the risk of being harsh and, if I may say so, silly. It is to its courage, I will say even its audacity, that we sometimes owe the redress of many abuses', so that the Ancien Régime had been 'a monarchy tempered by songs', and 'ever since people have sung in France, all the authorities have declared war on songs and songsters'.[61] Thus there were protest songs during the cholera of 1832, and in the

Lyons risings of 1831 and 1834. Political songs had much greater influence than the press, and were thus one of the chief weapons of the opposition. The malicious and satirical attacks on Restoration nobles, Jesuits, and police in Beranger's songs were a huge success, spread everywhere through hawkers, street and pub singers, and were sung all over France, a measure of his renown being the Jesuits' setting of new words to the tune of his celebrated song against them.[62] With the July Revolution popular songs were far more political than ever before, though the regime soon began to clamp down on street singers, and to forbid dinners where the radical songs of such composers as 'Burgundian the Genius' were sung:

> Without showing anger
> He displays profound contempt
>    For the mercenary creature
> Who works for a low price.
>
> In short, his existence
> Consists wholly of toil,
>    For competition
> Produces rivals without term;
>    But since France
> Has such a peerless code,
>    A hospital death
> Will be his just reward.[63]

Saint-Simonians and Icarians also made great use of songs.[64]

'I am bent on resuscitating Chartism in earnest, in London,' wrote the newly arrived Cooper to his fellow-poet, William Jones, in 1845, '. . . and, therefore, intend to introduce singing.'[65] Chartist songs played a vital part in Chartist meetings, both large and small, set to simple metres, often to tunes from Methodist revivalist sects. John Stafford, 'the Charleston poet', although illiterate, composed many successful Chartist songs in Lancashire,[66] and Bramwich's 'Britannia's Sons' was sung by Leicester Chartists, Staffordshire miners on strike in 1842, in West Yorkshire in 1848, in a Black Country miners' strike in 1858, and at a Leicestershire Reform demonstration in 1866. Chartist, Socialist, and friendly society song-books multiplied after 1839, and it was indicative of his links to popular culture that Reynolds later insisted on the need for radical songs.[67] Songs remained just as important among the republicans and Internationalists at the end of our period.

Songs were collective rather than private, whether indoors or outdoors, so here, again, the public-house or cabaret was a key location. A fundamental institution was thus the 'free and easy' convivial singing club, an informal and amateur sing-song involving songs, toasts, cheers, and the old tavern traditions of 'harmony' through collective reading or chanting. These occasions, sometimes all-male, sometimes mixed, were mainly on Saturday nights after pay, in which people took it in turns to sing or do a turn, and everyone joined in the choruses in an expression of unity. 'It is, briefly, a concert in a public-house, where everybody drinks what he likes, smokes what he likes, and either sings himself or listens to his neighbour singing, as it may please him.'[68] In time some became grander affairs, with pianos and semi-professional entertainers, and later developed into full singing saloons and music-halls, but the more informal gatherings, often with peculiar and strange names, kept their long popularity.[69]

Songs were particularly effective in times of repression, when the use of a universal medium, common tunes and a whole variety of forms, including elliptical, ironic, ambiguous, and humorous language, was very difficult to suppress. The potential of such mixed convivial and singing occasions as free and easies for radicals is clear, and they were used in London in the repression of the later 1790s: 'if the business transacted was treason, it was carefully wrapped up in the jokes and ribaldry, said or sung in such places'.[70] But it was Thomas Spence, the great pioneer of adapting traditional forms and methods to radical uses, for example cheap tracts, verses (many of his followers only wrote in verse), broad-sheets, handbills, posters, tokens, and wall-chalkings, who also set out to use songs, recitations, drinking, toasts, and singing in harmony at tavern free and easies during the wars, with a stress on radical solidarity and brotherhood. For, he said, 'cannot small meetings be effected where large ones durst not be attempted . . . Even under the modern tyrannies of China, France, Turkey, etc., what can hinder small companies from meeting in a free and easy convivial manner and singing their rights and instructing each other in their song?' As Iain McCalman has shown, the free and easy was one of the key channels of Jacobin cultural diffusion in post-war London.[71]

At the same time, after the defeat of Napoleon in 1815, the clericalist Restoration had clamped down on all expressions of opposition to the regime and so, 'as at the time of the Mazarinades, the people consoled and avenged themselves through singing'.[72] Radicals in Paris naturally used the developing popular free and easy (*goguette*) for singing, recitation, and dancing. As in England, there were exotic names (often the railing and carping Momus), rivalries and competitions, the swapping of tunes, collections for distressed comrades, and sensual, epicurean, bacchic, vulgar, bawdy, licentious, obscene, and Rabelaisian songs, but also waggish and satirical attacks on statesmen, government and church. Many were about the rigour, hardships, and sadness of life, to understand which 'you must have, like the artisan, constantly before your eyes the unhappy prospect of a sad morrow, and the fear of having to appeal to the charity of his brothers in adversity'.[73]

Some Paris Restoration free and easies were composed of members of particular trades who met at particular cafés, such as the Anacreon (mostly whitesmiths), Joyous Friends of Pleasure (shoemakers and tailors), the Little Goguette (printing workers). The repressive and clericalist nature of the Restoration reinforced their oppositional and radical stance, exemplified in the ironic notice, 'political topics are forbidden but smoking is allowed'.[74]

Nicholas Brazier was taken by a relative to the 'Children of Glory'. 'I forewarn you, added my cousin, that you will find yourself with working men, artisans, it is a wholly popular society.' They were, in fact, mainly building workers.[75] The free and easies worshipped Beranger, who had set out to elevate popular song from the bawdy, licentious, and drinking level, and popular songsters followed his models. Dominant themes in these songs were a very strong anticlericalism, and a popular religiosity devoid of church, hierarchy, Original Sin, miracles, divinity of Christ, evil, Hell, or all intermediaries between man and God (priests, monks, confessors, guardian angels, saints, Devil, dogmas, rites, or relics). God was seen as giving meaning to men's birth and death but not interfering too much in between, being basically a benevolent, understanding, good fellow who created wine, love, and friendship and wanted people to enjoy themselves (a view totally at variance with Tridentine Roman Catholicism and also distinct from much Christian radicalism, but having a lot in common with Chatel). There was also a strident patriotism and a populist cult of Napoleon:

> Ah! how proud one is to be French
> When one looks at the column!
>
> He will return, the little corporal
> Let the grey coat live forever!
> Honour, honour to our great emperor.

It was, in short, a negative liberalism, against nobles, courtiers, police, magistrates, censorship, repression, and Restoration, with the basic theme that people should be left alone by the authorities to enjoy themselves; in all, a heady subversive combination of hedonism, anticlericalism, and libertarianism. 'Make love, live in joy; spurn your grandees and hypocrites.'

Thus, in combining radicalism and popular sociability, the free and easies were important centres of opposition to the regime. 'And as for these singing meetings, or free and easies (*goguettes*), so criticised, so ridiculed since, it must nevertheless be recognised that they were, at this time, powerful schools of patriotic education. It was in these meetings that the Paris working men went to imbibe the love of our national glories and public liberties. It was in the beautiful pieces of Beranger that the people reinvigorated that heroic courage that enabled it to accomplish in three days that providential revolution of 1830, dealing the last blow to that old paraphernalia of hereditary monarchy', for 'all waged war against the Restoration, and all had soldiers under fire from the Swiss on the 28 and 29 July 1830'.[76]

The July Revolution led to a great expansion of free and easies, in Paris especially, where they numbered several hundreds. The Shepherds of Syracuse 'were men in blouses, in jackets, with horny hands and faces blackened by labour and sweat', and female workers too. In these free and easies radicals engaged in praise of the republican Bacchus, and in a populist Bonapartist critique of the conservative and craven regime (the emotion at the return of Napoleon's remains in 1840 was sustained through such songs as 'Napoleon and Jesus Christ'). They experienced increasing repression from 1832, but although all authorised meetings always solemnly announced that all political songs or songs attacking religion, the King, or morality were forbidden, this was often evaded, and the presence of policemen with the power to stop any songs was circumvented by hints, allusions and irony. One of the largest and more formal of the societies, the 'Songster's Tournament' ('Lice Chansonnière'), was overtly republican. The 'Infernals', composed of workmen and students, each with a special demon name, was more extreme and was repressed by the police. The unauthorised 'Animals', or 'Menagerie', under Charles Gille, admitted people after a Masonic-style baptism into an animal name, and opened with the announcement 'political songs are permitted, and one can say **** to the King', and had to keep moving premises to avoid suppression. Some set out explicitly to radicalise free and easies. Eugene Pottier, writer of plays for children's theatres and future author of the 'International', became a composer of free and easy songs after the July Revolution, many of them set to Beranger tunes. While he never renounced the epicureanism of his youth, he changed the genre of trite drinking songs into a sort of mystical communion with God through wine, excluded bawdy elements, and filled his songs with patriotic and radical sentiments, lamenting that the July Revolution had changed nothing and that winter had dried the flowers of July. When the other Saint-Simonians scattered, Jules Louis Vinçard kept the group of working men together and organised Sunday afternoon meetings at cafés. With Lachambeaudie and others he set out to spread the Saint-Simonian faith in the language of republican epicureanism at the expense of the blue elements in popular songs. (Similarly the Chartist Leno organised free and easy harmonic meetings at a pub in Uxbridge in the late 1840s, including impromptu songs, and managed to exclude blue ones.)[77] Pierre Dupont's famous 'Let us drink to the Independence of the World' was based on a Saint-Simonian song in his native Lyons and, like Dupont, Vinçard could compose tunes on the spot, and his songs and those of his companions spread in the free and easies, especially in the 1840s. Free and easies thus remained important in radicalism, the mood varying with circumstances, the dashing of the early hopes and the repression often leading to resignation and laments, as in Lapointe's 'Poverty is slavery' and 'All escapes us, alas!', Pottier's 'It is always the same', and Lachambeaudie's 'But I have suffered so much that I weep no more!' With the crushing of the 1839 Seasons' rising, only four secret societies remained in Paris, and one of them mainly for singing. According to Blanqui, the people who sang songs at free and easies were not the sort to join political societies, but this does not reduce the importance of this level of radicalism, especially in view of the relative unimportance of formal organisation, and Blanqui himself was prosecuted in 1847 for founding a revolutionary communist free and easy, the 'Goguette of the Sons of the Devil'.[78]

'The cruellest tyrant is infamous poverty / And it is that which must be overthrown.' The most popular of all the French religious communists was the abbé Constant, who had a greater rapport with popular culture then Chatel. He had, significantly, been a travelling comedian for a while (as had two of Chatel's priests), wrote short novels and was a popular illustrator, but it was especially his songs that had the impact, for he was master of the whole gamut of ballads, carols, odes, drinking songs, comic pieces, Rabelaisian humour, laments, revolutionary songs, and outrageous lampoons. Often they were set to popular airs, such as the 'Marseillaise':

> Yes, nature is our mother:
> We claim her rights for all.
> On the earth we wish to place
> Our feet and not our knees!
> Justice and not vengeance! . . .
> Work and freedom too!
> Fraternity or death!
> Deliverance or nothing!

Later he was also the writer on magic who had the most popular impact, again because of his songs, especially when in the 1860s he returned to his earlier Rabelaisianism.[79]

The 1848 revolution produced a new wave of songs, Lamennais

being one who saw their importance. 'Song being a powerful arm of popular opinion, we propose to gather, in the free and easies and political clubs, the progressive expression of the thought of the people.'[80] Pottier produced new songs about the hopes of bread and the promises of the vote, and Lachambeaudie was one of those arrested when a cook's association was raided for singing patriotic songs. Again, as open propaganda was closed down once more, songs retained their importance.

At a dinner of the Luxembourg delegates in November 1848, where the bread came from a co-operative bakers' association, the dinner was by a cooks' association, and the decorations by an upholsters' association, Lachambeaudie recited two of his fables and Dupont sang one of his songs.[81] Dupont was the outstanding songster of the Second Republic, with a prestige equal to Beranger's earlier. His 'Song of bread', 'Song of the peasants', 'Song of the soldiers', 'Song of the vote', 'Song of the labourers', and, above all, 'Let us drink to the Independence of the World', and 'Song of the working men', were on everyone's lips and captured the sentiments of those years of injustice and brotherhood, and the millennial hopes of the election due in 1852.

> It is two years, barely two years,
> Till the Gallic cock will crow;
> Stretch your ear towards the plain,
> Do you hear what he will say?
> He says to the children of the land
> Who are bent beneath their load
> 'Here is the end of poverty,
> Consumers of black bread and water.
> From the sacred mounts where the light
> Forges its light and its fires,
> Come, displaying your light,
> Eighteen hundred and fifty two.'[82]

When legal means of radical expression were steadily ended, singing become a more important form of protest and means of rallying the faithful. After the *coup* a determined effort was made to crush the free and easies, and, in Pottier's eyes, the Second Empire, by banning political songsters, froze political song. On the other hand, the authorities did allow the development of larger establishments, and full music-halls (*café-concerts*), seen, as in England, as easier to control.[83] Nevertheless, informal singing continued as a form of resistance, with singers moving from room to room as they sang, avoiding overt political content, and using caustic, satirical, ironical, and farcical language. One aspect of this was a retreat into dialect and non-French songs. In 1856

Constant was imprisoned for his song 'Caligula' attacking Napoleon III,[84] but Dupont's remained the most popular radical songs, and as the Imperial police recognised, 'the propaganda carried out through the medium of songs is very dangerous. Through this medium the worst doctrines are easily engraved on the memory of the population. These rhymed and sung forms are introduced into all meetings, are repeated by all and constitute a real evil.'[85]

The limited liberalisation of the 1860s led to the growth of cafés (and dance-halls) and more general singing, and Pyat saw the public-house ball and singing at cafés as the main forms of public meeting.[86]

## Clubs

Free and easies did overlap with popular theatre and dancing, but they were also just one example of the more general phenomenon, the club, often based in pub or café, that was such an important element in popular radicalism. The variety and specialisation of pubs and cafés, grouping people with similar interests, including members of a single occupation, meant that they often developed a private and even restricted, closed and exclusive character, and became almost private clubs, exemplified by the private nicknames by which members were known in the group.[87] These merged with such formal clubs as box, benefit, lottery, cutter (rowing), cock and hen (salacious for the young), Judge and Jury, athletic, singing, musical, saving (clothing, furniture, clocks), mutual aid, or trade ones. 'The English working man is by nature, one would think, the most social or sociable animal on earth. He joins clubs and associations almost by instinct.' But the contrast with France was rather the greater restriction on voluntary associations, for, when allowed, French working men also developed a rich associational life. Discussion and debates were a well-established feature of tavern radicalism, and convivial-debating clubs were an important radical institution in our period, combining reading aloud and songs, ballads, toasts, and jokes, though the 'debates' included much banter and chaffing and were not really structured, oratorical, or keeping to the topic in question, being as much concerned with debunking authority through shock, humour, and pathos.[88] The *clubs* in Paris in 1848, that is, really, political unions, were largely debating and discussion bodies, and the formal clubs that emerged in France in the 1860s were mainly discussion ones,[89] while the Christian Socialist the Marquis of Townsend, the founder of one of the precursors of the Reform League and International Working Men's Association, the Universal League, was forced against his wishes to include political discussions.[90]

Convivial groups could become the basis for political action, as with a singing society in Paris that became the secret society of Jacobins, or a café group in Lyons in the 1840s, the Voraces, who became in 1848 the notorious radical militia who seized control of the forts dominating the city.[91]

Social and convivial clubs with their own rented rooms or premises were a development of this, and were further bases of independence – free of the masters' control and pressure from landlords to drink too much, and free to smoke (an important issue – a radical paper in 1848 saw the new no-smoking rule in the Tuileries as a return to aristocratic ways),[92] freer also of drink taxes and bans on gambling, and indeed from the police generally. Clubs could thus become centres of radical political activity, or become radical through harassment by the authorities, as with the *chambrées* in France under the July Monarchy and Second Republic. Thus the Working Men's Electoral Association of Chelsea, formed to support Odger's candidacy in the 1868 election, became a discussion society meeting in the back room of a pub, but when they were expelled they clubbed together to rent a broken-down house, and profits from the sale of ale and tobacco enabled them to lease good premises in the King's Road and become the famous Eleusis club, the chief radical club in London. Similarly a group, mainly of shoemakers, formed a St James's club in 1864, the provision of liquor in 1867 guaranteeing the clubs' success.[93]

Such clubs engaged in political discussion and themselves accepted some of the criticism of pub culture (excessive drinking, rowdyism, links with the underworld, even Toryism), and some members of the middle classes therefore supported clubs as alternatives to the pub. In the 1860s, especially, there was in Britain liberal and reforming support for a significant movement to found working-men's clubs. But tension arose in these clubs through resentment aroused by patronage, efforts to change behaviour, Bible classes, religious exhortations, limitations on the reading matter and games allowed, hostility of many patrons to trade unions, ban on discussions of politics and religion, and exclusion of smoking and ale on the assumption that working-class drinking inevitably led to drunkenness. The patrons' original intentions were subverted within the clubs, and they came to encompass a whole range of activities, mostly continuations of pub activities, with beer on sale, games such as billiards, cards, dominoes, draughts, bagatelle, skittles, rowing, and quoits, Saturday evening concerts, free and easies, lectures on political economy, history, religion, literature, poetry, phrenology, mesmerism, and physiology, discussion classes, spelling bees, libraries, newspapers, a reading room, smoking room, philanthropic and sick funds, death money, benefits and donations for unemployed and distressed members and their families, subscriptions for winter coal, flour, blankets, boots, and Christmas geese, summer outings, children's Christmas parties, and brass bands. These all-male establishments, as they became independent, often became very political, especially in the 1870s, in opposition to Sabbatarianism, the anti-music hall lobby, Irish coercion, or grants to the Royal Family.[94]

We must therefore emphasis the continuity of radical groups based in cafés and pubs and mingling radical politics with conviviality, adopting different forms in different circumstances, the sites of small-scale and informal collective practices that made possible wider temporary mobilisation and organisation. The *Bee-Hive* attributed the Commune to a politicisation achieved, despite repression of political processions and societies, through talk at workshops and cabarets.[95] While in Britain, political parties outside London came to engage quite widely in clubs, lectures, galas, excursions, and friendly societies, this was mainly after 1867, when earnest liberals tended to leave the way clear for Tories to associate themselves with beer, pudding, enjoyment of life and sport and popular culture, but for most of our period cultural differences between liberals and conservatives were not marked and it was radicals that most associated themselves with these convivial activities.[96]

Thus the revival of popular radicalism in London in the early 1830s, particularly in the National Union of the Working Classes, incorporated debating clubs, bawdy literature, and meetings at pubs, coffee-houses and infidel-radical chapels, while the Society of the Rights of Man had sections meeting at bars, and engaged in drinking and singing.[97] The Chartist movement was a coming together of existing groups of radicals, and after the heady days of 1839 many branches were based on taverns and beer-houses and involved the usual tone and forms. Republican Solidarity in 1848–9 was based on a reds' network in already-existing associations, clubs, cabarets, salons, and beer-houses.[98] The Reform League in London brought together a number of existing, largely pub-based radical groups as branches, such as the Robin Hood Discussion Society in Leather Lane, though the numbers naturally expanded during the excitement over parliamentary reform. These branches, mainly meeting at pubs, engaged in the same activities as they had been doing before. While a systematic corps of lectures arranged by the Executive seems to have had a limited effect, the branches had lectures and discussions on a range of topics quite distinct from the official programme of the League, such as trade unions, the opening of museums on Sundays, republicanism, town and country life, Shake-speare's *Hamlet*, poetry of peasant life, Ireland, Cromwell, Instinct

against Reason, and compulsory education, while a shoemakers' branch
in Bloomsbury had a lecture on shoes from the time of Alfred to the
present.[99] For the Shoreditch branch, 'among the many advantages
arising from these branch unions may be mentioned that they are a first-
rate mutual instruction class. After the necessary business of the evening
is concluded, we discuss political questions.'[100] Many branches had
singing, the Marylebone branch resolving 'that this meeting views with
pleasure the introduction of Reform songs at the weekly meetings of this
branch', and the League, like the Spenceans earlier, produced its own
choir-book.[101] The North London branch had monthly entertainments,
involving songs, recitations, comic medleys, and the 'Reform Minstrels'
who also performed elsewhere, while the Clerkenwell branch methodi-
cally canvassed working men's clubs and held open-air rallies on
Clerkenwell Green, mixing business with pleasure, involving the
Garibaldi and Cubitt's bands.[102] As well as red flags, tricolours, and
caps of liberty, Reform League banners at demonstrations had
humorous, ribald, and carnivalesque slogans, especially puns.[103]

At other times, when such movements declined, these branches
unravelled into clusters of separate radical–convivial groups, as in
London in the 1820s. It was the club basis of London Chartism that
enabled it to survive the 1848 repression largely unscathed, in contrast
to the rest of the country, so that Chartism maintained a strong presence
in the metropolis right through the 1850s, its activities consisting mainly
of lectures, discussions, and debates at a number of locations, such as
secularist halls, educational premises but, above all, public-houses.
Sometimes these were separate societies, as with Codgers' at the Barley
Mow off Fleet Street, founded in 1755, of which Wilkes and Hunt had
been members, sometimes they were sections of the National Charter
Association, Boot and Shoemakers' Reform Association, the National
Union of 1858, or the later London Political Union, but basically
Chartism consisted of a set of pub-based clubs, discussions, and lecture
groups, mixing radicalism with conviviality and song in the traditional
way. The key figure in this milieu was John Leno, the 'king' of London
tavern radicalism, the fiery Uxbridge Chartist of 1848, who had come to
London in 1851 already an experienced pub reciter, lecturer, and singer,
and later printed the songs he performed in the clubs and pubs as *King
Labour's Song-Book*. He organised a group of young radicals called
'Propagandists', who led weekly discussions at the various locations. It
was in this 1850s Chartist milieu that the leading radicals of the 1860s
won their spurs, for example Odger, Cremer, Howell, and Henriette,
none of them as yet involved in trade unionism. But the great builders'
strike of 1859 aroused great emotion in these radical clubs (in the same

way that the Paris public meetings of the later 1860s were aroused by Paris strikes where the document was imposed), and it was through this *radical* support for the builders that Odger, Cremer, and Howell became prominent in the trade union world. It was the absence of this sub-culture that weakened such radicalism in the provinces. These younger club Chartists of the 1850s were to be the leaders of the Reform League in the mid-1860s, and, as Leno said of the League, 'that it was the outgrowth of the Chartist movement, there can be no manner of doubt'.[104]

With the break-up of the Reform League after the Reform Act and recriminations over further political reform, relations with the Gladsto-nian Liberals, the scandal of the secret election fund, and Fenianism, a number of branches resumed their activities as separate ultra-radical, anti-Gladstonian, republican, and largely secularist clubs, coming together at times in the Working Men's Reform League, Land and Labour League, Republican organisations, International Democratic Association, or Unemployed Poor Union. Thus the Robin Hood Discussion Society became a branch of, in turn, the Reform League and Land and Labour League. At the same time, as trade union affiliation to the IWMA fell away, this organisation also became mainly composed of these east London ultra-radical clubs.[105] Thereafter clubs remained important in London radicalism, in organisations such as the Manhood Suffrage League in the 1870s, the Democratic Federation in the early 1880s, and the Metropolitan Radical Federation of twenty-six clubs in 1886, all continuations of that Chartist, republican, and secularist tradition different from official liberalism.[106] There was thus basically a continuity of tavern and club radicalism, with an enduring tone and ideology, in London right through from the early to the late nineteenth century, occasionally coming together in wider movements and organi-sations, such as NUWC, ELDA, NCA, RL and LLL, but continuing when these came to an end. Throughout this period, in both Britain and France, criticism and disapproval and repression focused on their 'disorderly' character, as occasions of immorality and drunkenness that were a threat to family life, just like the 'intellectual Saturnalia' and 'socialist carnival' of the Paris public meetings.[107]

As we have seen with the free and easies, such clubs were a particularly important basis for radicalism in times of repression, as politics at convivial meetings was difficult to track down and suppress, while the possibility of discussion was far more attractive than military-style discipline and commands (it was the lack of debate and discussion that led to artisan withdrawals from the 'Families' and 'Seasons' secret societies, with their stress on strict discipline and passive obedience).[108]

During the French Wars and their aftermath, Spenceans and others used debating clubs, free and easies, popular chapels, and dinners. While the July Revolution led to open political activity for a while in France, repression after 1834 led to secret insurrection societies, and a reliance on benefit and co-operative societies, educational groups, free and easies, dinners, and private clubs. With arrests and the refusal of public spaces in later 1839, Chartists fell back on education, and cultural and co-operative activities (only a few engaging in insurrectionary conspiracies). M'Douall in 1840 suggested a regrouping of Chartists in 'reading clubs' to avoid prosecution.[109] The 1848 revolution brought political freedom to France for a while, and the secret societies became political unions, but increasing repression of meetings, organisations, and the press led to a falling back on social and benefit clubs, dinners, election meetings, co-operative societies, illegal secret societies, the use of traditional festivities, and meetings in bars and cafés to talk and sing, so that all of these experienced repression in turn, including forms of public entertainment and the cabarets, 'for there one could still converse on the criminal path followed by the president of the Republic and the majority of his monarchist acolytes'.[110] In Besançon 'some attempts at political associations, in the form of *Benefit Societies* have been tried'.[111] Radicals fell back increasingly on private clubs. 'The parties are still organised in the *Clubs* (*cercles*) and the *Chambers* (*chambrées*) which have replaced the political unions (*clubs*) – *There lies the danger.*' The authorities recognised the problem 'in the small towns and countryside, *Chambrées* held in the private houses and thus escaping surveillance'.[112]

With the *coup d'état*, the police state built up in the Second Republic was now used with full force against any kinds of popular independence – republican works, trade and benefit societies, combinations, or café meetings, even cafés themselves. 'The imperial fist presses everywhere down upon us. It has forced us out of sick clubs, because we sometimes talked in them about the state of the nation . . . but even our singing clubs are now suppressed, and we must not meet even to transact the business of a benefit society without giving notice of our design to the police, and receiving into our party at least two of its agents as lookers on. The result has been the decay of all such societies, and the extinction of most of them.'[113] Under the Empire, there were no civil liberties, no independent press, theatre, religious life, novels, public speaking, or organisational form of any kind, and order reigned on the outside, suspect taverns were closed, chapbook catalogues and teachers purged, street disorders prevented, and attempts were made to stop all autonomous working-class sociability. Radicals therefore used songs and singing clubs, underground distribution of tracts, sometimes handwritten, and private meetings at cafés, such as one in Paris where 'gather every evening, from 5 to 7 o'clock some veterans of 48, who come to chat about past times, the politics of the day, and also of hopes of a return to the Republic'.[114] Thus in the first election after the 1851 *coup* and its attendant terrible repression, clandestine propaganda in the working-class districts of Lyons, using natural networks of communication in workshops, homes, and cafés that the police could not penetrate, secured the election of the republican Hénon.[115] Later, when the Empire gave working-class sociability a certain space and liberty in an unsuccessful attempt to channel it, radicals used the three forms of formal organisation allowed: benefit, co-operative, and educational societies.[116] Thus in the 1863 election the Paris republicans' electoral committee included some working men, from an engineers' benefit society and two clubs. It was one of these clubs, the United Workers, led by Tolain, that set in motion the election of trades' delegates in 1862, the labour candidates in 1863 and 1864, and the French section of the International Working Men's Association in 1864.[117] After a brief period of freedom with the fall of the Empire, repression after the Commune meant another retreat into clubs, and 'the cafés resumed their old role of political haven'.[118]

In London, too, clubs were seen as a way of establishing political freedom, because of the hostility of authorities, especially magistrates, to the use of back rooms in pubs for red republicanism and secularism, their power of withholding licenses giving them great leverage, while the Fenian scare and consequent harassment and eviction of Reform League branches in 1868 led to a number of them forming overtly radical clubs on a more specialised, permanent footing – the Holborn and Clerkenwell branches forming the Patriotic Club, and the Chelsea branch eventually forming the Eleusis Club.[119]

Thus the form of organisation varied with circumstances. In the early 1830s a breakaway from the journeymen silk-weavers' compagnonnic trade society of Ferrandiniers led to a rival society condemned by the Ferrandiniers as Renegades. In the latter 1840s they had become a mainly convivial club under the name of Voraces, also engaged in protests against frauds in the weight of bread and quality of wine. In the freedom of early 1848 they operated openly as a political organisation and militia, but with the return of repression they became a secret society.[120]

These radical activities and milieux did not simply reflect elements in popular culture or male artisan culture; songsters such as Pottier, Vinçard, or Leno sought to reform and improve pub and café songs, and English working men's clubs rejected some aspects of pub life, but all retained the features of easy-going hedonism, epicureanism, and drink. Popular culture was not uniform, and not all radical artisans shared in an 'idealized artisan culture', consisting of 'a group of shoemakers or weavers disputing religion and politics over their work, and frequently adjourning to the pub to quaff whisky or ale, sing subversive songs, and debate the existence of God'.[121] Another development out of free and easies, apart from the music-hall, was choral societies (*orphéons*) of artisans, clerks, and shopkeepers, under a teacher who could read music, singing tunes printed by the growing sheet-music industry. These developed in the early 1830s, in France partly because of a clamp-down on free and easies and political songs, and in England in many cases growing from the Dissenting chapels, independent of elite musical life, and often able to use mechanics' institutions. A little later, and sometimes in tandem, developed amateur bands and orchestras.[122] These were usually far removed from the pub culture of the free and easies, and therefore more favoured by respectable opinion,[123] yet they were equally relevant to radicalism. Some of the early French ones, notably the Montagnards, were formed by radicals in response to repression, while the Children of Lutèce of the 1840s were very prominent at radical events in the Second Republic.[124] Most learned music through the rival Wilhelm and Mainzer methods, but in Paris the republican teacher Chevé used a special democratic elementary course aimed at enabling the masses to read and learn music without needing to cram or be 'turned into parrots'. It was through this method that Vinçard learned to write music, and he was prominent in organising the Saint-Simonian orchestra and choir that gave public performances. The Owenites and secularists were also keen on respectable vocal and instrumental music and concerts that the whole family could attend, the Hallelujah Chorus being a great favourite.[125] Radicals and Chartists also had harmonic meetings, soirées, and concerts, often to raise funds for individuals in distress, while trade organisations often held concerts in support of strikes, although Sabbatarian pressure suppressed the London radicals' Sunday Evenings for the People in the 1860s.[126] Choral and musical societies and concerts were also an important part of radical activity in the Second Republic.[127] Under the Empire, the rapidly spreading Orphéon choral societies tended to be republican, their organ was run by the republican Jules Simon and sometimes included political articles, and the token republican newspaper allowed by the regime, the *Siècle*, established a circulation through these societies. In the 1860s the republican Gallic Harmony in Lyons performed at liberal events.[128] In London, the German Working Men's Society was best known for its vocalist chorus, which officiated at radical and International occasions, as did the Garibaldian and Cubitt bands.[129]

These choral and musical clubs were rather different from the singing groups at pubs and cafés, even though some of these had formal organisation, and they indicate cultural differences and tensions within popular radicalism. The Owenites' and post-1839 Chartists' constant round of social activities of fellowship included respectable, non-pub forms such as temperance, soirées, tea-parties, excursions, and choral and musical events, in which the participation of women and families was specifically sought, although a move away from pubs and an encouragement of the participation of females was not usually a means of liberating them.[130] There were elements in radicalism and among trade union leaders that disapproved of what were regarded as 'rowdy' forms and sensational aspects inimical to rational debate – mass rallies, demonstrations, and processions; public meetings; street agitation; hero worship of political leaders with 'star' qualities; boisterous and often spontaneous tavern-, café-, or club-based 'debates' and sing-songs, that combined radical politics with conviviality, and reached a wider constituency. Leaders of a London shoemakers' trade society organised a meeting at the Mechanics' Institution, without refreshment, and were scandalised when members brought bottles, pipes, and tinder boxes.[131] William Lovett rejected the mass platform, cult of leaders, and meetings in pubs.[132] Benoit described how Lyons radicals disliked the way people brought food and drink to celebrations of trees of liberty. Skelton disapproved of Coffin's fairground and commercial devices. Jones objected to *Reynolds's* combination of sensationalism and radicalism, organised evening gatherings away from pubs, and in 1855 wanted the demonstrations in Hyde Park to be orderly and observe decorum, without organ grinders or banjo players. Republican deputies and provincial radicals disowned the Paris public meetings, while some of the leadership of the Reform League disapproved of its branches' appropriation of the customary culture of radical street-theatre.[133] Many Chartists thought that the special London characteristic of meeting in pubs, under the influence of drink and in the tobacco fumes, was useless in the work of rational radical education and understanding.[134] Much radical activity was not intellectual, sophisticated, or coherent enough for other radicals, who disapproved of the shallowness and sensation-alism of *Reynolds's Newspaper*, and the unreflective emotion that could easily be suborned and was open to appropriation by Toryism or Bonapartism. For a while Palmerston gained extensive appeal among groups of radicals, as the non-party opponent of legislative activism and supporter of parliamentary independence of government, the libertarian anti-authoritarian and patriotic friend of liberty, the victim of court and aristocracy, the virile, manly, womanising anti-Sabbatarian supporter of pleasure, of easy-going and approachable manners. Yet there is no doubt that these themes and styles were very effective in broadening appeal, and that they characterised a type of radicalism resistant to liberalism as these very appropriations indicated, encouraging support for republicanism, secularism, labour struggles, and irreverence, most evident in the two capital cities of London and Paris. They are not easy to access in the sources, especially in that of the press.[135] The concern to make radicalism more 'rational' grew in importance, but it tended to be relatively over-reported in the press, and the extent of the changes actually effected in popular radicalism during this period must not be exaggerated.

Thus, an obvious point, radicals drew on, used, and modified all aspects of popular culture, different groups selecting and appropriating the most pertinent and congenial cultural forms and idioms. The relative importance of *all* educational, cultural, and convivial activities rose when radical movements were in decline and no longer gathered great crowds, or when there was repression and radicals fell back on safer activities that were far more impervious to police control. We must, however, avoid a crude dualistic categorisation of popular culture, much of it based on the definitions of respectability made by people outside the world of labour. People were at home in several worlds, like the Saint-Simonian rule-maker Vinçard, or the secularist tailor Neesom, who was active in the tavern-based post-war Spencean activity and revolutionary London Democratic Association, and was a supporter of temperance, a schoolteacher, and a colleague of Lovett.[136]

Entertainment was important in most forms of radicalism, and all forms of it vexed some radical leaders. For some participants, the main or sole appeal of Owenite activities was enjoyment,[137] and just as Nonconformists were afraid that their choral concerts had become merely entertainment, so Owenites who rejected the urban leisure activity centred on the pub as destructive of brotherly love, worried that members were interested in dancing, entertainment, singing, and benefit societies rather than Owenism, and that, despite the ban on alcohol, members smuggled it in.[138] Educational events, such as science lectures with flash-bang experiments, were a form of entertainment, as the Owenites and mesmerists realised but many educators did not before the 1850s.[139] Much of the attraction of politics and religion was that they were controversial and thus entertaining subjects.[140] At the republican meetings at the Rotunda in 1831, many of the audience left after the speech by the star, Gale Jones.[141] Radicals were well aware of the attraction of staged debates, of Chartists with Socialists, Leaguers, or Temperance advocates, or between Socialists and Christians, and the Socialists saw the attraction of women lecturers.[142] Perhaps connected with this was the success of dialogues as a form of written propaganda. Thus Perdiguier, in seeking to reform the *compagnonnages*, relied on songs and a dialogue as the effective ways of moulding opinion, while one of the most successful radical almanacs of the Second Republic, by Joigneaux, contained brief didactic dialogues on such matters as indirect taxes, elections, and radicalism, and Wheeler composed a dialogue for use by the agents of his Friend-in-Need insurance society.[143] But these were different forms of entertainment, and the music-halls drew on Rabelaisian theatricals used in free and easies whose members were 'epicureans in jackets and blouses', where Pottier sang on love, wine, mistresses, laughter, and gaming, and against marriage and monasteries, for 'this life is a free and easy'.[144]

These elements are also evident in the wave of indoor public meetings in Paris in the last years of the Empire. While the initial ones, at the Waux-Hall in the centre of the city, took the form of lectures by liberals and economists, the tone soon changed and they were captured by the extreme left. The Pré-aux-Clercs was mainly the place for rowdy anti-Catholic and socialist students and shop assistants, with few working men. The largest was the Salle Molière, mainly attended by the middle and lower middle class. But soon the public meetings moved from the fine areas and the centre of the city to the working-class suburbs (meetings further out were not very successful). These meetings, each with a regular, largely local audience and speakers from a pool of twenty-five to thirty ultra-radicals who performed everywhere, became in effect political clubs, and exhibited the features we have come across. They grew increasingly radical, choosing provocative chairmen, for example extremists, political exiles such as Ledru-Rollin, Pyat, Raspail, Barbès, and Rochefort, or men in prison, and although they were supposed to be non-political, they adopted official topics such as 'Capital and Labour' or 'the struggle of men in nature and the means of remedying it' which they then proceeded to ignore in elliptical and allusive attacks on the regime, government, and its agents (and in direct attacks and open calls for revolt at the time of the trial of the Imperial murderer of Victor Noir in April 1870). A constant irritant was the presence of a policeman, who had powers to warn speakers and dissolve the meeting, and became the target of increasing insults, defiance, and threats. There was bitter antagonism to the liberal leaders and deputies who shunned and criticised the meetings, and strong support for groups on strike, above all, the Paris leather-dressers. Typically, it was the political aspect of the strikes, the repression by the regime, that was the chief focus. 'What they wanted the public above all to understand, was the collusion between the government, that is the Imperial State, and the employers. Labour conflict were treated from the political rather than industrial angle.'[145] These meetings had many of the features of convivial clubs and popular entertainment. The 933 meetings took place at 63 different places, of which 21 were ballrooms, 9 music-halls, 4 theatres, 2 circuses, and 18 wine-sellers. They imposed their own types of discussion, with open expressions of approval and disapproval through applause and hooting of speakers, so that each meeting became a popular jury, with votes often held. There was great intolerance of speakers who were not entertaining, and, as with the Spenceans after the wars, they were not real debates or focused on a topic, anyone who tried to read from books or notes was howled down, the stress being on extempore speaking. The tone of convivial clubs was also retained in the mockery of authorities, comical attacks on the police, humour and energy, extravagant opinions, grotesque topics, ridicule, and burlesque incidents.[146]

These meetings were not accurately reported in the press. The liberal Molinari attributed their content and tone to the lack of liberal freedoms in France, but in fact they were paralleled in British clubs. The radical press reports at the start of our period of the meetings of the National Union of the Working Classes in London give a different image, but there are indications in the sources that these meetings were not in fact very different (and this is clearer with the performances of Robert Taylor at the Rotunda and Benbow's Institution of the Working Classes). In both countries, in the taverns and café groups, free and easies, clubs, and the Paris public meetings of 1868–70, all composed of artisans and a sprinkling of middle-class people, we find a broad consistency in tone and ideas, overlapping with much of the older broadside literature and street ballads, and reproduced to a degree in *Reynolds's Newspaper* (which carried sensational and titillating reports, condemned the 'Saints' for their opposition to public amusements, music-halls, and dancing girls, backed the strikers in every single industrial dispute, and supported the Paris Commune). There was an often vague republicanism, consisting mostly of personal attacks and insults on monarchs such as Louis-Philippe, Victoria, and Napoleon III and members of their families, and denunciations of the costs of royalty. There was a basic desire to be left alone in freedom, a stress more on independence than participation. There was a bitter anticlericalism, with sizeable elements of secularism and scepticism (if the radical Jesus was invoked, it was not as a religious figure). There was condemnation of the rich and powerful, of corrupt place-seekers, and of politics as an organised swindle, often in the form of personal and colourful targets, and a concern, often salacious, with conspiracy and sex in high places. Thus the aristocracy was 'so steeped in lasciviousness, dissoluteness, and profligacy – it was so thoroughly rotten and corrupt, that it ought to be annihilated at once'.[147] As Constant sang:

> The great art, above all in our age,
> Is to steal without being caught,
> To lie without being detected
> To be esteemed without being wise.[148]

This cynical attitude to government was accompanied by a concern about social questions and poverty, some feeling that things were better in the past, a stress on the theft of the land from the people, resentment at the rich for abandoning their obligations for the poor, and insistence that the poor and unemployed needed public support. There was an often fierce patriotism, and support for strikes, especially when the masters used the document or discharge note or the authorities sided with them against the men. But very often the concern was less with systematic and social theory than with a rhetoric and theatre to impel action and debunk and puncture authority through shock, humour, and pathos. There was also a stress on collective participation, in collective reading of newspapers, criticism, and discussions, with open expressions of approval and disapproval. Blanqui's political club in early 1848, the Central Republican Society, was true to these characteristics. In contrast to those of Cabet or Raspail, which really consisted of lectures by the great men with no real discussion, or to the efforts in some clubs to impose order on proceedings through agreed agenda, prepared resolutions, and formal votes, Blanqui made no effort to dominate his, which was characterised by the rowdy give-and-take of debate, minimal organisation, a general ignoring of the agenda, and yet with no real disorder.[149] The assertion of independence from elites thus often took the theatrical form of a Grand Guignol style of extravagant, criminal, and seditious utterances, polemical directness, rhetorical bombast, low burlesque, ribaldry, blasphemy, ridicule, parody, satire, flouting of respectability, profanity, bawdy humour, laughter, and expressions of derision.

Thus different forms of radicalism were expressed in different cultural spheres. This was not a difference of technology, as print and song can express any type of view. While it is true that a newspaper forms, not a single source, but a group of sources, radical journalism on the whole presented a secular radicalism, in the form of political principles, personal arguments, and day-to-day political and economic issues, the balance varying partly with the strength of radical movements and the levels of freedom allowed. Public demonstrations and the related British set-piece meetings laid stress on unity, harmony, consensus, unifying leadership, and abiding principles (moral, religious, or legal/constitutional), and had greater reliance on religious and constitutional themes, partly because they drew on established models such as the British county and town meetings and evangelical religious camp-meetings, and French religious processions and official pageants. Such occasions also had a fairground and popular theatre element, which tends to be filtered out in the sources. Other, usually smaller meetings could have a more spontaneous give-and-take character, with free reign for personal differences, which do not come out very well in the sources, while at gatherings in elections a misleadingly exaggerated identification with the political system, emphasis on constitutionalism and legalism, and reformer/conservative dichotomies were displayed. Radicals in mutual improvement societies expressed an often earnest self-educated faith in progress through education, reason, and moralisation, and sought to distance themselves from many aspects of popular culture, as in trade society leaders' efforts to change and unite members and participate in public life and debate; their radicalism also embraced a concern with man's place in the world and universe, and often an involvement in unorthodox medicine and science. Autobiographies are one of the best sources for this kind of radicalism. Respectable, family-oriented radical occasions were another form again, and tended to be over-reported in the press. The usually tavern- or café-based radicalism of clubs, debating groups, and free and easies was different again, characterised by banter, participation, republicanism, anticlericalism (yet often with conceptions of a benign and indulgent deity), satire, abuse, hedonism and theatricality. This form of radicalism is least evident in the sources, the printed text alone of songs not always telling us much, and it is often contacted through the slanted content of police reports, prosecution dossiers, and trial reports.

None of these was a more real or essential radicalism, and the existence of these different radical forms, by no means mutually exclusive, makes it difficult to see radical language, particularly the language of the press, as itself determinant or constitutive of radicalism.[150] The sources thus have to be carefully assessed and used, and it has to be recognised that their nature means that the last form of radicalism is seriously underplayed in them.

# Conclusion

Plebeian radicals often admired Switzerland, where, a Chartist explained, the working classes had the vote and

> there are no legalised monopolies – no protecting duties – trade is free as the winds of heaven, her revenue scarcely amounts to four shillings a year to each of her population, while the taxes, direct and indirect, amount to nearly as many pounds. Switzerland has no National Debt – no bloated, tithe-gorging, state church; – she prosecutes no wars but those of self defence and in these the spirit of her noble Tell has been exhibited to the preservation of her unimpaired liberty for five hundred years. Her population mingle the peaceful pursuits of agriculture and manufacture in their mountain-homes, while the sweet stream of plenty rolls down her sequestered vales, diffusing health, morality, content and gladsomeness round the Swiss cottager's fireside: – what a contrast to *Coventry-Bastille Murders*! Aye, and all this without a Queen! – because the sovereign people maintain their legitimate ascendancy in the Swiss government.[1]

This was in many ways a classic idealised vision of a Paineite decentralised democracy, an artisan republic of independent men, that would have been familiar and attractive to urban artisans everywhere, although to see it as a specifically artisan ideal is to miss its appeal to a wide range of the poor, and this study of urban artisans who were involved in radical political activity confirms the great similarities in popular aspirations and ideals in European plebeian movements.[2]

The experiences of the various urban artisan trades also show many similarities – the expansion in step with population and economic growth, mainly in the form of a multiplication of small units of production nevertheless linked by credit, mercantile and production networks, pressures arising from cheaper, lower-quality production, greater intensity of work, sub-contracting, and a surplus of labour partly due to the amount of female and juvenile labour in the labour market. These problems were common to artisan trades on both sides of the Channel, so that 'all trades not producing any luxury articles are subject to the same regime'.[3] Artisan insecurity led to similar conflicts in the workshops, in which formal organisations were not usually involved, and to remarkably similar trade societies, involved in benefits, placement, tramping, and adjudication. The obvious differences lay in the political situation, in the usually greater legality or toleration of industrial action, strikes and societies in Britain, except during the early months of 1848 when fear of the people and the neutrality of the authorities meant unprecedented and unparalleled opportunities for industrial action in France.

The similarity between workplace experience and trades societies on both sides of the Channel, and the dissimilarities in their radicalism, is revealing of the connexions between these levels. The divisions and antagonisms in the workforce, and the exclusivities, rivalries, and hostilities of trade societies were not good bases in themselves for united movements of the people, which had to overcome and transcend work-related divisions. However, it is also important that common industrial action, involving different firms and societies, more often over wage rises than any other issue, could lead to radicalisation. Common action between trade societies was easiest over political issues, and the potential of the radical appeal through emphases on freedom, tyranny, slavery, manliness, equality, and justice, was displayed in the languages of disputes and in the fact that wide support among other trades for groups on strike occurred when there had been abuses of authority in the form of imposition by employers of the document or discharge note or intervention by public authorities in favour of the employers or against the strikers. Both the workplace and trade society could be important locations and bases for radical political activity and mobilisation. Furthermore, trade union leaders, themselves often political radicals, enunciated themes that were also persistent ones in radicalism: an impatience with sectional rivalries, disenchantment with popular attitudes, mentalities and practices, and the wish to educate workmen so as to participate fully in public life .

Radical political ideas also exhibited a broad similarity, resting on an opposition to privilege and ruling elites, and on a support for democracy and popular sovereignty, liberal freedoms, rights, patriotism, access to the land, no taxation of necessities, progressive direct taxation, and publicly funded education. There was broad continuity in these ideas during the period, with the incorporation of 'socialist' concerns with poverty, politically privileged and connected 'capitalists', and political economy, and a moral condemnation of competition as the enemy of harmony, unity, and happiness. Yet the very different political systems and situations meant very different forms of radical action and organisation, and radical practice was not determined mainly by political ideas. Similarly, artisans in radical organisation often engaged in actions and pursued concerns related to everyday life, such as relief and benefits, activities opposed by others holding the same radical opinions. There was similar support in both countries for co-operative trading, a growing interest after mid-century in mutualist credit and insurance, and, to a lower degree, involvement in co-operative production as a strike weapon, a means of unemployment relief, or a form of equitable sub-contracting. The greater apparent importance of co-operative production in France was not due to its advocacy by French republicans (something paralleled by British liberals in the 1860s), but to the political circumstances of the post-June 1848 Second Republic and the mid-1860s, when overt radical political and industrial activity were repressed but co-operation was allowed or encouraged, so that it flourished as a fall-back or front activity. The forms of radical activity, and the relative importance of public meetings and demonstrations, the press, national leaders, and formal organisation, similarly depended on the general political situation and institutions.

Similar 'front' or clandestine functions to those of work groups, and trade, benefit, and co-operative societies, were played by educational, religious, and convivial (usually pub- or café-based) groups. But each of these, with the exception of co-operative production societies, had an importance and vitality of its own, and thus demonstrate how radicalism, however much it distinguished between people and created its own loyalties and values, remained a part of everyday life with its concerns and tensions, and had to accommodate the demands of work, family, and leisure. Formal organisation was relative unimportant, and radic-alism drew on other sources, although the existence of an organisation could give members the confidence to retain independence of action, even if formal organisations were not always committed in fact to particular programmes. Education was a particular concern of auto-didact workmen who played such a disproportionate role in popular radicalism, yet who frequently felt alienated from popular culture and bitter at worker apathy, at the same time as wanting to improve and moralise their fellow-workmen, with a longing for a life not confined to work that would enable a participation in culture, a resentment at the prevailing contempt for manual labour and a demand for workers' place in public life and civil society. There were obvious differences between Roman Catholic France and Protestant and religiously pluralistic Britain, and the far greater hatred in France of the Church of Rome which fostered a more widespread rejection of even undenominational Christianity. Yet both French and British radicalism were similar in incorporating anticlericalism, radical lessons from the Bible, scepticism, provocative blasphemy, secularism, new religious prophets (often incorporating criticisms of existing social relations and the position of women), admiration of the life and teachings of Jesus the man, and millenarian upsurges at times of great political excitement. An interest in science, often unorthodox, led usually not to materialism but to a concern with invisible and even occult forces that could be investigated and manipulated, pantheistic notions, and older philosophical traditions that overlapped with or incorporated religion, theosophy, and magic. Plebeian radicalism also used the centres and forms of popular culture, especially convivial, singing, debating and discussion clubs, usually situated in cabarets or public-houses and sharing the modes of popular broadsides, theatre, journalism, and literature, although in Britain there were from the 1840s, especially in the provinces, much more widespread and determined efforts to locate radical activity away from pubs and to broaden family involvement, a process assisted by greater political freedom and by the availability of alternative premises.

Thus we should not seek to identify the distinctive features of French radicalism and British radicalism as entities and then identify the variables that explain the differences between them, for there were variations and differences within each country. The shared capacities, concerns and experiences led urban artisans, when allowed, to develop similar responses and institutions. Yet their political activities, despite broad similarities in radical ideas, exhibited great variety and fluctuations, mainly because of changing political situations. The importance of political circumstances, the extent of toleration or repression, the balance of political forces, the nature of elite politics, the strength and confidence of a movement, the ways in which people read the situation and responded to it, the possibilities and strategies they canvassed, need stressing as key factors in explaining radical actions. For activity was sometimes open, sometimes secret; after a revolution there were fears over reactionaries and the threat of losing the recently acquired liberties, there was political polarisation and social panic; liberals in office disappointed erstwhile allies; confidence and optimism gave movements a totally different character in England in 1839 or France in 1848; there was a tendency to condemn the moral failings of the people in periods of decline or defeat; the nature of religious radicalism changed with the situation; educational activities had different implications in the presence or absence of a strong radical movement; extensive repression led to radical strategies concentrating on abiding forms such as educational activities, front organisations, benefit and co-operative societies, and convivial groups, as well as conspiracies.

Radicalism was therefore characterised by diversity and variety, and radical movements were popular alliances, drawing on existing groups and bases for action, which persisted after the movement lapsed. This diversity in radicalism has always been recognised, but has tended to be seen in terms of ideological differences, or of differences in social composition, the two, of course, often being combined. But ideology and programmes do not in themselves explain support, movements were not ideologically uniform, the decline of a movement was not a reflection of a change in ideology, and political movements were never socially homogeneous. The differences within radicalism stemmed more from tactical choices and readings of the situation, and conceptions of what the movement was about – should it aim for mass support and mobilisation, or for the support of the discriminating or effective? Should it appeal to emotion and menace, or to reason and persuasion? Was it religious or secular? How exclusive should the focus on politics be? Should it accept people as they were, or seek to change them to fit them for success and power? These divisions were to be found *within* every radical movement and rested on differing conceptions of what radicalism was and meant, and how it should be achieved; they were thus cultural rather than ideological or social divisions.

Artisan and other working-class radicals pressed for civil liberties against arbitrary and unfair actions by authorities, police and agents of the law, employed radical and patriotic symbolism in emphasising their universalistic identity as citizens, and participated in heteregeneous alliances against conservatives and the politically powerful. There is therefore no single or simple answer to how and why artisans became radical. Yet we do find abiding artisan material concerns, over wages (in combinations and pressures for wage-fixing), food prices (exclusive dealing, co-operative stores, and opposition to tariffs), and unemployment (shorter hours, public works, and unemployment relief). Action was provoked not only by such material concerns, but also by conceptions of fairness, justice, and freedom (as in the freedom to talk, sing, or smoke at work, opposition to the document and to the authorities' siding with employers against the men), and by a challenge to social 'class' contempt for manual workers, and all such action met condemnation as subversive. The development of a liberal society, with its associations, educational expansion, wider political inclusion, and greater professionalisation, all affected popular political activity, particularly among the more educated leaders concerned with clearer and more regular organisation, legality, and the participation of working people in public life, including public acceptance and politics. Their efforts to change both public perceptions of working people and their institutions, and the attitudes and behaviour of working people themselves, led to tensions within the movements. Yet amongst these same people, in rejections of clear distinctions between the political and the social, and between the values and ethics of public life and the home, in some currents of religion and unorthodox medicine, there was also a challenge to liberal civil society. Such a challenge was also focused more widely in work practices and organisations and convivial practices.

The period was still one of informality but not spontaneity in political and industrial action, of part-time and voluntary schooling and mutual improvement rather than public education, of lay rather than professionalised religion, of unorthodox and amateur science and medicine, of free and easies rather than professional entertainers and music-halls. Hence the importance in plebeian radicalism of the medley of overlapping and often unspecialised benefit, trade, co-operative, credit, insurance, educational, religious and convivial groups and clubs, radicalism being part of wider social life and, to repeat, linked to and embodying individual and collective efforts, against frightful odds, to cope with uncertainty, endure hardship, pursue aspirations, secure respect, and enjoy life

It was thus a radicalism very much of its time, with a conception of democracy that was limited, socially and by gender. Yet other groups were to benefit from its thrust towards a more inclusive society, in which everyone belongs, has equal citizenship, and is guaranteed a minimum of rights. Only at the 'post-modern' end of the next century was this reversed in a return to the old vocabularies of exclusion and morally unworthy dangerous classes, to the pre-democratic view of whole classes as outlaws and threats to society.

# Notes

INTRODUCTION

1 McCalman, *Radical Underworld*, p. 93.
2 E.g. Sewell, 'Social change', 79–83; Hanagan, *Logic*, pp. 14–15.
3 See also van der Linden, 'Keeping distance'.


1. ARTISANS

1 *PMG* 20 Apr. 1833, p. 121.
2 *PMG* 8 Sept.1832, p. 523.
3 *PMG* 27 May 1831, p. 3.
4 *A* Sept. 1840, p. 1.
5 Blanqui to Uranie, BN NAF 9581, fol. 227.
6 E. Thompson, *Making*, pp. 189–207, 484–521; Magraw, 'Pierre Joigneaux', 599–602.
7 *PMG* 2 Nov. 1833, p. 350.
8 For a general survey, see: Breuilly, 'Artisan economy'.
9 Marseilles petition, *A* Apr. 1847, p. 487.
10 Lequin, *Ouvriers* I, p. 138.
11 Tartaret, *Commission Ouvrière*, p. 135.
12 *O* 5 July 1851, p. 1.
13 Sykes, 'Popular politics', chs. 3–6, esp. p. 266. See also Tilly and Lees, 'People of June', p. 193.
14 Little, 'Chartism and liberalism', pp. 90–2, 101–8, 126–31, 326–36; Sheridan, 'Social and economic foundations', p. 21; Monfalcon, *Histoire*, p. 33; Truquin, *Mémoires*, p. 135; Stewart-McDougall, *Artisan Republic*, p. 5.
15 *OSM* 6 Mar. 1836, p. 67.
16 J. L. and B. Hammond, *The Age of the Chartists* (1930), p. 270; Berenson, *Populist Religion*, p. 51.
17 *WM* 6 Oct.1866, p. 166.
18 *R* 15 July 1846, p. 98; *WM* 19 Oct. 1861, p. 123; *Bakers' Record* 24 June 1871, p. 5 [I am grateful to Ian McKay for drawing my attention to this source]; Nadaud, *Mémoires*, p. 192; Agulhon, *Ville ouvrière*, p. 169.
19 *St. Crispin* 30 Jan. 1869, p. 66.
20 E. Thompson, *Making*, pp. 55–9.

21  H. Arendt, *The Human Condition* (1958), pp. 79–93.
22  *C* 15 Dec.1866, p. 5.
23  *NP* May 1851, pp. 1–2; *PP* 29 May 1852, p. 6, 14 Aug. 1852, p. 3, 14 May 1853, p. 3; *Democrat* 3 Nov. 1855, p. 1.
24  T.Wright, *Habits*, p. 3; A. Reid, 'Intelligent artisans and aristocrats of labour: the essays of Thomas Wright', in J. Winter (ed.), *The Working Class in Modern British History. Essays in Honour of Henry Pelling* (Cambridge, 1983); Crossick, 'Gentlemen', pp. 168–9.
25  C. S., 'Ouvrier', in *Dictionnaire Politique*, p. 669; *Progrès Journal de Lyon, Politique Quotidien* 10 July 1861, p. 1; Molinari, *Mouvement socialiste*, esp. pp. xviii–xx; Poulot, *Question sociale*, pp. 206, 285–6, 341–5. See also Place, in Prothero, *Artisans*, pp. 173.


## 2. RADICALISMS

1  *BH* 14 Apr. 1866, p. 7.
2  *Les Sociétés Populaires*, p. 31; Raspail, *Avenues*, p. 200; *Crisis* 14 July 1832, p. 71; [Martin], *Nouveau catéchisme*, pp. 14, 40; *Tribune* 23 June 1832, p. 4, Sunday suppt., p. 1; Laponneraye, *Défense*, p. 5; *JP* July 1834, pp. 21–2; *NL* 2 Mar. 1839, p. 2; *TWM* 15 July 1848, p. 35, 29 July 1848, p. 43; *OT* 18 June 1848, p. 1; Reynolds, *RWN* 28 July 1850, p. 7; Elliott, *NS* 27 Mar. 1852, p. 7; *PP* 13 June 1857, p. 1; Rider, *MWA* 28 Jan. 1865, p. 8; Leno, *Aftermath*, p. 73; Rocher, *M* 20 Mar. 1870, p. 3.
3  NA MS 155, 11 Feb., fol. 283; see also Moreau, 20 Jan., fols. 195–6.
4  Bulletin, 22 Dec. 1831, F7 3885; 'Association libre pour l'instruction du peuple', 3 June, F11 6674; *JO* 19 Sept. 1830, p. 2, 21 Oct. 1830, p. 2, 28 Oct. 1830, p. 1; *Bon Sens* 25 Oct. 1832, p. 3; Newman, 'Blouse and the frock coat', 39–40, 54.
5  *A* Nov. 1843, p. 18; Cavaignac, *Opinion*, p. 4; *CP* 19 Mar. 1848, p. 1; Blanqui, NAF 9581, fol. 61.
6  *NS* 11 June 1842, p. 1.
7  Société Républicaine Centrale, 7, 14 Mar., and Blanqui, NAF 9581, fols. 41, 44, 112–3; *Tribune* 13 June 1830, p. 2; Coutant, *Ruche* Nov. 1840, pp. 1,3,6.
8  Rendall, *Origins*, ch. 17; Aminzade, *Ballots*, pp. 33–4; Belchem, 'Radical language', 249; Vernon, *Politics*, pp. 312–3.
9  Lamennais, *Peuple Constituant* 15 Apr. 1848, p. 1; Williams, *PP* 26 Nov. 1853, p. 1. See also *CP* 29 Mar. 1848, p. 1; *AR* 25 Nov. 1849, p. 1; Odger, *BH* 16 Sept. 1865, p. 1, 12 Mar. 1864, p. 6, 19 Mar. 1864, p. 7.
10  *P* 14 Apr. 1849, p. 2. See also *EO* June 1844, p. 16.
11  *NS* 16 Oct. 1841, p. 7, 28 Jan. 1843, p. 8; 'Veta', *NS* 21 Oct. 1843, p. 7; *R* 29 July 1846, p. 138; *RN* 30 Mar. 1851, p. 7, 22 June 1851, p. 7; Minck, NA MS 155, fol. 371; Lovett, *Life*, p. 141 n.1; Millière, *M* 15 Jan. 1870, p. 2; Biagini, *Liberty*, p. 272;.
12  Cossham, *BH* 28 Mar. 1863, p. 1.
13  *MWA* 18 Mar. 1865, p. 8, 25 Mar. 1965, p. 5; *BH* 18 Mar. 1865, p. 8; Gillespie, *Labor and Politics*, pp. 238–40, 244; Biagini, *Liberty*, pp. 267–74.
14  O'Connor, *NS* 15 Nov. 1845, p. 7, 11 July 1846, p. 4, 26 Sept. 1846, p. 7; *RWN* 25 Aug. 1850, p. 7.

15 Prothero, 'William Benbow', 155–62.
16 O'Connor, *NS* 27 May 1843, p. 1; *TWM* 15 July 1848, p. 35. See also Nantes, reply, *Pop.* 22 Nov. 1845, p. 203.
17 Mora, *Union* Jan. 1845, p. 3.
18 *RN* 2 Jan. 1859, p. 4.
19 Cabet, *République*, p. 3.
20 Lovett, *LD* 30 July 1837, p. 367; *CP* 14 May 1848, p. 1.
21 Dufraisse, *CP* 24 Mar. 1848, p. 3, 14 Mar. 1848, p. 4; Amann, *Revolution*, pp. 35–6, 42.
22 Blanqui to Nadaud, May 1850, NAF 9581, fol. 236; Benoit, *Confessions*, pp. 125–6; Lefrançais, *Souvenirs* II, pp. 25–6; Dommanget, *Idées politiques*, pp. 341–2, 348, 349; Loubere, *Louis Blanc*, p. 95; Amann, *Revolution*, pp. 33, 89.
23 Savina, CC 585; see also Raspail, *Avenues*, p. 206; Cour des Pairs, *Affaire* I, pp. 95, 128 (Guinard); Rittiez, *Histoire* I, p. 370; Weill, *Histoire*, pp. 32, 94, 251; Amann, *Revolution*, pp. 298–300; McPhee, 'Crisis'; Moss, 'June 13, 1849', 413–4; Berenson, *Populist Religion*, p. 106.
24 Cabet, *Salut*, p. 10; Cabet, *Ligne droite*, pp. 32, 49, 60; *A* 31 July 1850, p. 558; *M* 8 Jan. 1870, p. 2; C. Johnson, 'Etienne Cabet', 434; C. Johnson, *Utopian Communism*, pp. 134–5, 231.
25 *WM* 4 Aug. 1866, p. 50; *C* 27 Apr. 1867, p. 4, 4 May 1867, p. 4 (and Bradlaugh on same page).
26 Cabet, *République*, pp. 6–7; C. Johnson, *Utopian Communism*, p. 38; Cour des Pairs, *Affaire* II, pp. 415–16; M'Douall, *Pop.* 19 Aug. 1843, p. 106; Dawson, *MG* 17 May 1848, p. 6.
27 *PMG* 30 July 1831, p. 29; Wolstenholme, *Sheffield Iris* 16 July 1839, p. 2; Ashton, *NS* 20 July 1839, p. 5; Jones, 8 Apr. 1848, p. 7; Lowery, 'Passages' 122; Crossick, *Artisan Elite*, p. 209.
28 Donovan, Leach, *MG* 17 May 1848, p. 6; Margadant, *French Peasants*, pp. xxiv, 142, 230, 246, 249, 266.
29 Benoit, *Confessions*, p. 95.
30 Reports in C 932B; C 942, Luxembourg 2946; *OT* 7 June 1848, p. 1; 11 June, p. 1, 13 June 1848, p. 4, 15 June 1848, p. 4, 20 June 1848, p. 4; *RP* 8 June 1848, p. 1; *PD* 13–15 June 1848, p. 1; Girard, *Garde Nationale*, pp. 309, 311
31 For election disorders, see: Proc.-Gen. Limoges to Min., 8 and 11 May 1848, Delangell to Proc.-Gen., 3 Sept. 1848, *Arrêt d'Accusation dans l'Affaire de Limoges*, depositions in BB30 361, dos.II, 'Cour de Limoges. Evénements de Limoges au 27 avril 1848', fols. 131, 132, 163, 266, 272 ff.; Merriman, *Agony*, pp. 10–13; NA MS. 155, fols. 462–74, 795–7; *Commerce* 13 June 1869, p. 2; Dalotel, *Aux origines*, pp. 365–6.
32 *Pop.* 19 Aug. 1843, p. 106. See also Doyle, *NS* 6 Dec. 1845, p. 3.
33 Margadant, 'Modernisation', pp. 275–6; Margadant, *French Peasants*, pp. 267, 334–5
34 *C* 5 Jan. 1867, p. 4; 2 Mar. 1867, p. 4, Bradlaugh, 16 Mar. 1867, pp. 4–5, 27 Apr. 1867, p. 4, 4 May 1867, p. 4; Leno, *Aftermath*, p. 79; Broadhurst, *Story*, pp. 34–40; A. Taylor, 'Modes', pp. 32–3.

## 3. TRADE UNIONISM

1 O'Neill, *St. Crispin* 24 July 1869, p. 40.
2 *CC* 7 Sept. 1844, p. 98.
3 J. D. Devlin to J. E. Gray, 10 Mar. 1849, MS letter in [Devlin], *Strangers' Homes*, fol. 4; *CC* 24 Aug. 1844, p. 8; *St. Crispin* 20 Mar. 1869, pp. 157–8, 2 Oct. 1869, p. 160, 19 Feb. 1870, p. 86; T. Wright, *Romance*, p. 166.
4 *Bakers' Record* 1 July 1871, p. 5; *St. Crispin* 15 Jan. 1870, p. 27.
5 Tartaret, *Exposition Universelle*, p. 45.
6 *LL* 17 Mar. 1849, p. 249.
7 Dupont, *Histoire* II, p. 432.
8 P. Vinçard, *Ouvriers*, p. 85; *TA* 1 Apr. 1849, p. 5; Chambre de Commerce, *Statistique* I, p. 106; Mazuy, *Essai*, pp. 180–1; Nadaud, *Mémoires*, pp. 94, 117, 145; *Shipwrights' J* June 1858, p. 42; *LL* 19 Aug. 1848, p. 23; Lyons Police, 2 July 1848, AML I 2 47B, fol. 455. See also dock-workers and coal-whippers, 26 Apr. 1831, F7 3885, and 2 Jan. 1833, F7 3886.
9 BB24 489–493 1626 Rollin.
10 *Reminiscences of a Stonemason*, p. 100.
11 *Tailor* 25 Jan. 1868, pp. 125–6; *WM* 3 Apr. 1866, p. 1; *WA* 7 Oct. 1865, p. 4; *BH* 7 Apr. 1866, p. 5; *MG* 13 Apr. 1869, p. 5.
12 P. Vinçard, *Ouvriers*, pp. 45–7; *NR* 17 Apr. 1870, p. 254.
13 *TA* 7 Jan. 1849, p. 5.
14 Cochut, *Associations ouvrières*, p. 51. See also bakers, Faure, 'Mouvements populaires', 59.
15 Broadhurst, *Story*, pp. 6, 10; Gauny, *Philosophe plébéien*, p. 30; *Ruche* Nov. 1840, p. 13; *Pop.* 7 Aug. 1842, p. 71, 13 Nov. 1842, p. 84; *Union* Apr. 1844, p. 2; Cabet, *Ouvrier*, p. 17; Corbon, *Secret*, p. 85; Tartaret, *Exposition Universelle*, p. 252; T. Wright, *Habits*, pp. 105–7.
16 Levasseur, *Histoire* I, p. 65; *MG* 5 May 1869, p. 6. See also 'Au sublime ouvrier', 31–45.
17 Poulot, *Question sociale*, pp. 146, 266.
18 [Smith], *Working Man's Way*, pp. 252–7; *WM* 9 June 1866, p. 366; T. Wright, *Habits*, pp. 94–9; Chauvet, *Ouvriers*, p. 574; Rancière, *Nuit*, p. 179; *BBCU* Feb. 1852, p. 5; Prothero, *Artisans*, pp. 34–5.
19 T. Wright, *Habits*, pp. 82–4.
20 Webb Coll. A 13, fol. 192; McClelland, 'Time to work', p. 193; *BBCU* 29 Nov. 1851, p. 8; Broadhurst, *Story*, p. 6.
21 *TA* 4 May 1849, p. 4.
22 Leroux, *Aux ouvriers typographes*, p. 10. See also Perrot, *Ouvriers en grève*, pp. 108–9.
23 *FSA* Jan. 1836, p. 3; *EO* June 1844, p. 31; *Last* 8 Nov. 1844, p. 17; Tartaret, *Exposition Universelle*, pp. 79, 87, 105–6, 181; *Rapport des Délégués Dessinateurs et Tisseurs*, pp. 22–3; *St. Crispin* 7 Aug. 1869, p. 64; Corbon, *Secret*, p. 206. For general surveys of benefit societies, see: P. H. J. Gosden, *The Friendly Societies in England 1815–1875* (Manchester, 1961); Prothero, *Artisans*, pp. 28–30; Sibalis, 'Mutual aid societies'; G. S. Sheridan, 'Internal life and tradition in the mutual aid societies of Lyons, 1800–1870', in J. F. Sweets (ed.), *Proceedings of the Ninth Meeting of the*

*Western Society for French History, 1981* (Lawrence, Kansas, 1982); Robert, 'Cortèges', pp. 62–7.

24 *TA* 11 Feb. 1849, p. 3; *JTA* 2 Apr. 1860, p. 37, 1 Sept. 1860, p. 98; Tartaret, *Commission Ouvrière*, pp. 281, 293, 296; *BH* 13 June 1863, p. 4, 20 June 1863, p. 1; Musson, *Typographical Association*, pp. 30, 284–5.

25 Leroux, *Aux ouvriers typographes*, p. 9; *TAHP* 28 Sept. 1850, p. 110; *APOT*, pp. 7–8; Webb Coll. A 44, fol. 74; Broadhurst, *Story*, p. 23; T. Wright, *Habits*, p. 104.

26 Letter, 13 Feb. 1841, Christy Papers, B/55/6/16; *A* July 1841, p. 87; *Ruche* Feb. 1847, p. 63; *O* 18 Jan. 1851, p. 41; *JTA* 1 Feb. 1860, p. 24; *BH* 5 Mar. 1864, p. 4; *Tailor* 7 Dec. 1867, p. 72, 28 Dec. 1867, p. 93; Operative Bricklayers' Society, Annual Report (1864), p. 3; Lévy, Procès, p. 7; Tartaret, *Commission Ouvrière*, pp. 264–6; Tartaret, *Exposition Universelle*, p. 175; *Rapport des Délégués Mécaniciens*, pp. 33–4; *APOT*, p. 15.

27 Durand, in Tartaret, *Commission Ouvrière*, p. 287.

28 T. Wright, *Habits*, pp. 68–73, 80; *TAHP* 5 Oct. 1850; Audiganne, *Populations ouvrières* I, p. 35; *WM* 20 Oct. 1866, p. 189.

29 Place Coll. set 53 E, fol. 62; Société Philanthropique, *Rapports et Comptes Rendues pour l'Année 1835*, pp. 195–6; Carter, 'Plumber, Painter and Glazier', *Guide to Trade*, p. 83; P. Vinçard, *Ouvriers* pp. 95–6; *WM* 27 Oct. 1866, p. 202.

30 Tartaret, *Commission Ouvrière*, p. 287; Chauvet, *Ouvriers*, pp. 518, 529.

31 Tartaret, *Commission Ouvrière*, p. 266.

32 *LL* 21 Apr. 1849, p. 292; *TAHP* 19 Oct. 1850, p. 135; *M* 31 Dec. 1869, p. 2; E. Hunt, *British Labour History*, p. 287; Hanson, 'Craft unions', 244–6.

33 *Ruche* Apr. 1844, p. 105, Mar. 1847, p. 69; *NS* 4 May 1844, p. 1; *C* 7 Apr. 1866, p. 6.

34 Chauvet, *Ouvriers*, p. 551.

35 Barberet, *Mouvement ouvrier*, pp. 50–3; P. Vinçard, *Ouvriers* p. 84; *Tailor* 3 Nov. 1866, p. 53; *Journeyman* Oct. 1890, p. 7; *Times* 12 Aug. 1859, p. 10; *BH* 20 May 1865, p. 5; Tartaret, *Exposition Universelle*, pp. 163–4; Poulot, *Question sociale*, pp. 225–6; *OSM* 26 May 1837, p. 166; Broadhurst, *Story*, pp. 6, 52; Chauvet, *Ouvriers*, p. 549; Webb Coll. A 13, fol. 196; *NS* 23 Oct. 1841, p. 7; Dunning, *Trades' Unions and Strikes*, pp. 43–6.

36 *Birmingham Chron.* 29 Sept. 1825, p. 2; *ES* 24 Jan. 1843, p. 3; *BTC* Feb. 1851, p. 22; *JTA* 1 May 1860, p. 50, 1 Sept. 1860, p. 105, 1 Oct. 1860, p. 112; *TSMC* Apr. 1865, p. 1, May 1865, p. 3; *BH* 20 Jan. 1866, p. 5, 15 July 1866, p. 5; *Bakers' Record* 10 June 1871, p. 5; Festy, 'Dix années', 171 n. 2, 195.

37 Police, 27 May 1848, C 932A, 711; C 942, Luxembourg, 2950; Gossez, *Ouvriers*, pp. 190, 209, 212. See also Lyons tailors and shoemakers (*Glaneuse* 17 Nov. 1833, p. 3, 24 Nov. 1833, p. 3; *A* Nov. 1841, p. 24) and Paris farriers (BB18 1715 3113).

38 *SRI* 16 Mar. 1844, p. 4. See also other examples among tailors (*Birmingham Chron.* 29 Sept. 1825, p. 2; Webb Coll. A 14, fol. 85; 25, fols. 99, 117), shoemakers (Devlin, *Contract Reform*, p. 19) and lithographers (*Commerce* 1 Aug. 1869, p. 2).

39 *Crisis* 30 Nov. 1833, p. 109; *Man* 8 Dec. 1833, p. 173; *NS* 10 Aug. 1844, p. 4; Lowery, 'Passages', pp. 84–5.

40 *JTA* 1 Sept. 1860, pp. 14, 97; *Ruche* Apr. 1842, pp. 22, 24; MRC, MSS/28/CO/1/8/3/2; Child, *Industrial Relations*, p. 128.

41 Poulot, *Question sociale*, p. 200.

42 For *compagnonnages* see: F7 9786, 56820. O.G., Dossier, 'Police des ouvriers, coalitions et compagnonnages'; Gendarmerie, 4/5 Nov. 1847, ADR 4M 94; Perdiguier, 'Notice'; Moreau, *Travail* 29 Jan. 1842, pp. 4–5; 27 Mar. 1842, pp. 10–11; 16 May 1842, pp. 25–6; *Journal of the Working Classes*, pp. 44–6; Martin Saint-Léon, *Compagnonnage*; Coornaert, *Compagnonnages*; Truant, 'Solidarity and symbolism'; Sonenscher, 'Mythical work'.

43 Bulletins 21 May and 23 Aug. 1830, F7 3884; *Journal du Commerce et des Théâtres de Lyon* 25 Mar. 1836, p. 2.

44 Bulletins 4, 5 Apr. 1825, F7 3879; 14 June 1827, F7 38881; Prefect Bouches-du-Rhône, 1 Aug. 1820, F7 9786; Moreau, *Travail* 27 Mar. 1842, p. 12; *EO* Sept. 1844, p. 117.

45 Perdiguier, *A* May 1846, p. 318.

46 *GT* 22 Jan. 1837, p. 203; note in CC 595, Recurt; Gossez, *Ouvriers*, p. 125.

47 Pref. Pol., 16 July 1822, F7 9787.

48 OSM 12 Dec. 1834, p. 10.

49 Styles, *Crisis* 22 Sept. 1832, p. 113; *LD* 14 Jan. 1838, p. 555; *NS* 30 Dec. 1843, p. 4, 10 Aug. 1844, p. 4, 7 Sept. 1844, p. 8; Webb Coll. A 13, fol. 181; *BH* 2 Sept. 1863, p. 5, 23 Dec. 1865, p. 5; *Tailor* 7 Sept. 1867, p. 293.

50 P. Vinçard, *Ouvriers*, p. 68; *Innovator* Apr. 1857, p. 30; *Secret des Compagnons Cordonniers Dévoilé*, p. 3; Gossez, *Ouvriers*, pp. 174–6; Prefect Bouches-du-Rhône, 2 July 1819, F7 9786; Guillaumou, *Confessions*, pp. 51–3; *CC* July 1844, p. 4.

51 General Union of Operative House Painters, *Quarterly Jan. 1871*, pp. 7, 16; *BH* 26 Sept. 1863, p. 4.

52 Webb Coll. A 46, fols. 27, 28; Giles, 'Felt-hatting industry', 126–8; Bulletin, 14 June 1827, F7 3881; Perdiguier, *Mémoires*, p. 104; Vial, *Coutume chapelière*, pp. 21, 23.

53 Newton, *TC* 4 Feb. 1854, p. 10. See also E. Hunt, *British Labour History*, p. 155.

54 1 Aug. 1825, F7 3879; Barberet, *Mouvement ouvrier*, pp. 119–21; Webb Coll. A 22, fol. 94, A 44, fols. 70, 82; Allen, *TAHP* 27 July 1850, p. 39; Amalgamated Society of Engineers, *Abstract*, p. 69.

55 *BBCU* 25 Aug. 1850, p. 4; *C* 1 Sept. 1866, p. 5; *APOT*, p. 26; Barberet, *Mouvement ouvrier*, pp. 29–30.

56 Webb Coll. A 22, fols. 26–7; Howe and Child, *Society of London Bookbinders*, p. 139.

57 *CC* July 1844, p. 43; *OSM* 31 Mar. 1837, p. 153.

58 *Times* 12 Aug. 1859, p. 10; Guillaumou, *Confessions*, p. 41; *Last* 20 Dec. 1844, p. 69; *Innovator* Mar. 1857, p. 20; *C* 18 May 1866, p. 5.

59 *CC* July 1844, pp. 42–3.

60 *NS* 16 May 1846, p. 5; *St. Crispin* 29 May 1869, p. 278; Webb Coll. A 25, fols. 91, 97.

61 *Yearly Account of the Income and Expenditure of the Journeymen Cabinet Makers*,

*Carver, and Wood Turners' Friendly Society, 1847* (Manchester, 1848); *Bristol Mercury* 19 Feb. 1848, p. 3; *JT* 16 Mar. 1848, p. 44; *Reminiscences of a Stonemason*, p. 144; Broadhurst, *Story*, pp. 11–13, 16–22.

62  *WM* 25 Aug. 1866, p. 92; Broadhurst, *Story*, pp. 21–2; Perdiguier, 'Notice', pp. 67–9; Kiddier, *Old Trade Unions*, pp. 19, 23–8, 48; Hobsbawm, *Labouring Men*, ch. 4; Leeson, *Travelling Brothers*; Southall, 'Mobility'.

63  *Bristol Mercury* 24 June 1848; *RN* 6 Mar. 1859, p. 4; Guillaumou, *Confessions*, p. 29.

64  BB18 1366; *CC* 10 Aug. 1844, p. 69.

65  Broadhurst, *Story*, pp. 11, 16–17.

66  *Birmingham J* 11 Apr. 1846, p. 5; *TSMC* Apr. 1853, p. 3, and *passim*; *TPC passim*; *JTA* 1 Feb. 1860, p. 20, 1 May 1860, p. 55, 1 June 1860, pp. 63, 67, July 1861, p. 219.

67  *BH* 8 July 1865, p. 1; *Tailor* 24 July 1868, p. 291; Pollard, *History of Labour*, pp. 65–7, 73.

68  Howe and Waite, *London Society of Compositors*, pp. 87, 90, 167; *A* Oct. 1843, pp. 12–13, 19 Mar. 1848, p. 98; *Ruche* Oct. 1843, pp. 8–10; *CP* 15 May 1848, p. 4; Levy, *Procès*, p. 76; Parmentier, in *Deuxième Procès*, p. 36; *WA* 21 Oct. 1865, p. 6; *BH* 10 Oct. 1863, p. 1; Tartaret, *Commission Ouvrière*, p. 39.

69  E.g. *WA* 18 Nov. 1865, pp. 4–5; *CC* July 1844 suppt., p. 53; *WM* 14 July 1866, p. 17; *Tailor* 20 Oct. 1866, p. 23; Festy, 'Dix années', 175, 193.

70  See also Cottereau, 'Distinctiveness', pp. 143–4; Sewell, 'Artisans', p. 165.

71  Prothero, *Artisans*, pp. 164, 217; Webb Coll. A 44, fols. 84, 85, 92. See also *Bolton Chron.* 14 Mar. 1829, p. 1; Bulletin, 15 Aug. 1830, F7 3884; F12 3110, *Charpentiers*; Prothero, 'London Chartism and trades', 208, 219.

72  Bulletin, 14 Nov. 1830, F7 3884; *JO* 14 Nov. 1830, p. 5; *RP* 21 June 1848, p. 1; *Peuple Constituant* 4 Mar. 1848, p. 2; *VR* 21 June 1848, p. 2; *OT* 22 June 1848, p. 1; MRC MSS 28/CO/1/8/3/2; MS 39A/TA/1/1/1, 23 Oct. 1850; 5th, 6th, and 23rd Half-yearly reports PTA, MS 39A/TA/4/1/1; *TPC* Mar. 1850, p. 70, Aug. 1853, p. 256; *TAHP* 21 Sept. 1850, p. 100; *TSMC* Nov. 1852, p. 4, Dec. 1852, p. 3.

73  *WM* 25 Aug. 1866, p. 92.

74  *St. Crispin* 22 Jan. 1870, p. 37.

75  Ashton-Under-Lyne minute book 1856–1863, 5 Sept. 1856, 2 Mar. 1863, MRC MSS 78/GUC+J/6/1; Webb Coll. A 13, fol. 353; *BFFC* Feb. 1850, p. 145, Sept. 1850, p. 160; *Gauntlet* 9 Mar. 1834, p. 908; *Glaneuse* 18 Nov. 1832, p. 2; Perdiguier, 'Notice', p. 44; Perdiguier, *Mémoires*, p. 178; Postgate, *Builders' History*, p. 32; E. Yeo, 'Culture and constraint', p. 170; Robert, 'Cortèges', pp. 68–74.

76  Guépin, *Nantes*, p. 452; *BH* 28 Feb. 1863, p. 5, 12 Aug. 1865, p. 5, 23 Sept. 1865, p. 5; *Ashton Reporter* 24 Sept. 1870, p. 8; *BFP* 24 July 1841, p. 7; *MG* 13 July 1833, p. 3, 17 Aug. 1839, p. 2; *LD* 14 July 1839, p. 3; *NS* 31 Oct. 1840, p. 7; *BFFC* Feb. 1847, p. 54, Nov. 1847, p. 72; *BBCU* 5 May 1848, p. 11, 2 May 1849, p. 43, 25 Aug. 1850, p. 4; *BTC* Aug. 1850, p. 48; *JTA* 1 June 1860, p. 64; Gossez, *Ouvriers*, p. 167; *Journal du Commerce et des Théâtres de Lyon* 27 June 1841, p. 2, 26 Oct. 1841, p. 3; P. Vinçard to Platier, BHVP MS. 1043, fol. 387.

77 *APO* II p. 44.
78 *BFFC* Nov. 1847, p. 117, Sept. 1850, p. 160.
79 *BH* 5 Mar. 1864, p. 5.
80 *TC* 4 Feb. 1854, p. 10; Sibalis, 'Mutual aid societies', 29; Foulon, *Eugène Varlin*, p. 28; *Birmingham J* 11 Apr. 1846, p. 5; PTA 14th Quarterly, MS 39A/TA/4/1/1; *OBSTC* 1 Dec. 1861, pp. 34–5.
81 *WA* 7 Oct. 1865, p. 4; *BH* 23 June 1866, p. 4; Webb Coll. A 13, fol. 11; Vial, *Coutume chapelière*, p. 170.
82 T. Wright, *Habits*, pp. 46, 60.
83 *APO* I, pp. 90–192, II, pp. 13, 45; Berryer, *Affaire des charpentiers*, p. 12; *A* Mar. 1842, p. 5.
84 *OSM* 4 June 1840, p. 445.
85 *OSM* 14 Aug. 1836, p. 91, 25 Dec. 1835, p. 58; Webb Coll. A 13, fol. 194.
86 *CC* 14 Sept. 1844, p. 109; *APO* II, pp. 20–2.
87 *OSM* 29 Sept. 1837, p. 198; *Trade Report of the Cabinet-Makers' Society*, Oct. 1870.
88 *VP* 4 Jan. 1850, p. 1.
89 Guillaumou, *Confessions*, pp. 54, 243–4. See also *NS* 2 Mar. 1844, p. 6, 21 Sept. 1844, p. 6.
90 Webb Coll. A 32, fol. 130; N. G. Clarke *et al.*, *A Scale of Prices for Job Work* (1828).
91 *MG* 4 June 1834, p. 2. See also *Last* 20 Dec. 1844, p. 66.
92 *BH* 2 July 1864, p. 5.
93 *OBSTC* 1 Nov. 1, p. 22; Broadhurst, *Story*, p. 7.
94 *NS* 24 Oct. 1846, p. 8.
95 Prothero, *Artisans*, p. 167; *C* 14 Apr. 1866, p. 6.
96 *JTA* 1 May 1860, p. 50, 1 Sept. 1860, p. 105, 1 Oct. 1860, p. 112; *TSMC* Apr. 1865, p. 1, May 1865, p. 3.
97 Jefferys, *Story of the Engineers*, p. 70; Musson, *Typographical Association*, p. 106.
98 Tartaret, *Exposition Universelle*, p. 260; *BH* 16 July 1864, p. 5.
99 Webb Coll. A 44, fol. 142, A 22, fol. 78. See also ship joiners in royal dockyards, A 11, fols. 225–6.
100 Webb Coll. A 18, fols. 150–3, 170, 338; *Tailor* 23 Mar. 1867, p. 379; *WA* 4 Nov. 1865, p. 2; *C* 21 Apr. 1866, p. 3.
101 *OT* 15 June 1848, p. 7; Gossez, *Ouvriers*, p. 174.
102 J. D. Devlin to J. E. Gray, 10 Mar. 1844, in [Devlin], *Strangers' Homes*; PTA 17th, MS 39A/TA/4/1/1; *fondeurs, typographie parisienne*, F12 3121A; *ebénistes*, F12 3112; Davenport, *PMG* 29 Aug. 1833, p. 275; *Bristol Times* 24 June 1843, p. 4; *CC* 7 Sept. 1844, pp. 97–8; *BBCU* 26 Mar. 1856, p. 38; *BH* 20 Aug. 1864, p. 7; *C* 7 Apr. 1866, p. 4; *Tailor* 13 June 1868, p. 273; Boyer, *De l'état des ouvriers*, pp. 61–2; Tartaret, *Commission Ouvrière*, p. 58; Tartaret, *Exposition Universelle*, p. 306; Gossez, *Ouvriers*, p. 153.
103 *BH* 12 Nov. 1864, p. 5. See also Tartaret, *Commission Ouvrière*, p. 29.
104 Perdiguier, *Mémoires*, p. 196.
105 E.g. Lyons police, 24 Dec. 1859, AML I2 47B, 456.
106 PTA 13th Quarterly, MS 39A/TA/4/1/1; *Tailor* 30 Mar. 1867, p. 389; *RWN* 14 July 1850, p. 5; *TA* 1 Apr. 1849, p. 6, 4 May 1849, p. 4.

107 *BBCU* 10 Oct. 1846, pp. 4–5.
108 Place Coll. set 52, fol. 89; Webb Coll. A 22, fols. 26–7; Tartaret, *Commission Ouvrière*, p. 473; 'Rapport du délégué graveur sur bois', in *Rapports des Délégués Imprimeurs en Papiers Peints*, p. 35; Prothero, *Artisans*, p. 44.
109 Gossez, *Ouvriers*, p. 165.
110 *Bolton Chron.* 29 Mar. 1828, p. 3; *LL* 16 Sept. 1844, p. 55; *NP*, p. 282; *BH* 14 Oct. 1865, p. 5; *Echo de la Fabrique* 25 Mar. 1832, p. 3; Duchêne, *Actualités* p. 22; *APOT*, p. 11; *OSM* 22 July 1836, p. 86, 14 Mar. 1839, p. 329, 28 Mar. 1839, p. 331, 4 July 1839, p. 354; Webb Coll. A 13, fol. 271.
111 *Règlement de la Société de l'Union des Doreurs*, p. 5; *ebénistes*, F12 3112; *Commerce* 27 June 1869, p. 2; *TA* 1 Apr. 1849, p. 5; *OSM* 23 June 1837, p. 169, 22 June 1838, p. 268; *A* 31 May 1843, p. 70; *BH* 10 Oct. 1863, p. 1.
112 *A* May 1841, p. 70, July 1847, p. 540; *St. Crispin* 19 Feb. 1870, p. 89; Chauvet, *Ouvriers*, p. 280.
113 Webb Coll. A 44, fol. 78; *OSM* 28 Oct. 1836, p. 107; *WM* 9 Aug. 1861, p. 61; *JT* 1 Apr. 1848, p. 56.
114 *BTC* Oct. 1850, p. 5. See also *OSM* 23 June 1837, p. 169; *WA* 7 Oct. 1865, p. 4; Dunning, *Trades' Unions and Strikes*, p. 17; Gossez, *Ouvriers*, pp. 229–30; Child, *Industrial Relations*, p. 140; W. Fraser, *Trade Unions and Society*, pp. 37–9.
115 *O* 5 Apr. 1841, pp. 217–8; *OBS Quarterly* Dec. 1865, p. 3; *Tailor* 13 June 1868, p. 271; *St. Crispin* 10 July 1869, p. 13.
116 *APOT*, pp. 37–9.
117 Webb Coll. A 14, fols. 216–7.
118 Guépin, *Nantes*, p. 395; Prothero, *Artisans*, p. 25; 'Tailleurs', *Rapports des Délégués des Ouvriers Parisiens*, p. 341.
119 *RWN* 14 July 1850, p. 5; *GT* 30 Nov. 1833, p. 98; *Tailor* 25 Jan. 1868, p. 127; *Journeyman* Oct. 1890, p. 7; Webb Coll. A 14, fol. 212; Poulot, *Question sociale*, pp. 141, 225–6; Chauvet, *Ouvriers*, p. 549.
120 P. Vinçard, *Ouvriers*, p. 83; *BH* 20 May 1865, p. 5; *Tailor* 3 Nov. 1866, p. 53; *Times* 12 Aug. 1859, p. 10; Tartaret, *Exposition Universelle*, pp. 163–4; Poulot, *Question sociale*, pp. 225–6.
121 *GT* 28 Aug. 1833, p. 1063, 4 Oct. 1833, p. 1186; *Pop.* 6 Oct. 1833, p. 3. See also the notoriously brutal and vindictive 'Black Prince', George Allen, *OSM* 26 May 1837, p. 166; *NS* 23 Oct. 1841, p. 7; Dunning, *Trades' Union and Strikes*, pp. 43–6. See also *BH* 28 Apr. 1866, p. 7.
122 Perdiguier, *Mémoires*, p. 135.
123 *Ruche* Feb. 1841, p. 8.
124 *St. Crispin* 10 Jan. 1870, p. 27.
125 *NS* 16 Mar. 1844, p. 8; *A* July 1841, p. 87; *APO* II p. 674; *Ruche* Aug. 1847, p. 171; Gauny, *Philosophe Plébéien*, pp. 39, 47.
126 *TA* 22 Apr. 1849, p. 5.
127 Chauvet, *Ouvriers*, pp. 293, 553. See also BB18 1714 3007.
128 *TC* 4 Feb. 1854, p. 10.
129 *OSM* 31 Mar. 1837, p. 149; *A* July 1844, p. 154; President C. des

Prud'hommes in Metal to Pref. Seine, 28 July 1848, Seine Archives, DM12 23; *MG* 10 Apr. 1869, p. 5, 12 Apr. 1869, p. 2, 13 Apr. 1869, p. 5, 27 Oct. 1869, p. 5; Webb Coll. A 13, fols. 30, 198, 245–6, 254; Gossez, *Ouvriers*, p. 97.

130 *Workman* 5 July 1861, p. 22; *BH* 29 Aug. 1863, p. 4, 20 Mar. 1869, p. 7; Macdonald, *True Story*, p. 22.

131 Vial, *Coutume chapelière*, p. 50; *Tailor* 2 Oct. 1866, p. 26; Pref. Pol., 26 Jan. 1865, 45 AP 6, dos. III; Dunning, *Trades' Unions and Strikes*, p. 24.

132 *TA* 13 May 1849, p. 3.

133 *APOT*, pp. 37–9; *JTA* 1 Feb. 1860, p. 13.

134 *TPC* Feb. 1850, pp. 59–60, Oct. 1850, p. 104, Feb. 1852, p. 170; MRC MS 28/CO/1/8/7/1, fols. 41–63; *A* May 1841, p. 70; *Ruche* Sept. 1840, p. 5, Apr. 1842, p. 22; Chambre de Commerce de Paris, *Statistique* II, p. 889.

135 *M* 17 Apr. 1870, p. 2.

136 Ladies' boot and shoemakers, *PP* 19 Feb. 1853, p. 3. See also Clément, 45 AP 6, dos. IV, 3 Aug. 1868.

137 Foulon, *Eugène Varlin*, p. 23.

138 Webb Coll. A 14, fol. 214.

139 *BH* 18 July 1863, p. 5.

140 *O* 17 Apr. 1851, pp. 361–2. See also Labour League, *PP* 15 Jan. 1853, p. 2. For sweating in tailoring, see: *NS* 2 Dec. 1843, p. 1, 9 Dec. 1843, p. 7; *GS* 18 Oct. 1851, p. 3; Liverpool, Razzell and Wainwright, *Victorian Working Class*, pp. 274–80; Parssinen and Prothero, 'London tailors' strike'; C. Johnson, 'Economic change and artisan discontent'.

141 *BBCU* 17 May 1864, pp. 2–3.

142 *OSM* 6 June 1839, pp. 347–8.

143 Gossez, *Ouvriers*, pp. 99–101.

144 E.g. *Bristol Mercury* 25 Aug. 1838, p. 3; *Bath Guardian* 27 Apr. 1839, p. 3; *NAUT* 1 Dec. 1847, p. 7; *BH* 6 Dec. 1862, p. 5.

145 *WM* 17 Mar. 1866, p. 1735; *C* 24 Feb. 1866, p. 8.

146 *WM* 21 July 1866, p. 32.

147 Orléans report, 23 Apr. 1844, BB18 1421 8319; *Association des Ouvriers Ebénistes*, p. 3; *Projet d'Association* (bronze-workers), p. 17; Tartaret, *Commission Ouvrière*, pp. 39–40.

148 E.g. *Devizes and Wiltshire Gazette* 10 Sept. 1840, p. 3.

149 Cottereau in 'Au sublime ouvrier', 40.

150 *Man* 17 Nov. 1833, p. 147; *MG* 22 June 1833, p. 3, 29 June 1833, p. 1, 3 Nov. 1869, p. 7; *PMG* 17 Sept. 1831, p. 83, 30 Aug. 1834, p. 234, 11 Oct. 1834, pp. 284–5; *WTS* 5 Oct. 1834, p. 457; *BH* 27 June 1863, p. 1; *Tailor* 16 Mar. 1867, pp. 359–60; *St. Crispin* 9 Oct. 1868, p. 168; Howe and Waite, *London Society of Compositors*, p. 96.

151 BB24 467–477 2643, Dornier; *TC* 4 Feb. 1854, p. 15.

152 Report Rennes, 24 Oct. 1847, BB18 1447 2962.

153 *Tailor* 6 Apr. 1867, p. 406, 3 Nov. 1866, p. 54, 25 Jan. 1868, p. 125; Keszler, *Des grèves*, p. 31; Prothero, *Artisans*, p. 301.

154 Pref. Pol. to Min. of Int., 26 Jan. 1865 [*sic* = 1866] 45 AP 6, dos. III. For other examples of strikes in the brisk season, see: Stockport hatters, *MG* 23 Jan. 1830, p. 2; Paris paper-stainers, *GT* 1 July 1840, p. 847; Bristol

cabinet-makers, *NS* 15 Aug. 1846, p. 4; Paris carpenters, Lenoble, *Aux charpentiers*, p. 7; Faure, 'Mouvements populaires', 53.
155 *BH* 30 Apr. 1864, p. 5.
156 Pref. Pol. to Min. of Int., 26 Jan. 1865 [*sic* = 1866], 45 AP 6, dos. III; anon. letter, Nepireau dossier, CC 608; Leroux, *Aux ouvriers typographes*, p. 1; Faure, 'Mouvements populaires', 64; *Birmingham J* 23 Nov. 1844, p. 2; *PP* 17 Sept. 1853, p. 6.
157 *GT* 24 Dec. 1832, p. 182, 13 Oct. 1833, p. 1217; *A* July 1845, p. 149; Berryer, *Affaire*, p. 6; Bulletin, 9 Sept. 1830, F7 3884; *C* 1 Sept. 1866, p. 5; Perdiguier, *Biographie*, pp. 57, 111; Perdiguier, *Mémoires*, p. 24; Faure, 'Mouvements populaires', 68.
158 E.g. Paris and Dunkirk shoemakers, *Bon Sens* 20 Oct. 1833, p. 3; Lyons silk-weavers, report Lyons 5 Dec. 1833, BB18 1339 9718; Rochdale sawyers, *BFP* 5 Mar. 1836, p. 1; London shoemakers, *O* 25 Nov. 1838, p. 52; Denton hatters, *NS* 10 Feb. 1844, p. 5, 24 Feb. 1844, p. 5; Lyons metal-workers, *M* 30 Apr. 1870, p. 4.
159 *Pop.* 13 July 1845, p. 187; doc. 16 May 1834, HO 64/15; *Pioneer* 17 May 1834, p. 357. See also Paris building joiners, petition to Min. of Pub. Works, 1 Sept. 1840, F13 522; Paris hatters and joiners, *OT* 6 June 1848, p. 3; London builders, *Times* 12 Aug. 1859, p. 10; Leeds builders, *BH* 4 June 1864, p. 5.
160 See also Malepeyre, *Code*, p. 10; Faure, 'Mouvements populaires', 61.
161 *Echo de la Fabrique* 5 Feb. 1832, p. 2; Perdiguier, *Statistique*, p. 26; *RN* 14 July 1850, p. 5; Poulot, *Question sociale*, pp. 342–3. For *essayage* see: *A* Dec. 1841, p. 28; *TA* 7 Jan. 1849, p. 5; *M* 12 Mar. 1870, p. 2, 22 Apr. 1849, p. 2; Keszler, *Des grèves*, p. 23; Tartaret, *Commission Ouvrière*, p. 42.
162 Gossez, *Ouvriers*, p. 74; *Tailor* 25 Mar. 1867, p. 101; *BH* 2 Dec. 1865, p. 5, 7 Apr. 1866, p. 5. See also Clermont-Ferrand wallers and St-Etienne carpenters, reports Riom, 21 Aug. 1845, and Lyons, 27 Aug. 1845, BB18 1435; Bath carpenters, *BH* 14 Oct. 1865, p. 8.
163 Faure, 'Mouvements populaires', 62; Gossez, *Ouvriers*, pp. 94, 140–1.
164 *Règlement de la Société de l'Union des Doreurs*, p. 3; Grignon, *Réfléxions*, pp. 3, 4; Gossez, *Ouvriers*, pp. 92–6.
165 *LD* 8 Oct. 1836, p. 30; *LM* 9 Oct. 1836, p. 30; Place Coll. set 51, fols. 297–300; Pref. Pol., 27 May 1848, C 930, dos. VII, 673; police reports 27 and 28 May, C 932A, 654, 706; *TAHP* 2 Nov. 1850, p. 150; *O* 1851–2 *passim*.
166 *WTS* 2 Aug. 1835, p. 803; *WMA* 1 Aug. 1835, pp. 46–8; *NS* Dec. 1846–May 1847; *Bakers' Record* 24 June 1871, p. 5; *M* 1 Apr. 1870, p. 2.
167 See distinction by Jacobs, *NS* 17 Oct. 1846, p. 3.
168 Bulletin, 21 June 1845, F7 3893; *C* 11 May 1867, p. 1; *Tailor*, 11 Apr. 1868, p. 210; *Rapport des Délégués Ferblantiers*, p. 16; Tartaret, *Commission Ouvrière*, p. 48; Chauvet, *Ouvriers*, pp. 498–9.
169 *GT* 15 Oct. 1840, p. 1240; *A* Feb. 1846, p. 266, Feb. 1847, p. 463; *Union* Jan. 1846, p. 6.
170 *GT* 13 Oct. 1833, p. 1217; report Paris, 2 July 1845, BB18 1433 554; Bulletin, 5 July 1845, F7 3893; *A* July 1845, p. 149.
171 BB24 478–483, 4184 Merot.

172 20 Jan. 1831, F7 3885; *PMG* 30 Aug. 1834, pp. 233–5, 13 Sept. 1834, p. 249, 20 Sept. 1834, p. 257; *Pioneer* 7 Sept. 1833, p. 2, 26 Oct. 1833, p. 59; *Times* 25 Oct. 1834, p. 3; *Leeds Times* 1 Nov. 1834, p. 4; Gossez, *Ouvriers*, pp. 140–1.

173 *Bolton Chron.* 10 May 1828, p. 3; *MG* 3 May 1834, p. 3, 28 June 1834, p. 3; *ATWR* Nov. 1845, p. 221; *Tailor* 6 Oct. 1866, p. 6; H. Tacheux, MS 1052, fol. 372; Parssinen and Prothero, 'London tailors' strike', 70.

174 *OSM* 13 Oct. 1837, pp. 201–3.

175 *Bakers' Record* 24 June 1871, p. 5.

176 Charleville and Mezières tailors, *GT* 17 July 1834, p. 866; Dijon shoemakers, Proc.-Gen., 29 Nov. 1833, BB18 1220 9874; Lyons joiners, BB24 478–483 4184 Merot; Bulletin, 7 Nov. 1832, F7 3886. See also Hanagan, 'Proletarian families', p. 432.

177 *Tailor* 25 Jan. 1868, p. 125.

178 *GT* 30 Nov. 1833, pp. 98–9, 2 Dec. 1833, p. 105.

179 *PMG* 30 Nov. 1833, p. 387; *Pioneer* 10 May 1834, p. 338; *GT* 13 Oct. 1833, p. 1217; *Appel à Tous nos Frères*; Stewart-McDougall, *Artisan Republic*, p. 16; Sewell, *Work and Revolution*, p. 176. See also Lyons silk-weavers, 'Sociétés secrètes. Ferrandiniers et renégats', in 'Clubs et associations' (Cour de Lyon 1848–1850), BB18 1474B.

180 *LM* 9 Oct. 1836, p. 30; *LD* 23 Oct. 1836, p. 44; Place Coll. set 51, fol. 297; *NS* 15 Aug. 1846, p. 4, 10 Nov. 1849, p. 5; *TC* 4 Feb. 1854, p. 9.

181 LSC 59th Quarterly, Oct. 1862, 28/CO/1/8/7/1; Chauvet, *Ouvriers*, p. 303. For other examples, see: London farriers, *C* 31 Mar. 1866, p. 7; London stonemasons, *NS* 4 Dec. 1841, p. 5; Manchester carpenters, Manchester No. 1 branch minute book 1863–1868, 20 June 1864, MRC MSS 78/ASC+J/6/1/12/1; Leeds carpenters, *BH* 16 Apr. 1864, p. 5; Coventry builders, *BH* 31 Dec. 1865, p. 5; London shoemakers, *C* 25 Aug. 1866, p. 8; Webb Coll. A 25, fol. 105; London wireworkers, *OBSTC* 1 June 1866, p. 578; London carpenters, *OBSTC* 17 June 1865, p. 5, 5 Aug. 1865, p. 5; London pattern-makers and engineers, *WA* 4 Nov. 1865, p. 5; *WM* 27 Jan. 1866, p. 6; London cabinet-makers, *BH* 13 Jan. 1866, p. 5; north-east engineers, Jefferys, *Story of the Engineers*, p. 87; Burgess, *Origins*, p. 42.

182 *Tailor* 8 June 1866, p. 128, 16 Feb. 1867, p. 297, 27 Apr. 1867, pp. 41–2, 4 May 1867, p. 54, 1 June 1867, p. 110; *WA* 23 Dec. 1865, p. 5; *WM* 4 May 1867, pp. 4–6.

183 *Tailor* 6 Apr. 1867, p. 413; Gaillard, 'Associations de production', 71. See also Lyons hatters, Vial, *Coutume chapelière*, p. 170.

184 *PP* 19 Feb. 1853, p. 3, 30 Apr. 1853, p. 2, 16 July 1853, p. 3; Webb Coll. A 25, fol. 92. See also Nottingham carpenters, *TC* 11 Feb. 1854, p. 117.

185 Nadaud, *Mémoires*, pp. 231–2; Gossez, *Ouvriers*, p. 127. See also Birmingham coopers, Webb Coll. A 44, fol. 103.

186 Faure, 'Mouvements populaires', 65, 68, 70; Sibalis, 'Mutual aid societies', 26–7, 29; Cottereau, 'Distinctiveness', pp. 143–4; Perrot, *Ouvriers en grève*, pp. 74, 426–7, 430; L. Hunt and Sheridan, 'Corporation', 820–1.

187 E.g. Northampton, *Pioneer* 11 Jan. 1834, p. 152, 15 Mar. 1834, p. 246; Nottingham, *Pioneer* 25 Jan. 1834, p. 174; London painters, *BH* 17 June 1864, p. 5, 30 June 1866, p. 5; compositors, *BH* 31 Mar. 1866, p. 5;

chairmakers and carvers, *C* 17 Feb. 1866, p. 6, 7 July 1866, p. 8; cabinet-makers, *WA* 13 Jan. 1866, p. 8; *BH* 13 Jan. 1866, p. 5. See also Paris bookbinders, goldsmiths, bronze-workers, and leather-dressers: Pref. Pol. to Min. of State, 26 Jan., 45 AP 6, doc. III, fols. 6, 11; Archives de la Préfecture de Police Ba 439, 'La fédération des sociétés ouvrières'; *WM* 6 Apr. 1867, p. 3; *Travail* 12 Dec. 1869, p. 2.

188  S. and B. Webb, *History of Trade Unionism*, pp. 179–80.
189  F. Beesly, 'The Amalgamated Society of Carpenters', *Fortnightly Review* 1 (1867), 321–3.
190  *BH* 20 Jan. 1866, p. 5, 16 June 1866, p. 6, 21 Jan. 1865, p. 5, 30 May 1865, p. 5, 12 Nov. 1865, p. 5, 13 Jan. 1866, p. 5; Maidstone branch minute book, 7 June 1865, 9 Sept. 1865, 10 Mar. 1866, MRC MSS 78/ASC+J/6/1/10.
191  Webb Coll. A 18, fol. 125; Howe and Waite, *London Society of Compositors*, pp. 209–11; *BH* 26 Sept. 1865, p. 4; Humphrey, *Robert Applegarth*, pp. 10–14; Faure, 'Mouvements populaires', 69.
192  Vial, *Coutume chapelière*, pp. 141, 165, 168–9, 171–3.
193  *TAHP* 12 Oct. 1850, p. 127; *Tichborne News* 6 July 1872, p. 3; H. Collins and Abramsky, *Karl Marx*, p. 17.
194  E.g. Paris tailors in 1833, *APO* II, p. 602.
195  E.g. Manchester shoemakers, *MG* 17 Jan. 1829, p. 4; *CC* May 1844, p. 32, June 1844, p. 40; Manchester tailors, *MG* 2 Aug. 1834, p. 3; London shoemakers, *C* 2 June 1866, p. 6; 25 Aug., p. 8; Birmingham shoemakers, *PP* 2 July 1853, p. 3; builders, *NS* 9 May 1846, p. 5; *Morn. Advertiser* 24 Aug. 1859, p. 5; Lyons silk-weavers, Sheridan, 'Social and economic foundations', pp. 18, 301–2, 578.
196  *WM* 16 Aug. 1861, p. 70; Leventhal, *Respectable Radical*, pp. 32–3.
197  *TAHP* 3 Aug. 1850, p. 41; *O* 29 Mar. 1851, pp. 203–4; Robert, 'Cortèges', p. 220.
198  *MG* 7 July 1832, p. 3, 14 July 1832, p. 3, 2 Nov. 1839, p. 2, 15 Dec. 1840, p. 3, 7 Apr. 1841, pp. 2–3; Butterworth Diaries, Oldham Local Interest Centre, 22 and 23 Feb. 1834. See also Manchester brickmakers, *RN* 27 July 1851, p. 9; Sykes, 'Popular politics', pp. 332–8; Richard Price, 'Other face of respectability'.
199  *MG* 16 May 1829, p. 3; *JO* 26 Sept. 1830, p. 2; Faure, 'Mouvements populaires', 65–6; Robert, 'Cortèges', p. 221.
200  Ashton-under-Lyne carpenters' strike book, MRC MSS 78/GUC+J/6/3; Coventry No. 1 lodge members book, MSS 78/GUC+J/6/5; *Tailor* 27 Apr. 1867, p. 40, 7 Sept. 1867, p. 294.
201  *Charter* 26 May 1839, p. 276; *CC* June 1844, p. 38, July 1844, p. 43; Webb Coll. A 24, fols. 76–80.
202  *MG* 3 May 1834, p. 3.
203  *TC* 25 Feb. 1854, p. 1; *Tailor* 6 Apr. 1867, p. 406; Tartaret, *Commission Ouvrière*, p. 30; E. Hunt, *British Labour History*, p. 285; Gossez, *Ouvriers*, p. 201; Chauvet, *Ouvriers*, p. 437.
204  *O* 17 May 1851, p. 317; Haynes, 'Employers and trade unions', p. 241.
205  Letter to *Tribune*, CC 617, 3rd bundle; *PMG* 2 Aug.–4 Oct. 1834; 4 and 8 July 1845, F7 3893; *National* 4 Aug. 1845, p. 1; *Pop.* 16 Aug. 1845, p. 191; *WM* 12 Oct. 1861, p. 119.

206 Marie, *GT* 2 Dec. 1833, p. 109. See also Sewell, *Work and Revolution*, p. 182; Behagg, *Politics and Production*, p. 66–71.

207 *PP* 21 May 1853, p. 4; *MWA* 19 Aug. 1865, p. 3; Howe and Child, *Society of London Bookbinders*, p. 123; Bulletin, 4 July 1845, F7 3893; Paris carpenters, *Pop.* 16 Aug. 1845, p. 191; Manchester carpenters, *NS* 21 Mar. 1846, p. 1; *Ruche* Oct. Montpellier smiths, 1844, pp. 299–300; boot and shoemakers, *SRI* 25 June 1853, p. 5; London builders, *WM* 12 Oct. 1861, p. 119; Blackburn, *MWA* 22 Apr. 1865, p. 1; Manchester carpenters, *C* 22 Sept. 1866, p. 5.

208 Shipwrights, Prothero, *Artisans*, pp. 168–9; farriers, Bulletin, 10 Sept. 1830, F7 3884; *APO* II, p. 602; packing-case makers, *GT* 15 Nov. 1833, pp. 46–7; tailors, *GT* 30 Nov. 1833, p. 99; *CC* 17 Aug. 1844, p. 73; boot and shoemakers, Webb Coll. A 25, fols. 30, 74; builders, *NS* 9 May 1846, p. 5; engineers, *BTC* Feb. 1852, pp. 6, 7; boot and shoemakers, *PP* 30 July 1853, p. 2; builders, Webb Coll. A 10, fol. 97, A 13, fol. 209; *BH* 3 Dec. 1864, p. 4; *MWA* 28 Jan. 1865, p. 4; tailors, *Tailor* 6 Oct. 1867, p. 2; *C* 31 Mar. 1866, p. 6, 25 Aug. 1866, p. 8, 1 Sept. 1866, p. 5; *passementiers*, *M* 10 Mar. 1870, p. 2.

209 Parssinen and Prothero, 'London tailors' strike'; *Birmingham J* 11 Apr. 1846; *NS* 16 May 1846, p. 5; *M* 27 Dec. 1869, p. 2.

210 *MG* 17 Jan. 1835, p. 17; *NS* 9 May 1846, p. 5.

211 *Birmingham J.* 9 May 1846, p. 4; *PP* 5 Oct. 1861, p. 115; *BH* 30 Apr. 1864, p. 4.

212 *BBCU* 18 Aug. 1849, p. 52, 1 Nov. 1849, p. 59.

213 Holt Town, *MG* 29 Nov. 1837, p. 3.

214 See also also 10 Nov. 1832, F7 3886.

215 Bulletin, 4 Nov. 1830, F7 3884.

216 Reports Rennes, 21 Mar. 1837, BB18 1366 4838; Toulouse, 11 Nov. 1842, BB18 1407 5683.

217 Report Poitiers, 17 Apr. 1835, BB18 1230 1994.

218 Reports Angers, 29 Oct., 7 Nov. 1833, BB18 1339 9750; 4 Nov. 1841, BB18 1398 2824; Rennes, 17 Oct. 1845, BB18 1436 1021.

219 Report Lyons, 5 Dec. 1833, BB18 1339 9788. See also report in 'Clubs et associations', BB18 1474B.

220 Report Angers, 8 Oct. 1833, BB18 1339 9750.

221 Haynes, 'Employers and trade unions', p. 247.

222 *APOT*, p. 12; 1856 Yearly Account of Cabinet-Makers' Society, 1856, MRC MSS 78/CU/4/1/2.

223 58th Quarterly LSC, Aug. 1862, MS 28/CO/1/8/7/1, fols. 45–7, 55–7. See also *BH* 23 July 1864, p. 7; *M* 5 Apr. 1870, p. 7.

224 Guillaumou, *Confessions*, p. 116; Perdiguier, *Mémoires*, pp. 222, 280.

225 *APOT*, pp. 8–9.

226 *APOT*, p. 23; Chauvet, *Ouvriers*, p. 463; Vial, *Coutume chapelière*, pp. 66–7.

227 Reports Rennes, 12, 14, 15, 17, 18, 21, 25 Nov. 1846, BB18 1447 2962.

228 Bulletin, 12 Sept. 1830, F7 3884.

229 *Ruche* Aug. 1847, p. 171.

230 Pref. Pol., 45 AP 6, dos. III.

231 *TSMC* Nov. 1871.

232 E.g. Tours and Brest tailors, *Tribune* Sunday suppt., no. 1, p. 3; Reports Rennes, 15, 18 Sept., 12 Oct. 1840, BB18 1387 979.
233 *JTA* 1 Oct. 1860, pp. 111–2; *BH* 6 Jan. 1866, p. 4.
234 *C* 9 Mar. 1867, p. 1, 6 Apr. 1867, p. 1; *BH* 9 Mar. 1867, p. 6; *WM* 6 Apr. 1867, p. 3; Tartaret, *Commission Ouvrière* p. 52; *Commerce* 20 June 1869, p. 1, 18 July 1869, p. 1, 25 July 1869, p. 1, 1 Aug. 1869, p. 2, 22 Aug. 1869, p. 2, 12 Sept. 1869, p. 3; *Travail* 10 Oct. 1869, p. 3, 21 Nov. 1869, pp. 1, 2, 3, 12 Dec. 1869, p. 2; *M* 21 Dec. 1869, p. 3; NA MS 155, fols. 653, 670; Varlin to Richard, 1 Dec. 1869, AML I2 55, II.
235 *True Sun* 24 May 1834, p. 1; *Crisis* 31 May 1834, p. 62; *Pioneer* 14 June 1834, p. 406; *WTS* 15 June 1834, p. 330; Parssinen and Prothero, 'London tailors' strike', 79.
236 *A* Feb. 1846, p. 265.
237 *O* 7 Feb. 1852, p. 258.
238 MSS 78/TC/Pre/2/1, 78/TC/MISC/2/1.
239 *GT* 22 Oct. 1835, p. 1340. See also Nîmes strike, Perdiguier, *Mémoires*, p. 246; Faure, 'Mouvements populaires', 67.
240 Bulletins 21, 23 June, 25 Aug. 1845, F7 3893; *Pop.* 13 July 1845, p. 187, 16 Aug. 1845, p. 191, 18 Oct. 1845, p. 200; *ATWR* Sept. 1845, p. 90; P. Vinçard, *Ouvriers*, p. 157; Perdiguier, *Biographie*, pp. 110–12.
241 *WM* 19 July 1861, p. 38, 26 July 1861, p. 46.
242 Prothero, *Artisans*, pp. 168–9; *Pop.* 16 Aug. 1845, p. 191, 18 Oct. 1845, p. 200.
243 *Birmingham J* 2 May 1846, p. 6; *NS* 2 May 1846, p. 5; *LL* 23 Sept. 1848, p. 61; *O* 14 Feb. 1852, pp. 267–9; *Beacon* 2 Nov. 1853, p. 21.
244 *Tailor* 18 May 1867, p. 91.
245 Bulletins 15 and 16 Sept. 1840, F7 3890; *A* Oct. 1840, p. 14, Dec. 1840, p. 30; Nadaud, *Mémoires*, p. 229.
246 *Last* 22 Nov. 1844, p. 33; *BTC* Apr. 1850, p. 25; PTA 14th Half-yearly, MS 39A/TA/4/1/1, Newport. See also Jefferys, *Story of the Engineers*, pp. 70–1.
247 OSM 30 Oct. 1835, fol. 49; 1 Apr. 1836, p. 70.
248 *TAHP* 19 Sept. 1850, p. 95; *NS* 28 Oct. 1843, p. 5; *BH* 18 June 1864, p. 4, 25 June 1864, p. 5; Jefferys, *Story of the Engineers*, pp. 70–1.
249 See also *WM* 25 Aug. 1866, p. 92.
250 *BTC* Dec. 1850, p. 15; *BFFC* Feb. 1848, p. 83, Aug. 1848, p. 109, Nov. 1848, p. 117, Sept. 1850, p. 155; Howe and Child, *Society of London Bookbinders*, p. 139.
251 Vial, *Coutume chapelière*, pp. 141, 168–9, 171–3.
252 Stewart and Hunter, *Needle is Threaded*, p. 48; *Tailor* 27 Apr. 1867, pp. 41–2.
253 Child, *Industrial Relations*, p. 128; *A* 31 Mar. 1850, pp. 501–2.
254 *Pioneer* 8 Mar. 1834, p. 238, 15 March 1834, p. 249; *A* 21 May 1848, p. 154; *APO* II, pp. 17, 24, 465–6; *NS* 10 Nov. 1849, p. 5; Tartaret, *Commission Ouvrière*, p. 37; *St. Crispin* 11 Dec. 1869, p. 289; Webb Coll. A 25, fol. 112; *GS* 5 July 1851, p. 3; *Tailor* 15 Dec. 1866, p. 164, 27 Apr. 1867, p. 44, 4 May 1867, p. 54, 25 May 1867, p. 98; *Times* 26 Apr. 1867, p. 12; Lawrence, *WM* 22 June 1867, p. 10; *Commerce* 15 Aug. 1869, p. 2.

255 *BTC* 21 Jan. 1862, p. 16; Howe and Child, *Society of London Bookbinders*, pp. 157–9; Barberet, *Mouvement ouvrier*, p. 58; Tartaret, *Commission Ouvrière*, p. 232.

256 *Fédération de Tous les Ouvriers*, p. 2; *NS* 16 May 1846, p. 5; *TAHP* 21 Sept. 1850, p. 100; *BH* 21 Jan. 1865, p. 5.

257 Tolain, *Quelques vérités*, p. 31; Tartaret, *Commission Ouvrière*, p. 31.

258 *TSMC* Oct. 1852, p. 1, Apr. 1865, p. 4, Feb. 1866, p. 4, Mar. 1866, p. 4, June 1869, p. 4; MSS 39A/TA/4/1/1; 39A/TA/1/3, fol. 14; 28/CO/1/8/7/1; Tartaret, *Commission Ouvrière*, p. 37; Jefferys, *Story of the Engineers*, p. 70.

259 *OSM* 29 Sept. 1837, p. 198, 13 Oct. 1837, p. 201, 24 Nov. 1837, p. 213, 25 May 1838, p. 261.

260 *Tailor* 26 Jan. 1867, p. 247; *JTA* 1 Sept. 1860, p. 105; Moberg, 'George Odger', p. 10.

261 Musson, *Typographical Association*, p. 27; Sibalis, 'Mutual aid societies', 15; Webb Coll. A 22, fol. 13; *Règlement de la Société de l'Union des Doreurs*, p. 4.

262 *JTA* 1 Oct. 1860, p. 112.

263 Noble, Building Trades Conference, 24 June 1859, MS 78/OS/1/1/1; Clément in Tartaret, *Commission Ouvrière*, pp. 161–2.

264 *O* 5 Apr. 1851, pp. 217–8; Webb Coll. A 13, fol. 262; *St. Crispin* 10 July 1869, p. 13.

265 *O* 13 Mar. 1852, p. 308; Menuisiers en bâtiments Paris, F12 3117; *Workman* 5 July 1861, p. 22; *Charter* 14 Apr. 1839, p. 181.

266 Coulson in OBS, *Quarterly* Dec. 1865, p. 3; *WM* 15 May 1866, p. 3.

267 *Tailor* 13 June 1868, p. 271. See also Dunning, *BH* 19 Dec. 1863, p. 5; *LL* 7 Oct. 1844, p. 73.

268 *OSM* 16 July 1840, p. 457; 6 Feb. 1845, p. 3.

269 Clément, in Tartaret, *Commission Ouvrière*, p. 29.

270 T. Wright, *Habits*, p. 36; *St. Crispin* 13 Mar. 1869, p. 150.

271 *Tailor* 15 Dec. 1866, p. 152, 16 Mar. 1867, p. 360, 23 Mar. 1867, p. 378, 6 Apr. 1867, p. 413, 23 Jan. 1868, pp. 125–6.

272 See Auslander, 'Perceptions of beauty', p. 163; Hanagan, 'Commentary', p. 188.

273 *St. Crispin* 13 Feb. 1869, p. 85; Leno, *Aftermath*, pp. 58–9. See also Sonenscher, *Work and Wages*, p. 371.

274 See also *APOT*, pp. 9–10.

275 *OSM* 10 Oct. 1839, p. 386, 22 July 1836, p. 87, 4 June 1840, p. 445.

276 *BH* 4 July 1863, p. 5; *WM* 21 July 1866, p. 27, 25 Aug. 1866, p. 88.

277 *LD* 14 July 1839, p. 3; Howe and Waite, *London Society of Compositors*, p. 111.

278 *APOT*, pp. 24–5, 28.

279 *Tailor* 19 Sept. 1868, pp. 343–4.

280 *CC* July 1844, suppt., p. 55; *BH* 17 Jan. 1863, p. 5, 10 Feb. 1866, p. 5.

281 *A* Mar. 1842, p. 5; *NAUT*, 1 Dec. 1847, p. 4.

282 Minutes 31 May, 2 and 16 June 1848, and petition 12 June 1848, Luxembourg dossier, C 925, 2963, 7032, 8006, 9008; Pref. Pol. 14 June 1848, C 932B; Luxembourg dossier, C 942, 2941; *A Tous les Travailleurs*; *VR* 14 June 1848, p. 1, 21 June 1848, p. 2, 11 Aug. 1848, p. 2; *OT* 14 June 1848, p. 2, 20 June 1848, p. 1; *CP* 2 Apr. 1848, p. 4; *A* 12 Apr. 1848,

pp. 108–9; *RP* 22 Apr. 1848, p. 1; *Manifeste des Délégués*, p. 1; *Les Délégués (Ouvriers)*; *P* 18 Apr. 1849, p. 4, 28 May 1849, p. 6; *VP* 29 Nov. 1849, p. 2, 1 Dec. 1849, p. 3; Gossez, *Ouvriers*, pp. 242–63, 322; Rancière, 'Myth', 9–10.

283  *AR* 12 Apr. 1849, p. 3; *PS* 28 Jan. 1849, p. 1; Aminzade, 'Transformation', p. 89.

284  *NS* Mar.–Apr. and Nov.–Dec. 1848, Mar.–May and Nov.–Dec. 1849; *SA* 5 Aug. 1848, pp. 29–30, 2 Sept. 1848, p. 88; *LL* 11 Nov. 1848, p. 116, 25 Nov. 1848, pp. 130–1, 2 Dec. 1848, pp. 137–8; *Britannia* 20 Apr. 1850, p. 245, 15 Mar. 1851, p. 165; *NUTARLA* 13 May 1848, p. 55.

285  *WM* 28 Aug. 1861, pp. 77–8; *BH* 1 Nov. 1862, p. 5, 29 Nov. 1862, p. 5, 4 Apr. 1863, p. 5, 20 June 1863, p. 5, 19 Mar. 1864, p. 5, 26 Mar. 1864, p. 5, 7 May 1864, p. 5, 22 Oct. 1864, p. 5, 19 Nov. 1864, p. 5, 8 July 1865, p. 5; *MWA* 26 Aug. 1865, p. 1; *C* 24 Mar. 1866, p. 6, 14 Apr. 1866, p. 6, 23 Feb. 1867, p. 5, 20 July 1867, p. 2; Gillespie, *Labor and Politics*, p. 203.

286  *A* Mar. 1845, pp. 81–6, Apr. 1845, pp. 98–9, May 1845, p. 127, June 1845, p. 133, Feb. 1846, p. 264, Mar. 1846, p. 273, May 1846, p. 309, July 1846, p. 338, Sept. 1846, pp. 373–5, Mar. 1847, p. 466, Apr. 1847, pp. 486, 496, Aug. 1847, p. 588; *Ruche* Oct. 1841, p. 4, Apr. 1844, pp. 101–6, Oct. 1844, pp. 290–1, Nov. 1844, p. 322, Feb. 1845, p. 33, Feb. 1847, pp. 34–6, April–May 1847, pp. 99–100; *Union* Mar. 1845, p. 1, Feb. 1846, p. 11; *F 1845* May 1845, pp. 42–3, Mar. 1846, p. 128; Duchêne, *Actualités*; *APOT*, pp. 17–18.

287  Prothero, *Artisans*, ch. 12; *Bolton Chron.* 19 Apr. 1828, p. 3, 26 Apr. 1828, p. 4, 3 May 1828, p. 4; *Leeds Intelligencer* 23 Oct. 1828, p. 3, 30 Oct. 1828, p. 3, 20 Nov. 1828, p. 2; *Leeds Mercury* 26 Apr. 1828, p. 3, 23 Aug. 1828, p. 3, 25 Oct. 1828, p. 3, 1 Nov. 1828, p. 5; *PMG* 23 Nov. 1833, p. 379, 18 Jan. 1834, p. 442, 7 June 1834, p. 143, 27 Sept. 1834, p. 269, 7 Mar. 1835, p. 453, 18 July 1835, pp. 602–3; *Gauntlet* 15 Dec. 1833, p. 715; *Pioneer* 4 Jan. 1834, p. 141; *TAHP* 14 Sept. 1850, p. 90; *O* 8 Mar. 1851, p. 153; *TC* 25 Feb. 1854, p. 6; *BBCU* 26 June 1855, p. 9; *C* 9 Feb. 1867, p. 1; Webb Coll. A 13, fol. 333; Gillespie, *Labor and Politics*, p. 51; Jefferys, *Story of the Engineers*, p. 74.

## 4. WORK AND RADICALISM

1  Tailors, Webb Coll. A 14, fols. 85, 154; *NS* 2 Dec. 1843, p. 1; *PP* 27 Aug. 1853, p. 2, 3 Sept. 1853, p. 2, 10 Sept. 1853, p. 2, *BH* 3 Feb. 1867, p. 7; *Tailor* 23 Mar. 1867, p. 381; Holyoake and Le Blond, *Appeal*; Schmiechen, *Sweated Industries*, pp. 125, 134, 161; cabinet-makers, *NS* 2 May 1846, p. 5; carpenters, *PMG* 13 Aug. 1831, p. 45; *NS* 31 July 1847, p. 2; *TC* 18 Feb. 1854, p. 6; *PP* 31 Jan. 1857, p. 5, 28 Aug. 1858, p. 5.

2  Webb Coll. A 45, fol. 23; *NS* 5 Dec. 1846–1 May 1847; *PN* 18 July 1847, p. 3; *Times* 18 Mar. 1848, p. 7; *LL* 12 Aug. 1848, p. 11, 30 Dec. 1848, p. 163; *RWN* 5 May 1850, p. 8; *Workman* 21 June 1861, p. 3; *WM* 21 Apr. 1866, p. 241; *MWA* 4 Feb. 1865, p. 7; G. Read, *The Practical Baker* (1846).

3  Cheap labour: BB18 1202 6440, Agen; *Bolton Chron.* 21 Apr. 1827, p. 4; *A* June 1847, p. 521; Boyer, *De l'état des ouvriers*, p. 19; Tartaret, *Exposition*

*Universelle*, pp. 328, 330, 338–40. Orders: Webb Coll. A. 14, fol. 77; Lovett, *Hetherington's Dispatch* 6 July 1836, Place Coll. set 56, fol. 10; *ATWM* Nov. 1845, p. 221; *Ruche* Feb. 1847, p. 39; *Tailor* 15 Dec. 1866, p. 152; *St. Crispin* 15 May 1869, pp. 253–4; Devlin, *Contract Reform*, pp. 6–11; Prothero, *Artisans*, pp. 44–5.

4  *TN* 31 July 1825, p. 38; *OSM* 28 Apr. 1837, p. 156.

5  *O* 19 Jan. 1852, suppt., pp. 1–8; *TC* 11 Feb. 1854, p. 9; W. Fraser, *Trade Unions and Society*, pp. 60–4, 199–200.

6  *O* 19 Apr. 1851, pp. 250–1, 3 Jan. 1852, pp. 212–15, 3 Apr. 1852, p. 330; Burgess, 'Trade union policy', 656.

7  Humphrey, *Robert Applegarth*, p. 33; Prothero, *Artisans*, pp. 183–91, 317–8; Gossez, 'Presse parisienne', p. 127; Isambert, *Christianisme*, p. 218.

8  *TAHP* 3 Aug. 1850, p. 46; *NS* 13 June 1846, p. 6; *O* 4 Jan. 1851, p. 10; Humphrey, *Robert Applegarth*, pp. 126–30.

9  Biagini, *Liberty*, pp. 9, 148; *Progrès Journal de Lyon* 10 July 1861, p. 1; Molinari, *Mouvement socialiste*, pp. xviii–xx.

10  Dolléans, *Histoire*, p. 297; Dalotel, *Aux origines*, pp. 15–22.

11  Macdonald, *MG* 3 Nov. 1869, p. 7.

12  E.g., *Man* 29 Sept. 1833, p. 99; Prothero, *Artisans*, p. 185; Prothero, 'London Chartism and trades', 210.

13  ASCJ, *Monthly Report* June 1860, p. 12.

14  *OSM* 16 Mar. 1838, p. 236, 24 Apr. 1851, p. 2, 28 Apr./12 May 1859, p. 3.

15  3rd Half-yearly report, MS 39A/TA/4/1/1.

16  Moberg, 'George Odger', pp. 104–6; *Report of Manchester Operative House Painters' Alliance*, Dec. 1868/June 1869, p. 6, MRC MSS 78/MA/4/1/1; Webb Coll. A 10, fol. 343, A11, fol. 148; Biagini, *Liberty*, pp. 149–52.

17  Humphrey, *Robert Applegarth*, pp. 33, 52–6; S. Coltham, 'George Potter, the Junta, and the *Bee-Hive*', *International Review of Social History* 9 (1964), 10 (1965).

18  Postgate, *Builders' History*, pp. 264–5, 281–4; Webb, *History of Trade Unionism*, pp. 262–72.

19  Biagini, *Liberty*, pp. 149, 164, 329.

20  *O* 10 Jan. 1851, suppt. p. 7, 19 July 1851, pp. 17–18; see also Harry, ASCJ, *Monthly Report* Nov. 1866, p. 21.

21  *NP* p. 342.

22  MRC MSS 28/CO/1/8/9/1.

23  *Report of Manchester Operative House Painters' Alliance*, Dec. 1868/June 1869, p. 6, MRC MSS 78/MA/4/1/1; Gen. Union of Operative House Painters, Quarterly, Apr. 1871, pp. 9–11, Jan. 1874, p. 7; ASCJ, *Monthly Report* Oct. 1866, pp. 11–12; *AR* 1 July 1849, p. 3.

24  *BTC* 21 Jan. 1865, pp. 19–20.

25  *OSM*, 16 Feb. 1838, p. 236.

26  *Tailor* 9 Feb. 1867, p. 279; see also *NS* 24 Sept. 1842, p. 2.

27  Webb Coll. A 10, fol. 216; see also A 25, fol. 91; *BBCU* 18 Aug. 1849, p. 49.

28  see above, pp. 83–5.

29  Parssinen and Prothero, 'London tailors' strike', 72–3, 84; Prothero, 'London Chartism and trades', 212–13. See also also the radical Guillaumou's leadership of Paris shoemakers in 1848 and attempts to transform the

*compagnonnages*: *VR* 7 June 1848, p. 2; *P* 7 Dec. 1848, p. 3, 8 Dec. 1848, p. 2. See also Colin (Chauvet, *Ouvriers*, pp. 118, 159), Henriette (*Tailor* 20 Oct. 1866, p.23, 1 Dec. 1866, p. 122), and Varlin (Pref. Pol. to Min. of Ag., 31 Jan. 1865, 45 AP 6, dos. III). See also BB30 366, dos II, fols. 162, 165.

30  See also Faure, 'Mouvements populaires', 82.

31  *Tailor* 23 Feb. 1867, pp. 313–14; Bell, 'Reform League', pp. 99, 337; Dunsmore, 'Working classes', pp. 26–8, 31–2.

32  Humphrey, *Robert Applegarth*, pp. 2, 6–8, 10, 18; A. Taylor, 'Modes', p. 207. See also Leventhal, *Respectable Radical*, pp. 26–7.

33  See also Berridge, 'Popular journalism'.

34  E.g. Jador, *Procès*, p. 25; *GT* 2 Dec. 1833, p. 107 (Marie); *Indicateur* 19 Oct. 1834, p. 1; Monfalcon, *Histoire*, p. 144 (Favre); Berryer, *Affaire*; Rancière, 'Myth', 4.

35  *AR* 22 Nov. 1849, p. 1; Perdiguier, *Biographie*, p. 79.

36  E.g. Wall, *NS* 30 Oct. 1841, p. 6, Drake, 6 July 1844, p. 5, and 2 Nov. 1844, p. 7; *A* July 1841, p. 7; *Pop.* 16 Aug. 1845, p. 191; Paris carpenters, *National* 7 July 1845, p. 1, 19 Aug. 1845, p. 1; Stevens, *Memoir*, p. 54; Moutet, 'Mouvement ouvrier', 14.

37  *Last* 15 Nov. 1844, p. 26. See also *O* 10 Jan. 1852, p. 225.

38  Perron, 'Association libre pour l'instruction du peuple', 5 June, F17 6674; [Martin], Nouveau catéchisme, p. 17; Farren, *NS* 30 July 1842, p. 7.

39  *BTC* 23 Nov. 1868, p. 194.

40  ASCJ, *Monthly Report* Nov.1866, pp. 17–18.

41  Builders, *PMG* 2 Aug. 1834, p. 207; bakers, *ES* 5 Dec. 1842, p. 1; shoe-makers, *Bristol Times* 24 June 1843, p. 4; bakers, *NS* 5 Dec. 1846, p. 6; *Shipwrights' J* Apr. 1858, p. 7; Macdonald, *True Story*, pp. 11, 13.

42  *OSM* 9 Apr. 1840, p. 431; *NS* 4 May 1844, p. 1; *Last* 15 Nov. 1844, p. 29.

43  *OSM* 28 Oct. 1836, p. 108, 25 Nov. 1836, p. 113, 24 June 1836, p. 80.

44  York tailors, *O* 21 Feb. 1852, p. 275.

45  FSOC, *AR 1859–60*, p. 14; see also Druitt, *Tailor* 9 Mar. 1867, p. 342.

46  *GT* 13 June 1839, p. 817; *OSM* 6 Jan. 1837, p. 126, 22 Dec. 1837, p. 221, 5 Jan. 1838, pp. 224–5, 16 Feb. 1838, p. 236, 5 Dec. 1839, p. 398, 6 Feb. 1845, p. 2; Festy, 'Dix années', 181.

47  OBS, *Report and Balance Sheets, Ending 1862*, p. 2, MSS 78/OB/4/1/2/1.

48  *BH* 10 Dec. 1864, p. 5, 4 Feb. 1865, p. 5, 18 Mar. 1865, p. 5.

49  Chauvet, *Ouvriers*, p. 523.

50  Lawrence, *BH* 21 Apr. 1866, p. 5; see also *Travail* 10 Oct.1869, p. 1.

51  *Tailor and Cutter* 1 Aug. 1868, p. 307; *Fédération de Tous les Ouvriers*, p. 2.

52  E.g. Yearly Account of Cabinet-Makers' Society, 1845–6, MRC MSS 78/ CU/4/1/2; PTA 17th Half-yearly, MS 39A/TA/4/1/1; Minutes Manchester No. 1. ASCJ, 14 June 1865, MSS 78/ASC+J/6/1/12/1; *TSMC* Feb. 1866, p. 4, Mar. 1866, pp. 4, June 1869, p. 4, MS 39A/TA/1/3, fol. 14; OSM leaflet, 1836; Bristol cabinet-makers, *NS* 28 Oct.1843, p. 5; masons, *HHE* 4 May 1833, p. 3; Paris goldsmiths, *APO* III, pp. 20–1.

53  Maidstone carpenters' branch minute book, 21. Dec. 1867, MRC MSS 78/ ASC+J/6/1/10.

54  *Règlement de la Société de l'Union des Doreurs*, p. 11.

55  *GT* 24 Aug. 1840, p. 1039; Tartaret, *Commission Ouvrière*, p. 53.

56 'Rapport des délégués dessinateurs', in *Rapports des Délégués Dessinateurs et Tisseurs*, p. 22.
57 Cabinet Makers' Society, Report Dec. 1845; Liverpool plasterers, Webb Coll. A 12, fol. 12; *Pioneer* 25 Jan. 1834, p. 174; *OSM*, 9 Dec. 1836, p. 117; Oldham hatters, *NS* 20 Jan. 1838, p. 7; *OBSTC* 1 Dec. 1861, p. 33; Paris trades, Tartaret, *Commission Ouvrière*, p. 53.
58 *TAHP* 17 Aug. 1850, p. 63; *BH* 30 Sept. 1863, p. 5; Markley, *OBSTC* 1 Dec. 1864, p. 33; 'Menuisiers en sièges et fauteuils', in *Rapports des Délégués des Ouvriers*, p. 521; 'Manifeste', Tartaret, *Commission Ouvrière*, p. 44; Macdonald, *True Story*, p. 5; Gossez, *Ouvriers*, p. 56; ASE, *O* 7 Feb. 1852, p. 257.
59 *OSM* 10 Oct. 1839, p. 385; OBS, 14th *AR*, p. 3, and *Quarterly June 1863*, in MS 78/OB/1/2/1.
60 *Last* 1 Nov. 1844, p. 2; *ECC* II, p. 55; *TAHP* 20 July 1850, p. 25; *O* 4 Jan. 1851, p. 1; Sheffield building trades, *NS* 31 Jan. 1846, p. 1; masons, *Shipwrights' J* Apr. 1858, p. 9; *Times* 4 Aug. 1859, p. 10; *OBSTC* 1 Oct. 1861, pp. 9–10; *BH* 10 Feb. 1866, p. 5; Favre, *Coalition*, p. 15; Macdonald, *True Story*, p. 5; *Règlement de la Société de l'Union des Doreurs*, pp. 1–2.
61 *BBCU* 26 June 1855, p. 13.
62 Tartaret, *Exposition Universelle*, p. 158.
63 Druitt, *Tailor* 23 Feb. 1867, pp. 314–5.
64 Tartaret, *Exposition Universelle*, p. 164.
65 Potter, *Labour Question*, p. 14.
66 Grignon, *Réflexions*, p. 2; anon. letter, Nepireu dossier, CC 608.
67 *NS* 27 Feb. 1841, p. 5; see also Devlin, *CC* 31 Aug. 1844, p. 94; *RWN* 11 Aug. 1850, p. 5.
68 Oldham engineers, *O* 3 May 1851, pp. 281–2; *OSM* 3 Feb. 1837, p. 135; Manchester bricklayers, *NS* 23 Oct. 1841, p. 7; Bristol and Bath trades, 27 Nov. 1841, p. 8, and 29 Jan. 1842, p. 3; Exeter shoemakers, *PP* 30 Apr. 1853, p. 2.
69 *Bakers' Record* 24 June 1871, p. 5.
70 PTA 6th Half-yearly, MS 39A/TA/4/1/1; *BH* 15 July 1864, p. 5; Macdonald, *True Story*, pp. 3, 12.
71 *Report of Manchester Operative House Painters' Alliance*, July–Dec. 1868, pp. 4–5; 'Réunion générale des tisseurs', 15 Oct., AML I2 47B, 873; ASCJ, *Monthly Report* May 1864, p. 3.
72 *BBCU* Nov. 1852, p. 1.
73 *OSM* 9 Dec. 1836, p. 117.
74 *OSM* 5 Jan. 1838, pp. 224–5.
75 *OSM* 13 Oct. 1837, p. 201.
76 *Moniteur* 10 June 1832, p. 1307.
77 *A* Nov. 1840, p. 18, 28 Feb. 1843, p. 44, July 1845, p. 148; Brisset, 'L'ouvrier', p. 560; D. Vincent, *Testaments*, pp. 125, 135.
78 Cour des Pairs, *Affaire* VI, p. 280.
79 Amann, *Revolution*, p. 309; Dunsmore, 'Working classes', p. 42.
80 Proc. Imp. Bordeaux to Proc.-Gen., 27 June 1856, BB30 366, dos.II, fol. 165; Margadant, *French Peasants*, p. 160.
81 E.g., *JO* 14 Oct. 1830, p. 3, 17 Oct. 1830, p. 3; *G* 28 Apr. 1833, p. 190, 14

July 1830, p. 367; *Charter* 11 Aug. 1839, p. 464, 25 Aug. 1839, p. 491, 6 Oct. 1839, p. 585; *NS* 21 Feb. 1846, p. 6, 5 Aug. 1848, p. 5; *Tailor* 1 Dec. 1866, pp. 120–2. See also Rancière, 'Myth', 3–4.

82  E. S. Beesly, *The Amalgamated Society of Carpenters and Joiners* (1867), p. 8. See also Humphrey, *Robert Applegarth*, p. 8.

83  *O* 5 May 1839, p. 7; *Charter* 28 Apr. 1839, p. 215, 5 May 1839, p. 283, 12 May 1839, p. 246; Silver Cup, *NS* 22 Nov. 1845, p. 1; Paddington carpenters, 1 May 1847, p. 5; engineers-smiths, *C* 941; Bulletins 19 and 30 Oct., 4 Nov. 1848 'Clubs et associations' (Cour de Paris (1848–1850)), BB18 1474B; *Tailor* 9 Feb. 1867, p. 279; Lyons metal-workers, *Commerce* 29 Aug. 1869, p. 2; *St. Crispin* 22 Jan. 1870, p. 41; Prothero, 'London Chartism and trades', 202–3 ; Gillespie, *Labor and Politics*, p. 204; Sheridan, 'Social and economic foundations', p. 150.

84  Fomberteau in NAF 9581, fol. 355; *CP* 3 Apr. 1848, p. 4.

85  Webb, *History of Trade Unionism*, pp. 39–40; *VR* 22 Apr. 1848, p. 1; Lefrançais, *Souvenirs* I, p. 230; Loubere, *Radicalism*, p. 31; Stewart-McDougall, *Artisan Republic*, pp. 67–8, 111.

86  M. Goffin (ed.), *The Diaries of Absalom Watkin, a Manchester man 1787–1861* (Stroud, 1993), p. 51; *MG* 20 Aug. 1831, p. 2; Sykes, 'Early Chartism and trade unionism', pp. 159–62.

87  E.g., *Sheffield Mercury* 29 Sept. 1838, p. 5; *BH* 23 May 1863, p. 4; Stewart-McDougall, *Artisan Republic*, p. 12.

88  *ECC* I, p. 109; *NS* 21 Dec. 1844, p. 1; *NP*, p. 261.

89  *WM* 18 Aug. 1866, p. 71; Fletcher, Stepney Green meeting, 21 Feb. 1839, HO 44/52. See also Prothero, 'Chartism in London', 85; Prothero, 'London Chartism and Trades', 203.

90  *WFP* 12 Mar. 1831, 2 Apr. 1831; *Charter* 6 Oct. 1839, p. 585; *NS* 23 Apr. 1842, p. 4, 30 Apr. 1842, p. 1; Place Coll. set 56, vol. Sept.–Oct. 1842, fol. 9; *PP* 20 Feb. 1858, p. 1.

91  Holyoake, *EL* 9 July 1864, p. 4; Hartwell, *BH* 20 Aug. 1864, p. 4; Marx to Engels, 1 Feb. 1865, in Karl Marx Frederick Engels, *Collected Works* (1987) XLII, p. 74.

92  A. Taylor, 'Modes', pp. 36–8, 46, 199–200.

93  *CP* 18 Apr. 1848, p. 1; Police report 12 May 1848, C930, dos. VI, 639; *RP* 14 May 1848, p. 2; Pref. Pol., 7 July, C 934, dos. VIII, 2671; C 925, doss. Luxembourg; C 930, dos. V, 608; Gossez, *Ouvriers*, pp. 20–1, 233, 245–6, 262–3, 300–1, 361–4; Amann, *Revolution*, pp. 46, 96, 181.

94  *Tribune* 12 Sept. 1831, p. 1; Sunday suppt., p. 1; *Bon Sens* 15 July 1832, p. 5, 28 Oct., 1832, p. 2; *Echo des Travailleurs* 6 Nov. 1833, p. 4; *Les Sociétés Populaires*, pp. 10–14, 27–32; Roche, *Manuel*, pp. 158–9; Cour des Pairs, *Affaire* I, pp. 28, 46.

95  Bulletins 8 Oct., 5 Nov. 1831, F7 3885; Raspail, *Lettres* I, pp. 308, 326–7; Weill, *Histoire*, pp. 31, 60, 67–8.

96  Nadaud, *Mémoires*, p. 140.

97  25 Jan. 1831, F7 3885 ; *JO* 26 Sept. 1830, p. 3; *Artisan* 26 Sept. 1830, p. 3; *Bolton Chron.* 31 Mar. 1831, p. 2; de la Hodde, *Histoire des sociétés secrètes*, pp. 57–8; Faure, 'Mouvements populaires', 75; Newman, 'What the crowd wanted', 27–32, 34, 37, 47; Moss, 'Parisian workers', 210.

98  Faure, 'Mouvments populaires', 76–8.
99  Bulletin 14 Nov. 1832, F7 3886; Pref. Pol. 21 May 1834, and Desjardin,
    CC 585; Cour des Pairs, *Affaire* I, pp. 27–8; IV, p. 402; Rittiez, *Histoire* I,
    pp. 366–70; de la Hodde, *Histoire des sociétés secrètes*, pp. 114–16; Weill,
    *Histoire*, pp. 71–2, 86; Faure, 'Mouvements Populaires', 83–4.
100 Delente, CC 594; Desjardin, CC 585. See also *Tribune* 24 Aug. 1832, p. 1;
    Cabet, *Moyen d'ameliorer.*
101 See above pp. 69–75.
102 CC 608, Nepireu; CC 616, 5ème Liasse, registers 1, 3 (Grignon); CC 618,
    8ème Liasse (Grignon); Pref. Pol., Aa 421, dos. 9801, (Efrahem); *Lettres
    Adressées au Journal La Tribune*, pp. 6, 7; *GT* 30 Nov. 1833, p. 99, 2 Dec.
    1833, p. 107, 23 Jan. 1834, p. 280, 26 Apr. 1834, pp. 590–1; Maitron,
    *Dictionnaire* (Courtais, Royer, Pasquier-Labruyère, Perard, Bourrière,
    Dupuy).
103 CC 616, 1er Liasse, fol. 6 (Chapius, shoemaker); Savina, CC 585 (Fortin,
    tailor); Feodiere, Bardeau, tailors, CC 587; Aa 421, dos. 39505 (Duchaille,
    copper-founder), 39506 (Dubois, tailor), 40603 (Marchand, baker), 41473
    (Schaef, baker); Faure, 'Mouvements populaires', 86.
104 *GT* 26 Apr. 1834, pp. 590–1, 27 Apr. 1834, p. 593; Pref. Pol., 21 May
    1834, CC 585.
105 24 Nov. 1833, CC 585.
106 Min. of Int., 16 Dec. 1833, BB18 9788; *Tribune* Sunday suppt.; Weill,
    *Histoire* pp. 70, 97; Cour des Pairs, *Affaire* IV, p. 41.
107 *A* Sept. 1840, p. 4; Jardin and Tudesq, *Restoration and Reaction*, p. 114.
108 Didier, Lecalve, 'SDH 3) 11ème Arrondt.', CC 589.
109 Borderau, Beaudot, CC 585; Leydier, CC 587; Lavoix Beaudot, CC 589;
    Lasseau, CC 608.
110 Candre, CC 595; Pouchin, CC 608.
111 CC 587, 589, 616.
112 Leclerc, CC 585.
113 Bulletin, CC 585.
114 *GT* 2 Oct. 1833, p. 1180, 5 Oct. 1833, p. 1192, 13 Oct. 1833, p. 1217;
    Recurt, CC 595.
115 Vaux, CC 587; Billioux, Latour, Cassel, Moux, Knabe, CC 589.
116 Gaessmann, CC 587.
117 Missillier, Mezlord, Desdoids, Knabe CC 589.
118 Grevin, Bulletin, CC 585; Lavoix, Moura, 'SDH 3) 11ème Arrondt.', CC
    589; Lasseau, CC 608. See also Stewart-McDougall, *Artisan Republic*,
    p. 125.
119 Grignon, *Réfléxions*, p. 4; *GT* 3 Dec. 1833, p. 109, 27 Apr. 1834, pp. 593.
120 *GT*. 26 Apr. 1834, pp. 590–1, 27 Apr. 1834, pp. 593–4; Société des Droits
    de l'Homme, *Association des Travailleurs*, pp. 1–2; *Tribune* Sunday suppt.,
    p. 2; Faure, 'Mouvements populaires', 70, 89.
121 See below, chapter 6.
122 See also Rémusat, *Mémoires* III, p. 422.
123 *CP* 23 Mar. 1848, p. 5, 6 Apr. 1848, p. 3. See also *RP* 29 Feb. 1848, p. 1.
124 M'Douall, *NS* 5 Oct. 1844, p. 1. See also *Bon Sens* 15 July 1832, p. 5; *Beacon*
    26 Oct. 1853, p. 6; Wallarge, *WM* 1 Nov. 1861, p. 127; Petrie, *Works*, p. 6.

125 *RWN* 5 Jan. 1851, p. 10; *WM* 1 Mar. 1867, pp. 5–7, 20 July 1867, p. 3, 17
Aug. 1867, p. 3; *C* 23 Feb. 1867, p. 5; *International Courier* 15 Dec. 1866;
Fribourg, *Association Internationale*, p. 10.

126 Odger, *BH* 27 July 1863, p. 4, 5 Dec. 1863, p. 1; Odger, *WA* 7 Oct. 1865,
p. 5; Robinson, 'Karl Marx', pp. 51–4, 63.

127 *ON* 17 Oct. 1861, p. 1; Tolain, *Vérités*; Leroy, in introduction to Proudhon,
*De la capacité*, p. 9–18; Rougerie, 'Première Internationale', 41; Sancton,
'Myth', 68; Zeldin, *France* I, p. 465; Moss, *Origins*, p. 52.

128 *WM* 1 Sept. 1862, p. 227–30; *BH* 1 Oct. 1864, p. 1; Tolain, *Vérités*,
pp. 28–36.

129 Fribourg, *Association Internationale*, p. 10; Nadaud, *Mémoires*, pp. 444–5.

130 AML I2 55, I, docs. 5, 27; Richard examination, doc. 21; Rougerie,
'Première Internationale', 41; Weill, *Histoire*, p. 378.

131 *BH* 4 Mar. 1865, p. 6, 18 Mar. 1865, p. 4, 15 Apr. 1865, p. 1, 3 Mar.
1866, p. 1; *WA* 2 Dec. 1865, p. 5; *C* 3 Mar. 1866, p. 7, 14 Apr. 1866, p. 2;
*Morn. Star* 12 Apr. 1866, pp. 2–3.

132 *BH* 1 July 1864, p. 1; *C* 8 Dec. 1866, p. 7, 5 Jan. 1867, p. 4, 12 Jan. 1867,
p. 4, 19 Jan. 1867, pp. 4–5, 2 Feb. 1867, p. 4, 9 Feb. 1867, p. 4, 16 Feb.
1867, pp. 4–5; *EL* 1 Dec. 1866, p. 315, 8 Dec. 1866, p. 327; *WM* 1 Dec.,
1866, p. 258, 8 Dec. 1866, pp. 270–1; Broadhurst, *Story*, p. 34.

133 Bell, 'Reform League', pp. 151, 203.

134 *BH* 15 Apr. 1865, p. 1; *C* 7 July 1866, p. 8, 1 Sept. 1866, pp. 6, 8, 26 Jan.
1867, p. 1, 27 Apr. 1867, p. 1; *EL* 1 Sept. 1866, pp. 97–8; Bell, 'Reform
League', pp. 180–1, 243–53. See also Great Malvern painters (*WA* 11
Nov. 1865, p. 2).

135 E.g., Harry, ASCJ, Annual Report Nov. 1866, MRC MSS 78/ASC+J/4/1/1;
Leno, *BH* 18 Mar. 1865, p. 4; *MWA* 18 Mar. 1865, p. 8; Milne, *Tailor* 23
Feb. 1867, p. 313.

136 *BH* 13 May 1865, p. 1; *MWA* 3 June 1865, p. 5.

137 *BH* 25 June 1864, p. 1.

138 *MWA* 17 June 1865, p. 7; *BH* 17 June 1865, p. 1.

139 *BH* 16 Sept. 1865, p. 1.

140 *BH* 14 Apr. 1866, p. 1; *C* 14 Apr. 1866, p. 2; W. Fraser, *Trade Unions and
Society*, pp. 127–8.

141 MS 28/CO/1/8/9/1; see also *OBSTC* 1 Mar. 1865, p. 353. For trade society
support for the IWMA, see *C* 8 Sept. 1866, p. 8.

142 Société Typographique de Paris, 22 May and 7 July 1852, in LSC 16th and
18th. Quarterly, MS 28/CO/1/8/3; 58th Quarterly, Aug. 1862, fols. 41–63,
MS 28/CO/1/8/7/1; 59th, Oct. 1862, fols. 15–16, MS 28/CO/1/8/7/8. See
also Montreal letter to Midland Branch of NTA in MS 39A/TA/1/1/1, fol.
18.

143 *BH* 16 July 1864, p. 5.

144 *BH* 18 June 1864, p. 4, 25 June 1864, p. 5, 16 July 1864, p. 5, 23 July
1864, p. 7; Merriman, *Red City*, pp. 112–14.

145 *RN* 3 Aug. 1851, p. 6, 10 Aug. 1851, p. 14; *PP* 12 May 1855, p. 4; *Times*
10 Apr. 1861, p. 11; *Workman* 5 July 1861, p. 2; *Tichborne News* 6 July
1872, p. 3.

146 *Red Republican* 17 Aug. 1850, pp. 65–7.

147 Odger, *WM* 25 May 1867, p. 10; Cremer, *WM* 23 May 1867, pp. 9–10; See also *Times* 28 Mar. 1861, p. 10.

148 Pref. Pol. to Min. Int., 26 Jan. 1865, 45 AP 6, dos. III; Vial, *Coutume chapelière*, p. 169.

149 *C* 10 Feb. 1866, p. 6, 31 Mar. 1866, p. 6, 7 Apr. 1866, pp. 4, 6, 14 Apr. 1866, p. 6, 28 Apr. 1866, p. 6, 11 Aug. 1866, p. 8; *BH* 28 Apr. 1866, p. 5; *WM* 1 May 1866, p. 7; *Tailor* 27 Oct. 1866, p. 40, 24 Nov. 1866, p. 109, 1 Dec. 1866, p. 118.

150 H. Collins and Abramsky, *Karl Marx*, pp. 68–70, 82; Robinson, 'Karl Marx', pp. 80–89.

151 *Tailor* 6 Apr. 1867, p. 413, 12 Apr. 1867, pp. 5–8, 20 Apr. 1867, pp. 26–9, 27 Apr. 1867, p. 44, 11 May 1867, p. 66; *WM* 20 Apr. 1867, p. 4, 4 May 1867, p. 6; Tartaret, *Commission Ouvrière*, p. 44; Keszler, *Des grèves*, p. 47.

152 *Tailor* 1 June 1867, p. 110, 13 July 1867, p. 194, 20 July 1867, p. 209; *C* 13 Apr. 1867, p. 4, 4 May 1867, p. 5, 8 June 1867, p. 5; *WM* 13 July 1867, p. 7.

153 H. Collins and Abramsky, *Karl Marx*, pp. 61, 70, 96, 252; Gillespie, *Labor and Politics*, p. 225.

154 Schapper, *NS* 13 Feb. 1847, p. 6; Applegarth, *Times* 15 Sept. 1869; Odger, *C* 2 June 1866, p. 6; Cremer, *WM* 25 May 1867, pp. 9–10; Jung, ASCJ, *Monthly Report* July 1869, p. 149; H. Collins and Abramsky, *Karl Marx*, p. 91.

155 Rougerie, 'Première Internationale', 37; Varlin, *Mutualité* 15 Oct. 1866, p. 324; Varlin, *M* 20 Apr. 1870, p. 2; Dolléans, *Histoire*, pp. 292–8; Moss, *Origins*, p. 52. For the French IWMA, see esp. Ba 439, 'Dos. Internationale à Paris', 4788–4885; 'Dos. Internationale dans les départements', 5031–5643.

156 AML I2 55, I docs. 17, 27, 31; Richard, 'Débuts', 67–74; Gaumont, *Histoire*, p. 601; Lequin, *Ouvriers* II, p. 208.

157 Richard, 'Débuts', 69; Kelso, 'French labor movement', 102; Dolléans, *Histoire*, p. 298.

158 *WM* 6 Apr. 1867, pp. 4–5; Dolléans, *Histoire*, pp. 298–301.

159 *WM* 1 Mar. 1867, pp. 5–7, 6 Apr. 1867, p. 3; *C* 9 Mar. 1867, p. 4, 29 June 1867, p. 4; OBS, *AR 1866–7*, p. 63, MRC MSS 78/OB/4/2/1; Webb Coll. A 11, fol. 51; *Tailor* 20 Apr. 1867, p. 26; Keszler, *Des grèves*, p. 47; Dolléans, *Histoire*, p. 303; Kelso, 'French labor movement', 104; Zeldin, *France* I, p. 731.

160 See above, p. 114.

161 Webb Coll. A 25, fol. 107; Collins and Abramsky, *Karl Marx*, p. 173; Robinson, 'Karl Marx', p. 96.

162 For the French IWMA in 1869–70, see esp.: police, 27 Feb. 1870, tailors, 28 Mar. 1870, Varlin to Richard, 1 Dec. 1869, AML I2 55, I docs. 29, 39, II; Pref. Pol. Ba 439, 'La fédération des sociétés ouvrières'; Varlin, *Commerce* 29 Aug. 1869, p. 1, 12 Sept. 1869, p. 3; *Travail* 21 Nov. 1869, p. 1, 12 Dec. 1869, p. 2; *M* 19 Dec. 1869, p. 2, 21 Dec. 1869, p. 3, 6 Mar. 1870, p. 2, 20 Apr. 1870, p. 2, 8 May 1870, p. 3; Richard, 'Débuts', 77, 81–4; Lefrançais, *Souvenirs* II, p. 399; Poulot, *Question sociale*, p. 351;

Kelso, 'French labor movement', 112; Rougerie, 'Première Internationale', 32; Perrot, *Ouvriers en grève*, p. 78; Dalotel, *Aux origines*, pp. 112–17.
163 Ba 435, 956, 980, 1172; Shipton, *Republican* 1 Aug. 1871, p. 6; Robinson, 'Karl Marx', pp. 96, 179–85, 189.

## 5. SOCIALISM

1 Sewell, *Work and Revolution*, pp. 209–10, 213–16; Moss, *Origins*, pp. 23, 70; Hollis, *Pauper Press*, ch. 7.
2 *PMG* 8 Dec. 1832, p. 637, 15 Dec. 1832, pp. 645–6, 11 Oct. 1834, pp. 281–2, 11 Apr. 1835, pp. 489–91; Varlin, *M* 11 Mar. 1870, p. 2.
3 *A* 31 July 1850, p. 558; Benoit, *Confessions*, p. 73; Cabet, *Salut*, pp. 39–41; Cabet, *Ligne droite*, p. 49; Gossez, 'Presse parisienne', p. 133; C. Johnson, *Utopian Communism*, pp. 76, 101–2, 111, 116, 127–30, 143, 223; Stewart-McDougall, *Artisan Republic*, pp. 14, 27–8; Rancière, 'Myth', 43 n. 5.
4 Nadaud, *Mémoires*, p. 261; Weill, *Histoire*, p. 98; C. Johnson, *Utopian Communism*, p. 37.
5 Lechapt to Cabet, 9 May 1847, MS 1052, fol. 212.
6 *F 1845*, May 1847, p. 242; *Pop.* 18 Apr. 1841, p. 9, 12 July 1844, p. 140, 9 May 1847, pp. 297–8; Berrier-Fontaine to Cabet, 20 Aug. 1847, MS 1052, fol. 22; *R* 7 Dec. 1847, p. 16; Rancière, *Nuit*, pp. 360–2.
7 *Lion* 31 July 1829, p. 132; Belchem, 'Republicanism', 27–30; O'Brien, *NS* 27 May 1848, p. 8, 1 Dec. 1849, p. 7; *GS* 23 Aug. 1851, p. 4; *A Brief Inquiry*, p. 63; Finn, *After Chartism*, pp. 86–7. See also *WM* 3 Mar. 1866, pp. 5–6, 1 June 1867, p. 3.
8 Cuddon, *Tailor and Cutter* 1 Feb. 1865, pp. 134–6; Harris, *Tailor* 31 Aug. 1867, pp. 288–9, 12 Oct. 1867, p. 6; O'Brien, *NS* 22 June 1844, p. 1; *Social Reformer* 6 Oct. 1849, p. 65; *LN* 25 July 1858, p. 1.
9 BB18 1473 6817; *Voix des Femmes* 20 Mar. 1848, p. 4; *Peuple* 29 Nov. 1848, p. 4; C. Johnson, *Utopian Communism*, pp. 260, 269–70, 282, 291; Amann, *Revolution*, p. 93.
10 *JT* 1 Apr. 1848, p. 56; *Organisation du Travail Proposée par Confais* (1848); Corbon, *Secret*, p. 109; Nadaud, *Mémoires*, p. 361; Gossez, *Ouvriers*, esp. pp. 53–4, 59, 74, 80–4, 90, 261, 385.
11 'Relevé des pétitions adressés à la Commission du Gouvernement pour l'organisation du travail par les ouvriers de toutes les industries de France', 2 May 1848, AN C 934, dos.VIII; Blanqui, NAF 9581, fols. 48–50; *Démocratie Pacifique* 28 Feb. 1848, p. 1; *CP* 8 Apr. 1848, pp. 3–4; *Peuple Constituant* 2 May 1848, p. 2, 11 May 1848, p. 1; *VR* 26 Mar. 1848, p. 2, 28 Apr. 1848, p. 2, 3 May–12 June 1848; *VP* 1 Dec. 1849, p. 3, 3 Dec. 1849, p. 2, 1 Jan. 1850, p. 2; *Les Délégués (Ouvriers)*; Cochut, *Associations ouvrières*, pp. 10–15; Engländer, *BH* 26 Nov. 1864, p. 17; Loubere, *Louis Blanc*, pp. 81–5, 103, 113–4; Gossez, *Ouvriers*, esp. pp. 7–281, 366; Rancière, 'Myth', 9–10.
12 Milligan, *MG* 17 May 1848, p. 6.
13 O'Brien, *PP* 24 Dec. 1853, p. 1.
14 Reports in AN 45 AP 6, and BHVP NA MS 155. See also: Lefrançais, *Souvenirs* II, esp. pp. 324–30; Richard, 'Débuts', 85; Molinari, *Mouvement socialiste*, esp. pp. xvi–xviii, 8–14; Poulot, *Question sociale*, pp. 195–6, 204,

213; Weill, *Histoire*, pp. 351–2, 381; Gaillard, 'Associations de production' 75; Dalotel, *Aux origines*, esp. pp. 37–8, 67–8, 103, 121, 148, 165–7, 216–17, 224–5, 245–6, 258, 262.

15  L. Vinçard, *Mémoires*, pp. 255–6.

16  Quoted in Burns, 'Strategy', p. 160.

17  *VR* 3 May 1848, p. 2.

18  *TA* 22 Apr. 1849, p. 3.

19  Raspail, *Avenues*, pp. 329–30.

20  *Banquet des Travailleurs Socialistes*, pp. 1–11; *P* 15–21 Nov.–15 Dec. 1848; Benoit, *Confessions*, pp. 168–9; Weill, *Histoire*, p. 230; Moss, 'June 13, 1849', 394–6; Agulhon, *Republican Experiment*, p. 70; Agulhon, *Ville ouvrière*, p. 301; Stewart-McDougall, *Artisan Republic*, pp. 107, 112.

21  *TA* 8 Apr. 1849, p. 1; *Réforme* 20 Apr. 1849, p. 1; Weill, *Histoire*, pp. 240–1; Fasel, 'Wrong revolution', 672; Vigier, *Seconde République* II, pp. 386–7; Loubere, *Louis Blanc*, pp. 32–6, 61 n. 1; Merriman, *Agony*, p. xxi; Margadant, *French Peasants*, pp. 138–9.

22  Blanqui, NAF 9592, fol. 15; Varlin, *M* 20 Jan. 1870, p. 2.

23  E.g. [Martin], *Nouveau catéchisme*, p. 17; *WTS* 14 Sept. 1834, p. 431; Ironside, *Sheffield Iris* 25 Sept. 1838, p. 3; *JP* 17 Jan. 1839.

24  O'Connor, *NS* 24 Oct. 1846, p. 5, Dixon, 18 Mar. 1848, p. 5; *RWN* 25 Aug. 1850, p. 1; Bishop, *NR* 17 Apr. 1870, p. 254; Broadhurst, *Story*, p. 57.

25  Porter, *Progress of the Nation*, pp. 336–7; *WM* 21 Apr. 1866, p. 251; Claeys, *Citizens*, p. 314.

26  Searle, *Entrepreneurial Politics*, pp. 183, 316.

27  *Artisan* 6 Nov. 1842, p. 2; Duquesne, *Ruche* Oct. 1843, p. 11; Cochut, *Associations ouvrières*, pp. 12–13; Chazelas, 'Episode', 248; Agulhon, *Ville ouvrière*, p. 270; Christofferson, 'French national workshops', esp. 505–8; Gossez, *Ouvriers*, pp. 159–60.

28  *CP* 30 Mar. 1848, p. 3; *VR* 28 Apr. 1848, p. 2; *RP* 20 June 1848, p. 2; Engländer, *BH* 26 Nov. 1864, p. 17; Weill, *Histoire*, p. 225; Loubere, *Louis Blanc*, pp. 91–2; Agulhon, *Republican Experiment*, p. 56; Gossez, *Ouvriers*, pp. 215–16; Amalric, 'Révolution de 1848', 350–1; Finn, *After Chartism*, p. 77 n. 44.

29  *CP* 11 Apr. 1848, p. 3; *VR* 9 Apr. 1848, p. 1, 15 Apr. 1848, p. 1, 19 June 1848, p. 1; *OT* 21 June 1848; *AR* 15 July 1849, p. 1; Gossez, 'Presse parisienne', pp. 158–9; Gossez, *Ouvriers*, pp. 215–16, 285, 295–6, 381–5.

30  Fribourg, 4 Nov. 1868, 45 AP 6, dos. IV; Tolain, *Courrier Français* 10 Sept. 1867, p. 2; *Travail* 21 Nov. 1869, p. 2; Finn, *After Chartism*, p. 92.

31  J. B. O'Brien, *The Rise, Progress, and Phases of Human Slavery* (1885), p. 144; Finn, *After Chartism*, p. 114; Searle, *Entrepreneurial Politics*, p. 316.

32  Longson, *Bolton Chron.* 17 Jan. 1829, p. 4. See also NAUT, *NS* 10 Apr. 1847, p. 5.

33  *NS* 2 Mar. 1844, p. 6. See also *Rapport des Délégués Cordonniers*, p. 4.

34  Potter, *Labour Question*, p. 10.

35  *CC* 24 Aug. 1844, p. 83.

36  Joiner to Mayhew, *RWN* 14 July 1850, p. 5; *O* 15 Mar. 1851, p. 161; Boyer, *De l'état des ouvriers*, p. 48.

37  *Bristol Mercury* 24 June 1843; *Shipwrights' J* Apr. 1858, p. 2.

38 *BBCU* 26 June 1855, p. 12.
39 Bristol Co-op. Soc., *Crisis* 14 July 1832, pp. 71–2.
40 Vidal, *TA* 18 Feb. 1849, p. 1.
41 *PMG* 17 Sept. 1831, p. 83; *Union* Sept. 1844, pp. 1–2; Avoine, NA MS 155, fols. 282–3; *A* Oct. 1840, p. 11; Mayhew, *RWN* 10 Nov. 1850, p. 4; Blanc, *Révolution française* IV, p. 108.
42 Parrott, *ES* 24 Jan. 1843, p. 3; *Bristol Times* 24 June 1843, p. 4; Exeter shoemakers, *PP* 30 Apr. 1853, p. 2; 'Rapport des délégués imprimeurs en taille-douce', in *Rapports des Délégués Imprimeurs Lithographes*, p.33; *Indicateur* 28 Dec. 1834, p. 1; Langlois, *P* 22 Dec. 1848, p. 3; *TA* 11 Mar. 1849, p. 2; Boyer, *Conseils de Prud'hommes*, p. 1.
43 *NS* 15 May 1843, p. 1, 21 Oct. 1843, p. 4; *Labourer* II, p. 154.
44 *O* 11 Jan. 1851, p. 27; Tailors, *BH* 12 May 1866, p. 6; Potter, 16 Apr. 1864, p. 5; Prothero, *Artisans*, p. 205; Dunning, *Morn. Advertiser* 17 Aug. 1859, p. 3; Kydd, *TC* 4 Feb. 1854, p. 10; Gillespie, *Labor and Politics*, pp. 11–12; Clements, 'British trade unions'; W. Fraser, *Trade Unions and Society*, pp. 170–83; McClelland, 'Time to work', p. 188.
45 *Times* 13 Sept. 1869, p. 8, Odger, 21 Sept. 1869, pp. 6, 7, 16 Nov. 1869, p. 6; *St. Crispin* 14 Aug. 1869, pp. 73–4, 23 Apr. 1870, p. 193.
46 Ferdinando, *NS* 1 Dec. 1849, p. 5; Bloomfield, *Times* 4 Aug. 1859, p. 10; *LL* 23 Sept. 1848, p. 57.
47 Cremer, *NR* 17 Apr. 1870, p. 253.
48 *Advocate* 9 Mar. 1833, p. 26; *BTC* 23 Sept. 1861, p. 97; *TC* 4 Feb. 1854, p. 8. See also *A* May 1844, p. 120, Nov. 1846, p. 406; Newton, *Political Examiner* 23 Mar. 1853, p. 51; *Ashton and Stalybridge Reporter* 26 Jan. 1861, p. 2; *BH* 18 Oct. 1862, p. 4; *M* 27 Jan. 1870, p. 3; Lefrançais, *Souvenirs* II, pp. 311–12; Lockwood, *Tools*, p. 84.
49 Kydd, *RWN* 30 Mar. 1851, p. 14. See also *BH* 12 May 1866, p. 6; Macdonald, *True Story*, p. 11.
50 *O* 11 Oct. 1851, p. 120; *Ashton and Stalybridge Reporter* 26 Jan. 1861, p. 2; *JTA* Oct. 1861, p. 249.
51 *Advocate* 9 Mar. 1833, p. 28. See also Tartaret, *Exposition Universelle*, p. 155.
52 *Règlement pour les Ouvriers Imprimeurs en Taille-douce*, p. 1. See also *O* 8 Mar. 1851, p. 156; PTA 6th Half-yearly report, 1852, MS 39A/TA/4/1/1.
53 Dunning, *Trades' Unions and Strikes*, p. 4; *BTC* 12 Feb. 1861, p. 69, 21 Nov. 1861, p. 101, 21 Jan. 1862, p. 110; *Glaneuse* 3 Nov. 1833, p. 3. See also *TAHP* 27 July 1850, p. 33, 24 Aug., p. 65; *OBSTC* 1 Oct. 1861, pp. 9–10.
54 *BTC* May 1854, p. 177, 23 Sept. 1861, p. 96, 21 Jan. 1865, p. 17; ASCJ, *Monthly Report* Nov. 1866, pp. 17–18; Macdonald, *True Story*, p. 11; Devlin, *CC* June 1844, p. 36; *O* 15 May 1852, p. 432; Dunning, *Trades' Unions and Strikes*, pp. 23–4.
55 *P* 8–15 Nov. 1848, p. 1.
56 *Times* 19 Feb. 1857, p. 8.
57 Skelton, *Last* 8 Nov. 1844, p. 18.
58 Noiret, *Aux travailleurs*, p. 5; Kydd, *NS* 26 Sept. 1846, p. 8; Cantagrel, *Travail* 12 Dec. 1869, p. 3.
59 '2ème Lettre à Curie', 30 Aug. 1829, CP 3706, fol. 201; Leroux, *Prolétaire et*

*bourgeois* , pp. 16, 21, 32; *Last* 20 Dec. 1844, pp. 66–7; *Union* June 1845, p. 1; Dommanget, *Idées politiques*, pp. 72–8, 234, 242.

60 Building: *MG* 22 June 1833, p. 3, 29 June 1833, p. 1, 3 Nov. 1869, p. 7; *Man* 17 Nov. 1833, p. 147; *WTS* 5 Oct. 1834, p. 457; *PMG* 30 Aug. 1834, p. 234, 10 Oct. 1834, pp. 284–5; *BH* 27 June 1863, p. 1. Tailoring: Petrie, *Man* 10 Nov. 1833, p. 5; *CC* May 1844, p. 31; Shorrocks, *Tailor* 16 Mar. 1867, pp. 359–60; *Journeyman* Aug. 1890, p. 1. Shoemakers: *Last* 13 Dec. 1844, p. 62, 3 Jan. 1845, p. 82; *St. Crispin* 9 Oct. 1869, p. 168. Silk: *NS* 19 Aug. 1843, p. 1; Sheridan, 'Social and economic foundations', p. 459. Books: Howe and Waite, *London Society of Compositors*, p. 96. See also Coignet to Comité du Travail, 29 July (1848), C 943, 31, 34; F. Coignet, *Projets d'association libre et volontaire entre les chefs d'industrie et les ouvriers et de réformation commerciale* (Lyons, 1848).

61 Pref. Pol., 9 Oct. 1856, BB30 366, dos. II, fol. 167; Dupeux, *French Society*, p. 126; Plessis, *Rise and Fall*, p. 125.

62 O'Brien, *GS* 23 Aug. 1851, p. 4; O'Brien, *PP* 3 Dec. 1853, p. 2, Murray, 24 Dec. 1853, p. 1; *Workman* 21 June 1861, p. 6; *WM* 1 Nov. 1861, p. 127, 15 May 1866, p. 1; Harris and Cudden in *Tailor* 31 Aug. 1867, p. 288, 12 Oct. 1867, p. 6, 2 Nov. 1867, pp. 30–1, 23 Nov. 1867, p. 50, 14 Dec. 1867, p. 78, 4 Jan. 1868, p. 102, 1 Feb. 1868, p. 134.

63 *Republican* 1 Sept. 1870, p. 3, 1 Nov. 1870, p. 6.

64 *Pioneer* 5 Apr. 1834, p. 284, 12 Apr. 1834, pp. 289–90, 19 Apr. 1834, pp. 305, 308, 3 May 1834, p. 330; *Crisis* 3 May 1834, p. 28; Harney, *Red Republican* 17 Mar. 1850, p. 1

65 NA MS 155, fol. 188 See also Pastelot, *JO* 7 Nov. 1830, p. 1; Osborne, Davis, *NR* 12 June 1870, p. 381.

66 Cavaignac, *Opinion*, p. 12; *Libérateur* 2 Feb. 1834, *RWN* 30 Mar. 1851, p. 14; Claeys, *Citizens*, pp. 178, 217; Prothero, 'William Benbow', 155–9 ; Sewell, *Work and Revolution*, p. 267; Rougerie, 'Mil huit cent soixante et onze', 71.

67 Gast, *Penny Papers* 18 June 1831, p. 3.

68 Gautier, *PD* 6–8 June 1848, p. 2.

69 Biagini, *Liberty*, pp. 186–8; Finn, *After Chartism*, pp. 267–8.

70 O'Connor, *NS* 13 May 1843, p. 1, 21 Oct. 1843, p. 4, 2 Nov. 1844, p. 1, 26 Apr. 1845, p. 6. See also Parker, *Workman* 21 June 1861, p. 4.

71 *A Brief Inquiry*, p. 45.

72 Coutant, *Ruche* Nov. 1840, p. 2; *F* May 1841, p. 1; *F 1845* May 1845, p. 42; T.-M., *Aux travailleurs*, p. 12; *NP*, pp. 111, 120; *PP* 5 June 1852, p. 4; Ducasse, NA MS 155, fol. 223; Humphrey, *Robert Applegarth*, pp. 104–6; H. Collins and Abramsky, *Karl Marx*, pp. 149, 154; Sewell, *Work and Revolution*, p. 233; Chase, *People's Farm*, esp. pp. 106, 183–4, 188.

73 O'Brien, *NS* 17 Apr. 1841, p. 1.

74 Gaumont, *Histoire*, p. 357; Stewart-McDougall, *Artisan Republic*, p. 60.

75 See also Corbon, *Secret*, p. 112; Chase, *People's Farm*, p. 187.

76 Lovett in Carpenter, *Proceedings*, p. 6.

77 *F 1845* Jan. 1845, pp. 3–4; Dupuy, *Ruche* Aug. 1841, p. 9, Gilland, Sept., p. 5, Alais, Dec. 1848, p. 342; *Travail* Sept. 1841, p. 18; *Travail* (Lyons), prospectus, p. 2; *PD* 22–4 Aug. 1848, p. 1; *RWN* 21 July 1850, p. 7;

Lahautière, *Loi sociale*, p. 8; L. Vinçard, *Mémoires*, pp. 236–7; Loubere, *Louis Blanc*, p. 23; Sewell, *Work and Revolution*, pp. 232, 279; Lockwood, *Tools*, p. 95; Claeys, *Citizens*, esp. pp. 58, 60–1, 176–7; Biagini, *Liberty*, p. 144.

78 See also Searle, *Entrepreneurial Politics*, pp. 289, 304; B. Taylor, *Eve*, p. 244.

79 Nadaud, *Mémoires*, p. 186.

80 See also E. Yeo, 'Robert Owen', p. 85; Claeys, *Citizens*, pp. 75, 176; Rancière, *Nuit*, pp. 123–4.


6. CO-OPERATION

1 *Projet d'Association* pp. 3–4; *TAHP* 21 Sept. 1850, p. 99. See also: *Economist* 27 Jan. 1821, p. 15, 5 May 1821, p. 234, 1 Sept. 1821, p. 89, 20 Oct., pp. 202–3, 27 Oct. 1821, p. 217, 8 Dec. 1821, p. 315; *Co-operator* Jan. 1863, p. 130; *Association des Ouvriers Bijoutiers*, p. 3; *Projet d'Association Fraternelle de l'Industrie Française*, p. 2; *Association Fraternelle des Ouvriers Menuisiers de la Ville de Lyon* (Lyons, n.d.)

2 Chabaud in Tartaret, *Commission Ouvrière*, p. 165. See also *WM* 13 Jan. 1866, p. 29, 19 May 1866, p. 308; *C* 8 Dec. 1866, p. 1.

3 Pollard, 'Nineteenth-century co-operation'; Holyoake, *History of Co-operation* I.

4 Lequin, *Ouvriers* II, pp. 187, 190; Furlough, *Consumer Cooperation*, p. 27.

5 *Union* July 1846, p. 51; Robson, *NS* 6 June 1846, p. 8; *C* 4 Oct. 1862, p. 3, 13 Sept. 1867, p. 3; Noiret, *Aux travailleurs*, p. 16; Noiret, *Deuxième lettre*, p. 3; Noiret, *Mémoire*, pp. 59, 64–73; Cochut, *Associations ouvrières*; Parent, in Tartaret, *Commission Ouvrière*, p. 159; Oliver, 'Labour Exchange Phase'; Moss, 'Parisian workers', p. 205; Hobsbawm, *Worlds*, pp. 260–1; L. Hunt and Sheridan, 'Corporation', 839–40; Furlough, *Consumer Cooperation*, pp. 15–28, 47.

6 *NS* 21 June 1845, p. 4; Carson to Owen, 1 Mar. 1832, Owen Coll. no. 522; Musson, *Trade Union and Social History*, p. 184; *C* 17 Nov. 1866, p. 4; Cole, *Century*, p. 161; *EO* July 1844, pp. 41–2.

7 *J. des Sciences Morales et Politiques* 17 Dec. 1831, pp. 36–9; *A* Oct. 1840, p. 12; Coutant, *Ruche* Nov. 1847, pp. 246–51; *Mutualité* 15 Oct. 1866, p. 307; Dupas in Tartaret, *Commission Ouvrière*, p. 165; Heftler, *Associations coopératives*, p. 287; Moss, 'Parisian workers', p. 209; Moss, 'Parisian producers' associations', pp. 77–9; C. Johnson, *Utopian Communism*, p. 162.

8 Moss, *Origins*, esp. pp. 22, 69–70; Hobsbawm, *Worlds*, pp. 223–4; C. Johnson, *Utopian Communism*, p. 17; Geary, *European Labour Protest*, p. 44.

9 Seine Prefect to Mayor 6th district, 15 Jan. 1839, Paris City Archives, Q1f 4826, 1 Apr. 1832, 4829, 20 Apr 1832, 4833; Truquin, *Mémoires*, p. 65; *P* 22 Jan. 1849, p. 3; *M* 20 Apr. 1870, p. 1; Sheridan, 'Social and economic foundations', p. 142.

10 *EO* June 1844, p. 20; Cochut, *Associations ouvrières*, pp. 95–6; Flotard, *Mouvement coopératif*, p. 10; Cole, *Century*, p. 63.

11 *O* 2 Aug. 1851, pp. 39–40; *BH* 20 Feb. 1864, p. 8; Leno, *Aftermath*, p. 81; *AR* 11 Sept. 1849, p. 3; Gaumont, *Histoire*, pp. 390–6; Stewart-McDougall, *Artisan Republic*, p. 121.

12 Carson to Owen, 1 Mar. 1832, Owen Coll. no. 522; Lambeth, *WFP* 20 June 1829; Nantes, *P* 1 Jan. 1849, pp. 3–4, 8 Jan. 1849, p. 3; *AR* 11 Mar. 1849, p. 3, 15 Apr. 1849, p. 3; Lincoln, *TAHP* 7 Sept. 1850, p. 80, London, 28 Sept. 1850, p. 111; Greenwich, *O* 1 Feb. 1851, p. 71, Leeds, 26 July 1851, p. 30; Rochdale, *Shipwrights' J* June 1858, p. 39; London, *Tailor* 30 Nov. 1867, p. 58; Paris, *Commerce* 1 Aug. 1869, p. 2, 15 Aug. 1869, p. 2, 22 Aug. 1869, p. 2; *M* 19 Mar. 1870, p. 3; Tartaret, *Commission Ouvrière*, p. 239; Cochut, *Associations ouvrières*, pp. 95–6; Gaumont, *Histoire*, p. 542; Cole, *Century*, pp. 84–5; Crossick, *Artisan Elite*, p. 170; Leeds, Dunsmore, 'Working classes', p. 157.

13 *WM* 3 Mar. 1866, p. 3.

14 *Felix Farley's Bristol J* 21 Mar. 1840, p. 2; *TAHP* 28 Sept. 1850, p. 111; *O* 12 July 1851, p. 16; *Cooperator* July 1860, p. 17; Mar. 1863, p. 161; Furlough, *Consumer Cooperation*, p. 54.

15 *Commerce* 22 Aug. 1869, p. 2.

16 *O* 26 Apr. 1851, p. 265.

17 *EL* 15 Oct. 1864, p. 1; *Indicateur* 12 Oct. 1834, p. 2; O'Neill, *St. Crispin* 15 Jan. 1870, p. 28; Tourneur, Tartaret, in Tartaret, *Commission Ouvrière*, pp. 33, 135; Lowery, 'Passages', p. 143; Nadaud, *Mémoires*, p. 137; Flotard, *Mouvement coopératif*, p. 10.

18 *WM* 4 Apr. 1861, p. 6, 4 Apr. 1863, p. 6; *P* 17 Jan. 1849, p. 4, 20 Feb. 1849, p. 4; *PP* 7 May 1853, p. 6; Engländer, *BH* 17 Dec. 1864, p. 1; Poulot, *Question sociale*, p. 240; Heftler, *Associations coopératives*, pp. 194–5; Gossez, *Ouvriers*, pp. 117–20; Agulhon, *Ville ouvrière*, p. 321; Merriman, *Agony*, p. 76.

19 *Shipwrights' J* June 1858, p. 39; *TAHP* 21 Sept. 1850, p. 100; *BH* 5 June 1875, p. 3; Cole, *Century*, esp. pp. 59–61, 75, 78, 84–5, 100, 111; Crossick, *Artisan Elite*, pp. 168–9.

20 *O* 26 Apr. 1851, p. 265.

21 Sheppard, *LD* 26 Nov. 1837, p. 498; Prothero, *Artisans*, pp. 247–8.

22 *Bolton Chron.* 12 Apr. 1828, p. 3; Gaumont, *Histoire*, p. 113; Stewart-McDougall, *Artisan Republic*, p. 121; Cole, *Century*, p. 67; Pollard, 'Nine-teenth-century co-operation', p. 96.

23 *Times* 11 Nov. 1869, p. 10; *Commerce* 11 July 1869, p. 2; *M* 14 Mar. 1870, p. 2; Tartaret, *Commission Ouvrière*, pp. 134, 136–7, 150–3, 159; Gaumont, *Histoire*, pp. 483–95, 500, 536–7, 557; Furlough, *Consumer Cooperation*, pp. 48–9. See also Sheridan, 'Social and economic founda-tions', pp. 518–9.

24 *Lion* 16 Oct. 1829, p. 481; *British Co-operator* Sept. 1830, p. 130; *Report of the Committee, and Proceedings*, p. 10.

25 Coutant, *Ruche* Nov. 1847, p. 247; *RWN* 15 Sept. 1850, p. 11; *TAHP* 21 Sept. 1850, pp. 99, 100; *PP* 31 July 1852, pp. 2–3; *WM* 1 Oct. 1862, pp. 265–9; *Cooperator* Mar. 1863, pp. 161–2, 165, May 1868, p. 193; *C* 17 Nov. 1866, p. 4; Cole, *Century*, pp. 66, 86, 114, 117–25, 127; Furlough, *Consumer Cooperation*, pp. 44 n. 46, 53; Sheridan, 'Social and economic foundations', pp. 518–19.

26 Tartaret, *Commission Ouvrière*, p. 135; Gaumont, *Histoire*, pp. 414, 428, 500; Stewart-McDougall, *Artisan Republic*, p. 119; Sheridan, 'Social and eco-

nomic foundations', pp. 119, 426–7; *Times* 11 Nov. 1869, p. 10; *TAHP* 21 Sept. 1850, p. 100; Cole, *Century*, pp. 87, 91, 104.

27 Tartaret, *Commission Ouvrière*, pp. 135, 137; *WM* 21 Sept. 1861, p. 107; Furlough, *Consumer Cooperation*, pp. 21–2.

28 *TAHP* 19 Oct. 1850, p. 134; *Cooperator* June 1860, pp. 2–3, Jan. 1861, p. 110, Mar. 1863, p. 162; *WM* 12 July 1861, p. 28; *EL* 27 Aug. 1864, p. 5, 15 Oct. 1864, p. 1; *BH* 29 Oct. 1864, p. 1, 14 Oct. 1865, p. 1; Cole, *Century*, pp. 79, 92–3, 133, 153–7, 176–7; Pollard, 'Nineteenth-century cooperation', pp. 98, 107; Pollard, *History of Labour*, p. 108; Gillespie, *Labor and Politics*, p. 35; Kirk, *Growth*, pp. 149–52, 157–9, 166–7; Garrard, *Leadership and Power*, pp. 178–9.

29 Rheims, *AR* 25 Jan. 1849, p. 3, 18 Aug. 1849, p. 2; Merriman, *Agony*, pp. 70–1; Lille, *P* 12 Mar. 1849, p. 4; *TA* 11 Mar. 1849, p. 7; Cochut, *Associations ouvrières*, pp. 95–6; Merriman, *Agony*, pp. 159–60; Furlough, *Consumer Cooperation*, p. 23; Rouen, *P* 2 Apr. 1849, p. 2; Amiens, 16 Jan., 10 Feb., 10 Mar. 1851, BB30 394; *WM* 25 May 1867, p. 10; Gaumont, *Histoire*, p. 515.

30 Proc. Lyons to Min. of Justice, 13 July 1849, Prefect Rhône to Min. of Int., 27 Aug. 1849, 'Cour de Lyon 1848–1850', BB18 1474B; Talandier to Holyoake, 26 Jan. 1861, 5 Oct. 1862, Holyoake Coll. nos. 1274, 1444; *Progrès Journal de Lyon*, *passim*; Gaumont, *Histoire*, pp. 396, 400–17, 420–1, 459, 571–85, 597, 606; Lequin, *Ouvriers* II, pp. 184–7; Stewart-McDougall, *Artisan Republic*, pp. 117–19, 122; Kelso, 'French labor movement', p. 103.

31 *WM* 7 Sept. 1861, p. 95, 1 Mar. 1862, p. 57, 1 July 1862, p. 194, 1 May 1866, p. 5, 22 Sept. 1866, p. 136, 13 Oct. 1866, p. 169; *Mutualité* 15 Sept. 1866, pp. 273–4; *Tailor* 8 Dec. 1866, p. 142, 23 Feb. 1867, p. 318; *Times* 11 Nov. 1869, p. 10; Tartaret, *Commission Ouvrière*, pp. 135, 150ff. 158–9; Gaumont, *Histoire*, p. 597; Cole, *Century*, p. 156; Kelso, 'French labor movement', p. 102; Crossick, *Artisan Elite*, p. 173.

32 Gaumont, *Histoire*, pp. 441–4.

33 *RWN* 9 June 1850, p. 5; *FLA* 15 Feb. 1862, p. 4; *Cooperator*, *passim*; *WM* 1 Mar. 1862, pp. 57–8, 1 Apr. 1862, pp. 85–6, 95, 99, 103–4, 1 May 1862, pp. 113–14, 1 June 1862, p. 142; *C* 17 Nov. 1866, p. 4; Cole, *Century*, pp. 103, 139, 142–6; *WM* 5 May 1866, p. 284.

34 Moral Union, *PMG* 11 Oct. 1834, p. 285; Tower Hamlets, *NS* 13 Mar. 1841, p. 5, Bermondsey, 31 July, p. 7, Lambeth, 15 Jan. 1842, p. 1, 5 Feb. 1842, p. 1, Golden Square, 11 May 1844, p. 6, Convention, 3 May 1845, p. 1, M'Grath, 10 May, p. 6, Skelton, 29 May 1847, p. 1.

35 *Cooperator* Mar. 1865, p. 167.

36 *WFP* 27 Dec. 1828; *Leeds Mercury* 18 July 1829; Penn, *WFP* 18 Oct. 1828, p. 516; *Associate* 1 Apr. 1829, p. 22; Tucker, *Crisis* 9 Nov. 1833, p. 85; *Carpenter's Political Letters* 24 Apr. 1831, p. 16; King, *FSA* Aug. 1836, p. 120, Sept. 1836, p. 137, Oct. 1836, pp. 150, 152; Heywood, *TAHP* 19 Oct. 1850, p. 134; Gaumont, *Histoire*, pp. 515, 572, 576; Cole, *Century*, pp. 69–70, 92; Merriman, *Agony*, pp. 71–2, 77–8; Prothero, *Artisans*, p. 253; Furlough, *Consumer Cooperation*, p. 23.

37 *SS* 3 May 1840, p. 1, Cameron, 5 July, p. 1.

38  Wolverhampton, *PMG* 28 Apr. 1832, p. 373, Macclesfield, 18 Aug. 1832,
    p. 497; Huddersfield, *BO* 27 July 1837, p. 205; Cleave, *NS* 5 June 1841,
    p. 6; Foster, *Class Struggle*, pp. 52–6.
39  *TAHP* 21 Sept. 1850, p. 100. See also Bell, 19 Oct. 1850, p. 134.
40  Thompson, *PP* 27 June 1857, p. 4.
41  *WTS* 27 July 1834, p. 379; *PMG* 9 Aug. 1834, p. 212; *GT* 2 Dec. 1833,
    p. 105, 24 Jan. 1834, p. 285; *A* Feb. 1846, p. 266; *TA* 7 Jan. 1849, p. 5;
    Blanc, *Révolution française* IV, p. 107; *BH* 14 Oct. 1865, p. 1; Gaumont,
    *Histoire*, pp. 526–9; Merriman, *Agony*, p. 74; Moutet, 'Mouvement ouvrier',
    37.
42  *TAHP* 21 Sept. 1850, p. 100; *RWN* 27 Apr. 1851, p. 14; *O* 3 May 1851,
    p. 284; Cole, *Century*, p. 62.
43  Murray, *WM* 21 Sept. 1861, p. 107.
44  See also P. Clark, *English Alehouse*, p. 321; Chase, *People's Farm*, p. 214;
    Prothero, *Artisans*, pp. 229, 382 n. 53.
45  *NS* 21 June 1845, p. 4; *Cooperator* May 1863, p. 198; Potter, *MWA* 18 Mar.
    1865, p. 5; H.Collins and Abramsky, *Karl Marx*, pp. 173–4; *NR* 20 Feb.
    1870, p. 125; Davies, *Heterodox London*, pp. 234–7; Shipley, *Club Life*,
    pp. 80–1. For French examples, see: *P* 7 Apr. 1849, p. 4; *VP* 14 Jan. 1850,
    p. 4, 21 Jan. 1850, p. 4; *AR* 20 Oct. 1849, p. 3; K. P., *Moyen*, p. 2.
46  Compositors: 7th and 10th Half-yearly PTA, MS 39A/TA/4/1/1; *TSMC*
    Nov. 1853, p. 3; *BH* 10 Oct. 1863, p. 1. Swindon iron trades, *TAHP* 20 July
    1850, p. 30; ASE, *O* 5 June 1852, p. 460. London Tailors: *Tailor* 29 June
    1867, p. 168, 6 July 1867, p. 180, 3 Aug. 1867, p. 231; *BH* 2 May 1868,
    p. 6; *BBCU* 1 Nov. 1848, pp. 25–6; Morgan, *St. Crispin* 27 Feb. 1869,
    p. 123.
47  *BH* 13 Jan. 1866, p. 4; Prothero, *Artisans*, pp. 252–3; Gaumont, *Histoire*,
    p. 4; Chase, *People's Farm*, pp. 168, 171.
48  *NS* 19 Aug. 1843, p. 2, 26 Aug. 1843, p. 1, 2 Sept. 1843, p. 2; *R* 21 Oct.
    1846, p. 270; *BH* 7 Mar. 1863, p. 1, 26 Apr. 1863, p. 1, 17 Oct. 1863, p. 4;
    *MWA* 15 July 1865, p. 1; *C* 18 Aug. 1866, p. 1; *WM* 8 June 1867, p. 11; *NR*
    3 Apr. 1870, p. 221, 5 June 1870, p. 365; *Republican* 1 Jan. 1871, p. 4;
    S. Newens, 'Thomas Edward Bowkett: nineteenth century pioneer of the
    working-class movement in East London', *History Workshop* no. 9 (1980).
49  *R* 26 Aug. 1846–11 Aug. 1847; Clark, *RWN* 2 Feb. 1851, p. 10; *BH* 1 Aug.
    1863, p. 8, 19 Sept. 1863, p. 1, 24 Oct. 1863, p. 1; Leventhal, *Respectable
    Radical*, pp. 132–3.
50  *BH* 6 Feb. 1864, p. 2, 18 Mar. 1864, p. 7; *R* 18 Nov. 1846, p. 303; *O* 22
    Mar. 1851, pp. 187–8; *MWA* 15 July 1865, p. 1; *VP* 11 Dec. 1849, p. 4, 12
    Dec., p. 4, 24 Dec, 1849 p. 4; *Socialiste* Oct. 1849, p. 3; NA MS 155, fol.
    89; Cole, *Century*, pp. 75, 92.
51  *Pioneer* 14 June 1834, p. 406; Place Papers, Add. MS 37, 773, fol. 128; *NS*
    15 Apr. 1843, p. 2, 8 Feb. 1845, p. 4, 2 Aug. 1845, p. 2, 11 July 1846, p. 4,
    26 June 1847, p. 5; *PN* 27 June 1847, p. 7; *RWN* 23 June 1850, p. 1; *RN* 15
    June 1851, p. 16, 15 June 1851, p. 15; *PP* 12 July 1856, p. 4, 22 Nov. 1856,
    p. 8; *BH* 8 Nov. 1862, p. 5, 25 June 1864, p. 5.
52  *PMGRF*, p. 50; *NS* 22 Jan. 1848, p. 4; *Vanguard* 29 Jan. 1853, p. 13.
53  E.g. Ireland, *NS* 18 Apr. 1846, p. 6; Newton, *O* 10 May 1851, p. 289,

17 May 1851, pp. 305–6, 15 Nov. 1851, p. 156, 22 May 1852, p. 448; Murray, *BH* 28 Nov. 1863, p. 4, 16 Jan. 1864, p. 4; Potter, *C* 23 Mar. 1867, p. 4, 20 Apr. 1867, p. 4. See *MWA* 18 Feb. 1865, p. 4

54 *NS* 8 Feb. 1845, p. 4, 2 Aug. 1845, p. 2, 7 Feb. 1846, p. 8, 24 Apr. 1847, p. 4, 1 Jan. 1848, p. 4; *PP* 8 Oct. 1853, p. 5; *BH* 5 Mar. 1864, p. 1; *MWA* 18 Feb. 1865, p. 4; Stevens, *Memoir*, pp. 61, 70, 79, 91.

55 *PP* 10 Feb. 1855, pp. 4–5, 24 Feb. 1855, p. 5, 7 Apr. 1855, p. 1, 21 Apr. 1855, p. 4, 25 Aug. 1855, p. 2, 27 Oct. 1855, p. 2, 1 Dec. 1855, p. 5, 29 Aug., 1857, p. 1, 5 Sept. 1857, p. 4, 3 Apr. 1858, p. 4.

56 *NU* May 1858, pp. 6, 8; *EL* 30 June 1866, p. 364; *BH* 8 Nov. 1862, p. 5, 25 June 1862, p. 2, 6 Feb. 1864, p. 6; *MWA* 22 Apr. 1865, p. 5, 29 Apr. 1865, p. 4; Stevens, *Memoir*, esp. pp. 63–6, 68, 78–86. For similar Chartist societies, see Finsbury Mutual Life Assurance Association, *PP* 22 May 1852, p. 4; Integrity Life Assurance, *NU* May 1858, p. 8.

57 *NS* 2 Aug. 1845, p. 2; *BH* 5 Mar. 1864, p. 1, 12 Mar. 1864, p. 6; Humphrey, *Robert Applegarth*, pp. 52–5; Prothero, *Artisans*, p. 237; P. Johnson, 'Class law', 151–4.

58 *PP* 1 Dec. 1855, p. 5; Stevens, *Memoir*, p. 65.

59 Tartaret, *Exposition Universelle*, p. 106; *Travail* 10 Oct. 1869, p. 3.

60 *MG* 21 Nov. 1835, p. 3; *FSA* Dec. 1836, p. 186; *TC* 11 Feb. 1854, p. 8; *PP* 10 Mar. 1855, p. 4; *BH* 1 Nov. 1862, p. 1, 3 Mar. 1866, p. 1; Prothero, *Artisans*, p. 382 n. 53; Berridge, 'Popular journalism', pp. 201–2.

61 Webb Coll. A 11, fol. 307, *APOT*, p. 26; *BH* 24 Oct. 1863, p. 5, 29 Oct. 1864, p. 5.

62 *BH* 8 July 1865, p. 5, 3 Mar. 1866, p. 1

63 *NU* Oct. 1858, p. 47, Nov. 1858, p. 54; *FLA* passim, esp. Mar. 1859, p. 2, June 1859, p. 2, July 1860, pp. 1–11; July 1861, p. 3, 1 Apr. 1862, p. 5, 1 June 1862, p. 3; *BH* 24 Feb. 1866, p. 7, 7 Apr. 1866, p. 7, 12 May 1866, p. 1.

64 *WM* 13 Jan. 1866, p. 29.

65 *FLA*, esp. Nov. 1859, p. 12, Dec. 1860, p. 1, May 1861, July 1861, p. 1, 15 Feb. 1862, p. 6, 1 May 1862, 1 Sept. 1862, p. 3; *NU* Nov. 1858, p. 54; *Morn. Advertiser* 24 Aug. 1859, p. 6.

66 *M* 20 Dec. 1869, p. 2, 22 Mar. 1870, p. 3; 'Cour de Lyon', 1 Dec. 1849, BB30 394.

67 *APO* II, p. 23; *M* 21 Dec. 1869, p. 3, 2 Mar. 1870, p. 2.

68 Gaumont, *Histoire*, pp. 473–4, 519–20; Lequin, *Ouvriers* II, p. 187; Gaillard, 'Associations de production', 79.

69 *A* May 1842, p. 68; *NS* 19 Sept. 1846, p. 5; *O* 8 Mar. 1851, p. 153; *BH* 12 Mar. 1864, p. 6, 19 Mar. 1864, p. 4; Noiret, *Mémoires*, p. 47; Nadaud, *Mémoires*, p. 197; Cole, *Century*, pp. 121, 146; C. Johnson, *Utopian Communism*, p. 166; C. Johnson, 'Revolution of 1830', p. 167; Rancière, *Nuit*, pp. 55, 273; Berridge, 'Popular journalism', pp. 201–5, 231, 383.

70 Pref. Pol. to Min. of Int., 26 Jan. 1865, 45 AP 6, dos. III.

71 E.g. London type-founders, *NS* 24 Feb. 1844, p. 6; Wolverhampton basketmakers, *NS* 14 Nov. 1846, p. 6; London brass-cock founders, *PN* 13 June 1847, p. 7; Paris paper-stainers, *OT* 3 June 1848, p. 4; Manchester wiredrawers, *C* 17 Nov. 1866, p. 4; Pimlico (London) builders, *O* 2 Aug. 1851,

pp. 39–40; *PP* 31 July 1852, pp. 2–3; London engineers, *O* 10 Jan. 1852, p. 224, 17 Jan 1852, pp. 233–4, 7 Feb. 1852, p. 265, 28 Feb. 1852, pp. 287–8; *PP* 31 July 1852, p. 2; *C* 16 Feb. 1867, p. 1; London cork-cutters, *TC* 25 Feb. 1854, p. 1; Manchester coach-makers, Webb Coll. A 45, fol. 379; Paris compositors and lithographers, Chauvet, *Ouvriers*, pp. 357–9, 424; Paris cabinet-makers, Tartaret, *Commission Ouvrière*, p. 194; Sheffield file-makers, *BH* 5 May 1866, p. 8; Birmingham coopers, Webb Coll. A 44, fol. 103; Bradford, Chester and Paris painters, Manchester Operative House Painters' Alliance, *Report Jan.–June 1868*, p. 4; *July–Dec. 1868*, p. 5; General Union of Operative House Painters, *Quarterly Jan. 1871*, p. 11; Webb Coll. A 13, fol. 13; Gaillard, 'Associations de production', 82; Paris leather-dressers, *Travail* 12 Dec. 1869, p. 2. See also: Varlin, *Travail* 12 Dec. 1869, p. 2; Moss, *Origins*, p. 53; Faure, 'Mouvements populaires', 87–8; Postgate, *Builders' History*, pp. 139, 244; Prothero, 'London Chartism and trades', 215; Prothero, *Artisans*, pp. 250–1, 301, 317; Gaillard, 'Associations de production', 71.

72 Tailors, *JT* 16 Mar. 1848, p. 44. E.g. Paris 1833, 1867, and 1869; London 1834 and 1867; Tours 1834; Montpellier, Rennes, and Leeds 1836; Middlesbrough and Darlington 1866: CC 618, 8ème Liasse: *Lettres Adressées au Journal La Tribune*, p. 6; *GT* 2 Dec. 1833, p. 105; *Tribune*, Sunday suppt., p. 1; *Pioneer* 3 May 1834, p. 334, 10 May 1834, p. 338; *BH* 20 May 1865, p. 5; *LT* 26 Nov. 1836, p. 5; *Tailor* 20 Oct. 1866, p. 20, 3 Nov. 1866, p. 57, 27 Apr. 1867, p. 44, 8 June 1867, p. 123, 6 July 1867, pp. 179–80, 19 Oct. 1867, p. 14; Festy, 'Dix années', 171, 175, 187; Parssinen and Prothero, 'London tailors' strike', 75 n. 3, 78; shoemakers, Ashton, *Stockport Advertiser* 28 May 1830, p. 6; Marseilles, Sewell, *Work and Revolution*, p. 177; London strong boots and shoemakers, *NS* 18 Apr. 1846, p. 6, 16 May 1846, p. 6, 23 May 1846, p. 8, 6 June 1846, p. 5; *LL* 11 Nov. 1848, p. 114; Toulon, Agulhon, *Ville ouvrière*, p. 292; Paris, *EL* 6 Aug. 1864, p. 4.

73 Blanc, *Révolution française* IV, p. 107; Gossez, *Ouvriers*, p. 17.

74 Whitehead, *Crisis* 4 May 1833, p. 131. See also *Tribune* Sunday suppt., p. 2; *Pioneer* 28 Dec. 1833, p. 135, 22 Feb. 1834, p. 215, 5 Apr. 1834, p. 288, 3 May 1834, p. 335; *Glaneuse* 12 Nov. 1833, p. 4; Efrahem, *De l'Association*, p. 2; Cabet, *Moyen d'améliorer*, p. 8; Gaumont, *Histoire*, p. 199.

75 *Leicestershire Movement* no.7, p. 53.

76 E.g. Homfirth woollen-weavers, *Crisis* 4 May 1833, pp. 131–2; Stalybridge cotton-spinners, *Ashton and Stalybridge Reporter* 1 June 1861, p. 3; London hairdressers, *WM* 27 Oct. 1866, p. 197; Colne cotton weavers, *C* 17 Nov. 1866, p. 4; Paris shop assistants, Gaumont, *Histoire*, pp. 566–7.

77 *O* 31 Mar. 1839, p. 5, 9 June 1839, p. 8; Drake, *NS* 25 Jan. 1845, p. 8, 2 May 1846, p. 5; Robson, 26 Sept. 1846, p. 2; *PN* 30 May 1847, p. 3; *TAHP* 20 July 1850, p. 31; *O* 27 Mar. 1852, pp. 326–8; *Tailor* 8 June 1867, p. 130, 2 Nov. 1867, pp. 26–7; *M* 12 May 1870, p. 2; Chauvet, *Ouvriers*, pp. 455, 502–3, 516; Lequin, *Ouvriers* II, p. 187; Gaillard, 'Associations de production', 71; Parssinen and Prothero, 'London tailors' strike', 72; Prothero, 'London Chartism and Trades', 215.

78 Wolfe, *BH* 27 Aug. 1864, p. 5.

79 Webb Coll. A 10, fol. 190; *TN* 3 Dec. 1826, p. 166; *WFP* 22 Aug. 1829,

12 Sept. 1829, 17 Oct. 1829, 24 July 1830; *Carpenter's Political Letters* 26 Mar. 1831, p. 16; Lovett, Place Papers, Add. MS 27, 822, fol. 18; *WM* 28 Sept. 1861, p. 110, 14 Apr. 1861, p. 233; Prothero, *Artisans*, pp. 251–2.

80 E.g. Paris shoemakers, *Fédération de Tous les Ouvriers*, p. 1; London brass-workers, *Official Gazette of Trades' Unions* 14 and 21 June 1834; London shoemakers, *O* 9 Dec. 1838, p. 83; Oldham iron trades, *Christian Socialist* II, pp. 138, 266, 292; Paris chair turners, Decamps in Tartaret, *Exposition Universelle*, p. 185; Moutet, 'Mouvement ouvrier', 36; Birmingham basket-makers, *C* 26 Jan. 1867, p. 1. See also *TAHP* 20 July 1850, p. 30, 31 Aug. 1850, p. 74; Heftler, *Associations coopératives*, p. 245; Agulhon, *Republic in the Village*, p. 212; Gossez, *Ouvriers*, pp. 169, 213, 317; Pollard, *History of Labour*, pp. 149–50; W. Fraser, *Trade Unions and Society*, p. 183; B. Taylor, *Eve*, pp. 89–90.

81 *ECC* II, p. 64; Webb Coll. A 11, fols. 303, 331. See also London brush-makers, Webb Coll. A 45, fols. 215–6.

82 Gossez, *Ouvriers*, p. 202; *WM* 1 Sept. 1861, p. 107; *NS* 11 Sept. 1841, p. 6; Vial, *Coutume chapelière*, p. 167.

83 *Crisis* 19 Jan. 1833, p. 13; *Birmingham Labour Exchange Gazette* 9 Feb. 1833, p. 20; Prothero, *Artisans*, pp. 251–2.

84 *PN* 21 Aug. 1847, p. 1; Musson, *Typographical Association*, p. 73; *APOT* pp. 17, 23–4; Chauvet, *Ouvriers*, pp. 351–2; Gossez, 'Presse parisienne', p. 176; Gossez, *Ouvriers*, pp. 200, 285; Rancière, *Nuit*, pp. 319, 321. See also Carpentier to Min. of J., 28 Nov. 1833, BB18 9788.

85 *Birmingham Labour Exchange Gazette* 9 Feb. 1833, p. 20; Prothero, *Artisans*, p. 253; Sanders, 'Working class movements', pp. 243, 246.

86 *Association Laborieuse et Fraternelle*, pp. 1–4; *APO* II, pp. 17–19; Gossez, *Ouvriers*, pp. 174–6; M. Sibalis, 'Shoemakers and Fourierism in nineteenth-century Paris: the *Société Laborieuse des Cordonniers-Bottiers*', *Histoire Sociale/Social History* 20 (1987); Rancière, *Nuit*, 319.

87 *TA* 1 Apr. 1849, p. 7; *PS* 5 Apr. 1849, p. 2; *APO* II, p. 19; *Association Fraternelle des Ouvriers Cordonniers de Bar*.

88 *Echo des Travailleurs* 6 Nov. 1833, p. 4. See also: Manchester, *TAHP* 21 Sept. 1850, p. 100; *RWN* 27 Apr. 1851, p. 14; *Cooperator* June 1860, p. 2, Mar. 1863, p. 175; Paris, *Union* Jan. 1846, p. 4, July 1846, p. 51; *Tailor* 20 Apr. 1867, p. 27; *M* 11 Apr. 1870, p. 2; Barberet, *Mouvement ouvrier*, pp. 61–2; *APO* II, p. 605; London, *Tailor* 3 Nov. 1866, p. 52, 10 Nov. 1866, pp. 77–8, 8 Dec. 1866, p. 142, 3 Aug. 1867, pp. 234–5, 8 Aug. 1868, p. 312, 15 Aug. 1868, p. 316. See also Gaumont, *Histoire*, pp. 227, 319; Gossez, *Ouvriers*, p. 161.

89 *Echo des Travailleurs* 6 Nov. 1833, p. 4; *ECC* II, p. 70; *O* 1 May 1852, p. 393, 8 May 1852, p. 416; Gossez, *Ouvriers*, p. 174; Sibalis, 'Shoemakers', 46.

90 Hirst, *LYC* New series no. 10, p. 16; Fox, *TAHP* 27 July 1850, p. 39; Walton, *C* 2 Feb. 1867, p. 1; *O* 31 Jan. 1852, p. 246.

91 *P* 1 Jan. 1849, pp. 3–4; *TAHP* 21 Sept. 1850, p. 100.

92 Prothero, *Artisans*, pp. 25, 250, 256; Agulhon, *Ville ouvrière*, pp. 166–9, 304.

93 *OSM* 11 Oct. 1838, pp. 293–4, 9 May 1839, p. 341, 23 May 1839, p. 345, 6 June 1839, pp. 347–8, 15 Aug. 1839, p. 375.

94 Edwards, 'The disease and the remedy', *TPC* Feb. 1850, pp. 57–62; *BH* 11 Apr. 1863, p. 5; *Rapport des Délégués de la Typographie*, p. 17; F12 3117 *menuisiers en bâtiments*; Cotterau, 'Denis Poulot's *Le Sublime*', pp. 151–2.

95 *TA* 13 May 1849, p. 1; Heftler, *Associations coopératives*, pp. 88–9, 267; Gossez, *Ouvriers*, pp. 100, 104–5, 167.

96 Cochut, *Associations ouvrières*, pp. 75–6; Engländer, *BH* 26 Nov. 1864, p. 1.

97 Marcroft, *Co-operative Village*, pp. 10–11.

98 *A* 26 Mar. 1848, p. 10. See also Merriman, *Agony*, p. 52; Welskopp, 'Defensive elitism', 13–18.

99 *CP* 26 Mar. 1848, p. 2, 30 Mar. 1848, p. 4; *VR* 27 Mar. 1848, p. 2, 30 Mar. 1848, p. 2; Heftler, *Associations coopératives*, pp. 41–3; Gossez, *Ouvriers*, pp. 106–8.

100 *A* Sept. 1840, p. 5, Oct. 1840, p. 12, 26 Mar. 1848, p. 101.

101 Pare, *TC* 4 Feb. 1854, p. 10; Cole, *Century*, pp. 159–61

102 *Shipwrights' J* June 1858, p. 39; *WM* 1 Apr. 1862, pp. 94–5; *Cooperator* Jan. 1863, p. 131; Pollard, *History of Labour*, p. 97.

103 *WA* 4 Nov. 1865, p. 3; *VP* 27 Oct. 1849, p. 4; Cole, *Century*, pp. 90–1, 159. See also: shoemakers, *Ruche* Feb. 1844, p. 36; smiths, *A* May 1841, p. 71.

104 *A* Apr. 1844, pp. 107–8; *Voix des Femmes* 31 Mar. 1848, p. 3; *VR* 15 May 1848, pp. 2–3; Tartaret, *Exposition Universelle*, p. 282; E. Carpenter, *Co-operative Production with reference to the Experiment of Leclaire* (1883); Gaillard, 'Associations de production', 60; Rancière, *Nuit*, pp. 429–30, 445. For the profit-sharing at the *Presse* newspaper, see: *Peuple Constituant* 22 Mar. 1848, pp. 2–3; *TA* 15 Apr. 1849, p. 7; Havard, in Tartaret, *Exposition Universelle*, p. 289.

105 *OT* 9 June 1848, p. 3, 20 June 1848, p. 1; Gossez, *Ouvriers*, p. 167.

106 *TA* 15 Apr. 1849, p. 7; Debock in Lévy, *Procès*, p. 7. Rancière, *Nuit*, p. 350.

107 Webb Coll. A 13, fol. 330; *VR* 15 May 1848, pp. 2–3; *O* 8 Mar. 1851, p. 155; Malon, *M* 24 July 1870, p. 2; Brossiers, F12 3109; Tartaret, *Exposition Universelle*, p. 232; *APOT*, p. 10; Gaillard, 'Associations de production', 60, 64, 69.

108 *Crisis* 19 Dec. 1833, p. 122; Heftler, *Associations coopératives*, pp. 251–2; Behagg, *Politics and Production*, pp. 81–2.

109 *Crisis* 20 Oct. 1833, p. 130; *NS* 21 Mar. 1846, p. 2; *P* 12 Mar. 1849, p. 4; *TAHP* 21 Sept. 1850, p. 99; *RWN* 27 Apr. 1851, p. 14; *PP* 31 July 1852, p. 2; *EL* 29 Sept. 1866, p. 173; *St. Crispin* 9 Jan. 1869, p. 28; *Almanach des Associations*, p. 152; Gossez, *Ouvriers*, pp. 147–9, 158, 161. See also Sheridan, 'Social and economic foundations', pp. 74, 132, 290, 300.

110 Sheridan, 'Social and economic foundations', pp. 111–12, 118; Webb Coll. A 11, fol. 307; Festy, 'Dix années', 186; Gaumont, *Histoire*, p. 596; *M* 17 Apr. 1870, p. 7.

111 See also Heftler, *Associations coopératives*, p. 42; Faure, 'Mouvements populaires', 88; Gossez, *Ouvriers*, p. 108.

112 6 Apr., C 930, dos. V, 624; *CP* 23 Mar. 1848, p. 1; Chambre de Commerce, *Statistique I*, p. 73; Engländer, *BH* 26 Nov. 1864, p. 1; *JTA*

1 Feb. 1860, p. 14; *APOT*, pp. 7, 10, 21; Heftler, *Associations coopératives*, pp. 172–6; Gossez, *Ouvriers*, pp. 159–60; Rancière, *Nuit*, pp. 322–5, 350; Agulhon, *Republic in the Village*, p. 214.

113 Petition, BB30 316 28b; reports 23 Apr. and 25 July 1848, C 930, dos. V, 626 and II, dos. IV, 'Ateliers de Clichy', fol. 604; *CP* 28 Mar. 1848, p. 1, 2 May 1848, p. 4; *VR* 29 Mar. 1848, p. 2; *Peuple Constituant* 2 May 1848, p. 2, 11 May, p. 1; *Travail* 28 May 1848, p. 2; *VP* 27 Nov. 1849, p. 2; Wahry, 4 Jan. 1850, p. 1, 20 Jan 1850, p. 2. Cochut, *Associations ouvrières*, pp. 33–6; Heftler, *Associations coopératives*, pp. 44–9, 52–4, 196–7; Loubere, *Louis Blanc*, pp. 86–7; Gossez, *Ouvriers*, pp. 164–6; Rancière, *Nuit*, pp. 319, 332–3; Agulhon, *Ville ouvrière*, p. 274. For relief cooperation more generally, see: *CP* 16 Mar. 1848, p. 4; Lefrançais, *Souvenirs I*, p. 76; Gossez, *Ouvriers*, pp. 160, 169, 319; Rancière, *Nuit*, p. 320.

114 See above, pp. 109–11.

115 E.g. [Martin], *Nouveau catéchisme*, p. 80; *Tribune* suppt., p. 1; Bernard, *Revue Républicaine* Oct.–Dec. 1834, pp. 289–301; Moss, *Origins*, pp. 38–39.

116 *J des Sciences Morales et Politiques* 17 Dec. 1831, pp. 36–7.

117 Buchez, '2ème lettre à Curie', 30 Aug. 1829, CP 3706, fol. 201; *J des Sciences Morales et Politiques* 17 Dec. 1831, pp. 37, 39; *A* 21 May 1848, p. 152; Leader, *TAHP* 19 Oct. 1850, p. 134; Duval, 'Origines', 217–19; Heftler, *Associations coopératives*, p. 3; *APO* IV, pp. 93–4; Gaumont, *Histoire*, pp. 116, 361; Dolléans, *Histoire*, pp. 74–7; Moss, 'Parisian workers', p. 209; Moss, 'Parisian producers' associations', pp. 74–5.

118 Leroux, *Aux ouvriers typographes*, p. 15; Gossez, *Ouvriers*, p. 197; Moss, *Origins*, p. 35; Faure, 'Mouvements populaires', 87–9; Sewell, *Work and Revolution*, p. 210; Rancière, *Nuit*, pp. 113–14.

119 Leroux, *Prolétaire et bourgeois*, pp. 6–7; Scott, 'Men and women', p. 84.

120 Heftler, *Associations coopératives*, p. 242; Rancière, *Nuit*, p. 319; Sonenscher, *Work and Wages*, p. 349.

121 C 925 dos. Luxembourg, 2989; Min. of Int. to Min. Travaux Publics, 4 June 1848, C 930, dos. V, 613; C 942, dos. 'Commission des délégués du Luxembourg', 2926; *Manifeste des Délégués*; *J des Travailleurs* 8–11 June 1848, p. 1, 11–15 June 1848, pp. 1–2, 22–25 June 1848, p. 1; Duchêne, *VP* 27 Nov. 1849, pp. 2–3, 7; Cochut, *Associations ouvrières*, pp. 11–12, 15; Heftler, *Associations coopératives*, p. 39; Gaumont, *Histoire*, pp. 245–6, 258–61; Gossez, 'Pré-syndicalisme', 69, 73, 77–8; Gossez, *Ouvriers*, pp. 294–6.

122 Webb Coll. A 45, fol. 362.

123 Abrahams, *Cleave's Weekly Police Gazette*, 26 Dec. 1835; Skelton, *NS* 25 Oct. 1845, p. 7; *O* 11 Jan. 1851, p. 26, 8 Mar. 1851, p. 145, 12 Apr. 1851, p. 234, 28 June 1851, pp. 408–9.

124 *NAUT* 1 Mar. 1848, pp. 30–3; *ATWR* Sept. 1845, pp. 109–10; *NS* 21 Mar. 1846, p. 3, 6 June 1846, p. 5; Parker, 29 May 1847, p. 7. See also *O* 4 Jan. 1851, p. 2, 22 Mar. 1851, pp. 185–6; Prothero, 'London Chartism and trades', 217–8.

125 *NS* 25 Jan. 1845, p. 8, 26 Apr. 1851, p. 1, 24 Jan. 1846, p. 1; Prothero, 'Chartism in London', 99; Prothero, 'London Chartism and trades', 215;

Flotard, *Mouvement coopératif*, pp. 5–25; Stewart-McDougall, *Artisan Republic*, p. 101.

126 E.g. *Association des Ouvriers Ebénistes*; *Association des Ouvriers Bijoutiers*; *Association Fraternelle* (Limoges); Lion, *Plus de patrons*; Agulhon, *Republican Experiment*, p. 116. For accounts and estimates of numbers, see: Lefrançais, *Souvenirs* I, pp. 74–6; Engländer, serialised in translation *BH* 29 Oct. 1864, p. 1–4 Feb. 1865, p. 1; Cochut, *Associations ouvrières*, pp. 16–17; Flotard, *Mouvement coopératif*, p. 86; Heftler, *Associations coopératives*, pp. 190–6, 239–40; Gaumont, *Histoire*, pp. 255–7, 279–82, 370; Gossez, *Ouvriers*, pp. 320–1; Lequin, *Ouvriers* II pp. 186–7; Stewart-McDougall, *Artisan Republic*, pp. 101–2; Rancière, *Nuit*, pp. 327–8. Lists of Parisian societies are frequently given in the radical and workers' press.

127 Prothero, *Artisans*, p. 297; Newbridge, *NS* 7 Nov. 1839, p. 7; E. Yeo, 'Robert Owen', p. 7; Cole, *Century*, p. 61; Heywood, *Cooperator* Apr. 1863, p. 182; *NU* Oct. 1858, p. 48; A. Taylor, 'Modes', pp. 212–14; Claeys, *Citizens*, p. 263.

128 *AR* 18 Mar. 1849, p. 1, 4 Mar., p. 1; *P* 8–15 Nov. 1848, p. 2; Benoit, *Confessions*, p. 119; Cochut, *Associations ouvrières*, pp. 16, 51–3; Heftler, *Associations coopératives*, pp. 60–9, 72–4, 139–50; Gaumont, *Histoire*, pp. 361, 368, 381; Gossez, *Ouvriers*, pp. 106, 143, 158, 200, 299, 315, 319; Gossez, 'Pré-syndicalisme', 74–5; Moss, 'Parisian producers' associations', p. 80; Agulhon, *Republican Experiment*, pp. 115–16; Stewart-McDougall, *Artisan Republic*, pp. 18, 20, 59, 101–2.

129 Lefrançais, *Souvenirs* I, pp. 73–5, II, pp. 333–5; Oct. 1848, Aa 428; Pref. Pol. to Garde des Sceaux, 7 and 11 Sept. 1850, BB18 1487, 9074; *TA* 11 Mar. 1849, p. 8, 1 Apr. 1849, p. 8; *APO* III, p. 530; Furlough, *Consumer Cooperation*, pp. 15, 21 n. 13.

130 *AR* 28 Jan. 1849, pp. 2–3; Heftler, *Associations coopératives*, pp. 204, 254; Agulhon, *Republican Experiment*, pp. 18, 91–2; Stewart-McDougall, *Artisan Republic*, pp. 100–1.

131 Proc.-Gen. Lyons to Garde des Sceaux, quoted in Tchernoff, *Parti républicain*, p. 148; Proc. Lyons to Min. of J., 13 July 1849, and Pref. Rhône to Min. of Int., 27 Aug., 'Cour de Lyon 1848–1850', BB18 1474B; Gaumont, *Histoire*, pp. 383–6, 390, 394–5; Stewart-McDougall, *Artisan Republic*, pp. 117, 120–1; Sheridan, 'Social and economic foundations', pp. 119, 149.

132 *Man* 8 Sept. 1833, p. 77; Nadaud, *Mémoires*, p. 373; Heftler, *Associations coopératives*, p. 238; Gaumont, *Histoire*, pp. 416–17.

133 *VP* 6 Dec. 1849, p. 2. See also *P* 25 Nov. 1848, p. 1, 26 Mar. 1849, p. 7; *VP* 9 Dec. 1849, p. 1; Heftler, *Associations coopératives*, p. 56.

134 *P* 8–15 Nov. 1848, p. 4, 18 Jan. 1849, pp. 1–2, 4 Apr. 1849, p. 2, 10 Apr. 1849, p. 4; *Commune Sociale* Dec. 1848, pp. 7–8; *TA* 7 Jan. 1849, p. 8, 21 Jan. 1849, p. 4; Lefrançais, *Souvenirs* I, pp. 131–2; Gossez, *Ouvriers*, pp. 321–2.

135 Engländer, *BH* 26 Nov. 1864, p. 1; *A* 7 Aug. 1848, p. 195; *P* 8 Sept. 1850, p. 4; Heftler, *Associations coopératives*, pp. 85–6, 91–3, 276; Gaumont, *Histoire*, pp. 275, 400–3; Merriman, *Agony*, p. 78; Gossez, *Ouvriers*, p. 317; Stewart-McDougall, *Artisan Republic*, p. 142.

136 *O* 7 Feb. 1852, pp. 254–5, 15 May 1852, p. 430; *BH* 23 July 1864, p. 7; Cohadon, *Mutualité* 15 Sept. 1866, p. 277; *Commerce* 26 Sept. 1869, p. 2; Heftler, *Associations coopératives*, p. 253; Gaumont, *Histoire*, pp. 319, 432–5, 571; Kelso, 'French labor movement', 100; Gossez, *Ouvriers*, p. 320; Agulhon, *Republic in the Village*, p. 209; Stewart-McDougall, *Artisan Republic*, p. 150.

137 *Commerce passim*, esp. 15 Aug. 1869, p. 2, 22 Aug. 1869, p. 2, 29 Aug. 1869, p. 2, 26 Sept. 1869, p. 2; *Mutualité* 15 Sept. 1866, pp. 286–97; *M* 21 Dec. 1869, p. 3, 12 May 1870, pp. 2, 3, 17 May 1870, p. 3, 21 July 1870, p. 2; Tartaret, *Commission Ouvrière*, pp. 163, 188, 194–5, 201–6, 211; *APO* II, p. 23; Gaumont, *Histoire*, pp. 497–8; Dolléans, *Histoire*, pp. 282–3; Kelso, 'French labor movement', 100; Moss, *Origins*, p. 5; Furlough, *Consumer Cooperation*, p. 62; Sheridan, 'Social and economic foundations', pp. 2–3, 14–15.

138 Delescluze to Ledru-Rollin, 11 Mar. 1852, MS 2015, fol. 786; *Cooperator* Nov. 1860, p. 71, Jan. 1863, p. 134; *WM* 19 May 1866, p. 308; *Mutualité* 15 Oct. 1866, p. 327; Tartaret, *Commission Ouvrière*, pp. 150ff.; Gaumont, *Histoire*, pp. 450, 499–500, 521, 571, 597–8; Furlough, *Consumer Cooperation*, p. 8.

139 F12 3110 *charpentiers, cloutiers pour meubles, couvreurs, cuirs et peaux*; 3115, *maçons*; 3121A, *imprimeurs*; 3112 *ébénistes*; 3109, *brossiers*; 3120, *tailleurs*; 3117 *menuisiers en bâtiments*; Gaillard, 'Associations de production', 61.

140 *WM* 25 May 1867, p. 9; Gaumont, *Histoire*, pp. 473, 508, 575; Lequin, *Ouvriers* II, p. 190; Plessis, *Rise and Fall*, p. 161; Stewart-McDougall, *Artisan Republic*, p. 159.

141 Tartaret, *Commission Ouvrière*, p. 163; Gaumont, *Histoire*, pp. 463–7, 474, 496–7, 535, 572–4; Kelso, 'French labor movement', pp. 100–1; Moss, *Origins*, pp. 49–50; Lequin, *Ouvriers* II, pp. 187–90; Dalotel, *Aux origines*, pp. 234–6, 257; Gaillard, 'Asssociations de production', 63–4, 74–5; Furlough, *Consumer Cooperation*, pp. 34–5, 42–5, 48–50; Sheridan, 'Social and economic foundations', p. 150.

142 *Travail* 21 Nov. 1869, p. 2; Simon in Tartaret, *Commission Ouvrière*, p. 214; Flotard, *Mouvement coopératif*, p. 3; Gaumont, *Histoire*, pp. 511, 516–18; Jardin and Tudesq, *Restoration and Reaction*, p. 308; C. Johnson, 'Revolution of 1830', p. 169; Roger Price, *French Second Republic*, pp. 57, 59; Perrot, 'Nineteenth-century work experience', pp. 281–2; Furlough, *Consumer Cooperation*, pp. 40–1; Sheridan, 'Social and economic foundations', p. 467.

143 45 AP 6, dos. 4, 27 Nov. 1868; *Commerce* 29 Aug. 1869, p. 2; *BH* 24 Sept. 1864, p. 5; *WM* 7 July 1866, p. 3; *C* 21 July 1866, p. 5; *APO* III, pp. 529–30; Gaumont, *Histoire*, pp. 473, 502–4, 590–1; Weill, *Histoire*, p. 378; Lequin, *Ouvriers* II, pp. 189–90; Moss, *Origins*, p. 50; Gaillard, 'Associations de production', 65, 72–4; Dalotel, *Aux origines*, p. 20; Furlough, *Consumer Cooperation*, pp. 38–9, 44–5.

144 *M* 3 Mar. 1870, p. 3, 22 Mar. 1870, p. 3, 31 Mar. 1870, p. 3; Gaumont, *Histoire*, pp. 544–5; Furlough, *Consumer Cooperation*, pp. 51, 53–4, 58 n. 77, 62.

145 BHVP NA MS 155, fols. 64–7; Bell, *Cooper's J* 4 May 1850, p. 273; *WM*

7 Apr. 1866, pp. 218–19; G. J. Holyoake, *Inaugural Address Delivered at the Nineteenth Annual Co-operative Congress . . . Carlisle, . . . 1887* (Manchester, 1887); Cochut, *Associations ouvrières*, p. 8; Gaumont, *Histoire*, pp. 468, 521–2, 552, 560, 574, 587, 598–9; Duval, 'Origines', 228; Moss, *Origins*, pp. 49; Rougerie, 'Commune', 60; Gaillard, 'Associations de production', 68, 74; Furlough, *Consumer Cooperation*, pp. 37–8, 42–3, 45; Sheridan, 'Social and economic foundations', pp. 15, 428.

146 Tartaret, *Commission Ouvrière*, pp. 194–5; Gaumont, *Histoire*, pp. 277, 522; Gaillard, p. 65; Moutet, 'Mouvement ouvrier', 27; Sheridan, 'Social and economic foundations', pp. 85, 110.

147 J. M. Ludlow and L. Jones, *Progress of the Working Classes 1832–1867* (1867), p. 296; Cole, *Century*, pp. 70–1, 82, 170; Agulhon, *Republican Experiment*, p. 97; Hanagan, *Logic*, p. 21; Sheridan, 'Social and economic foundations', p. 548.

148 Austin, *Crisis* 21 Dec. 1833, p. 131; *F* Nov. 1841, pp. 2–3; Jones, *NS* 15 Jan. 1848, p. 8; Jones, *NP*, pp. 27–31; *PP* 13 June 1857, p. 1; Cuddon, *WM* 12 Oct. 1861, p. 119; *BH* 26 Nov. 1864, p. 1; Tartaret, *Commission Ouvrière*, pp. 102, 135, 161, 183–4; Macdonald, *True Story*, pp. 11, 21; Cuddon, *Tailor* 14 Dec. 1867, p. 78; *M* 6 Mar. 1870, p. 2, Malon, 24 July 1870, p. 2; Noiret, *Deuxième lettre*, p. 10; Gaumont, *Histoire*, p. 477; Stewart-McDougall, *Artisan Republic*, pp. 117–18; Sheridan, 'Social and economic foundations', p. 110.

149 *O* 5 July 1851, pp. 4–5, 12 July 1851, pp. 12–16, 9 July 1851, p. 21, 17 Jan. 1852, pp. 233–4, 7 Feb. 1852, p. 265, 28 Feb. 1852, pp. 287–8, 1 May 1852, p. 393, 8 May 1852, p. 416; *WM* 21 July 1866, p. 34, Greening, 17 Aug. 1867, pp. 4–5; Humphrey, *Robert Applegarth*, p. 45; *Cooperator* Dec. 1860, p. 99; ASCJ, *Monthly Report* Feb. 1869, pp. 37–8; Broadhurst, *Story*, pp. 47–50.

150 Cole, *Century*, pp. 102–4, 110–11, 131–3.

151 *M* 6 Mar. 1870, p. 3, 31 Mar. 1870, p. 3.

152 Dupas, Barbier in Tartaret, *Commission Ouvrière*, pp. 161, 165; *Commerce* 12 Sept. 1869, p. 2; *M* 16 Dec. 1869, p. 1, 7 Jan. 1870, p. 3, 27 Jan. 1870, p. 3, 11 Apr. 1870, p. 2, 17 Apr. 1870, p. 12; Gaumont, *Histoire*, pp. 533–4, 568, 603–5, 612; Kelso, 'French labor movement', 102, 106; Chauvet, *Ouvriers*, p. 516; Gaillard, 'Associations de production', 70, 83–4; Lequin, *Ouvriers* II, p. 190; Dalotel, *Aux origines*, pp. 259–60; Sheridan, 'Political economy', 235; Sheridan, 'Social and economic foundations', pp. 17, 235.

153 *WM* 22 Sept. 1866, p. 136; Société d'Economie Politique (Lyons), *Compte-Rendu* (1881–2), p. 23; Gaumont, *Histoire*, pp. 497–8, 588; Moss, *Origins*, pp. 53–4; Gaillard, 'Associations de production', 61, 68–9, 79; Sheridan, 'Social and economic foundations', pp. 19, 521.

154 Rougerie, 'Commune', 61; Moss, *Origins*, p. 69; Moutet, 'Mouvement ouvrier', 26–8; Furlough, *Consumer Cooperation*, pp. 55 n. 73, 56 n. 73, 58 n. 78, 59–61.

155 *TAHP* 31 Aug. 1850, p. 74; *PP* 26 May 1855, p. 1; *WM* 17 Aug. 1867, pp. 4–5; Gaumont, *Histoire*, pp. 595, 611; Lequin, *Ouvriers* II, pp. 189–90. For a few that did last a long time, see: *APO* II, pp. 605, 676;

Heftler, *Associations coopératives*, pp. 251–2, 281, 283; Gaumont, *Histoire*, pp. 395–6.

156 G.J. Holyoake, *The Policy of Commercial Co-operation as Respects and Including the Consumer* (Manchester, 1873), p. 7 and preface; S. Yeo, 'Three socialisms', pp. 108–9.

157 *VR* 8 May 1848, p. 4; Pollard, *History of Labour*, pp. 101, 111; Tholfsen, *Working Class Radicalism*, pp. 162, 253; Hanagan, *Nascent Proletarians*, p. 12; Furlough, *Consumer Cooperation*, pp. 2, 6, 8–9, 29, 47–8, 55.

## 7. CLASS AND RADICALISM

1 Sweet, *Chartist Pilot* 20 Jan. 1844, p. 2.

2 *NS* 10 Nov. 1849, p. 5.

3 See also Aminzade, 'Class analysis', pp. 90–4.

4 See also Joyce, *Visions*; Finn, *After Chartism*, pp. 7, 9, 11; Sheridan, 'Social and economic foundations', pp. 24–5, 30.

5 See also Fomberteau, NAF 9581, fol. 355; *Les Sociétés Populaires*, p. 32; J. Vincent, *Formation*, pp. 36–9; Agulhon, *Ville ouvrière*, pp. 299–300, 311; Nossiter, 'Shopkeeper radicalism'; Nossiter, 'Middle class', pp. 79–80; Loubere, *Radicalism*, p. 76; Roger Price, *French Second Republic*, pp. 114, 151–2, 165–6, 238, 241; Lequin, *Ouvriers* II, pp. 161, 167; Christofferson, 'Urbanization', 202–3; L. Hunt and Sheridan, 'Corporation', 836; Perrot, 'Formation', p. 87; Biagini, *Liberty*, pp. 11, 13.

6 Agulhon, *Republic in the Village*, pp. 249–50; Margadant, 'Modernisation', p. 256. See also Sewell, *Work and Revolution*, pp. 283–4; Hanagan, *Nascent Proletarians*, pp. 16–18.

7 E.g. Reform League, *BH* 10 Dec. 1864, p. 1, 13 May 1865, p. 1, 20 May 1865, p. 6; *MWA* 3 June 1865, p. 5, 20 May 1865, p. 5; *Journal du Faubourg Saint-Antoine*, CC 613, 2ème Liasse; Varlin, *TO* 4 June 1865, p. 2; Cabet, *Guide*, p. 19; Gossez, 'Presse parisienne'; J. Vincent, *Formation*, p. 189; Finn, *After Chartism*, pp. 253–4.

8 *Lettres d'un Républicain sur la Misère des Ouvriers et les Moyens de la Faire Cesser*, CC 585; Desplanche, *Ruche* Aug. 1841, p. 5; Perdiguier, Apr. 1844, p. 101; Gaumont, *Union* Apr. 1845, p. 1; *A* Mar. 1847, p. 467; Cottereau, 'Distinctiveness', p. 151.

9 *Dictionnaire Politique*, pp. 669–70; *National* 3 July 1845, p. 1; Duquene, *Ruche* Feb. 1847, p. 36; *Réforme* 30 Apr. 1848, p. 1; Churchill, *NS* 29 Apr. 1848, p. 1; Reynolds, *RN* 11 July 1858, p. 7; *BH* 26 Aug. 1864, p. 4; Molinari, *Mouvement socialiste*, pp. xviii–xx; Girard, *Garde Nationale*, p. 258; Amann, *Revolution*, p. 52; Biagini, *Liberty*, p. 152; Finn, *After Chartism*, p. 301.

10 Nepireu dossier, CC 608; *Indicateur* 9 Oct. 1834, pp. 1, 2; *Ruche*, Apr.–May 1848, p. 70; [Martin], *Nouveau catéchisme*, p. 9; Richard, 'Débuts', 77; Weill, *Histoire*, p. 70; Amann, *Revolution*, pp. 166–9.

11 Prothero, 'Chartism in London', 94–6, 103–5; Goodway, *London Chartism*, pp. 14–18; Sykes, 'Popular politics', pp. 147–67, 572–3; Gossez, 'Presse parisienne', p. 159; Merriman, *Agony*, p. 150.

12 Bouillon, 'Démocrates-socialistes', esp. 87; Agulhon, *Ville ouvrière*, pp.

302–3, 309; Roger Price, *French Second Republic*, pp. 137, 223, 239; Moss, 'June 13, 1849', 397.

13  Aguet, *Grèves*, pp. 1–14; Fasel, 'Urban workers', 663–8; Stewart-McDougall, *Artisan Republic*, p. 127.

14  *PP* 3 Nov. 1855, p. 1, 11 Nov. 1855, p. 1.

15  *JO* 19 Sept. 1830, p. 2, 28 Feb., 11, 12 Mar., 12 July 1831, F7 3881; Faure, 'Mouvements populaires', 55, 73–7.

16  Police report, 6 Mar. 1848, C 930 dos. VI, 648; Christofferson, 'French national workshops', 510–12; Rancière, *Nuit*, p. 211; D. Thompson, *Chartists*, pp. 30–2; O'Neill, *St. Crispin* 7 Aug. 1869, p. 64; Tyrrell, 'Class consciousness', 110–13; *PP* 17 Jan.–7 Mar. 1857; M. Rose, 'Rochdale man'; *PMG* 3 Nov. 1832, pp. 593–600; Behagg, *Politics and Production*, p. 180.

17  *O* 10 Apr. 1852, pp. 347–50, 17 Apr. 1852, p. 373; Gillespie, *Labor and Politics*, pp. 101–3. See also Biagini, *Liberty*, p. 148.

18  Jacobs, *Bath Guardian* 4 Nov. 1837, p. 3. See also Prosser, *Last* 24 Jan. 1845, p. 106; Nadaud, *PP* 6 Nov. 1852, p. 3.

19  E.g. Thomas, *JO* 28 Oct. 1830, p. 3; Perdiguier, *Mémoires*, pp. 109, 114.

20  *JO* 19 Sept. 1830, p. 2.

21  *NS* 5 Feb. 1842, p. 4.

22  *PMG* 7 Jan. 1832, p. 235, 27 Oct. 1832, p. 577; Hetherington, 12 Oct. 1833, p. 327; Prothero, 'William Benbow', 144–5; Prothero, *Artisans*, p. 334; Sykes, 'Some aspects', 178.

23  *NS* 20 Feb. 1841, p. 4.

24  Skelton, *NS* 10 Feb. 1844, p. 6; *NL* 20 July 1839, p. 5; Cardiff, *NS* 24 Apr. 1841, p. 1, Trowbridge, 1 May 1841, p. 3, O'Connor, Ridley, 5 Mar. 1842, p. 1, 10 Feb. 1844, p. 6.

25  Dixon, *BH* 23 Apr. 1864, p. 1.

26  *Organisateur* 15 Aug. 1830, pp. 2–3; Hibbert, *PMG* 5 Nov. 1831, p. 149; Laponneraye, 21 Nov. 1831, F7 3885; *A* July 1844, p. 153, June 1846, p. 321; *Peuple Souverain. Journal des Travailleurs* 26 Mar. 1848, p. 1; *CP* 24 May 1848, p. 1; Gautier, *PD* 15–18 June 1848, p. 2; Toussenel, *TA* 4 May 1849, p. 2; *AR* 17, 19, and 21 June 1849, p. 2; C. Johnson, *Utopian Communism*, p. 227.

27  *Réforme* 30 Apr. 1848, p. 1.

28  Williams, *LD* 17 Sept. 1836, p. 3.

29  Ragon, *Histoire*, p. 81.

30  O'Connor, *NS* 3 May 1845, p. 1; Reynolds, *RN* 22 June 1851, p. 14; Laponneraye, *Défense*, pp. 5–6; Soul, *LD* 14 July 1839, p. 3; Mason, *Chartist Pilot* 23 Dec. 1843, p. 2; *Peuple Constituant* 18 Mar. 1848, p. 2; *TWM* 17 June 1848, p. 18; *Positif* July 1849, p. 3; Roger Price, *French Second Republic*, pp. 232–4; D. Fraser, *Urban Politics*, p. 15.

31  *NS* 15 May 1841, p. 1.

32  *PMG* 9 Aug. 1834, p. 212; *NS* 11 Sept. 1841, p. 1, 18 Sept. 1841, p. 1, 18 June 1842, p. 1, 2 July 1842, p. 4, 9 July 1842, p. 1, 5 Aug. 1843, p. 8; Doyle, 11 Mar. 1848, p. 1; Jones, *PP* 13 Jan. 1855, p. 1; *NP*, p. 152; *PP* 29 Oct. 1853, p. 1, 6 June 1857, p. 1.

33  *AR* 11 Jan. 1849, p. 3.

34 Henriette, *BH* 13 Oct. 1866, p. 1; Benbow, *NS* 8 Sept. 1849, p. 5; Fussell, *PP* 2 Oct. 1852, p. 3, April–Sept. 1857, Hooson, 5 Dec. 1857, p. 4; *C* 21 Apr. 1866, p. 4.

35 Devlin to Gray, 10 Mar. 1849, in [Devlin], *Strangers' Homes*; Davenport, *PMG* 24 Aug. 1833, p. 275; Concord, *Pioneer* 7 Sept. 1833, p. 3; shoemakers, *Bristol Times* 24 June 1843, p. 4; NAUT, *NS* 10 Apr. 1847, p. 5; *BH* 2 June 1866, p. 5 (Drake); Hennock, 'Finance and politics', 216; Morris, 'Voluntary societies', 292, 297–8; Gossez, *Ouvriers*, p. 103.

36 Dubois, Nepireu dossier; Maurice, Giroux, CC 608; Gossez, 'Diversité', 442.

37 6 Apr. 1848, C 930, dos. V, 624; 10, 12 Oct. 1856, BB30 366, dos. II, fol. 168; NA MS 155, fols. 527, 758; *NS* 7 Nov. 1846, p. 2; *Ruche* Dec. 1848, p. 324; *WM* 8 Sept. 1866, p. 107, 15 Sept. 1866, p. 122; *M* 22 Dec. 1869, p. 2; Durand, Tartaret, in Tartaret, *Commission Ouvrière*, pp. 240–1; Tartaret, *Exposition Universelle*, p. 124; Poulot, *Question sociale*, pp. 146–7; Gossez, 'Diversité', 453–4; Amann, *Revolution*, pp. 7, 166–7; Plessis, *Rise and Fall*, pp. 116, 124; Dalotel, *Aux origines*, p. 75; Moore, *Injustice*, p. 203.

38 *PMG* 17 Aug. 1833, p. 262.

39 *Pop.* 22 Nov. 1845, pp. 203–4; Cabet, *Salut*, p. 22; *RP* 1 May 1848, p. 1; *NU* May 1858, p. 4; Crossick, *Artisan Elite*, pp. 163–4; C. Johnson, *Utopian Communism*, pp. 225–6; Dalotel, *Aux origines*, p. 159.

40 Mrs Grote to Place, 16 Aug. 1837, 11 Mar. 1840, Place Papers, Add. MSS 35,150, fol. 279 and 35,151, fol. 291.

41 See also Crossick, 'Gentlemen', pp. 152, 153; Moore, *Injustice*, p. 146.

42 Leroux, *Prolétaire et bourgeois*, p. 4; *CP* 6 May 1848, p. 1; Santerre, C 925, Luxembourg dossier, 2997. See also Aix Proc.-Gen. to Keeper of Seals, 29 Jan. 1849, BB30 358, dos. II (Aix), fol. 210; C. Jones, *Political Secret*, p. 3; Moss, 'Parisian workers', p. 208.

43 Dommanget, *Idées politiques*, pp. 232–3; *Artisan* 10 Oct. 1830, p. 3; *Union* Aug. 1846, p. 61; Constant, *Règne*, p. 1; Dalotel, *Aux origines*, pp. 156–7; Vernon, *Politics*, pp. 266–70, 290, 310.

44 *Constitution of the London Democratic Association*, HO 44/52.

45 *C* 10 Feb. 1866, p. 4; *M* 24 Dec. 1869, p. 2; *AR* 11 Mar. 1849, p. 1.

46 Dennis, *Cri du Peuple* 8 Apr. 1871, p. 1, 20 Apr. 1871, p. 1.

47 Pillot, *Ni châteaux*, p. 22.

48 Jouy, *Adresse*, pp. 14–15, 28; Crossick, 'Gentlemen', p. 157; Dalotel, *Aux origines*, pp. 159–63.

49 Laponneraye, *Cours*, pp. 13, 36–7; *Artisan* 22 Sept. 1830, p. 1, 26 Sept. 1830, p. 1; *Les Sociétés Populaires*, p. 31; [Martin], *Nouveau catéchisme*, p. 9; *Tribune* suppt., pp. 1, 3; Desjardin, CC 585; Boyer, *De l'état des ouvriers*, p. 15; *Travail* Sept. 1841, p. 22; *Artisan* 13 Sept. 1842, p. 1; *Travail* 28 May 1848, p. 1; *AR* 14 Jan. 1849, p. 1; *PS* 1 Mar. 1849, p. 2; Lemaire, Mollet, in Tartaret, *Commission Ouvrière*, pp. 136–7; C. Jones, *Political Secret*, p. 3; Vallès, *Cri du Peuple* 22 Mar. 1871, p. 1; Agulhon in Nadaud, *Mémoires*, pp. 23, 94n.; Amann, *Revolution*, p. 42; Perrot, 'Formation', p. 98.

50 Dalotel, *Aux origines*, p. 163.

51 E. London Female Total Abstinence Association, *NS* 30 Jan. 1841, p. 1.

52 *Chartist Pilot* 9 Dec. 1843, p. 3.

53 *Artisan* 3 Oct. 1830, pp. 1, 2; *Travail* (Lyons), Prospectus, p. 1; Skelton, *NS* 2 Apr. 1842, p. 7, 3 Sept. 1842, p. 1, O'Brien, 1 Dec. 1849, p. 7; *Red Republican* 6 July 1850, p. 21; Lucraft, *BH* 23 Sept. 1865, p. 1, Beales, 14 Apr. 1866, p. 17; Sewell, *Work and Revolution*, pp. 282–3; Joyce, *Visions*, p. 65; Finn, *After Chartism*, pp. 251, 264, 300.

54 Searle, *Entrepreneurial Politics*, pp. 25–30.

55 *FLA* Jan. 1860, pp. 4, 12.

56 Prothero, *Artisans*, pp. 216–17; *LL* 21 Oct. 1848, p. 92; *WM* 3 Jan. 1866, p. 1; Tolain, *Quelques vérités*, p. 23; Crossick, *Artisan Elite*, p. 222; Crossick, 'Gentlemen', p. 153.

57 *BH* 20 Jan. 1866, p. 6; R. J. Halliday, *John Stuart Mill* (1976), pp. 35–6; Auslander, 'Perceptions of beauty', p. 163.

58 *Artisan* 22 Sept. 1830, p. 1; *Tait's* in *O* 5 July 1851, p. 6; *BBCU* Nov. 1852, pp. 2–3; Drake, *PP* 27 Feb. 1858, p. 1; Perdiguier, *Mémoires*, pp. 232, 319; Guépin, *Nantes*, p. 478; T. Wright, *Habits*, p. vii; J. Vincent, *Formation*, p. 80; Bédarida, *Social History*, p. 52; Gossez, 'Diversité', 448; Plessis, *Rise and Fall*, pp. 126–8; Crossick, 'Gentlemen', p. 154; Moore, *Injustice*, p. 127; Sewell, *Work and Revolution*, pp. 282–3.

59 Lefrançais, *Souvenirs* I, p. 133.

60 G. J. Holyoake, *Moral Errors which Endanger the Permanence of Co-operative Societies* (Huddersfield, 1863), p. 3.

61 Berthaut, *Ruche* Feb. 1841, pp. 8, 10; *RP* 10 Apr. 1848, p. 1; Rancière, *Nuit*, pp. 217.

62 *CP* 3 Apr. 1848, p. 4; Agulhon, *Ville ouvrière*, p. 318; Rancière, *Nuit*, p. 111; 'Organisation des associations ouvrières', 29 Aug. 1849, Aa 432, fol. 418; Barthélemy to Blanqui, 4 July 1850, NAF 9581, fol. 209.

63 *Indicateur* 9 Oct. 1834, p. 3; Perdiguier, *Ruche* Apr. 1844, p. 102; Perdiguier, *Mémoires*, pp. 156–7; Raspail, *Avenues*, p. 121; Gossez, 'Diversité', 441–4; Roger Price, *French Second Republic*, p. 181; Varlin, *Commerce* 20 June 1869, p. 1.

64 Savinien-Lapointe, *Union* July–Aug–Sept. 1845, p. 1.

65 *TAHP* 19 Oct. 1850, p. 133.

66 Little, 'Chartism and Liberalism', p. 323; *TC* 25 Feb. 1859, p. 6; P. Johnson, 'Class law', esp. 147–9, 155–8, 165–8; Poulot, *Question sociale*, pp. 158–9; Tholfsen, *Working Class Radicalism*, pp. 246–7; Biagini, *Liberty*, p. 146.

67 Hogg, *Bolton Chron.* 19 Mar. 1831, p. 3.

68 *Bell's New Weekly Messenger*, quoted in *Destructive* 1 June 1833, p. 134.

69 Wakley, *PMG* 20 Sept. 1834, p. 262; E. Thompson, *Making*, p. 90; Nadaud, *Mémoires*, p. 386; Agulhon, *Republican Experiment*, p. 126; Gillespie, *Labor and Politics*, p. 262; Crossick, *Artisan Elite*, p. 221; Biagini, *Liberty*, pp. 259–65. The verse is quoted in A. Taylor, 'Modes', p. 458.

70 Harney, *NS* 26 Feb. 1848, p. 3. See also Doyle, 28 Mar. 1846, p. 1.

71 Nadaud, *Mémoires*, p. 229; Loubere, *Louis Blanc*, p. 57; Mitard, 'Ledru-Rollin'.

72 Joyce, *Visions*, p. 52–3; Nadaud, *Mémoires*, pp. 29–30, 140, 262n., 301 and n., 302–3; Weill, *Histoire*, pp. 155–6; Mitard, 'Ledru-Rollin'; Agulhon, *Republic in the Village*, p. 153; Rancière, *Nuit*, pp. 167–8.

73  *BH* 5 Mar. 1864, p. 4, 23 Apr. 1864, p. 7.

74  E. Thompson, *Making*, p. 623; Epstein, *Lion*, pp. 91–3; Belchem, 'Henry Hunt'; Joyce, *Visions*, pp. 38–40; Kersosie, 4 May 1834, CC 590; *Ruche* Apr.–May 1847, p. 110; Zeldin, *France* I, pp. 484–6; Truquin, *Mémoires*, p. 66; Wilkes, *BH* 25 June 1864, p. 1, 9 Sept. 1871, p. 11; Finlen, *C* 30 June 1866, p. 5; Crossick, *Artisan Elite*, pp. 216, 223–6.

75  *Bath Journal* 27 Mar. 1837, p. 4; *Bath Chronicle* 23 Mar. 1837, p. 3, 6 Apr. 1837, p. 3; Crossick, *Artisan Elite*, pp. 199, 222–3.

76  Webber, *Cleave's Weekly Police Gazette* 5 Mar. 1836; *O* 10 Apr. 1852, pp. 347–50, 17 Apr. 1852, p. 373; Gillespie, *Labor and Politics*, p. 125, 294; Tolain, *Quelques vérités*, esp. pp. 9, 11, 16–18; Manifeste, Tartaret, *Commission Ouvrière*, pp. 43–50; *BH* 30 May 1863, p. 4, 14 May 1864, p. 1, 14 Apr. 1866, p. 1, 21 Apr. 1866, p. 1, 28 Apr. 1866, p. 1, 9 Sept. 1871, p. 11; *P* 26 Apr. 1849, p. 4; Gaumont, *Histoire*, p. 575; Foulon, *Eugène Varlin*, pp. 28–9; *St. Crispin* 6 Feb. 1869, p. 71; Leventhal, *Respectable Radical*, p. 128; Shipton, *Centaur* 17 May 1879, p. 5; Moss, *Origins*, p. 65; Crossick, *Artisan Elite*, pp. 222–3.

77  Lefrançais, *Souvenirs* I, p. 267; Soutter, *Recollections*, pp. 29, 45–6.

78  Tolain, *Quelques vérités*, p. 35.

79  *Artisan* 22 Sept. 1830, p. 1; Kydd, *NS* 27 May 1848, p. 8; Vermorel, Tartaret, *Exposition Universelle*, p. 15; Rancière, *Nuit*, pp. 54, 167, 176–7, 219; Crossick, *Artisan Elite*, pp. 219–20; *EO* Oct. 1844, p. 147 (charity); *OSM* 10 Sept. 1840, p. 473 (Poor Law); O'Neill, *St. Crispin* 7 Aug. 1869, p. 64.

80  Coutant, *Ruche* Oct. 1843, p. 4; Prothero, *Artisans*, pp. 185–6. See also *JO* 19 Sept. 1830, p. 1; *RP* 14 Oct. 1847, p. 1.

81  *Bon Sens* 28 Oct 1832, p. 3.

82  Searle, *Entrepreneurial Politics*, pp. 129, 266–8.

83  *Artisan* 22 Sept. 1830, p. 1, 26 Sept. 1830, p. 1, 10 Oct. 1830, p. 2; *JO* 19 Sept. 1830, p. 1, 28 Oct. 1830, p. 1; *Ruche* Dec. 1839, p. 1; *Pop.* 30 Jan, 1842, p. 46; *EO* June 1844, p. 8; Marseilles, *A* Apr. 1847, p. 487. See also Isambert, *Christianisme*, p. 228; J. Vincent, *Formation*, pp. xii, xiv; Rancière, *Nuit*, pp. 270–1.

84  *Ruche* Dec. 1839, p. 5.

85  *AR*, Prospectus.

86  'Dessinateurs et tisseurs', in *Rapports des Délégués Dessinateurs et Tisseurs*, p. 22. See also Gast, in Prothero, *Artisans*, p. 332.

87  Nadaud, *Mémoires*, p. 196; *Artisan* 26 Sept. 1830, p. 1; Murray, *WM* 28 Aug. 1861, p. 77; *BH* 10 Oct. 1863, p. 1; *PS* 4 Mar. 1849, p. 2; Corbon, *Secret*, pp. 76–8; *St. Crispin* 2 Apr. 1870, p. 159; Moore, *Injustice*, pp. 160, 167; Biagini, *Liberty*, p. 339.

88  Perdiguier, *Mémoires*, p. 243. See also Mora, *Union* Oct. 1844, p. 1; *Pop.* 22 Nov. 1845, p. 204; Nadaud, *Mémoires*, p. 282n.

89  Lowery, 'Passages', pp. 90, 97–8; Nadaud, *Mémoires*, p. 229; Soutter, *Recollections*, p. 29; Little, 'Chartism and Liberalism', p. 216. See above, p. 99.

90  *OSM* 4 June 1840, p. 446; *Artisan* 22 Sept. 1830, p. 1; *JO* 19 Sept. 1830, p. 1; *AR*, Prospectus; Vernon, *Politics*, pp. 310–13; McCalman, *Radical Underworld*, p. 48; Rancière, *Nuit, passim*; Perrot, 'Formation', p. 96.

91 Rancière, 'Good times', p. 50; Rancière, 'Myth', 10.

92 *MWA* 20 May 1865, p. 5; *BH* 14 Apr. 1866, p. 1. See also C. Johnson, *Utopian Communism*, p. 67; Tyrrell, 'Class consciousness', 104.

93 Girard, *Garde Nationale* , p. 363; Ranciere, *Nuit*, pp. 256ff.

94 Arlès-Dufour to Enfantin, 25 Mar. 1848, Enfantin Papers, Bibliothèque de l'Arsénal, 7683

95 *National* 3 July 1845, p. 1; Ridley, *NS* 5 Mar. 1842, p. 1; J. Vincent, *Formation*, p. 125; Agulhon, *Republican Experiment*, p. 96; Sewell, *Work and Revolution*, pp. 269–71; Reddy, *Rise of Market Culture*, pp. 148–82; Storch, 'Plague', p. 62; D. Thompson, *Chartists*, pp. 243–51; Joyce, *Visions*, p. 77.

96 28 Sept. 1840, F7 3890; Dalotel, *Aux Origines*, p. 37.

97 7 Nov. 1832, F7 3886.

98 Alison, quoted in P. Hollis (ed.), *Class and Conflict in Nineteenth-Century England 1815–1850* (1973), p. 215; D. Thompson, *Chartists*, p. 271.

99 Elt, *Morning Advertiser*, in Place Coll. set 56, vol. Jan.–Aug. 1844, fol. 180; Epstein, *Lion*, p. 276; G. Jones, 'Language of Chartism', p. 44.

100 Belchem, 'Feargus O'Connor', pp. 276–8; D. Thompson, *Chartists*, p. 233.

101 Jador, *Procès*, p. 3; *GT* 8 Mar. 1834, p. 422; Favre, *De la coalition*, p. 7; Nadaud, *Mémoires*, p. 262; C. Johnson, 'Revolution of 1830', pp. 155–6.

102 Monfalcon, *Histoire*, p. 100.

103 Dalotel, *Aux origines*, pp. 331–40.

104 *RWN* 22 Sept. 1850, p. 5.

105 Police, 14 Mar. 1848, C 930, dos. VI, 645.

106 *OT* 3 June 1848, p. 4.

107 Le Havre, *CP* 14 Apr. 1848, p. 4; *RP* 14 May 1848, p. 2, 3 July 1848, p. 2; Taylor, *MWA* 20 May 1865, p. 8; Mazuy, *Essai*, p. 54; Molinari, *Mouvement socialiste*, p. 2; Weill, *Histoire*, pp. 213, 222; Chazelas, 'Episode', 241, 247, 336–7; Gossez, *Ouvriers*, pp. 48–9, 69–73, 90–1, 232; Agulhon, *Republic in the Village*, p. 259; Agulhon, *Republican Experiment*, pp. 94–6, 99; Roger Price, *French Second Republic*, pp. 110–13, 149, 179; Amann, *Revolution*, p. 184; Merriman, *Agony*, pp. 7–9; Christofferson, 'Urbanization', 196.

108 *TP* 16 Mar. 1848, p. 1.

109 Gautier, *VR* 3 May 1848, p. 2.

110 *CP* 23 Mar. 1848, p. 3, 1 May 1848, p. 3; *AR* 1 July 1849, p. 2; Pottier, *Œuvres*, p. 55; Agulhon, *Ville ouvrière*, p. 288.

111 Roger Price, *French Second Republic*, p. 151; Vigier, *Seconde République* II, p. 338; Margadant, *French Peasants*, pp. 301–2.

112 *A* Sept. 1840, pp. 5–6; *Peuple Constituant* 3 Mar. 1848, p. 1. For an excellent account of the National Guard, see Girard, *Garde Nationale*.

113 Chazelas, 'Episode', 174–6, 179–80; Merriman, *Agony*, p. 5.

114 *VR* 18 May 1848, p. 1; *P* 3 Dec. 1848, p. 1; Chazelas, 'Episode', 252–4; Gaumont, *Histoire*, pp. 354–5; Gossez, *Ouvriers*, pp. 223–4; Agulhon, *Ville ouvrière*, pp. 270, 280, 287; House, 'Civil–military relations', esp. pp. 151, 156–7, 163; Girard, *Garde Nationale*, pp. 173, 363; Amann, *Revolution*, p. 81; Merriman, *Agony*, p. 133; Margadant, *French Peasants*, pp. 287–8; Stewart-McDougall, *Artisan Republic*, pp. 33, 35, 37, 40, 42, 66; Fasel, 'Urban workers', 671–2.

115 Gossez, 'Diversité', 449, 455; Agulhon, *Republic in the Village*, p. 280;

Agulhon, *Republican Experiment*, pp. 92, 105–6; Margadant, *French Peasants*, p. 325.

116 Perrot, 'Formation', p. 95.

117 *RN* 10 Apr. 1859, p. 7; Lockwood, *Tools*, p. 94; Agulhon, *Ville ouvrière*, p. 192; Berridge, 'Popular journalism', pp. 69, 96, 343–6, 355–8, 361, 363, 376, 378.

## 8. POLITICAL ACTION AND ORGANISATION

1 *Bon Sens* 28 Oct. 1832, p. 2, 23 May 1834, p. 3; Proc.-Gen. Lyons, July 1857, BB30 379.

2 Berjeau, *VP* 10 Dec. 1849, pp. 3–4.

3 Morris, 'Voluntary societies'; Molinari, *Mouvement socialiste*, p. 29; Dalotel, *Aux origines*, p. 17.

4 Grey to William IV, 19 June 1832, in Henry Earl Grey (ed.), *The Reform Act, 1832. The Correspondence of the Late Earl Grey with his Majesty King William IV and with Sir Herbert Taylor from Nov. 1830 to June 1832* (1867), 2 vols., I, p. 472.

5 O'Connor, *NS* 10 Feb. 1838, p. 3; P. Fraser, 'Public petitioning and Parliament before 1832', *History* 46 (1961).

6 3 Oct. 1843, F7 3892; Nadaud, *Mémoires*, p. 303; Stewart-McDougall, *Artisan Republic*, p. 25; C. Johnson, *Utopian Communism*, p. 106; Merriman, *Agony*, p. 136.

7 Lefrançais, *Souvenirs* II, p. 295.

8 NA MS 155, fols. 6–8, 11–47; 474–6; Dalotel, *Aux origines*, pp. 18, 22–4, 29–30, 39–43; Truquin, *Mémoires*, pp. 157, 161.

9 *BH* 25 Nov. 1865, p. 4; Garrard, *Leadership and Power*, p. 116; Vernon, *Politics*, ch. 1 and pp. 64–70.

10 *MG* 26 Sept. 1838, p. 2.

11 *NS* 1 Nov. 1845, p. 1; see also Lowery, 'Passages', p. 166.

12 Robert, 'Cortèges', pp. 46, 48.

13 CC 612, registers 1, 2, 3, 5; 614, 3ème Liasse; 615; 1er and 2ème Liasses; Weill, *Histoire*, pp. 84–5.

14 Epstein, 'Radical dining', 282–4.

15 Elland, *NS* 3 Mar. 1838, p. 5, Halifax, 5 Jan. 1839, p. 8, London, 28 Sept. 1844, p. 1, 27 Sept. 1845, p. 5; *A* Oct. 1844, p. 5; E. Yeo, 'Culture and constraint', p. 168.

16 Weill, *Histoire*, pp. 141–2; Stewart-McDougall, *Artisan Republic*, p. 26.

17 Blanqui, Nov. 1848, NAF 9581, fols. 143–4; *P* 29 Nov. 1848, p. 1, 19 Jan. 1849, p. 4, 24 Jan. 1849, p. 2, 3 Mar. 1849, p. 4; *PS* 8 Apr. 1849, p. 3; *Banquet des Travailleurs Socialistes*; Agulhon, *Ville ouvrière*, p. 301; Merriman, *Agony*, pp. 84–5; Berenson, *Populist Religion*, pp. 76, 95–6; Dalotel, *Aux origines*, p. 18; Baugham, 'French Banquet campaign'.

18 Robert, 'Cortèges', pp. 20–1, 104–6; Merriman, *Agony*, p. 83.

19 Robert, 'Cortèges', pp. 119, 154–61; Agulhon, *Republican Experiment*, pp. 90–1; Tilly, 'Cake of custom'; Merriman, *Agony*, pp. 86, 88.

20 *Political Examiner* 30 Mar. 1853, pp. 67–8; Raspail, *Avenues*, p. 340; Weill, *Histoire*, pp. 316–7.

21 *Pioneer* 29 Mar. 1834, p. 272, 5 Apr. 1834, p. 288; *G* 23 Mar. 1834, p. 944; *PMG* 12 Apr. 1834, p. 78; Huggett, *NS* 28 Nov. 1840, p. 5, 23 July 1842, p. 5, 30 July 1842, p. 1, 12 Aug. 1843, p. 2.

22 Tartaret, *Exposition Universelle*, p. 152; *BH* 30 May 1863, p. 4.

23 Poulot, *Question sociale*, p. 206; Cottereau, 'Denis Poulot's *Le Sublime*', pp. 163–8; Dalotel, *Aux origines*, pp. 22, 108.

24 *Annuaire du Rhône* (1842), p. 100; *M* 31 Jan. 1870, p. 3.

25 *NS* 17 May 1842, p. 7.

26 *C* 16 Mar. 1867, p. 1, 13 Apr. 1867, p. 1; *WM* 22 Sept. 1866, p. 131.

27 Vernon, *Politics*, pp. 64–70.

28 *NS* 9 Feb. 1839, p. 3; D. Vincent, *Testaments*, p. 135; Epstein, *Lion*, pp. 90–1, 110–16; D. Jones, *Chartism*, p. 80.

29 Vernon, *Politics*, pp. 209–11, 232–4; Prothero, 'William Benbow', 150–3; Belchem, 'Henry Hunt'; Belchem, 'Feargus O'Connor', pp. 269–71; Epstein, *Lion*, pp. 110–23, 157–64; Finn, *After Chartism*, p. 106; *WM* 14 July 1866, p. 13.

30 Molinari, *Mouvement socialiste*, pp. 29–30; Poulot, *Question sociale*, p. 400. See also *P* 21 Nov. 1848, p. 8.

31 Garrard, *Leadership and Power*, pp. 124, 211; Vernon, *Politics*, pp. 18–47, 155–8.

32 *OT* 16 June 1848, p. 1; Soutter, *Recollections*, p. 36; Lefrançais, *Souvenirs* II, p. 314; Robert, 'Cortèges', p. 44; Vernon, *Politics*, pp. 66–7, 125–6, 150–1, 225–8.

33 Finn, *After Chartism*, pp. 295–7.

34 *NS* 31 Aug. 1844, p. 1, Clark, 11 Mar. 1848, p. 1; *LL* 16 Sept. 1848, p. 51; Lucraft, *PP* 13 Feb. 1858, p. 4; D. Thompson, *Chartists*, p. 129; Finn, *After Chartism*, p. 85.

35 Vilain, *CP* 15 Apr. 1848, p. 4.

36 Reports 4, 12 June, C 930, dos. V, 681, 697; June reports, C 932B; Nadaud, *Mémoires*, pp. 342, 351–2.

37 NA MS 155, fol. 60; Dalotel, *Aux origines*, pp. 26, 39–40, 349; Richard, 'Débuts', 85.

38 Garibaldian committee, *WM* 1 Nov. 1862, p. 286.

39 *BH* 2 Apr. 1864, pp. 1, 4, 23 Apr. 1864, p. 1, 30 Apr. 1864, pp. 1, 4, 6, 7 May 1864, p. 1, 14 May 1864, p. 3, 28 May, p. 1; Bell, 'Reform League', pp. 47–9; A. Taylor, 'Modes', pp. 333–4, 451, 453, 483.

40 *BH* 7 June 1873, pp. 7, 9–10; *People's Advocate* 31 July 1875, p. 2; A. Taylor, ' "Commons-stealers" '; Moberg, 'George Odger', p. 347; Marlow, 'London working men's clubs', p. 30.

41 Hamer, *Politics of Electoral Pressure*.

42 NA MS 155, fol. 462; Dalotel, *Aux origines*, pp. 34, 39–41, 125–6, 292, 296, 298.

43 Pilbeam, *Republicanism*, p. 11.

44 Pref. Pol. to Min. of Int., 9 Sept. 1848, and Parquet letter 30 Oct. 1848, in 'Clubs et associations' (Cour de Paris (1845–1850)), BB18 1474B; Berenson, *Populist Religion*, p. 94; Merriman, *Agony*, p. 55; Margadant, *French Peasants*, p. 111.

45 Tolain, *Quelques vérités*, p. 20; Lefrançais, *Souvenirs* II, p. 349; Dalotel, *Aux origines*, pp. 38–9.

46  NA MS 155, fols. 468–71; Dalotel, *Aux origines*, p. 39.

47  *BH* 14 May 1864, pp. 1, 4, 21 May 1864, p. 4, 28 May 1864, p. 1, 11 June 1864, p. 1, 25 June 1864, p. 1, 2 July 1864, p. 1, 23 July 1864, p. 1.

48  *JP* June 1834, p. 3.

49  J. Vincent, *Formation*, pp. 58, 60, 82–3; Phillips, *Great Reform Bill*, p. 48; Finn, *After Chartism*, pp. 105–18; Vernon, pp. 106, 131–2, 142–51.

50  Cooper, *Life*, p. 171.

51  Coutant, *Ruche* May 1844, p. 134; Raspail, *Avenues*, p. 109.

52  Dupont, *Histoire*, pp. 335–6; I. Collins, *Government and Newspaper Press*, esp. pp. 62, 72, 86, 99; Zeldin, *France* II, p. 496; Jardin and Tudesq, *Restoration and Reaction*, p. 185; Touchard, *Gloire* II, p. 66.

53  Humphrey, *Robert Applegarth*, p. 119.

54  See Hollis, *Pauper Press*; Wiener, *War of the Unstamped*.

55  *Glaneuse* 18 Dec. 1831, pp. 1–3; I. Collins, *Government and Newspaper Press*, p. 72; Raspail, *Avenues*, pp. 154–5; Weill, *Histoire*, pp. 89–90; *Bon Sens* prospectus, p. 3.

56  Laponneraye, Aa 421, dos. 41365; Leneveux, *TO* 4 June 1865, p. 3; *O* 5 Apr. 1851, p. 223; Raspail, *Avenues*, pp. 243, 251n.; Gossez, *Ouvriers*, p. 291; D. Thompson, 'Presse de la classe ouvrière', pp. 17–19.

57  2 Mar. 1848, NAF 9951, fols. 111–12.

58  C 934, 'Enquête', dos. VIII (8), 692; *A* 12 Mar. 1848, p. 83, 20 June 1848, p. 179, 10 July 1848, p. 188; *RP* 27 Feb. 1848, p. 1; Lefrançais, *Souvenirs* I, p. 64; I. Collins, *Government and Newspaper Press*, p. 101; Vigier, *Seconde République* II, pp. 270, 272; Knight, Place Coll. set 70, fol. 420; Lowery, 'Passages', pp. 93–4; Weill, *Histoire*, p. 238; Merriman, 'Radicalisation', p. 215; Merriman, *Agony*, p. 25.

59  Monckton Deverill, *NS* 13 Nov. 1841, p. 4; *BTC* June 1850, p. 35.

60  Tailors, *WA* 23 Dec. 1865, p. 8; *Glaneuse* 22 Dec. 1832, p. 3; [C. M. Smith], *Working Man's Way*, p. 188; Nadaud, *Mémoires*, pp. 140–1; Rémusat, *Mémoires* III, p. 420; Poulot, *Question sociale*, p. 239; C. Johnson, *Utopian Communism*, p. 146; Agulhon, *Ville ouvrière*, p. 318; Humphrey, *Robert Applegarth*, p. 2; J. Vincent, *Formation*, p. 58; Gibson, *Social History*, p. 97; Merriman, *Agony*, p. 28; *JP*, Prospectus, p. 1; Biagini, *Liberty*, p. 26.

61  Vernon, *Politics*, pp. 142–7, 159–60, 180–1.

62  'Propagande démocratique et sociale', Aa 432, fol. 409; Carlile, *Prompter* 20 Aug. 1831, p. 734; Cleave, *PMG* 29 Sept. 1832, p. 547; Epstein, *Lion*, pp. 68–77; Delente, CC 594; de la Hodde, *Histoire des sociétés secrètes*, p. 133; Monfalcon, *Histoire*, p. 146; Amann, *Revolution*, pp. 48–9.

63  Dunsmore, 'Working Classes', pp. 59–60.

64  Agulhon, *Ville ouvrière*, p. 314; Berenson, *Populist Religion*, pp. 81–2, 174–5, 182–3.

65  Cabet, *Salut*, pp. 17–18; McPhee, 'Crisis', 75; Raspail, *Avenues*, p. 230; Weill, *Histoire*, pp. 76–7; Agulhon, *Republican Experiment*, p. 19; Vigier, *Seconde République* I, p. 308; Berenson, *Populist Religion*, p. 99; Stewart-McDougall, *Artisan Republic*, p. 111; Leventhal, *Respectable Radical*, p. 45; J. Vincent, *Formation*, p. 178.

66  Cooper, *Life*, pp. 179–80; Colley, 'Whose nation?', 105; Vernon, *Politics*, ch. 7; Epstein, *Lion*, pp. 92–3, 216–9.

67  *C* 8 Sept. 1866, p. 4; *WM* 11 Aug. 1866, p. 58; *WM* 5 Sept. 1866, pp. 111–12; *EL* 3 Nov. 1866, pp. 245–6.

68  D. Johnson, *Guizot*, pp. 197–9, 244; Agulhon, *Ville ouvrière*, pp. 254, 258–60.

69  Epstein, *Lion*, p. 71; *C* 22 Sept. 1866, 29 Sept. 1866, p. 4.

70  Nadaud, *Mémoires*, p. 242; *Ami de la Charte* 14 Sept. 1829, p. 2; Bouillon, 'Démocrates-socialistes', 80; Agulhon, *Ville ouvrière*, p. 310; Agulhon, *Republican Experiment*, pp. 85–8; Berenson, *Populist Religion*, p. 132.

71  Weill, *Histoire*, p. 365.

72  NA MS 155, fol. 643.

73  Biagini, *Liberty*, pp. 4, 106–7, 114, 356, 371–2, 381, 396.

74  E. London females, *Charter*, 27 Oct. 1839, p. 640; Cameron, *NS* 7 Nov. 1840, p. 1; Lovett, *NS* 1 May 1841, p. 3; Lowery, ' Passages', p. 173; Prothero, *Artisans*, pp. 326–7; Epstein, *Lion*, pp. 220–35; Sykes, 'Popular politics', pp. 606–22.

75  Philp, *NS* 15 Aug. 1840, p. 7, Philp, 15 May 1841, p. 7.

76  D. Jones, *Chartism*, p. 103.

77  E. Yeo, 'Culture and constraint', p. 170; E. Yeo, 'Robert Owen', pp. 104–5; Epstein, 'Organisational and cultural aspects'; D. Jones, *Chartism*, pp. 78–9; Sykes, 'Popular politics', pp. 623–33.

78  O'Connor, *NS*, 18 Jan. 1851, p. 1; C. Johnson, *Utopian Communism*, pp. 209–13.

79  'Propagande démocratique et sociale', Aa 432, fol. 410; *P* 29 Mar. 1849, p. 4; Weill, *Histoire*, p. 259; Berenson, *Populist Religion*, pp. 79–81.

80  Margadant, *French Peasants*, p. 165; Gaumont, *Histoire*, pp. 271–2; Vigier, *Seconde République* II, p. 263; Roger Price, *French Second Republic*, pp. 202–4; Merriman, *Agony*, p. 43; Berenson, *Populist Religion*, pp. 85–94; Stewart-McDougall, *Artisan Republic*, pp. 117, 123, 125–6.

81  Margadant, *French Peasants*, p. 163.

82  *Ballot* 11 Feb. 1860, p. 3; Potter, *BH* 25 Feb. 1865, p. 4, 22 July 1865, p. 1, 23 Sept. 1865, p. 1, 7 Oct. 1865, p. 1, 9 Mar. 1867, p. 1; *MWA* 3 June 1865, p. 5, 22 July 1865, pp. 4–5; Bell, 'Reform League', p. 144; *WA* 9 Dec. 1865, pp. 4–5; *NR* 6 Feb. 1870, p. 95; A. Taylor, 'Modes', pp. 586.

83  *BH* 1 Apr. 1865, pp. 1, 2, 15 Apr. 1865, p. 1; *PP* 16 Jan. 1858, p. 1; *NR* 27 Oct. 1860, p. 5; Gillespie, *Labor and Politics*, p. 279; Leventhal, *Respectable Radical*, p. 92; Bell, 'Reform League'; Dunsmore, 'Working classes'.

84  Searle, *Entrepreneurial Politics*, p. 223 n. 108; Dunsmore, 'Working classes', pp. 133–4.

85  *Newcastle Chronicle* 26 May 1832.

86  *Tribune* 10 June 1832, p. 3. See also Strasbourg, 24 Apr. 1834, CC 590; *Voix des Femmes* 21 Apr. 1848, p. 2; Moore, *Injustice*, p. 368; Perrot, *Ouvriers en grève*, p. 76.

87  Perdiguier, *Mémoires*, p. 152.

88  D. Thompson, *Chartists*, pp. 121–4, 132, 135; Stewart-McDougall, *Artisan Republic*, pp. 23, 136–7.

89  *NU* May 1858, p. 2.

90  D. Thompson, *Chartists*, pp. 120–34; J. Vincent, *Formation*, pp. 8, 48; Owen, *Darkened Room*, p. 15; B. Taylor, *Eve*, p. 81; Vernon, *Politics*, pp. 233, 238, 249; A. Clark, *Struggle*, pp. 220–52.

91  Soutter, *Recollections*, pp. 33–6; Gillespie, *Labor and Politics*, pp. 260–1; Bell, 'Reform League', pp. 71, 130–1; Moberg, 'George Odger', pp. 145, 245–6; 295–6; Dunsmore, 'Working classes', pp. 42, 211; Leventhal, *Respectable Radical*, pp. 71, 81–2; E. Yeo, 'Culture and constraint', p. 163.

92  There is an excellent account of the strikes in Sykes, 'Popular politics', ch. 15.

## 9. EDUCATION AND CIVILISATION

1  Raspail, *Avenues*, p. 157.

2  Jouy, *Adresse*, p. 9.

3  [Martin], *Nouveau catéchisme*, p. 7; Carlile, *G* 21 Apr. 1833, p. 161; Neesom, *Charter* 8 Sept. 1839, p. 527; E. Thompson, *Making*, p. 733; *CP* 9 Mar. 1848, p. 1; Prothero, *Artisans*, pp. 193–4, 297–8.

4  Wallarge, *WM* 1 Nov. 1861, p. 127; Petrie, *Works*, pp. 5, 6, 8–9; *Glaneuse* 29 Nov. 1832, p. 2.

5  *NS* 22 June 1839, p. 4.

6  *JO* 4 Nov. 1830, p. 2; *Projet de Petition des Petits Commerçants*; *Bon Sens* 28 Oct. 1832, p. 3; Société des Droits de l'Homme, *Education Nationale*, pp. 13–15; *LD* 12 Nov. 1837, p. 481; *M* 4 Feb. 1870, p. 1; Biagini, *Liberty*, p. 169.

7  Wood, *SA* 23 Sept. 1848, p. 140.

8  *JP* prospectus, p. 1.

9  SDH, *Education Nationale*, p. 13.

10  Devlin, *CC* 14 Sept. 1844, p. 117; Lockwood, *Tools*, p. 113.

11  Broadhurst, *Story*, p. 22; Lovett, *Life*, pp. 9–11, 17–19, 26, 51; Perdiguier, *Mémoires*, pp. 29–30, 305; Agulhon, 'Martin Nadaud', pp. 10, 21; D. Vincent, *Bread*, p. 113.

12  *Menuisiers carossiers*, F12 3117; *NS* 26 Dec. 1840, p. 3; Dupuy, *Ruche* Aug. 1841, p. 9.

13  'Athenée des ouvriers', Feb. 1831, CP 3706, fol. 202. See also *JO* 21 Nov. 1830, pp. 1–2, 28 Nov. 1830, p. 1; Prothero, *Artisans*, pp. 191–203, 297–8.

14  *Bon Sens* prospectus, p. 1; Weill, *Histoire*, p. 44.

15  Lechevalier to Committee, CC 615, 1ère Liasse; Bibliothèque populaire, CC 617 3ème Liasse; *Tribune* 3 June 1832, p. 2; Raspail, *Avenues*, p. 211; Weill, *Histoire*, p. 57–8.

16  *Glaneuse* 29 Nov. 1832, p. 2, 3.

17  Raspail, *Avenues*, pp. 153–9, 187; Raspail, *Lettres* I, pp. 326–7; Aa 421, dos. 14639; Laponneraye, *Défense*, pp. 2–3; Verax, *Crisis* 14 June 1834, pp. 78–80; Agulhon, 'Problème', 59.

18  Cagniard, CC 595; *Glaneuse* 24 Oct. 1833, p. 3, 5 Nov. 1833, p. 3; Faure, 'Mouvements populaires', 85–6. See above, p. 109.

19  Lovett, Place Papers, Add. MS 27,822, fol. 25; Lovett, *Life*, p. 55.

20  E.g. Marylebone, *NS* 26 Dec. 1840, p. 2, Wall, 6 Feb. 1841, p. 1; north London, 20 Mar. 1841, p. 1, Bermondsey, 31 July 1841, p. 7, City of London, 18 Sept. 1841, p. 7, 13 Nov. 1841, p. 2, Dockhead, 28 May 1842, p. 2, Marylebone, 18 June 1842, p. 5, Finsbury, 26 Sept. 1846, p. 6, Soho, 10 Oct. 1846, p. 8, 17 Oct. 1846, p. 8, Finsbury, 18 Sept. 1847, p. 1.

21 *RP* 9 June 1848, p. 3; *A* 11 June 1848, p. 178; *P* 3 Mar. 1849, p. 4.

22 *M* 29 Dec. 1869, p. 3, 7 Jan. 1870, p. 3; Gaumont, *Histoire*, pp. 518–9; K. Auspitz, *The Radical Bourgeoisie. The Ligue de l'Enseignement and the Origins of the Third Republic 1866–1885* (Cambridge, 1982), chs.1–2.

23 Raspail, *Avenues*, pp. 229–31.

24 Burns, 'Strategy', p. 166; Finn, *After Chartism*, p. 85.

25 BB24 419–430, 1467 Fabre, 431–9, 3089 Boins; Weill, *Histoire*, pp. 248, 310–11, 354.

26 T. Wright, *Habits*, pp. 11–13, 18–19.

27 *NS* 22 June 1839, p. 4; Pilling, in *Trial of Feargus O'Connor, Esquire, and 58 other Chartists* (Manchester, 1843), p. 252.

28 Tartaret, *Commission Ouvrière*, pp. 80–107; CP 3706, fol. 202; *BH* 28 Nov. 1863, p. 6; Humphrey, *Robert Applegarth*, pp. 173, 192–6; Lockwood, *Tools*, p. 71; R. D. Anderson, *Education in France 1848–1870* (Oxford, 1975), pp. 195–6; Sheridan, 'Social and economic foundations', p. 470.

29 Truquin, *Mémoires*, p. 61; Nadaud, *Mémoires*, pp. 149, 156–7, 329–30. See also Berenson, *Populist Religion*, p. 50.

30 Lovett, *Life*, p. 28–9; *Republican* 27 May 1825, pp. 668–9, 29 Dec. 1826, pp. 791–2; McCalman, *Radical Underworld*, p. 197.

31 Lovett, *Life*, pp. 17, 28–30, 32, 71–2; Perdiguier, *Mémoires*, p. 137; Gauny, *Philosophe plébéien*, p. 27; *Bakers' Record* 6 May 1871, p. 5; *St. Crispin* 5 June 1869, p. 289 (Odger); *BH* 7 June 1873, p. 1; Lefrançais, *Souvenirs* II, p. 316 (Tolain); Gaumont, *Histoire*, p. 527 (Malon); Lockwood, *Tools*, pp. 23, 49; Ragon, *Histoire*, p. 82; Leventhal, *Respectable Radical*, p. 9; Rancière, *Nuit*, p. 62; Moore, *Injustice*, p. 211.

32 *NS* 6 Mar. 1841, p. 8; Foulon, *Eugène Varlin*, pp. 16–24.

33 Roe, *Lamennais*, p. 5; Cholvy and Hilaire, *Histoire religieuse*, p. 170.

34 *WM* 28 Apr. 1866, p. 255 (Massey); T. Wright, *Habits*, p. 11; Poulot, *Question sociale*, pp. 139–40, 156–7; Perdiguier, *Mémoires*, p. 200; Leno, *Aftermath*, p. 20; B. Harrison, *Peaceable*, p. 163; D. Vincent, *Bread*, pp. 110–31, 177–8; Berenson, *Populist Religion*, pp. 50, 70; Pichois, 'Cabinets', 529–30; Leventhal, *Respectable Radical*, p. 8; Perrot, 'Formation', p. 99; Lockwood, *Tools*, pp. 30, 104, 108, 192; Chase, *People's Farm*, p. 19; Ragon, *Histoire*, p. 77.

35 Lockwood, *Tools*, p. 113.

36 D. Vincent, *Bread*, pp. 172–4.

37 Ragon, *Histoire*, p. 114; B. Harrison, *Peaceable*, p. 162; D. Vincent, *Bread*, p. 140–8; *St. Crispin* 5 June 1869, pp. 289–90 (Odger).

38 *Bakers' Record* 1 July 1871, p. 5; D. Vincent, *Bread*, pp. 181–3; Cameron, *BTC* 23 Sept. 1861, p. 98; Perdiguier, *Mémoires*, pp. 77, 158–9, 195.

39 D. Vincent, *Bread*, pp. 44, 127–8, 131.

40 Westminster, *G* Jan.–Mar. 1834; *Crisis* Jan.–Apr. 1834; *O* 16 June 1839, p. 33; *FSA* June 1836, pp. 83–4; *Cleave's* 27 Aug. 1836, p. 35; *O* 10 Jan. 1852 suppt, p. 7; Geary, *European Labour Protest*, p. 43.

41 *BTC* Oct. 1850, p. 51; *O* 20 Mar. 1852, pp. 318–19; Chauvet, *Ouvriers*, p. 478.

42 *Ruche* Apr.–May 1847, p. 112; *EL* 27 Aug. 1864, p. 2; *MWA* 25 Mar. 1865, p. 5; *BH* 27 May 1865, p. 4, 3 Sept. 1865, p. 1, 9 Dec. 1865, p. 1; 13 Jan. 1866, p. 7; *WM* 6 Jan. 1866, p. 6; *M* 29 Dec. 1869, p. 3.

43 T. Wright, *Habits*, pp. 11–12; Gossez, *Ouvriers*, pp. 29–30; D. Vincent, *Bread*, pp. 175–6.

44 Perdiguier, *Mémoires*, p. 299; Nadaud, *Mémoires*, p. 157; Dessolaire to Lamennais, 29 Dec. 1844, *Nouvelle Revue Rétrospective* 6 (1897), p. 296; Poulot, *Question sociale*, p. 135; Leno, *Aftermath*, p. 20; D. Vincent, *Bread*, pp. 160, 166–95; McCalman, *Radical Underworld*, pp. 256–7; Newman, 'Blouse and frock coat', 43; Bruhat, 'Anticléricalisme', p. 97; Vernon, *Politics*, pp. 288–9.

45 Brand, 'Conversion', 255.

46 *A* Aug. 1847, p. 558; Chauvet, *Ouvriers*, pp. 169–70; Leno, *Aftermath*, p. 42.

47 Nepireu, CC 608; E. Thompson, *Making*, pp. 88–9; D. Vincent, *Bread*, p. 133.

48 D. Vincent, *Bread*, pp. 133, 175–6; Gossez, *Ouvriers*, pp. 29–30; Moore, *Injustice*, p. 211; Vernon, *Politics*, p. 252.

49 Rancière, 'Reply', 45; Rancière, 'Good times', p. 50.

50 D. Vincent, *Bread*, pp. 170–1, 181–5; Lovett, *WMF* 13 Apr. 1833, p. 131, 18 May 1833, p. 176; Lovett, *Life*, pp. 24–5; Perdiguier, *Mémoires*, p. 137; Agulhon, 'Martin Nadaud', p. 21; Leno, *Aftermath*, p. 62.

51 *JO* 4 Nov. 1830, p. 2; Perdiguier, *Biographie*, p. 108; Perdiguier, *Mémoires*, pp. 7, 34, 94; D. Vincent, *Bread*, pp. 190–1.

52 E. Thompson, *Making*, p. 766.

53 E.g. Lovett, *Life*, pp. 147, 194, 202–7, 259; Prothero, *Artisans*, pp. 298–9.

54 Rancière, *Nuit*, p. 130.

55 Rancière, 'Myth', 6; Rancière, *Nuit*, p. 165, 201; *P* 11 Feb. 1849, p. 4.

56 Quoted in Lockwood, *Tools*, p. 115; D. Vincent, *Bread*, pp. 153–4.

57 Pottier, *Œuvres*, p. 55; Lockwood, *Tools*, p. 30; *A* 28 Feb. 1843, p. 44; *TO* 4 June 1865, p. 1; McClelland, 'Time to work', pp. 205–6; D. Vincent, *Bread*, pp. 147–85; Rancière, *Nuit*, pp. 20, 68, 353; Rancière in Gauny, *Philosophe plébéien*, p. 7.

58 *Bakers' Record* 1 July 1871, p. 5; O'Neill, *St. Crispin* 20 Feb. 1869, p. 100; D. Vincent, *Bread*, pp. 186–7; Moberg, 'George Odger', p. 9.

59 Perdiguier, *Mémoires*, pp. 158–9, 301; Rancière, in Gauny, *Philosophe plébéien*, p. 8.

60 *NS* 11 May 1844, p. 4.

61 D. Vincent, *Bread*, p. 186; I. V. Kovalev, *An Anthology of Chartist Literature* (Moscow, 1956); *WM* Apr. 1866, p. 255; *Tailor* 12 Jan. 1867, p. 213, 28 Dec. 1867, p. 96; *NR* 11 Aug. 1860, p. 8, 5 Jan. 1861, p. 2; *Ruche, passim*; *Union* Jan. 1845, p. 4 and *passim*; *Artisan* 8 Dec. 1842, p. 4; *Travailleur* (Liège) 24 Jan. 1849, p. 3; Perdiguier, *Biographie*, p. 106; Weill, *Histoire*, p. 172; Agulhon, *Ville ouvrière*, p. 191. The authoritative survey of worker-poetry in the 1840s is Lockwood, *Tools*. See also: Ragon, *Histoire*; Brochon, in Pottier, *Œuvres*; Newman, '*L'arme du siècle*'; D. Vincent, *Bread*, pp. 185, 192; Weill, *Histoire*, pp. 92, 169, 173; Agulhon, *Ville ouvrière*, pp. 189–92, 235, 237, 241; Agulhon, 'Problème', 57; Allen, 'Social history', 267; Little, 'Chartism and Liberalism', ch. 5.

62 Whitmore, quoted in Little, 'Chartism and Liberalism', p. 248.

63 *NS* 23 Dec. 1843, p. 3; *TA* 4 Mar. 1849, p. 7; *NR* 8 Jan. 1865, p. 20.

64 Chauvet, *Ouvriers*, pp. 605, 607, 610.

65 Maidment, 'Essayists and artizans'; Maidment, 'Class and cultural production'.
66 *L'Illustration* 29 Nov. 1845, p. 203, quoted in Briquet, *Agricol Perdiguier*, p. 147.
67 *Artisan* 6 Oct. 1842, p. 3; Lockwood, *Tools*, p. 128; Agulhon, *Ville ouvrière*, pp. 238–9, 252–3; Poncy, *Chanson de chaque métier*.
68 Lockwood, *Tools*, p. 307.
69 Lockwood, *Tools*, pp. 176–7, 230; Nadaud, *Mémoires*, pp. 283, 321–4, 331 and n.; Sewell, *Work and Revolution*, p. 236; Rancière, 'Myth', 7; Rancière, 'Reply', 43.
70 Cooper, *Purgatory*, quoted in Lockwood, *Tools*, p. 37. See also p. 193.
71 Lockwood, *Tools*, p. 118; Agulhon, *Ville ouvrière*, pp. 143, 186–7, 237; Ragon, *Histoire*, pp. 92, 96.
72 E. Thompson, *Making*, p. 55.

## 10. RELIGIONS AND PHILOSOPHY

1 Cooper, *Life*, esp. pp. 42–3, 47, 55–71, 95, 103, 107–11, 169, 313–15, 320–1, 347; *R* 8 Mar. 1848, p. 30; Massey *WM* 28 Apr. 1866, p. 255; Skelton, *NS* 1 Jan. 1848, p. 3, 8 Jan. 1848, p. 5, 19 Feb. 1848, p. 5, 8 Apr. 1848, p. 3; Devlin to Gray, 10 Mar. 1849, in [Devlin], *Strangers' Homes*; *St. Crispin* 20 Mar. 1869, pp. 157–8, 8 Jan. 1870, p. 13, 19 Feb. 1870, pp. 85–6; Devlin's friend O'Neill's autobiography serialised in *St. Crispin*, 2 Oct. 1869–12 Feb. 1870.
2 *NS* 27 Feb. 1841, p. 4, 2 Sept. 1843, p. 2, 17 May 1848, p. 8; *R*, e.g., 15 Sept. 1847, pp. 504–7, 13 Sept. 1848, p. 251; J. Devlin, *The Sydenham Sunday* (1853); *PP* 19 Feb. 1853, p. 6.
3 *NS* 29 May 1847, p. 1; *Sheffield Times* 24 Feb. 1849, p. 2; *PP* 23 May 1857, p. 4, 14 Nov. 1857, p. 5; *WM* 1 Mar. 1862, p. 83, 1 Apr. 1862, pp. 108–9, 1 May 1862, p. 125; *NR* 3 Dec. 1864, p. 624; *People's Advocate* 26 June 1875, p. 5, 17 July 1875, p. 6; J. Skelton, *A Plea for the Botanic Practice of Medicine* (1853); J. Skelton, *The Epitome of the Botanic Practice of Medicine* (Leeds, 1855).
4 Cooper, *Life*, p. 311; Oppenheim, *Other World*, pp. 233–5.
5 Oppenheim, *Other World*, pp. 40–1, 234–5; J. Harrison, 'Early Victorian radicals', p. 207.
6 McLeod, *Religion and the People*, ch. 7.
7 Vigier, *Seconde République* II, p. 115; Obelkevich, *Religion and Rural Society*, p. 275; Bédarida, *Social History*, p. 92.
8 *TAHP* 28 Sept. 1850, p. 107.
9 McLeod, *Religion*, pp. 39–40; Obelkevich, *Religion and Rural Society*, p. 307; J. Harrison, *Second Coming*, pp. 41–2; McCalman, *Radical Underworld*, p. 58; Joutard, 'Protestantisme', 145–64.
10 T. Tackett, *Religion, Revolution and Regional Culture in Eighteenth-Century France. The Ecclesiastical Oath of 1791* (Princeton, 1986), pp. 229–48.
11 Gibson, *Social History*, p. 54.
12 Normanby, *The English at Home*, pp. 241, 244, quoted in J. Phillips, *Great Reform Act*, p. 284.

13 Biagini, *Liberty*, pp. 197–8, 211, 217–9, 22–6, 229–33, 239–40.

14 Corbon, *Secret*, pp. 302–3.

15 *PMG* 30 Nov. 1833, p. 381.

16 Murray, *People's Advocate* 6 May 1876, p. 3.

17 *Times* 27 Nov. 1839, p. 6; Epstein, 'Organisational and cultural aspects', p. 255.

18 William Jones, *Chartist Pilot* 16 Dec. 1843, p. 4.

19 D. Jones, *Chartism*, pp. 49–57; Epstein, 'Organisational and cultural aspects', pp. 233–4, 249–55; McNulty, 'Working class movements', pp. 155–89; Isambert, *Christianisme*, pp. 230–1; E. Yeo, 'Robert Owen', p. 107; E. Yeo, 'Christianity', 123–37; D. Thompson, *Chartists*, pp. 116–17, 260–1, 278; Berenson, *Populist Religion*.

20 E.g. *NS* 6 Feb. 1841, p. 2.

21 Little, 'Chartism and Liberalism', pp. 228–30.

22 Mercier, *Eliphas Lévi*, p. 52; Perdiguier, *Biographie*, p. 82; Raspail, *Avenues*, p. 156; *Echo des Travailleurs* 1 Jan. 1834, p. 1; *Montagne de la Fraternité* 5 May 1848, p. 2; Blanqui toast, NAF 951, fol. 2; *EO* Aug. 1844, p. 77; Laponneraye, *Cours*, p. 3; *O* 12 July 1851, p. 9, 29 Nov. 1851, p. 168; Pottier, *Œuvres*, pp. 48, 49, 67; Blanqui, Salières, Pardigon, in *Banquet des Travailleurs Socialistes*, pp. 5, 13, 19; *A* Nov. 1846, p. 413; Desplanches, *Ruche* Apr. 1840, p. 28, Vannostal, May 1840, p. 1; Savage, *PP* 19 June 1852, p. 6; *RN* 9 Jan. 1859, p. 1; E. Yeo, 'Robert Owen', p. 107; E. Yeo, 'Christianity'; Bowman, *Eliphas Lévi*, pp. 37–8; Berenson, *Populist Religion*; Biagini, *Liberty*, pp. 14–16, 31–41, 57.

23 *Trades' J* 4 July 1840, p. 8; Legallois, *TP* 30 Mar. 1848, p. 1; Bowman, *Christ romantique*, pp. 116–17; Chase, *People's Farm*, p. 102; E. Yeo, 'Culture and constraint', p. 157; Berenson, *Populist Religion*, pp. 102, 194; Rancière, *Nuit*, pp. 254–588.

24 *Bolton Chron.* 16 Aug. 1834, p. 3; D. Jones, *Chartism*, p. 54.

25 E.g. London *NS* 6 Feb. 1841, p. 1, 27 Feb. 1841, p. 5, 13 Mar. 1841, p. 1, 20 Mar. 1841, p. 1, 21 Aug. 1841, p. 2, 2 Oct. 1841, p. 1, 9 Oct. 1841, p. 7, 16 Oct. 1841, p. 1, 13 Nov. 1841, p. 2, 22 Oct. 1842, p. 8, 7 Jan. 1843, p. 7.

26 E.g. *P* 24 Feb. 1849, p. 4.

27 E. Yeo, 'Culture and constraint', p. 170.

28 D. Thompson, *Early Chartists*, p. 218.

29 D. Thompson, *Chartists*, pp. 238–9.

30 *Réformateur* June 1835, pp. 18–19; Gibson, *Social History*, pp. 252–3; Lammenais, *Words*, p. 6; Gilbert, *Religion and Society*, p. 183; McCalman, *Radical Underworld*, p. 148.

31 Quoted in McNulty, 'Working class movements', p. 178.

32 E.g. pamphlet cited in Weill, *Histoire*, p. 221 (BN code Lb54 117); F. K. S., *Trades' Triumphant!*

33 Corbon, *Secret*, p. 303.

34 Corbon, *Secret*, p. 305.

35 Biagini, *Liberty*, pp. 35, 382, 389, 391–2, 401.

36 McNulty, 'Working class movements', pp. 156–7.

37 See also McNulty, 'Working class movements', pp. 156–8; J. Harrison, 'Early Victorian radicals', p. 208; Agulhon, *Ville ouvrière*, pp. 191–2.

38 Cooper, *Life*, p. 211; E. Yeo, 'Christianity', 118–23.

39  Cholvy and Hilaire, *Histoire religieuse*, p. 167.
40  E. Yeo, 'Christianity', 123.
41  Lévy, *P* 4 Jan. 1849, p. 2, Proudhon, 7 May 1849, p. 1; Cholvy and Hilaire, *Histoire religieuse*, pp. 168–9.
42  Bowman, *Christ romantique*, ch. 2.
43  14 Jan. 1831, F7 3885; Perdiguier, *Mémoires*, p. 30; *GT* 15 Nov. 1830, p. 51.
44  Bowman, *Eliphas Lévi*, pp. 23, 49–51; Webb, *Flight*, pp. 164–71, 222; Mercier, *Eliphas Lévi*, pp. 9, 11–12; Kselman, *Miracles*, p. 80; C. Johnson, *Utopian Communism*, p. 71.
45  Jowell, 'Thoré-Bürger', pp. 3–4.
46  *Republican* 18 June 1831, p. 3; *Prompter* 27 Aug. 1831, p. 772; E. Thompson, *Making*, pp. 779–800; J. Harrison, *Second Coming*, pp. 154–6; Oliver, *Prophets*, ch. 7.
47  Ganneau, *Manifeste*; C. Johnson, *Utopian Communism*, pp. 66–78.
48  *Montagne de la Fraternité* 7 May 1848, p. 1.
49  BB24 409–18, 5755 19 Nov. 1852; Pujol, *Prophétie*.
50  *LL* 30 Sept. 1848, p. 72; Sobrier, *Cette page prophétique*, in Ganneau, *Waterloo*; de la Hodde, *Histoire des sociétés secrètes*, pp. 120, 128, 147; Erdan, *France mistique* II, pp. 620–1; Amann, *Revolution*, p. 50; Webb, *Flight*, pp. 194–6, 198–9; Bowman, *Eliphas Lévi*, p. 11; Mercier, *Eliphas Lévi*, p. 41; Kselman, *Miracles*, p. 79.
51  Mapah, *Montagne de la Fraternité* 5 May 1848, pp. 3–4, 11 May 1848, p. 3; Bowman, *Eliphas Lévi*, pp. 104–5; Manuel, *Prophets*, p. 4; Webb, *Flight*, p. 199.
52  C 941; *TP* 23 Mar. 1848, p. 2, 26 Mar. 1848, pp. 1–2; *Montagne de la Fraternité* 5 May 1848, p. 2, 7 May 1848, pp. 2–3; *Voix des Femmes* 28 Apr. 1848, p. 3; Dautry, *1848*, p. 90; Bowman, *Eliphas Lévi*, p. 17; Bowman, *Christ romantique*, pp. 87, 105, 111–13; Webb, *Flight*, p. 199; Mercier, *Eliphas Lévi*, p. 41.
53  Cholvy and Hilaire, *Histoire religieuse*, p. 170; Margadant, *French Peasants*, p. 145.
54  Obelkevich, *Religion and Rural Society*, pp. 274–5, 302; McCalman, *Radical Underworld*, p. 46; E. Yeo, 'Culture and constraint', p. 162; B. Taylor, *Eve*, pp. 142–3; E. Yeo, 'Christianity', 126.
55  Erdan, *France mistique*, I, pp. 183–204, 386; P. Joutard, 'Réveils et vitalité du protestantisme français', in J. Joutard (ed.), *Du roi très chrétien à la laïcité républicaine* (1991).
56  Gisquet, *Mémoires* III, p. 177.
57  For Chatel's church, see esp. Bulletin 28 Sept. 1831, F7 3885; *Réformateur* (1834–5); *Eglise Française* (1835–6); *Réformateur Religieux* (1843); *Réformateur* (1843–4); *GT* 12 July 1833, p. 902, 21 Apr. 1834, p. 573, 15 Nov. 1834, p. 57, 5 Apr. 1835, p. 617, 14 Mar. 1836, p. 472, 24 Feb. 1843, p. 471, 1 June 1843, p. 809; *P* 20 Dec. 1848, p. 4, 17 Mar. 1849, p. 4; Chatel, *Sermon*; Chatel, *Code*; Chatel, *A la Chambre*, pp. 2–4; Auzou, *Bon Sens* 20 Oct. 1833, p. 3; Auzou, *Oraison*; Auzou, *Observations*; Calland and Le Rousseau, *Profession de foi*; Gisquet, *Mémoires* III, pp. 179–80; Lefrançais, *Souvenirs* I, p. 129; Champfleury, *Excentriques*, pp. 262–5, 284–5, 295; Erdan, *France mistique* I, pp. 211–13; Mirecourt, *Contemporains*, pp. 42–54;

Isambert, *Christianisme*, pp. 167, 200; Hornus, 'Petites églises', 271; Auzou, Bruley, Calland, Chatel, Le Rousseau, Pillot, Robert du Var, in Maitron, *Dictionnaire*.

58 Hetherington, *Principles and Practice*; Prothero, *Artisans*, pp. 259–60; McCalman, *Radical Underworld*, pp. 73–6; Chase, *People's Farm*, pp. 109–10; Brooke, *Democrats*, pp. 46, 52, 57.

59 *Man* 24 Nov. 1833, p. 156.

60 *Isis* 15 Sept. 1832, pp. 415, 495.

61 D. Vincent, *Bread*, pp. 167, 172–4, 179–80.

62 *PMG* 19 Nov. 1831, p. 174.

63 'Agrarius' (Petrie), *Man* 28 July 1833, p. 26.

64 NA MS 155, fol. 123.

65 Lovett, Place Papers, Add. MS 27,822, fol. 18; *PMG* 7 Sept. 1831, p. 85, 29 Sept. 1832, p. 548, 6 Oct. 1831, p. 556, 24 Nov. 1831, p. 619; *Destructive* 7 Dec. 1833, p. 356.

66 Cooper, *Life*, pp. 260–3, 316, 352–8, 361–7.

67 Weill, *Histoire*, pp. 186, 330–1; Agulhon, *Republican Experiment*, p. 44.

68 *Political Examiner* 2 Mar. 1853, p. 4; *NR* 27 Oct. 1860, p. 8, 2 Feb. 1861, p. 6, 10 Dec. 1861, p. 623; *BH* 3 Sept. 1865, p. 1, 9 Sept. 1865, p. 1, 3 Mar. 1866, p. 1, 24 Mar. 1866, p. 1, 9 Mar. 1867, p. 1, 7 July 1867, p. 1; Soutter, *Recollections*, pp. 23–4.

69 Benbow, *Crimes*; McCalman, *Radical Underworld*, pp. 189–90.

70 *Prompter* 10 Sept. 1831, p. 782; *G* 30 Mar. 1834, p. 953; *PMG* 3 Sept. 1831, p. 782, Apr. 1832–June 1833; Prothero, *Artisans*, pp. 258–64, 290, 294–7; *NS* 16 Oct 1841, p. 1, 13 Nov. 1841, p. 2.

71 *Republican* 2 July 1831, p. 6, 9 July 1831, pp. 5–6; Prothero, *Artisans*, p. 294; Royle, *Victorian Infidels*, pp. 31–43; Cooter, *Cultural Meaning*, pp. 216–19; *PMG* 20 July 1833, p. 236, 3 Aug. 1833, p. 252, 17 Aug. 1833, p. 268, 4 Jan. 1834, p. 436, 11 Jan. 1834, p. 112, 10 May 1834, p. 136; *Destructive* 4 May 1833, p. 108, 20 July 1833, pp. 196, 200, 27 July 1833, p. 208, 3 Aug. 1833, p. 216, 17 Aug. 1833, p. 232; *NS* 24 May 1845, p. 3; Roe, *Lamennais*, pp. 164, 177, 199–205.

72 McCalman, *Radical Underworld*, ch. 7; Chase, *People's Farm*, pp. 88–9.

73 *Republican* 11 Aug. 1826, pp. 129–30; *Lion* 25 Jan. 1828, p. 114; HO 40/25, 10 and 15 Nov. 1830, fols. 421, 553; *Prompter* 4 Dec. 1830, pp. 52–4, 9 July 1831, pp. 561–4; 8 Oct., 12 and 27 Nov. 1832, HO 64/12; 14, 22 Apr. 1833, 24 Feb. 1834, HO 64/15; *PMG* 22 Sept. 1832, p. 544, 29 Sept. 1832, p. 552; *NS* 24 May 1845, p. 3; McCalman, *Radical Underworld*, esp. pp. 195–203; McCalman, 'Popular irreligion', pp. 63–4.

74 *Réf* Apr. 1835, pp. 4–8; Erdan, *France mistique* I, p. 212.

75 Pillot to Enfantin, Enfantin Papers, Bibliothèque de l'Arsénal, 7606, fols. 91, 92; *Ami de la Religion* 28 June 1835, p. 597; *A Tous*, pp. 4, 28, 40–3; Agulhon, *Ville ouvrière*, p. 225.

76 Chatel, *Code*, esp. pp. 266, 268, 443, 449.

77 *Réf* 1 Feb. 1844, pp. 489, 492; Duquesne, *Ruche* Feb. 1844, p. 51; Bowman, *Christ romantique*, p. 130.

78 Desage, *P* 25 Dec. 1848, p. 1, 'X' (Chevé), 12 Feb. 1849, p. 6, 25 Apr. 1849, p. 4, 2 May 1849, p. 3; *TP* 19 Mar. 1848, p. 1; *Vérité* no. 1, p. 3; *Petit*

*Messager du Village* 1 June 1849, p. 18; Benoit, *Confessions*, p. 76; Rancière, *Nuit*, pp. 300–1.

79  *P* 20 Dec. 1848, p. 4; Champfleury, *Excentriques*, p. 295–6.

80  Robert, *Ruche* Apr. 1844, p. 119.

81  *Eglise Française* Aug. 1835, pp. 12–13, Aug. 1836, p. 29; *GT* 10 Aug.–9 Sept. 1836, 11 June 1841, pp. 809–10, 24 Feb. 1843, p. 471; Pillot, *Le code religieux*; Pillot, *Ni châteaux*; Bulletins 18 and 22 June, 1 July 1840, F7 3890; de la Hodde, *Histoire des sociétés secrètes*, pp. 268–9; *Premier Banquet Communiste*; *Humanitaire* July 1841, p. 7, Aug. 1841, p. 11; *F* July 1841, pp. 11–12, Aug. 1841, p. 15; Weill, *Histoire*, p. 162; Aa 366 (1848); BB24 778, 10948; Ba 435, dos. 5171, 5393.

82  Benoit, *Confessions*, pp. 37–41.

83  Cabet, *Salut*, pp. 2–3; Cabet, *Vrai Christianisme*; Dubeau to Cabet, 26 July 1847, MS 1052, fol. 133; C. Johnson, *Utopian Communism*, pp. 92–4, 128–30, 173–4, 213–16, 231–4.

84  *PMG* 14 July 1832–19 Apr. 1834; *WMF* 19 Jan. 1833, p. 40, 26 Jan. 1833, p. 48, 23 Mar. 1833, p. 108, 8 June 1833, p. 199; *Destructive* 15 June 1833, pp. 155–6, 14 Sept. 1833, pp. 259–60.

85  J. W. Scott, *Gender and the Politics of History* (New York, 1988), pp. 77, 83.

86  *Eglise Française* Oct. 1835, pp. 12–16, 29; Chatel, *Code*, pp. 309, 374; Erdan, *France mistique* I, p. 217.

87  *P* 20 Dec. 1848, p. 4; Mirecourt, *Contemporains*, p. 53; Bowman, *Eliphas Lévi*, p. 106.

88  *Crisis* 4 May 1833, p. 133; Saville, 'J. E. Smith', p. 118; B. Taylor, *Eve*, pp. 168–71; Darnton, *Mesmerism*, pp. 143–4; Oppenheim, *Other World*, p. 188.

89  Owen, *Darkened Room*, pp. 7–12, 112–38.

90  Bowman, *Eliphas Lévi*, pp. 25, 28–32; *TP* 30 Mar. 1848, p. 2; B. Taylor, *Eve*, p. 171; Rendall, *Origins*, p. 106; Moses, 'Saint-Simonian men'; Owen, *Darkened Room*, p. 16.

91  Lamennais, *Words*, pp. 22, 56.

92  Chase, *People's Farm*, pp. 47–57, 61, 79–86; Preston, *Life*, p. 24; McCalman, *Radical Underworld*, pp. 98–106.

93  O'Brien, *NS* 9 June 1838, p. 4, Harney, 23 June 1838, p. 6; *LD* 24 June 1838, p. 739, 1 July 1838, p. 746.

94  For the Spenceans, see: Chase, *People's Farm*; for O'Brien and O'Brienites, see: Plummer, *Bronterre*; Shipley, *Club Life*; M. Bevir, 'The British Social Democratic Federation 1880–1885. From O'Brienism to Marxism', *International Review of Social History* 37 (1992).

95  O'Brien to Owen, 27 May 1832, Owen Coll. no. 546; *NS* 17 Feb. 1838, p. 5; Burns, 'Strategy', p. 61; *Social Reformer* 11 Aug.–8 Sept. 1849, 15 Sept. 1849, p. 44, 20 Oct. 1849, p. 84; *PP* 8 May 1852, p. 5; O'Brien, *Vision of Hell*, esp. pp. 6–8; *RN* 3 Aug. 1851, p. 14.

96  *Crisis* 22 Mar. 1834, p. 242.

97  *A Brief Inquiry*, esp. title page and pp. 24, 26, 30–1, 62A, 65, 69, 72; for William Neale, see: *Social Reformer* 1 Sept. 1849, p. 25; *NR* 5 Jan. 1868, p. 7; for Harris see: Harris to Owen, 5 and 26 Mar. 1854, Owen Coll. nos. 2246, 2763; *NR* 5 Mar. 1865, pp. 157–8, 26 Mar. 1865, p. 204, 3 Dec. 1865,

p. 771, 12 Jan. 1868, p. 29, 19 Jan. 1868, p. 44, 23 June 1868, p. 6; H. Collins and Abramsky, *Karl Marx*, p. 248; Shipley, *Club Life*, p. 6.

98  *RWN* 2 June 1850, p. 7; Jones, *Political Secret*; Finlen, *PP* 23 June 1855, p. 2; *WM* 1 Jan. 1867, p. 1, 4 May 1867, p. 3, 13 July 1867, p. 8; Davies, *Heterodox London*, pp. 210–30; *Republican*, esp. 1 Feb. 1872, p. 1; Royle, *Victorian Infidels*, pp. 158–9, 195.

99  *Eglise Française* Aug. 1835, pp. 17–18; 22–9, Aug. 1836, p. 27; *RR* 7 May 1843, pp. 88–9; *Réf* 1 Aug. 1843, pp. 74–91; Auzou, *Oraison*, p. 5; Chatel, *Eloge*.

100 Touchard, *Gloire*, p. 242; Rude, *Mouvement ouvrier*, pp. 615–6.

101 *Tribune* 6 Aug. 1832, p. 3; Touchard, *Gloire*, p. 258.

102 Ganneau, *Waterloo*.

103 Bulletin, 16 Nov. 1840, F7 3890; 'Sociétés secrètes. Ferrandiniers et renégats', 'Clubs et associations' (Cour de Lyon 1848–1850), BB18 1474B; *A* Dec. 1840, p. 27; Galle, *Ruche* Mar. 1841, p. 31; *Peuple* 29 May 1849, p. 4; Ganneau, *Manifeste*; Ganneau, *Waterloo*; Coutant, *Ruche* Nov. 1840, p. 3; de la Hodde, *Histoire des sociétés secrètes*, pp. 268–9; Nadaud, *Mémoires*, p. 224n; Bernstein, 'Néo-babouvisme', p. 261; Jardin and Tudesq, *Restoration and Reaction*, pp. 124, 127; C. Johnson, *Utopian Communism*, pp. 65–75; Webb, *Flight*, pp. 195–7; Kselman, *Miracles*, p. 78.

104 Erdan, *France mistique* I, p. 228.

105 Constant, 'Le tombeau de Napoleon' and 'Le Dieu du peuple' in *Trois harmonies* pp. 19–22, 85–7; *TP* 19 Mar. 1848, p. 2, 23 Mar. 1848, p. 2, 30 Mar. 1848, p. 2; Erdan, *France mistique* I, pp. 249–51, 289–90; Darnton, *Mesmerism*, p. 139n; Manuel, *Prophets*, p. 4; Webb, *Flight*, pp. 196–7, 221; Bowman, *Eliphas Lévi*, pp. 15–16; Mercier, *Eliphas Lévi*, pp. 64–5; Agulhon, 'Problème', 59.

106 See also McCalman, *Radical Underworld*, pp. 4, 114–15, 183–201.

107 Lockwood, *Tools*, p. 228.

108 Obelkevich, *Religion and Rural Society*, p. 311; D. Vincent, *Bread*, p. 177; Plessis, *Rise and Fall*, p. 112; Bédarida, *Social History*, pp. 90–2.

109 Bauberot, 'Conversions', pp. 167–8; Hilaire, 'Notes', pp. 196–8; Gibson, *Social History*, pp. 139–57, 254–6; Phayer, 'Politics and popular religion', 361; Mercier, *Eliphas Lévi*, p. 43; Bruhat, 'Anticléricalisme', p. 82; Magraw, *France*, p. 138.

110 Cantagrel, *Commerce* 12 Sept. 1869, pp. 3–4; 45 AP 6, dos. IV, 6 July, 18 Nov. 1868; Weill, *Histoire*, p. 320; NA MS 155, fols. 70, 175–6, 561; Lefrançais, *Souvenirs* II, pp. 310, 318, 338; Dalotel, *Aux origines*, pp. 104–5, 139, 200–5, 213–15.

111 Quoted in Rancière, *Nuit*, p. 432; Richard, 'Débuts', 85. See also Aminzade, *Ballots*, pp. 50–1.

112 S. Yeo, 'A new life. The religion of socialism in Britain, 1883–1896', *History Workshop* no. 4 (1977).

113 Lefrançais, *Souvenirs* I, p. 3. See also Weill, *Histoire*, p. 406.

114 Erdan, *France mistique* I, p. 213; Mirecourt, *Contemporains*, p. 53; *A Tous*; J. Le Rousseau, *Notions*; Pillot entry in Maitron, *Dictionnaire*.

115 Desmond, 'Artisan resistance', esp. 77, 80–90, 94, 97; Bowler, *Invention of Progress*, pp. 88–9, 136–8, 143, 171; Oppenheim, *Other World*, pp. 272–7.

116 Barker, *NR* 4 Aug. 1860, p. 4.
117 D. Vincent, *Bread*, pp. 172–4; Barrow, *Independent Spirits*, pp. 66–73, 85, 155–7, 160, 187; Rancière, *Nuit*, p. 180.
118 Quoted in J. Harrison, 'Early Victorian radicals', p. 202.
119 Rancière in Gauny, *Philosophe plébéien*, p. 92.
120 *Co-op Mag.* July 1828, p. 111; *British Co-operator* May 1830, pp. 40–3; *WFP* 3 July 1830; *NR* 19 Jan. 1868, p. 44; J. Harrison, *Robert Owen*, pp. 239–43; Lechevalier to Comité de l'Association pour l'Instruction du Peuple, CC 615, 1ère Liasse; Gabriel, *Ruche* Oct. 1843, p. 31; Jowell, 'Thoré-Bürger', pp. 3–5. For the movements looked at in the following pages, see: Darnton, *Mesmerism*; Parssinen, 'Popular science'; Parssinen, 'Mesmeric performers'; Parssinen, 'Professional deviants'; Cooter, *Cultural Meaning*; Oppenheim, *Other World*; Barrow, *Independent Spirits*; Owen, *Darkened Room*; Brown, 'Social context'. See also: Agulhon, *Ville ouvrière*, pp. 213, 317; Bowler, *Invention of Progress*, pp. 88–9; Rancière, *Nuit*; Rancière in Gauny, *Philosophe plébéien*.
121 *Ruche* Jan. 1844, p. 27; adverts in *P* 27 Apr. 1849, p. 4, 6 May 1849, p. 4, 20 May 1849, p. 4, 21 May 1849, p. 4; *VP* 11 Nov. 1849, p. 4; *NR* 28 July 1860, p. 6; Carmarthen, *BH* 10 Feb. 1866, p. 2;
122 Havret, Bernard, Tartaret, in Tartaret, *Exposition Universelle*, pp. 64–6.
123 Weill, *Histoire*, pp. 41–2, 199; *LL* 30 Sept. 1848, p. 72; *VP* 10 Oct. 1849, p. 4; *Peuple de 1850* 1 Sept. 1850, p. 8, Ragon, p. 102.
124 *NS* 26 Oct. 1842, p. 5; *Sheffield Times* 24 Feb. 1849, p. 2; *PP* 23 May 1857, p. 4, 14 Nov. 1857, p. 5; *WM* 1 Mar. 1862, p. 83; 1 Apr. 1862, pp. 108–9, 1 May 1862, p. 125; *BH* 19 Sept. 1863, p. 6; *NR* 3 Dec. 1864, p. 624; *People's Advocate* 26 June 1875, p. 5, 17 July 1875, p. 6.
125 *P* 10 Feb. 1849, p. 4, 27 Apr. 1849, p. 4, 16 May 1849, p. 4, 20 May 1849, p. 4, 21 May 1849, p. 4; *VP* 12 Nov. 1849, p. 4; Truquin, *Mémoires*, pp. 141–2; Mercier, *Eliphas Lévi*, p. 43.
126 Jennerson, *NR* 15 Dec. 1860, p. 7; Wallace, *EL* 21 July 1866, p. 9, 29 Sept. 1866, p. 171; Smith, *NR* 5 Jan. 1868, pp. 6–7. See also Webb, *Flight*, p. 16.
127 Eg. *NR* 24 Sept. 1865, p. 616, 17 Apr. 1870, p. 250.
128 Darnton, *Mesmerism*, p. 127; J. Harrison, *Second Coming*, p. 70; E. Thompson, *Witness*, pp. xiv–xv.
129 Oppenheim, *Other World*, pp. 3, 39–40, 224; Barrow, *Independent Spirits*, p. 32; J. Harrison, *Second Coming*, p. 222; McCalman, *Radical Underworld*, pp. 83–4, 93.
130 Manuel, *Prophets*, ch. 5; Darnton, *Mesmerism*, pp. 143–4; Brochon in Pottier, *Œuvres*, pp. 23–5; Cooter, 'Bones of contention', p. 209; Le Rousseau, *Notions*; Rancière, *Nuit, passim*; Bowman, *Eliphas Lévi*, p. 34; Lefrançais, *Souvenirs* I, pp. 80, 96; Webb, *Flight*, pp. 221–2; B. Taylor, *Eve*, pp. 169–71.
131 *Voix des Femmes* 4 Apr. 1848, p. 2; Webb, *Flight*, pp. 150–2, 220; Jacob, *Radical Enlightenment*, p. 36; Jowell, 'Thoré-Bürger', pp. 141, 353n63.
132 *M* 21 Jan. 1870, p. 2, 22 Jan. 1870, p. 2, 23 Jan. 1870, p. 1, 25 Jan. 1870, p. 2; *CP* 3 Apr. 1848, p. 3; Weill, *Histoire*, pp. 130, 345; Lefrançais, *Souvenirs* II, pp. 310, 318; C. Johnson, *Utopian Communism*, pp. 252–3.
133 Letter 5 Jan. 1849, BHVP MS 1043, fol. 52.

134 J. Harrison, 'Early Victorian radicals'; Barrow, *Independent Spirits*, pp. 97, 145–8.

135 *Crisis* 8 June 1833, p. 171. See also D. Vincent, *Bread*, p. 188; Chase, *People's Farm*, pp. 18–19, 162–4, 166–7, 177; Pottier, *Œuvres*, p. 63.

136 See also Manuel, *Prophets*, p. 143; Darnton, *Mesmerism*, pp. 127, 149–56; Isambert, *Christianisme*, pp. 223, 228; Bowman, *Eliphas Lévi*, pp. 18, 41.

137 See also McCalman, *Radical Underworld*, pp. 60–72, 144–8.

138 E. Douka Kabiloglou, *Plato and the English Romantics* (London, 1990).

139 Royle, *Victorian Infidels*, p. 20; Jacob, *Radical Enlightenment*, pp. 22, 31, 47; E. Thompson, *Witness*, pp. 26–7, 158.

140 W. R. Newman, *Gehennical Fire: the Lives of George Starkey, an American Alchemist in the Scientific Revolution* (Harvard, 1995).

141 E. Thompson, *Witness*, pp. xiv–xv.

142 NAF 9581 fols. 112, 123; Blanqui, *Eternité*; Raspail, *Avenues*, pp. 349–50; Wassermann, *Clubs*, pp. 13, 15–16; Hutton, *Cult*, pp. 38, 46–7.

143 J. L. Brooke, *The Refiner's Fire. The Making of Mormon Cosmology, 1644–1844* (Cambridge, 1995).

144 J. Harrison, *Second Coming*, pp. 39–40; Webb, *Flight*, pp. 122–30.

145 Nadaud, *Mémoires*, p. 60; Darnton, *Mesmerism*, p. 140; J. Harrison, *Second Coming*, pp. 21, 39–40; Oppenheim, *Other World*, pp. 213, 222–3; Barrow, *Independent Spirits*, p. 165.

146 B. Taylor, *Eve*, pp. 160–1; J. Harrison, *Second Coming*, p. 221; J. Harrison, 'Early Victorian radicals', p. 206; Barrow, *Independent Spirits*, p. 91; Shipley, *Club Life*, pp. 41–4.

147 Rancière in Gauny, *Philosophe plébéien*, pp. 6, 89, 92.

## 11. THE CULTURE OF RADICAL CLUBS

1 Quoted in M. Bouloiseau, *The Jacobin Republic 1792–1794* (Cambridge, 1972), p. 169.

2 Quoted in Behagg, *Politics and Production*, p. 109.

3 Corbon, *Secret*, pp. 182–5.

4 *BTC* Feb. 1851, pp. 20–2; *Reminiscences of a Stonemason*, p. 76.

5 Morrell, *BH* 13 Jan. 1866, p. 7.

6 Perdiguier, *Mémoires*, p. 156.

7 E. Yeo, 'Robert Owen', p. 14; E. Yeo, 'Culture and constraint', p. 170; Bailey, *Leisure*, p. 26; Chase, *People's Farm*, pp. 186–7; B. Harrison, 'The Sunday trading riots of 1855', *Historical Journal* 8 (1965).

8 *Pioneer* 19 Oct. 1833, p. 41; Debock, *TO* 11 June 1865, p. 6.

9 Mora, *Union* Jan. 1845, p. 4.

10 *Artisan* 10 Oct. 1830, p. 3; *A* Sept. 1840, p. 1, 28 Feb. 1843, p. 43, Mar. 1844, p. 95, July 1849, pp. 375–6; *PP* 14 Feb. 1857, p. 1; Hartwell, *BH* 25 Oct. 1862, p. 1; Murray, 14 Mar. 1863, p. 1; Dumas, *TO* 4 June 1865, p. 2, Tolain, 18 June 1865, p. 9; Guile, *WM* 29 Sept. 1866, p. 154; P. Vinçard, *Nouvelle des Abonnés* 5 Jan. 1867, p. 37; *St. Crispin* 19 Mar. 1870, pp. 145–6; Perdiguier, *Mémoires*, p. 232; E. Yeo, 'Robert Owen', p. 95; Stewart-McDougall, *Artisan Republic*, p. 20; I. Collins, *Government and Newspaper*

*Press*, pp. 91–2; Ragon, *Histoire*, p. 96; Rancière, 'Good times', pp. 47, 66–7; Vernon, *Politics*, pp. 215–17, 235–8.

11 *P* 21 Dec. 1848, p. 2.

12 *NS* 28 Nov. 1840, p. 4; *FSA* Aug. 1836, p. 121; *RWN* 26 May 1850, p. 7; *PP* 23 May 1857, p. 1, 18 July 1857, p. 1; *NU* May 1858, p. 2, Nov. 1858, p. 54; *BH* 4 July 1863, p. 6; *C* 22 Dec. 1866, p. 4, 5 Jan. 1867, p. 4; Flotard, *Mouvement coopératif*, pp. 14, 21; Stevens, *Memoir*, p. 93; E. Yeo, 'Robert Owen', pp. 84, 86; E. Yeo, 'Culture and constraint', p. 169; Finn, *After Chartism*, p. 129.

13 Jouy, *Adresse*, p. 21.

14 Raspail, *Avenues*, pp. 121–2.

15 E. Yeo, 'Christianity', 122; Faure, *Paris Carême-prenant*, ch. 3; Berenson, *Populist Religion*, p. 212; Robert, 'Cortèges', pp. 53, 104, 122–3; Metz, *Tribune* 1 June 1832, p. 4.

16 Brazier, *Histoire* I, p. v ; T. Wright, *Habits*, pp. 156–62; Poulot, *Question sociale*, pp. 149, 257; Perdiguier, *Mémoires*, pp. 159, 215, 232; Lyon, *Lyre*, p. 103; Corbon, *Secret*, p. 327; Agulhon, *Republic in the Village*, pp. 116–18; Agulhon, 'Problème', 52; Rancière, *Nuit*, pp. 36–7; Rancière, 'Good times', p. 53; Reddy, 'Moral sense', p. 384; Crump, 'Popular audience', pp. 275, 278–9; Vinçard, *TA* 25 Feb. 1849, p. 7; McCalman, 'Popular irreligion', p. 61.

17 Hartwell, *TPC* Apr. 1852, p. 178, Jan. 1853, p. 221, Apr. 1853, p. 233; *Ruche* Feb. 1847, p. 63; Chauvet, *Ouvriers*, p. 586.

18 Vinçard, *TA* 25 Feb. 1849, p. 7; Loubere, *Louis Blanc*, p. 45.

19 *JO* 7 Nov. 1830, p. 3; *Glaneuse*, 4 Nov. 1832, p. 4; *OT* 3 June 1848, p. 1; Brazier, *Histoire* I, p. 185; McCalman, 'Popular irreligion', p. 61.

20 Bulletin 30 Sept. 1830, F7 3884; *PMG* 23 July 1831, p. 21; *BH* 9 Sept. 1865, p. 1; *WM* 20 Oct. 1866, p. 187; Rancière, 'Good times', pp. 52, 54, 56, 59–60; Biagini, *Liberty*, p. 45.

21 *NS* 4 Aug. 1838, p. 6; *Voix des Femmes* 25 Mar. 1848, p. 2; Dalotel, *Aux origines*, p. 45; Robert, 'Cortèges', p. 44.

22 Ragon, *Histoire*, p. 96. See also E. Thompson, *Making*, p. 58; J. Vincent, *Formation*, p. 78; B. Harrison, 'Pubs', pp. 50–7; Duveau, *Vie*, p. 186; *Commerce* 1 Aug. 1869, p. 3; Perdiguier, *Mémoires*, p. 215; Nadaud, *Mémoires*, p. 417.

23 Bulletin 5 Jan. 1829, F7 3883; *CC* 24 Aug. 1844, p. 85; Broadhurst, *Story*, p. 7; *JTA* 1 May 1860, p. 52; Chambre de Commerce, *Statistique* I, p. 71; T. Wright, *Habits*, pp. 124–30, 133–4; Chauvet, *Ouvriers*, pp. 419, 570, 573; E. Thompson, *Making*, p. 317; Bailey, *Leisure*, p. 111; McClelland, 'Time to work', p. 207; Cottereau, 'Denis Poulot's *Le Sublime*', p. 116; Agulhon, 'Working class and sociability', p. 41; Prestwich, 'French workers', 39.

24 Poulot, *Question sociale*, pp. 181–2, 188, 233–9, 255; Agulhon, *Republic in the Village*, p. 126; Berenson, *Populist Religion*, p. 187.

25 *Artisan* 2 Oct. 1842, p. 2; Nadaud, *Mémoires*, pp. 164, 195; *Tailor* 25 May 1867, p. 98; Beesly, *BH* 6 Feb. 1864, p. 1; Chambre de Commerce, *Statistique* I, pp. 70–1; Poulot, *Question sociale*, p. 266; P. Clark, *English Alehouse*, p. 312; Agulhon, 'Problème', 51; Agulhon, 'Working class and

sociability', pp. 41–3; B. Harrison, 'Pubs', pp. 172, 174; Cottereau, 'Denis Poulot's *Le Sublime*', p. 118; Haine, 'Café friend', p. 618; Haine, *World*, pp. 184–206.

26 Haine, 'Café friend', 610.

27 Lowery, 'Passages', p. 82; Loubere, *Radicalism*, p. 17; Merriman, 'Radicalisation', p. 217; Weill, *Histoire*, p. 77; Haine, 'Café friend', 607–10, 612, 615–17.

28 E.g. Paris smiths, *GT* 28 Oct. 1840, p. 1283; Toulouse tailors, Report 11 Nov. 1842, BB18 1407, 5683; Rouen woolcombers, *AR* 14 Jan. 1849, p. 4; engineers, *TAHP* 17 Aug. 1850, p. 61.

29 Raspail, *Avenues*, p. 122.

30 McCalman, *Radical Underworld*, p. 138; Merriman, *Agony*, pp. 100–1; Dolléans, *Histoire*, p. 257; Hanagan, *Nascent Proletarians*, p. 84; Haine, 'Café friend', 608–11, 619.

31 Agulhon, 'Working class and sociability', p. 43.

32 *Pioneer* 10 May 1834, p. 351; *TC* 11 Feb. 1854, p. 9; D. Vincent, *Testaments*, pp. 135, 186–7; P. Clark, *English Alehouse*, p. 297; Agulhon, 'Working class and sociability', pp. 40–1; Prothero, *Artisans*, pp. 271, 275; McCalman, *Radical Underworld*, pp. 195–8; Nadaud, *Mémoires*, p. 197; Finn, *After Chartism*, p. 134.

33 *NS* 12 Apr. 1845, p. 1; *BTC* Oct. 1850, p. 1; *BH* 10 Oct. 1863, p. 1; *C* 8 June 1867, p. 1; Howe and Waite, *London Society of Compositors*, pp. 102–3; Child, *Industrial Relations*, p. 86; Chauvet, *Ouvriers*, pp. 216–17, 258; P. Clark, *English Alehouse*, p. 294; E. Yeo, 'Robert Owen', p. 96; Finn, *After Chartism*, p. 129; Vernon, *Politics*, pp. 216–19, 229–30.

34 Nadaud, *Mémoires*, p. 269; Epstein, 'Cap of Liberty'.

35 *CC* May 1844, p. 31, 24 Aug. 1844, p. 84; *NS* 8 Sept. 1849, p. 1.

36 Gisquet, *Mémoires* III, p. 180; *NS* 26 Oct. 1842, p. 5; Barrow, *Independent Spirits*, pp. 181–2. See also Oppenheim, *Other World*, p. 212.

37 Lyons Police Lieut. to Min. of Int., 27 July 1819, F7 9787; Berenson, *Populist Religion*, p. 80; Magraw, *France*, pp. 148–9; Vernon, *Politics*, pp. 256–8.

38 Bruhat, 'Anticléricalisme', p. 91; Report Lyons, 7 Oct. 1851, BB30 394, no. 365P, 8634; *F 1845* Oct. 1845, p. 2; *A* Nov. 1846, p. 414; *VP* 1 Oct. 1849, p. 4; Weill, *Histoire*, p. 171; Gaumont, *Histoire*, p. 255; Gossez, *Ouvriers*, pp. 354–60; Merriman, *Agony*, pp. 25, 41–3; J. Harrison, *Second Coming*, pp. 50–1; Berenson, *Populist Religion*, p. 128.

39 *MG* 19 Dec. 1855, p. 4; *Freelance* (Manchester) 26 Jan. 1867.

40 Touchard, *Gloire* I, pp. 242–3; Magraw, *History*, pp. 35–7; Roger Price, *French Second Republic*, p. 209; *AR* 8 Nov. 1849, p. 2; Lefrançais, *Souvenirs* I, pp. 69–71; I. Collins, *Government and Newspaper Press*, p. 108.

41 *Ruche* Oct. 1843, p. 23, June 1844, p. 161; *Pop.* 8 May 1842; *Qui Vive!* 3 Oct. 1871, p. 1; D. Johnson, *Guizot*, p. 243; C. Johnson, *Utopian Communism*, p. 84; Gibson, *Social History*, p. 111; Allen, 'Social history', 267; Magraw, *France*, p. 86; Agulhon, 'Problème', 58; I. Collins, *Government and Newspaper Press*, pp. 88–92.

42 *Last* 1 Nov. 1844, pp. 7, 8.

43 Berridge, 'Popular journalism'; Joyce, *Visions*, pp. 66–9; A. Taylor, 'Reynolds's Newspaper'.

44 *Glaneuse* 4 Dec 1832, p. 3; McCalman, *Radical Underworld,* pp. 146–50, 167–76; Weill, *Histoire,* p. 170–1; I. Collins, *Government and Newspaper Press,* pp. 85–6.

45 Lefrançais, *Souvenirs* I, p. 281; Weill, *Histoire,* pp. 355–6; I. Collins, *Government and Newspaper Press,* pp. 155–6, 160; Kelso, 'French labor movement', 110.

46 Pref. Pol., 10 and 16 Oct. 1856, BB30 366, dos. II, fols. 168, 177; *G* 3 Nov. 1833, p. 624; Nadaud, *Mémoires,* pp. 140, 306–7; Weill, *Histoire,* pp. 296, 313; Touchard, *Gloire,* p. 201; E. Yeo, 'Culture and constraint', p. 163; Pichois, 'Cabinets'; Allen, 'Social history', 264, 359; BB18 1472 6733; Merriman, *Agony,* pp. 25, 41–2, 47; Agulhon, *Republic in the Village,* p. 264; Agulhon, 'Problème', 54–6; Berenson, *Populist Religion,* pp. 49, 83, 90, 128, 132, 134, 138, 182; Plessis, *Rise and Fall,* p. 139; Bell, 'Reform League', p. 140.

47 Perrot, 'Nineteenth-century work experience', p. 305.

48 Chase, *People's Farm,* pp. 47, 73; *NS* 3 Mar. 1849, p. 1; Foulon, *Eugène Varlin,* p. 21.

49 Orleans, BB18 1472 6733; Loubere, *Radicalism,* p. 71; Merriman, *Agony,* p. 28; Margadant, *French Peasants,* p. 163; *NS* and *R passim.*

50 *Réf* May 1835, p. 21.

51 *AR* 18 Feb. 1849, p. 3; Sykes, 'Popular politics', p. 625.

52 Perdiguier, *Mémoires,* p. 137; Agulhon, 'Problème', 55; *TPC* Jan. 1851, p. 114; *St. Crispin* 16 Oct. 1869, p. 183; Leno, *Aftermath,* p. 37.

53 Dessolaire to Lamennais, 3 Nov. 1844, *Nouvelle Revue Rétrospective* 6 (1897), p. 291; Nadaud, *Mémoires,* p. 141; Rémusat, *Mémoires* IV, pp. 165–6; Audiganne, *Populations ouvrières* I, p. 52; Weill, *Histoire,* p. 87; Cottereau, 'Denis Poulot's *Le Sublime*', p. 165; Vernon, *Politics,* pp. 144–6.

54 *Ruche* May 1841, p. 30; *F 1845* Aug. 1846, p. 171; Feb. 1847, p. 224; *A* July 1847, p. 543; *P* 19 Feb. 1849, p. 8, 4 Apr. 1849, p. 2; Lockwood, *Tools,* pp. 105–6; Ragon, *Histoire,* p. 84.

55 *A* Aug. 1844, p. 174. See also Droux, 'Chanson', 121–5.

56 Brazier, *Histoire* II, p. 230; Phayer, 'Politics and popular religion', 349.

57 Rancière, 'Good times', p. 50; Lockwood, *Tools,* pp. 192, 226, 228.

58 Perdiguier, *Biographie,* pp. 9–10; Perdiguier, *Mémoires,* pp. 87–8; Lyon, *Lyre,* p. 13; Lockwood, *Tools,* p. 22.

59 F. Gendron, *La jeunesse dorée* (Quebec, 1979), pp. 110–15; *JO* 11 Nov. 1830, p. 2.

60 C. Kingsley, 'Burns and his school', *Miscellanies* I (1859), p. 404, quoted in Little, 'Chartism and Liberalism', p. 231.

61 Brazier, *Histoire* I, pp. 191–2, 204–5. See also Touchard, *Gloire* I, p. 115; Summerfield, 'Effingham Arms', p. 231.

62 Pref. of Var to Min. Finance, 11 Aug. 1825, F7 9787; Perdiguier, *Mémoires,* pp. 46, 48, 52; Brazier, *Histoire* I, p. 291, II, pp. 24, 197; Berthaud, 'Goguettier', p. 514; Droux, 'Chanson', 121; Touchard, *Gloire* I, pp. 200–1, 387, 436; Ragon, *Histoire,* pp. 93–4; Gibson, *Social History,* p. 242.

63 Lyon, *Lyre,* pp. 115–17.

64 Aa 421, Pref. Pol., and dos. 5021; CC 585; 595, Candre; Bulletins 16 Sept. 1845, 2, 3 Oct. 1846, F7 3893; *JO* 7 Nov. 1830, p. 3, 18 Nov. 1830, p. 3, 12

Dec. 1830, p. 3; *Tribune* 19 Sept. 1831, p. 4; *Glaneuse* 8 Dec. 1832, p. 3, 15
Jan. 1833, p. 3, 28 Apr. 1833, pp. 1, 3; *Bon Sens* 3 Feb. 1833, p. 1; *GT* 18
Oct. 1837, p. 1230; *Ruche* [Dec. 1839], p. 4, Vinçard, May 1842, p. 11,
Coutant, Oct. 1843, p. 4, Oct. 1847, p. 238, Feb.–March 1848, pp. 47–8; *A*
Aug. 1844, p. 173, Aug. 1846, p. 363, Oct. 1846, p. 396; Duchamp, *Union*
Oct. 1845, p. 4; *Travail* 24 Feb. 1848, p. 2, no. 1, p. 2; *Peuple Constitant* 23
Mar. 1848, p. 3; *PD* 14 May 1848, p. 1; *Beacon* 7 Dec. 1853, p. 111; Brazier,
*Histoire* II, p. 224; L. Vinçard, *Mémoires*, pp. 44, 49; Truquin, *Mémoires*,
p. 36; Raspail, *Avenues*, p. 171; Droux, 'Chanson', 122–4; Weill, *Histoire*,
pp. 24, 72–3, 189; Rude, *Mouvement ouvrier*, pp. 607–8; Ragon, *Histoire*,
p. 84; Touchard, *Gloire* I, pp. 200, 382, 426.

65 Cooper to Jones, 4 Mar., 30 June 1845, Leicestershire Record Office Misc.
Papers, quoted in Little, 'Chartism and Liberalism', p. 231.

66 Jones, *Chartism*, p. 78; Epstein, 'Radical dining', 280 n. 32.

67 Lockwood, *Tools*, pp. 161, 226; E. Yeo, 'Culture and constraint', p. 169;
Little, 'Chartism and Liberalism', p. 225; *PP* 31 Dec. 1853, p. 3; Reynolds,
*RWN* 22 Sept. 1850, p. 1; *WM* 25 Aug. 1866, p. 90.

68 *Freelance* 2 Mar. 1867.

69 Nadaud, *Mémoires*, p. 417; *BH* 2 May 1863, p. 1; *Freelance* 7 Dec. 1867,
p. 181; *All the Year Round* 11 (1873), pp. 175–6; *City Lantern* (Manchester)
30 Oct. 1874, p. 40; Storch, 'Policeman', 493; Bailey, *Leisure*, pp. 16–17,
32; Summerfield, 'Effingham Arms', pp. 211, 231–2.

70 *Personal Recollections of the Life and Times, with Extracts from the Correspondence, of Valentine Lord Cloncurry* (Dublin, 1849), p. 64.

71 *Spence's Songs*, quoted in McCalman, *Radical Underworld*, p. 22; see also
pp. 49, 153–4; Chase, *People's Farm*, pp. 101, 112.

72 Berthaud, 'Goguettier', p. 514.

73 *Artisan* 2 Oct. 1842, p. 1.

74 Pref. Pol. 29 Mar. 1820, and 5 Jan. 1822, D/b 173; Aug. 1827, F7 6700 [I
owe these references to Michael Sibalis]. For the *goguettes*, see also: Crochon,
BHVP MS 1025, fol. 698; *JO* 2 Dec. 1830, p. 2; *Artisan* Oct.–Dec. 1842; *A*
May 1844, pp. 125–8, Aug. 1844, pp. 172–6, Oct. 1844, pp. 11–12; *EO*
Oct. 1844, p. 139; Brazier, *Histoire* II, pp. 215–24; Brazier, *Chansons
nouvelles*, pp. 12–30; Berthaud, 'Goguettier'; G. de Nerval, *Œuvres* (1985) I,
pp. 412, 460; Dinaux, *Sociétés badines* II, pp. 86–8, 449; L. Vinçard,
*Mémoires*, pp. 24–6, 30, 213–14, 217–19, 227–30, 232–3, 236–7; Raspail,
*Avenues*, p. 245; Cim, *Chansonnier*, pp. 33–42, 46–55, 60, 155; Lockwood,
*Tools*, pp. 40, 107–8, 170, 192, 227; Agulhon, *Republic in the Village*,
pp. 146–7; Agulhon, 'Problème', 39, 56; Touchard, *Gloire* I, pp. 168–9,
177, 182, 189–91, 202–26, 229–32, 416; Agulhon, *Republican Experiment*,
p. 114; Agulhon, 'Working class and sociability', pp. 46–7, 58; Brochon, in
Pottier, *Œuvres*, pp. 8–9, 11, 14, 22–3, 33–9; Ragon, *Histoire*, pp. 84, 117;
Rancière, *Nuit*, pp. 8, 39, 49, 246–9; Rancière, 'Good times', pp. 49–51, 69,
71; Droux, 'Chanson', 123.

75 Brazier, *Histoire* II, pp. 216, 218.

76 L. Vincard, *Mémoires*, p. 26.

77 Leno, *Aftermath*, pp. 20–1.

78 *CP* 3 Apr. 1848, p. 3. The attribution to Blanqui is contentious.

79  Constant, *Trois harmonies*; Constant, *Règne*; Constant, *Marseillaise*; Erdan, *France mistique* I, p. 290; Mercier, *Eliphas Lévi*, pp. 25, 32, 38–9, 41, 47, 66–8.

80  *TP* 16 Mar. 1848, pp. 1–2.

81  *P* 8–15 Nov. 1848, p. 4.

82  *P* 5 Dec. 1848, p. 3, 4 Apr. 1849, p. 2, 16 Apr. 1849, p. 4; *Travailleur* (Liège) 24 Jan. 1849, p. 3; Weill, *Histoire*, pp. 265–6; Lockwood, *Tools*, pp. 132–3, 168, 173, 196, 227; Ragon, *Histoire*, pp. 94, 119–22; Berenson, *Populist Religion*, p. 53.

83  Poulot, *Question sociale*, pp. 139, 277; Cim, *Chansonnier*, p. 35; Droux, 'Chanson', 129; E. Weber, *Peasants*, pp. 436–7; Brochon, in Pottier, *Œuvres*, pp. 14, 15, 19; Reddy, 'Moral sense', p. 387; Rancière, 'Good times', pp. 45–6, 51, 57, 60–1, 63; T. Clark, *Painting*, pp. 210–13, 230–33, 236, 304 n. 11; Cunningham, *Leisure*, p. 171.

84  Pref. Pol. 16 Oct. 1856, BB30 366, dos. II, fol. 177; Mercier, *Eliphas Lévi*, p. 45.

85  Berthaud, 'Goguettier'; Agulhon, 'Working class and sociability', p. 47; Merriman, *Agony*, p. 90; Reddy, *Rise of Market Culture*, pp. 257–61, 280, 287; Sancton, 'Myth', 72; Pref. Pol. 10, 13 and 16 Oct. 1856, BB30 366, dos. II, fols. 168, 171, 177.

86  Dalotel, *Aux origines*, p. 44

87  Poulot, *Question sociale*, pp. 243–6; Agulhon, *Ville Ouvrière*, p. 151; Agulhon, 'Problème', 51; Agulhon, 'Working class and sociability', p. 57; Berenson, *Populist Religion*, p. 147; Haine, 'Café friend', p. 616.

88  *Chartist Pilot* 16 Dec. 1843, p. 2; *CC* 24 Aug. 1844, p. 85; *Last* 10 Jan. 1845, p. 96; *NS* 1 Jan. 1845, p. 3, 8 Jan. 1845, p. 5, 19 Feb. 1845, p. 5, 8 Apr. 1845, p. 3; *NR* 19 Jan. 1868, p. 44; Poulot, *Question sociale*, p. 243; Lowery, 'Passages', pp. 22–3; Leno, *Aftermath*, pp. 74–5; E. Thompson, *Making*, p. 617; Agulhon, 'Working class and sociability', p. 57; McCalman, *Radical Underworld*, pp. 49, 148–50; Chase, *People's Farm*, p. 88; Shipley, *Club Life*, pp. 51–5; Berenson, *Populist Religion*, p. 147; Biagini, *Liberty*, p. 27.

89  Nantes, *TA* 21 Jan. 1849, p. 6; Agulhon, *Republic in the Village*, pp. 148–9; Agulhon, 'Working class and sociability', p. 49; Sheridan, 'Social and economic foundations', p.15; Lequin, *Ouvriers* II, p. 190. For the distinction between *clubs* (political unions) and clubs *(cercles)* see *Peuple Constituant* 24 Mar. 1848, p. 1; Dinaux, *Sociétés badines* I, p. 161.

90  Bell, 'Reform League', pp. 25–6.

91  Rémusat, *Mémoires* III, p. 391; Agulhon, 'Working class and sociability', pp. 47–8.

92  *CP* 7 May 1848, p. 4.

93  Agulhon, 'Working class and sociability', pp. 51–6; Agulhon, *Republic in the Village*, pp. 125–8, 134–7, 140, 143; Zeldin, *France* I, pp. 477–8; Margadant, *French Peasants*, p. 155; *BH* 31 Jan. 1863, p. 1, 4 Apr. 1863, p. 1, 2 May 1863, p. 1, 3 Sept. 1863, p. 1; *Echo* 25 Mar. 1884, p. 1; S. Yeo, 'Three socialisms', p. 109; S. Yeo, 'Notes', p. 251; Marlow, 'London working men's clubs', pp. 15, 93–4.

94  *TAHP* 26 Oct. 1850, p. 144; *BH* 14 Mar. 1863, p. 1, 2 Sept. 1865, p. 1; *MWA* 3 June 1865, p. 5, 24 June 1865, p. 5; *WM* 21 July 1866, p. 33, 29

Sept. 1866, p. 154; *NR* 3 Apr. 1870, p. 222; Postgate, *Builders' History*, pp. 199–200; Bailey, *Leisure*, pp. 106–22; Richard Price, 'Working men's club movement'; Shipley, *Club Life*, esp. pp. 3, 20–2, 26–7, 41–8; Biagini, *Liberty*, pp. 176–7; Marlow, 'London working men's clubs'.

95 McCalman, *Radical Underworld*, p. 5; Cotterau, 'Denis Poulot's *Le Sublime*' pp. 165–6; Haine, 'Café friend', 621.

96 Garrard, *Leadership and Power*, p. 47; Joyce, *Work*, pp. 282–303; Cunningham, 'Patriotism', 20; Vernon, *Politics*, pp. 235–45.

97 *PMG passim*; McCalman, *Radical Underworld*, p. 245; Musillier, 'Société des Droits de l'Homme, 1) 7ème Arrondisement', CC 589; Report 24 Apr. 1834, CC 590; Cour des Pairs, *Affaire* IV, p. 424.

98 Agulhon, *Republican Experiment*, p. 102.

99 *BH* 2 Sept. 1865, p. 1, 4 Nov. 1865, p. 7, 13 Oct. 1866; *C* 10 Nov. 1866, p. 5, 22 Dec. 1866, p. 5, 16 Mar. 1867, p. 5, 27 Apr. 1867, p. 4.

100 *C* 16 Mar. 1867, p. 3.

101 *C* 9 Mar. 1867, p. 4, 16 Mar. 1867, p. 5; A. Taylor, 'Modes', p. 480.

102 *BH* 28 Apr. 1866, p. 1; *C* 9 Feb. 1867, p. 5, 30 June 1867, pp. 1, 5.

103 For the League's cultural activities, see A. Taylor, 'Modes', pp. 474–81; Bell, 'Reform League', pp. 103, 165, 167; Finn, *After Chartism*, pp. 242, 247.

104 *R* 22 July 1846, p. 124, 29 July 1846, p. 142, 8 Mar. 1848, p. 207; *NS* 1 Apr. 1848, p. 1, 29 Apr. 1848, p. 2; *RWN* 12 Jan. 1851, p. 10; *Political Examiner* 2 Mar. 1853, p. 4; *PP* 3 July 1858, p. 5; *London News, passim*; *NU passim*; Davies, *Heterodox London*, pp. 264–6; Leno, *Aftermath*, pp. 55, 73, 75; Leventhal, *Respectable Radical*, pp. 7, 20, 22, 26–7; B. Harrison, 'Pubs', pp. 179–80; Finn, *After Chartism*, pp. 131–5; Shipley, *Club Life*; Little, 'Chartism and Liberalism', p. 348; A. Taylor, 'Modes', pp. 195, 206–9, 391–2.

105 *WM* 10 Aug. 1867, p. 10; *BH* 20 Mar. 1869, p. 1; *NR passim*; *Republican, passim*; H. Collins and Abramsky, *Karl Marx*, pp. 164–5, 252; Leventhal, *Respectable Radical*, pp. 92–4; Finn, *After Chartism*, pp. 281–2; Robinson, 'Karl Marx', pp. 96–8, 179–222; A. Taylor, 'Modes', pp. 631–46, 680, 687–90, 708–14.

106 *People's Advocate*, 1876, *passim*; P. Thompson, 'Liberals, radicals and labour in London 1880–1900', *Past and Present* no. 27 (1964), 75–8; Shipley, *Club Life*, pp. 50–6; Biagini, *Liberty*, pp. 176–7; Marlow, 'London working men's clubs', pp. 31, 40–49.

107 *City Lantern* (Manchester) 12 Mar. 1875, p. 186; McCalman, *Radical Underworld*, ch. 9; Agulhon, in Nadaud, *Mémoires*, p. 387; Margadant, *French Peasants*, p. 220; Dalotet, *Aux origines*, pp. 64–5, 103.

108 de la Hodde, *Histoire des sociétés secrètes*, p. 275.

109 Burns, 'Strategy', p. 136.

110 Naudaud, *Mémoires*, p. 387; Agulhon, *Republic in the Village*, p. 244; Lequin, *Ouvriers* II, pp. 163–5; Merriman, *Agony* pp. 59–60, 91, 95; Machin, 'Prefects', p. 287; Margadant, *French Peasants*, pp. 156–60, 220, 226; Stewart-McDougall, *Artisan Republic*, pp. 122, 135; Christofferson, 'Urbanization', 204; Rancière, 'Good times', pp. 56–7.

111 Besançon, 10 Aug. 1850, BB30 394.

112 Reports Aix, 17 Jan. and 10–13 Dec. 1850, BB30 394. See also Proc.-Gen.

to Garde des Sceaux, 26 May 1851, BB30 379, p. 4; Benoit, *Confessions*, p. 74; Agulhon, *Republic in the Village*, p. 134; Richard, 'Débuts', 85.

113 Duthie, *Tramp's Wallet*, pp. 146–7.

114 Lefrançais, *Souvenirs* I, pp. 287–8; Agulhon, *Republican Experiment*, p. 179; Plessis, *Rise and Fall*, pp. 132–3, 138–9; Reddy, 'Moral sense', p. 392; Robert, 'Cortèges', pp. 210–12.

115 Agulhon, *Republican Experiment*, pp. 175–6.

116 Police, 'Cercle Progressif des Travailleurs des Brotteaux', 21 Mar. 1867, 6 June 1868, 'Cercle de la Solidarité', 11 Mar. 1868, 5 Dec. 1873, in ADR 4M 630; Gaumont, *Histoire*, pp. 585–6; Lequin, *Ouvriers* II, p. 190; Sheridan, 'Social and economic foundations', p. 15.

117 *Credo des Travailleurs-Unis*, C 925, dos. IV.; 'Dos. Commission des délégués du Luxembourg', 2963 and dos. IV, C 942; Tolain, *Quelques vérités*, p. 16; *M* 27 Jan. 1870, p. 3.

118 Perrot, *Ouvriers en grève*, p. 189.

119 A. Taylor, 'Modes', p. 554; Marlow, 'London working men's clubs', p. 15

120 'Sociétés secrètes. Ferrandiniers et renégats', in 'Clubs et assocations' (Cour de Lyon 1848–1850), BB18 1474B; Report 11 Jan. 1850, Cour de Lyon, and Lyon Soc., BB30 394; *Journal de la Guillotière* 18 Aug. 1844, p. 4, 14 Aug. 1845, p. 2; *Gazette de Lyon* 5 Mar. 1848, p. 1; Benoit, *Confessions*, p. 122; Lévy-Schneider 'Journal', 457; Gaumont, *Histoire*, p. 355; Stewart-MacDougall, *Artisan Republic*, pp. xiii–xiv, 29, 43, 51, 56, 80, 155.

121 A. Clark, *Struggle*, p. 25.

122 Corbon, *Secret*, p. 27; Simon, *Histoire générale*, pp. 32–45; P. Clark, *English Alehouse*, p. 323; W. Weber, 'Artisans'; E. Weber, *Peasants*, pp. 438–42; Agulhon, *Republic in the Village*, pp. 120–1, 138; Agulhon, 'Working class and sociability', p. 47; Hanagan, *Nascent Proletarians*, p. 85.

123 *City Lantern* (Manchester) 15 Jan. 1875, pp. 123–4.

124 *Ruche* Oct.–Nov. 1848, p. 314; *Voix des Femmes* 27 Mar. 1848, p. 3; *P* 27 Dec. 1848, p. 2, 19 Jan. 1849, p. 4, 24 Jan. 1849, p. 2; Simon, *Histoire générale*, pp. 33, 36; Gossez, *Ouvriers*, p. 29; Amann, *Revolution*, p. 30; W. Weber, 'Artisans', 258.

125 X [Chevé], *Peuple* 12 Feb. 1849, p. 6; L. Vinçard, *Mémoires*, pp. 114–15, 266; *TO* 4 June 1865, p. 3, 18 June 1865, p. 10; *Crisis* 23 Mar. 1833, p. 88; *Charter* 16 Feb. 1840, p. 14; *RWN* 19 May 1850, p. 7, 25 May 1851, p. 14; *NR* 23 Apr. 1865, p. 270, 8 Jan. 1865, p. 28, 17 Dec. 1865, p. 808; E. Yeo, 'Robert Owen', p. 86, 98–9; S. Yeo, 'Notes', p. 269 n. 80; Simon, *Histoire générale*, p. 38; W. Weber, 'Artisans', 257.

126 *Doreurs en bois*, F12 3111; Lee, *Pioneer* 5 July 1834, p. 5; Marylebone, *NS* 6 Feb. 1841, p. 1, Bermondsey, 8 May 1841, p. 1, O'Brien, 14 Aug. 1841, p. 4, masons, 11 Dec. 1841, p. 6, Stallwood, 23 July 1842, p. 7, Durham, 10 Aug. 1844, p. 8, Somers Town, 12 Oct. 1844, p. 1; *Ruche* April–May 1847, p. 116; Preston, *TC* 11 Feb. 1854, p. 9, 18 Feb. 1854, p. 9; Tower Hamlets, *PP* 9 Aug. 1856, p. 1; *People* 18 Apr. 1857, p. 4; *NU* May 1858, pp. 2, 3; Arnott, *NR* 8 Sept. 1860, p. 5; IWMA, 8 Oct. 1865, p. 647; Universal League, *BH* 19 Mar. 1864, p. 5, 22 Oct. 1864, p. 1, Sunday League, 27 Jan. 1866, p. 1; *EL* 24 Feb. 1866, p. 83; *C* 10 Nov. 1866, p. 4; Chauvet, *Ouvriers*, p. 586; *St. Crispin* 26 Feb. 1870, p. 108.

127 E.g. *P* 20 Jan. 1849, p. 4, 24 Jan. 1849, p. 2, 11 Feb. 1849, p. 4, 12 Feb. 1849, p. 4, 27 May 1849, p. 4, 30 Aug. 1850, p. 8; Champfleury, *Excentriques*, p. 295.

128 Pref. Pol. 23 Oct. 1856, BB30 366, dos. II, fol. 185; *Progrès* (Lyons) 28 July 1861, p. 2.

129 *WA* 7 Oct. 1865, p. 5; *C* 17 Feb. 1866, p. 6. See also Biagini, *Liberty*, p. 421 and n. 294.

130 D. Jones, *Chartism*, pp. 78–81; B. Taylor, *Eve*, p. 229; Vernon, *Politics*, pp. 229–30.

131 *FSA* Jan. 1836, p. 11.

132 Lovett, *Life*, pp. 75, 76, 134; *NS* 17 Feb. 1838, p. 1. See also Belchem, 'Radical language', 256; Vernon, *Politics*, pp. 217, 235.

133 Benoit, *Confessions*, p. 61; Barrow, *Independent Spirits*, pp. 181–2; *PP* 24 May 1855, p. 1, 14 Feb. 1857, p. 1; NA MS 155, fols. 205–7, 222; Vernon, *Politics*, pp. 142, 235–6.

134 Farren, *NS* 30 July 1842, p. 7, Clark, M'Grath, 15 Aug. 1846, p. 5.

135 *NS* 15 Aug. 1846, p. 5; Richard, 'Débuts', 85; Vernon, *Politics*, p. 246; A. Taylor, 'Modes', pp. 645–6, 708–14, 740–6.

136 *NR* 20 July 1861, p. 6; Lovett, *Life*, p. 208; Poulot, *Question sociale*, pp. 134–40.

137 E. Yeo, 'Robert Owen', pp. 98–9.

138 E.g. J. B., *NMW* 4 Feb. 1843, p. 255, Cooper, 18 Feb. 1843, p. 273; E. Yeo, 'Robert Owen', pp. 87, 95; W. Weber, 'Artisans', p. 260.

139 *Journal du Commerce et des Théâtres de Lyon* 17 Apr. 1836, p. 4; *NMW* 1 Nov. 1834, p. 8, 19 Jan. 1839, p. 203, 13 Apr., p. 394, Oldham, 13 Feb. 1841, p. 104; *Artisan* 9 Oct. 1842, p. 1; Oppenheim, *Other World*, pp. 216–7; Parssinen, 'Mesmeric performers'.

140 *Artisan* 12 Jan. 1843, p. 1; D. Vincent, *Bread*, p. 157; Prothero, *Artisans*, p. 200; Marlow, 'London working men's clubs', pp. 4–5.

141 Cleave, *Republican* 11 June 1831, p. 6.

142 B. Taylor, pp. 141, 185.

143 J. Leroux, *Prolétaire et bourgeois*; *Banquet des Travailleurs Socialistes*, p. 24; Merriman, *Agony*, p. 43; Stevens, *Memoir*, p. 64.

144 Pottier, *Œuvres*, pp. 33–9, 64; Berthaud, 'Goguettier', p. 514; B. Harrison, 'Pubs', p. 172; Summerfield, 'Effingham Arms', p. 233.

145 Dalotel, *Aux origines*, pp. 264–9.

146 For these meetings see: AN 45 AP 6, dos. 4; NA MS 155; *Commerce* 4 July 1869, p. 1; *M* 23 Jan. 1870, p. 3, 16 Apr. 1870, pp. 2–3; Lefrançais, *Souvenirs* II, pp. 320ff.; Molinari, *Mouvement socialiste*; Dalotel, *Aux origines*; Cottereau, 'Denis Poulot's *Le Sublime*', pp. 163–8. For music-halls used in Lyons, see police, 27 Feb. 1870, and Min. of Int. to Pref. Rhône, 9 Mar. 1870, AML I2 55, I, docs. 29, 30.

147 Reynolds, *RWN* 9 June 1850, p. 7.

148 Constant, 'La politique', in *Trois harmonies*, p. 121.

149 *RP* 27 Apr. 1848, p. 3, 3 May 1848, p. 2; Benoit, *Confessions*, p. 126; C. Johnson, *Utopian Communism*, p. 267; Wassermann, *Clubs*, pp. 31–2, 35–8; Amann, *Revolution*, pp. 62–3.

150 G. Jones, 'Language of Chartism'; D. Thompson, 'The languages of class', *Bulletin of the Society for the Study of Labour History* 52 (1987), 56.

## CONCLUSION

1 *Chartist Pilot* 9 Dec. 1843, p. 3.
2 Biagini, *Liberty*, pp. 11, 67–8, 86, 139, 174.
3 Brossiers, F12 3109.

# Select bibliography

This is a select bibliography, in which the lists of books, pamphlets, and articles include only works that are cited in the footnotes. A few works cited only once are not included in the bibliography, and in these cases full title and publication details are given in the footnote reference
  > denotes change of title

## PRIMARY

### MANUSCRIPT

*Archives de la Préfecture de Police, Paris*
Aa
366, 421, 428, 432
Ba
435, 439
D/b
173

*Archives de la Ville de Paris, Paris*
DM12 23
Q 1f

*Archives Départmentales du Rhône, Lyons*
4M
94, 629–630

*Archives Municipales de Lyon*
I2 47B
I2 55 Police Politique. Association Internationale des
Travailleurs (1864–1870)

*Archives Nationales, Paris*
BB18 Correspondence Générale de la Division Criminelle 1230, 1239, 1245,
  1252, 1262, 1368, 1382, 1384–1385, 1387, 1398, 1402, 1407–1408, 1415,
  1420–1421, 1429, 1433–1436, 1444, 1447, 1472–1473, 1474B, 1487,
  1714–1715, 1791
BB21 Graces Accordées
566–574

BB24 Graces Demandées ou Accordées
409–418,  419–430,  431–439,  440–447,  467–477,  478–483,  489–493,
    591–604, 778
BB30 Versements de 1904 et 1905
301, 306, 316, 358, 358, 361, 366, 394
C Assemblées Nationales
930, 932–934, 939, 941–3, 966, 2242
CC Cour des Pairs. Procès Politiques
585–587, 589–590, 593–595, 608, 612–618, 670
F7 Police Générale
3879, 3881, 3883–3886, 3890, 3892–3, 6682, 6685–6686, 6694, 6700,
    6782–4, 9786–7,
F9 Affaires Militaires
1156
F12 Commerce et Industrie
2354, 3105–3106, 3109–3112, 3115–3117, 3121A, 3120
F13 Travaux Publics
522
F17 Sciences et Lettres, Ministère de l'Instruction Publique
6674
45 AP 6 Papiers Rouher

*Bibliothèque de l'Arsénal*
Enfantin Papers

*Bibliothèque Historique de la Ville de Paris*
CP 3706
MS 1025
MS 1043 Révolution de 1848
MS 1052 Papiers Cabet
MS 2015–6 Papiers Ledru-Rollin
NA MS 153–4
NA MS 155 Réunions Publiques à Paris 1868–1870

*Bibliothèque Nationale, Paris*
II NAF 9581 Papiers Blanqui

*British Library, London*
Place Papers
Place Collection

*Co-operative Union Library, Manchester*
Holyoake Collection
Owen Collection

*Library of Political and Economic Science, London School of Economics*
Webb Collection of Trade Union Manuscripts
A 10–14, 18, 22, 24, 25, 44–46

*Modern Records Centre, University of Warwick*
28/CO/1/8/3
28/CO/1/8/7/1
28/CO/1/8/9/1
28/CO/1/10/4
39A/TA/1/1/1
39A/TA/1/3
39A/TA/4/1/1
39A/TA/4/7/1
78/ASC+J/4/1/1
78/ASC+J/6/1/10
78/ASC+J/6/1/12/1,2
78/CU/4/1–3
78/GUC+J/6/1,3,5
78/MA/4/1/1
78/MB/4/1/1
78/OB/4/1/2/1
78/OB/4/2/1
78/OS/1/1/1
78/OS/2/1/8
78/OS/4/1/1,5,6,10,13,17,20,30,34
78/TC/Pre/2/1
78/TC/MISC/2/1


*National Library of Australia*
Linton Papers
MS 1698
MS 1776


*Public Record Office, London*
Home Office Papers


*Stockport Public Library*
Christy Collection
B/JJ/5/16,17,23
B/P/2/1,2,5,12,18,21
B/PP/4/30,32
B/SS/6/16
B/UU/4/4
B/VV/4/9

PRINTED

## Newspapers and periodicals

Dates are given to distinguish works with similar or common titles or, when the whole run has not been read, to indicate the years consulted.

*Advocate; or, Artizans' and Labourers' Friend*
*Amalgamated Society of Carpenters and Joiners' Monthly Report*
*Apprentice and Trades' Weekly Register* > *Trades' Weekly Register and Apprentice*
*Artisan Journal des Classes Laborieuses* (1836)
*Artisan, Journal de la Classe Ouvrière* (1830)
*Artisan, Moniteur Ouvrier de Paris et des Départements* (1842–3)
*Association Rémoise, Journal du Travail, de l'Industrie, de l'Agriculture et du Commerce, Fondé par les Corporations* (1849)
*Atelier. Organe des intérêts Moraux et Matériels des Ouvriers*
*Beacon: a Weekly Journal of Politics and Literature* (1853)
*Bee-Hive*
*Birmingham Labour Exchange Gazette*
*Book-Binders' Consolidated Union. Friendly Circular*
*Book-Finishers' Friendly Circular*
*Bookbinders' Consolidated Union Circular*
*Bookbinders' Trade Circular*
*Bronterre's National Reformer, in Government, Law, Property, Religion, and Morals*
*Carpenter's Political Letters*
*Charter*
*Cleave's Weekly Police Gazette*
*Co-Operator. A Record of Co-operative Progress: Conducted Exclusively by Working Men* (1860–63)
*Commerce. Journal Commercial, Politique, Scientifique & Littéraire*
*Commune de Paris. Moniteur des Clubs*
*Commune Sociale, Journal Mensuel des Travailleurs* (1848–9)
*Cordwainers' Companion: a Miscellany of Trade and General Information*
*Courrier de l'Assemblée Nationale. Journal Politique et Littéraire (1848)*
*Courrier Français* (1867)
*Crisis; or the Change from Error and Misery, to Truth and Happiness*
*Democrat and Labour Advocate* (1855)
*'Destructive' and Poor Man's Conservative* (1833) > *People's Conservative and Trade Union Gazette* (1833–4) > *Hetherington's Twopenny Dispatch* (1834–6) > *London Dispatch* (1836–9)
*Early Closing Advocate, and Commercial Reformer*
*Echo de la Fabrique, Journal Industriel de Lyon et du Département du Rhône*
*Echo des Ouvriers*
*Echo des Travailleurs. Journal de la Fabrique de Lyon et du Progrès*
*Egalitaire, Journal de l'Organisation Sociale*
*English Chartist Circular* (1841–44)
*English Leader* (1864, 1866–7)
*Evening Star* (1842)
*Fraternité* (1841–3)
*Fraternité de 1845* (1845–8)
*Friendly Societies' Advocate and Journal of Useful Information for the Industrious Classes*
*Friends of Labour Association's Monthly Circular of General Information, and Working Man's Advocate* (1859–63)
*Gauntlet*

*Gazette des Tribunaux*
*Glaneuse*
*Humanitaire, Organe de la Science Sociale*
*Indicateur, Journal Industriel de Lyon* (1834–5)
*Innovator or Boot-and-Shoemaker's Monitor*
*International Courier*
*Journal des Ouvriers. Liberté. Ordre Public!* (1830)
*Journal des Tailleurs*
*Journal du Peuple*
*Journal of the Typographic Arts*
*Journal of the Working Classes*
*Journeyman. An Organ Devoted to the Interests of Working Tailors*
*Labour League, or Journal of the National Association of United Trades*
*Labourer*
*Laboureur Journal Politique de l'Agriculture et des Campagnes* (1849)
*Lancashire and Yorkshire Co-operator*
*Last*
*Libérateur* (1834)
*London News*
*Man. A Rational Advocate*
*Marseillaise*
*Miner and Workman's Advocate* (1865) > *Workman's Advocate* (1865–66) >
     *Commonwealth* (1866–67)
*Montagnard Satirique. Journal Politico-Littéraire-Charivarique* (1849)
*Montagne de la Fraternité. Tribune des Représentants Amis du Peuple*
*Monthly Report of the National Association of United Trades for the Protection of
     Industry* > *National United Trades' Association Report and Labour's Advocate*
*Mutualité. Revue du Travail & des Sociétés Coopératives* (1866)
*National Reformer* (1860–70)
*National Union*
*New Moral World, a London Weekly Publication, Developing the Principles of the
     Rational System of Society*
*Northern Liberator*
*Northern Star*
*Notes to the People*
*Nouveau Monde* (1849–50)
*Nouvelle des Abonnés. Journal pour Rien*
*Nouvelle Revue Rétrospective* (1897)
*Operative. Established by the Working Classes for the Defence of the Rights of Labour*
     (1838–9)
*Operative* (1851–2)
*Operative Bricklayers' Society's Trade Circular and General Reporter*
*Operative. Devoted to the Classes Connected with the Constructive and Decorative Arts*
     (Dublin, 1862)
*Opinion Nationale. Journal du Soir* (1861, 1865)
*Organisation du Travail, la Vérité aux Ouvriers* (1848)
*Organisation du Travail. Journal des Ouvriers* (1848)
*Paris Sun-Beam* (1837)

*People* (1857–8)

*People's Advocate and National Vindicator of Right v Wrong* (1875) > *People's Advocate* (1876)

*People's Newspaper*

*People's Paper. The Champion of Political Justice and Universal Right*

*Père Duchêne, Gazette de la Révolution* (1848)

*Petit Messager du Village* (1849)

*Peuple Constituant* (1848)

*Peuple Souverain. Journal des Travailleurs* (Bordeaux, 1849)

*Peuple Souverain. Journal des Travailleurs* (1848)

*Pioneer: or Trades' Union Magazine*

*Political Examiner: a Weekly Democratic Journal* (1853)

*Poor Man's Guardian* (1831–35)

*Poor Man's Guardian and Repealer's Friend* (1843)

*Populaire* (1833–4)

*Populaire de 1841. Journal de Réorganisation Sociale et Politique* (1841–7)

*Positif, Journal des Travailleurs* (1849)

*Power of the Pence*

*Qui Vive! Journal Quotidien. Organe de la Démocratie Universelle* (1871)

*Reasoner* (1846–8)

*Red Republican* > *Friend of the People*

*Réformateur Religieux ou l'Echo de l'Eglise Française*

*Réformateur, Journal Religieux Consacré au Développement de la Doctrine de l'Eglise Française et du Christianisme Unitaire* > *L'Eglise Française, Journal Religieux*

*Réformateur, ou l'Echo de l'Eglise Française*

*Représentant du Peuple* (1848) > *Peuple. Journal de la République Démocratique et Sociale* (1848–9) > *Voix du Peuple* (1849–50) > *Peuple de 1850* (1850)

*Republican. A Monthly Advocate and Record of Republican and Democratic Principles and Movements* (1870–72)

*Revue Républicaine. Journal des Doctrines et des Intérêts Démocratiques* (1834)

*Reynolds's Weekly Newspaper; a Journal of Democratic Progress and General Intelligence* (1850–51) > *Reynolds's Newpaper* (1851, 1857–9)

*Ruche Populaire, Journal des Ouvriers, Redigé et Publié par Eux-mêmes*

*Shipwrights' Journal*

*Social Reformer* (1849)

*Socialiste, Journal de l'Etat-Echange* (1849)

*Solidarité* (1849)

*Southern Star*

*St. Crispin, a Weekly Journal, Devoted to the Interest of Boot and Shoe Makers, and All Engaged in the Leather Trades*

*Tailor. A Weekly Trades Journal & Advertiser*

*Tichborne News and Anti-Oppression Journal* (1872)

*Tocsin des Travailleurs* (1848)

*Trades' Advocate and Herald of Progress. Established by the Iron Trades* (1850)

*Trades' Chronicle* (1854)

*Trades' Journal* (1840–1)

*Trades' Weekly Messenger* (1848)

*Travail* (1869)

*Travail Affranchi* (1849)
*Travail, Journal des Classes Ouvrières* (1842)
*Travail. Journal du Travailleur Electeur et Eligible* (1848)
*Travail. Organe de la Rénovation Sociale* (Lyons, 1841)
*Travail. Véritable Organe des Intérêts Populaires* (1848)
*Travailleur. Journal des Associations. Echange, Vente en Gros et en Détail de Tous les Produits de l'Industrie parisienne*
*Tribun du Peuple. Organe des Travailleurs* (1848)
*Tribune*
*Tribune Ouvrière* (1865)
*True Sun* (1834)
*Typographical Protection Circular*
*Typographical Societies' Monthly Circular*
*Union. Bulletin des Ouvriers Redigé et Publié par Eux-mêmes* (1843–46)
*Vanguard, a Weekly Journal of Politics, History, Biography, and General Literature*
*Vérité. Feuille Mensuelle Illustrée de la Religion Socialiste*
*Voyant-Pourvoyeur de Travail, d'Emploi et de Crédit aux Travailleurs Abonnés*
*Vraie République* (1848)
*Weekly True Sun* (1834–7)
*Working Man's Friend and Political Magazine* (1832–3)
*Working Man: a Weekly Record of Social and Industrial Progress* (1866)
*Workman Co-operative Newspaper* (1861) > *Working Man Co-operative Newspaper* (1861–62) > *Working Man. A Political and Social Advocate of the Rights of Labour* (1866, 1867)

In addition, a large number of newspapers have been consulted very selectively, notably *The Times* and other London dailies, Paris dailies such as *National* and *Réforme, Manchester Guardian*, and other local papers (especially in Manchester, Leeds, Birmingham, Bristol, and Lyons)

**Contemporary published works**
Works in English published in London and in French in Paris, unless otherwise stated.

*A Brief Inquiry into the Natural Rights of Man; his Duties and Interests* (1852)
*A Tous Le Philosophone et l'Eglise Française* (Nantes, 1830)
*A Tous les Travailleurs* [Luxembourg delegates] (1848)
*Almanach des Associations Ouvrières pour 1850 Publié sous les Auspices de l'Union Essénienne* (1849)
Amalgamated Society of Engineers, *Abstract Report of the Council's Proceedings* (1862)
*Appel à Tous nos Frères de la Corporation des Ouvriers Cordonniers et Bottiers de la Ville de Paris, sans Distinction de Société* (n.d.=1848)
*Association des Ouvriers Bijoutiers* (n.d.=1850)
*Association des Ouvriers Ebénistes sous la Raison Sociale Drien et Cie* (n.d.)
*Association Fraternelle des Ouvriers Cordonniers* (Limoges, 1850)
Audiganne, A., *Les populations ouvrières et les industries de la France dans le mouvement social du XIXe siècle* (1854), 2 vols.

Auzou, L.-N., *Observations sur une lettre de M. l'abbé Chatel* (1832)
   *Oraison funèbre de Napoleon II, duc de Reichstadt* (1832)
Banquet des Travailleurs Socialistes. *Président Auguste Blanqui Détenu à Vincennes* (1849)
Barberet, J., *Le mouvement ouvrier à Paris de 1870 à 1873* (1874)
   *Le travail en France. Monographies professionelles* III (1887); V (1889)
Benbow, W., *The Crimes of the Clergy, or the Pillars of Priest-Craft Shaken* (1823)
Benoit, J., *Confessions d'un prolétaire* (1968)
Berryer, M., *Affaire des charpentiers* (1845)
Berthaud, L. A., 'Le Goguettier', in *Les Français Peints par Eux-mêmes, Encyclopédie Morale du Dix-Neuvième Siècle* IV (1842)
Blanc, L., *Révolution française. Histoire de dix ans 1830–1840* (1841–55), 5 vols.
Blanqui, A., *L'éternité par les astres. Hypothèse astronomique* (1872)
Boyer, A., *De l'état des ouvriers et de son amélioration par l'organisation du travail* (1841)
   *Les conseils de prud'hommes au point de vue de l'intérêt des ouvriers, et de l'égalité de droits* (n.d.=1841)
Brazier, N., *Chansons nouvelles* (1836)
   *Histoire des petits théâtres de Paris depuis leur origine* (1838), 2 vols.
Brisset, M., 'L'ouvrier de Paris', in *Les Français Peints par Eux-mêmes, Encyclopédie Morale du Dix-Neuvième Siècle* V (1842)
Broadhurst, H., *Henry Broadhurst M.P. The Story of his Life from a Stonemason's Bench to the Treasury Bench* (1901)
Brooke, J. W., *The Democrats of Marylebone* (1839)
Cabet, E., *Guide du citoyen aux prises avec la police et la justice* (1842)
   *L'ouvrier; ses misères actuelles, leur cause et leur remède; son futur bonheur dans la communauté; moyens de l'établir* (1844)
   *La République du populaire* (1833)
   *Le vrai Christianisme Suivant Jésus-Christ* (1846)
   *Ma ligue droite ou le vrai chemin du salut pour le peuple* (1847)
   *Moyen d'améliorer l'état déplorable des ouvriers* (n.d.)
   *Salut par l'Union, ou ruine par la division* (1845)
Calland, V., and Le Rousseau, J., *Eglise catholique française. Profession de foi* (1834)
Carpenter, W., *Proceedings of the Third Co-operative Congress; Held in London* (1832)
[Carter, T., and others], *The Guide to Trade* (1838–9)
Cavaignac, G., *Opinion de G. Cavaignac sur le droit d'association* (n.d.)
Chambre de Commerce de Paris, *Statistique de l'Industrie à Paris Résultant de l'Enquête Faite par la Chambre de Commerce pour les Années 1847–1848* (1851)
Champfleury, *Les excentriques* (1855)
Chatel, F.-F., *A la Chambre des députés* (1843)
   *Eloge de Napoléon* (1841)
   *Le code de l'humanité, ou l'humanité ramenée à la connaissance du vrai Dieu et au véritable socialisme* (1838)
   *Sermon de M. l'abbé Chatel, à l'ouverture de la Nouvelle Eglise Française, rue de la Sourdière, no.23* (1831)

Cochut, A., *Les associations ouvrières. Histoire et théorie des tentatives de réorganisation industrielle operées depuis la révolution de 1848* (1851)

Constant, A., *La Marseillaise du peuple* (1848)
  *Le règne du peuple* (1848)
  *Les trois harmonies, chansons & poésies* (1845)

Cooper, T., *The Life of Thomas Cooper, Written by Himself* (1872)

Corbon, A., *Le secret du peuple de Paris* (1863)

Cour des Pairs, *Affaire du Mois d'Avril 1834. Rapport Fait à la Cour par M. Girard (de l'Ain)* (1834), 4 vols.

Davies, C. M., *Heterodox London: or, Phases of Freethought in the Metropolis* (1874)

*Deuxième Procès des Ouvriers Typographes en Première Instance et en Appel* (1862)

Devlin, J. D., *Strangers' Homes; or, the Model Lodging Houses of London* (1853)
  *Contract Reform* (1856)

*Dictionnaire Politique Encyclopédie du Langage et de la Science Politiques* (1842)

Dinaux, A., *Les sociétés badines, bachiques, chantantes et littéraires. Leur histoire et leurs travaux* (1867) 2 vols.

Duchêne, G., *Actualités. Livrets et prud'hommes* (1847)

Dunning, T. J., *Trades' Unions and Strikes: their Philosophy and Intention* (1860)

Dupont, P., *Histoire de l'imprimerie* (1854)

Duthie, W., *A Tramp's Wallet; Stored by an English Goldsmith During his Wanderings in Germany and France* (1858)

Duval, J., 'Les origines du mouvement coopératif', *Journal des Economistes* 8 (1867)

Efrahem, *De l'association des ouvriers de tous les corps d'état*

Erdan, A., *La France mistique, tableau des excentricités religieuses de ce temps*, 2 vols. (1855)

Esquiros, A., *L'évangile du peuple* (1840)

F. K. S., *Trades' Triumphant! or, Unions' Jubilee!!* (n.d.)

Favre, J., *De la coalition des chefs d'atelier de Lyon* (Lyons, 1833)

*Fédération de Tous les Ouvriers de France. Règlement de la Corporation des Ouvriers Cordonniers* (n.d.)

Flotard, E., *Le mouvement coopératif à Lyon et dans le Midi de la France* (1867)

Fribourg, E. E., *L'Association Internationale des Travailleurs* (1871)

Ganneau, *Manifeste en faveur d'une association* (1840)
  *Waterloo 18 Juin 1815* (1840)

Gauny, L. G., *Le philosophe plébéien. Textes presentés et rassemblés par Jacques Rancière* (1983)

Gisquet, H., *Mémoires de M. Gisquet, ancien préfet de police* III (1840)

Grignon, *Réflexions d'un ouvrier tailleur sur la misère des ouvriers en général, la durée des journées de travail, le taux des salaires* (n.d.)

Guépin, A., and Bonamy, E., *Nantes au XIXe siècle; statistique topographique, industrielle et morale, faisant suite à l'histoire des progrès de Nantes* (Nantes, 1835)

Guillaumou, T., *Les confessions d'un compagnon* (1864)

Hetherington, H., *Principles and Practice Contrasted; or, a Peep into 'The Only True Church of God upon Earth', Commonly Called Freethinking Christians* (1828)

Hodde, L. de la, *Histoire des sociétés secrètes et du parti républicain de 1830 à 1848* (1850)

[Holyoake, G. J., and Leblond, R.], *The Appeal of the Distressed Operative Tailors to the Higher Classes and the Public* (1850)

Holyoake, G. J., *The History of Co-operation in England: its Literature and Advocates* (1875, 1879), 2 vols

Jador, H., *Procès de la Commission des Ouvriers Typographes. Au bénéfice de la Caisse de Secours Mutuels pour les typographes sans ouvrage* (1830)

Jones, C.[C. Inglis], *The Political Secret; or, the Bible not What It Is Represented to Be. An Address to the People* (1866)

Jouy, *Adresse aux prolétaires et ouvriers français sur la situation présente de la France* (1839)

K. P., *Moyen infallible de donner du travail et de l'aisance a l'ouvrier et de faire cesser les sociétés ou prétendues coalitions* (n.d.)

Keszler, *Des grèves à propos de celle des ouvriers tailleurs en avril 1867* (1867)

la Mennais, F. de, *The Words of a Believer* (Paris, 1834)

Lahautière, R., *De la loi sociale* (1841)

Laponneraye, A., *Cours public d'histoire de France, depuis 1789 jusqu'en 1830* (n.d.)
*Défense du citoyen Laponneraye, prononcé aux Assises du Département de la Seine, le 21 avril 1832* (1832)

Le Rousseau, J., *Notions de phrénologie* (1847)

*Le Secret des Compagnons Cordonniers Dévoilé* (1858)

Lefrançais, G., *Souvenirs d'un révolutionnaire* (Brussels, n.d.) 2 vols

Leno, J. B., *The Aftermath: with Autobiography of the Author* (1892)

Lenoble, A., *Aux charpentiers de Paris (maîtres et ouvriers)* (1845)

Leroux, J., *Aux ouvriers typographes. De la nécessité de fonder une association ayant pour but de rendre les ouvriers propriétaires des instrumens de travail* (1833)
*Le prolétaire et le bourgeois. Dialogue sur la question des salaires, où l'on démontre que la baisse des salaires ne profite à personne* (1840)

*Les Délégués (Ouvriers)* [Luxembourg delegates] (1848)

*Les Sociétés Populaires de 1830, par un Negociant, Officier de la Garde Nationale* (1830)

*Lettres Adressées au Journal La Tribune pour les Ouvriers Tailleurs, Boulangers, Cordonniers, Concernant leurs Demandes en Augmentation de Salaire, et Règlement des Ouvriers Tailleurs pour Former des Compagnies d'Ouvriers* (n.d.)

Lévy, A., *Procès des ouvriers typographes* (1862)

Lion, *Plus de patrons! Association des ouvriers cordonniers-bottiers de toute la France sous le concours du Gouvernement* (1848)

Lovett, W., *The Life and Struggles of William Lovett in Search of Bread, Knowledge and Freedom* (1876)

Lowery, R., 'Passages in the life of a temperance lecturer', in B. Harrison and P. Hollis (eds.), *Robert Lowery. Radical and Chartist* (1979)

Lyon, L. J., *La lyre du devoir* (1846)

Macdonald, W., *The True Story of Trades' Unions Contrasted with the Caricatures and Fallacies of the Pretended Economists* (Manchester, 1867)

Malepeyre, M., *Code des ouvriers ou recueil méthodique des lois et règlements, concernant les ouvriers, chefs d'atelier, contremaîtres, compagnons et apprentis, avec des notes explicatives* (1833)

*Manifeste des Délégués des Corporations (ayant siégé au Luxembourg) aux Ouvriers du Département de la Seine* (n.d.=1848)

Marcroft, W., *A Co-operative Village: How to Make it and Where to Form it* (Manchester, n.d.)

[Martin, P.], *Nouveau cathéchisme républicain, indiquant à tout citoyen ses droits, ses devoirs, et la forme de gouvernement qui convient le mieux à la dignité et au bonheur d'un peuple. Par un prolétaire* (Lyons, 1833)

Mazuy, F., *Essai historique sur les moeurs et coutumes de Marseille au dix-neuvième siècle* (Marseilles, 1853)

Mirecourt, E. de, *Les contemporains. Portraits et silhouettes au XIXe siècle.* no. 138. *Renan. L'abbé Chatel* (1871)

Molinari, G. de, *Le mouvement socialiste et les réunions publiques avant la révolution du 4 Septembre 1870* (1872)

Monfalcon, J. B., *Histoire des insurrections de Lyon, en 1831 et en 1834, d'après des documents authentiques* (Lyons, 1834)

Nadaud, M., *Mémoires de Léonard ancien garçon maçon* (1976)

Noiret, C., *Aux travailleurs* (Rouen, 1840)
  *Deuxième lettre aux travailleurs* (Rouen, 1841)
  *Mémoires d'un ouvrier rouennais* (Rouen, 1836)

O'Brien, J. B., *A Vision of Hell* (1859)
  *The Rise, Progress, and Phases of Human Slavery* (1885)

Perdiguier, A., 'Notice sur le compagnonnage', in his *Le livre du compagnonnage* (1840; 2nd edition, 1841)
  *Biographie de l'auteur du livre du compagnonnage et réflexions diverses* (1846)
  *Mémoires d'un compagnon* (Moulins, 1914)
  *Statistique du salaire des ouvriers en réponse à M. Thiers et autres économistes de la même école* (1849)

Pillot, J.-J., *Le code religieux. Le culte chrétien* (1837)
  *Ni châteaux ni chaumières, ou état de la question sociale en 1840* (1840)

Poncy, C., *La chanson de chaque métier* (1850)

Porter, G. R., *The Progress of the Nation, in its Various Social and Economical Relations, from the Beginning of the Nineteenth Century* (1847)

Potter, G., *The Labour Question. An Address to Capitalists, and Employers, of the Building Trades* (1861)

Pottier, E., *Eugène Pottier, ouvrier, poète, communard, auteur de l'Internationale. Œuvres complètes* (ed. P. Brochon) (1966)

Poulot, D., *Question sociale. Le sublime ou le travailleur comme il est en 1870 et ce qu'il peut être* (1980)

*Premier Banquet Communiste, le 1er Juillet 1840* (n.d.)

Preston, T., *The Life and Opinions of Thomas Preston, Patriot and Shoemaker* (1817)

*Projet d'Association Destiné a l'Industrie du Bronze* (1850)

*Projet d'Association Fraternelle de l'Industrie Française* (Lyons, 1848)

*Projet de Pétition des Petits Commerçants, des Chefs d'Atelier et les Ouvriers de Nantes* (Nantes, n.d.)

Proudhon, P.-J., *De la capacité politique des classes ouvrières* (1865; edition, 1924)

Pujol, L., *Prophétie des jours sanglants* (1848)

*Rapport des Délégués Cordonniers Publié par la Commission Ouvrière* (1863)
*Rapport des Délégués Ferblantiers* (n.d.)
*Rapport des Délégués Mécaniciens* (1863)
*Rapport des Délégués Tanneurs, Corroyeurs et Maroquiniers* (1862)
*Rapports des Délégués des Ouvriers Parisiens à l'Exposition de Londres en 1862. Publié par la Commission Ouvrière* (1862–4)
*Rapports des Délégués Dessinateurs et Tisseurs en Châles et des Délégués Tisseurs en Nouveautés Publiés par la Commission Ouvrière* (1863)
*Rapports des Délégués Imprimeurs en Papiers Peints, du Délégué pour les Papiers de Couleurs et de Fantaisie, et des Délégués Graveurs sur Bois pour Etoffes et pour Papiers Peints, Publiés par la Commission Ouvrière* (1863)
*Rapports des Délégués Imprimeurs Lithographes et des Délégués Imprimeurs en Taille-Douce, Publiés par la Commission Ouvrière* (1863)
Raspail, F.-V., *Les avenues de la République. Souvenirs de F.-V. Raspail sur sa vie et sur son siècle 1794–1878* (1984)
  *Lettres sur les prisons de Paris* (1839), 2 vols
Razzell, P. E., and Wainwright, R. W., *The Victorian Working Class. Selections from Letters to the Morning Chronicle* (1973)
*Règlement de la Société de l'Union des Doreurs* (n.d.)
*Règlement pour les Ouvriers Imprimeurs en Taille-Douce* (n.d.)
*Reminiscences of a Stonemason, by a Working Man* (1908)
Rémusat, C. de, *Mémoires de ma vie*; III *Des luttes parlementaires. La question d'Orient. Le Ministère Thiers-Rémusat (1832–1841)* (1960); IV *Les dernières années de la monarchie. La révolution de 1848. La Seconde République (1841–1852)* (1962)
*Report of the Committee, and Proceedings at the Fourth Quarterly Meeting, of the British Association for Promoting Co-operative Knowledge* (1830)
Richard, A., 'Les débuts du parti socialiste français', *Revue Politique et Parlementaire* 11 (1897)
Rittiez, F., *Histoire du regne de Louis-Philippe Ier 1830–1848* I (1858)
Roche, A., *Manuel du prolétaire* (1833)
[Smith, C. M.], *The Working Man's Way in the World: Being the Autobiography of a Journeyman Printer* (1853)
Société des Droits de l'Homme, *Association des Travailleurs* (n.d.)
Société des Droits de l'Homme et du Citoyen, *De l'Education Nationale* (n.d.)
*Société Laborieuse des Ouvriers Cordonniers-Bottiers* (n.d.)
Société Philanthropique, *Rapports et Comptes-Rendus pour l'Année 1835* (1836)
Soutter, F. W., *Recollections of a Labour Pioneer* (1923)
Stevens, W., *A Memoir of Thomas Martin Wheeler* (1862)
Tartaret, E., *Commission Ouvrière de 1867* (1868)
  *Exposition Universelle de 1867. Commission Ouvrière de 1867 2ème recueil des procès-verbaux des assemblées générales des délégués et des membres des bureaux électoraux* (1869)
Tolain, H., *Quelques vérités sur les elections de Paris (31 mai 1863)* (1863)
Truquin, N., *Mémoires et aventures d'un prolétaire à travers la révolution. L'Algérie, la République argentine et le Paraguay* (1977)
Vinçard, L., *Mémoires episodiques d'un vieux chansonnier Saint-Simonien* (1878)
Vinçard, P., *Appel à tous les travailleurs. Par le citoyen Vinçard, typographe* (n.d.)

*Les ouvriers de Paris. Etudes de moeurs, types, caractères, travail, salaire, dangers,*
   *etc.* (n.d.=1850)
Vincent, D. (ed.), *Testaments of Radicalism. Memoirs of Working Class Politics*
   *1790–1885* (1977)
Wright, T., *Some Habits and Customs of the Working Classes, by a Journeyman*
   *Engineer* (1867; reprint New York, 1967)


SECONDARY


PRINTED

Aguet, J.-P., *Les grèves sous la Monarchie de Juillet (1830–1847)* (Geneva, 1954)
Agulhon, M., 'Le problème de la culture populaire en France autour de 1848',
   *Romantisme. Revue de la Société des Etudes Romantiques* no. 9 (1975)
   'Martin Nadaud, témoin du XIXe siècle', introduction to M. Nadaud,
   *Mémoires de Léonard, ancien garçon maçon* (1976)
   'Working class and sociability in France before 1848', in P. Thane,
   G. Crossick, and R. Floud (eds.), *The Power of the Past. Essays for Eric*
   *Hobsbawm* (Cambridge, 1984)
   *The Republic in the Village. The People of the Var from the French Revolution to the*
   *Second Republic* (Cambridge, 1982)
   *The Republican Experiment, 1848–1852* (Cambridge, 1983)
   *Une ville ouvrière au temps du socialisme utopique. Toulon de 1815 à 1851* (1970)
Allen, J. S., 'Toward a social history of French romanticism: authors, readers,
   and the book trade in Paris, 1820–1840', *Journal of Social History* 13
   (1979)
Amalric, J.-P., 'La Révolution de 1848 chez les cheminots de la compagnie du
   Paris-Orléans', *Revue d'Histoire Economique et Sociale* 41 (1963)
Amann, P., *Revolution and Mass Democracy. The Paris Club Movement in 1848*
   (1975)
Aminzade, R., 'Class analysis, politics and French labor history', in L. R.
   Berlanstein (ed.), *Rethinking Labor History* (Urbana, 1993)
   'The transformation of social solidarities in nineteenth-century Toulouse', in
   J. M.Merriman (ed.), *Consciousness and Class Experience in Nineteenth-*
   *Century Europe* (1979)
   *Ballots and Barricades. Class Formation and Republican Politics in France,*
   *1830–1871* (Chicago, 1993)
'Au sublime ouvrier. Entretien avec Alain Cottereau', *Les Révoltes Logiques* no.
   12 (1980)
Auslander, L., 'Perceptions of beauty and the problem of consciousness: Parisian
   furniture makers', in L. R. Berlanstein (ed.), *Rethinking Labor History*
   (Urbana, 1993)
Bailey, P., *Leisure and Class in Victorian England. Rational Recreation and the*
   *Contest for Control, 1830–1885* (1978)
Barrow, L., *Independent Spirits. Spiritualism and English Plebeians, 1850–1910*
   (1986)

Bauberot, J., 'Conversions collectives au Protestantisme et religion populaire en France au XIXe siècle', in *La religion populaire* (Colloques Internationaux du Centre National de la Recherche Scientifique) (1979)

Baughman, J. J., 'The French Banquet campaign of 1847–48', *Journal of Modern History* 31 (1959)

Bédarida, F., *A Social History of England 1851–1975* (1979)

Behagg, C., *Politics and Production in the Early Nineteenth Century* (1990)

Belchem, J., '1848: Feargus O'Connor and the collapse of the mass platform', in J. Epstein and D. Thompson (eds.), *The Chartist Experience: Studies in Working-Class Radicalism and Culture, 1830–60* (1982)

'Henry Hunt and the evolution of the mass platform', *English Historical Review* 93 (1978)

'Radical language and ideology in early nineteenth-century England: the challenge of the platform', *Albion* 20 (1988)

'Republicanism, popular constitutionalism and the radical platform in early nineteenth-century England', *Social History* 6 (1981)

Berenson, E., 'A new religion of the left: Christianity and social radicalism in France, 1815–1848', in F. Furet and M. Ozouf (eds.), *The Transformation of Political Culture 1789–1848* (Oxford, 1989)

*Populist Religion and Left-Wing Politics in France, 1830–1852* (Guildford, 1984)

Bernstein, S., 'Le néo-babouvisme d'après le presse (1837–1848)', in *Babeuf et les problèmes du babouvisme* (Colloque International de Stockholm, 1960) (1963)

Biagini, E. F., *Liberty, Retrenchment and Reform. Popular Liberalism in the Age of Gladstone, 1860–1880* (Cambridge, 1992)

Bouillon, J., 'Les démocrates-socialistes aux élections de 1849', *Revue Française de Science Politique* 6 (1956)

Bowler, P. J., *The Invention of Progress. The Victorians and the Past* (Oxford, 1989)

Bowman, F. P., *Eliphas Lévi, visionnaire romantique* (1969)

*Le Christ romantique* (Geneva, 1973)

Brand, C. F., 'The conversion of the British trade-unions to political action', *American Historical Review* 30 (1925)

Breuilly, J., 'Artisan economy, ideology and politics: the artisan contribution to the mid-nineteenth-century European labour movement', in his *Labour and Liberalism in Nineteenth-Century Europe. Essays in Comparative History* (Manchester, 1994)

Briquet, J., *Agricol Perdiguier. Compagnon du Tour de France et représentant du Peuple 1805–1875* (1955)

Brown, P. S., 'Social context and medical theory in the demarcation of nineteenth-century boundaries', in W. F. Bynum and R. Porter (eds.), *Medical Fringe and Medical Orthodoxy 1750–1850* (1987)

Bruhat, J., 'Anticléricalisme et mouvement ouvrier en France avant 1914. Esquisse d'une problematique', in F. Bédarida, and J. Maitron (eds.), *Christianisme et monde ouvrier* (1971)

Burgess, K., 'Trade union policy and the 1852 lock-out in the British engineering industry', *International Review of Social History* 17 (1972)

*The Origins of British Industrial Relations. The Nineteenth Century Experience* (1975)

Chase, M., *'The People's Farm'. English Radical Agrarianism 1755–1840* (Oxford, 1988)

Chauvet, P., *Les Ouvriers du Livre en France de 1789 à la constitution de la Fédération du Livre* (1956)

Chazelas, V., 'Un episode de la lutte de classe à Limoges', *La Révolution de 1848* 7 (1910–11)

Child, J., *Industrial Relations in the British Printing Industry. The Quest for Security* (1967)

Cholvy, G. and Hilaire, Y.-M., *Histoire religieuse de la France contemporaine* (Toulouse, 1985)

Christofferson, T. R., 'The French national workshops of 1848: the view from the provinces', *French Historical Studies* 11 (1980)

'Urbanization and political change: the political transformation of Marseille under the Second Republic', *Historian* 36 (1974)

Cim, A., *Le chansonnier Emile Debraux, roi de la goguette (1796–1831)* (1910)

Claeys, *Citizens and Saints. Politics and Anti-Politics in Early British Socialism* (Cambridge, 1989)

Clark, A., *The Struggle for the Breeches. Gender and the Making of the British Working Class* (1995)

Clark, P., *The English Alehouse: a Social History 1200–1830* (1983)

Clark, T. J., *The Painting of Modern Life. Paris in the Art of Manet and his Followers* (1984)

Clements, R. V., 'British trade unions and popular political economy 1850–1875', *Economic History Review* 14 (1961)

Cole, G. D. H., *A Century of Co-operation* (Manchester, 1944)

Colley, 'Whose nation? Class and national consciousness in Britain 1750–1830', *Past and Present* no. 113 (1986)

Collins, H. and Abramsky, C., *Karl Marx and the British Labour Movement. Years of the First International* (1965)

Collins, I., *The Government and the Newpaper Press in France 1814–1881* (Oxford, 1959)

Coornaert, E., *Les compagnonnages en France du Moyen Age à nos jours* (1966)

Cooter, R. 'Bones of contention? Orthodox medicine and the mystery of the bone-setter's craft', in W. F. Bynum and R. Porter (eds.), *Medical Fringe and Medical Orthodoxy 1750–1850* (1987)

*The Cultural Meaning of Popular Science. Phrenology and the Organization of Consent in Nineteenth-Century Britain* (Cambridge, 1984)

Cottereau, A., 'Denis Poulot's *Le Sublime* – a preliminary study', in A. Rifkin and R. Thomas (eds.), *Voices of the People. The Social Life of 'La Sociale' at the End of the Second Empire* (1988)

'The distinctiveness of working-class cultures in France, 1848–1900', in I. Katznelson and A. R. Zolberg (eds.), *Working-Class Formation. Nineteenth-Century Patterns in Western Europe and the United States* (Princeton, 1986)

Crossick, G., 'From gentlemen to the residuum: languages of social description in Victorian Britain', in P. J. Corfield (ed.), *Language, History and Class* (Oxford, 1991)

*An Artisan Elite in Victorian Society. Kentish London 1840–1880* (1978)

Crump, J., 'The popular audience for Shakespeare in nineteenth-century Leicester', in *Shakespeare and the Victorian Stage* (Cambridge, 1986)

Cunningham, H., 'The language of patriotism, 1750–1914', *History Workshop* no. 12 (1981)

*Leisure in the Industrial Revolution c1780–c1880* (1980)

Dalotel, A., Faure, A., and Freiermuth, J.-C., *Aux origines de la Commune. Le mouvement des réunions publiques à Paris 1868–1870* (1980)

Darnton, R., *Mesmerism and the End of the Enlightenment in France* (Cambridge, Mass., 1968)

Dautry, J., *1848 et la Deuxième République* (1957)

Desmond, A., 'Artisan resistance and evolution in Britain, 1819–1848', *Osiris* 3 (1987)

Dolléans, E., *Histoire du mouvement ouvrier. 1830–1871* (1936)

Dommanget, M., *Les idées politiques et sociales d'Auguste Blanqui* (1957)

Droux, G., 'La chanson lyonnaise', *Revue d'Histoire de Lyon* 6 (1907)

Dupeux, G., *French Society 1789–1970* (1976)

Duveau, G., *La Vie ouvrière en France sous le Second Empire* (1946)

Epstein, J., 'Radical dining, toasting and symbolic expression in early nineteenth-century Lancashire: rituals of solidarity', *Albion* 20 (1988)

'Some organisational and cultural aspects of the Chartist movement in Nottingham', in J. Epstein and D. Thompson (eds.), *The Chartist Experience: Studies in Working-Class Radicalism and Culture, 1830–60* (1982)

'Understanding the cap of liberty: symbolic practice and social conflict in early nineteenth-century England', *Past and Present* no. 122 (1989)

*The Lion of Freedom: Feargus O'Connor and the Chartist Movement, 1832–1842* (1982)

Fasel, G., 'The wrong revolution: French republicanism in 1848', *French Historical Studies* 8 (1974)

'Urban workers in provincial France, February–June 1848', *International Review of Social history* 17 (1972)

Faure, A., 'Mouvements populaires et mouvement ouvrier à Paris (1830–1834)', *Mouvement Social* no. 88 (1974)

*Paris Carême-prenant. Du Carnaval à Paris au XIXe siècle 1800–1914* (1978)

Fédération Française des Travailleurs du Livre, *Les Associations Professionnelles Ouvrières Typographiques* (1900)

Festy, O., 'Dix années de l'histoire corporative des ouvriers tailleurs d'habits, (1830–1840)', *Revue d'Histoire des Doctrines Economiques et Sociales* 5 (1912)

Finn, M. C., *After Chartism. Class and Nation in English Radical Politics, 1848–1874* (Cambridge, 1993)

Foster, J., *Class Struggle and the Industrial Revolution. Early Industrial Capitalism in Three English Towns* (1974)

Foulon, M., *Eugène Varlin, relieur et membre de la Commune* (Clermont-Ferrand, 1934)

Fraser, D., *Urban Politics in Victorian England. The Structure of Politics in Victorian Cities* (Leicester, 1976)

Fraser, W. H., *Trade Unions and Society. The Struggle for Acceptance 1850–1880* (1974)

Furlough, E., *Consumer Cooperation in France. The Politics of Consumption, 1834–1930* (Ithaca, 1991)

Gaillard, J., 'Les associations de production et la pensée politique en France (1852–1870)', *Le Mouvement Social* no. 52 (1965)

Garrard, J., *Leadership and Power in Victorian Industrial Towns 1830–80* (Manchester, 1983)

Gasnault, F., *Guinguettes et Lorettes. Bals publics et danse sociale à Paris entre 1830 et 1870* (1986)

Gaumont, J., *Histoire générale de la coopération en France. Les idées et les faits. Les hommes et les œuvres* I *Précurseurs et premises* (1924)

Geary, D., *European Labour Protest 1848–1939* (1981)

Gibson, R., *A Social History of French Catholicism 1789–1914* (1989)

Gilbert, A. D., *Religion and Society in Industrial England. Church, Chapel and Social Change, 1740–1914* (1976)

Giles, P. M., 'The felt-hatting industry, c.1500–1850 with particular reference to Lancashire and Cheshire', *Transactions of the Lancashire and Cheshire Antiquarian Society* 49 (1959)

Gillespie, F. E., *Labor and Politics in England 1850–1867* (1966)

Girard, L., *La Garde Nationale 1814–1871* (1964)

Goodway, D., *London Chartism 1838–1848* (Cambridge, 1982)

Gossez, R., 'Diversité des antagonismes sociaux vers le milieu du XIXe siècle', *Revue Economique* (1956)

'Pré-syndicalisme ou pré-coopération? L'organisation ouvrière et ses phases dans le département de la Seine de 1834 à 1851', *Archives Internationales de Sociologie de la Coopération* no. 6 (1959)

'Presse parisienne à destination des ouvriers 1848–1851', in J. Godechot (ed.), *La presse ouvrière 1819–1850* (1966)

*Les ouvriers de Paris* I *L'organisation 1848–1851* (1967)

Haine, W. S., ' "Café friend": friendship and fraternity in Parisian working class cafés, 1850–1914', *Journal of Contemporary History* 27 (1992)

*The World of the Paris Café. Sociability among the French Working Class, 1789–1914* (1996)

Hamer, D. A., *The Politics of Electoral Pressure: a Study in the History of Victorian Reform Agitations* (Hassocks, Sussex, 1977)

Hanagan, M. P., 'Commentary: for reconstruction in labor history', in L. R. Berlanstein (ed.), *Rethinking Labor History* (Urbana, 1993)

'Proletarian families and social protest: production and reproduction as issues of social conflict in nineteenth-century France', in S. L. Kaplan and C. J. Koepp (eds.), *Work in France. Representation, Meaning, Organization, and Practice* (1986)

*Nascent Proletarians. Class Formation in Post-Revolutionary France* (Oxford, 1989)

*The Logic of Solidarity. Artisans and Industrial Workers in Three French Towns 1871–1914* (Chicago, 1980)

Hanson, C. G., 'Craft unions, welfare benefits, and the case for trade union law reform, 1867–75', *Economic History Review* 28 (1975)

Harrison, B., 'Pubs', in H. J. Dyos and M. Wolff (eds.), *The Victorian City. Images and Realities* I (1973)

*Peaceable Kingdom. Stability and Change in Modern Britain* (Oxford, 1982)

Harrison, J. F. C., 'Early Victorian radicals and the medical fringe', in W. F. Bynum and R. Porter (eds.), *Medical Fringe and Medical Orthodoxy 1750–1850* (1987)

*Robert Owen and the Owenites in Britain and America: the Quest for a New Moral Worlds* (1969)

*The Second Coming. Popular Millenarianism 1780–1850* (1979)

Haynes, M., 'Employers and trade unions, 1824–1850', in J. Rule (ed.), *British Trade Unionism 1750–1850. The Formative Years* (1988)

Heftler, E., *Les associations coopératives de production sous la Deuxième République* (1899)

Hennock, E. P., 'Finance and politics in urban local government in England, 1835–1900', *Historical Journal* 6 (1963)

Hilaire, Y.-M., 'Notes sur la religion populaire au XIXe siècle', in *La religion populaire* (Colloques Internationaux du Centre National de la Recherche Scientifique) (1979)

Hobsbawm, E. J., *Labouring Men. Studies in the History of Labour* (1965)

*Worlds of Labour. Further Studies in the History of Labour* (1984)

Hollis, P., *The Pauper Press. A Study in Working-Class Radicalism of the 1830s* (Oxford, 1970)

Hornus, J.-M., 'Les petits églises catholiques non romaines', *Revue d'Histoire et de Philosophie Religieuses* 50 (1970)

House, J. H., 'Civil–military relations in Paris, 1848', in R. Price (ed.), *Revolution and Reaction. 1848 and the Second French Republic* (1975)

Howe, E., and Child, J., *The Society of London Bookbinders 1780–1951* (1952)

Howe, E., and Waite, H. E., *The London Society of Compositors (Re-established 1848)* (1948)

Humphrey, A. W., *Robert Applegarth, Trade Unionist, Educationalist, Reformer* (Manchester, 1913; reprint, 1984)

Hunt, E. H., *British Labour History 1815–1914* (1981)

Hunt, L., and Sheridan, G., 'Corporation, association, and the language of labor in France, 1750–1850', *Journal of Modern History* 58 (1986)

Hutton, P. H., *The Cult of the Revolutionary Tradition. The Blanquists in French Politics, 1864–1893* (1981)

Isambert, F.-A., *Christianisme et classe ouvrière. Jalons pour une étude de sociologie historique* (Tournai, 1961)

Jacob, M., *The Radical Enlightenment. Pantheists, Freemasons and Republicans* (1981)

Jardin, A., and Tudesq, A.-J., *Restoration and Reaction, 1815–1848* (Cambridge, 1983)

Jefferys, J. B., *The Story of the Engineers 1800–1945* (1946)

Johnson, C. H., 'Economic change and artisan discontent: the tailors' history, 1800–48', in R. Price (ed.), *Revolution and Reaction. 1848 and the Second French Republic* (1975)

'Etienne Cabet and the problem of class antagonism', *International Review of Social History* 11 (1966)

'The revolution of 1830 in French economic history', in J. M. Merriman (ed.), *1830 in France* (New York, 1975)

*Utopian Communism in France. Cabet and the Icarians 1839–1851* (1974)

Johnson, D., *Guizot. Aspects of French History 1787–1874* (1963)

Johnson, P., 'Class law in Victorian England', *Past and Present* no. 141 (1993)

Jones, D., *Chartism and the Chartists* (1975)

Jones, G. S., 'The language of Chartism', in J. Epstein and D. Thompson (eds.), *The Chartist Experience: Studies in Working-Class Radicalism and Culture, 1830–60* (1982)

Joutard, P., 'Protestantisme populaire et univers magique: le cas cévenol', in *Le monde alpin et rhodanien* (1977)

Joyce, P., *Visions of the People. Industrial England and the Question of Class* (Cambridge, 1991)

   *Work, Society and Politics. The Culture of the Factory in later Victorian England* (Brighton, 1980)

Kelso, M. R., 'The French labor movement during the last years of the Second Empire', in D. C. McKay (ed.), *Essays in the History of Modern Europe* (New York, 1936)

Kiddier, W., *The Old Trade Unions, from Unpublished Records of the Brushmakers* (1931)

Kirk, N., *The Growth of Working Class Reformism in Mid-Victorian England* (1985)

Kselman, T. A., *Miracles and Prophecies in Nineteenth-Century France* (New Brunswick, N. J., 1983)

Leeson, R. A., *Travelling Brothers. The Six Centuries' Road from Craft Fellowship to Trade Unionism* (1979)

Lequin, Y., *Les Ouvriers de la région lyonnaise (1848–1914)* (Lyons, 1980), 2 vols.

Levasseur, E., *Histoire des classes ouvrières en France depuis 1789 à nos jours* (1867), 2 vols.

Leventhal, F. M., *Respectable Radical. George Howell and Victorian Working Class Politics* (1971)

Lévy-Schneider, L., 'Le journal d'un bourgeois de Lyon en 1848 et la question des Voraces', *La révolution de 1848* vol. 21 (1925)

Linden, M. van der, 'Keeping distance: Alf Lüdtke's "decentred" labour history', *International Review of Social History* 40 (1995)

Lockwood, H. D., *Tools and the Man. A Comparative Study of the French Workingman and the English Chartists in the Literature of 1830–1848* (New York, 1927)

Loubere, L. A., *Louis Blanc. His Life and his contribution to the Rise of French Jacobin-Socialism* (Evanston, Ill., 1961)

   *Radicalism in Mediterranean France. Its Rise and Decline, 1848–1914* (Albany, N. Y., 1974)

Machin, H., 'The prefects and political repression: February 1848 to December 1851', in R. Price (ed.), *Revolution and Reaction. 1848 and the Second French Republic* (1975)

Magraw, R., 'Pierre Joigneaux and socialist propaganda in the French countryside, 1849–1851', *French Historical Studies* 10 (1978)

   *A History of the French Working Class* I *The Age of Artisan Radicalism, 1815–1871* (Oxford, 1992)

   *France 1814–1915. The Bourgeois Century* (Oxford, 1983)

Maidment, B. E., 'Class and cultural production in the industrial city: poetry in

Victorian Manchester', in A. J. Kydd and K. W. Roberts (eds.), *City, Class and Culture. Studies of Social Policy and Cultural Production in Victorian Manchester* (Manchester, 1985)

'Essayists and artizans – the making of nineteenth-century self-taught poets', *Literature and History* 9 (1983)

Maitron, J. (ed.), *Dictionnaire Biographique du Mouvement ouvrier Français. Première Partie: 1789–1864* (1964), 3 vols.; *Deuxième Partie: 1864–1871* (1968), 6 vols.

Manuel, F. E., *The Prophets of Paris. Turgot, Condorcet, Saint-Simon, Fourier, and Comte* (New York, 1962)

Margadant, T. W., 'Modernisation and insurgency in December 1851: a case study of the Drome', in R. Price (ed.), *Revolution and Reaction. 1848 and the Second French Republic* (1975)

*French Peasants in Revolt. The Insurrection of 1851* (Princeton, 1979)

Martin Saint-Léon, E., *Le compagnonnage. Son histoire. Ses coutumes. – ses règlements. Ses rites* (1901)

McCalman, I. D., 'Popular irreligion in early Victorian England: infidel preachers and radical theatricality in 1830s London', in R. W. Davis and R. J. Helmstadter (eds.), *Religion and Irreligion in Victorian Society* (1992)

*Radical Underworld. Prophets, Revolutionaries and Pornographers in London, 1795–1840* (Cambridge, 1988)

McClelland, K., 'Time to work, time to live: some aspects of work and the re-formation of class in Britain, 1850–1880', in P. Joyce (ed.), *The Historical Meanings of Work* (Cambridge, 1987)

McLeod, H., *Religion and the People of Western Europe 1789–1970* (Oxford, 1981)

McPhee, P., 'The crisis of radical republicanism in the French Revolution of 1848', *Historical Studies* (Australia and New Zealand) 16 (1974)

Mercier, A., *Eliphas Lévi et la pensée magique au XIXe siècle* (1974)

Merriman, J. M., 'Radicalisation and repression: a study of the demobilisation of the "democ-socs" during the Second French Republic', in R. Price (ed.), *Revolution and Reaction. 1848 and the Second French Republic* (1975)

*The Agony of the Republic. The Repression of the Left in Revolutionary France 1848–1851* (1978)

*The Red City. Limoges and the French Nineteenth Century* (Oxford, 1985)

Ministère de Commerce, de l'Industrie, des Postes et des Télégraphes. Office du Travail, *Les Associations Professionnelles Ouvrières* (1894–1904), 4 vols.

Mitard, S., 'Ledru-Rollin et la question sociale en 1841', *Revue d'Histoire Economique et Sociale* 30 (1952)

Moore, B., *Injustice: the Social Bases of Obedience and Revolt* (1978)

Morris, R.J ., 'Voluntary societies and British urban elites, 1780–1850: an analysis', *Historical Journal* 26 (1983)

Moses, C., 'Saint-Simonian men/Saint-Simonian women', *Journal of Modern History* 54 (1982)

Moss, B. H., 'June 13, 1849: the abortive rising of French radicalism', *French Historical Studies* 13 (1984)

'Parisian producers' associations (1830–51): the socialism of skilled workers', in R. Price (ed.), *Revolution and Reaction. 1848 and the Second French Republic* (1975)

'Parisian workers and the origins of republican socialism, 1830–1833', in J. M. Merriman (ed.), *1830 in France* (New York, 1975)

*The Origins of the French Labor Movement 1830–1914. The Socialism of Skilled Workers* (Berkeley, 1976)

Moutet, A., 'Le mouvement ouvrier à Paris du lendemain de la Commune au premier congrès syndical en 1876', *Mouvement Social* no. 58 (1967)

Musson, A. E., *The Typographical Association. Origins and History up to 1949* (1954)

*Trade Union and Social History* (1974)

Newman, E. L., '*L'arme du siècle, c'est la plume.* The French worker poets of the July Monarchy and the spirit of revolution and reform', *Journal of Modern History* 51 (1979), suppt

'The blouse and the frock coat: the alliance of the common people of Paris with the liberal leadership of the middle class during the last years of the Bourbon Restoration', *Journal of Modern History* 46 (1974)

'What the crowd wanted in the French revolution of 1830', in J. M. Merriman (ed.), *1830 in France* (New York, 1975)

Nossiter, T. J., 'Shopkeeper Radicalism in the 19th. century', in T. J. Nossiter, A. H. Hanson and S. Rokkan (eds.), *Imagination and Precision in the Social Sciences* (1972)

'The middle class and nineteenth century politics: notes on the literature', in J. Garrard, D. Jary, M. Goldsmith, and A. Oldfield (eds.), *The Middle Class in Politics* (Farnborough, 1978)

Obelkevich, J., *Religion and Rural Society: South Lindsey 1825–1875* (Oxford, 1976)

Oliver, W. H., 'The Labour Exchange phase of the co-operative movement', *Oxford Economic Papers* 10 (1958)

*Prophets and Millennialists. The Usages of Biblical Prophecy in England from the 1790s to the 1840s* (Oxford, 1978)

Oppenheim, J., *The Other World. Spiritualism and Psychical Research in England, 1850–1914* (Cambridge, 1985)

Owen, A., *The Darkened Room. Women, Power, and Spiritualism in Late Nineteenth Century England* (1989)

Parssinen, T. M., 'Mesmeric performers', *Victorian Studies* 21 (1977)

'Popular science and society: the phrenology movement in early Victorian Britain', *Journal of Social History* 8 (1974)

'Professsional deviants and the history of medecine: medical mesmerists in Victorian Britain', *Sociological Review*, monograph 26 (1979)

Parssinen, T. M., and Prothero, I. J., 'The London tailors' strike of 1834 and the collapse of the Grand National Consolidated Trades' Union: a police spy's report', *International Review of Social History* 22 (1977)

Perrot, M., 'A nineteenth-century work experience as related in a worker's autobiography: Norbert Truquin', in S. L. Kaplan and C. J. Koepp (eds.), *Work in France. Representation, Meaning, Organization and Practice* (1986)

'On the formation of the French working class', in I. Katznelson and A. R. Zolberg (eds.), *Working-Class Formation. Nineteenth-century Patterns in Western Europe and the United States* (Princeton, 1986)

*Les ouvriers en grève en France 1871–1890* (1974)

Phayer, J. M., 'Politics and popular religion: the cult of the Cross in France, 1815–1840', *Journal of Social History* 11 (1978)

Phillips, J. A., *The Great Reform Bill in the Boroughs. English Electoral Behaviour, 1818–1841* (Oxford, 1992)

Pichois, C., 'Les cabinets de lecture à Paris durant la première moitié du XIXe siècle', *Annales* 14 (1959)

Pilbeam, P. M., *Republicanism in Nineteenth-Century France, 1814–1871* (1995)

Plessis, A., *The Rise and Fall of the Second Empire* (Cambridgs, 1985)

Plummer, A., *Bronterre. A Political Biography of Bronterre O'Brien 1804–1864* (1971)

Pollard, S., 'Nineteenth-century co-operation: from community building to shopkeeping', in A. Briggs and J. Saville (eds.), *Essays in Labour History* I (1960)

*A History of Labour in Sheffield* (Liverpool, 1959)

Postgate, R. W., *The Builders' History* (1923)

Prestwich, P. E., 'French workers and the temperance movement', *International Review of Social History* 25 (1980)

Price, Richard, 'The other face of respectability: violence in the Manchester brickmaking trade 1859–1870', *Past and Present* no. 66 (1975)

'The working men's club movement and Victorian social reform ideology', *Victorian Studies* 15 (1971)

*Masters, Unions and Men. Work Control in Building and the Rise of Labour 1830–1914* (Cambridge, 1980)

Price, Roger, *An Economic History of Modern France, 1730–1914* (1981)

*The French Second Republic. A social history* (1972)

Prothero, I., 'Chartism in London', *Past and Present* no. 44 (1969)

'London Chartism and the trades', *Economic History Review* 24 (1971)

'William Benbow and the concept of the "general strike"', *Past and Present* no. 63 (1974)

*Artisans and Politics in Early Nineteenth-Century London. John Gast and his Times* (Folkestone, 1979)

Ragon, M., *Histoire de la littérature prolétarienne en France. Littérature ouvrière, littérature paysanne, littérature d'expression populaire* (1974)

Rancière, J., 'A reply', *International Labor and Working Class History* no. 25 (1984)

'Good times or pleasure at the barriers', in A.Rifkin and R.Thomas (eds.), *Voices of the People. The Social Life of 'La Sociale' at the End of the Second Empire* (1988)

'The myth of the artisan. Critical reflections on a category of social history', *International Labor and Working Class History* no. 24 (1983)

*La nuit des prolétaires* (1981)

Reddy, W. M., 'The moral sense of farce: the patois literature of Lille factory laborers, 1848–70', in S. L. Kaplan and C. J. Koepp (eds.), *Work in France. Representation, Meaning, Organization, and Practice* (1986)

*The Rise of Market Culture. The Textile Trade and French Society, 1750–1900* (Cambridge, 1984)

Rendall, J., *The Origins of Modern Feminism: Women in Britain, France and the United States 1780–1860* (Basingstoke, 1985)

Roe, W. G., *Lamennais and England. The Reception of Lamennais' Religious Ideas in England in the Nineteenth Century* (Cambridge, 1985)

Rose, M., 'Rochdale man and the Stalybridge riot. The relief and control of the unemployed during the Lancashire Cotton Famine', in A. P. Donajgrodzki, *Social Control in Nineteenth Century Britain* (1977)

Rougerie, J., 'La Commune de 1871. Problèmes d'histoire sociale', *Archives Internationales de Sociologie de la Coopération* no. 8 (1960)

'Mil huit cent soixante et onze', *Mouvement Social* no. 79 (1972)

'Sur l'histoire de la Première Internationale', *Mouvement Social* no. 51 (1965)

Royle, E., *Victorian Infidels. The Origins of the British Secularist Movement 1791–1866* (Manchester, 1974)

Rude, F., *Le mouvement ouvrier à Lyon de 1827 à 1832* (1944)

Sancton, T. A., 'The myth of French worker support for the North in the American Civil War', *French Historical Studies* 11 (1979)

Saville, J., 'J. E. Smith and the Owenite movement, 1833–4', in S. Pollard and J. Salt (eds.), *Robert Owen. Prophet of the poor* (1971)

Schmiechen, J. A., *Sweated Industries and Sweated Labour. The London Clothing Trades 1860–1914* (1984)

Scott, J. W., 'Men and women in the Parisian garment trades: discussions of family and work in the 1830s and 1840s', in P. Thane, G. Crossick, and R. Floud (eds.), *The Power of the Past. Essays for Eric Hobsbawm* (Cambridge, 1984)

Searle, G. R., *Entrepreneurial Politics in Mid-Victorian Britain* (Oxford, 1993)

Sewell, W. H., 'Social change and the rise of working-class politics in nineteenth-century Marseille', *Past and Present* no. 65 (1974)

*Work and Revolution in France. The Language of Labor from the Old Regime to 1848* (Cambridge, 1980)

Sheridan, G. J., 'The political economy of artisan industry: government and the people in the silk trade of Lyon, 1830–1870', *French Historical Studies* 11 (1979)

Shipley, S., *Club Life and Socialism in Mid-Victorian London* (1971)

Sibalis, M. D., 'The mutual aid societies of Paris, 1789–1848', *French History* 3 (1989)

Simon, H.-A., *Histoire générale documentaire, philosophique. anecdotique & statistique de l'Institution Orphéonique Française* (1909)

Sonenscher, M., 'Mythical work: workshop production and the *compagnonnages* of eighteenth-century France', in P. Joyce (ed.), *The Historical Meanings of Work* (Cambridge, 1987)

*Work and Wages: Natural Law, Politics and the Eighteenth-Century French Trades* (Cambridge, 1989)

Southall, H., 'Mobility, the artisan community and popular politics in early nineteenth-century England', in G. Kearns and C. W. J. Withers (eds.), *Urbanising Britain. Essays on Class and Community in the Nineteenth Century* (Cambridge, 1991)

Stewart, M., and Hunter, L., *The Needle is Threaded. The History of an Industry* (1964)

Stewart-McDougall, M. L., *The Artisan Republic. Revolution, Reaction and Resistance in Lyon 1848–1851* (Gloucester, 1984)

Storch, R. D., 'The plague of the blue locusts. Police reform and popular resistance in Northern England, 1840–57', *International Review of Social History* 20 (1975)

'The policeman as domestic missionary: urban discipline and popular culture in Northern England, 1850–1880', *Journal of Social History* 9 (1976)

Summerfield, P., 'The Effingham Arms and the Empire: deliberate selection in the evolution of music hall in London', in E. and S. Yeo (eds.), *Popular Culture and Class Conflict 1590–1914: Explorations in the History of Labour and Leisure* (Brighton, 1981)

Sykes, R., 'Early Chartism and trade unionism in South-East Lancashire', in J. Epstein and D. Thompson (eds.), *The Chartist Experience: Studies in Working-Class Radicalism and Culture, 1830–60* (1982)

'Some aspects of working-class consciousness in Oldham, 1830–1842', *Historical Journal* 23 (1980)

Taylor, A., ' "Commons-stealers", "land-grabbers" and "jerry-builders": space, popular radicalism and the politics of public access in London', *International Review of Social History* 40 (1995)

'*Reynolds's Newspaper*, opposition to monarchy and the radical anti-jubilee: Britain's anti-monarchist tradition reconsidered', *Historical Research* 68 (1995)

Taylor, B., *Eve and the New Jerusalem. Socialism and Feminism in the Nineteenth Century* (1983)

Tchernoff, I., *Le parti républicain sous la Monarchie de Juillet. Formation et évolution de la doctrine républicaine* (1901)

Tholfsen, T. R., *Working Class Radicalism in Mid-Victorian England* (1976)

Thompson, D. (ed.), *The Early Chartists* (1971)

Thompson, D., 'La presse de la classe ouvrière anglaise 1836–1848', in J. Godechot (ed.), *La presse ouvrière 1819–1850* (1966)

*The Chartists. Popular Politics in the Industrial Revolution* (New York, 1984)

Thompson, E. P., *The Making of the English Working Class* (1963)

*Witness against the Beast. William Blake and the Moral Law* (Cambridge, 1993)

Tilly, C., 'Did the cake of custom break?', in J. M.Merriman (ed.), *Consciousness and Class Experience in Nineteenth-Century Europe* (1979)

Tilly, C., and Lees, L. H., 'The people of June, 1848', in R. Price (ed.), *Revolution and Reaction. 1848 and the Second French Republic* (1975)

Tilly, C., L. and R., *The Rebellious Century 1830–1930* (1975)

Touchard, J., *La gloire de Béranger* (1968), 2 vols.

Truant, C. M., 'Solidarity and symbolism among journeymen artisans: the case of *Compagnonnage*', *Comparative Studies in Society and History* 21 (1979)

Tyrrell, A., 'Class consciousness in Early Victorian Britain: Samuel Smiles, Leeds politics, and the self-help creed', *Journal of British Studies* 9 (1970)

Vernon, J., *Politics and the People. A Study in English Political Culture, c. 1815–1867* (Cambridge, 1993)

Vial, J., *La coutume chapelière. Histoire du mouvement ouvrier dans la chapellerie* (1941)

Vigier, P., *La Seconde République dans la région alpine. Etude politique et sociale* (1963), 2 vols.

Vincent, D. (ed.), *Testaments of Radicalism. Memoirs of Working Class Politics 1790–1885* (1977)

Vincent, D., *Bread, Knowledge and Freedom. A Study of Nineteenth-Century Working-Class Autobiography* (1982)

Vincent, J., *The Formation of the British Liberal Party* (New York, 1966)

Wassermann, S., *Les clubs de Barbès et de Blanqui en 1848* (Geneva, 1978)

Webb, J., *The Flight from Reason* (1971)

Webb, S. and B., *The History of Trade Unionism, 1666–1920* (1920)

Weber, E., *Peasants into Frenchmen. The Modernization of Rural France 1870–1914* (1977)

Weber, W., 'Artisans in concert life of mid-nineteenth-century London and Paris', *Journal of Contemporary History* 13 (1978)

Weill, G., *Histoire du parti républicain en France (1814–1870)* (1928)

Welskopp, T., ' "Defensive elitism" and early craft unions in the wrought iron industry after 1850: Britain, the USA and Germany in comparative perspective', *Labour History Review* 58 (1995)

Wiener, J. H., *The War of the Unstamped: the Movement to Repeal the British Newspaper Tax, 1830–1836* (Ithaca, New York, 1969)

Wright, T., *The Romance of the Shoe* (1922)

Yeo, E., 'Christianity in Chartist struggle 1838–1842', *Past and Present* no. 91 (1981)

'Culture and constraint in working-class movements, 1830–1855', in E. and S. Yeo (eds.), *Popular Culture and Class Conflict 1590–1914: Explorations in the History of Labour and Leisure* (Brighton, 1981)

'Robert Owen and radical culture', in S. Pollard and J. Salt (eds.), *Robert Owen. Prophet of the Poor* (1971)

Yeo, S., 'Notes on three socialisms – collectivism, statism and associationism – mainly in late-nineteenth- and early-twentieth-century Britain', in C. Levy (ed.), *Socialism and the Intelligentsia 1880–1914* (1987)

'Three Socialisms: Statism, Collectivism, Associationism', in W. Outhwaite and M. Hulkay (eds.), *Social Theory and Social Criticism* (Oxford, 1982)

Zeldin, T., *France 1848–1945. I Ambition, Love and Politics* (Oxford, 1973)

DISSERTATIONS

Bell, A. D., 'The Reform League from its origins to the Reform Act of 1867' (D.Phil., Oxford, 1961)

Berridge, V. S., 'Popular journalism and working class attitudes 1854–1886: a study of Reynolds's Newspaper, Lloyd's Weekly Newspaper and the Weekly Times' (Ph.D., London, 1976)

Burns, T. R., 'Strategy, language and leadership in the British working-class movement, 1832–1875' (Ph.D., Manchester, 1994)

Dunsmore, M. R., 'The working classes, the Reform League and the Reform Movement in Lancashire and Yorkshire' (M.A., Sheffield, 1961)

Jowell, F. S., 'Thoré-Bürger and the art of the past', (Ph.D., Harvard, 1971)

Little, A., 'Chartism and Liberalism. Popular politics in Leicestershire 1842 to 1874' (Ph.D., Manchester, 1991)

Marlow, L., 'London working men's clubs: some aspects of their history, 1860–1890' (M.A., Warwick, 1972)

McNulty, D., 'Working class movements in Somerset and Wiltshire, 1837–1848' (Ph.D., Manchester, 1981)

Moberg, D. R., 'George Odger and the English working class movement: 1860–1877' (Ph.D., London, 1953)

Robert, V., 'Cortèges et manifestations à Lyon (1848–1914)' (DES, Lyons II, 1991)

Robinson, K., 'Karl Marx, the International Working Men's Association, and London radicalism, 1864–1872' (Ph.D., Manchester, 1976)

Sanders, J. R., 'Working class movements in the West Riding Textile District 1829–1839, with emphasis on local leadership and organisation' (Ph.D., Manchester, 1984)

Sheridan, G. J., 'The social and economic foundations of association among the silk-weavers of Lyons, 1852–1870' (Ph.D., Yale, 1978)

Sykes, R. A., 'Popular politics and trade unionism in South-East Lancashire, 1829–42' (Ph.D., Manchester, 1982)

Taylor, A., 'Modes of political expression and working-class radicalism 1848–1874: the London and Manchester examples' (Ph.D., Manchester, 1992)

# Index